By the Editors of
CONSUMER GUIDE®

PRESCRIPTION DRUGS

Drug Consultants:
Cheryl Nunn-Thompson, Pharm.D., BCPS
Mary Lynn Moody, R.Ph.
Joan Stachnik, Pharm.D., BCPS

Publications International, Ltd.

Drug Consultants:
Cheryl Nunn-Thompson, Pharm.D., BCPS, is a doctor of pharmacy and is on faculty at the University of Illinois (Chicago) College of Pharmacy. She is a member of several pharmacy organizations and has published and lectured extensively on drug information topics.

Mary Lynn Moody, R.Ph., is coordinator of the Drug Information Center at Columbia-Michael Reese Hospital and is a clinical assistant professor at the University of Illinois (Chicago) College of Pharmacy.

Joan Stachnik, Pharm.D., BCPS, is a clinical assistant professor and drug information specialist at the University of Illinois College of Pharmacy (Chicago).

Photography: Sam Griffith Studios, Inc.

Editorial Assistance: St. Joseph Hospital (Elgin, Illinois), Office Building Pharmacy

Contents

Introduction

The right drug for the right patient in the right dose by the right path at the right time: This rule sums up the decisions made when your doctor gives you a prescription. You've helped to make these decisions by giving your doctor a complete medical history, which should include any previous allergic reactions you've suffered, any other drugs you may be taking, any chronic health problems you may have, and whether you are pregnant or breast-feeding an infant. Once you leave your doctor's office with your prescription in hand, however, you have still more to do as a responsible patient and informed consumer.

Drug therapy is an important component of health care. When you receive a prescription, you must know how and when to properly administer your medication. You must understand and comply with your dosage schedule. You must know what to do to prevent certain side effects and how to handle any side effects that might occur. You must recognize the signals that indicate the need to call your doctor.

Yet all too often, patients leave their doctors' offices without a full understanding of the drug therapy they're about to start. This may result in a failure to fully comply with their doctors' instructions. For example, patients may stop taking the medication too soon because it doesn't seem to work or because they feel better or because it causes bothersome side effects. They may take the drug improperly, at the wrong time, too often, or not often enough. They may continue drinking alcohol or taking other drugs when they shouldn't be. Perhaps they don't even realize that taking cold pills, oral contraceptives, aspirin, or vitamins could affect the action of the prescribed drug. The end result may be that they do not get better; they may get worse and may even suffer a dangerous reaction.

Few of us would buy a car without shopping around, a house or condominium without an appraisal or an appliance without knowing how to work it. Prescription medications should be approached like these other purchases: with understanding. You will be the end user. As an informed consumer you should know what you are buying and how to get the most out of your purchase.

Prescription drugs are dispensed on the basis of two assumptions: 1) instructions for proper use are provided, and 2) those instructions will be followed. In many states, pharmacists are required to provide drug information for each prescription medication by means of written information, verbal counseling, or both. Nevertheless, as a consumer, you have the responsibility to understand your own drug therapy. The National Council of Patient Information and Education (NCPIE) is made up of health-care professionals, lay people, and consumer advocates. It has published guidelines to provide consumers with the information they need regarding proper drug therapy. This is important since the Council estimates that half of all prescriptions dispensed in one year are taken incorrectly. Moreover, almost 40 million prescriptions go unclaimed every year (11 percent of women and 7 percent of men don't fill or don't pick up their prescription medication). This leads to unnecessary side effects, worsening of illnesses, and, in rare cases, even death. The economic losses from taking medicine incorrectly and not filling prescriptions have been estimated at 1.5 billion dollars annually for lost workdays due to preventable illness. NCPIE recommends that you ask your health-care professional the following questions about each prescription medication you receive:

1. What is the name of the drug and what is it supposed to do for you?

2. How and when should it be taken?

3. What other medications, foods, drinks, or activities should be avoided while taking the drug?

4. Are any side effects likely, and what should be done if they occur?

Prescription Drugs provides the information you need to take prescription medications safely and effectively. Along with general information on how to read a prescription and how to buy, store, and administer drugs, this publication provides an introduction to the action of drugs—how they work to stop infection, to lower blood pressure, and to relieve pain. It then provides detailed information on hundreds of the most commonly prescribed drugs. Included in the drug profiles is information on how to alleviate certain side effects, whether the drug should be taken on an empty stomach or with meals, whether it is likely to affect your ability to drive, and whether generic equivalents are available for a prescribed trade-name medication. You will discover which side effects are common to some medications and which side effects present danger signals that require immediate attention from your physician.

Of course, *Prescription Drugs* is not a substitute for consulting your doctor, pharmacist, or other health-care provider. They are your primary reference sources on the use of prescription drugs. To assure that you receive the best health care possible, however, you, too, must be informed and knowledgeable about the prescription drugs you use.

Filling Your Prescription

While you're having your prescription filled, you should make sure you understand what the drug is used for, your dosage schedule, and how to store the medication properly. You should be clear about what kinds of precautions to take to prevent or reduce side effects, whether you should restrict your diet or drinking habits while taking the drug, which side effects are expected or unavoidable, and which side effects signal a need for a doctor's attention. Your first step in having your prescription filled is reading and understanding what your doctor has written.

READING YOUR PRESCRIPTION

Prescriptions are not mysterious—they contain no secret messages. Many of the symbols and phrases doctors use on prescriptions are abbreviated Latin or Greek words; they are holdovers from the days when doctors actually wrote in Latin. For example, *gtt* comes from the Latin word *guttae*, which means *drops,* and *bid* is a shortened version of *bis in die,* which is Latin for *twice a day.*

You do not have to be a doctor, nurse, or pharmacist to read a prescription. You can (and should) learn how to read one yourself—after all, the prescription describes the drug you will be taking. You should understand what your doctor has written on the prescription blank to be sure that the label on the container you receive from your pharmacist coincides with your prescription.

The accompanying table lists the most common prescription symbols and abbreviations. Use it as a guide to read the sample prescriptions that follow.

Common Abbreviations and Symbols Used in Writing Prescriptions

Abbreviation	Meaning	Derivation and Notes
aa	of each	*ana* (Greek)
ac	before meals	*ante cibum* (Latin)
AD	right ear	*auris dextra* (Latin)
AL	left ear	*auris laeva* (Latin)
AM	morning	*ante meridiem* (Latin)
AS	left ear	*auris sinistra* (Latin)
au	both ears	*auris* (Latin)
bid	twice a day	*bis in die* (Latin)
C	100	—
c̄	with	*cum* (Latin)
cap	capsule	—
cc or cm³	cubic centimeter	30 cc equals one ounce
disp	dispense	—
dtd#	give this number	*dentur tales doses* (Latin)
ea	each	—
ext	for external use	—
gtt	drops	*guttae* (Latin)
gt	drop	*gutta* (Latin)
h	hour	*hora* (Latin)
hs	at bedtime	*hora somni* (Latin)
M ft	make	*misce fiat* (Latin)
mitt#	give this number	*mitte* (Latin)
mL	milliliter	30 mL equals one ounce (1 mL=1 cc)

Abbreviation	Meaning	Derivation and Notes
O	pint	*octarius* (Latin)
OD	right eye	*oculus dexter* (Latin)
OL	left eye	*oculus laevus* (Latin)
OS	left eye	*oculus sinister* (Latin)
OU	each eye	*oculus uterque* (Latin)
pc	after meals	*post cibum* (Latin)
PM	evening	*post meridiem* (Latin)
po	by mouth	*per os* (Latin)
prn	as needed	*pro re nata* (Latin)
q̄	every	*quaqua* (Latin)
qd	once a day; every day	*quaqua die* (Latin)
qid	four times a day	*quater in die* (Latin)
qod	every other day	—
s̄	without	*sine* (Latin)
sig	label as follows	*signa* (Latin)
sl	under the tongue	*sub lingua* (Latin)
SOB	shortness of breath	—
sol	solution	—
ss	half unit	*semis* (Latin)
stat	at once; first dose	*statim* (Latin)
susp	suspension	—
tab	tablet	—
tid	three times a day	*ter in die* (Latin)
top	apply topically	—
ung or ungt	ointment	*unguentum* (Latin)
UT	under the tongue	—
ut dict or UD	as directed	ut dictum (Latin)
x	times	—

John D. Jones MD
Anytown, U.S.A.

DEA# 123456789   PHONE# 123-4567

NAME *Your Name*   AGE *47*
ADDRESS *Anytown, U.S.A.*   DATE *5/10/92*

℞ *Fiorinal*
    # 24
    Sig: caps i q̄ 4 h prn pain

REFILLS *5x*   DISPENSE AS WRITTEN
LABEL *yes*   *John D. Jones M.D.*
                                              SUBSTITUTION

The first sample prescription is for a medication called
Fiorinal. The prescription tells the pharmacist to give you 24
capsules (#24), and it tells you to take one capsule (caps i)
every four hours (q 4h) as needed (prn) for pain. The prescription indicates that you may receive five refills (5x), that
the label on the drug container should state the name of the
drug (yes), and that the pharmacist may substitute (substitution) a less expensive equivalent generic product.

Look at the second prescription. It shows that you will receive 100 (dtd C) tablets of Lanoxin, 0.125 mg. You will take

---

John D. Jones MD
Anytown, U.S.A.

DEA# 123456789   PHONE# 123-4567

NAME *Your Name.*   AGE *55*
ADDRESS *Anytown, U.S.A.*   DATE *5/23/92*

℞ *Lanoxin 0.125*
    dtd C
    Sig: iii stat, ii tomorrow AM,
    then i q̄ AM c̄ OJ

                                        John D. Jones, M.D.
                                        DISPENSE AS WRITTEN
REFILLS *prn*
LABEL *✓*   _____

                                              SUBSTITUTION

three tablets at once (iii stat), then two (ii) tomorrow morning (AM), and one (i) every (q) morning (AM) thereafter with (c) orange juice (OJ). You will receive the specific brand noted (dispense as written), you may receive refills as needed (prn), and the name of the drug will be on the package (✔).

Remember to check the label on the drug container when you receive your medicine. If the information on the label differs from what is written on the prescription, ask your pharmacist for an explanation. Be certain that you are receiving the right medication and the correct instructions for taking it.

TALKING TO YOUR PHARMACIST

Once you have read the prescription, its directions may seem clear enough, but will they seem clear when you get home? For example, the prescription for the Fiorinal states that you should take one capsule every four hours as needed. How many capsules can you take each day—four, six, . . . more? The phrase "as needed" is not clear, and unless you understand what it means, you don't know how much medication you can take per day. What if your prescription instructs you to take "one tablet four times a day?" What does "four times a day" mean? For some antibiotics, it may mean one tablet every six hours around the clock. For other medications, it may mean one tablet in the morning, one at noon, one in the early evening, and one at bedtime. For still others, it may mean one tablet every hour for the first four hours after you get up in the morning. Don't leave the pharmacy with unanswered questions; ask your pharmacist for an explanation of any confusing terms on your prescription.

Your pharmacist is a valuable resource in your health care. He or she should have a record of ALL the prescription and over-the-counter (see below) drugs you receive in order to detect any possible life-threatening drug interactions. It is therefore a good idea to choose a pharmacy that maintains careful records and then to stick with that pharmacy.

The pharmacist will be able to tell you if your medication is likely to cause drowsiness or nausea and if your therapy may be affected by smoking tobacco, eating certain foods, or drinking alcohol. He or she can tell you what to expect from the medication and about how long you will have to take it. Of course, treatments vary tremendously, but you should ask whether you will have to take medication for five to ten days (to treat a mild respiratory infection, for example) or for a few months (which might be necessary for a kidney infection).

You should discuss with your pharmacist the possible side effects of your medication and ask for a description of symptoms. The pharmacist can tell you which side effects require prompt attention from your physician. For example, one of the major side effects of the drug carbamazepine is the development of a blood disorder. Since a sore throat can be one of the early symptoms of a blood disorder, your pharmacist may instruct you to consult your physician if this symptom occurs.

Your pharmacist can also explain how to take your medicine. You need to know whether to take the drug before or after a meal or along with it. The timing of doses of a drug can make a big difference, and the effectiveness of each drug depends on following the directions for its use. Your pharmacist can tell you what is meant by the phrases "as needed," "as directed," and "take with fluid." For example, you may take water, but not milk, with some drugs. With other drugs, you should drink milk. Your pharmacist can also tell you how many refills you may have and whether you may need them.

OVER-THE-COUNTER DRUGS

Drugs that can be purchased without a prescription are referred to as over-the-counter (OTC) drugs. The largest selection is found in drugstores, of course, but they are also sold in grocery and convenience stores, airports, and even hotel lobbies. There are no legal requirements or limitations as to who may buy or sell them.

Products sold OTC contain amounts of active ingredients considered safe for self-treatment by consumers when instructions on the label are followed. Many people visit a doctor for ailments that can be treated effectively by taking nonprescription drugs. Actually, prescriptions are sometimes written for such drugs. Your pharmacist will be able to recommend appropriate OTC medications and how to use them.

On the other hand, if your pharmacist urges you to not take certain OTC drugs, follow the advice. For one thing, OTC drugs could affect the way your body reacts to prescription drugs you may be taking. For instance, people taking tetracycline should avoid taking antacids or iron-containing products at the same time; their use should be separated by an interval of at least two hours. Antacids and iron interfere with the body's absorption of tetracycline, thereby decreasing its effectiveness. So be sure you know what you are taking. If you are unsure of the type or contents of your medications, ask your doctor or pharmacist.

In the last several years, many medicines that formerly could be obtained only through a doctor's prescription have become available over the counter. These medicines can now be purchased OTC because of their established history of safety and efficacy. The Food and Drug Administration understands that certain medications, if available OTC, allow consumers to self-treat minor health problems, thereby reducing the nation's health-care costs. Accordingly, important medicines such as clotrimazole (a medicine to treat fungal infections), ibuprofen and naproxen (pain relievers), and nicotine gum (to help patients stop smoking) have been "switched" from prescription to OTC availability. Some medicines now available OTC are not identical to the prescription form, however. For example, cimetidine, famotidine, and ranitidine have been available for several years by prescription only to treat stomach ulcers. These medicines are now OTC, but the OTC form is designed for a different health problem (the prevention and treatment of heartburn) and offered at a reduced dosage. Therefore, if you need medication for stomach ulcer disease, a prescription is still required in order to provide the correct dosage. Note also that OTC availability of a medicine you've been taking through prescription does not mean you should stop the prescription form and change to the less expensive OTC form. If this situation arises, be sure to discuss the matter with your doctor or pharmacist.

GENERIC DRUGS

One way your pharmacist can help you save money is by dispensing generic drugs. *Generic* means not protected by trademark registration. The generic name of a drug is usually a shortened form of its chemical name. Any manufacturer can use the generic name when marketing a drug.

Usually a manufacturer uses a trade name (or brand name) as well as a generic name for a drug. A trade name is registered, and only the manufacturer who holds the trademark can use the trade name when marketing a drug. For example, only SmithKline Beecham can call their amoxicillin product

Amoxil, and only Squibb Pharmaceuticals can use the trade name Capoten for captopril. Most trade names are capitalized in print and usually include the registered symbol (®) after them. You should know both the generic and trade name of every drug you take.

Many people think that drugs with trade names are made by large manufacturers and generic drugs are made by smaller companies. In fact, a manufacturer may market large quantities of a drug under a brand name and also sell the base chemical to several other companies, some of which then sell the drug under its generic name and some of which sell it under their own brand name. For example, the antibiotic ampicillin is the base for over 200 different products, yet all ampicillin is produced by only a few dozen drug companies.

Generic drugs are generally priced lower than their trademarked equivalents, largely because they are not as widely advertised. Not every drug is available generically, however, and not every generic is significantly less expensive than its trademarked equivalent. Nevertheless, consumers may be able to save money by purchasing a generic product. To cite one example, 100 tablets of Inderal (40 mg) costs about $53, while the same quantity of the generic equivalent costs about $10— a savings of $43 or an impressive 80 percent.

For some drugs, it's inadvisable to shop around for a generic equivalent. Although the FDA has stated that no evidence exists to suspect serious differences between trade-name drugs and generic drugs, some differences are seen when the two types of drugs are compared. For example, because of variations in the way they are made or the fillers (nonactive ingredients) used, capsules from different manufacturers may not dissolve in the stomach at the same rate or to the same extent. This is especially true for the various generic carbamazepine, digoxin, phenytoin, and warfarin products. It is therefore important to discuss the advantages or disadvantages of any particular generic product with your doctor and pharmacist.

All states have some form of substitution law that allows pharmacists to fill prescriptions with the least expensive equivalent product. However, your doctor can authorize the use of a specific brand of medication on the prescription form (see the sample prescriptions on page 10). You should be aware that certain patients can sometimes respond in different ways to various equivalent products, and your doctor may have good reasons for being specific. Again, discuss this with your doctor.

MAIL-ORDER PRESCRIPTION DRUGS

Traditionally, Americans have purchased prescription medication at their neighborhood drugstore. Today this is no longer always the case. Some patients—especially those who may be very ill or unable to get around easily—simply find it more convenient to have their medications mailed directly to their homes. There are also many people who take medication on a regular basis for a chronic disease, such as high blood pressure or heart disease, who prefer home delivery. Actually, mail-order pharmacies are not all that new. The Veteran's Administration (VA) started a mail-order operation in the late 1940s. And the American Association of Retired Persons Pharmacy Service, which provides both OTC and prescription medication by mail, has been supplying medication to its members for more than 35 years. Still, the majority of people who get their medication by mail have been encouraged to do so because of group contracts with employers and insurers.

Most mail-order pharmacies maintain toll-free telephone lines to respond to questions from patients and physicians. And they may provide printed information about your prescription, just as many local pharmacies do. But when you do business by mail, there is an unavoidable loss of face-to-face interaction with your pharmacist, which is important to many people. Thus, before deciding whether buying prescription medications by mail is best for you and your family, carefully consider the various advantages and drawbacks.

HOW MUCH TO BUY

On a prescription, your doctor specifies exactly how many tablets or capsules or how much liquid medication you will receive. But if you must take a drug for a long period of time or if you are very sensitive to drugs, you may want to consider purchasing more or less than the amount specified.

The amount of medication to buy depends on several factors. One is the condition being treated. For example, medications to treat heart disease, high blood pressure, diabetes, or a thyroid condition may be purchased in large quantity because patients with such chronic conditions take medication for long periods. Chances are they will pay less per dose by purchasing in volume. In most cases the price per dose decreases with the amount purchased. In other words, a drug that usually costs six cents per tablet may cost four or five cents per tablet if you buy 100 at a time. Another factor is how much you can afford or—for those whose prescriptions are covered by insurance—how much your insurance company will pay. A third factor is the length of time your medication can be stored. Nitroglycerin tablets, for example, lose their effectiveness after about six months and should be replaced with a fresh supply. There is no reason to ask for more nitroglycerin in tablet form than will be needed during that period of time.

Many doctors prescribe only a single month's supply of a drug, even if it will be taken for a long time. If you wish to buy more, check with your pharmacist. It is also important to have enough medication on hand so you'll be covered—if you're away from your pharmacy while traveling, for example. Serious side effects could occur if you miss even a few doses of drugs such as propranolol or prednisone.

If you have been plagued by annoying side effects or have had allergic reactions to some drugs in the past, you may want to ask your pharmacist to dispense only enough medication on an initial prescription for a few days or a week. That way you can determine how your body reacts to the drug. Pharmacists cannot allow the return of a prescription medication once it has left the pharmacy. You may have to pay more per dose if the pharmacist dispenses a small quantity, but at least you will not be paying for a supply of medication your body can't tolerate. Be sure you can get the remainder of the prescribed amount of the drug if no serious or intolerable side effects occur. With some drugs, after you have received part of the intended amount, you cannot receive the remainder without another prescription.

STORING YOUR DRUGS

Before you leave the pharmacy, find out how you should store your medication. If drugs are stored in containers that do not protect them from heat or moisture, they may lose potency.

All medications should be kept in their original containers. One reason for this is that some drugs may lose potency when stored with other medications. A more important reason is to prevent confusion about which drug is being taken. And never remove the label from a prescription vial. It contains the name of the medication, directions for proper use, and the prescription number (which is helpful when the time comes for a refill).

You can safely store most prescription drugs at room temperature and out of direct sunlight. But even drugs dispensed in colored bottles or in containers that reflect light should be kept out of direct sunlight.

Some drugs require storage in the refrigerator; others should not be refrigerated. For example, some liquid cough suppressants thicken as they become cold and will not pour from the bottle. Some people keep nitroglycerin tablets in the refrigerator in the mistaken belief that the drug will be more stable when kept cold. This is not the case, however: Nitroglycerin should not be stored in the refrigerator.

Even if the label on your medication states "keep refrigerated," this does not mean you can keep the drug in the freezer compartment. If a drug is frozen and then thawed, coated tablets may crack and some liquids may separate into layers that can't be remixed.

Many people keep prescription drugs and other medications in the bathroom medicine cabinet, but this is one of the worst places to keep drugs. Small children can easily climb onto the sink and reach drugs stored above it. Meanwhile, the temperature and humidity changes in the bathroom may adversely affect the stability of prescription and OTC medication.

It is required by law that all prescription medications for oral use must be dispensed in childproof containers. If you find the container difficult to open AND if there are no small children in your home, ask your pharmacist to dispense your medication in a container that is not childproof.

Definitions Used to Describe Storage Temperatures

Excessive Cold	Less than 36°F (2°C)
Refrigerated	Between 36°F and 46°F (2°–8°C)
Cool	Between 46°F and 59°F (8°–15°C)
Room temperature	Between 59°F and 86°F (15–30°C)
Excessive heat	More than 104° F (40° C)

Do not keep unused prescription drugs. Flush leftover medication down the toilet or pour it down the sink, then wash and discard the empty container. Regularly clean out your medicine cabinet, and remove any drugs that are not being used or that have expired (the expiration date is sometimes shown on the container label). Such drugs can be dangerous to your children and guests, and you might be tempted to take them yourself if you develop similar symptoms in the future. Similar symptoms may not be due to the same disease, and you may be denied proper medication or even make your condition worse by taking the wrong medication.

It cannot be repeated too often: KEEP ALL MEDICATIONS AWAY FROM CHILDREN. If a child accidentally swallows medication or receives too much of a prescribed medication, IMMEDIATELY CALL YOUR LOCAL POISON CONTROL CENTER, A NEARBY EMERGENCY ROOM, OR YOUR DOCTOR for instructions and recommendations. These phone numbers should be written down in a readily accessible place. (For safety's sake, it is wise to keep a list of these and other important telephone numbers—such as those for the police and fire departments—near every telephone in your home.) You should also have an emetic (a vomit-inducing agent) such as syrup of ipecac on hand in case you are directed to empty a child's stomach. But do not administer an emetic (available without a prescription at your local drugstore) unless specifically instructed to do so by a medical professional.

Administering Medication Correctly

To derive the maximum benefit, you must use your medicine correctly. If you use drugs improperly, you may not receive their full therapeutic effects. Indeed, improper administration can be dangerous, since some drugs may become toxic if used incorrectly.

Before administering medications to older adults (that is, people 65 years of age or older) or children, ask your doctor for specific instructions. These groups of patients can be more sensitive to dosage amounts and side effects of medications than young and middle-aged adults.

As a person ages, the function of the kidneys, liver, and other organ systems in the body slows down. Compared with younger adults, people over 65 may have a reduced capacity to break down and remove medicines from their bodies. Therefore, it is sometimes recommended that older people receive lower initial doses of drugs, and that drug dosages be increased more slowly. In other cases, a different drug within the same class of medication may be administered because the side effects from the alternative drug may be less bothersome. For example, in the elderly population with diabetes, the oral antidiabetic agent glyburide may be more appropriate than chlorpropamide (another oral antidiabetic agent), which is associated with an increased chance of dangerously low blood sugar in the elderly. In general, physicians "start low and go slow" when prescribing medications and adjusting dosages for older patients. The drug profiles in this book will indicate in the WARNINGS section when caution is warranted for drugs given to older adults.

Infants and children also differ from adults in terms of how their bodies respond to medication. Depending on age and weight, the best dose of a medicine for a younger patient may be different from an adult dose. Accordingly, children may be given lower dosages of some medications (including antibiotics) and higher dosages of other medications (including phenytoin, carbamazepine, and phenobarbital) than adults.

AEROSOL SPRAYS

Many topical (applied to the skin) medications are packaged as pressurized aerosol sprays. These sprays usually cost more than the cream or ointment form of the same product. They are especially useful on very tender or hairy areas of the body where it is difficult to apply a cream or ointment. Aerosols can have a cooling effect on burns or rashes.

Before using an aerosol, shake the can to evenly disperse the particles of medication. Hold the container upright four to six inches from the skin. Press the nozzle for a few seconds, then release.

Never use an aerosol around the face or eyes. If your doctor tells you to treat part of your face, simply spray the solution onto your hand, then rub it in. If you get it into your eyes or on a mucous membrane, pain may result. It may even damage the eyes.

Aerosol sprays may feel cold when applied. If this sensation bothers you, ask your pharmacist or doctor whether another form of the same product is available.

BUCCAL TABLETS

A few drugs, including some forms of nitroglycerin, are prepared as tablets that must be placed under the lip or in the cheek. These products are designed to release a dose of the drug over a period of time. To take a buccal tablet properly, place it between the upper lip and gum (above the front teeth) or between the cheek and gum. If you eat or drink during the three to five hours it takes for the tablet to dissolve, place the tablet between the upper lip and gum. Do not go to sleep with a tablet in your mouth because it could slip down your throat and cause choking.

CAPSULES, TABLETS, AND ORAL POWDERS

Many people find it hard to swallow a tablet or capsule. If tablets or capsules tend to catch in your throat, rinse your mouth with water, or at least wet your mouth, before attempting to swallow them. Then place the tablet or capsule on the back of your tongue, take a drink, and gulp it down. If it seems too large to swallow or tends to stick in your throat, there is another possible option: Empty the capsule or crush the tablet in a spoon and mix it with applesauce, soup, or even chocolate syrup. But BE SURE TO CHECK WITH YOUR PHARMACIST BEFOREHAND, since some tablets and capsules must be swallowed whole and should not be crushed or opened. Your pharmacist can tell you which ones can and cannot be taken this way.

If you have trouble swallowing a tablet or capsule and prefer to not mix the medication with food, ask your doctor to prescribe an alternative in the form of a liquid or a chewable tablet instead.

Occasionally medications come in oral powder form (for example, cholestyramine and colestipol). Such preparations should be carefully mixed with liquids, then swallowed; they are not meant to be swallowed dry.

EAR DROPS

Ear drops must be administered so they fill the ear canal. To use ear drops properly, tilt your head to one side, turning the affected ear upward. Grasp the earlobe and gently pull it toward the ceiling and back to straighten the ear canal. When administering ear drops to a child, gently pull the child's earlobe downward and back. Fill the dropper and place the prescribed number of drops (usually a dropperful) into the ear. Be careful to avoid touching the sides or edge of the ear canal, because the dropper can easily become contaminated by such contact.

Keep the ear tilted upward for five to ten seconds while continuing to hold the earlobe. Your doctor may want you to gently insert a small wad of clean cotton into the ear to prevent the medication from seeping out. Do not wash or wipe the dropper after use; replace it in the bottle and tightly close the bottle to keep out moisture.

Before administering ear drops, you may warm the container by simply rolling it back and forth between your hands to bring the solution to body temperature. Do not place the bottle in boiling water, however: The ear drops may become so hot that they cause pain when placed in the ear. Boiling water can also cause the label to loosen or peel off and might even ruin the medication.

EYE DROPS AND EYE OINTMENTS

Before administering eye drops or ointments, wash your hands. Then sit or lie down and tilt your head back. Using your thumb and forefinger, gently and carefully pull your lower eyelid down to form a pouch. Hold the dropper close to your eyelid without touching it. Squeeze the prescribed amount of medicine into this pouch and slowly close your eye. Try not to blink. Keep your eye closed, and place one finger at the corner of the eye next to your nose for a minute or two, applying slight pressure (this prevents loss of medication through the duct that drains fluid from the surface of the eye into the nose and throat). Then wipe away any excess with a clean tissue. Do not wash or wipe the dropper before replacing it in the bottle—you might accidentally contaminate the rest of the medication. Close the bottle tightly to keep out moisture.

To administer an eye ointment, squeeze a line of ointment in the prescribed amount into the pouch formed as described above for administering eye drops (avoid touching the tube to your eyelid), and close your eye. Roll your eye a few times to spread the ointment.

Be sure the drops or ointments you apply are intended for use in the eye (all products manufactured for use in the eye must be sterilized to prevent eye infections). And check the expiration date on the label or container. Don't use a drug product after the specified date, and never use any eye product that has changed color. If it appears that your medication contains particles that weren't visible at the time of purchase, discard it.

LIQUIDS

Liquid medications are used in several different ways. Some are intended to be used externally on the skin; some are placed in the eye, ear, nose, or throat; still others are taken internally. Before taking or using any liquid medication, carefully read the label for specific directions.

A suspension is a liquid product containing particles that settle to the bottom of the container. It must be shaken before use so each application contains the right proportion of ingredients. If you don't shake it well each time, you may not get the correct amount of the active ingredient, and as the amount of liquid remaining in the bottle becomes smaller, the drug could become more concentrated. Thus, you may be getting more of the active ingredient than you need. A dose could even reach toxic levels.

When opening a bottle of liquid medication, point it away from you. Some of these solutions build up pressure inside the bottle. When opened, the liquid could spurt out and stain your clothing. If the medication is for application to the skin, pour a small quantity onto a cotton pad or a piece of gauze. (Don't use a large piece of cotton or gauze, since that will absorb more medication than is needed, resulting in waste.) Don't pour the medication into your cupped hand; you may spill some of it. If you're treating only a small area, spread the medication with your finger or a cotton-tipped applicator. But never dip cotton-tipped applicators or pieces of cotton or gauze into the bottle itself.

Liquid medications that are to be swallowed must be measured accurately. When your doctor prescribes one teaspoonful of medication, he or she is thinking of a 5-milliliter (mL) medical spoon. The ordinary teaspoons you have at home can hold anywhere from 2 to 10 mL of liquid. If you use one of these to measure your medication, you may get too little or too much drug with each dose. Ask your pharmacist for a medical teaspoon or one of the other plastic devices for accurately measuring liquid medications. Most of these items cost only a few cents; they are well worth their cost in ensuring accurate dosage. Incidentally, while it's true that many children balk at medication taken from a teaspoon, they often enjoy taking it from a "special" spoon.

NOSE DROPS AND SPRAYS

Before using nose drops or sprays, gently blow your nose if you can. To administer nose drops, fill the dropper, tilt your head back, and place the prescribed number of drops into your nose. To prevent contamination of the rest of the medicine, do not touch the dropper to the nasal membranes. Keep your head tilted for five to ten seconds, and sniff gently two or three times.

When using a nasal spray, do not tilt your head back. Insert the sprayer into the nose, but try to avoid touching the inner nasal membranes. Sniff and squeeze the sprayer at the same time. Do not release your grip on the sprayer until you have withdrawn it from your nose (to prevent nasal mucus and bacteria from entering the plastic bottle and contaminating its contents). After you have sprayed the prescribed number of times in one or both nostrils, gently sniff two or three times.

Unless your doctor has told you otherwise, you should not use nose drops or sprays for more than two or three days at a time. If they have been prescribed for a longer period, do not administer nose drops or sprays from the same container for more than one week. Bacteria from your nose can easily enter the container and contaminate the solution. If you must take medication for more than a week, purchase a new container. Never allow anyone else to use your nose drops or spray.

RECTAL SUPPOSITORIES

Rectal suppositories are used to deliver various types of medication. They may be used as laxatives, sleeping aids, tranquilizers, or preparations to relieve the itching, swelling, and pain of hemorrhoids. Regardless of the reason for their use, all rectal suppositories are inserted in the same way.

In extremely hot weather, a suppository may become too soft to handle properly. If this happens, place it in the refrigerator, in a glass of cool water, or under running cold water until it becomes firm. (A few minutes is usually sufficient.) Before inserting a suppository, remove any aluminum wrappings. Rubber finger coverings or disposable rubber gloves may be worn when inserting a suppository, but they are not necessary unless your fingernails are unusually long or sharp.

To insert a suppository, lie on your left side with your right knee bent. Push the suppository, pointed end first, into the rectum as far as is comfortable. You may quickly feel as if you want to have a bowel movement, but ignore that feeling and lie still for a few minutes. Delay trying to have a bowel movement for at least an hour. If you have trouble inserting a suppository or if the process is painful, coat the suppository with a thin layer of petroleum jelly or mineral oil.

Some manufacturers of suppositories used for hemorrhoids suggest that their product should be stored in the refrigerator. But don't assume that this is always the case. Ask your pharmacist for advice about proper storage.

SUBLINGUAL TABLETS

Some drugs, such as nitroglycerin, are prepared as tablets that must be placed under the tongue. Such medications are more rapidly or more completely absorbed into the bloodstream from the lining of the mouth than they are from the stomach and intestinal tract.

To take a sublingual tablet properly, place it under your tongue, close your mouth, and hold the saliva under your tongue for as long as you can before swallowing to allow the tablet to dissolve. A bitter taste in your mouth five minutes after taking a nitroglycerin tablet indicates that the drug has not yet been completely absorbed. Wait at least five minutes longer before drinking liquids. Drinking too soon may wash the medication into the stomach before it has been completely absorbed. Do not smoke, eat, or chew gum while the medication is dissolving.

THROAT LOZENGES AND DISCS

Both lozenges and discs contain medication that is released in the mouth to soothe a sore throat, to reduce coughing, or to treat laryngitis. Neither should be chewed; they should be allowed to dissolve in the mouth. After the lozenge or disc has dissolved, try not to swallow or drink any fluids for a while.

THROAT SPRAYS

To administer a throat spray, open your mouth fully and spray the medication as far back as possible. Hold the spray in your mouth for as long as you can, try not to swallow, and do not drink any fluids for several minutes. Swallowing a throat spray is not harmful, but if you find that your throat spray upsets your stomach, don't swallow it; simply spit it out.

TOPICAL OINTMENTS AND CREAMS

Most topical (applied to the skin) ointments and creams exert only local effects—that is, they affect only the area to which they are directly applied. Most creams and ointments are expensive (especially steroid products) and should be applied to the skin in as thin a layer as possible. A thin layer is just as effective as a thick layer, but less expensive. Moreover, some steroid-containing creams and ointments can cause toxic side effects if applied too heavily.

Before applying the medication, moisten the skin by immersing it in water or by dabbing the area with a clean, wet cloth. Blot the skin almost dry and apply the medication as directed. Gently massage it into the skin until the cream or ointment disappears.

If your doctor has not indicated whether you should receive a cream or an ointment, ask your pharmacist for the one you prefer. Creams are greaseless and do not stain your clothing; they are best to use on the scalp or other hairy areas of the body. However, if your skin is dry, ask for an ointment. Ointments help keep skin soft.

If your doctor tells you to place a wrap on the skin after the cream or ointment has been applied, you may use transparent plastic film like that used for wrapping food. A wrap holds the medication close to the skin and helps to keep the skin moist so the drug can be absorbed. To use a wrap correctly, apply the cream or ointment as directed, then wrap the area with a layer of transparent plastic film. Follow your doctor's directions EXACTLY, and keep the wrap in place only as long as you are told to do so. If you keep a wrap on the skin too long, too much of the drug may be absorbed, which may lead to increased side effects. Do not use a wrap without your doctor's approval, and never use one for an oozing lesion.

TRANSDERMAL PATCHES

Transdermal patches allow controlled, continuous release of medication. They are convenient and easy to use. Apply the patch to a hairless or clean-shaven area of skin, avoiding scars and wounds. Choose a site, such as the chest or upper arm, that is not subject to excessive movement. For best results and to minimize skin irritation, each time you replace a patch, apply the new patch to a different area of the body. Ask your doctor or pharmacist for guidance if necessary. In the event that a patch becomes dislodged, discard and replace it promptly to maintain the flow of medication. It is all right to bathe or shower with a patch in place.

If redness or irritation develops at the application site, consult your physician. Some people are sensitive to the materials used to make patches.

VAGINAL OINTMENTS AND CREAMS

Most vaginal products are packaged with complete instructions for use. If a woman is not sure how to administer vaginal medication, she should ask her pharmacist.

Before using any vaginal ointment or cream, read the directions. They will probably tell you to attach the applicator to the top of the tube and to squeeze the tube from the bottom until the applicator is completely filled. Then lie on your back with your knees drawn up. Hold the applicator horizontally or pointed slightly downward, and insert it into the vagina as far as it will go comfortably. Press the plunger down to empty the cream or ointment into the vagina. Withdraw the plunger and wash it in warm, soapy water. Rinse it thoroughly and allow it to dry completely.

VAGINAL TABLETS AND SUPPOSITORIES

Most packages of vaginal tablets or suppositories include complete directions for use, but you may wish to review these general instructions.

Remove any foil wrapping. Place the tablet or suppository in the applicator that is provided. Lie on your back with your knees drawn up. Hold the applicator horizontally or tilted slightly downward, and insert it into the vagina as far as it will comfortably go. Depress the plunger slowly to release the tablet or suppository into the vagina. Withdraw the applicator and wash it in warm, soapy water. Rinse it and let it dry completely.

Unless your doctor has told you otherwise, do not douche two to three weeks before or after you use vaginal tablets or suppositories. Be sure to ask your doctor for specific recommendations on douching.

Coping with Side Effects

Drugs are prescribed and taken precisely because they have certain desirable effects on the human body. The desirable reaction to a drug is known as the drug's activity or therapeutic effect. But drugs sometimes have undesirable effects as well. These unwanted effects are referred to side effects, adverse reactions, or, in some rare cases, lethal effects.

Even if you experience minor side effects, it is very important that you continue to take your medication exactly as it was prescribed. You should take the full dose at the appropriate times throughout the day for the length of time prescribed by your doctor. It is simply not appropriate to take a lesser amount of medication to avoid side effects or because your condition appears to be improving. It not valid to assume that taking half of the regular dose will provide half of the therapeutic effects. Indeed, a smaller dose may not provide any benefit whatsoever.

Some side effects are expected and unavoidable, but others may surprise the doctor as well as the patient. Such unexpected reactions may be due to an individual's peculiar response to the drug.

Side effects generally fall into one of two major categories—those that are obvious, and those that can be detected only through laboratory testing. Discussion between you and your doctor about your medication should not be limited to the most easily recognized side effects. Other, less obvious, side effects may also be harmful, and you should be sure you understand what they are.

If you know a particular side effect is expected from a specific drug, you can relax a little. Most expected side effects are temporary and need not cause alarm. You'll merely experience discomfort or inconvenience for a short time. For example, you may become drowsy after taking an antihistamine or develop an upset stomach after taking the antibiotic erythromycin. Of course, if you find minor side effects especially bothersome, you should discuss them with your doctor, who may be able to prescribe another drug or at least assure you that the benefits of the drug you are taking far outweigh its side effects. Sometimes side effects can be minimized or eliminated by changing your dosage schedule or taking the drug with meals. Be sure to consult your doctor or pharmacist if you have questions.

Some side effects signal a serious, perhaps even a dangerous, problem. If such side effects appear, you should notify your doctor immediately. The discussion that follows should help you determine whether any side effects you experience require attention.

OBVIOUS SIDE EFFECTS

Some side effects are obvious to the patient; others can be discerned only through laboratory testing. We divided our discussion according to the body parts affected by the side effects, then we arranged the topics in alphabetical order.

Circulatory System

Drugs may slow down or speed up the heartbeat. If a drug slows the heartbeat, you may feel drowsy and tired or even dizzy. If a drug accelerates the heartbeat, you probably will experience palpitations (thumping in the chest). You may feel as though your heart is skipping a beat occasionally. For most people, these symptoms do not indicate a serious problem. If they occur frequently, however, consult your doctor, who may prescribe other medication or adjust your dosage.

Some drugs can cause edema (fluid retention), in which fluid from the blood collects outside the blood vessels. Ordinarily, edema is not a serious condition. But if you are steadily gaining weight or have gained more than three pounds within a week, be sure to consult your doctor.

Drugs may decrease or increase blood pressure. When blood pressure decreases, you may feel drowsy or tired; you may become dizzy, or even faint, especially when you rise suddenly from a sitting or reclining position. If a drug makes you dizzy or light-headed, sit or lie down for a while. To avoid light-headedness when you stand, contract and relax the muscles of your legs for a few moments before rising. Push one foot against the floor while raising the other foot slightly, alternating feet so you are "pumping" your legs in a pedaling motion. Get up slowly, and be careful on stairs. When blood pressure increases, you may feel dizzy, have a headache or blurred vision, hear a ringing or buzzing in your ears, or experience frequent nosebleeds. If these symptoms occur, contact your doctor.

Ears

Although a few drugs may cause loss of hearing if taken in large quantities, hearing loss is uncommon. Drugs that are used to treat problems of the ear may cause dizziness, and many drugs produce tinnitus (a sensation of ringing, buzzing, thumping, or hollowness in the ears). Discuss any persistent hearing or ear problem with your doctor.

Eyes

Blurred vision is a common side effect of many drugs. Medications such as digoxin may cause you to see a halo around a lighted object, such as a television screen or a traffic light, and other drugs may cause night blindness. Chlordiazepoxide and clidinium combination makes it difficult to judge distance accurately while driving and also makes the eyes sensitive to sunlight. While the effects caused by chlordiazepoxide and clidinium combination are to be expected, the effects on the eyes caused by digoxin are danger signs of toxicity. In any case, if an eye-related problem occurs while you are taking medication, contact your physician.

Gastrointestinal System

The gastrointestinal system includes the mouth, esophagus, stomach, small and large intestines, and rectum. A side effect that affects this system can be expected from almost any drug. Many drugs produce diarrhea, constipation, dry mouth, mouth sores, difficulty in swallowing, heartburn, nausea, vomiting, loss of appetite, or abnormal cramping. Other drugs cause bloating and gas, and some cause rectal itching.

Diarrhea can be expected after taking many drugs, but in most cases it is temporary and self-limiting; that is, it should stop within three days. During this time, do not take any diarrhea remedy, and drink liquids to replace the fluid you are losing. If the diarrhea lasts more than three days or is accompanied by fever, call your doctor.

In some cases, diarrhea signals a problem. For example, some antibiotics can cause severe diarrhea. When diarrhea is severe—that is, diarrhea that lasts for several days, or stools that contain blood, pus, or mucus—the intestine may become ulcerated and begin to bleed. If severe diarrhea develops while taking antibiotics, contact your doctor.

As a side effect of drug use, constipation is more common but less serious than diarrhea. It occurs when a drug slows down the activity of the bowel. Medications such as amitriptyline and chlorpromazine have this effect. Constipation also develops when drugs cause moisture to be absorbed from the bowel, resulting in a more solid stool. Finally, constipation may arise if a drug acts on the nervous system to decrease nerve impulses to the intestine—an effect produced, for example, by methyldopa. Constipation caused by a drug can last for several days.

You may help relieve constipation by drinking eight to ten glasses of water a day, including more fiber in your diet, and getting plenty of exercise (unless your doctor directs you to do otherwise). Do not take laxatives unless your doctor directs you to do so. If constipation continues for more than three days, call your doctor.

Nervous System

Drugs that act on the nervous system may cause drowsiness or stimulation. If a drug causes drowsiness, you may become dizzy or your coordination may become impaired. If a drug causes stimulation, you may become nervous or have insomnia or tremors. Neither drowsiness nor stimulation is cause for concern for most people. When you are drowsy, however, you should be careful around machinery and should avoid driving. Some drugs cause throbbing headaches, and others produce tingling in the fingers or toes. If these symptoms don't disappear in a few days to a week, notify your doctor.

Respiratory System

Side effects common to the respiratory system include stuffy nose, dry throat, shortness of breath, and slowed breathing. A stuffy nose and dry throat usually disappear several days after starting a medication. If these side effects are bothersome, you may use nose drops (consult your doctor first) or throat lozenges, or you may gargle with warm salt water to relieve them. Shortness of breath is a characteristic side effect of some drugs (for example, propranolol). If shortness of breath occurs frequently, check with your doctor. It may be a sign of a serious side effect, or you may simply be overexercising.

Skin

Skin reactions include itching, swelling, rash, and sweating. Itching, swelling, and rash frequently indicate a drug allergy. You should not continue to take a drug if you develop an allergy to it, but be sure to contact your doctor before you stop taking the drug.

Some drugs increase sweating; others decrease it. Drugs that decrease sweating may cause problems during exercise or hot weather when your body needs to sweat to reduce body temperature.

If you have a minor skin reaction not diagnosed as an allergy, ask your pharmacist for a soothing cream. Your pharmacist may also suggest that you take frequent baths or dust the sensitive area with a suitable powder.

Another type of skin reaction is photosensitivity (also called phototoxicity or sun toxicity)—that is, unusual sensitivity to the sun. Tetracyclines can cause photosensitivity. If, while taking such a drug, you are exposed to the sun for even a brief period of time (10 or 15 minutes), you may experience a severe sunburn. This doesn't mean you have to stay indoors while taking these drugs, but you should be fully clothed while outside, and you should not remain in the sun too long. You should also use a protective sunscreen while in the sun—ask your pharmacist to help you choose one. Since medications may remain in your bloodstream after you stop taking them, you should continue to follow these precautions for two days after ending treatment with drugs that lead to photosensitivity.

SUBTLE SIDE EFFECTS

Some side effects are difficult to detect. You may not be aware of any symptoms at all, or you may notice only slight ones. Therefore, your doctor may want you to have periodic blood tests or eye examinations to ensure that no subtle damage is occurring while you are on certain medications.

Blood

A great many drugs affect the blood and the circulatory system but do not produce noticeable symptoms for some time. Some drugs decrease the number of red blood cells—the cells responsible for carrying oxygen and nutrients throughout the body. If you have too few red blood cells, you become anemic; you appear pale and feel tired, weak, dizzy, and perhaps hungry. Other drugs decrease the number of white blood cells—the cells responsible for combating infection. Having too few white blood cells increases susceptibility to infection and may prolong illness. If a sore throat or a fever begins after you start taking a drug and continues for a few days, you may have an infection and too few white blood cells to fight it. Call your doctor.

Kidneys

If one of the side effects of a drug is to reduce the kidneys' ability to remove chemicals and other substances from the blood, these substances begin to accumulate in body tissues. Over a period of time, this accumulation may cause vague symptoms, such as swelling, fluid retention, nausea, headache, or weakness. Obvious symptoms, especially pain, are rare.

Liver

Drug-induced liver damage may result in the accumulation of fat within the liver. Since the liver is responsible for converting many drugs and body chemicals into compounds that can be eliminated by other organs of the body (kidneys, lungs, gastrointestinal tract), drug-induced liver damage can result in a buildup of these substances. Because liver damage may be quite advanced before it produces any symptoms, periodic blood tests of liver function are recommended during therapy with certain drugs.

DRUG USE DURING PREGNANCY AND BREAST-FEEDING

Before taking any medication, it is very important to tell your doctor if you are pregnant (or planning to become pregnant) or are breast-feeding an infant. For most drugs, complete information on safety during pregnancy and while breast-feeding is lacking. This is not due to negligence or lack of concern on the part of regulatory agencies, but to the fact that it would be unethical to conduct drug experiments on pregnant and nursing women. With this in mind, you and your doctor should discuss the risks versus benefits of taking any medications during pregnancy or while nursing an infant.

MANAGEMENT OF SIDE EFFECTS

Consult the drug profiles to determine whether the side effects you are experiencing are minor (relatively common and usually not serious) or major (symptoms that indicate the need to consult your doctor). If your side effects are minor, you may be able to compensate for them (see the following table for suggestions). However, notify your doctor if you consider minor side effects to be persistent or particularly bothersome.

If you experience any major side effects, contact your doctor immediately. Your dosage may need adjustment, or you may have developed a sensitivity to the drug. Your doctor may want to switch you to an alternative medication. In any case, never stop taking a prescribed medication unless you discuss it with your doctor first.

Common Minor Side Effects

Side Effect	Management
Constipation	Increase the amount of fiber in your diet; drink plenty of fluids*; exercise*
Decreased sweating	Avoid working or exercising in the sun or under warm conditions
Diarrhea	Drink lots of water to replace lost fluids; if diarrhea lasts longer than three days, call your doctor
Dizziness	Avoid operating machinery or driving a car
Drowsiness	Avoid operating machinery or driving a car
Dry mouth	Suck on candy or ice chips, or chew sugarless gum
Dry nose and throat	Use a humidifier or vaporizer
Fluid retention (mild)	Avoid adding salt to foods; keep legs raised, if possible
Headache	Remain quiet; take aspirin* or acetaminophen*
Insomnia	Take the last dose of the drug earlier in the day*; drink a glass of warm milk at bedtime; ask your doctor about an exercise program
Itching	Take frequent baths or showers, or use wet soaks
Nasal congestion	If necessary, use nose drops*
Palpitations (mild)	Rest often; avoid tension; do not drink coffee, tea, or cola; stop smoking
Upset stomach	Take the drug with milk or food*

*Consult your doctor first

How Drugs Work

Prescription drugs fall into a number of categories according to the conditions for which they are given. In the following pages, we will provide you with a better understanding of the types of medications that are prescribed for different medical conditions.

CARDIOVASCULAR DRUGS

Antianginals

Since the heart is a muscle that must work continuously, it requires a constant supply of nutrients and oxygen. The chest pain known as angina can occur when there is an insufficient supply of blood, and consequently of oxygen, to the heart. There are several types of antianginal drugs. These include beta blockers (acebutolol, atenolol, betaxolol, bisoprolol, labetalol, metoprolol, nadolol, pindolol, propranolol, timolol), calcium channel blockers (diltiazem, nifedipine, verapamil), and vasodilators (nitroglycerin, isosorbide dinitrate). These drugs act by increasing the amount of oxygen that reaches the heart muscle.

Antiarrhythmics

If the heart does not beat rhythmically or smoothly (a condition called arrhythmia), its rate of contraction must be regulated. Antiarrhythmic drugs (disopyramide, mexiletine, procainamide, propranolol, quinidine, tocainide) prevent or alleviate cardiac arrhythmias by altering nerve impulses within the heart.

Anticoagulants

Drugs that prevent blood clotting are called anticoagulants (blood thinners). Anticoagulants fall into two categories.

The first category contains only one drug, heparin. Heparin must be given by injection, so its use is generally restricted to hospitalized patients.

The second category includes oral anticoagulants, principally derivatives of the drug warfarin. Warfarin may be used in the treatment of conditions such as stroke, heart disease, and abnormal blood clotting. It is also used to prevent the movement of a clot, a development that could cause serious problems. It acts by preventing the liver from manufacturing the proteins responsible for blood clot formation.

People taking warfarin must be careful to avoid using many other drugs (including some doses of aspirin) because the interaction of the other drugs with the anticoagulant could cause internal bleeding. Indeed, patients on warfarin should check with their pharmacist or physician before using any other medications, including over-the-counter products for coughs or colds. They should also have their blood checked frequently by their physician to ensure that the correct degree of blood thinning is maintained.

Antihyperlipidemics

Drugs for treating atherosclerosis, or hardening of the arteries, act to reduce the serum (the liquified portion of blood) levels of cholesterol and triglycerides (fats), which form plaques (deposits) on the walls of arteries. Some antihyperlipidemics, such as cholestyramine and colestipol, bind to bile acids in the gastrointestinal tract, thereby decreasing the body's production of cholesterol. Clofibrate, lovastatin, and pravastatin also decrease the body's production of cholesterol. Use of such drugs is generally recommended only after diet and lifestyle changes have failed to lower blood lipids to desirable levels. Even then, diet therapy should be continued.

Antihypertensives

Basically, high blood pressure is a condition in which the pressure of the blood against the walls of the blood vessels is higher than what is considered normal. High blood pressure, or hypertension, which can eventually cause damage to the brain, eyes, heart, or kidneys, is controllable. If medication for high blood pressure has been prescribed, it is very important that you continue to take it regularly, even if you don't notice any symptoms of hypertension. If hypertension is controlled, other damage can be prevented. Drugs that counteract or reduce high blood pressure can prolong the life of a hypertensive patient.

Several different drug actions produce an antihypertensive effect. Some drugs block nerve impulses that cause arteries to constrict; others slow the heart rate and decrease its force of contraction; still others reduce the amount of a certain hormone (aldosterone) in the blood that causes blood pressure to rise. The effect of any of these is to reduce blood pressure. The mainstay of antihypertensive therapy is often a diuretic, a drug that reduces body fluids. Examples of antihypertensive drugs include beta blockers, calcium channel blockers, ACE (angiotensin-converting enzyme) inhibitors (including benazepril, captopril, enalapril, lisinopril, and quinapril), and the agents clonidine, hydralazine, losartan, prazosin, and terazosin.

Beta Blockers

Beta-blocking drugs block the response of the heart and blood vessels to nerve stimulation, thereby slowing the heart rate and lowering blood pressure. They are used in the treatment of a wide range of diseases, including angina, hypertension, migraine headaches, arrhythmias and glaucoma. Metoprolol and propranolol are two examples of beta blockers.

Calcium Channel Blockers

Calcium channel blockers (diltiazem, nifedipine, verapamil) are used for the prevention of angina (chest pain). Verapamil is also useful in correcting certain arrhythmias (heartbeat irregularities) and lowering blood pressure. This group of drugs is thought to prevent angina and arrhythmias by blocking or slowing calcium flow into muscle cells, which results in vasodilation (widening of the blood vessels) and greater oxygen delivery to the heart muscle.

Cardiac Glycosides

Cardiac glycosides include drugs that are derived from digitalis (digoxin is an example). This type of drug slows the rate of the heart but increases its force of contraction. Cardiac glycosides act as both heart depressants and stimulants: They may be used to regulate irregular heart rhythm or to increase the volume of blood pumped by the heart in heart failure.

Diuretics

Diuretic drugs, such as chlorothiazide, chlorthalidone, furosemide, hydrochlorothiazide, and spironolactone, promote the loss of water and salt from the body (which is why they are sometimes called water pills). This loss of water and salt results in lower blood pressure. They also lower blood pressure by increasing the diameter of blood vessels. Because many antihypertensive drugs cause the body to retain salt and water, they are often used concurrently with diuretics. Most diuretics act directly on the kidneys, but there are different types of diuretics, each with different actions. This allows therapy for high blood pressure to be adjusted for individual patients.

Thiazide diuretics, such as chlorothiazide, chlorthalidone, and hydrochlorothiazide, are the most commonly prescribed water pills available today. They are generally well tolerated and can be taken once or twice a day. Since patients do not develop a tolerance to their antihypertensive effect, they can be taken for prolonged periods. However, a major drawback to thiazide diuretics is that they often deplete the body of potassium. This can be compensated for with a potassium supplement. Potassium-rich foods and liquids, such as apricots, bananas, and orange juice, can also be used to help correct a potassium deficiency. Salt substitutes are another source of potassium. If necessary, your doctor will direct you to a source of potassium appropriate for you.

Loop diuretics, such as furosemide, act more vigorously than thiazide diuretics. (Loop refers to the structures in the kidneys on which these medications act.) Loop diuretics promote more water loss than thiazide diuretics but they also deplete more potassium.

To remove excess water from the body but retain its store of potassium, manufacturers developed potassium-sparing diuretics. Drugs such as amiloride, spironolactone, and triamterene are effective in treating potassium loss, heart failure, and hypertension. Potassium-sparing diuretics are combined with thiazide diuretics in medications such as amiloride and hydrochlorothiazide combination, spironolactone and hydrochlorothiazide combination, and triamterene and hydrochlorothiazide combination. Such blends of drugs enhance the antihypertensive effect and reduce the loss of potassium.

Vasodilators

Vasodilating drugs cause the blood vessels to dilate (widen). Some of the antihypertensive agents, such as hydralazine and prazosin, lower blood pressure by dilating the arteries or veins. Other vasodilators are used in the treatment of stroke and diseases characterized by poor circulation. Ergoloid mesylates, for example, are used to reduce the symptoms of senility by increasing blood flow to the brain.

DRUGS FOR THE EARS

For an ear infection, a physician usually prescribes an antibiotic and a steroid, or a medication that contains a combination of the two. The antibiotic attacks the infecting bacteria, and the steroid reduces the inflammation and pain. Often a local anesthetic, such as benzocaine or lidocaine, may also be prescribed to relieve pain.

DRUGS FOR THE EYES

Almost all drugs that are used to treat eye problems can be used to treat disorders of other parts of the body as well.

Glaucoma is one of the major disorders of the eye, causing increased pressure within the eyeball. It is of special concern to people over 40 years of age. Although glaucoma is sometimes treated surgically, pressure in the eye can usually be reduced, and blindness prevented, through use of eye drops. Three drugs frequently prescribed for this purpose are epinephrine, pilocarpine, and timolol.

Epinephrine is another name for the body chemical called adrenaline. Epinephrine is secreted in the body when one must flee from danger, resist attack, or combat stress. It increases the amount of sugar in the blood, accelerates the heartbeat, and dilates the pupils. The mechanism by which epinephrine lowers pressure within the eye is not completely understood, but it appears to involve both a decrease in the production of aqueous humor (fluid) and an increase in the outflow of this fluid from the eye.

Pilocarpine is a cholinergic drug. As such it acts by stimulating parasympathetic nerve endings, which alter the activity of many organs throughout the body. For example, a cholinergic drug can cause the heart rate to decrease, intestinal activity to increase, and the bronchioles within the lungs to constrict. When used in the eyes, pilocarpine causes constriction of the pupils and increases the flow of aqueous humor (fluid) out of the eye, thereby reducing the pressure.

Timolol is a beta-blocking drug that works against glaucoma by decreasing the production of aqueous humor (fluid) in the eye. Unless they have a history of heart failure or asthma, most patients with glaucoma can use this medicine. Indeed, timolol accounts for about 70 percent of all glaucoma medications sold.

Steroids can be used to treat noninfectious eye inflammations as long as they are not used for an extended period of time. Pharmacists carefully monitor refill requests for eye drops, particularly if the drops contain steroids. They may refuse to refill such prescriptions until you have revisited your doctor. This is because with long-term use such products can cause further eye problems. Antibiotics are also used to treat bacterial eye infections.

GASTROINTESTINAL DRUGS

Anticholinergics

Anticholinergic drugs—for example, dicyclomine—slow the action of the bowel and reduce the amount of stomach acid. Because these drugs slow the action of the bowel by relaxing the muscles and relieving spasms, they are said to have an antispasmodic action.

Antidiarrheals

Diarrhea may be caused by many conditions, including influenza and ulcerative colitis, and it can sometimes occur as a side effect of drug therapy. Narcotics and anticholinergics slow the action of the bowel and can thereby help alleviate diarrhea. A medication such as diphenoxylate and atropine combination contains both a narcotic and an anticholinergic.

Antinauseants

Antinauseants reduce the urge to vomit. One of the most effective antinauseants is the phenothiazine derivative prochlorperazine. This medication acts on the vomiting center in the brain. It is often administered rectally and usually alleviates nausea and vomiting within a few minutes to an hour. Antihistamines are also commonly used to prevent nausea and vomiting, especially when these problems are caused by motion sickness. This type of medication may also work on the vomiting center in the brain.

Antiulcer Medications

Antiulcer medications are prescribed to relieve the symptoms and promote the healing of peptic ulcers. The antisecretory ulcer medications cimetidine, famotidine, nizatidine, and ranitidine work by suppressing the production of excess stomach acid. Another antiulcer drug, sucralfate, works by forming a chemical barrier over an exposed ulcer that protects the ulcer from stomach acid, much as a bandage protects a wound from debris. These drugs provide sustained relief from ulcer pain and promote healing. Omeprazole is a third type of antiulcer drug. It works by blocking acid production in the stomach.

HORMONES

Hormones are substances produced and secreted by a gland and act to stimulate and regulate body functions. Hormone drugs are given to mimic the effects of naturally produced hormones and are commonly given when naturally occurring hormones are not being produced in sufficient amounts to regulate specific body functions. This category of medication also includes oral contraceptives and certain types of drugs that are used to combat inflammatory reactions.

Antidiabetic Drugs

Insulin, which is secreted by the pancreas, regulates the level of glucose (a form of sugar) in the blood, as well as the metabolism of carbohydrates and fats. Insulin's counterpart, glucagon, stimulates the liver to release stored glucose. Both insulin and glucagon must be present in the right amounts to maintain the proper blood-sugar levels.

Treatment of diabetes mellitus (inability of the body to produce and/or utilize insulin) may involve an adjustment of diet and/or the administration of insulin or oral antidiabetic drugs. Glucagon is given only in emergencies, such as insulin shock, when blood-sugar levels must be raised quickly.

Oral antidiabetic medications induce the pancreas to secrete more insulin by acting on small groups of cells within the pancreas that make and store insulin. Oral antidiabetic medications are prescribed for diabetic patients who are not able to regulate their blood-sugar levels through diet modification alone. These medicines can be used by patients with both type I (insulin-dependent) and type II (non–insulin-dependent) diabetes. In patients with type I diabetes, these oral medicines (including glyburide or a newer medicine called metformin) are given in addition to insulin injections.

Sex Hormones

Although small amounts of sex hormones are secreted by the adrenal glands, for the most part these hormones are produced by the sex glands. Estrogens are the female hormones responsible for secondary sex characteristics such as development of the breasts and maintenance of the lining of the uterus. Testosterone (androgen) is the corresponding male hormone. It is responsible for secondary sex characteristics such as facial hair, a deepened voice, and the maturation of external genitalia. Progestin is also produced in females: It prepares the uterus for pregnancy.

Testosterone reduces elimination of protein from the body, thereby producing an increase in muscle size. Athletes sometimes take drugs called anabolic steroids (chemicals similar to testosterone) for this effect, but using medication this way is dangerous, since anabolic steroids can adversely affect the heart, nervous system, and kidneys.

Most oral contraceptives (birth control pills) combine estrogen and progestin, but some contain only progestin. Examples of progestin-only contraceptives include the Norplant implant and the Depo-Provera contraceptive device. Progestin aids in preventing ovulation, alters the lining of the uterus, and thickens cervical mucus—processes that help to prevent conception and implantation. The estrogen in birth control pills prevents egg production. Oral contraceptives have many side effects, so their use should be discussed with a physician.

Conjugated estrogens are used in replacement therapy to treat symptoms of menopause in women whose bodies are no longer able to produce estrogen in sufficient quantities. Medroxyprogesterone is used to treat uterine bleeding because of its ability to induce and maintain a lining in the uterus that resembles the lining produced during pregnancy. It also suppresses the release of the pituitary-gland hormone that initiates ovulation, and it is used for menstrual problems.

Steroids

The pituitary gland secretes adrenocorticotropic hormone (ACTH), which directs the adrenal glands to produce adrenocorticosteroids, such as cortisone. Oral steroid preparations (prednisone, for example) may be used to treat poison ivy, hay fever, or insect bites as well as inflammatory diseases such as arthritis. How these drugs relieve inflammation is currently unknown.

Steroids may also be applied to the skin to deal with certain inflammatory skin conditions. Triamcinolone and the combination of fluocinonide, hydrocortisone, and iodochlorhydroxyquin are examples of steroid hormone creams or ointments.

Thyroid Drugs

In the past, thyroid preparations were made by drying and pulverizing the thyroid glands of animals and then forming them into tablets. That medication is in minimal use today because people who are unable to produce a sufficient amount of thyroid hormone usually turn to a synthetic form, such as levothyroxine. In fact, thyroid hormone was one of the first hormone drugs to be produced synthetically.

ANTI-INFECTIVES

Antibiotics

Antibiotics are used to treat a wide variety of bacterial infections. Most antibiotics are either derived from molds or produced synthetically. They inhibit the growth of bacteria by interfering with the production of certain biochemicals necessary to sustain the bacteria's life or by interfering with the bacteria's ability to use nutrients. The body's defenses then have a much easier time eliminating the infection.

When used properly, antibiotics are usually effective. To treat an infection adequately, however, antibiotics must be taken regularly for a specific period of time. If they are not taken for the prescribed period, microorganisms resistant to the antibiotic are given the opportunity to continue growing, and the infection could recur. Aminoglycosides, cephalosporins, erythromycins, penicillins (including ampicillin and amoxicillin), quinolones, and tetracyclines are some examples of antibiotics.

Antibiotics do not counteract viruses, such as those causing the common cold, so their use in cold therapy is inappropriate.

Antivirals

Antiviral drugs are used to combat viral infections. An antiviral called acyclovir is being used in the management of herpes. This medication reduces the reproduction of the herpes virus in initial outbreaks, lessens the number of outbreaks of recurrent infection, and speeds the healing of herpes blisters. Acyclovir does not cure the disease, however.

Vaccines

Vaccines were used long before antibiotics became available. A vaccine contains weakened or dead disease-causing microorganisms or parts of such organisms, which activate the body's immune system to produce a natural defense against a particular disease (such as polio or measles). A vaccine is usually given to prevent a specific disease, but it may also be used to alleviate or treat an infectious disease.

Other Anti-infectives

Drugs called anthelmintics are used to treat worm infestations. Fungal infections are treated with antifungals, such as nystatin, that destroy and prevent the growth of fungi.

A pediculicide is a drug used to treat a person infested with lice, while a scabicide is prescribed to deal with scabies.

ANTINEOPLASTICS

Antineoplastic drugs are used in the treatment of cancer. Most of the drugs in this category prevent the growth of rapidly dividing cells, such as cancer cells. Antineoplastics are, without exception, extremely toxic and can cause serious side effects. But for many cancer victims, the benefits derived from chemotherapy with antineoplastic drugs far outweigh the risks.

TOPICAL DRUGS

Drugs are often applied topically (locally to the skin) to treat skin disorders so there are minimal systemic (throughout the body) side effects. Antibiotic creams or ointments are prescribed for skin infections; adrenocorticosteroids are used to treat inflammatory skin conditions.

Another common dermatologic (skin) problem is acne. Acne is often treated with over-the-counter drugs, but it sometimes requires prescription medication. Antibiotics such as clindamycin, erythromycin, and tetracycline are used orally or applied topically to slow the growth of the bacteria that play a role in the formation of acne pustules. Keratolytics (agents that soften the skin and cause the outer cells to slough off) are also sometimes prescribed.

Some medications that are applied to the skin have more far-reaching effects in the body. For example, nitroglycerin can be placed on the skin in the form of an ointment or patch and then absorbed into the bloodstream. The absorbed nitroglycerin dilates blood vessels and alleviates the chest pain known as angina. Clonidine, estrogen, and scopolamine, are also available in the form of transdermal patches.

CENTRAL NERVOUS SYSTEM DRUGS

Amphetamines

Amphetamines or adrenergic drugs are commonly used as anorectics (drugs used to reduce the appetite). These drugs temporarily quiet the part of the brain that causes hunger, but they also keep a person awake, speed up the heart, and raise blood pressure. After two to three weeks, these medications begin to lose their effectiveness as appetite suppressants.

Amphetamines stimulate most people, but they have the opposite effect on hyperkinetic children. Hyperkinesis (the condition of being highly overactive) is difficult to diagnose or define and requires a specialist to treat. But when hyperkinetic children take amphetamines or the adrenergic drug methylphenidate, their level of activity diminishes. Most likely, amphetamines quiet these youngsters by selectively stimulating parts of the brain that ordinarily control activity.

Analgesics

Pain is not a disease, but a symptom of some other problem. Drugs used to relieve pain are called analgesics, which form a rather diverse group. We do not fully understand how most analgesics work. In fact, whether or not they all act on the brain is unknown. In any case, analgesics fall into two categories: They may be either narcotic or nonnarcotic.

Narcotics are derived from the opium poppy. They act on the brain to relieve pain, often bringing on drowsiness and a feeling of well-being. Some narcotics relieve coughing spasms and are used in cough syrups. Unfortunately, narcotics are addictive. To date, attempts by manufacturers to produce nonaddictive synthetic narcotic derivatives have not succeeded.

Nonnarcotic pain relievers are also used. Salicylates (aspirin) and nonsteroidal anti-inflammatory drugs (NSAIDs) are the most frequently administered pain relievers in the United States today. While aspirin ordinarily does not require a prescription, doctors often write prescriptions for it to treat diseases such as arthritis.

Acetaminophen may be used in place of aspirin to relieve pain, but it does not reduce inflammation.

A number of analgesics contain codeine or other narcotics combined with nonnarcotic analgesics (such as aspirin or acetaminophen). These analgesics are not as potent as pure narcotics but are frequently as effective. Because these medications contain narcotics, however, they have the potential for abuse and must be used with caution.

Antianxiety/sedatives

Medications used in the treatment of anxiety, panic disorder, and insomnia selectively reduce the activity of certain chemicals in the brain. Drugs formulated to relieve anxiety include barbiturates, benzodiazepines, and buspirone. These drugs are not offered to relieve the stresses of everyday life; they are used only when indicated by your doctor. Drugs used to induce sleep in insomniacs include diphenhydramine, doxepin, hydroxyzine, and triazolam.

Anticonvulsants

Drugs such as carbamazepine and phenytoin are used to control seizures and other symptoms of epilepsy. They selectively reduce excessive stimulation in the brain.

Antidepressants

Tricyclic antidepressants (such as amitriptyline), selective serotonin reuptake inhibitors (such as fluoxetine, paroxetine, and sertraline) tetracyclic antidepressants (such as maprotiline), and monoamine oxidase (MAO) inhibitors (such as phenelzine) are used to combat depression. Antidepressants are also used in the preventive treatment of migraine headaches and other types of pain, although the manner in which they help to provide relief is not clearly understood.

Antidepressants may produce serious side effects, and they can interact with other drugs. MAO inhibitors can also mix with certain foods, resulting in dangerous increases in blood pressure. Therefore, they should be used very carefully.

Anti-inflammatory Drugs

Inflammation is the body's response to injury. It causes swelling, pain, fever, redness, and itching. Aspirin is one of the most effective anti-inflammatory drugs. Other drugs, called non-steroidal anti-inflammatory drugs (for example, fenoprofen, ibuprofen, indomethacin, naproxen, and tolmetin), relieve inflammation and may be more effective than aspirin in certain individuals. Steroids are also used to treat inflammatory diseases.

When sore muscles tense, they cause pain, inflammation, and spasm. Skeletal muscle relaxants (for example, aspirin, orphenadrine, and caffeine combination, as well as meprobamate and aspirin combination) can relieve these symptoms. Skeletal muscle relaxants are often given in combination with an anti-inflammatory drug such as aspirin. Some doctors believe that aspirin and rest are better than skeletal muscle relaxants for alleviating the symptoms of muscle strain.

Antiparkinsonism Agents

Parkinson's disease is a progressive disorder caused by a chemical imbalance in the brain. Victims of Parkinson's disease have uncontrollable tremors, develop a characteristic stoop, and eventually become unable to walk. Drugs such as benztropine, bromocriptine, levodopa, selegiline, and trihexyphenidyl are used to correct the chemical imbalance, thereby relieving the symptoms of the disease. Benztropine and trihexyphenidyl are also used to relieve tremors brought on by other medications.

Antipsychotics

Major tranquilizers or antipsychotic agents are usually prescribed for patients with psychoses (certain types of mental disorders). These drugs calm certain areas of the brain but permit the rest of the brain to function normally. They act as a screen that allows transmission of some nerve impulses but restricts others. The drugs most frequently used are phenothiazines, such as chlorpromazine and thioridazine.

RESPIRATORY DRUGS

Antihistamines

Histamine is a body chemical that, when released in the body, typically causes swelling and itching. Antihistamines counteract these allergy symptoms by blocking the effects of histamine and are used for mild respiratory allergies, such as hay fever. Diphenhydramine and other antihistamines are relatively slow-acting. Severe allergic reactions sometimes require the use of epinephrine (which is not an antihistamine). In its injectable form, epinephrine acts very quickly.

Some types of antihistamines are also used to prevent or treat the symptoms of motion sickness. Diphenhydramine and meclizine are used specifically for this purpose.

Antitussives

Antitussives control coughs. There are many over-the-counter (nonprescription) antitussives available, most of which contain dextromethorphan. Codeine is a narcotic antitussive that is an ingredient in many prescription cough medications. Before they can relieve a cough, these preparations must be absorbed into the blood, circulate through the system, and then act on the brain.

Bronchodilators

Bronchodilators (agents that open airways in the lungs) and medications that relax smooth-muscle tissue (such as that found in the lungs) are used to improve breathing. Aminophylline and theophylline are oral bronchodilators commonly used to relieve the symptoms of asthma and pulmonary emphysema. Albuterol and metaproterenol are bronchodilators available orally or as inhalants and act directly on the muscles of the bronchi (breathing tubes).

Decongestants

Decongestants constrict blood vessels in the nose and sinuses to open air passages. They are available in different forms: as oral preparations, nose drops, and nose sprays. Oral decongestants are slow-acting but do not interfere with the production of mucus or movement of the cilia (hairlike structures) of the respiratory tract. They can increase blood pressure, however, so they should be used cautiously by patients who have high blood pressure. Topical decongestants (nose drops or spray) provide almost immediate relief. They do not increase blood pressure as much as oral decongestants, but they do slow the movement of the cilia. People who use these products may develop a tolerance for them. (Tolerance can be described as a need for ever-increasing dosages to achieve a beneficial effect.) One disadvantage of developing a tolerance is that as the dosage increases, the risk of side effects also increases. Topical decongestants should not be used for more than a few days at a time.

Expectorants

Expectorants are used to change a nonproductive cough to a productive one (that is, one that brings up phlegm). Expectorants are supposed to increase the amount of mucus produced, but drinking water or using a vaporizer or humidifier is probably more effective. The only expectorant judged to be safe and effective is guaifenesin. Older products that contain expectorants such as ammonium chloride and terpin hydrate have been removed from the OTC market.

VITAMINS AND MINERALS

Vitamins and minerals are chemical substances that are vital to the maintenance of normal body function. Most of us obtain enough vitamins and minerals in our regular diet, but some people develop vitamin deficiencies. Serious nutritional deficiencies lead to diseases such as pellagra and beriberi, which must be treated by a physician. People who have an inadequate or restricted diet, people who have certain disorders or debilitating illnesses, and women who are pregnant or breast-feeding are among those who may benefit from taking supplemental vitamins and minerals. Even these people should consult a doctor to verify the need for supplements.

Drug Profiles

On the following pages are drug profiles for the most commonly prescribed drugs, as well as a few selected over-the-counter medications. These profiles are arranged alphabetically according to the generic name.

A drug profile summarizes the most important information about a particular drug. By studying a drug profile, you will learn what to expect from your medication, when to be concerned about possible side effects, which drugs interact with the drug you are taking, and how to take the drug to achieve its maximum benefit. Each profile includes the following information:

generic name

The drugs profiled in this book are listed by generic names. You should know both the generic and the trade names of all of the medications you are taking. If you don't know the contents of your medication, check with your pharmacist.

BRAND NAMES (Manufacturers)
The most common trade names of each generic product are listed, along with the manufacturers' names. Not every available trade name is included, but as many as possible have been listed. "Various manufacturers" is listed for some of the generic names—this indicates that there are generic products available.

TYPE OF DRUG
The chemical or pharmacologic class or pharmacological effect is listed for each generic drug.

INGREDIENTS
The components of each drug product are itemized. Many drugs contain several active chemical components; all are included under this category.

DOSAGE FORMS
The most common forms (for example, tablets, capsules, liquid, suppositories) of each profiled drug are listed, as well as

the drug's alcohol content, if any. Strengths or concentrations are also provided.

STORAGE

Storage requirements for each of the dosage forms listed are discussed. These directions should be followed carefully in order to ensure the potency of your medications.

USES

It is important that you understand why you are taking each of your medications. This section includes the most important and most common clinical uses for each drug profiled. Your doctor may prescribe a drug for a reason that does not appear on this list. The exclusion does not mean that your doctor has made an error. However, if the use for which you are taking a drug does not appear in this category and if you have any questions about why the drug was prescribed, consult your doctor. A description of how the drug is thought to work is also given in this section.

TREATMENT

Instructions are provided on how to take each profiled medication in order to obtain its maximum benefit. Information can be found on whether the drug can be taken with food; how to apply the ointment, cream, ear drops, or eye drops; how to insert suppositories; and recommendations for what to do if you miss a dose of your medication.

SIDE EFFECTS

Minor. The most common and least serious reactions to a drug are listed in this section. Most of these side effects, if they occur, disappear in a day or two. Do not expect to experience these side effects; but if they occur and are particularly annoying, do not hesitate to seek medical advice.

Suggestions for preventing or relieving some of these side effects are also provided.

Major. Major side effects are less common than minor side effects, and you will probably never experience them. However, should any of the reactions listed in this section occur, you should call your doctor. These reactions indicate that something may be going wrong with your drug therapy. You may have developed an allergy to the drug, or some other problem could have occurred. If you experience a major side effect, it may be necessary to adjust your dosage or to substitute a different medication in your treatment. It is important to discuss this with your doctor.

New side effects are being reported daily. If you experience a reaction that is bothersome or severe, consult your doctor immediately, even if the side effect is not mentioned in this publication.

INTERACTIONS

This section lists the medications (both prescription and over-the-counter drugs) and foods that can interact with the profiled drug. Certain drugs are safe when used alone but may cause serious reactions when taken in combination with other drugs or chemicals or certain foods. A description of how the profiled drug interacts with other drugs or foods and what to expect if the two are taken together is also provided. Not all possible drug combinations have been tested. So it is important that your pharmacist and health care providers be aware of all the drugs you are taking (including prescription, over-the-counter, homeopathic, and natural product remedies).

WARNINGS

This section lists the precautions necessary for safe use of the profiled drug. It provides information on drugs that should be avoided if you have had a previous allergic reaction or severe drug reaction, as well as information on the conditions or disease states that require close monitoring while this drug is being taken. In this section you will also find out whether the profiled drug is likely to affect your driving ability, whether you are likely to become tolerant to its effects, if it is dangerous to stop taking the drug abruptly, and if you should discuss with your doctor stopping the drug before having surgery or any other medical or dental procedure.

Certain individuals are allergic to the color additive FD&C Yellow No. 5 (tartrazine). This section provides information on the tartrazine content of the various dosage forms.

Other information included in this category might concern supplemental therapy—for example, drinking extra fluids while treating a urinary tract infection or wearing cotton underpants while treating a vaginal infection.

A discussion of the known risks of treatment with this drug during pregnancy or while breast-feeding an infant is provided. It should be kept in mind that for the majority of drugs available, the risks to a fetus or nursing infant are not known. Experiments are not usually conducted on pregnant women and infants (for ethical reasons). You should therefore discuss the risks and benefits of any particular drug therapy with your doctor if you are pregnant, are planning to become pregnant, or are nursing an infant.

---

acarbose

BRAND NAME (Manufacturer)
Precose (Bayer)
TYPE OF DRUG
Oral antidiabetic
INGREDIENT
acarbose
DOSAGE FORM
Tablets (50 mg and 100 mg)
STORAGE
This medication should be stored at room temperature in a tightly closed container. It should not be refrigerated or frozen. Discard any outdated medication.

USES
Acarbose is used for the treatment of the form of diabetes mellitus that appears in adulthood and cannot be managed by exercise and control of diet alone. This kind of diabetes is known as type II or non–insulin-dependent diabetes. Acarbose works differently from other antidiabetic medications: It does not act to lower your blood sugar. Instead, it works to reduce the amount of sugar that your body can absorb from food. Acarbose can be used alone or with other oral antidiabetic agents (such as sulfonylureas).

TREATMENT
In order for this medication to work correctly, it must be taken at the beginning of each main meal, as directed by your doctor. It is important to avoid missing any doses of acarbose. However, if you have already finished a meal and forgot to take your dose, do not take the missed dose at all. Just return

to your regular dosing schedule, taking the next dose at the beginning of your next main meal. Do not double the dose.

SIDE EFFECTS

Minor. Abdominal pain, diarrhea, and stomach gas. These side effects are common with acarbose and tend to lessen as your body adjusts to the medication.

Major. You should tell your doctor about any side effects that are persistent or particularly bothersome. IT IS ESPECIALLY IMPORTANT TO TELL YOUR DOCTOR about severe abdominal pain or discomfort as well as persistent diarrhea or stomach gas.

INTERACTIONS

Acarbose interacts with several types of medications:

1. Acarbose may reduce the effectiveness of digestive enzymes.

2. Drugs such as charcoal or other absorbents may interfere with the action of acarbose.

WARNINGS

• It is important to tell your doctor if you have ever had an unusual or allergic reaction to any medication, especially to acarbose.

• It is also important to tell your doctor if you now have or have ever had anemia or liver disease, any type of stomach or intestinal disorders, or any complications from diabetes.

• Before having surgery or any other medical or dental treatment, be sure to tell your doctor or dentist that your are taking acarbose.

• Follow the special diet provided by your doctor. This is an important part of controlling your blood sugar and is necessary in order for this medication to work properly.

• Test for sugar in your urine as directed by your doctor. It is a convenient way to determine whether your diabetes is being controlled by this medication.

• Acarbose does not cause hypoglycemia (low blood sugar), even if it is taken without food. However, acarbose is sometimes used with other antidiabetic agents that may cause hypoglycemia. IT IS IMPORTANT TO REMEMBER THAT acarbose will interfere with your body's ability to absorb table sugar. If you experience symptoms of hypoglycemia (such as anxiety, chills, cold sweats, cool or pale skin, drowsiness, excessive hunger, headache, nausea, nervousness, rapid heartbeat, shakiness, or unusual tiredness or weakness), you need to eat or drink something containing GLUCOSE OR DEXTROSE right away. Table sugar will not be absorbed by your body if you are taking acarbose. It is important for your family and friends to know the symptoms of low blood sugar. They should understand what to do if they observe any of these symptoms in you.

• Be sure to tell your doctor if you are pregnant or plan to become pregnant. This drug has not been studied for use during pregnancy. Your doctor may switch you to insulin while you are pregnant. Also be sure to tell your doctor if you are breast-feeding an infant. Small amounts of acarbose may pass into breast milk.

acetaminophen and codeine combination

BRAND NAMES (Manufacturers)
acetaminophen with codeine (various manufacturers)
Capital with Codeine (Carnrick)
Phenaphen-650 with Codeine (Robins)
Phenaphen with Codeine (Robins)
Tylenol with Codeine (McNeil)
TYPE OF DRUG
Analgesic combination
INGREDIENTS
acetaminophen and codeine
DOSAGE FORMS
Tablets (300 mg acetaminophen with 15 mg, 30 mg, or
   60 mg codeine; 325 mg acetaminophen with 30 mg
   or 60 mg codeine; 650 mg acetaminophen with
   30 mg codeine)
Capsules (325 mg acetaminophen with 15 mg, 30 mg,
   or 60 mg codeine)
Oral elixir (120 mg acetaminophen and 12 mg codeine
   per 5-mL spoonful, with 7% alcohol)
On the label of the vial of tablets or capsules, the name of
   this drug may be followed by a number that refers to the

amount of codeine present (#2 has 15 mg codeine, #3 has 30 mg codeine, and #4 has 60 mg codeine).

STORAGE

This medication should be stored at room temperature. It should never be frozen.

USES

Acetaminophen and codeine combination is used to relieve mild to severe pain (formulations of this medication with higher codeine contents are used to relieve more severe pain). Codeine is a narcotic analgesic that acts upon on the central nervous system (brain and spinal cord) to relieve pain.

TREATMENT

In order to avoid stomach upset, you can take this medication with food or milk.

This medication works most effectively if you take it at the onset of pain, rather than waiting until the pain becomes intense.

Measure the dose of the liquid form of this medication carefully with a specially designed 5-mL measuring spoon. An ordinary kitchen teaspoon is not accurate enough for measuring the dosage.

If you are taking this medication on a regular schedule and you miss a dose, take the missed dose as soon as possible, unless it is almost time for the next dose. In that case, don't take the missed dose at all; just return to your regular dosing schedule. Do not double the next dose.

SIDE EFFECTS

Minor. Constipation, dizziness, drowsiness, dry mouth, false sense of well-being, flushing, light-headedness, loss of appetite, nausea, painful or difficult urination, or sweating. These side effects should disappear as your body adjusts to the medication.

If you are constipated, increase the amount of fiber in your diet (fresh fruits and vegetables, salads, bran, and whole-grain breads), exercise, and drink more water (unless your doctor directs you to do otherwise).

To reduce mouth dryness, chew sugarless gum or suck on ice chips or hard candy.

If you feel dizzy or light-headed, sit or lie down for a while; get up slowly from a sitting or reclining position; and be careful on stairs.

Major. Tell your doctor about any side effects that are persistent or particularly bothersome. IT IS ESPECIALLY IMPORTANT TO TELL YOUR DOCTOR about anxiety, difficulty in breathing, excitation, fatigue, palpitations, rash, restlessness, sore throat and fever, tremors, unusual bleeding or bruising, weakness, or yellowing of the eyes or skin.

INTERACTIONS

This medication interacts with several other types of drugs:

1. Concurrent use with other central nervous system depressants (such as alcohol, antihistamines, barbiturates, benzodiazepine tranquilizers, muscle relaxants, and phenothiazine tranquilizers) or with tricyclic antidepressants can cause extreme drowsiness.

2. A monoamine oxidase (MAO) inhibitor taken within 14 days of this medication can lead to unpredictable and severe side effects.

3. Long-term use and high doses of the acetaminophen portion of this medication can increase the effects of oral anticoagulants (blood thinners, such as warfarin); this combination may lead to bleeding complications.

4. Anticonvulsants (antiseizure medications), barbiturates, and alcohol can increase the liver toxicity caused by large doses of the acetaminophen portion of this medication.

BE SURE TO TELL YOUR DOCTOR about any medications you are currently taking, especially any listed above.

WARNINGS

• Tell your doctor about unusual or allergic reactions you have had to any medications, especially to acetaminophen, codeine, or other narcotic analgesics (such as hydrocodone, hydromorphone, meperidine, methadone, morphine, oxycodone, and propoxyphene).

• Tell your doctor if you now have or if you have ever had an acute abdominal condition, asthma, a blood disorder, brain disease, colitis, epilepsy, gallstones or gallbladder disease, head injuries, heart disease, kidney disease, liver disease, lung disease, mental illness, prostate disease, thyroid disease, or urethral strictures.

• If this drug makes you dizzy or drowsy, do not take part in any activity that requires alertness, such as driving a car or operating potentially dangerous equipment.

• Before having surgery or any other medical or dental treatment, be sure to tell your doctor or dentist that you are taking this medication.

• Because this product contains codeine, it has the potential for abuse and must be used with caution. Usually, it should not be taken on a regular schedule for longer than ten days at a time. Tolerance develops quickly; do not increase the dosage or stop taking the drug abruptly unless you first consult your doctor. If you have been taking large amounts of this medication for long periods, you may experience a withdrawal reaction (diarrhea, excessive yawning, gooseflesh, irritability, muscle aches, nausea, runny nose, shivering, sleep disorders, stomach cramps, sweating, trembling, vomiting, or weakness). Your doctor may, therefore, want to reduce the dosage gradually.

• Because this product contains acetaminophen, additional drugs that contain acetaminophen should not be taken without first getting your doctor's approval. Be sure to check the labels on over-the-counter pain, sinus, allergy, asthma, diet, cough, and cold products before you use them in order to see if they also contain acetaminophen.

• Be sure to tell your doctor if you are pregnant. The effects of this medication during pregnancy have not been thoroughly studied in humans. Codeine used regularly in large doses during pregnancy can result in addiction of the fetus, leading to withdrawal symptoms (diarrhea, excessive crying, excessive yawning, irritability, fever, sneezing, tremors, or vomiting) at birth. Also tell your doctor if you are breast-feeding an infant. Small amounts of this drug may pass into breast milk and cause drowsiness in the nursing infant.

---

acetaminophen and hydrocodone combination

BRAND NAMES (Manufacturers)
acetaminophen with hydrocodone (various manufacturers)
Anexsia (Mallinckrodt)

Co-Gesic (Central)
Hy-Phen (Ascher)
Lortab (Russ)*
Lorcet (UAD)
Vicodin (Knoll)
Vicodin ES (Knoll)
Zydone (DuPont)
*Available in different strengths
TYPE OF DRUG
Analgesic combination
INGREDIENTS
acetaminophen and hydrocodone
DOSAGE FORMS
Tablets (500 mg acetaminophen with 2.5 mg, 5 mg, or
  7.5 mg hydrocodone; 650 mg acetaminophen with
  7.5 mg hydrocodone; 650 mg acetaminophen with
  10 mg hydrocodone, 750 mg acetaminophen with
  7.5 mg hydrocodone)
Capsules (500 mg acetaminophen with 5 mg hydrocodone)
Liquid (167 mg acetaminophen with 2.5 mg hydrocodone
  per 5-mL spoonful, with 7% alcohol)
STORAGE
Acetaminophen and hydrocodone combination tablets, capsules, and liquid should be stored at room temperature in
tightly closed, light-resistant containers.

USES

This medication is used to relieve moderate to severe pain.
Hydrocodone is a narcotic analgesic that acts on the central
nervous system (brain and spinal cord) to relieve pain.

TREATMENT

To avoid stomach upset, take this drug with food or milk.

Each dose of the oral liquid form of this medication should
be measured carefully with a specially designed 5-mL measuring spoon, not with an ordinary kitchen teaspoon.

This medication works most effectively if you take it at the
onset of pain, rather than waiting until it becomes intense.

If you are taking this medication on a regular schedule and
you miss a dose, take the missed dose as soon as possible,
unless it is almost time for your next dose. In that case, don't

take the missed dose at all; just return to your regular dosing schedule. Do not double the next dose.

SIDE EFFECTS

Minor. Constipation, dizziness, dry mouth, false sense of well-being, flushing, light-headedness, loss of appetite, nausea, painful or difficult urination, or sweating. These side effects should disappear as your body adjusts to the medication.

If you are constipated, increase the amount of fiber in your diet (fresh fruits and vegetables, salads, bran, and whole-grain breads), exercise, and drink more water (unless your doctor directs you to do otherwise).

To reduce mouth dryness, chew sugarless gum or suck on ice chips or hard candy.

If you feel dizzy, sit or lie down for a while; get up from a sitting or reclining position slowly; and be careful on stairs.

Major. Tell your doctor about any side effects that are persistent or particularly bothersome. IT IS ESPECIALLY IMPORTANT TO TELL YOUR DOCTOR about anxiety, difficulty in breathing, excitation, fatigue, palpitations, rash, restlessness, sore throat and fever, tremors, unusual bleeding or bruising, weakness, or yellowing of the eyes or skin.

INTERACTIONS

This medication interacts with several other types of drugs:

1. Concurrent use of this medication with other central nervous system depressants (such as alcohol, antihistamines, barbiturates, benzodiazepine tranquilizers, muscle relaxants, and phenothiazine tranquilizers) or with tricyclic antidepressants can cause extreme drowsiness.

2. A monoamine oxidase (MAO) inhibitor taken within 14 days of this drug can lead to severe side effects.

3. Long-term use and high doses of the acetaminophen portion of this medication can increase the effects of oral anticoagulants (blood thinners, such as warfarin); this combination may lead to bleeding complications.

4. Anticonvulsants (antiseizure medications), barbiturates, and alcohol can increase the liver toxicity caused by large doses of the acetaminophen portion of this medication.

TELL YOUR DOCTOR about any medications you are currently taking, especially any of those listed above.

WARNINGS

• Tell your doctor about unusual or allergic reactions you have had to any medications, especially to acetaminophen, hydrocodone, or other narcotic analgesics (such as codeine, hydromorphone, meperidine, methadone, morphine, oxycodone, and propoxyphene).

• Tell your doctor if you now have or if you have ever had acute abdominal conditions, asthma, blood disorders, brain disease, colitis, epilepsy, gallstones or gallbladder disease, a head injury, heart disease, kidney disease, liver disease, lung disease, mental illness, prostate disease, thyroid disease, or urethral strictures.

• If this drug makes you dizzy or drowsy, do not take part in any activity that requires you to remain alert, such as driving an automobile or operating potentially dangerous equipment.

• Before having surgery or any other medical or dental treatment, be sure to tell your doctor or dentist that you are taking this medication.

• Because this product contains hydrocodone, it has the potential for abuse and must be used with caution. Usually, it should not be taken on a regular schedule for longer than ten days at a time. Tolerance develops quickly; do not increase the dosage or stop taking the drug abruptly unless you first consult your doctor. If you have been taking large amounts of this medication for long periods, you may experience a withdrawal reaction (diarrhea, excessive yawning, gooseflesh, irritability, muscle aches, nausea, runny nose, shivering, sleep disorders, stomach cramps, sweating, trembling, vomiting, or weakness). Your doctor may, therefore, want to reduce the dosage gradually.

• Because this product contains acetaminophen, additional medications that contain acetaminophen should not be taken without your doctor's approval. Check the labels on over-the-counter (nonprescription) pain, sinus, allergy, asthma, diet, cough, and cold products to see if they contain acetaminophen.

• Be sure to tell your doctor if you are pregnant. The effects of this medication during pregnancy have not been thoroughly studied in humans. Regular use of hydrocodone in large doses during pregnancy can result in addiction of the fetus, leading to withdrawal symptoms (diarrhea, excessive crying, excessive yawning, fever, irritability, sneezing, tremors, or vomiting) at birth. Also be sure that you tell your doctor if you are breast-feeding an infant. Small amounts of this medication may pass into breast milk and cause excessive drowsiness in the nursing infant.

---

acetaminophen and oxycodone combination

BRAND NAMES (Manufacturers)
oxycodone hydrochloride with acetaminophen
   (various manufacturers)
Percocet (DuPont)
Roxicet (Roxane)
TYPE OF DRUG
Analgesic combination
INGREDIENTS
acetaminophen and oxycodone
DOSAGE FORMS
Tablets (325 mg acetaminophen with 5 mg oxycodone;
   500 mg acetaminophen with 5 mg oxycodone)
Capsules (500 mg acetaminophen with 5 mg oxycodone)
Oral liquid (325 mg acetaminophen with 5 mg oxycodone
   per 5-mL spoonful, with 0.4% alcohol)
STORAGE
Acetaminophen and oxycodone tablets should be stored at room temperature in a tightly closed container.

USES

Acetaminophen and oxycodone combination is used to relieve moderate to severe pain. Oxycodone is a narcotic analgesic that acts on the central nervous system (brain and spinal cord) to relieve pain.

TREATMENT

In order to avoid stomach upset, you can take this medication with food or milk.

This medication works most effectively if you take it at the onset of pain, rather than waiting until the pain becomes intense.

If you are taking this medication on a regular schedule and you miss a dose, take the missed dose as soon as possible, unless it is almost time for your next dose. In that case, don't take the missed dose at all; just return to your regular dosing schedule. Do not double the next dose.

SIDE EFFECTS

Minor. Constipation, dizziness, drowsiness, dry mouth, false sense of well-being, flushing, light-headedness, loss of appetite, nausea, painful or difficult urination, or sweating. These side effects should disappear as your body adjusts to the medication.

If you are constipated, increase the amount of fiber in your diet (fresh fruits and vegetables, salads, bran, and whole-grain breads), exercise, and drink more water (unless your doctor directs you to do otherwise).

To reduce mouth dryness, chew sugarless gum or suck on ice chips or hard candy.

If you feel dizzy or light-headed, sit or lie down for a while; get up from a sitting or reclining position slowly; and be careful on stairs.

Major. Tell your doctor about any side effects that are persistent or particularly bothersome. IT IS ESPECIALLY IMPORTANT TO TELL YOUR DOCTOR about anxiety, difficulty in breathing, excitation, fatigue, palpitations, rash, restlessness, sore throat and fever, tremors, unusual bleeding or bruising, weakness, or yellowing of the eyes or skin.

INTERACTIONS

This medication interacts with several other types of drugs:

1. Concurrent use of this medication with other central nervous system depressants (such as alcohol, antihistamines, barbiturates, benzodiazepine tranquilizers, muscle relaxants, and phenothiazine tranquilizers) or with tricyclic antidepressants can cause extreme drowsiness.

2. A monoamine oxidase (MAO) inhibitor taken within 14 days of this medication can cause severe side effects.

3. Long-term use and high doses of the acetaminophen portion of this medication can increase the effects of oral anticoagulants (blood thinners, such as warfarin); the combination of these drugs may lead to bleeding complications.

4. Anticonvulsants (antiseizure medications), barbiturates, and alcohol can increase the liver toxicity caused by large doses of the acetaminophen portion of this medication.

BE SURE TO TELL YOUR DOCTOR about any medications you are currently taking, especially any listed above.

WARNINGS

• Tell your doctor about unusual, unexpected, or allergic reactions you have had to any medications, especially to acetaminophen, oxycodone, or other narcotic analgesics (such as codeine, hydrocodone, hydromorphone, meperidine, methadone, morphine, and propoxyphene).

• Tell your doctor if you now have or if you have ever had an acute abdominal condition, asthma, blood disorders, brain disease, colitis, epilepsy, gallstones or gallbladder disease, head injuries, heart disease, kidney disease, liver disease, lung disease, mental illness, prostate disease, thyroid disease, or urethral strictures.

• If this drug makes you dizzy or drowsy, do not take part in any activity that requires alertness, such as driving a car or operating potentially dangerous equipment.

• Before having surgery or any other medical or dental treatment, be sure to tell your doctor or dentist that you are taking this medication.

• Because this product contains oxycodone, it has the potential for abuse and must be used with caution. Usually, it should not be taken on a regular schedule for longer than ten days at a time. Tolerance develops quickly; do not increase the dosage or stop taking the drug abruptly unless you first consult your doctor. If you have been taking large amounts of this medication for long periods, you may experience a withdrawal reaction (muscle aches, diarrhea, gooseflesh, runny nose, nausea, vomiting, shivering, trembling, stomach cramps, sleep disorders, irritability, weakness, excessive yawning, or sweating). Your doctor may, therefore, want to reduce the dosage gradually.

• Because this product contains acetaminophen, additional medications that contain acetaminophen should not be taken without your doctor's approval. Check the labels on over-the-counter (nonprescription) pain, sinus, allergy, asthma, diet, cough, and cold products to see if they contain acetaminophen.

• Be sure to tell your doctor if you are pregnant. The effects of this medication during pregnancy have not been thoroughly studied in humans. Oxycodone, used regularly in large doses during pregnancy, can result in addiction of the fetus, leading to the appearance of withdrawal symptoms (such as irritability, excessive crying, tremors, fever, vomiting, diarrhea, sneezing, or excessive yawning) at birth. Also tell your doctor if you are breast-feeding an infant. Small amounts of this medication may pass into breast milk and cause excessive drowsiness in the nursing infant.

acetaminophen and propoxyphene combination

BRAND NAMES (Manufacturers)
Darvocet-N 50 (Lilly)
Darvocet-N 100 (Lilly)
propoxyphene hydrochloride with acetaminophen
    (various manufacturers)
propoxyphene napsylate with acetaminophen
    (various manufacturers)
Wygesic (Wyeth-Ayerst)
TYPE OF DRUG
Analgesic combination
INGREDIENTS
acetaminophen and propoxyphene
DOSAGE FORM
Tablets (325 mg acetaminophen with 50 mg propoxyphene napsylate; 650 mg acetaminophen with 100 mg propoxyphene napsylate; 650 mg acetaminophen with 65 mg propoxyphene hydrochloride)
STORAGE
Acetaminophen and propoxyphene combination tablets and capsules should be stored at room temperature in tightly closed containers.

USES
This medication is used to relieve moderate to severe pain. Propoxyphene is a narcotic analgesic that acts on the central nervous system (brain and spinal cord) to relieve pain.

TREATMENT

In order to avoid stomach upset, you can take this medication with food or milk.

This medication will work best if you take it at the onset of pain, rather than waiting until the pain has become intense.

If you are taking this acetaminophen and propoxyphene combination on a regular schedule and you miss a dose, take the missed dose as soon as possible, unless you are nearing the time for the next dose. In that case, do not take the missed dose at all; just return to your regular dosing schedule. It is important that you do not double the next dose.

SIDE EFFECTS

Minor. Constipation, dizziness, drowsiness, dry mouth, false sense of well-being, flushing, light-headedness, headache, loss of appetite, nausea, painful or difficult urination, or sweating. These side effects should disappear as your body adjusts to the drug.

If you are constipated, increase the amount of fiber in your diet (fresh fruits and vegetables, salads, bran, and whole-grain breads), exercise and drink more water (unless your doctor directs you to do otherwise).

To reduce excessive mouth dryness, you may want to chew sugarless gum or you may want to suck on ice chips or hard candy.

If you feel dizzy or light-headed, sit or lie down for a while; get up from a sitting or lying position slowly; and be careful on stairs.

Major. Tell your doctor about any side effects that are persistent or particularly bothersome. IT IS ESPECIALLY IMPORTANT TO TELL YOUR DOCTOR about anxiety, difficulty in breathing, excitation, fatigue, palpitations, rash, restlessness, sore throat and fever, tremors, unusual bleeding or bruising, weakness, or yellowing of the eyes or skin.

INTERACTIONS

This medication interacts with several other types of drugs:

1. Concurrent use of acetaminophen and propoxyphene combination with other central nervous system depressants (such as alcohol, antihistamines, barbiturates, benzodiazepine tranquilizers, muscle relaxants, and phenothiazine tranquilizers) or with tricyclic antidepressants can possibly cause extreme drowsiness.

2. A monoamine oxidase (MAO) inhibitor taken within 14 days of this medication can lead to unpredictable and severe side effects.

3. Long-term use and high doses of acetaminophen can increase the effects of oral anticoagulants (blood thinners, such as warfarin), which may lead to bleeding complications.

4. Anticonvulsants (antiseizure medication), barbiturates, and alcohol can increase the liver toxicity caused by large doses of the acetaminophen portion of this medication.

5. The propoxyphene portion of this medication decreases the elimination of carbamazepine, warfarin, and tricyclic antidepressants from the body, which can lead to an increase in side effects.

Before starting to take this medication, BE SURE TO TELL YOUR DOCTOR about any medications you are currently taking, especially any of those listed above.

WARNINGS

• Tell your doctor about unusual or allergic reactions you have had to any medications, especially to acetaminophen, propoxyphene, or other narcotic analgesics (such as codeine, hydrocodone, hydromorphone, meperidine, methadone, morphine, and oxycodone).

• Tell your doctor if you now have or if you have ever had an acute abdominal condition, asthma, blood disorders, brain disease, colitis, epilepsy, gallstones or gallbladder disease, head injuries, heart disease, kidney disease, liver disease, lung disease, mental illness, prostate disease, thyroid disease, or urethral strictures.

• If this drug makes you dizzy or drowsy, do not take part in any activity that requires alertness, such as driving a car.

• Before having surgery or any other medical or dental treatment, be sure to tell your doctor or dentist that you are taking this medication.

• Because this product contains propoxyphene, it has the potential for abuse and must be used with caution. Usually, it should not be taken on a regular schedule for longer than ten days at a time. Tolerance develops quickly; do not increase the dosage or stop taking the drug abruptly unless you first consult your doctor. If you have been taking large amounts of this medication for long periods, you may experience a withdrawal reaction (muscle aches, diarrhea, gooseflesh, runny nose, nausea, vomiting, shivering, trembling, stomach cramps, sleep disorders, irritability, weakness, excessive yawning, or sweating). Your doctor may, therefore, want to reduce the dosage gradually to prevent or minimize this response.

• Because this product contains acetaminophen, additional medications that contain acetaminophen should not be taken without your doctor's approval. Check the labels on over-the-counter (nonprescription) pain, sinus, allergy, asthma, diet, cough, and cold products to see if they contain acetaminophen.

• Be sure to tell your doctor if you are pregnant. The effects of this medication during pregnancy have not been thoroughly studied in humans. Propoxyphene used regularly in large doses during pregnancy can result in addiction of the fetus, leading to withdrawal symptoms (irritability, excessive crying, tremors, fever, vomiting, diarrhea, sneezing, or excessive yawning) at birth. Also tell your doctor if you are breast-feeding an infant. Small amounts of this medication may pass into the mother's breast milk and cause excessive drowsiness in the nursing infant.

acetazolamide

BRAND NAMES (Manufacturers)
acetazolamide (various manufacturers)
AK-Zol (Akorn)
Dazamide (Major)
Diamox (Lederle)
Diamox Sequels (Lederle)
TYPE OF DRUG
Carbonic anhydrase inhibitor
INGREDIENT
acetazolamide
DOSAGE FORMS
Tablets (125 mg and 250 mg)
Sustained-release capsules (500 mg)
STORAGE
Acetazolamide tablets and capsules should be stored at room temperature in tightly closed containers.

USES

This medication is used to treat glaucoma and epilepsy and to prevent or treat the symptoms of mountain sickness.

TREATMENT

In order to avoid stomach irritation, you can take acetazolamide with food or with a full glass of water or milk (unless your doctor directs you to do otherwise).

The sustained-release form of this medication should be swallowed whole. Chewing, crushing, or breaking these capsules destroys their sustained-release activity and possibly increases the side effects.

If you miss a dose of this medication, take the missed dose as soon as possible, unless it is almost time for the next dose. In that case, do not take the missed dose; just return to your regular dosing schedule. Do not double the next dose.

SIDE EFFECTS

Minor. Confusion, drowsiness, increased urination, loss of appetite, or a tingling feeling. These side effects should disappear as your body adjusts to the medication.

Major. Tell your doctor about any side effects that are persistent or particularly bothersome. IT IS ESPECIALLY IMPORTANT TO TELL YOUR DOCTOR about back pain; bloody or black, tarry stools; blurred vision; convulsions; difficult or painful urination; fever; rash; unusual bleeding or bruising; or yellowing of the eyes or skin.

INTERACTIONS

Acetazolamide interacts with other types of medications:
1. Acetazolamide can decrease the excretion through the kidneys of amphetamines, ephedrine, flecainide, mexiletine, pseudoephedrine, tocainide, and quinidine, which can lead to an increased risk of side effects with these medications. Acetazolamide can also increase the side effects (to the bones) of carbamazepine, phenobarbital, phenytoin, and primidone.
2. Dosage adjustments of insulin or oral antidiabetic medications may be necessary when this medication is started.
3. The therapeutic benefits of lithium, methenamine, or methotrexate may be decreased by acetazolamide.

Before starting to take acetazolamide tablets or capsules, BE SURE TO TELL YOUR DOCTOR about any medications that you are currently taking, especially any of the medications that are listed above.

WARNINGS

• Tell your doctor about unusual or allergic reactions you have had to any medications, especially to acetazolamide, methazolamide, sulfonamide antibiotics, diuretics (water pills), oral antidiabetics, dapsone, sulfone, or sulfoxone.

• Before starting to take this medication, be sure to tell your doctor if you now have or if you have ever had acidosis, Addison's disease (underactive adrenal gland), chronic lung disease, diabetes mellitus, electrolyte disorders, gout, kidney disease, or liver disease.

• If this drug makes you dizzy or drowsy, avoid taking part in any activity that requires alertness.

• Although several generic versions of this drug are available, you should not switch from one brand to another without your doctor's or pharmacist's approval. Not all of these products are equivalent.

• Tolerance to this drug can develop quickly. Check with your doctor if you feel this drug is losing effectiveness.

• Be sure to tell your doctor if you are pregnant. Although this drug appears to be safe in humans, birth defects have been reported in the offspring of animals that received large doses during pregnancy. Also tell your doctor if you are breast-feeding an infant. Although acetazolamide passes into breast milk, the effects on the infant are not known.

---

acyclovir

BRAND NAME (Manufacturer)
Zovirax (Burroughs Wellcome)
TYPE OF DRUG
Antiviral
INGREDIENT
acyclovir
DOSAGE FORMS
Capsules (200 mg)
Ointment (5%)
Oral Suspension (200 mg per 5-mL spoonful)
Tablets (200 mg, 400 mg, and 800 mg)

STORAGE
Acyclovir ointment, capsules, and tablets should be stored in a cool, dry place. The suspension form should be kept in the refrigerator.

USES
Acyclovir is used to treat genital herpes and herpes infections of the skin including chicken pox. Acyclovir prevents the growth and multiplication of the herpes virus. This drug does not cure a herpes infection, but may relieve the pain associated with the viral infection and may shorten its duration.

TREATMENT
Take oral acyclovir or apply topical acyclovir as soon as possible after the symptoms of a herpes infection appear. Wash the infected area with soap and water, and allow it to dry. To avoid spreading the infection, use a rubber glove or a finger cot to apply the ointment. Apply enough acyclovir so that you completely cover the area of the infection.

Complete the full course of therapy, even if your symptoms disappear sooner. The full course usually lasts about ten days.

If you miss a dose of this medication, take or apply the missed dose as soon as possible. However, if you do not remember until it is almost time for the next dose, do not apply the missed dose at all; just return to your regular dosing schedule. Do not use a double dose of the medication at the next application.

SIDE EFFECTS
Minor. You may experience temporary pain, burning, stinging, itching, or rash when this medication is applied topically. This sensation should disappear as your body adjusts to the medication.

After oral therapy, you may experience diarrhea, difficulty sleeping, dizziness, fatigue, headache, rash, upset stomach, or vomiting. These side effects should disappear as your body adjusts to the medication.

Major. Tell your doctor about any side effects that are persistent or particularly bothersome. IT IS ESPECIALLY IMPORTANT TO TELL YOUR DOCTOR about fever or muscle pain.

INTERACTIONS
Acyclovir should not interact with other medications if it is used according to directions.

WARNINGS
• Be sure to tell your doctor about unusual or allergic reactions you have had to any medications.
• Acyclovir ointment is intended for use on the skin only; it should not be used in or around the eyes.
• Try to avoid sexual activity while you have signs or symptoms of genital herpes; this medication does not prevent the transmission of herpes to other individuals, nor does it prevent recurrences.
• This medication has been prescribed for your current infection only. A subsequent infection, or one that someone else has, may require a different medication. Do not use your medication to treat other infections, unless your doctor directs you to do so.
• Be sure to tell your doctor if you are pregnant. Although this drug appears to be safe in animals, studies in humans during pregnancy have not been conducted. Also tell your doctor if you are breast-feeding an infant. Although acyclovir passes into breast milk, no toxicity has been observed in any infants.

---

albuterol

BRAND NAMES (Manufacturers)
Proventil (Schering)
Ventolin (Glaxo)
TYPE OF DRUG
Bronchodilator
INGREDIENT
albuterol
DOSAGE FORMS
Tablets and extended-release tablets (2 mg and 4 mg)
Inhalation aerosol (each spray delivers 90 mcg)
Inhalation solution (0.5% and 0.083%)
Oral syrup (2 mg per 5-mL spoonful)
Rotocaps for inhalation (200 mcg)

STORAGE

Albuterol tablets and oral syrup should be stored at room temperature in a tightly closed, light-resistant container. The inhalation aerosol should be stored away from excessive heat—the contents are pressurized and can explode if heated.

USES

Albuterol is used to relieve wheezing and shortness of breath caused by lung diseases such as asthma, bronchitis, and emphysema. This drug acts directly on the muscles of the bronchi (breathing tubes) to relieve bronchospasms (muscle contractions of the bronchi), which allows air to move more freely to and from the lungs.

TREATMENT

To lessen stomach upset, take albuterol tablets and oral syrup with food (unless your doctor directs you to do otherwise).

Each dose of oral syrup should be measured carefully with a 5-mL measuring spoon designed for that purpose. Ordinary kitchen teaspoons are not accurate enough.

The inhalation aerosol form of this medication is usually packaged with an instruction sheet. Read the directions carefully before using this medication. You may wish to consult your doctor or pharmacist about the proper administration of this drug. The container should be shaken well just before each use. The contents tend to settle on the bottom, so it is necessary to shake the bottle in order to distribute the ingredients evenly and equalize the doses. If more than one inhalation is necessary, wait at least one full minute between doses, in order to receive the full benefit of the first dose.

If you miss a dose of this medication and remember within an hour, take the missed dose immediately; then follow your regular dosing schedule for the next dose. If you miss the dose by more than an hour, just wait until the next scheduled dose. Do not double the dose.

SIDE EFFECTS

Minor. Anxiety, dizziness, flushing, headache, insomnia, irritability, loss of appetite, muscle cramps, nausea, nervousness, restlessness, sweating, tremors, vomiting, weakness, or dryness or irritation of the mouth or throat (from the inhalation aerosol). These side effects should disappear as your body adjusts to the medication.

To help prevent dryness or irritation of the mouth or throat, rinse your mouth with water after each dose of the inhalation aerosol.

In order to avoid difficulty in falling asleep, check with your doctor to see if you can take the last dose of this medication several hours before bedtime each day.

If you feel dizzy, sit or lie down for a while; get up from a sitting or reclining position slowly; and be careful on stairs.

Major. Tell your doctor about any side effects that are persistent or particularly bothersome. IT IS ESPECIALLY IMPORTANT TO TELL YOUR DOCTOR about chest pain, difficult or painful urination, itching, palpitations, or rash.

INTERACTIONS

Albuterol interacts with several other types of drugs:

1. The beta blockers (acebutolol, atenolol, labetalol, metoprolol, nadolol, pindolol, propranolol, timolol) antagonize (act against) this medication, decreasing its effectiveness.

2. Monoamine oxidase (MAO) inhibitors, tricyclic antidepressants, antihistamines, levothyroxine, and over-the-counter (nonprescription) cough, cold, asthma, allergy, diet, and sinus medications may increase the side effects of this medication.

3. There may be a change in the dosage requirements of insulin or oral antidiabetic medications when albuterol is started.

4. The blood-pressure-lowering effects of guanethidine may be decreased by this medication.

5. The use of albuterol with other bronchodilator drugs (either oral or inhalant drugs) can have additive side effects. Discuss this with your doctor.

BE SURE TO TELL YOUR DOCTOR about any medications you are taking, especially any listed above.

WARNINGS

• Tell your doctor about unusual or allergic reactions you have had to medications, especially to albuterol or any related drug (amphetamines, ephedrine, epinephrine, isoproterenol, metaproterenol, norepinephrine, phenylephrine, phenylpropanolamine, pseudoephedrine, terbutaline).

• Tell your doctor if you now have or if you have ever had diabetes mellitus, an enlarged prostate gland, epilepsy, glaucoma, heart disease, high blood pressure, or thyroid disease.
• This medication can cause dizziness. Your ability to perform tasks that require alertness, such as driving a car or operating potentially dangerous equipment, may be decreased. Appropriate caution should, therefore, be taken.
• Before having surgery or any other medical or dental treatment, be sure to tell the doctor or dentist that you are taking this medication.
• Do not exceed the recommended dosage of this medication; excessive use may lead to an increase in side effects or a loss of effectiveness.
• Avoid contact of the aerosol inhalation with your eyes.
• Do not puncture, break, or burn the aerosol container. The contents are under pressure and may explode.
• Contact your doctor if you do not respond to the usual dose of this medication. It may be an indication that your asthma is getting worse, which may require additional therapy.
• Be sure to tell your doctor if you are pregnant. The effects of this medication during pregnancy have not been thoroughly studied in humans, but it has caused side effects in the offspring of animals that received large doses during pregnancy. Also tell your doctor if you are breast-feeding an infant. It is not known if albuterol passes into breast milk.

alendronate

BRAND NAME (Manufacturer)
Fosamax (Merck)
TYPE OF DRUG
Bone resorption inhibitor
INGREDIENT
alendronate
DOSAGE FORM
Tablets (10 mg and 40 mg)
STORAGE
Store alendronate at room temperature in a tightly closed container.

USES

Alendronate represents a new class of drug that works by increasing the development of new bone growth in the body and preventing the weakening and breakdown of bones. This medication is used in the treatment of post-menopausal osteoporosis and for patients with Paget's disease.

TREATMENT

Alendronate must be taken with a full glass (6 to 8 ounces) of water only (not coffee, mineral water, tea, or juice) on an empty stomach. Because food, certain beverages, and other medications will decrease the amount of alendronate absorbed from the body, you should take this medication at least 30 minutes before the first food, beverage, or medication of the day. In addition, to avoid irritation or pain in your esophagus, it is very important that you not lie down for at least 30 minutes after taking alendronate.

If you miss a dose of alendronate, take the missed dose as soon as possible, unless it is later in the day. In that case, do not take the missed dose at all; just wait until the next scheduled dose. Do not double the next dose.

SIDE EFFECTS

Minor. Abdominal pain, muscle pain, nausea, and skin rash.
Major. Tell your doctor about any side effects that are persistent or particularly bothersome. IT IS ESPECIALLY IMPORTANT TO TELL YOUR DOCTOR about constipation, diarrhea, difficulty swallowing, gas, headache, heartburn, irritation or pain in your esophagus, and unusually full or bloated feelings in your stomach.

INTERACTIONS

Alendronate can only be absorbed by your body when your stomach is empty. Therefore it is very important that you do not take any other medications (including antacids) or foods for at least 30 minutes after your morning dose of alendronate. This drug can interact with aspirin and aspirin-containing medications, increasing the frequency of problems with stomach upset or heartburn.

WARNINGS
• Tell your doctor about any unusual allergic reactions you have had to any medications, especially to alendronate. Also be sure to tell your doctor if you have ever had kidney disease, peptic ulcer disease, esophageal reflux disease, low blood calcium, or a deficiency of vitamin D.
• Be sure to tell your doctor if you are pregnant. The effects of this medication have not been thoroughly studied in humans. Also notify your doctor if you are breast-feeding an infant. It is not known if alendronate is distributed into breast milk.

---

allopurinol

BRAND NAMES (Manufacturers)
allopurinol (various manufacturers)
Lopurin (Boots)
Zyloprim (Burroughs Wellcome)
TYPE OF DRUG
Antigout
INGREDIENT
allopurinol
DOSAGE FORM
Tablets (100 mg and 300 mg)
STORAGE
Allopurinol tablets should be stored at room temperature in a tightly closed container.

USES
This medication is used to treat chronic gout and to lower blood uric acid levels. Allopurinol blocks the body's production of uric acid. Allopurinol should not be used to treat acute gout attacks.

TREATMENT
In order to avoid stomach irritation, you can take allopurinol with food or with a full glass of water or milk. It may take one to three weeks before the full effects of this medication are observed.

Drink at least 10 to 12 glasses (eight ounces each) of fluids per day while taking this medication in order to prevent the formation of kidney stones.

If you miss a dose of this medication, take the missed dose as soon as possible, unless it is almost time for the next dose. In that case, do not take the missed dose at all; just return to your regular dosing schedule. Do not double the next dose.

Take this drug for the full duration of prescribed therapy, as the full benefit of allopurinol may be delayed for several weeks.

SIDE EFFECTS

Minor. Diarrhea, drowsiness, nausea, stomach upset, or vomiting. These side effects should disappear as your body adjusts to the medication.

Major. Tell your doctor about any side effects that are persistent or particularly bothersome that may be the result of this medication. IT IS ESPECIALLY IMPORTANT TO TELL YOUR DOCTOR about blurred vision, chills, difficult or painful urination, fatigue, fever, loss of hair, muscle aches, numbness or tingling sensations, paleness, rash, sore throat, unusual bleeding or bruising, or yellowing of the eyes or skin.

INTERACTIONS

Allopurinol interacts with several other types of drugs:

1. Alcohol, diuretics (water pills), and pyrazinamide can increase blood uric acid levels, thus decreasing the effectiveness of allopurinol.

2. Allopurinol can increase the body's store of iron salts, which can lead to iron toxicity.

3. When combined with allopurinol, ampicillin can increase the chance of skin rash; thiazide diuretics and captopril can increase the chance of allergic reactions; and cyclophosphamide can increase the chance of blood disorders. Allopurinol can also increase the blood levels and side effects of mercaptopurine, azathioprine, oral anticoagulants (blood thinners), and theophylline.

4. Vitamin C can make the urine acidic, which can increase the risk of kidney stone formation with this medication.

Before starting to take allopurinol, BE SURE TO TELL YOUR DOCTOR about any medications you are currently taking, especially any of those listed above.

WARNINGS

• Tell your doctor about unusual or allergic reactions you have had to any medications, especially to allopurinol.

• Tell your doctor if you now have or if you have ever had blood disorders, kidney disease, or liver disease. Also tell your doctor if you have a relative with idiopathic hemochromatosis (a disorder of iron metabolism).
• This drug may cause dizziness or drowsiness. Do not take part in any activity that requires alertness, such as driving a car or operating potentially dangerous equipment.
• Be sure to tell your doctor if you are pregnant. Although this drug appears to be safe in animals, studies in pregnant women have not been conducted. Also tell your doctor if you are breast-feeding an infant. Although allopurinol passes into breast milk, no problems have been observed in nursing infants.

alprazolam

BRAND NAMES (Manufacturers)
alprazolam (various manufacturers)
Xanax (Upjohn)
TYPE OF DRUG
Benzodiazepine sedative/hypnotic
INGREDIENT
alprazolam
DOSAGE FORMS
Oral solution (0.1% and 1%)
Tablets (0.25 mg, 0.5 mg, 1 mg, and 2 mg)
STORAGE
This medication should be stored at room temperature in a tightly closed, light-resistant container. If medicine is stored so that it is not protected from heat and moisture, potency could be impaired.

USES
Alprazolam is prescribed to treat symptoms of anxiety and anxiety associated with depression. It may work by acting as a depressant of the central nervous system. This drug is currently used to relieve nervousness and panic disorder. Alprazolam is effective for this purpose for short periods, but it is important to try to identify and remove the cause of the anxiety as well.

TREATMENT

This drug should be taken exactly as directed by your doctor. It can be taken with food or a full glass of water if stomach upset occurs.

If you are taking this medication regularly and you miss a dose, take the missed dose immediately if you remember within an hour of the scheduled dose. If more than an hour has passed, skip the dose you missed and wait for the next scheduled dose. Do not double the dose.

SIDE EFFECTS

Minor. Bitter taste in mouth, constipation, diarrhea, dizziness, drowsiness (after a night's sleep), dry mouth, excessive salivation, fatigue, flushing, headache, heartburn, loss of appetite, nausea, nervousness, sweating, or vomiting. As you adjust to the drug, these effects should disappear.

To relieve constipation, increase the amount of fiber in your diet (fresh fruits and vegetables, salads, bran, and whole-grain breads), exercise, and drink more water (unless your doctor directs you to do otherwise).

Dry mouth can be relieved by chewing sugarless gum or by sucking on ice chips.

If you feel dizzy, sit or lie down for a while; get up slowly from a sitting or reclining position; and be careful on stairs.

Major. Tell your doctor about any side effects that are persistent or particularly bothersome. IT IS ESPECIALLY IMPORTANT TO TELL YOUR DOCTOR about blurred or double vision, chest pain, severe depression, difficulty in urinating, fainting, falling, fever, hallucinations, joint pain, mouth sores, nightmares, palpitations, rash, shortness of breath, slurred speech, sore throat, uncoordinated movements, unusual excitement, unusual tiredness, or yellowing of the eyes or skin.

INTERACTIONS

Alprazolam interacts with several other types of drugs:

1. To prevent oversedation, this drug should not be taken with alcohol, other sedative drugs, central nervous system depressants (such as antihistamines, barbiturates, muscle relaxants, pain medications, narcotics, medicines for seizures, and phenothiazine tranquilizers), or antidepressant medications.

2. This medication may decrease the effectiveness of carbamazepine, levodopa, and oral anticoagulants (blood thinners).

3. Disulfiram, oral contraceptives (birth control pills), isoniazid, and cimetidine can increase the blood levels of alprazolam, which can lead to toxic effects.

4. Concurrent use of rifampin may decrease the effectiveness of alprazolam.

Before starting to take alprazolam, BE SURE TO TELL YOUR DOCTOR about any medications you are currently taking, especially any of those listed above.

WARNINGS

• Tell your doctor about unusual or allergic reactions you have had to any medications, especially to alprazolam or other benzodiazepine tranquilizers (such as chlordiazepoxide, clorazepate, diazepam, flurazepam, halazepam, lorazepam, oxazepam, prazepam, temazepam, or triazolam).

• Tell your doctor if you now have or if you have ever had liver disease, kidney disease, epilepsy, lung disease, myasthenia gravis, narrow-angle glaucoma, porphyria, mental depression, mental illness, or sleep apnea.

• This medicine can cause drowsiness. Avoid tasks that require mental alertness, such as driving a car or using potentially dangerous equipment.

• This medication has the potential for abuse and must be used with caution. Tolerance may develop quickly; do not increase the dosage of the drug without first consulting your doctor. It is also important not to stop this drug suddenly if you have been taking it in large amounts or if you have used it for several months. Your doctor will want to reduce the dosage gradually.

• This is a safe drug when used properly. When it is combined with other sedative drugs or alcohol, however, serious side effects can develop.

• Be sure to tell your doctor if you are pregnant. This medicine may increase the chance of birth defects if it is taken during the first three months of pregnancy. In addition, too much use of this medicine during the last six months of pregnancy may result in addiction of the fetus—leading to withdrawal side effects in the newborn. Use of this medicine during the last weeks of pregnancy may cause drowsiness, slowed heartbeat, and breathing difficulties in the infant. Also tell your doctor if you are breast-feeding an infant. This medicine can pass into breast milk and cause excessive drowsiness, slowed heartbeat, and breathing difficulties in nursing infants.

---

amantadine

BRAND NAMES (Manufacturers)
amantadine hydrochloride (various manufacturers)
Symadine (Reid-Rowell)
Symmetrel (DuPont)
TYPE OF DRUG
Antiparkinsonism agent and antiviral
INGREDIENT
amantadine
DOSAGE FORMS
Capsules (100 mg)
Oral syrup (50 mg per 5-mL spoonful)
STORAGE
Amantadine should be stored at room temperature in a tightly closed container. This medication should never be frozen.

USES

Amantadine is used to treat the symptoms of Parkinson's disease and to prevent or treat respiratory tract infections caused by influenza A virus. It is thought to relieve the symptoms of Parkinson's by increasing the levels of dopamine, an important chemical in the brain, which is lacking in these patients. Amantadine is also an antiviral agent that slows the growth of the influenza virus.

TREATMENT

Amantadine can be taken on an empty stomach or with food or milk.

Each dose of the oral syrup should be measured carefully with a specially designed 5-mL measuring spoon. If you are taking amantadine to treat a viral infection, you should start taking it as soon as possible after exposure to the infection. Continue to take this medication for the entire time prescribed by your doctor (usually seven to 14 days), even if the symptoms of infection disappear before the end of that period. If you stop taking the drug too soon, the virus is given a chance to continue growing and the infection could recur.

Amantadine works best when the level of medicine in your bloodstream is kept constant. Therefore, take the doses at evenly spaced intervals day and night. For example, if you are to take two doses a day, the doses should be spaced 12 hours apart.

If you are taking amantadine to treat Parkinson's disease, you should know that the full effects of this medication may not become apparent for several weeks.

If you miss a dose of this medication, take the missed dose as soon as possible, unless it is almost time for the next dose. In that case, don't take the missed dose at all; just return to your regular dosing schedule. Do not double the next dose.

SIDE EFFECTS

Minor. Constipation, dizziness, dry mouth, fatigue, headache, insomnia, loss of appetite, nausea, or vomiting. These side effects should gradually disappear.

To relieve constipation, increase the amount of fiber in your diet (fresh fruits and vegetables, salads, bran, and whole-grain breads), exercise, and drink more water (unless your doctor directs you to do otherwise).

If you feel dizzy, sit or lie down for a while; get up slowly from a sitting or reclining position; and be careful on stairs.

To relieve mouth dryness, chew sugarless gum or suck on ice chips or hard candy.

Major. Tell your doctor about any side effects that are persistent or particularly bothersome. IT IS ESPECIALLY IMPORTANT TO TELL YOUR DOCTOR about anxiety, confusion, convulsions, depression, difficulty urinating, fluid retention, hallucinations, purplish-red spots on the skin, shortness of breath, skin rash, slurred speech, or visual disturbances.

INTERACTIONS

Amantadine interacts with several other types of drugs:

1. Concurrent use of amantadine and alcohol can lead to dizziness, fainting, and confusion.

2. Phenothiazine tranquilizers and tricyclic antidepressants in combination with amantadine can lead to confusion, hallucinations, and nightmares.

BE SURE TO TELL YOUR DOCTOR about any medications you are currently taking, especially any of those listed above.

WARNINGS

• Tell your doctor about unusual or allergic reactions you have had to any medications, especially to amantadine.

• Before starting to take amantadine, tell your doctor if you now have or if you have ever had epilepsy, heart or blood vessel disease, kidney disease, liver disease, mental disorders, or stomach ulcers.

• If this drug makes you dizzy, avoid taking part in any activity that requires alertness, such as driving a car or operating potentially dangerous equipment.

• If you are taking amantadine to treat Parkinson's disease, do not stop taking the medication unless you first consult your doctor. Stopping the drug abruptly may lead to a worsening of the disease. Your doctor may, therefore, want to reduce your dosage gradually to prevent this from occurring. In addition, tolerance to the benefits of amantadine can develop in several months. If you notice a loss of effectiveness, BE SURE TO CONTACT YOUR DOCTOR.

• Be sure to tell your doctor if you are pregnant. Although amantadine appears to be safe in humans, birth defects have been reported in the offspring of animals that received large doses during pregnancy. Also tell your doctor if you are breast-feeding an infant. Small amounts of amantadine pass into breast milk and may cause side effects in the nursing infant.

---

amitriptyline

BRAND NAMES (Manufacturers)
amitriptyline hydrochloride (various manufacturers)
Elavil (Stuart)
Endep (Roche)
Enovil (Hauck)
TYPE OF DRUG
Tricyclic antidepressant
INGREDIENT
amitriptyline
DOSAGE FORM
Tablets (10 mg, 25 mg, 50 mg, 75 mg, 100 mg, and 150 mg)
STORAGE
Store at room temperature in a tightly closed container.

USES

Amitriptyline is used to relieve the symptoms of mental depression. This medication belongs to a group of drugs referred to as the tricyclic antidepressants. These medicines are thought to relieve depression by increasing the concentration of certain chemicals necessary for nerve transmission in the brain.

TREATMENT

This medication should be taken exactly as your doctor prescribes. It can be taken with water or with food to lessen the chance of stomach irritation, unless your doctor tells you to do otherwise.

The effects of therapy with this medication may not become apparent for two or three weeks.

If you miss a dose of this medication, take the missed dose as soon as possible, and then return to your regular dosing schedule. However, if the dose you missed was a once-a-day bedtime dose, do not take that dose in the morning; check with your doctor instead. If the dose is taken in the morning, it may cause some unwanted side effects. Never double the dose of amitriptyline.

SIDE EFFECTS

Minor. Constipation, cramps, diarrhea, dizziness, drowsiness, dry mouth, fatigue, heartburn, loss of appetite, nausea, peculiar tastes in the mouth, restlessness, sweating, vomiting, weakness, or weight gain or loss. As your body adjusts to the medication, these side effects should disappear.

This medication may cause increased sensitivity to sunlight. You should, therefore, avoid prolonged exposure to sunlight and sunlamps. Wear protective clothing and use an effective sunscreen.

Amitriptyline may cause your urine to turn blue-green; this effect is harmless.

Dry mouth can be relieved by chewing sugarless gum or by sucking on ice chips or hard candy.

To relieve constipation, increase the amount of fiber in your diet (fresh fruits and vegetables, salads, bran, and whole-grain breads), exercise, and drink more water (unless your doctor directs you to do otherwise).

To avoid dizziness when you stand, contract and relax the muscles of your legs for a few moments before rising. Do this by alternately pushing one foot against the floor while raising the other foot slightly, so that you are "pumping" your legs in a pedaling motion.

Major. Tell your doctor about any side effects that are persistent or particularly bothersome. IT IS ESPECIALLY IMPORTANT TO TELL YOUR DOCTOR about agitation, anxiety, blurred vision, chest pain, confusion, convulsions, difficulty in urinating, enlarged or painful breasts (in both sexes), fainting, fever, fluid retention, hair loss, hallucinations, headaches, impotence, mood changes, mouth sores, nervousness, nightmares, numbness in the fingers or toes, palpitations, ringing in the ears, seizures, skin rash, sleep disorders, sore throat, tremors, uncoordinated movements or balance problems, unusual bleeding or bruising, or yellowing of the eyes or skin.

INTERACTIONS

Amitriptyline interacts with a number of other types of medications:

1. Extreme drowsiness can occur when this medicine is taken with central nervous system depressants (such as alcohol, antihistamines, barbiturates, benzodiazepine tranquilizers, muscle relaxants, narcotics, pain medications, phenothiazine tranquilizers, and sleeping medications) or with other antidepressants.

2. Amitriptyline may decrease the effectiveness of antiseizure medications and may block the blood-pressure-lowering effects of clonidine and guanethidine.

3. Oral contraceptives (birth control pills) or estrogen-containing drugs can increase the side effects and reduce the effectiveness of the tricyclic antidepressants (a drug type that includes amitriptyline).

4. Cimetidine can decrease the elimination of amitriptyline from the body, thus increasing the possibility of side effects.

5. Tricyclic antidepressants may increase the side effects of thyroid medication and of over-the-counter (nonprescription) cough, cold, allergy, asthma, sinus, and weight-control medications.

6. The concurrent use of tricyclic antidepressants and monoamine oxidase (MAO) inhibitors should be avoided because the combination may result in fever, convulsions, or high blood pressure. At least 14 days should separate the use of amitriptyline and the use of an MAO inhibitor.

Before starting to take amitriptyline, BE SURE TO TELL YOUR DOCTOR about any medications you are currently taking, especially any of those listed above.

WARNINGS

• Tell your doctor if you have had unusual or allergic reactions to medications, especially to amitriptyline or any of the other tricyclic antidepressants (imipramine, doxepin, trimipramine, amoxapine, protriptyline, desipramine, maprotiline, nortriptyline).

• Tell your doctor if you have a history of alcoholism, or if you have ever had asthma, diabetes, high blood pressure, liver or kidney disease, heart disease, a heart attack, circulatory disease, stomach problems, intestinal problems, difficulty in urinating, enlarged prostate gland, epilepsy, glaucoma, thyroid disease, mental illness, or electroshock therapy.

• If this drug makes you dizzy or drowsy, do not take part in any activity that requires alertness, such as driving a car or operating potentially dangerous equipment.

• Before having surgery or other medical or dental treatment, tell your doctor or dentist you are taking this drug.

• Do not stop taking this drug suddenly. Abruptly stopping it can cause nausea, headache, stomach upset, fatigue, or a worsening of your condition. Your doctor may want to reduce the dosage gradually.

• The effects of this medication may last as long as seven days after you have stopped taking it, so continue to observe all precautions during that period.

• Be sure to tell your doctor if you are pregnant. Studies have not been done in humans; however, studies in animals have shown that this type of medication can cause side effects to the fetus when given to the mother in large doses during pregnancy. Also tell your doctor if you are breast-feeding an infant. Small amounts of this drug can pass into breast milk and may cause unwanted side effects, such as irritability or sleeping problems, in nursing infants.

amlodipine

BRAND NAME (Manufacturer)
Norvasc (Pfizer)

TYPE OF DRUG
Antianginal and antihypertensive
INGREDIENT
amlodipine
DOSAGE FORM
Tablets (2.5 mg, 5 mg, and 10 mg)
STORAGE
This medication should be stored at room temperature in a tightly closed container away from heat and direct sunlight.

USES

Amlodipine belongs to a group of drugs known as calcium channel blockers and is used to prevent the symptoms of angina (chest pain). It can also be used to treat high blood pressure. Amlodipine dilates the blood vessels of the heart and increases the amount of oxygen that reaches the heart muscle, though it is unclear exactly how it operates.

TREATMENT

This medication should be taken exactly as prescribed by your doctor. Amlodipine can be taken with meals or with a full glass of water if stomach upset occurs. Try to develop a set schedule for taking it.

Amlodipine does not relieve chest pain once it has begun; it is only used to prevent angina attacks.

If you miss a dose and remember within four hours, take the missed dose and resume your regular schedule. If more than four hours have passed, skip the dose you missed and then take your next dose as scheduled. Do not double the next dose.

This medication does not cure angina or high blood pressure, but it can help to control the condition as long as you continue to take it.

SIDE EFFECTS

Minor. Constipation, diarrhea, dizziness, drowsiness, headache, insomnia, light-headedness, nausea, nervousness, stomach pain, or vomiting.

To relieve constipation, increase the amount of fiber in your diet (fresh fruits and vegetables, salads, bran and whole-grain breads), exercise, and drink more water (unless your doctor directs you to do otherwise).

Major. Tell your doctor about any side effects that are persistent or particularly bothersome. IT IS ESPECIALLY IMPORTANT TO TELL YOUR DOCTOR about confusion, depression, eye pain, or visual changes, fatigue, fluid retention, flushing, palpitations, skin rash.

INTERACTIONS

At this time, amlodipine does not appear to interact with other drugs when used according to directions.

WARNINGS

• Tell you doctor about unusual or allergic reactions you have had to any medications, especially amlodipine.

• Tell your doctor if you have ever had liver disease, obstructive coronary artery disease, or heart failure.

• If this drug makes you drowsy or dizzy, avoid taking part in any activity that requires alertness, such as driving a car or operating potentially dangerous equipment.

• Be sure to tell your doctor if you are pregnant. Extensive studies in pregnant women have not been conducted, but side effects have been reported in the offspring of animals that received large doses of amlodipine during pregnancy. Also be sure to tell your doctor if you are breast-feeding an infant. It is not known if amlodipine passes into breast milk.

---

amoxapine

BRAND NAMES (Manufacturers)
amoxapine (various manufacturers)
Asendin (Lederle)
TYPE OF DRUG
Tricyclic antidepressant
INGREDIENT
amoxapine
DOSAGE FORM
Tablets (25 mg, 50 mg, 100 mg, and 150 mg)
STORAGE
This medication should be stored at room temperature in a tightly closed container.

USES

Amoxapine is used to relieve the symptoms of mental depression. This medication belongs to a group of drugs referred to as the tricyclic antidepressants. These medicines are thought to relieve depression by increasing the concentration of certain chemicals necessary for nerve transmission in the brain.

TREATMENT

This medication should be taken exactly as your doctor prescribes. It can be taken with water or with food to lessen the chance of stomach irritation, unless your doctor tells you to do otherwise.

If you miss a dose of this medication, take the missed dose as soon as possible, then return to your regular dosing schedule. However, if the dose you missed was a once-a-day bedtime dose, do not take that dose in the morning; check with your doctor instead. If the dose is taken in the morning, it may cause some unwanted side effects. Never double the dose.

SIDE EFFECTS

Minor. Constipation, cramps, diarrhea, dizziness, drowsiness, dry mouth, fatigue, heartburn, loss of appetite, nausea, peculiar tastes in the mouth, restlessness, sweating, vomiting, weakness, or weight gain or loss. As your body adjusts to the medication, these side effects should disappear.

This medication may cause increased sensitivity to sunlight. Avoid prolonged exposure to sunlight and sunlamps. Wear protective clothing, and use an effective sunscreen.

Dry mouth can be relieved by chewing sugarless gum or by sucking on ice chips or hard candy.

To relieve constipation, increase the amount of fiber in your diet (fresh fruits and vegetables, salads, bran, and whole-grain breads). You can also increase your exercise and drink more water (unless your doctor directs you to do otherwise).

To avoid dizziness or light-headedness when you stand, contract and relax the muscles of your legs for a few moments before rising. Do this by alternately pushing one foot against the floor while raising the other foot slightly, so that you are "pumping" your legs in a pedaling motion.

Major. Tell your doctor about any side effects that are persistent or particularly bothersome. IT IS ESPECIALLY IMPORTANT TO TELL YOUR DOCTOR about agitation, anxiety, blurred vision, chest pains, confusion, convulsions, difficulty in urinating, enlarged or painful breasts (in both sexes), fainting, fever, fluid retention, hair loss, hallucinations, headaches, impotence, mood changes, mouth sores, nervousness, nightmares, numbness in the fingers or toes, palpitations, ringing in the ears, seizures, skin rash, sleep disorders, sore throat, tremors, uncoordinated movements or balance problems, unusual bleeding, or yellowing of the eyes or skin.

INTERACTIONS

Amoxapine interacts with a number of other types of drugs:
1. Extreme drowsiness can occur when this medicine is taken with central nervous system depressants, including alcohol, antihistamines, barbiturates, benzodiazepine tranquilizers, muscle relaxants, narcotics, pain medications, phenothiazine tranquilizers, and sleeping medications, or with other antidepressants.
2. Amoxapine may decrease the effectiveness of antiseizure medications and may block the blood-pressure-lowering effects of clonidine and guanethidine.
3. Birth control pills or estrogen-containing drugs can increase the side effects and reduce the effectiveness of the tricyclic antidepressants (including amoxapine).
4. Cimetidine can decrease the elimination of amoxapine from the body, increasing the possibility of side effects.
5. Tricyclic antidepressants may increase the side effects of thyroid medication and over-the-counter (nonprescription) cough, cold, allergy, asthma, sinus, and diet medications.
6. The concurrent use of tricyclic antidepressants and monoamine oxidase (MAO) inhibitors should be avoided, because the combination may result in fever, convulsions, or high blood pressure. At least 14 days should separate the use of amoxapine and the use of an MAO inhibitor.
   BE SURE TO TELL YOUR DOCTOR about any medications you are currently taking, especially any of those listed above.

WARNINGS

• Tell your doctor if you have had unusual or allergic reactions to medications, especially to amoxapine or any of the other tricyclic antidepressants (amitriptyline, imipramine, doxepin, trimipramine, protriptyline, desipramine, maprotiline, nortriptyline).

• Tell your doctor if you have a history of alcoholism, or if you now have or ever had asthma, high blood pressure, liver or kidney disease, heart disease, a heart attack, circulatory disease, stomach problems, intestinal problems, difficulty in urinating, enlarged prostate gland, epilepsy, glaucoma, thyroid disease, mental illness, or electroshock therapy.

• If this drug makes you dizzy or drowsy, do not take part in any activity that requires alertness, such as driving a car or operating potentially dangerous equipment.

• Before having surgery or other medical or dental treatment, tell your doctor or dentist you are taking this drug.

• Do not stop taking this drug suddenly. Abruptly stopping it can cause nausea, headache, stomach upset, fatigue, or a worsening of your condition. Your doctor may want to reduce the dosage gradually.

• The effects of this medication may last as long as seven days after you have stopped taking it, so continue to observe all precautions during that period.

• Be sure to tell your doctor if you are pregnant. Studies have not been done in humans; however, studies in animals have shown that this type of medication can cause side effects to the fetus when large doses are given to the mother during pregnancy. Also tell your doctor if you are breast-feeding an infant. Small amounts of this drug can pass into breast milk and may cause unwanted effects, such as irritability or sleeping problems, in nursing infants.

---

amoxicillin

BRAND NAMES (Manufacturers)
amoxicillin (various manufacturers)
Amoxil (SmithKline Beecham)
Polymox (Bristol)
Trimox (Squibb)
Wymox (Wyeth-Ayerst)
TYPE OF DRUG
Antibiotic
INGREDIENT
amoxicillin
DOSAGE FORMS
Capsules (250 mg and 500 mg)

Chewable tablets (125 mg and 250 mg)
Oral suspension (125 mg and 250 mg per 5-mL spoonful)
Oral suspension drops (50 mg per mL)

STORAGE

Amoxicillin tablets and capsules should be stored at room temperature in tightly closed containers. The oral-suspension form should be stored at room temperature or in the refrigerator in a tightly closed container. Any unused portion of the suspension should be discarded after 14 days because the drug loses its potency after that time. This medication should never be frozen.

USES

Amoxicillin antibiotic is used to treat a wide variety of bacterial infections, including infections in the middle ear, skin, upper and lower respiratory tracts, and urinary tract. Amoxicillin acts by severely injuring the cell walls of the infecting bacteria, thereby preventing them from growing and multiplying.

Amoxicillin kills susceptible bacteria but is not effective against viruses, parasites, or fungi.

TREATMENT

Amoxicillin can be taken either on an empty stomach or with food or milk (in order to prevent stomach upset).

The suspension form of this medication should be shaken well just before measuring each dose. The contents tend to settle on the bottom of the bottle, so it is necessary to shake the container to distribute the ingredients evenly and equalize the doses. Each dose should then be measured carefully with a specially designed 5-mL measuring spoon or the 1-mL dropper provided, as directed by your doctor or pharmacist. An ordinary kitchen teaspoon is not accurate enough.

It is important to continue to take this medication for the entire time prescribed by your doctor (usually seven to 14 days), even if the symptoms of infection disappear before the end of that period. If you stop taking the drug too soon, resistant bacteria are given the chance to continue growing, and the infection could recur.

Amoxicillin works best when the level of medicine in your bloodstream is kept constant. It is best, therefore, to take the doses at evenly spaced intervals day and night. For example, if you are to take three doses a day, the doses should be spaced eight hours apart.

If you miss a dose of this drug, take the missed dose immediately. If you don't remember to take the missed dose until it is almost time for your next dose, take the missed dose and space the following dose about halfway through the regular interval between doses, then return to your regular schedule. Do not skip any doses.

SIDE EFFECTS

Minor. Diarrhea, heartburn, nausea, or vomiting. These side effects should disappear as your body adjusts to the drug.
Major. Tell your doctor about any side effects that are persistent or particularly bothersome. IT IS ESPECIALLY IMPORTANT TO TELL YOUR DOCTOR about bloating, chills, cough, darkened tongue, difficulty in breathing, fever, irritation of the mouth, muscle aches, rash, rectal or vaginal itching, severe or bloody diarrhea, or sore throat. If your symptoms of infection seem to be getting worse rather than improving, you should contact your doctor.

INTERACTIONS

Amoxicillin interacts with other types of medications:
1. Probenecid can increase the blood concentration of this medication.
2. Amoxicillin may decrease the effectiveness of oral contraceptives (birth control pills), and pregnancy could result. You should, therefore, use a different or additional (barrier) form of birth control while taking this medication. Discuss this with your doctor.
3. The concurrent use of amoxicillin and allopurinol can increase the risk of developing a rash.

BE SURE TO TELL YOUR DOCTOR about any medications you are currently taking.

WARNINGS

• Tell your doctor about unusual or allergic reactions you have had to any medications, especially to amoxicillin, ampicillin, or penicillin or to cephalosporin antibiotics, penicillamine, or griseofulvin.

• Tell your doctor if you now have or if you have ever had kidney disease, asthma, or allergies.
• This medication has been prescribed for your current infection only. Another infection later on, or one that someone else has, may require a different medicine. You should not give your medicine to other people or use it for other infections, unless your doctor specifically directs you to do so.
• People with diabetes taking amoxicillin should know that this drug may cause a false-positive sugar reaction with a Clinitest urine glucose test. To avoid this problem while taking amoxicillin, you should switch to Clinistix or Tes-Tape to test your urine for sugar.
• Be sure to tell your doctor if you are pregnant. Although amoxicillin appears to be safe during pregnancy, extensive studies in humans have not been conducted. Also tell your doctor if you are breast-feeding an infant. Small amounts of this medication pass into breast milk and may temporarily alter the bacterial balance in the intestinal tract of the nursing infant, resulting in diarrhea.

amoxicillin and clavulanic acid combination

BRAND NAME (Manufacturer)
Augmentin (SmithKline Beecham)
TYPE OF DRUG
Antibiotic
INGREDIENTS
amoxicillin and clavulanic acid
DOSAGE FORMS
Tablets (250 mg amoxicillin and 125 mg clavulanic acid;
    500 mg amoxicillin and 125 mg clavulanic acid)
Chewable tablets (125 mg amoxicillin and 31.25 mg
    clavulanic acid; 250 mg amoxicillin and 62.5 mg
    clavulanic acid)
Oral suspension (125 mg amoxicillin and 31.25 mg clavu-
    lanic acid per 5-mL spoonful; 250 mg amoxicillin and
    62.5 mg clavulanic acid per 5-mL spoonful)

STORAGE

Amoxicillin and clavulanic acid tablets should be stored at room temperature in a tightly closed container. The oral suspension should be stored in the refrigerator in a tightly closed container. Any unused portion of the suspension should be discarded after ten days because the drug loses its potency after that time. This drug should never be frozen.

USES

Amoxicillin and clavulanic acid combination is used to treat a wide variety of bacterial infections, including infections of the middle ear, skin, sinuses, lower respiratory tract, and urinary tract. Amoxicillin is an antibiotic that acts by severely injuring the cell membranes of infecting bacteria, thereby preventing them from growing and multiplying. Clavulanic acid has no antibacterial activity. It acts to prevent the breakdown of amoxicillin in the body.

Amoxicillin and clavulanic acid combination kills susceptible bacteria, but it is not effective against viruses, parasites, or fungi.

TREATMENT

Amoxicillin and clavulanic acid combination can be taken either on an empty stomach or with food or milk in order to prevent stomach upset.

The suspension form of this medication should be shaken well just before measuring each dose. The contents tend to settle on the bottom of the bottle, so it is necessary to shake the container to distribute the ingredients evenly and to equalize the doses. Each dose should then be measured carefully with a specially designed 5-mL measuring spoon. An ordinary kitchen teaspoon is not accurate enough.

It is important to continue to take this medication for the entire time prescribed by your doctor (usually seven to ten days), even if the symptoms of infection disappear before the end of that period. If you stop taking the drug too soon, resistant bacteria are given the chance to continue growing, and the infection could recur.

Amoxicillin and clavulanic acid combination works best when the level of medicine in your bloodstream is kept constant. It is best, therefore, to take the doses of this medication at evenly spaced intervals throughout the day and night. For example, if you are to take three doses a day, the doses should be spaced eight hours apart.

If you miss a dose of amoxicillin and clavulanic acid combination, take the missed dose of this medication immediately. However, if you do not remember to take the missed dose until it is almost time for your next dose, take the missed dose; space the next dose about halfway through the regular interval between doses; and then return to your regular schedule. Try not to skip any doses.

SIDE EFFECTS

Minor. Abdominal discomfort, bloating, diarrhea, gas, headache, heartburn, nausea, or vomiting. These side effects should disappear as your body adjusts to this medication.

Major. Tell your doctor about any side effects that are persistent or particularly bothersome. IT IS ESPECIALLY IMPORTANT TO TELL YOUR DOCTOR about bloody or prolonged diarrhea, chills, cough, darkened tongue, difficulty in breathing, fever, irritation of the mouth, itching, muscle aches, rash, rectal or vaginal itching, sore throat, or unusual bleeding or bruising. If your symptoms of infection seem to be getting worse rather than improving, you should contact your doctor.

INTERACTIONS

Amoxicillin and clavulanic acid can interact with several other types of medications:

1. Probenecid can increase the blood concentration of amoxicillin.

2. Amoxicillin may decrease the effectiveness of oral contraceptives (birth control pills), and pregnancy could result. You should, therefore, use a different or additional (barrier) form of birth control while taking this medication. Discuss this with your doctor.

3. Amoxicillin and clavulanic acid can increase the risk of side effects with disulfiram (Antabuse).

4. The risk of skin rash is increased when amoxicillin and allopurinol are taken concurrently.

Before starting this medication, BE SURE TO TELL YOUR DOCTOR about any medications you are currently taking, especially any of the medications listed above.

WARNINGS

• Tell your doctor about unusual or allergic reactions you have had to any medications, especially to penicillin, amoxicillin, ampicillin, cephalosporin antibiotics, penicillamine, griseofulvin, or clavulanic acid.

• Tell your doctor if you now have or if you have ever had allergies, asthma, kidney disease, or mononucleosis.

• This medication has been prescribed for your current infection only. A subsequent infection, or one that someone else has, may require an entirely different medication. You should not give your medicine to other people for their use, nor should you use it to treat other infections, unless your doctor specifically indicates that is all right to do so.

• People with diabetes taking amoxicillin should know that this drug may cause a false-positive sugar reaction with a Clinitest urine glucose test. To avoid this problem while taking amoxicillin, you should switch to Clinistix or Tes-Tape to test your urine for sugar.

• Be sure to tell your doctor if you are pregnant. Although amoxicillin and clavulanic acid combination appears to be safe during pregnancy, studies in humans have not been conducted. Also tell your doctor if you are breast-feeding an infant. Small amounts of this medication pass into breast milk and may cause diarrhea in the nursing infant.

---

ampicillin

BRAND NAMES (Manufacturers)
ampicillin (various manufacturers)
Omnipen (Wyeth-Ayerst)
Polycillin (Apothecon)
Principen (Apothecon)
Totacillin (SmithKline Beecham)
TYPE OF DRUG
Antibiotic
INGREDIENT
ampicillin
DOSAGE FORMS
Capsules (250 mg and 500 mg)
Oral suspension (125 mg and 250 mg per 5-mL spoonful)
Oral suspension drops (100 mg per mL)

STORAGE

Ampicillin capsules should be stored at room temperature; ampicillin liquid suspension and drops should be refrigerated but should never be frozen. Do not keep any of these medications beyond the expiration date written on the container. All containers should be closed tightly to keep out moisture.

USES

Ampicillin is used to treat a wide variety of bacterial infections, including middle ear infections in children and infections of the respiratory, urinary, and gastrointestinal tracts. This type of antibiotic acts by severely injuring the cell walls of the infecting bacteria, thereby preventing them from growing and multiplying. Ampicillin kills susceptible bacteria but is not effective against viruses, parasites, or fungi.

TREATMENT

It is best to take ampicillin on an empty stomach (one hour before or two hours after a meal) with a full glass of water (not juice or soda pop). Always follow your doctor's directions.

If you have been prescribed the liquid-suspension form of ampicillin, be sure to shake the bottle well before taking this medication. The contents tend to settle on the bottom of the bottle, so it is necessary to shake the container to distribute the ingredients evenly and equalize the doses. Be sure to use specially marked droppers or spoons in order to accurately measure the correct amount of liquid. Household teaspoons vary in size and may not give you the correct dosage.

Ampicillin works best when the level of medicine in your bloodstream is kept constant. It is, therefore, best to take the doses at evenly spaced intervals day and night. For example, if you are to take four doses a day, the doses should be spaced six hours apart.

If you miss a dose, take it as soon as possible. If it is already time for the next dose, take it; space the next two doses at half the normal time interval (for example, if you were supposed to take one capsule every six hours, take your next two doses every three hours); then resume your normal dosing schedule.

Please remember that it is very important that you continue to take this medication for the entire duration prescribed to you by your doctor (usually seven to 14 days), even if the symptoms are no longer apparent before the end of that period. If you stop taking this medication too soon, resistant bacteria are given a chance to continue growing, and the infection could recur.

SIDE EFFECTS

Minor. Diarrhea, nausea, or vomiting. These side effects should disappear as your body adjusts to the medication.

Major. Tell your doctor about any side effects that are persistent or particularly bothersome. IT IS ESPECIALLY IMPORTANT TO TELL YOUR DOCTOR about darkened tongue, difficulty in breathing, fever, joint pain, mouth sores, rash, rectal or vaginal itching, severe or bloody diarrhea, or sore throat. If your symptoms of infection seem to be getting worse rather than improving, you should contact your doctor.

INTERACTIONS

This drug interacts with other types of medications:

1. Ampicillin interacts with allopurinol, chloramphenicol, erythromycin, paromomycin, tetracycline, and troleandomycin.

2. Ampicillin may decrease the effectiveness of oral contraceptives (birth control pills), and pregnancy could result. You should, therefore, use a different or additional (barrier) form of birth control while taking ampicillin.

   BE SURE TO TELL YOUR DOCTOR about any medications you are currently taking, especially any of the drugs listed above.

WARNINGS

• Tell your doctor about unusual or allergic reactions you have had to any medications, especially to penicillin, ampicillin, amoxicillin, cephalosporin antibiotics, penicillamine, or griseofulvin.

• Tell your doctor if you have or have ever had liver or kidney disease, asthma, hay fever, or other allergies.

• This medication has been prescribed for your current infection only. Another infection later on, or one that someone else has, may require a different medicine. Do not give your medicine to other people or use it for other infections unless your doctor directs you to do so.

• People with diabetes taking ampicillin should know that this drug may cause a false-positive sugar reaction with a Clinitest urine glucose test. To avoid this problem while taking ampicillin, you should switch to Clinistix or Tes-Tape to test your urine for sugar.
• Be sure to tell your doctor if you are pregnant. Although ampicillin appears to be safe during pregnancy, extensive studies in humans have not been conducted. Also tell your doctor if you are breast-feeding an infant. Small amounts of this medication pass into breast milk and may temporarily alter the bacterial balance in the intestinal tract of the nursing infant, resulting in diarrhea.

aspirin

BRAND NAMES (Manufacturers)
aspirin* (various manufacturers)
Bayer* (Glenbrook)
Bayer Children's* (Glenbrook)
Easprin (Parke-Davis)
Ecotrin* (SmithKline Beecham)
Empirin* (Burroughs Wellcome)
ZORprin (Boots)
*Available over the counter (without a prescription)
TYPE OF DRUG
Analgesic and anti-inflammatory
INGREDIENT
aspirin
DOSAGE FORMS
Tablets (81 mg, 162.5 mg, 325 mg, 500 mg, and 650 mg)
Chewable tablets (81 mg)
Chewing gum (227 mg)
Enteric-coated tablets (81 mg, 162 mg, 325 mg, 500 mg, 650 mg, and 975 mg)
Sustained-release tablets (650 mg, 800 mg, and 950 mg)
Suppositories (60 mg, 120 mg, 125 mg, 130 mg, 195 mg, 200 mg, 300 mg, 325 mg, 600 mg, 650 mg, and 1.2 g)
STORAGE
Store at room temperature in a tightly closed container. Moisture causes aspirin to decompose. Discard the medicine if it has a vinegary odor.

USES

Aspirin is used to treat mild to moderate pain, fever, and inflammatory conditions, such as rheumatic fever, rheumatoid arthritis, and osteoarthritis. Because it prevents the formation of blood clots, aspirin has also been shown to be effective in reducing the risk of transient ischemic attacks (small strokes) and to have a protective effect against heart attacks in men with angina (chest pain).

Aspirin is a useful medication that is utilized in the treatment of a wide variety of diseases. Because it is so common and so readily available, you may not think of it as "real medicine." This is a common misconception; aspirin certainly is "real medicine." If your doctor prescribes or recommends aspirin for your condition, it is for a good reason. FOLLOW YOUR DOCTOR'S DIRECTIONS CAREFULLY!

TREATMENT

To avoid stomach irritation, you should take aspirin with food or with a full glass of water or milk.

Chewable aspirin tablets may be chewed, dissolved in fluid, or swallowed whole.

Be sure to swallow the sustained-release or enteric-coated tablets whole. Crushing, chewing, or breaking these tablets destroys their sustained-release activity and increases their side effects.

To use the suppository, remove the foil wrapper and moisten the suppository with water (if it is too soft to insert, refrigerate the suppository for half an hour or run cold water over it before you remove the wrapper). Lie on your left side with your right knee bent. Push the suppository into the rectum, pointed end first. Lie still for a few minutes. Avoid having a bowel movement for at least an hour in order to give the drug time to be absorbed into your system.

If you are using aspirin to treat an inflammatory condition, it may take two or three weeks until the full benefits are observed.

If you are taking aspirin on a regular schedule and you miss a dose, take the missed dose as soon as possible, unless it is almost time for the next dose. In that case, do not take the missed dose at all; just return to your regular dosing schedule. Do not double the next dose.

SIDE EFFECTS

Minor. Heartburn, nausea, or vomiting. These side effects should disappear as your body adjusts to the medication.

Major. Tell your doctor about any side effects that are persistent or particularly bothersome. IT IS ESPECIALLY IMPORTANT TO TELL YOUR DOCTOR about any loss of hearing or ringing in the ears; bloody or black, tarry stools; confusion; difficult or painful urination; difficulty in breathing; dizziness; severe stomach pain; skin rash; or unusual weakness.

INTERACTIONS

Aspirin interacts with a number of other types of medications:

1. Aspirin can increase the effects of anticoagulants (blood thinners), such as warfarin, leading to bleeding complications.
2. The antigout effects of probenecid and sulfinpyrazone may be blocked by aspirin.
3. Aspirin can increase the gastrointestinal side effects of nonsteroidal anti-inflammatory drugs, alcohol, phenylbutazone, and adrenocorticosteroids (cortisonelike medicines).
4. Ammonium chloride, methionine, and furosemide can increase the side effects of aspirin.
5. Acetazolamide, methazolamide, antacids, and phenobarbital can decrease the effectiveness of aspirin.
6. Aspirin can increase the side effects of methotrexate, penicillin, thyroid hormone, phenytoin, sulfinpyrazone, naproxen, valproic acid, insulin, and oral antidiabetic medications.
7. Aspirin can decrease the effects of spironolactone.

Before starting to take aspirin, BE SURE TO TELL YOUR DOCTOR about any medications you are currently taking, especially any of those listed above.

WARNINGS

• Tell your doctor about unusual or allergic reactions you have had to any medications, especially to aspirin, methyl salicylate (oil of wintergreen), tartrazine, diclofenac, diflunisal, flurbiprofen, fenoprofen, ibuprofen, indomethacin, ketoprofen, meclofenamate, mefenamic acid, naproxen, piroxicam, sulindac, tolmetin, or etodolac.

• Before starting to take aspirin, be sure to tell your doctor if you now have or if you have ever had asthma, bleeding disorders, congestive heart failure, diabetes, glucose-6-phosphate dehydrogenase (G6PD) deficiency, gout, hemophilia, high blood pressure, kidney disease, liver disease, nasal polyps, peptic ulcers, or thyroid disease.

• Before having surgery or any other medical or dental treatment, be sure to tell your doctor or dentist that you are taking aspirin. Aspirin is usually discontinued five to seven days before surgery, in order to prevent bleeding complications.

• The use of aspirin in children (about 16 years of age or less) with the flu or chicken pox has been associated with a rare, life-threatening condition called Reye's syndrome. Aspirin should, therefore, not be given to children with signs of an infection.

• Large doses of aspirin (greater than eight 325-mg tablets per day) can cause erroneous urine glucose test results. People with diabetes should, therefore, check with their doctor before changing insulin doses while taking this medication.

• Additional medications that contain aspirin should not be taken without your doctor's approval. Be sure to check the labels on over-the-counter (nonprescription) pain, sinus, allergy, asthma, cough, and cold preparations to see if they contain aspirin.

• Be sure to tell your doctor if you are pregnant. Aspirin has been shown to cause birth defects in the offspring of animals that received large doses during pregnancy. Large doses of aspirin given to a pregnant woman close to term can prolong labor and cause bleeding complications in the mother and heart problems in the infant. Also tell your doctor if you are breast-feeding an infant. Small amounts of aspirin pass into breast milk.

---

aspirin and codeine combination

BRAND NAMES (Manufacturers)
aspirin with codeine (various manufacturers)
Empirin with Codeine (Burroughs Wellcome)
TYPE OF DRUG
Analgesic combination
INGREDIENTS
aspirin and codeine

DOSAGE FORM
Tablets (325 mg aspirin with 15 mg, 30 mg, or 60 mg of
  codeine)
Note that on the label of the vial of tablets, the name of this
  drug is followed by a number. This number refers to the
  amount of codeine: #3 contains 30 mg of codeine;
  #4 contains 60 mg.

STORAGE
Aspirin and codeine combination tablets should be stored at
room temperature in a tightly closed container. Care should be
taken to prevent moisture from entering the container, as it
will cause the aspirin in this product to decompose. Discard
the medicine if it has a vinegary odor.

USES
This medication is used to relieve tension headaches and mild
to severe pain. Codeine is a narcotic analgesic that acts on
the central nervous system to relieve pain.

TREATMENT
In order to avoid stomach upset, you can take this medication with food or milk.

This medication works best if you take it at the onset of pain
rather than when the pain becomes intense.

If you are taking this medication on a regular schedule and
you miss a dose, take the missed dose as soon as possible,
unless it is almost time for your next dose. In that case, don't
take the missed dose at all; just return to your dosing schedule.
Do not double the next dose.

SIDE EFFECTS
Minor. Constipation, dizziness, drowsiness, dry mouth, false
sense of well-being, flushing, indigestion, light-headedness,
loss of appetite, nausea, sweating, and vomiting. These side
effects should disappear over time as your body adjusts to the
medication.

If you are constipated, increase the amount of fiber in your
diet (fresh fruits and vegetables, salads, bran, and whole-grain
breads), drink more water, and exercise (unless your doctor
directs you to do otherwise).

Chew sugarless gum or suck on ice chips or a piece of hard
candy to reduce mouth dryness.

If you feel dizzy or light-headed, sit or lie down for a while; get up from a sitting or lying position slowly; and be careful on stairs.

Major. Tell your doctor about any side effects that are persistent or particularly bothersome. IT IS ESPECIALLY IMPORTANT TO TELL YOUR DOCTOR about severe abdominal pain; bloody or black, tarry stools; chest tightness; difficult or painful urination; difficulty in breathing; fatigue; itching; palpitations; rash; ringing in the ears; tremors; or yellowing of the eyes or skin.

INTERACTIONS

Aspirin and codeine combination interacts with several other types of drugs:

1. Concurrent use of it with other central nervous system depressants (such as alcohol, antihistamines, barbiturates, benzodiazepine tranquilizers, muscle relaxants, and phenothiazine tranquilizers) or with tricyclic antidepressants can cause extreme drowsiness.

2. The concurrent use of aspirin and codeine combination and monoamine oxidase (MAO) inhibitors should be avoided. At least 14 days should separate the use of aspirin and codeine combination and the use of an MAO inhibitor.

3. Alcohol and anti-inflammatory medication can increase the gastrointestinal side effects of this medication.

4. The side effects of anticoagulants (blood thinners, such as warfarin), oral antidiabetic agents, phenytoin, and methotrexate may be increased by the aspirin in this product.

5. Large doses of antacids increase the elimination of the aspirin portion of this medication from the body and decrease its effectiveness.

6. Aspirin may decrease the antigout effects of probenecid and sulfinpyrazone.

BE SURE TO TELL YOUR DOCTOR about any medications you are currently taking, especially any listed above.

WARNINGS

• Tell your doctor about unusual or allergic reactions you have had to medications, especially to aspirin, methyl salicylate (oil of wintergreen), diclofenac, diflunisal, flurbiprofen, fenoprofen, ibuprofen, indomethacin, ketoprofen, meclofenamate, mefenamic acid, naproxen, piroxicam, sulindac, tolmetin, and etodolac or to codeine or other narcotic analgesics (such as hydrocodone, hydromorphone, meperidine, methadone, morphine, oxycodone, and propoxyphene).

• Tell your doctor if you now have or if you have ever had abdominal disease, Addison's disease, bleeding or blood disorders, brain disease, colitis, epilepsy, gallstones or gallbladder disease, head injuries, heart disease, hemophilia, kidney disease, liver disease, lung disease, peptic ulcers, porphyria, enlarged prostate gland, or thyroid disease.

• If this drug makes you dizzy or drowsy, do not take part in any activity that requires alertness, such as driving a car or operating potentially dangerous equipment.

• Before having surgery or any other medical or dental treatment, be sure to tell your doctor or dentist that you are taking this medication. Aspirin-containing medication is usually discontinued five to seven days before surgery, to prevent bleeding complications.

• The use of aspirin in children (about 16 years of age or less) in an attempt to treat the flu or chicken pox has been associated with a rare, life-threatening condition called Reye's syndrome. Aspirin-containing products should therefore not be given to children with signs of infection.

• Because this drug contains codeine, it has the potential for abuse and must be used with caution. Usually, it should not be taken on a regular schedule for longer than ten days at a time. Tolerance for codeine develops quickly; do not increase the dosage or stop taking the drug abruptly unless you first consult your doctor. If you have been taking large amounts of this medication for long periods, you may experience a withdrawal reaction (muscle aches, diarrhea, gooseflesh, runny nose, nausea, vomiting, shivering, trembling, stomach cramps, sleep disorders, irritability, weakness, excessive yawning, or sweating). Your doctor may, therefore, want to reduce the dosage gradually.

• Because this product contains aspirin, additional medications that contain aspirin should not be taken without your doctor's approval. Check the labels on over-the-counter (nonprescription) pain, sinus, allergy, asthma, cough, and cold products to see if they contain aspirin.

• People with diabetes should be aware that large doses of aspirin (more than eight 325-mg tablets per day) may inter-

fere with urine sugar testing. They should check with their doctor before changing their insulin dose.
• Be sure to tell your doctor if you are pregnant. The effects of this medication during pregnancy have not been thoroughly studied in humans. If used regularly in large doses during pregnancy, codeine may result in addiction of the fetus, leading to withdrawal symptoms (irritability, excessive crying, tremors, fever, vomiting, diarrhea, sneezing, or excessive yawning) at birth. Large amounts of aspirin taken close to the end of pregnancy may prolong labor and cause bleeding problems in the mother and heart problems in the newborn infant. Also tell your doctor if you are breast-feeding an infant. Small amounts of this medication may pass into breast milk and cause excessive drowsiness in the nursing infant.

aspirin and oxycodone combination

BRAND NAMES (Manufacturers)
oxycodone hydrochloride, oxycodone terephthalate, and aspirin (various manufacturers)
Percodan (DuPont)
Percodan-Demi (DuPont)
TYPE OF DRUG
Analgesic combination
INGREDIENTS
aspirin and oxycodone
DOSAGE FORM
Tablets (325 mg aspirin with 2.25 mg oxycodone hydrochloride and 0.19 mg oxycodone terephthalate; 325 mg aspirin with 4.5 mg oxycodone hydrochloride and 0.38 mg oxycodone terephthalate)
STORAGE
Store at room temperature in a tightly closed container. Moisture causes the aspirin in this product to decompose. Discard the medicine if it has a vinegary odor.

USES
This combination medication is used to relieve moderate to severe pain. Oxycodone is a narcotic analgesic that acts upon

the central nervous system (brain and spinal cord) to alleviate pain.

TREATMENT

In order to avoid stomach upset, you can take this medication with food or milk.

This medication works most effectively if you take it at the onset of pain, rather than waiting until the pain becomes intense.

If you are taking this medication on a regular schedule and you miss a dose, take the missed dose as soon as possible, unless it is almost time for your next dose. In that case, don't take the missed dose at all; just return to your regular dosing schedule. Do not double the next dose.

SIDE EFFECTS

Minor. Constipation, dizziness, drowsiness, dry mouth, false sense of well-being, flushing, indigestion, light-headedness, loss of appetite, nausea, sweating, or vomiting. These side effects should disappear over time as your body adjusts to the medication.

If you are constipated, increase the amount of fiber in your diet (fresh fruits and vegetables, salads, bran, and whole-grain breads), drink more water, and exercise (unless your doctor directs you to do otherwise).

Chew sugarless gum or suck on ice chips or a piece of hard candy to reduce mouth dryness.

If you feel dizzy, light-headed, or nauseated, sit or lie down for a while; get up from a sitting or lying position slowly; and be careful on stairs.

Major. Tell your doctor about any side effects that are persistent or particularly bothersome. IT IS ESPECIALLY IMPORTANT TO TELL YOUR DOCTOR about bloody or black, tarry stools; chest tightness; difficult or painful urination; difficulty in breathing; fatigue; itching; palpitations; rash; ringing in the ears; severe abdominal pain; tremors; or yellowing of the eyes or skin.

INTERACTIONS

This medication interacts with several other types of drugs:
1. Concurrent use of this medication with other central nervous system depressants (such as alcohol, antihistamines, barbitu-

rates, benzodiazepine tranquilizers, muscle relaxants, and phenothiazine tranquilizers) or with tricyclic antidepressants can cause extreme drowsiness.

2. The concurrent use of aspirin and oxycodone combination and monoamine oxidase (MAO) inhibitors should be avoided. At least 14 days should separate the use of this drug and the use of an MAO inhibitor.

3. Alcohol and anti-inflammatory medications can increase the gastrointestinal side effects of this medication.

4. The side effects of anticoagulants (blood thinners, such as warfarin), oral antidiabetic agents, phenytoin, and methotrexate may be increased by the aspirin in this product.

5. Large doses of antacids increase the elimination of the aspirin portion of this medication from the body and decrease its effectiveness.

6. The aspirin portion of this medication may decrease the antigout effects of probenecid and sulfinpyrazone.

BE SURE TO TELL YOUR DOCTOR about any medications you are currently taking.

WARNINGS

• Tell your doctor about unusual or allergic reactions you have had to medications, especially to aspirin, methyl salicylate (oil of wintergreen), diclofenac, diflunisal, flurbiprofen, fenoprofen, ibuprofen, indomethacin, ketoprofen, meclofenamate, mefenamic acid, naproxen, piroxicam, sulindac, or tolmetin or to oxycodone or other narcotic analgesics (such as codeine, hydrocodone, hydromorphone, meperidine, methadone, morphine, or propoxyphene).

• Tell your doctor if you now have or if you have ever had abdominal disease, Addison's disease, bleeding or blood disorders, brain disease, colitis, epilepsy, gallstones or gallbladder disease, head injuries, heart disease, hemophilia, kidney disease, liver disease, lung disease, peptic ulcers, porphyria, enlarged prostate gland, or thyroid disease.

• If this drug makes you dizzy or drowsy, do not take part in any activity that requires alertness, such as driving an automobile or operating any potentially dangerous equipment.

• Before having surgery or any other medical or dental treatment, tell your doctor or dentist that you are taking this drug. Aspirin-containing medications are usually stopped five to seven days before surgery in order to prevent complications.

• The use of aspirin in children (about 16 years of age or less) with the flu or chicken pox has been associated with a rare, life-threatening condition called Reye's syndrome. Aspirin-containing products should, therefore, not be given to children who show any signs of having an infection.

• Because this drug contains oxycodone, it has the potential for abuse and must be used with caution. Usually, it should not be taken on a regular schedule for longer than ten days at a time. Tolerance develops quickly; do not increase the dosage or stop taking the drug abruptly, unless you first consult your doctor.

• If you have been taking large amounts of this medication for long periods, you may experience a withdrawal reaction (muscle aches, diarrhea, gooseflesh, runny nose, nausea, vomiting, shivering, trembling, stomach cramps, sleep disorders, irritability, weakness, excessive yawning, or sweating). Your doctor may, therefore, want to reduce the dosage gradually to prevent or minimize this response.

• Because this product contains aspirin, additional medications that contain aspirin should not be taken without your doctor's approval. Check the labels on over-the-counter (nonprescription) pain, sinus, allergy, asthma, cough, and cold products to see if they contain aspirin.

• People with diabetes should be aware that large doses of aspirin (more than eight 325-mg tablets per day) may interfere with urine sugar testing. Such individuals should check with their doctor before making adjustments to their dosage of insulin.

• Be sure to tell your doctor if you are pregnant. The effects of this medication during pregnancy have not been thoroughly studied in humans. Oxycodone, used regularly in large doses during pregnancy, may result in addiction of the fetus, leading to withdrawal symptoms (irritability, excessive crying, tremors, fever, vomiting, diarrhea, sneezing, or excessive yawning) at birth. Large amounts of aspirin taken close to the end of pregnancy may prolong labor and cause bleeding problems in the mother and heart problems in the newborn infant. Also tell your doctor if you are breast-feeding an infant. Small amounts of this medication may pass into breast milk and cause excessive drowsiness in the nursing infant.

aspirin, caffeine, and butalbital combination

BRAND NAMES (Manufacturers)
butalbital with aspirin and caffeine (various manufacturers)
Fiorgen (Goldline)
Fiorinal (Sandoz)
Isollyl (Rugby)
Lanorinal (Lannett)
Marnal (Vortech)
TYPE OF DRUG
Analgesic combination and sedative
INGREDIENTS
aspirin, caffeine, and butalbital
DOSAGE FORMS
Tablets (325 mg aspirin, 40 mg caffeine, and 50 mg
butalbital)
Capsules (325 mg aspirin, 40 mg caffeine, and 50 mg
butalbital)
STORAGE
Aspirin, caffeine, and butalbital combination tablets and cap-
sules should be stored at room temperature in tightly closed
containers. Moisture causes the aspirin in this product to de-
compose. Discard the medicine if it has a vinegary odor.

USES

This combination medication is used to relieve tension
headaches and mild to moderate pain. Butalbital belongs to a
group of drugs known as barbiturates. The barbiturates act on
the central nervous system (brain and spinal cord) to produce
relaxation. Caffeine is a central nervous system stimulant. It
constricts blood vessels in the head, which may help to relieve headaches.

TREATMENT

To avoid stomach upset, take this drug with food or milk. This
drug works most effectively if you take it at the onset of pain,
rather than waiting until the pain is intense. If you are taking
this medication on a regular schedule and you miss a dose,

take the missed dose as soon as possible, unless it is almost time for your next dose. In that case, don't take the missed dose at all; just return to your regular dosing schedule. Do not double the next dose.

SIDE EFFECTS

Minor. Dizziness, drowsiness, gas, loss of appetite, nausea, nervousness, sleeping disorders, or vomiting. These side effects should disappear over time as your body adjusts to the medication.

If you feel dizzy or light-headed, sit or lie down for a while; get up slowly from a sitting or lying position; and be especially careful on stairs.

Major. Tell your doctor about any side effects that are persistent or particularly bothersome. IT IS ESPECIALLY IMPORTANT TO TELL YOUR DOCTOR about bloody or black, tarry stools; chest tightness; confusion; difficult or painful urination; light-headedness; loss of coordination; palpitations; rash; ringing in the ears; severe abdominal pain; shortness of breath; sore throat and fever; or yellowing of the eyes or skin.

INTERACTIONS

This medication interacts with several other types of drugs:

1. Concurrent use of this medication with other central nervous system depressants (such as alcohol, antihistamines, barbiturates, benzodiazepine tranquilizers, muscle relaxants, and phenothiazine tranquilizers) or with tricyclic antidepressants can cause extreme drowsiness.

2. Alcohol and anti-inflammatory medications can increase the gastrointestinal side effects of this medication.

3. The side effects of anticoagulants (blood thinners, such as warfarin), oral antidiabetic agents, phenytoin, and methotrexate may be increased by the aspirin in this product.

4. Large doses of antacids increase the elimination of the aspirin portion of this medication from the body and decrease its effectiveness.

5. Aspirin may decrease the antigout effects of probenecid and sulfinpyrazone.

6. Butalbital can increase the elimination from the body of oral contraceptives (birth control pills), carbamazepine, adrenocorticosteroids (cortisonelike drugs), digoxin, doxycycline, tricyclic antidepressants, griseofulvin, metronidazole, theophylline, aminophylline, and quinidine, thereby decreasing the effectiveness of these medications.

7. The side effects of cyclophosphamide may be increased by butalbital.

BE SURE TO TELL YOUR DOCTOR about any medications you are currently taking, especially any of those listed above.

WARNINGS

• Tell your doctor about unusual or allergic reactions you have had to medications, especially to aspirin, methyl salicylate (oil of wintergreen), diclofenac, diflunisal, flurbiprofen, fenoprofen, ibuprofen, indomethacin, ketoprofen, meclofenamate, mefenamic acid, naproxen, piroxicam, sulindac, or tolmetin; to caffeine; or to butalbital or other barbiturates (such as phenobarbital, pentobarbital, or secobarbital).

• Tell your doctor if you now have or if you have ever had bleeding problems, blood disorders, diabetes mellitus, heart disease, hemophilia, hyperactivity, kidney disease, liver disease, mental depression, peptic ulcers, or thyroid disease.

• If this drug makes you dizzy or drowsy, do not take part in any activity that requires alertness, such as driving a car or operating potentially dangerous equipment.

• Before having surgery or any other medical or dental treatment, be sure to tell your doctor or dentist that you are taking this medication. Aspirin-containing medication is usually discontinued five to seven days before surgery in order to prevent bleeding complications.

• The use of aspirin in children (about 16 years of age or less) in an attempt to treat the symptoms of the flu or chicken pox has been associated with a rare, life-threatening condition called Reye's syndrome. Therefore, it is very important that aspirin-containing products should not be given to children with the signs of these infections.

• Because this drug contains butalbital, it has the potential for abuse and must be used with caution. Tolerance develops quickly; do not increase the dosage or stop taking the drug abruptly, unless you first consult your doctor. If you have been taking large amounts of this medication for long periods, you may experience a withdrawal reaction (muscle aches, diarrhea, convulsions, sleep disorders, nervousness, irritability, or weakness). Your doctor may, therefore, want to reduce the dosage gradually.

• Because this product contains aspirin, additional medications that contain aspirin should not be taken without your physician's approval. Check the labels on over-the-counter (nonprescription) pain, sinus, allergy, asthma, cough, and cold products to see if they contain aspirin.

• You should not take more than six tablets or capsules of this drug in one day, unless your doctor specifically directs you to do so.

• People with diabetes should be aware that large doses of aspirin (more than eight 325-mg tablets or capsules per day) may interfere with urine sugar testing. They should check with their doctor before changing their insulin dose.

• Be sure to tell your doctor if you are pregnant. The effects of this medication during pregnancy have not been thoroughly studied in humans. Butalbital, used regularly in large doses during pregnancy, may result in addiction of the fetus, leading to withdrawal symptoms (irritability, excessive crying, tremors, fever, vomiting, diarrhea, sneezing, or excessive yawning) at birth. Large amounts of aspirin taken close to the end of pregnancy may prolong labor and cause bleeding problems in the mother and heart problems in the newborn infant. Also tell your doctor if you are breast-feeding an infant. Small amounts of this medication may pass into breast milk and cause excessive drowsiness in the nursing infant.

---

aspirin, caffeine, and dihydrocodeine combination

BRAND NAME (Manufacturer)
Synalgos-DC (Wyeth-Ayerst)
TYPE OF DRUG
Analgesic combination
INGREDIENTS
aspirin, caffeine, and dihydrocodeine
DOSAGE FORM
Capsules (356.4 mg aspirin, 30 mg caffeine, and 16 mg dihydrocodeine)
STORAGE
This medication should be stored at room temperature in a tightly closed container. Moisture causes the aspirin in this

product to decompose. Do not keep any medication beyond the expiration date written on the containter.

USES

Aspirin, caffeine, and dihydrocodeine combination is used to relieve mild to moderate pain. Dihydrocodeine is a narcotic analgesic that acts on the central nervous system (brain and spinal cord) to relieve pain. Caffeine is a central nervous system stimulant. It constricts the blood vessels in the head, which may help to relieve headaches.

TREATMENT

In order to avoid stomach upset, you can take this medication with food or milk.

This medication works most effectively if you take it at the onset of pain, rather than waiting until the pain becomes intense.

If you are taking this drug on a schedule and you miss a dose, take the missed dose as soon as possible, unless it is almost time for your next dose. In that case, don't take the missed dose at all; just return to your regular dosing schedule. Do not double the next dose.

SIDE EFFECTS

Minor. Constipation, dizziness, drowsiness, dry mouth, false sense of well-being, headache, indigestion, loss of appetite, nausea, nervousness, restlessness, sleep disorders, sweating, or vomiting. These side effects should disappear as your body adjusts to the medication.

If you are constipated, increase the amount of fiber in your diet (fresh fruits and vegetables, salads, bran, and whole-grain breads), drink more water, and exercise (unless your doctor directs you to do otherwise).

Chew sugarless gum or suck on ice chips or a piece of hard candy to reduce mouth dryness.

If you feel dizzy or light-headed, sit or lie down for a while; get up from a sitting or lying position slowly; and be careful on stairs.

Major. Tell your doctor about any side effects that are persistent or particularly bothersome. IT IS ESPECIALLY IMPORTANT TO TELL YOUR DOCTOR about black, tarry stools; blurred vision; chest tightness; difficult or painful urination;

difficulty in breathing; fainting; itching; light-headedness; loss of coordination; palpitations; ringing in the ears; severe abdominal pain; skin rash; sore throat and fever; or unusual bleeding or bruising.

INTERACTIONS

This medication interacts with several other types of drugs:

1. Concurrent use of this medication with other central nervous system depressants (such as alcohol, antihistamines, barbiturates, benzodiazepine tranquilizers, muscle relaxants, and phenothiazine tranquilizers) or with tricyclic antidepressants can cause extreme drowsiness.

2. Concurrent use of this drug and monoamine oxidase (MAO) inhibitors should be avoided. At least 14 days should separate the use of aspirin, caffeine, and dihydrocodeine combination and the use of an MAO inhibitor.

3. Alcohol and anti-inflammatory medication can increase the gastrointestinal side effects of this medication.

4. The aspirin in this product may increase the side effects of anticoagulants (blood thinners, such as warfarin), oral antidiabetic agents, phenytoin, and methotrexate.

5. Large doses of antacids increase the elimination of the aspirin portion of this medication from the body and decrease its effectiveness.

6. The aspirin portion of this medication may decrease the antigout effects of probenecid and sulfinpyrazone.

BE SURE TO TELL YOUR DOCTOR about any medications you are currently taking, especially any of the medications listed above.

WARNINGS

• Tell your doctor about unusual or allergic reactions you have had to medications, especially to aspirin, methyl salicylate (oil of wintergreen), diclofenac, diflunisal, flurbiprofen, fenoprofen, ibuprofen, indomethacin, ketoprofen, meclofenamate, mefenamic acid, naproxen, piroxicam, sulindac, tolmetin, or etodolac; to dihydrocodeine or other narcotic analgesics (such as codeine, hydrocodone, hydromorphone, meperidine, methadone, morphine, oxycodone, and propoxyphene); or to caffeine.

• Tell your doctor if you now have or if you have ever had abdominal disease, Addison's disease, bleeding or blood disorders, brain disease, colitis, epilepsy, gallstones or gallbladder disease, head injuries, heart disease; hemophilia, kidney disease, liver disease, lung disease, peptic ulcers, prostate disease, or thyroid disease.

• If this drug makes you dizzy or drowsy, do not take part in any activity that requires alertness, such as driving an automobile or operating potentially dangerous equipment or machinery.

• Before having surgery or any other medical or dental treatment, be sure to tell your doctor or dentist that you are taking this medication. Aspirin-containing medication is usually discontinued five to seven days before surgery in order to prevent bleeding complications.

• The use of aspirin in children (about 16 years of age or less) in an attempt to treat the symptoms of the flu or chicken pox has been associated with a rare, life-threatening condition called Reye's syndrome. Therefore, it is very important that aspirin-containing products should not be given to children with the signs of these infections.

• Because this drug contains dihydrocodeine, it has the potential for abuse and must be used with caution. Usually, it should not be taken on a regular schedule for longer than ten days at a time. Tolerance develops quickly; do not increase the dosage or stop taking the drug abruptly, unless you first consult your doctor. If you have been taking large amounts of this medication for long periods, you may experience a withdrawal reaction (muscle aches, diarrhea, gooseflesh, runny nose, nausea, vomiting, shivering, trembling, stomach cramps, sleep disorders, irritability, weakness, excessive yawning, or sweating). Your doctor may, therefore, want to reduce the dosage gradually.

• Because this product contains aspirin, additional medications that contain aspirin should not be taken without your doctor's approval. Check the labels on over-the-counter (nonprescription) pain, sinus, allergy, asthma, cough, and cold products to see if they contain aspirin.

• People with diabetes should be aware that large doses of aspirin (more than eight 325-mg tablets of aspirin per day) may interfere with urine sugar testing and should check with their doctor before changing their insulin dose.

• Be sure to tell your doctor if you are pregnant. The effects of this medication during pregnancy have not been thoroughly studied in humans. Dihydrocodeine, used regularly in large doses during pregnancy, may result in addiction of the fetus, leading to withdrawal symptoms (irritability, excessive crying, tremors, fever, vomiting, diarrhea, sneezing, or excessive yawning) at birth. Large amounts of aspirin taken close to the end of pregnancy may prolong labor and cause bleeding problems in the mother and heart problems in the newborn infant. Also tell your doctor if you are breast-feeding an infant. Small amounts of this medication may pass into breast milk and cause excessive drowsiness in the nursing infant.

aspirin, caffeine, butalbital, and codeine combination

BRAND NAME (Manufacturer)
Fiorinal with Codeine (Sandoz)
TYPE OF DRUG
Analgesic combination and sedative
INGREDIENTS
aspirin, caffeine, butalbital, and codeine
DOSAGE FORM
Capsules (325 mg aspirin, 40 mg caffeine, 50 mg butalbital, and 30 mg codeine)
Note that on the label of the vial of capsules the name of this drug is followed by a number. This number refers to the amount of codeine present (#3 contains 30 mg codeine).
STORAGE
Aspirin, caffeine, butalbital, and codeine combination tablets and capsules should be stored at room temperature in tightly closed containers. Moisture causes the aspirin in this product to decompose. Discard the medicine if it has the odor of vinegar.

USES
This combination medication is used to relieve tension headaches and mild to moderate pain. Codeine is a narcotic analgesic that acts on the central nervous system (brain and spinal cord) to relieve pain. Butalbital belongs to a group of drugs known as barbiturates. The barbiturates act on the cen-

tral nervous system to produce relaxation. Caffeine is a central nervous system stimulant. It constricts blood vessels in the head, which may help to relieve headaches.

TREATMENT

In order to avoid stomach upset, you can take this medication with food or milk.

This medication works most effectively if you take it at the onset of pain, rather than waiting until the pain becomes intense.

If you are taking this medication on a regular schedule and you miss a dose, take the missed dose as soon as possible, unless it is almost time for your next dose. In that case, don't take the missed dose at all; just return to your regular dosing schedule. Do not double the next dose.

SIDE EFFECTS

Minor. Constipation, dizziness, drowsiness, flushing, headache, indigestion, loss of appetite, nausea, nervousness, sleep disorders, sweating, tiredness, or vomiting. These side effects should disappear as your body adjusts to the medication.

If you feel dizzy or light-headed, sit or lie down for a while; get up from a sitting or lying position slowly; and be careful on stairs.

If you are constipated, increase the amount of fiber in your diet (fresh fruits and vegetables, salads, bran, and whole-grain breads), drink more water, and exercise (unless your doctor directs you to do otherwise).

Major. Tell your doctor about any side effects that are persistent or particularly bothersome. IT IS ESPECIALLY IMPORTANT TO TELL YOUR DOCTOR about bloody or black, tarry stools; blurred vision; chest tightness; confusion; difficult or painful urination; loss of coordination; palpitations; rash; ringing in the ears; shortness of breath; severe abdominal pain; sore throat and fever; or yellowing of the eyes or skin.

INTERACTIONS

This combination medication interacts with several other types of drugs:

1. Concurrent use of this medication with other central nervous system depressants (such as alcohol, antihistamines, barbiturates, benzodiazepine tranquilizers, muscle relaxants, or phenothiazine tranquilizers) or with tricyclic antidepressants can cause extreme drowsiness.

2. Alcohol and anti-inflammatory medications can increase the gastrointestinal side effects of this medication.

3. The side effects of anticoagulants (blood thinners, such as warfarin), oral antidiabetic agents, phenytoin, and methotrexate may be increased by the aspirin content in this combination medication.

4. Large doses of antacids increase the elimination of the aspirin portion of this medication from the body and decrease its effectiveness.

5. Aspirin may decrease the antigout effects of probenecid and sulfinpyrazone.

6. Butalbital can increase the elimination from the body of oral contraceptives (birth control pills), carbamazepine, adrenocorticosteroids (cortisonelike drugs), digoxin, doxycycline, tricyclic antidepressants, griseofulvin, metronidazole, theophylline, aminophylline, and quinidine, thereby decreasing the effectiveness of these drugs.

7. The side effects of cyclophosphamide may be increased by butalbital.

8. This medication may interact with monoamine oxidase (MAO) inhibitors.

BE SURE TO TELL YOUR DOCTOR about any medications you are currently taking, especially any of those listed above.

WARNINGS

• Tell your doctor about unusual or allergic reactions you have had to medications, especially to aspirin, methyl salicylate (oil of wintergreen), diclofenac, diflunisal, flurbiprofen, fenoprofen, ibuprofen, indomethacin, ketoprofen, meclofenamate, mefenamic acid, naproxen, piroxicam, sulindac, tolmetin, or etodolac; to codeine or other narcotic analgesics (such as hydrocodone, hydromorphone, meperidine, methadone, morphine, oxycodone, and propoxyphene); to caffeine; or to butalbital or other barbiturates (such as phenobarbital, pentobarbital, and secobarbital).

• Tell your doctor if you now have or if you have ever had abdominal disease, Addison's disease, bleeding or blood disorders, brain disease, colitis, epilepsy, gallstones or gallbladder disease, head injuries, heart disease, hemophilia, kidney disease, liver disease, lung disease, peptic ulcers, porphyria, prostate disease, or thyroid disease.

• If this drug makes you dizzy or drowsy, do not take part in any activity that requires alertness, such as driving a car or operating potentially dangerous equipment.

• Before having surgery or any other medical or dental treatment, be sure to tell your doctor or dentist that you are taking this medication. Aspirin-containing medication is usually discontinued five to seven days before surgery in order to prevent bleeding complications.

• The use of aspirin in children (about 16 years of age or less) with the flu or chicken pox has been associated with a rare, life-threatening condition called Reye's syndrome. Aspirin-containing products should, therefore, not be given to children with signs of infection.

• Because this drug contains codeine and butalbital, it has the potential for abuse and must be used with caution. Usually, it should not be taken on a regular schedule for longer than ten days at a time. Tolerance develops quickly; do not increase the dosage or stop taking the drug abruptly, unless you first consult your doctor. If you have been taking large amounts of this medication for long periods, you may experience a withdrawal reaction (muscle aches, diarrhea, gooseflesh, runny nose, nausea, vomiting, shivering, trembling, stomach cramps, sleep disorders, irritability, weakness, excessive yawning, or sweating). Your doctor may, therefore, want to reduce the dosage gradually.

• Because this product contains aspirin, additional medications that contain aspirin should not be taken without your doctor's approval. Check the labels on over-the-counter (non-prescription) pain, sinus, allergy, asthma, cough, and cold products to see if they contain aspirin.

• You should not take more than six tablets or capsules of this drug in one day, unless your doctor specifically directs you to do so.

• People with diabetes should be aware that large doses of aspirin (more than eight 325-mg tablets or capsules per day) may interfere with urine sugar testing. They should, therefore, check with their doctor before attempting to adjust their insulin dose.

• Be sure to tell your doctor if you are pregnant. The effects of this medication during pregnancy have not been thoroughly studied in humans. Codeine and butalbital, used regularly in large doses during pregnancy, may result in addiction of the fetus, leading to withdrawal symptoms (irritability, excessive crying, tremors, fever, vomiting, diarrhea, sneezing, or excessive yawning) at birth. Large amounts of aspirin taken close to the end of pregnancy may prolong labor and cause bleeding problems in the mother and heart problems in the newborn infant. Also tell your doctor if you are breast-feeding an infant. Small amounts of this medication may pass into breast milk and cause excessive drowsiness in the nursing infant.

---

astemizole

BRAND NAME (Manufacturer)
Hismanal (Janssen)
TYPE OF DRUG
Antihistamine
INGREDIENT
astemizole
DOSAGE FORM
Tablets (10 mg)
STORAGE
Store this medication in a tightly closed container in a cool, dry place, away from heat or direct light, and out of the reach of children.

USES
Astemizole is indicated for the treatment of the allergic symptoms of conditions such as hay fever or hives. It belongs to a group of drugs known as antihistamines, which act by blocking the action of histamine, a chemical that is released by the body during an allergic reaction. It may be useful in patients unable to tolerate side effects, such as sedation, that other antihistamines may produce.

TREATMENT
Astemizole should be taken only as needed, and the prescribed dose should not be exceeded.

Because food significantly impairs the absorption of this medication, the drug should be taken on an empty stomach, at least two hours after a meal. No additional food should be taken for at least an hour after a dose is taken.

It may take up to two days for astemizole to achieve its full therapeutic effect.

If you miss a dose of this medication, take the missed dose as soon as possible, unless it is almost time for your next dose. In that case, do not take the missed dose at all; just wait until the scheduled dose at all; just wait until the next scheduled dose. Do not double the dose.

SIDE EFFECTS

Minor. Abdominal pain, diarrhea, drowsiness, dry mouth, gas, headache, increased appetite, nervousness, increased sensitivity to sunlight, or weight gain.

To relieve mouth dryness, chew sugarless gum or suck on ice chips or hard candy.

Major. Tell your doctor about any side effects that are persistent or particularly bothersome. It is ESPECIALLY IMPORTANT TO TELL YOUR DOCTOR about symptoms of a hypersensitivity reaction such as shortness of breath or rash.

INTERACTIONS

Although clinical studies with astemizole have not shown significant interactions with central nervous system depressants, such as alcohol or diazepam, it is important to be aware of the possibility of interactions. BE SURE TO TELL YOUR DOCTOR about all medications you are taking before starting astemizole.

Astemizole should not be taken with erythromycin, ketoconazole, or itraconazole, as an irregular heartbeat (arrhythmia) may develop.

Fluconazole, metronidazole, clarithromycin, azithromycin, and troleandomycin can increase the possibility of irregular heart rate when taken with astemizole.

WARNINGS

• Tell your doctor about unusual or allergic reactions you have had to any medication, especially to astemizole.

• Before taking this medication, be sure to tell your doctor about any heart disease (especially irregular heartbeat) that you now have or have ever had.

• Do not increase the dose of astemizole in attempts to gain quicker relief. Take this medication regularly as recommended by your doctor (do not skip doses) to achieve best results.

• Although astemizole is a less-sedating antihistamine, some patients may be more sensitive to its effects. Until you are familiar with how astemizole affects you, be cautious in performing tasks that require alertness.

• Tell your physician of any known liver ailments. Patients with diseases of the liver may not eliminate astemizole as rapidly as those with normal liver function.

• Be sure to tell your doctor if you are pregnant or plan to become pregnant. The safety of astemizole in pregnant women has not been established. In animal studies in which administered doses of astemizole exceeded dosage levels used in humans, an increased incidence of low birth weight and risk of infant death was noted. Since breakdown products of the drug may remain in the body for up to four months after use, this fact should be taken into consideration if pregnancy is being planned.

• Because babies are more sensitive to the side effects of antihistamines, such as excitement or irritability, astemizole is not recommended in nursing mothers until its effects upon infants are more fully established.

---

atenolol

BRAND NAMES (Manufacturers)
atenolol (various manufacturers)
Tenormin (ICI Pharma)
TYPE OF DRUG
Beta-adrenergic blocking agent
INGREDIENT
atenolol
DOSAGE FORM
Tablets (25 mg, 50 mg, and 100 mg)
STORAGE
Atenolol should be stored at room temperature in a tightly closed, light-resistant container.

USES

Atenolol is used to treat high blood pressure and angina (chest pain). It belongs to a group of medicines known as beta-adrenergic blocking agents or, more commonly, beta blockers. These drugs work by controlling impulses along certain nerve pathways. The result is a decreased workload for the heart.

TREATMENT

Atenolol can be taken with a glass of water, with meals, immediately following meals, or on an empty stomach, depending on your doctor's instructions. Try to take the medication at the same time(s) each day.

Try not to miss any doses of this medication. If you do miss a dose, take the missed dose as soon as possible. However, if the next scheduled dose is within eight hours (if you are taking this medicine only once a day) or within four hours (if you are taking this medicine more than once a day), do not take the missed dose at all; just return to your regular dosing schedule. Do not double the next dose.

It is important to remember that atenolol does not cure high blood pressure, but it will help to control the condition as long as you continue to take it.

SIDE EFFECTS

Minor. Anxiety; constipation; decreased sexual ability; diarrhea; difficulty in sleeping; drowsiness; dryness of the eyes, mouth, and skin; headache; nausea; nervousness; stomach discomfort; tiredness; or weakness. These side effects should disappear as your body adjusts to the medicine.

If you are extra-sensitive to the cold, be sure to dress warmly during cold weather.

To relieve constipation, increase the amount of fiber in your diet (fresh fruits and vegetables, salads, bran, and whole-grain breads), and drink more water (unless your doctor directs you to do otherwise).

Plain, nonmedicated eye drops (artificial tears) may help to relieve eye dryness.

Sucking on ice chips or chewing sugarless gum helps relieve mouth or throat dryness.

Major. Tell your doctor about any side effects that are persistent or particularly bothersome. IT IS ESPECIALLY IMPORTANT TO TELL YOUR DOCTOR about breathing difficulty or wheezing; cold hands or feet (due to decreased blood circulation to skin, fingers, and toes); confusion; dizziness; fever and sore throat; hair loss; hallucinations; light-headedness; mental depression; nightmares; reduced alertness; skin rash; swelling of the ankles, feet, or lower legs; or unusual or unexplained bleeding or bruising.

INTERACTIONS

Atenolol interacts with a number of other medications:

1. Indomethacin and other nonsteroidal anti-inflammatory drugs (including diclofenac, etodolac, ibuprofen, ketoprofen, naproxen, and piroxicam) have been shown to decrease the blood-pressure-lowering effects of the beta blockers. This may also happen with aspirin or other salicylates.

2. Concurrent use of beta blockers and calcium channel blockers (diltiazem, nifedipine, and verapamil) or disopyramide can lead to heart failure or very low blood pressure.

3. Cimetidine and oral contraceptives (birth control pills) can often increase the side effects of beta-adrenergic blocking agents.

4. Side effects may also be increased when beta blockers are taken with clonidine, digoxin, epinephrine, phenylephrine, phenylpropanolamine, phenothiazine tranquilizers, prazosin, or monoamine oxidase (MAO) inhibitors. At least 14 days should separate the use of a beta blocker and the use of an MAO inhibitor.

5. Alcohol, barbiturates, and rifampin can decrease the effectiveness of atenolol.

6. Beta blockers may antagonize (work against) the effects of theophylline, aminophylline, albuterol, isoproterenol, metaproterenol, and terbutaline.

7. Beta blockers can also interact with insulin or oral antidiabetic agents—raising or lowering blood-sugar levels or masking the symptoms of low blood sugar.

8. The action of beta blockers may be increased if they are used with chlorpromazine, furosemide, or hydralazine, which may have a negative effect.

9. In patients who have congestive heart failure treated with digitalis glycosides (for example, digoxin or digitoxin), caution should be used as both atenolol and digitalis products may slow heart conduction.

BE SURE TO TELL YOUR DOCTOR about any medications you are currently taking, especially any of those listed above.

WARNINGS

• Before starting to take this medication, it is important to tell your doctor if you have ever had unusual or allergic reactions to any beta blocker (acebutolol, atenolol, betaxolol, bisoprolol, carteolol, esmolol, labetalol, metoprolol, nadolol, penbutolol, pindolol, propranolol, and timolol).

• Tell your doctor if you now have or if you have ever had allergies, asthma, hay fever, eczema, slow heartbeat, bronchitis, diabetes mellitus, emphysema, heart or blood vessel disease, kidney disease, liver disease, thyroid disease, or poor circulation in the fingers or toes.

• In people with diabetes, atenolol may block some of the warning signs of low blood sugar, such as rapid pulse rate, but not others, such as dizziness or sweating.

• You may want to check your pulse while taking this medication. If your pulse is much slower than your usual rate (or if it is less than 50 beats per minute), check with your doctor. A pulse rate that is too slow may cause circulation problems.

• Atenolol may affect your body's response to exercise. Make sure you discuss with your doctor a safe amount of exercise for your medical condition.

• It is important that you do not stop taking this medicine without first checking with your doctor. Some conditions may become worse when the medicine is stopped suddenly, and the danger of a heart attack is increased in some patients. Your doctor may want you to gradually reduce the amount of medicine you take before stopping completely. Make sure that you have enough medicine on hand to last through vacations and holidays.

• Before having surgery or any other medical or dental treatment, tell the physician or dentist that you are taking this medicine. Often, this medication will be discontinued 48 hours prior to any major surgery.

• This medicine can cause dizziness, drowsiness, light-headedness, or decreased alertness. Therefore, exercise caution while driving a car or operating any potentially dangerous equipment.

• While taking this medicine, do not use any over-the-counter (nonprescription) asthma, allergy, cough, cold, sinus, or diet preparations unless you first check with your pharmacist or doctor. Some of these medicines can cause high blood pressure when taken at the same time as a beta blocker.

• Be sure to tell your doctor if you are pregnant. Animal studies have shown that some beta blockers can cause problems in pregnancy when used at very high doses. Adequate studies have not been done in humans, but there has been some association between beta blockers used during pregnancy and low birth weight, as well as breathing problems and slow heart rate in the newborn infants. However, other reports have shown no effects on newborn infants. Also tell your doctor if you are breast-feeding an infant. Small amounts of atenolol may pass into breast milk.

---

atenolol and chlorthalidone combination

BRAND NAMES (Manufacturers)
atenolol and chlorthalidone (various manufacturers)
Tenoretic (ICI Pharma)
TYPE OF DRUG
Beta-adrenergic blocking agent and diuretic
INGREDIENTS
atenolol and chlorthalidone
DOSAGE FORM
Tablets (50 mg atenolol and 25 mg chlorthalidone; 100 mg atenolol and 25 mg chlorthalidone)
STORAGE
Atenolol and chlorthalidone combination tablets should be stored at room temperature in a container that is tightly closed and resistant to light. The tablets should be protected from moisture during storage.

USES
Atenolol and chlorthalidone combination is prescribed to treat high blood pressure. Chlorthalidone is a diuretic, which reduces fluid accumulation in the body by increasing the elimination of salt and water through the kidneys. Atenolol belongs to a group of medicines known as beta-adrenergic blocking agents or, more commonly, beta blockers. They work

by controlling impulses along certain nerve pathways, thereby decreasing the workload on the heart and lowering blood pressure.

TREATMENT

This medication can be taken with a glass of water, with meals, immediately following meals, or on an empty stomach, depending on your doctor's instructions.

Try to take the medication at the same times(s) each day. Avoid taking a dose after 6:00 P.M.; otherwise, you may have to get up during the night to urinate.

If you miss a dose of this medication, take the missed dose as soon as possible, unless it is almost time for your next dose. In that case, do not take the missed dose at all; just wait until the next scheduled dose. Do not double the dose.

Atenolol and chlorthalidone combination does not cure high blood pressure, but it will help to control the condition as long as you continue to take it.

SIDE EFFECTS

Minor. Anxiety, constipation, cramps, decreased sexual ability, diarrhea, difficulty in sleeping, dizziness, drowsiness, dryness of the eyes and skin, gas, headache, heartburn, loss of appetite, nervousness, restlessness, stomach discomfort, sweating, or tiredness. These side effects should disappear as your body gets accustomed to the medication.

Chlorthalidone can cause increased sensitivity to sunlight. It is important, therefore, to avoid prolonged exposure to sunlight and sunlamps. Wear protective clothing and sunglasses, and use an effective sunscreen.

If you become extra-sensitive to the cold, be sure to dress warmly during cold weather.

Plain, nonmedicated eye drops (artificial tears) may help to relieve eye dryness.

To relieve constipation, increase the amount of fiber in your diet (fresh fruits and vegetables, salads, bran, and whole-grain breads) unless your doctor directs you to do otherwise.

Sucking on ice chips or chewing sugarless gum helps to relieve mouth and throat dryness.

To avoid dizziness or light-headedness when you stand that may be a result of taking atenolol and chorthalidone combination, contract and relax the muscles of your legs for a few moments before rising. Do this by alternately pushing one foot against the floor while raising the other foot slightly, so that you are "pumping" your legs in a pedaling motion. This will increase the blood flow through your body.

Major. Tell your doctor about any side effects that are persistent or particularly bothersome. IT IS ESPECIALLY IMPORTANT TO TELL YOUR DOCTOR about blurred vision, cold hands and feet, confusion, depression, difficulty in breathing, dry mouth, excessive thirst, excessive weakness, fever, hair loss, hallucinations, itching, joint pain, mood changes, muscle pain or spasms, nausea, nightmares, numbness or tingling in the fingers or toes, palpitations, rapid weight gain (three to five pounds within a week), reduced alertness, ringing in the ears, skin rash, sore throat, swelling, unusual bleeding or bruising, vomiting, or yellowing of the eyes or skin.

INTERACTIONS

Atenolol and chlorthalidone combination can interact with other types of medications:

1. Indomethacin and other nonsteroidal anti-inflammatory drugs (including diclofenac, etodolac, ibuprofen, ketoprofen, naproxen, and piroxicam), aspirin, and other salicylates may decrease the blood-pressure-lowering effects of beta blockers such as atenolol and chlorthalidone combination.

2. Concurrent use of atenolol and calcium channel blockers (diltiazem, nifedipine, verapamil) or disopyramide can lead to heart failure or very low blood pressure.

3. Cimetidine can increase blood levels of atenolol, resulting in greater side effects. Side effects may also be increased when atenolol is taken with clonidine, digoxin, epinephrine, phenylephrine, phenylpropanolamine, phenothiazine tranquilizers, prazosin, reserpine, oral contraceptives (birth control pills), or monoamine oxidase (MAO) inhibitors. At least 14 days should separate the use of atenolol and the use of an MAO inhibitor.

4. Atenolol can antagonize (act against) the effects of theophylline, aminophylline, albuterol, isoproterenol, metaproterenol, and terbutaline.

5. Alcohol, barbiturates, and rifampin can decrease blood levels of beta blockers, resulting in decreased effectiveness.

6. The action of beta blockers may be increased if they are used with chlorpromazine, furosemide, or hydralazine, which may have a negative effect.

7. Atenolol and chlorthalidone can interact with insulin and oral antidiabetic agents—raising or lowering blood-sugar levels and masking the symptoms of low blood sugar.

8. Chlorthalidone can decrease the effectiveness of oral anticoagulants (blood thinners, such as warfarin), antigout medications, and methenamine.

9. Fenfluramine may increase the blood-pressure-lowering effects of this drug, which can be dangerous.

10. Cholestyramine and colestipol can decrease the absorption of chlorthalidone from the gastrointestinal tract. Chlorthalidone should, therefore, be taken one hour before or four hours after a dose of cholestyramine or colestipol (if you have also been prescribed one of these medications).

11. Chlorthalidone may increase the side effects of amphotericin B, calcium supplements, cortisonelike steroids (such as cortisone, dexamethasone, hydrocortisone, prednisone, and prednisolone), digoxin, digitalis, lithium, quinidine, sulfonamide antibiotics, and vitamin D.

BE SURE TO TELL YOUR DOCTOR about all of the medications you are currently taking, especially any of the ones listed above.

WARNINGS

• Tell your doctor about unusual or allergic reactions you have had to medications, especially to atenolol or any other beta blocker (acebutolol, betaxolol, carteolol, esmolol, labetalol, metoprolol, nadolol, penbutolol, pindolol, propranolol, and timolol), to chlorthalidone or other diuretics (such as bendroflumethiazide, benzthiazide, chlorothiazide, cyclothiazide, hydrochlorothiazide, hydroflumethiazide, methyclothiazide, metolazone, polythiazide, and furosemide), or to any sulfa drug, including oral antidiabetic medications and sulfonamide antibiotics.

• Tell your doctor if you now have or if you have ever had asthma, diabetes mellitus, heart disease, gout, kidney disease or problems with urination, liver disease, lung disease, pancreatitis, poor circulation in the fingers or toes, systemic lupus erythematosus, or thyroid disease.

• Chlorthalidone can cause potassium loss. Signs of potassium loss include dry mouth, thirst, weakness, muscle pain or cramps, nausea, and vomiting. If you experience any of these symptoms, call your doctor. To help prevent this problem, your doctor may have blood tests performed periodically to monitor your potassium levels. To help avoid potassium loss, take this medication with a glass of fresh or frozen orange juice or cranberry juice, or eat a banana every day. The use of a salt substitute also helps to prevent potassium loss. Do not change your diet until you discuss it with your doctor. Too much potassium may also be dangerous.

• While taking this medication, limit your intake of alcohol in order to prevent dizziness and light-headedness.

• Do not take any over-the-counter (nonprescription) medications for weight control or for allergy, asthma, cough, cold, or sinus problems unless you first check with your doctor.

• To prevent severe water loss (dehydration) while taking this drug, check with your doctor if you have any illness that causes severe or continuous nausea, vomiting, or diarrhea.

• This medication can raise blood-sugar levels in people with diabetes. Blood sugar should be monitored carefully with blood or urine tests when this medication is being taken.

• You may want to check your pulse while taking this medication. If your pulse is much slower than your usual rate (or if it is less than 50 beats per minute), check with your doctor; a pulse rate that slow may cause circulation problems.

• Atenolol can affect your body's response to exercise. Make sure that you ask your doctor what an appropriate amount of exercise would be for you, taking into account your medical condition.

• Before having surgery or any other medical or dental treatment, tell your doctor or dentist that you are taking this medicine. Often, this medication will be discontinued 48 hours prior to any major surgery.

• This medication can cause dizziness, drowsiness, light-headedness, or decreased alertness. Therefore, exercise caution whenever driving a car or operating potentially dangerous equipment.

• A doctor does not usually prescribe a "fixed-dose" drug like this as the first choice in the treatment of high blood pressure. Usually the patient first receives each ingredient singly. If there is an adequate response to the fixed dose contained in this product, it can then be substituted. The advantage of a combination product is increased convenience and (often) decreased cost.

• It is important that you do not stop taking this medicine unless you first check with your doctor. Some conditions worsen when this medicine is stopped suddenly, and the danger of a heart attack is increased in some patients. Your doctor may, therefore, want you to gradually reduce the amount of medicine you take before stopping completely. Make sure that you have enough medicine on hand to last through vacations, holidays, and weekends.

• Be sure to tell your doctor if you are pregnant. Animal studies have shown that some beta blockers can cause problems in pregnancy when used at very high doses. Studies have not been conducted in humans, but there has been some association between use of beta blockers during pregnancy and low birth weight, as well as breathing problems and slow heart rate in newborn infants. However, other reports have shown no effects on newborn infants. Also tell your doctor if you are breast-feeding an infant. Although problems in humans have not been reported, small amounts of this medication may pass into breast milk, so caution is warranted.

---

atropine, scopolamine, hyoscyamine, and phenobarbital combination

BRAND NAMES (Manufacturers)
Barophen (various manufacturers)
belladonna alkaloids with phenobarbital
   (various manufacturers)
Donnamor (H.L. Moore)
Donna-Sed (Vortech)
Donnatal (Robins)
Hyosophen (Rugby)
Kinesed (Stuart)
Malatal (Mallard)
Spasmolin (various manufacturers)
Spasmophen (Lannett)

Spasquid (Geneva Generics)
Susano (Halsey)
TYPE OF DRUG
Anticholinergic and sedative
INGREDIENTS
atropine, scopolamine, hyoscyamine, and phenobarbital
DOSAGE FORMS
Tablets (0.0194 mg atropine, 0.0065 mg scopolamine,
    0.104 mg hyoscyamine, and 16 mg phenobarbital)
Capsules (0.0194 mg atropine, 0.0065 mg scopolamine,
    0.104 mg hyoscyamine, and 16 mg phenobarbital)
Oral elixir (0.0194 mg atropine, 0.0065 mg scopolamine,
    0.104 mg hyoscyamine, and 16 mg phenobarbital,
    with 23% alcohol)
Chewable tablets (0.12 mg atropine, 0.007 mg
    scopolamine, 0.12 mg hyoscyamine, and 16 mg
    phenobarbital)
Extended-release tablets (0.058 mg atropine, 0.0195 mg
    scopolamine, 0.311 mg hyoscyamine, and 48.6 mg
    phenobarbital)
STORAGE
The medication should be stored at room temperature (never
frozen) in a tightly closed, light-resistant container. Do not
keep any medication beyond the expiration date.

USES

Atropine, scopolamine, hyoscyamine, and phenobarbital combination is used to treat stomach and intestinal disorders.
    Atropine, scopolamine, and hyoscyamine belong to a group
of drugs known as belladonna alkaloids or anticholinergic
agents. These drugs block certain nerve pathways, thereby
slowing the gastrointestinal tract and decreasing urination.
Phenobarbital is a sedative that acts directly on the brain to
slow the activity of the nervous system.

TREATMENT

Take this medication 30 minutes to one hour before meals
(unless your doctor says otherwise). To reduce stomach upset,
take it with food or with a glass of water or milk.
    At least one hour should separate administration of this
medication from the administration of either antacids or an-

tidiarrheal medications—they may prevent gastrointestinal absorption of this drug.

Measure the liquid form of this medication carefully with a specially designed 5-mL measuring spoon. An ordinary kitchen teaspoon is not accurate enough.

If you miss a dose, don't take the missed dose; just return to your regular dosing schedule. Don't double the next dose.

SIDE EFFECTS

Minor. Confusion; constipation; decreased sexual desire; dizziness; drowsiness; dry mouth, nose, and throat; headache; insomnia; loss of taste; muscle pain; nausea; nervousness; reduced sweating; sensitivity of eyes to sunlight; vomiting; or weakness. These side effects should disappear as your body adjusts to the medication.

If you are constipated, increase the amount of fiber in your diet (fresh fruits and vegetables, salads, bran, and whole-grain breads), exercise, and drink more water (unless your doctor directs you to do otherwise).

Chew sugarless gum or suck on ice chips or a piece of hard candy to reduce mouth dryness.

Wear sunglasses if your eyes become sensitive to light.

To avoid dizziness or light-headedness when you stand, contract and relax the muscles of your legs for a few moments before rising. Do this by pushing one foot against the floor while raising the other foot slightly, alternating feet so that you are "pumping" your legs in a pedaling motion.

Major. Tell your doctor about any side effects that are persistent or particularly bothersome. IT IS ESPECIALLY IMPORTANT TO TELL YOUR DOCTOR about blurred vision, difficulty in breathing, difficulty in urinating, hallucinations, hot and dry skin, palpitations, rash, slurred speech, sore throat, or yellowing of the eyes or skin.

INTERACTIONS

Atropine, scopolamine, hyoscyamine, and phenobarbital combination interacts with several other types of drugs:

1. This medication can cause extreme drowsiness when combined with central nervous system depressants (such as alcohol, antihistamines, barbiturates, benzodiazepine tranquilizers, muscle relaxants, narcotics, and pain medications) or with tricyclic antidepressants.

2. Amantadine, antihistamines, haloperidol, monoamine oxidase (MAO) inhibitors, phenothiazine tranquilizers, procainamide, quinidine, and tricyclic antidepressants can increase the side effects of the belladonna alkaloids. At least 14 days should separate the use of this drug and the use of an MAO inhibitor.

3. The phenobarbital content in this drug can decrease the effectiveness of oral anticoagulants (blood thinners, such as warfarin), cortisonelike medications, digoxin, griseofulvin, doxycycline, metronidazole, phenytoin, and tricyclic antidepressants.

WARNINGS

• Tell your doctor about unusual or allergic reactions you have had to any medications, especially to atropine, scopolamine, hyoscyamine, phenobarbital, or to other barbiturates (such as butalbital, pentobarbital, primidone, and secobarbital).

• Tell your doctor if you now have or if you have ever had enlarged prostate gland, glaucoma, heart disease, hiatal hernia, high blood pressure, internal bleeding, kidney disease, liver disease, lung disease, myasthenia gravis, porphyria, obstructed bladder, obstructed intestine, ulcerative colitis, or thyroid disease.

• If this medication makes you dizzy or drowsy or blurs your vision, do not take part in any activity that requires alertness, such as driving a car or operating potentially dangerous equipment. Be careful on stairs, and avoid getting up suddenly from a lying or sitting position.

• This medication can decrease sweating and heat release from the body. Avoid strenuous exercise in hot weather, and avoid taking hot baths, showers, and saunas.

• Before having surgery or any other medical or dental treatment, tell the doctor or dentist that you are taking this drug.

• Be sure to tell your doctor if you are pregnant. This medication crosses the placenta. Phenobarbital given to the mother close to term can cause breathing problems and bleeding complications in the newborn infant. Also tell your doctor if you are breast-feeding an infant. Small amounts of this medication pass into breast milk and may cause excessive drowsiness or irritability in the nursing infant.

azithromycin

BRAND NAME (Manufacturer)
Zithromax (Pfizer)
TYPE OF DRUG
Antibiotic
INGREDIENT
azithromycin
DOSAGE FORM
Capsules (250 mg)
STORAGE
This product should be stored at room temperature in a closed, light-resistant container.

USES

Azithromycin is used to treat a wide variety of bacterial infections, including those of the upper and lower respiratory tracts and skin and certain sexually transmitted diseases. This medicine acts by preventing bacteria from manufacturing protein and thereby preventing their growth. Azithromycin kills certain bacteria but is not effective against viruses, parasites, or fungi.

TREATMENT

It is best to take azithromycin on an empty stomach (one hour before and two hours after a meal). Azithromycin works best when the level of medicine in your bloodstream is kept constant. Therefore, it is best to take the doses at the same time every day.

If you miss a dose, take it immediately. However, if you don't remember to take your scheduled dose until the next day, skip the missed dose and go back to your regular dosing schedule. Do not double the next dose.

It is important to continue to take this medicine for the entire time period prescribed by the doctor (usually five days), even if the symptoms disappear before the end of that period. If you stop taking this drug too soon, resistant bacteria (bacteria that will not be killed by the antibiotic) are given a chance to continue to grow and infection could recur.

SIDE EFFECTS

Minor. Diarrhea, nausea, vomiting, headache, dizziness, abdominal pain. These effects should disappear as your body adjusts to the medication.

This medication can cause increased sensitivity to sunlight. It is important to avoid prolonged exposure to sunlight and sunlamps. Wear protective clothing and use an effective sunscreen.

If you feel dizzy or light-headed, sit or lie down for a while; get up slowly from a sitting or reclining position; and be careful on stairs.

Major. Tell your doctor about any side effects that are persistent or particularly bothersome. IT IS ESPECIALLY IMPORTANT TO TELL YOUR DOCTOR about fever, palpitations, rash, shortness of breath, swelling of the face or neck, sore throat, rectal or vaginal itching, unusual bruising or bleeding, or yellowing of the eyes or skin. If your symptoms of infection seem to be getting worse rather than improving, you should contact your doctor.

INTERACTIONS

Azithromycin interacts with several medications:

1. Azithromycin potentially can increase blood levels of aminophylline, theophylline, carbamazepine, cyclosporin, phenytoin, digoxin, triazolam, phenobarbital, ergotamine, dihydroergotamine, or oral anticoagulants (blood thinners, such as warfarin); this may lead to serious side effects.

2. Antacids containing aluminum and magnesium will decrease the efficacy of azithromycin. Take antacids one hour before, or two hours after your dose of azithromycin.

3. Astemizole, loratidine, and terfenadine may cause irregular heart rate when taken with azithromycin.

BE SURE TO TELL YOUR DOCTOR about any medications you are currently taking, especially any listed above.

WARNINGS

• Tell your doctor about any unusual reactions you have to any medications, especially to azithromycin, clarithromycin, or erythromycin.

• Tell you doctor if you have or ever had kidney disease, liver disease, or heart disease.

• This medication has been prescribed for your current infection only. Another infection later on, or one that someone else has, may require a different medicine. You should not give your medication to other people or use it for other infections, unless your doctor specifically directs you to do so.

• Before having surgery or any other medical or dental treatment, be sure to tell your doctor or dentist you are taking azithromycin.

• Be sure to tell your doctor if you are pregnant. The effects of this medicine during pregnancy have not been thoroughly studied in humans. Also tell your doctor if you are breast-feeding an infant. It is not known if azithromycin passes into breast milk.

---

benazepril

BRAND NAME (Manufacturer)
Lotensin (Ciba-Geigy)
TYPE OF DRUG
Antihypertensive
INGREDIENT
benazepril
DOSAGE FORM
Tablets (5 mg, 10 mg, 20 mg, and 40 mg)
STORAGE
Store benazepril at room temperature in a tightly closed container.

USES
Benazepril is used to treat high blood pressure and congestive heart failure. It is a vasodilator (it widens the blood vessels) that acts by blocking the production of chemicals that may be responsible for constricting, or narrowing, the blood vessels.

TREATMENT
Benazepril can be taken with food if it causes irritation or on an empty stomach. To become accustomed to taking this medication, try to take it at the same time(s) every day.

It may be several weeks before you notice the full effects of this medication.

If you miss a dose of benazepril, take the missed dose as soon as possible, unless it is almost time for the next dose. In that case, do not take the missed dose at all; just wait until the next scheduled dose. Do not double the dose.

Benazepril does not cure high blood pressure, but it will help control the condition as long as you continue to take it.

SIDE EFFECTS

Minor. Abdominal pain, cough, diarrhea, dizziness, drowsiness, fatigue, headache, insomnia, nausea, nervousness, sweating, or vomiting. These side effects should disappear as your body adjusts to the medication. To avoid dizziness when you stand, contract and relax the muscles of your legs for a few moments before rising. Do this by alternately pushing one foot against the floor while lifting the other foot slightly.

Major. Tell your doctor about any side effects that are persistent or particularly bothersome. IT IS ESPECIALLY IMPORTANT TO TELL YOUR DOCTOR about chest pain; difficulty breathing; fainting; fever; itching; light-headedness (especially during the first few days); muscle cramps; palpitations; rash; sore throat; swelling of the face, eyes, lips, or tongue; tingling in the fingers and toes; or yellowing of the eyes or skin.

INTERACTIONS

Benazepril interacts with several other types of medications:

1. Diuretics and other antihypertensive medications can cause an excessive drop in blood pressure when they are combined with benazepril (especially with the first dose).

2. The combination of benazepril with amiloride, potassium supplements, salt substitutes, spironolactone, or triamterene can lead to hyperkalemia (dangerously high levels of potassium in the bloodstream).

3. Nonsteroidal anti-inflammatory agents (including ibuprofen, indomethacin, and naproxen) may reduce the effectiveness of this medication.

Before starting to take benazepril, BE SURE TO TELL YOUR DOCTOR about any medications you are currently taking, especially any of those listed above.

WARNINGS

• Tell your doctor about any unusual allergic reactions you have had to any medications, especially to benazepril.

• Tell your doctor if you now have or if you have ever had blood disorders, heart failure, renal disease, or systemic lupus erythematosus.

• Excessive perspiration, dehydration, or prolonged vomiting or diarrhea can lead to an excessive drop in blood pressure while you are taking this medication. Contact your doctor if you have any of these symptoms.

• Before having surgery or other medical or dental treatment, tell your doctor or dentist you are taking this drug.

• If this drug makes you dizzy or drowsy, do not take part in any activity that requires alertness, such as driving a car or operating potentially dangerous equipment, and avoid handling hazardous material.

• If you have high blood pressure, do not take any over-the-counter (nonprescription) medications for weight control or for asthma, sinus, cough, cold, or allergy problems unless you first check with your doctor.

• Be sure to tell your doctor if you are pregnant. Drugs in the same class as benazepril have been shown to cause birth defects, including kidney damage, low blood pressure, improper skull development, and death when taken in the second and third trimesters. Also tell your doctor if you are breast-feeding an infant. Small amounts of benazepril may be distributed into breast milk.

benztropine

BRAND NAMES (Manufacturers)
benztropine (various manufacturers)
Cogentin (Merck Sharp & Dohme)
TYPE OF DRUG
Anticholinergic and antiparkinsonism agent
INGREDIENT
benztropine
DOSAGE FORM
Tablets (0.5 mg, 1 mg, and 2 mg)
STORAGE
Benztropine tablets should be stored at room temperature in a tightly closed container. This medication should not be refrigerated.

USES

Benztropine is used to treat the symptoms of Parkinson's disease or to control the side effects of phenothiazine tranquilizers. It is not understood how this medication works, but it may act by balancing certain chemicals in the brain.

TREATMENT

In order to reduce the possibility of stomach irritation, you can take benztropine tablets with food or just after a meal.

Antacids and antidiarrheal medicines prevent the absorption of this medication, so at least one hour should separate doses of benztropine and one of these medicines.

If you miss a dose of this medication, take the missed dose as soon as possible, unless it is within two hours of your next dose. In that case, don't take the missed dose at all; just return to your regular dosing schedule. Do not double the next dose.

SIDE EFFECTS

Minor. Bloating; blurred vision; constipation; dizziness; drowsiness; dry mouth, throat, and nose; false sense of well-being; headache; increased sensitivity of the eyes to light; muscle cramps; nausea; nervousness; reduced sweating; or weakness. These side effects should disappear as your body adjusts to the medication.

If you are constipated, increase the amount of fiber in your diet (fresh fruits and vegetables, salads, bran, and whole-grain breads), exercise, and drink more water (unless your doctor directs you to do otherwise).

Chew sugarless gum or suck on ice chips or a piece of hard candy to reduce mouth dryness.

If your eyes become sensitive to light, avoid exposure to the sun or wear sunglasses.

To avoid dizziness and light-headedness when you stand, contract and relax the muscles of your legs for a few moments before rising. Do this by pushing one foot against the floor while raising the other foot slightly, alternating feet so that you are "pumping" your legs in a pedaling motion.

Major. Tell your doctor about any side effects that are persistent or particularly bothersome. IT IS ESPECIALLY IMPORTANT TO TELL YOUR DOCTOR about depression, difficulty sleeping, difficulty in urinating, hallucinations, involuntary muscle movements, loss of balance, memory loss, mood changes, numbness of the fingers, palpitations, or unusual excitement.

Some side effects may occur for a short time after discontinuing this drug. Consult your doctor if they become bothersome.

INTERACTIONS
Benztropine can interact with several other types of medications:
1. It can cause extreme drowsiness when combined with alcohol or other central nervous system depressants (such as antihistamines, barbiturates, benzodiazepine tranquilizers, muscle relaxants, narcotics, and pain medications) or with tricyclic antidepressants.
2. Amantadine, antihistamines, haloperidol, monoamine oxidase (MAO) inhibitors, phenothiazine tranquilizers, procainamide, quinidine, and tricyclic antidepressants can increase the side effects of benztropine. At least 14 days should separate the use of this drug and the use of an MAO inhibitor.

Before starting to take this medication, BE SURE TO TELL YOUR DOCTOR about any medications you are currently taking, especially any of those drugs that are listed above.

WARNINGS
• Be sure to tell your doctor about unusual or allergic reactions you have had to any medications, especially to benztropine.
• Tell your doctor if you now have or if you have ever had achalasia (difficulty in relaxing certain muscles), glaucoma, heart disease, high blood pressure, kidney disease, liver disease, myasthenia gravis, blockage of the intestinal tract or urinary tract, enlarged prostate gland, stomach ulcers, or thyroid disease.
• If this drug makes you dizzy or drowsy, be sure to avoid any activity that requires alertness, such as driving a car or operating potentially dangerous equipment. Be careful on stairs, and avoid getting up suddenly from a lying or sitting position.
• This medication can decrease sweating and heat release from the body. You should, therefore, avoid getting overheated

by strenuous exercise in hot weather and should avoid taking hot baths, showers, and saunas.

• Elderly patients are more sensitive to the effects of benztropine. Contact your doctor if confusion, disorientation, agitation, or hallucinations occur.

• Be sure to tell your doctor if you are pregnant. Extensive studies of the use of benztropine during pregnancy have not been conducted. Also tell your doctor if you are breast-feeding an infant. Small amounts of this medication may pass into breast milk. In addition, benztropine can reduce milk formation in lactating women.

---

betamethasone dipropionate (topical)

BRAND NAMES (Manufacturers)
Alphatrex (Savage)
betamethasone dipropionate (various manufacturers)
Diprolene (Schering)
Diprosone (Schering)
Maxivate (Westwood)
TYPE OF DRUG
Adrenocorticosteroid hormone
INGREDIENT
betamethasone
DOSAGE FORMS
Ointment (0.05%)
Cream (0.05%)
Lotion (0.05%)
Aerosol (0.1%)
Gel (0.05%)
STORAGE
Betamethasone dipropionate ointment, cream, and lotion should be stored at room temperature in tightly closed containers. This medication should never be frozen.

The aerosol form of this medication is packaged under pressure. It should not be stored near heat or an open flame or in direct sunlight, and the container should never be punctured.

USES

Your adrenal glands naturally produce certain cortisonelike chemicals. These chemicals are involved in various regulatory processes in the body (such as those involving fluid balance, temperature, and reaction to inflammation). Betamethasone dipropionate belongs to a group of drugs known as adrenocorticosteroids (or cortisonelike medications). It is used to relieve the skin inflammation (redness, swelling, itching, and discomfort) associated with conditions such as dermatitis, eczema, and poison ivy. How betamethasone dipropionate acts to relieve these dermatological conditions is not completely understood.

TREATMENT

Before applying this medication, wash your hands. Then, unless your doctor gives you different instructions, gently wash the area of the skin where the medication is to be applied. With a clean towel, pat the area until it is almost dry; it should be slightly damp when you put the medicine on it.

If you are using the lotion form of this medication, shake it well before pouring it out. The contents tend to settle on the bottom of the bottle, so it is necessary to shake the container to distribute the ingredients evenly and equalize the doses.

Apply a small amount of the medication to the affected area in a thin layer. Do not bandage the area unless your doctor tells you to do so. If you are to apply an occlusive dressing (like kitchen plastic wrap), be sure you understand the instructions. Wash your hands again after application.

Shake the aerosol spray form of this medication in order to disperse the medication evenly. Hold the can upright, six to eight inches from the area to be sprayed, and spray the area for one to three seconds. DO NOT SMOKE while you are using the aerosol spray; the contents are under pressure and may explode when exposed to heat or flames.

Avoid applying this medication to areas with cuts or open wounds.

If you miss a dose of this medication, apply the dose as soon as possible, unless it is almost time for the next application. In that case, do not apply the missed dose; just return to your regular schedule. Do not put twice as much of the medication on your skin at the next application.

SIDE EFFECTS

Minor. Acne, burning sensation, itching, skin dryness, or rash.

If the affected area is extremely dry or scaling, the skin may be moistened before applying the medication by soaking in water or by applying water with a clean cloth. The ointment form is probably most appropriate for dry skin.

A mild, temporary stinging sensation may occur after this medication is applied. If this persists, contact your doctor.

Major. Tell your doctor about any side effects that are persistent or particularly bothersome. IT IS ESPECIALLY IMPORTANT TO TELL YOUR DOCTOR about blistering, increased hair growth, irritation of the affected area, loss of skin color, secondary infection in the area being treated, or thinning of the skin with easy bruising.

INTERACTIONS

This medication should not interact with any other medications as long as it is used according to directions.

WARNINGS

• Tell your doctor about unusual or allergic reactions you have had to any medications, especially to betamethasone dipropionate or any other adrenocorticosteroid (such as amcinonide, clocortolone, cortisone, desonide, desoximetasone, dexamethasone, diflorasone, flumethasone, fluocinolone, fluocinonide, fluorometholone, flurandrenolide, halcinonide, hydrocortisone, methylprednisolone, prednisolone, prednisone, and triamcinolone).

• Tell your doctor if you now have or if you have ever had blood vessel disease, chicken pox, diabetes mellitus, fungal infection, peptic ulcer, shingles, tuberculosis, tuberculosis of the skin, or any other type of infection, especially at the site currently being treated.

• If irritation develops while using this drug, immediately discontinue its use and notify your doctor.

• This product is not for use in the eyes or on mucous membranes; contact may result in side effects.

• Do not use this product with an occlusive wrap unless your doctor directs you to do so. Systemic absorption of this drug is increased if extensive areas of the body are treated, particularly if occlusive bandages are used. If it is necessary for you to

use this drug under a wrap, follow your doctor's instructions exactly; do not leave the wrap in place longer than specified.
• If you are using this medication on a child's diaper area, do not put tight-fitting diapers or plastic pants on the child. This may lead to increased systemic absorption of the drug and a possible increase in side effects.
• Elderly patients and younger children have thinner skin, and, therefore, betamethasone dipropionate is more likely to be absorbed. Report any adverse effects to your doctor.
• In order to avoid freezing skin tissue when using the aerosol form of betamethasone dipropionate, make sure that you do not spray for more than three seconds, and hold the container at least six inches from the skin.
• When using the aerosol form of this medication on the face, cover your eyes and do not inhale the spray.
• Use this medication only for your current condition. Do not use it for another problem later or give it to other people to use.
• Tell your doctor if you are pregnant. If large amounts of this drug are applied for prolonged periods, some of it may cross the placenta. Although studies in humans have not been conducted, birth defects have been observed in the offspring of animals that were given large oral doses of this type of drug during pregnancy. Also tell your doctor if you are breast-feeding an infant. If absorbed through the skin, small amounts of the drug may pass into breast milk and may cause growth suppression or a decrease in natural adrenocorticosteroid production in the nursing infant.

---

betamethasone dipropionate and clotrimazole combination (topical)

BRAND NAME (Manufacturer)
Lotrisone (Schering)
TYPE OF DRUG
Adrenocorticosteroid hormone and antifungal
INGREDIENTS
betamethasone dipropionate and clotrimazole

DOSAGE FORM

Topical cream (0.05% betamethasone dipropionate and 1% clotrimazole)

STORAGE

This medication should be stored at room temperature (never frozen) in a tightly closed container. Discard any outdated or unneeded medication.

USES

This combination drug is used to treat fungal infections of the skin. Clotrimazole is an antifungal agent that prevents the growth and multiplication of a wide range of fungi and yeast. Betamethasone dipropionate belongs to a group of drugs known as adrenocorticosteroids (or cortisonelike medications). Your adrenal glands naturally produce certain cortisonelike chemicals. These chemicals are involved in various regulatory processes in the body. Betamethasone dipropionate is added to this combination to relieve skin inflammation (redness, swelling, itching, and discomfort).

TREATMENT

Before applying betamethasone dipropionate and clotrimazole combination, you should wash your hands. Then, unless your doctor tells you to do otherwise, cleanse the affected area with soap and water. Pat the skin with a clean towel until it is almost dry. Gently massage a small amount of the cream over the entire affected area and the skin immediately surrounding. Avoid applying the medication to areas with cuts or open wounds. Don't bandage or cover the area after applying the medication, unless your doctor instructs you to do so. Wash your hands again after application.

Improvement in your condition may not become apparent for as long as a week after you begin treatment with this drug. However, you should be sure to complete the full course of medication. If you stop using this drug too soon, resistant fungi are given a chance to continue growing, and the infection could recur. If your condition has not improved after four weeks, CONTACT YOUR DOCTOR. Clotrimazole may not be effective against the organism causing your infection.

If you miss a dose of this drug, apply the dose as soon as possible, unless it is almost time for the next application. In that case, do not apply the missed dose; just return to your regular schedule. Do not put twice as much of the drug on your skin at the next application.

SIDE EFFECTS

Minor. Acne and burning sensation. You may also experience some burning, itching, redness, or stinging when this drug is applied to the skin. These side effects should disappear as your body adjusts to this medication.

Major. Tell your doctor about any side effects that are persistent or particularly bothersome. IT IS ESPECIALLY IMPORTANT TO TELL YOUR DOCTOR about blistering, increased hair growth, irritation, loss of skin color, peeling of the skin, swelling, or thinning of the skin with easy bruising.

INTERACTIONS

Betamethasone dipropionate and clotrimazole combination should not interact with other medications as long as it is used according to directions.

WARNINGS

• Tell your doctor about unusual or allergic reactions you have had to any medications, especially to betamethasone dipropionate or other adrenocorticosteroids (amcinonide, clocortolone, cortisone, desonide, desoximetasone, dexamethasone, diflorasone, flumethasone, fluocinolone, fluocinonide, fluorometholone, flurandrenolide, halcinonide, hydrocortisone, methylprednisolone, prednisolone, prednisone, and triamcinolone) or to clotrimazole.

• Tell your doctor if you now have or if you have ever had blood-vessel disease, chicken pox, diabetes mellitus, fungal infection, peptic ulcers, pulmonary tuberculosis, shingles, tuberculosis of the skin, or any other type of infection, especially at the site being treated.

• If irritation develops while using this drug, immediately discontinue its use and notify your doctor.

• This product is not for use in the eyes or on mucous membranes; contact may result in side effects.

• Do not use this product with an occlusive wrap unless your doctor directs you to do so. Systemic absorption of this drug is increased if extensive areas of the body are treated, particularly if occlusive bandages are used. If it is necessary for you to use this drug under a wrap, follow your doctor's instructions exactly; do not leave the wrap in place longer than specified.

• If you are using this medication on a child's diaper area, do not put tight-fitting diapers or plastic pants on the child. This may lead to increased systemic absorption of the drug and a possible increase in side effects.

• Elderly patients and younger children have naturally thinner skin, and therefore the drug is more likely to be absorbed. Report any adverse effects to your doctor.

• This medication has been prescribed for your current infection only. A subsequent infection, or one that someone else has, may require a different medication. Therefore, you should not give your medicine to other people or use it for other infections, unless directed to do so by your doctor.

• To avoid reinfection, keep the affected area clean and dry, wear freshly laundered clothing, and avoid tight-fitting clothes.

• Be sure to tell your doctor if you are pregnant. If large amounts of this drug are applied for prolonged periods, some of it will be absorbed and may cross the placenta. Although studies in humans have not been conducted, birth defects have been observed in the offspring of animals that were given large oral doses of adrenocorticosteroids during pregnancy. Also tell your doctor if you are breast-feeding an infant. Small amounts of this type of drug may pass into breast milk and cause growth suppression or a decrease in adrenocorticosteroid production in the nursing infant.

---

betamethasone valerate (topical)

BRAND NAMES (Manufacturers)
betamethasone valerate (various manufacturers)
Betatrex (Savage)
Beta-Val (Lemmon)
Valisone (Schering)
Valisone Reduced Strength (Schering)
TYPE OF DRUG
Adrenocorticosteroid hormone

INGREDIENT
betamethasone
DOSAGE FORMS
Cream (0.01% and 0.1%)
Lotion (0.1%)
Ointment (0.1%)
STORAGE
This medication should be stored at room temperature (never frozen) in a tightly closed container.

USES

Your adrenal glands naturally produce certain cortisonelike chemicals. These chemicals are involved in various regulatory processes in the body (such as those involving fluid balance, temperature, and reaction to inflammation). Betamethasone valerate belongs to a group of drugs known as adrenocorticosteroids (or cortisonelike medications). It is used to relieve the skin inflammation (redness, swelling, itching, and discomfort) associated with conditions such as dermatitis, eczema, and poison ivy. How this drug acts to relieve these disorders is not completely understood.

TREATMENT

Before applying this medication, wash your hands. Then, unless your doctor gives you different instructions, gently wash the area of the skin where the medication is to be applied. With a clean towel, pat the area almost dry; it should be slightly damp when you put the medicine on.

If you are using the lotion form of this drug, shake it well before pouring out the medicine to distribute the ingredients evenly and equalize the doses.

Apply a small amount of the medication to the affected area in a thin layer. Avoid applying medication to cuts or open wounds. Do not bandage the area unless your doctor tells you to do so. If you are to apply an occlusive dressing (like kitchen plastic wrap), be sure you understand the instructions. Wash your hands again after application.

If you miss a dose of this medication, apply the dose as soon as possible, unless it is almost time for the next application. In that case, do not apply the missed dose; just return to your regular dosing schedule. Do not put twice as much on your skin at the next application.

SIDE EFFECTS

Minor. Acne, burning sensation, itching, rash, or skin dryness.

If the affected area is extremely dry or scaling, the skin may be moistened before applying the medication by soaking in water or by applying water with a clean cloth. The ointment form is probably better for dry skin than other forms.

A mild, temporary stinging sensation may occur after this medication is applied. If this persists, contact your doctor.

Major. Tell your doctor about any side effects that are persistent or particularly bothersome. IT IS ESPECIALLY IMPORTANT TO TELL YOUR DOCTOR about blistering, increased hair growth, irritation of the affected area, loss of skin color, secondary infection of the area being treated, or thinning of the skin with easy bruising.

INTERACTIONS

This medication should not interact with any other medications as long as it is used according to directions.

WARNINGS

• Tell your doctor about unusual or allergic reactions you have or have had to any medications, especially to betamethasone valerate or other adrenocorticosteroids (such as amcinonide, clocortolone, cortisone, desonide, desoximetasone, dexamethasone, diflorasone, flumethasone, fluocinolone, fluocinonide, fluorometholone, flurandrenolide, halcinonide, hydrocortisone, methylprednisolone, prednisolone, prednisone, and triamcinolone).

• Tell your doctor if you now have or if you have ever had blood-vessel disease, chicken pox, diabetes mellitus, fungal infection, peptic ulcers, shingles, tuberculosis, tuberculosis of the skin, or any other type of infection, especially at the site currently being treated.

• If irritation develops while using this drug, immediately discontinue its use and notify your doctor.

• This product is not for use in the eyes or on mucous membranes; contact may result in side effects.

• Use this drug only for your current condition. Do not use it for another problem or give it to others to use.

• Do not use this product with an occlusive wrap unless your doctor directs you to do so. Systemic absorption of this drug is increased if extensive areas of the body are treated, particularly if occlusive bandages are used. If it is necessary for you to use this drug under a wrap, follow your doctor's instructions exactly.

• If you are using this medication on a child's diaper area, do not put tight-fitting diapers or plastic pants on the child. This may lead to increased systemic absorption of the drug and a possible increase in side effects.

• Elderly patients and younger children have naturally thinner skin, and, therefore, the drug is more likely to be absorbed. Report any adverse effects.

• Be sure to tell your doctor if you are pregnant. If large amounts of this drug are applied for prolonged periods, some of it will be absorbed and may cross the placenta. Although studies in humans have not been conducted, birth defects have been observed in the offspring of animals that were given large oral doses of this type of drug during pregnancy. Also tell your doctor if you are breast-feeding an infant. If absorbed through the skin, small amounts of this type of drug pass into breast milk and may cause growth suppression or a decrease in natural adrenocorticosteroid production in the nursing infant.

---

betaxolol (ophthalmic)

BRAND NAMES (Manufacturers)
Betoptic (Alcon)
Betoptic S (Alcon)
TYPE OF DRUG
Antiglaucoma ophthalmic solution
INGREDIENT
betaxolol
DOSAGE FORM
Ophthalmic drops (0.25% and 0.5% betaxolol)
STORAGE
Store at room temperature in a tightly closed container. Discard any outdated medication.

USES

Betaxolol is used to reduce pressure in the eye caused by glaucoma or other eye conditions. This medication belongs to a group of drugs known as beta blockers. When applied to

the eye, betaxolol reduces pressure within the eye, perhaps
by decreasing eye fluid (aqueous humor) production and by increasing the outflow of fluid from the eye.

TREATMENT

Wash your hands with soap and water before applying ophthalmic betaxolol. To avoid contamination of the drops, do
not touch the tube portion of the dropper with your fingers
or let it touch your eye; do not wipe off or rinse the dropper
after use.

To apply the drops, tilt your head back and pull down your
lower eyelid with one hand to make a pouch below the eye.
Drop the prescribed amount of medicine into this pouch and
slowly close your eyes. Try not to blink. Keep your eyes closed,
and place one finger at the corner of the eye next to your nose
for a minute or two, applying slight pressure (this is done to
prevent loss of medication into the nose and throat canal).
Then wipe away any excess with a clean tissue. Since administering the drug is somewhat difficult, you may want to
have someone else apply the drops for you.

If you miss a dose of this medication, apply the missed dose
as soon as possible, then return to your regular dosing schedule. However, if it is almost time for the next dose, skip the
dose you missed. Do not double the next dose.

SIDE EFFECTS

Minor. When you first apply this medication, it may sting or
burn your eyes. This should stop in a few minutes. You may
also notice sensitivity of your eyes to bright lights or sunlight.
Wearing sunglasses and avoiding excessive exposure to sunlight may help relieve this sensitivity.

Major. Tell your doctor about any side effects that are persistent or particularly bothersome. IT IS ESPECIALLY IMPOR-
TANT TO TELL YOUR DOCTOR about hives, irritation of the
eye that lasts more than a few minutes after application, itching, or skin rash. Major side effects are rare when this product
is used correctly. However, depression, fluid accumulation,
insomnia, shortness of breath, decreased heart rate, or swelling
of the feet may occur. If you have any of these symptoms,
contact your doctor.

INTERACTIONS

Ophthalmic betaxolol has been known to increase the side effects of reserpine and oral beta blockers. BE SURE TO TELL YOUR DOCTOR about any medications you are currently taking.

WARNINGS

• Tell your doctor about unusual or allergic reactions you have had to any medications, especially to betaxolol or to any other beta blocker (acebutolol, atenolol bisoprolol, carteolol, esmolol, labetalol, metoprolol, nadolol, penbutolol, pindolol, propranolol, and timolol).

• Be sure to tell your doctor if you now have or if you have ever had asthma, diabetes mellitus, heart failure, lung disease, slow or abnormal heartbeat, or thyroid disease.

• Before having surgery or any other medical or dental treatment, tell your doctor or dentist that you are taking this medication. Your doctor or dentist may want to gradually withdraw this medication prior to the procedure.

• Be sure to tell your doctor if you are pregnant. Although betaxolol appears to be safe in animals, studies in pregnant women have not been conducted. Also tell your doctor if you are breast-feeding an infant. Small amounts of betaxolol may pass into breast milk.

betaxolol (systemic)

BRAND NAME (Manufacturer)
Kerlone (Searle)
TYPE OF DRUG
Beta-adrenergic blocking agent
INGREDIENT
betaxolol
DOSAGE FORM
Tablets (10 mg and 20 mg)
STORAGE
Betaxolol should be stored at room temperature in a tightly closed container.

USES

Betaxolol is prescribed for the treatment of high blood pressure. Betaxolol belongs to a group of medicines known as beta-adrenergic blocking agents or, more commonly, beta blockers. These drugs work by controlling impulses along certain nerve pathways. This results in a decreased workload for the heart.

TREATMENT

Betaxolol can be taken with a glass of water, with meals, immediately following meals, or on an empty stomach, depending on your doctor's instructions. It is important that you try to take the medication at the same time(s) each day.

Try not to miss any doses of this medication. If you do miss a dose of the medication, take the missed dose as soon as possible. However, if the next scheduled dose is within eight hours (if you are taking this medication only once a day) or within four hours (if you are taking this medication more than once a day), do not take the missed dose at all; just return to your regular dosing schedule. Do not double the next dose of the medication.

It is important to remember that betaxolol does not cure high blood pressure.

SIDE EFFECTS

Minor. Decreased sexual ability, diarrhea, fatigue, headache, indigestion, or nausea. These side effects should diminish as your body becomes accustomed to the medication.

Major. Tell your doctor about any side effects that are persistent or particularly bothersome. IT IS ESPECIALLY IMPORTANT TO TELL YOUR DOCTOR about breathing difficulty or wheezing; cold hands or feet due to decreased blood circulation to the skin, fingers, and toes; confusion; dizziness; fever and sore throat; hair loss; hallucinations; light-headedness; mental depression; nightmares; reduced alertness; skin rash; swelling of the ankles, feet, or lower legs; or unusual bleeding or bruising.

INTERACTIONS

Betaxolol interacts with a number of other medications:
1. Indomethacin, other nonsteroidal anti-inflammatory agents (including diclofenac, etodolac, ibuprofen, ketoprofen,

naproxen, and piroxicam) aspirin, and other salicylates may decrease the blood-pressure-lowering effects of beta blockers.
2. Calcium channel blockers (nifedipine, verapamil, and diltiazem) may be used with beta blockers such as betaxolol unless the patient has heart trouble. Very low blood pressure
and heart failure have been observed in patients with impaired
heart function who take beta blockers.
3. Side effects may also be increased if beta blockers are taken
with epinephrine, phenylephrine, phenylpropanolamine, phenothiazine tranquilizers, reserpine, clonidine, prazosin, or
monoamine oxidase (MAO) inhibitors. At least 14 days should
separate the use of a beta blocker and the use of an MAO inhibitor.
4. Beta blockers may antagonize (work against) the effects of
theophylline, aminophylline, albuterol, isoproterenol, metaproterenol, and terbutaline.
5. Beta blockers can also interact with insulin or oral antidiabetic agents—raising or lowering blood-sugar levels or masking symptoms of low blood sugar.
6. Furosemide, hydrochlorothiazide, or hydralazine may increase the blood-pressure-lowering effects of beta blockers.
7. Alcohol, barbiturates, and rifampin can decrease blood
concentrations of this drug, which can result in a decrease in
effectiveness.
8. If you are on both betaxolol and clonidine, and both of
these medications are to be discontinued, it is recommended
that the betaxolol be tapered off over several days before the
gradual reduction of clonidine.
9. In patients who have congestive heart failure treated with
digitalis glycosides (for example, digoxin or digitoxin), caution should be used as both betaxolol and digitalis products
may slow heart conduction.
   Before starting to take betaxolol, BE SURE TO TELL YOUR
DOCTOR about any medications you are already taking—including over-the-counter products—especially any of the medications listed above.

WARNINGS
• Tell your doctor about any unusual or allergic reactions you
have had to any medications, especially to betaxolol or any
other beta blocker (acebutolol, atenolol, bisoprolol, carteolol,

esmolol, labetolol, metoprolol, nadolol, penbutalol, pindolol, propranolol, and timolol).

• Be sure to tell your doctor if you now have or if you have ever had asthma, bronchitis, diabetes mellitus, heart block, heart failure, kidney disease, liver disease, peripheral vascular disease (poor circulation in the fingers or toes), severe brady-cardia (slowed heart rate), or thyroid disease.

• Betaxolol therapy may increase the risk of cardiac failure in some patients. Report any abnormal heart function to your doctor.

• Patients with severe bronchospastic disease (such as asthma) should, in general, not receive beta blockers. Inform your physician if breathing is difficult.

• In people with diabetes, betaxolol may block some of the warning signs of low blood sugar (hypoglycemia), such as a rapid pulse rate, but not others, such as sweating or feelings of dizziness.

• You may want to check your pulse while taking this drug. If your pulse is much slower than usual or less than 50 beats per minute, check with your doctor. A pulse that is too slow may cause circulation problems.

• This medication may affect your body's response to exer-cise. Ask your doctor what an appropriate amount of exercise would be for you.

• It is important that you do not stop taking this drug without first checking with your doctor. Some conditions, such as angina pectoris, may become worse when the drug is stopped suddenly, and the danger of a heart attack is increased in some patients. Your doctor may want you to gradually reduce the amount of the drug you take before stopping completely. Make sure that you have enough medication on hand to last through vacations and holidays.

• Tell your doctor or dentist that you are taking this drug before having surgery or any other medical or dental treatment. Often, this medication will be discontinued 48 hours prior to any major surgery.

• While taking this drug, do not use any over-the-counter (nonprescription) allergy, asthma, cough, cold, sinus, or diet preparations without first checking with your doctor or phar-macist. The combination of these medications with a beta blocker can result in high blood pressure.

• Betaxolol may reduce intraocular pressure and give a misleading negative glaucoma test.
• Be sure to tell your doctor if you are pregnant. Animal studies have shown that some beta blockers can cause problems in pregnancy when used at very high doses. Adequate studies have not been conducted in humans, but there has been some association between beta blockers used during pregnancy and low birth weight, breathing problems, and slow heart rate in the newborn. Also tell your doctor if you are breast-feeding an infant. Although this medication has not been shown to cause problems in breast-fed infants, it may pass into breast milk, so caution is warranted.
• The safety of this medication has not been established in children.

---

brompheniramine

BRAND NAMES (Manufacturers)
Bromphen (various manufacturers)
brompheniramine maleate (various manufacturers)
Brotane* (Halsey)
Dimetane* (Robins)
Dimetane Extentabs* (Robins)
*Available over the counter (without a prescription)
TYPE OF DRUG
Antihistamine
INGREDIENT
brompheniramine
DOSAGE FORMS
Tablets (4 mg and 8 mg)
Capsules (4 mg)
Sustained-release tablets (8 mg and 12 mg)
Oral elixir (2 mg per 5-mL spoonful, with 3% alcohol)
STORAGE
Brompheniramine tablets and oral elixir should be stored at room temperature in tightly closed containers.

USES
This medication is an antihistamine (antihistamines block the action of histamine, a chemical released by the body during an

allergic reaction). Brompheniramine is used to treat or prevent symptoms of allergy.

TREATMENT

To avoid stomach upset, take brompheniramine with food or with a full glass of milk or water (unless your doctor directs you to do otherwise).

The elixir form should be measured carefully with a specially designed 5-mL measuring spoon. An ordinary kitchen teaspoon is not accurate enough.

The sustained-release tablets should be swallowed whole. Breaking, chewing, or crushing them destroys their sustained-release activity and may increase side effects.

If you miss a dose, take the missed dose as soon as possible, unless it is almost time for your next dose. In that case, don't take the missed dose at all; just return to your regular dosing schedule. Do not double the next dose.

SIDE EFFECTS

Minor. Blurred vision; confusion; constipation; diarrhea; difficult or painful urination; dizziness; dry mouth, throat, or nose; headache; irritability; loss of appetite; nausea; restlessness; ringing or buzzing in the ears; stomach upset; or unusual increase in sweating. These side effects should disappear as your body adjusts to the medication.

This medication can cause increased sensitivity to sunlight. It is, therefore, important to avoid prolonged exposure to sunlight and sunlamps. Wear protective clothing and use an effective sunscreen.

If you are constipated, increase the amount of fiber in your diet (fresh fruits and vegetables, salads, bran, and whole-grain breads), exercise, and drink more water (unless your doctor tells you not to do so.)

Chew sugarless gum, or suck on ice chips or a piece of hard candy to reduce mouth dryness.

If you feel dizzy or light-headed, sit or lie down for a while; get up slowly; and be careful on stairs.

Major. Tell your doctor about any side effects that are persistent or particularly bothersome. IT IS ESPECIALLY IMPORTANT TO TELL YOUR DOCTOR about a change in menstruation, clumsiness, feeling faint, flushing of the face, hallucinations, palpitations, rash, seizures, shortness of breath, sleeping disorders, sore throat or fever, tightness in the chest, unusual bleeding or bruising, or unusual tiredness or weakness.

INTERACTIONS

Brompheniramine interacts with several other drugs:

1. Concurrent use of it with central nervous system depressants (such as alcohol, barbiturates, benzodiazepine tranquilizers, muscle relaxants, narcotics, pain medications, and phenothiazine tranquilizers) or with tricyclic antidepressants can cause extreme drowsiness.

2. Monoamine oxidase (MAO) inhibitors (isocarboxazid, pargyline, phenelzine, and tranylcypromine) can increase the side effects of this medication. At least 14 days should separate the use of this drug and the use of an MAO inhibitor.

3. Brompheniramine can decrease the activity of oral anticoagulants (blood thinners, such as warfarin).

BE SURE TO TELL YOUR DOCTOR about any medications you are currently taking.

WARNINGS

• Tell your doctor about unusual or allergic reactions you have had to medications, especially to brompheniramine or to any other antihistamine (such as carbinoxamine, chlorpheniramine, clemastine, cyproheptadine, dexchlorpheniramine, dimenhydrinate, dimethindene, diphenhydramine, diphenylpyraline, doxylamine, hydroxyzine, promethazine, pyrilamine, terfenadine, trimeprazine, tripelennamine, and triprolidine).

• Tell your doctor if you now have or if you have ever had asthma, blood-vessel disease, glaucoma, high blood pressure, kidney disease, peptic ulcers, enlarged prostate gland, or thyroid disease.

• Brompheniramine can cause drowsiness or dizziness. Your ability to perform tasks that require alertness, such as driving a car or operating potentially dangerous machinery, may be decreased. Appropriate caution should be taken.

• Be sure to tell your doctor if you are pregnant. The effects of this medication during pregnancy have not been thoroughly studied in humans. Also tell your doctor if you are breastfeeding an infant. Small amounts of brompheniramine pass into breast milk and may cause unusual excitement or irritability in nursing infants.

bumetanide

BRAND NAME (Manufacturer)
Bumex (Roche)
TYPE OF DRUG
Diuretic and antihypertensive
INGREDIENT
bumetanide
DOSAGE FORM
Tablets (0.5 mg, 1 mg, and 2 mg)
STORAGE
Bumetanide should be stored at room temperature in a tightly closed, light-resistant container.

USES

Bumetanide is prescribed to treat high blood pressure. It is also used to reduce fluid accumulation in the body caused by conditions such as heart failure, cirrhosis of the liver, kidney disease, and the long-term use of some medications. This medication reduces fluid accumulation by increasing the elimination of salt and water through the kidneys.

TREATMENT

To decrease stomach irritation, you can take this medication with a glass of milk or with a meal (unless your doctor directs you to do otherwise). Try to take it at the same time every day. Avoid taking a dose after 6:00 P.M.; otherwise you may have to get up during the night to urinate.

If you miss a dose of this medication, take the missed dose as soon as possible, unless it is almost time for the next one. In that case, do not take the missed dose at all; just wait until the next scheduled dose. Do not double the next dose.

This medication does not cure high blood pressure, but it will help to control the condition as long as you continue to take it.

SIDE EFFECTS

Minor. Blurred vision, constipation, cramps, diarrhea, dizziness, headache, loss of appetite, sore mouth, or stomach upset. As your body adjusts to the medication, these side effects should disappear.

This medication causes an increase in the amount of urine or frequency of urination when you first begin to take it. It may also cause you to have an unusual feeling of tiredness. These effects should begin to lessen after several days.

This medication can cause increased sensitivity to sunlight. It is, therefore, important to avoid prolonged exposure to sunlight and sunlamps. Wear protective clothing and use an effective sunscreen.

To relieve constipation, increase the amount of fiber in your diet (fresh fruits and vegetables, salads, bran, and whole-grain cereals and breads) and exercise (unless your doctor directs you to do otherwise).

To avoid dizziness or light-headedness when you stand, contract and relax the muscles of your legs for a few moments before rising. Do this by pushing one foot against the floor while raising the other foot slightly, alternating feet.

Major. Tell your doctor about any side effects that are persistent or particularly bothersome. IT IS ESPECIALLY IMPORTANT TO TELL YOUR DOCTOR about abdominal pain, confusion, difficulty in breathing, dry mouth, fainting, itching, joint pains, loss of appetite, mood changes, muscle pain and cramps, nausea, palpitations, rash, ringing in the ears, sore throat, thirst, tingling in the fingers and toes, unusual bleeding or bruising, vomiting, weakness, or yellowish discoloration of the eyes or skin.

INTERACTIONS

Bumetanide interacts with several other types of drugs:

1. It can increase the side effects of alcohol, barbiturates, narcotics, cephalosporin antibiotics, chloral hydrate, cortisone and cortisonelike steroids (such as dexamethasone, hydrocortisone, prednisone, and prednisolone), digoxin, digitalis, lithium, amphotericin B, cisplatin, mercaptopurine, and polymyxin B.

2. Probenecid and indomethacin (and other nonsteroidal antiinflammatory agents, including diclofenac, etodolac, ibuprofen, ketoprofen, naproxen, and piroxicam) may decrease the diuretic effectiveness of this medication.

Before taking bumetanide, BE SURE TO TELL YOUR DOCTOR about any medications you are currently taking, especially any of those listed above.

WARNINGS

• Tell your doctor about unusual or allergic reactions you have had to any medications, especially to bumetanide, other diuretics, or any other sulfa drugs, including oral antidiabetic medicines or sulfonamide antibiotics.

• Before you start taking this medication, tell your doctor if you now have or if you have ever had kidney disease or problems with urination, diabetes mellitus, gout, liver disease, or asthma.

• Bumetanide can cause potassium loss. Signs of potassium loss include dry mouth, thirst, weakness, muscle pain or cramps, nausea, and vomiting. If you experience any of these symptoms, call your doctor. Your doctor may want to have blood tests performed periodically in order to monitor your potassium levels. To help avoid potassium loss, take this medication with a glass of fresh or frozen orange or cranberry juice, or eat a banana every day. The use of a salt substitute also helps prevent potassium loss. Do not make any changes to your diet or use a salt substitute, however, without first discussing it with your doctor. Taking too much potassium may also be dangerous.

• Before having surgery or any other medical or dental treatment, be sure to tell your doctor or dentist that you are taking bumetanide.

• In order to avoid dizziness or fainting while taking this medication, try not to stand for long periods of time; avoid drinking excessive amounts of alcohol; and avoid strenuous exercise in hot weather, as well as hot baths, showers, and saunas.

• If you have high blood pressure, do not take any over-the-counter (nonprescription) medication for weight control or for cough, cold, allergy, asthma, or sinus problems, unless you first check with your doctor.

• To prevent severe water loss (dehydration) while taking this drug, check with your doctor if you have any illness that causes severe or continuous nausea, vomiting, or diarrhea.

• This medication can raise blood-sugar levels in patients with diabetes. Therefore, blood sugar should be monitored carefully with blood or urine tests when this medication is being taken.

• Be sure to tell your doctor if you are pregnant. This drug crosses the placenta. Although studies in humans have not been conducted, adverse effects have been reported in the offspring of animals that were given large doses of this drug during pregnancy. Also tell your doctor if you are breast-feeding an infant. Although problems in humans have not been reported, it is not known if bumetanide passes into breast milk.

---

bupropion

BRAND NAME (Manufacturer)
Wellbutrin (Burroughs Wellcome)
TYPE OF DRUG
Antidepressant
INGREDIENT
bupropion hydrochloride
DOSAGE FORM
Tablets (75 mg and 100 mg)
STORAGE
Store at room temperature in a tightly closed container.

USES
Bupropion is used to relieve the symptoms of mental depression in patients who cannot take other medications. The exact mechanism of action of bupropion is unknown, but it is thought to relieve depression by altering the concentration of certain chemicals that are necessary for nerve transmission in the brain.

TREATMENT
It is important to take your medication on a regular schedule as recommended by your physician. If you miss a dose and the next regular dose should be taken in less than six hours, skip the missed dose and take the next at the scheduled time. Never double the dose.

The effects of this medication may not become apparent for several weeks.

SIDE EFFECTS
Minor. Constipation, decreased appetite, decreased sexual ability, diarrhea, dizziness, dry mouth, excessive sweating, fatigue, headache, irregular heartbeat, insomnia, nausea, se-

dation, or vomiting. These side effects should decrease or disappear as your body adjusts to the medication.

To relieve constipation, increase the amount of fiber in your diet (fresh fruits and vegetables, salads, bran, and whole-grain breads). You can also increase your exercise level and drink more water (unless your doctor directs you to do otherwise).

To decrease dry mouth, chew sugarless gum or suck on ice chips or hard candy.

To avoid dizziness or light-headedness when you stand, contract and relax the muscles in your legs for a few moments before rising from a sitting or reclining postion. Do this by pushing one foot against the floor while raising the other foot slightly, alternating feet so that you are "pumping" your legs in a pedaling motion.

Major. Tell your doctor about any side effects that are persistent **or** particularly bothersome. IT IS ESPECIALLY IMPORTANT TO TELL YOUR DOCTOR about agitation, blurred vision, movement disorders, rash, tremors, or seizures.

INTERACTIONS

1. Bupropion may decrease the effectiveness of carbamazepine, phenobarbital, or phenytoin, which may lead to more seizures.

2. Bupropion can interact with monoamine oxidase (MAO) inhibitors. At least 14 days should separate the use of this drug and the use of an MAO inhibitor.

3. Bupropion may decrease the effectiveness of cimetidine.

4. Alcohol may increase the side effects of bupropion.

Be sure to tell your doctor about any medications you are currently taking, especially any of those listed above.

WARNINGS

• Tell your doctor about unusual or allergic reactions you have had to any medications, especially to bupropion.

• Tell your doctor if you now have or have ever had cataracts or vision problems, seizures or epilepsy, bulimia, anorexia nervosa, mania, liver or kidney disease, or respiratory disorders.

• This medication may make you tired or drowsy or affect your thinking ability. You should not operate potentially dangerous equipment or drive an automobile until you know how this drug affects you.

• Do not stop taking this medication abruptly or increase the dose unless so directed by your physician. Stopping abruptly or increasing your dose in large amounts can lead to increased side effects.

• Do not take any over-the-counter (nonprescription) medication or new prescription drug without discussing it with your doctor or pharmacist. Many over-the-counter preparations and some prescription medications may interact with bupropion.

• Tell your doctor if you are pregnant. In high doses, bupropion has caused chromosomal changes in animals, but the effects in humans are unknown. Also tell your doctor if you are breast-feeding an infant. This medication can pass into the breast milk and lead to adverse effects in the infant.

---

buspirone

BRAND NAME (Manufacturer)
BuSpar (Mead Johnson)
TYPE OF DRUG
Antianxiety agent
INGREDIENT
buspirone hydrochloride
DOSAGE FORM
Tablets (5 mg and 10 mg)
STORAGE
Buspirone should be stored at room temperature in a tightly closed container. Avoid exposure to high temperatures (greater than 86°F).

USES
This medication is prescribed as a treatment for the symptoms of anxiety. It is not yet understood exactly how this medication works. Buspirone has been shown to be effective in relieving symptoms of anxiety, but it is important that you try to identify and remove the cause of the anxiety as well.

TREATMENT
Buspirone should be taken exactly as directed by your doctor. It can be taken with food or a full glass of water if stomach upset occurs.

If you are taking this drug regularly and miss a dose, take the missed dose immediately if you remember within an hour. If more time has passed, however, skip the dose you missed and wait for the next scheduled dose. Do not double the dose.

SIDE EFFECTS

Minor. Diarrhea, dizziness, excitement, fatigue, headache, light-headedness, nasal congestion, nausea, nervousness, sleeping problems, sweating, or weakness. These side effects should disappear as your body adjusts to this medication.

If you feel dizzy or light-headed, sit or lie down for a while; get up slowly from a sitting or reclining position; and be careful on stairs.

Major. Tell your doctor about any side effects that are persistent or particularly bothersome. IT IS ESPECIALLY IMPORTANT TO TELL YOUR DOCTOR about chest pain, confusion, feelings of anger, lack of coordination, muscle pain, numbness, rash, ringing in the ears, sore throat, tingling in your fingers or toes, or tremors.

INTERACTIONS

Although extensive studies on buspirone have not yet been completed, this drug may interact with several other medications.

To prevent oversedation, this drug should not be taken with alcohol or other central nervous system depressants (such as antihistamines, barbiturates, muscle relaxants, pain medicines, narcotics, medicines for seizures, phenothiazine tranquilizers, and antidepressants).

Before starting buspirone, BE SURE TO TELL YOUR DOCTOR about any medications you are currently taking, especially any of those listed above.

WARNINGS

• Before starting buspirone, be sure to tell your doctor about any unusual or allergic reactions you have had to any medications, especially to buspirone.

• Be sure to tell your doctor if you now have or if you have ever had kidney disease, liver disease, or any type of psychiatric disorder.

• Until you experience how this medication affects you, do not drive a car or operate potentially dangerous machinery.

• Be sure to tell your doctor if you are pregnant. Although buspirone does appear to be safe in animals, complete studies in pregnant women have not been conducted. Also be sure to tell your doctor if you are breast-feeding an infant. Small amounts of buspirone have been shown to pass into the milk of animals.

calcifediol

BRAND NAME (Manufacturer)
Calderol (Organon)
TYPE OF DRUG
Vitamin D analog
INGREDIENT
calcifediol (25-hydroxycholecalciferol)
DOSAGE FORM
Capsules (20 mcg and 50 mcg)
STORAGE
Calcifediol capsules should be stored at room temperature in a tightly closed, light-resistant container. This medication should not be refrigerated.

USES
Vitamin D is essential to many body systems, including bone structure, regulation of blood calcium levels, and heart and muscle contraction. Since vitamin D is activated in the kidneys, patients with chronic (long-term) kidney failure are unable to produce enough active vitamin D on their own. Calcifediol is one of the active forms of vitamin D. This medication is used to treat bone disease and hypocalcemia (low blood-calcium levels) in patients on dialysis.

TREATMENT
Calcifediol can be taken either on an empty stomach or with food or milk (as directed by your doctor). The capsules should be swallowed whole; do not crush or chew them.

If you miss a dose of this drug, take the missed dose as soon as possible, unless it is almost time for the next dose. In that case, do not take the missed dose at all; return to your regular dosing schedule. Do not double the next dose.

SIDE EFFECTS

Minor. None, at the dosages normally prescribed.

Major. The side effects associated with calcifediol therapy are usually the result of too much medication (vitamin D toxicity). Tell your doctor about any side effects that are persistent or particularly bothersome. IT IS ESPECIALLY IMPORTANT TO TELL YOUR DOCTOR about blurred vision, bone pain, constipation, dry mouth, headache, irritability, loss of appetite, mental disorders, metallic taste in the mouth, muscle pain, nausea, palpitations, runny nose, increased thirst, increased urination, vomiting, weakness, or weight loss.

INTERACTIONS

Calcifediol interacts with several types of medications:

1. The dosage of calcifediol may need to be altered if anticonvulsant medication (such as phenytoin, phenobarbital, and primidone) is started.

2. Cholestyramine, colestipol, and mineral oil can decrease the absorption of calcifediol from the gastrointestinal tract.

3. Use of magnesium-containing antacids along with calcifediol may cause high blood levels of magnesium.

4. Calcifediol may lower the effectiveness of verapamil.

5. Corticosteroids may counteract the effects of Vitamin D analogs such as calcifediol.

6. Digoxin and digitoxin can cause irregular heart rate when taken with calcifediol.

7. Be sure to tell your doctor if you are taking a thiazide diuretic (water pill); some patients may experience elevated calcium levels when thiazide diuretics are combined with calcifediol.

BE SURE TO TELL YOUR DOCTOR about any medications you are currently taking, especially any of those listed above.

WARNINGS

• Be sure to tell your doctor about unusual or allergic reactions you have had to any medications, especially to calcifediol, calcitriol, dihydrotachysterol, ergocalciferol, or vitamin D.

• Before starting to take this medication, be sure to tell your doctor if you now have or if you have ever had heart or blood-vessel disease, hypercalcemia (high levels of calcium in the bloodstream), hyperphosphatemia (high levels of phosphate in the bloodstream), kidney disease, vitamin D intoxication, or sarcoidosis.

• Before taking over-the-counter (nonprescription) products that contain calcium, phosphates, magnesium, or vitamin D, consult your doctor. These ingredients can increase the side effects of calcifediol.

• Be sure to tell your doctor if you are pregnant. Although calcifediol (in normal doses) appears to be safe during pregnancy, extensive studies in humans have not been conducted. Birth defects have been reported in the offspring of animals that received large doses of this medication during pregnancy. Also tell your doctor if you are breast-feeding an infant. Small amounts of calcifediol pass into breast milk.

---

calcitriol

BRAND NAME (Manufacturer)
Rocaltrol (Roche)
TYPE OF DRUG
Vitamin D analog
INGREDIENT
calcitriol (1.25-dihydroxycholecalciferol)
DOSAGE FORM
Capsules (0.25 mcg and 0.5 mcg)
STORAGE
Calcitriol should be stored at room temperature in a tightly closed, light-resistant container.

USES

Vitamin D is essential to bone structure, regulation of blood calcium levels, and heart and muscle contraction. Since vitamin D is activated in the kidneys, patients with chronic kidney failure are unable to produce enough active vitamin D on their own. Calcitriol is one of the active forms of vitamin D. This drug is used to treat bone disease and hypocalcemia (low blood-calcium levels) in dialysis patients.

TREATMENT

Calcitriol can be taken either on an empty stomach or with food or milk (as directed by your doctor). The capsules should be swallowed whole.

If you miss a dose of this drug, take the missed dose as soon as possible, unless it is almost time for the next dose. In that case, do not take the missed dose at all; return to your regular dosing schedule. Do not double the next dose.

SIDE EFFECTS

Minor. None, at the dosages normally prescribed.
Major. Side effects result from too much medication (vitamin D toxicity). Tell your doctor about any side effects that are persistent or particularly bothersome. IT IS ESPECIALLY IMPORTANT TO TELL YOUR DOCTOR about appetite loss, blurred vision, bone pain, constipation, dry mouth, headache, irritability, mental disorders, metallic taste, muscle pain, nausea, palpitations, runny nose, increased thirst, increased urination, vomiting, weakness, or weight loss.

INTERACTIONS

Calcitriol interacts with several types of medications:
1. The dosage of calcitriol may need to be adjusted if anticonvulsant medication (phenytoin, phenobarbital, or primidone) is started.
2. Cholestyramine, colestipol, and mineral oil can decrease the absorption of calcitriol from the gastrointestinal tract.
3. Use of magnesium-containing antacids along with calcitriol may cause high blood levels of magnesium.
4. Calcitriol may lower the effectiveness of verapamil.
5. Corticosteroids may counteract the effects of Vitamin D analogs such as calcifediol.
6. Digoxin and digitoxin can cause irregular heart rate when taken with calcifediol.
7. Be sure to tell your doctor if you are taking a thiazide diuretic (water pill); some patients may experience elevated calcium levels when thiazide diuretics are combined with calcifediol.
   BE SURE TO TELL YOUR DOCTOR about any medications you are currently taking, especially any of those listed above.

WARNINGS

• Be sure to tell your doctor about unusual or allergic reactions you have had to any medications, especially to calcitriol, calcifediol, dihydrotachysterol, ergocalciferol, or vitamin D.

• Before starting to take this drug, tell your doctor if you have ever had heart or blood vessel disease, hypercalcemia (high levels of blood calcium), hyperphosphatemia (high levels of blood phosphate), kidney disease, vitamin D intoxication, or sarcoidosis.

• Before taking any over-the-counter (nonprescription) products that contain calcium, phosphates, magnesium, or vitamin D, check with your doctor. These ingredients can increase the side effects of calcitriol.

• Be sure to tell your doctor if you are pregnant. Although calcitriol appears to be safe during pregnancy in humans, birth defects have been reported in the offspring of animals that received large doses during pregnancy. Also be sure to tell your doctor if you are breast-feeding an infant. Studies have shown that small amounts of calcitriol may pass into breast milk.

---

captopril

BRAND NAMES (Manufacturers)
Capoten (Squibb)
captopril (various manufacturers)
TYPE OF DRUG
Antihypertensive
INGREDIENT
captopril
DOSAGE FORM
Tablets (12.5 mg, 25 mg, 50 mg, and 100 mg)
STORAGE
Captopril should be stored at room temperature in a tightly closed container.

USES
Captopril is used to treat high blood pressure and heart damage after a heart attack. It is also used to slow the development of kidney disease in patients with diabetes. Captopril is a vasodilator (it dilates the blood vessels) that acts by blocking the production of chemicals that may be responsible for constricting or narrowing blood vessels.

TREATMENT

To obtain maximum benefit from captopril, you should take it on an empty stomach one hour before meals. In order to become accustomed to taking this medication, try to take it at the same time(s) every day.

It may be several weeks before you notice the full effects of this medication.

If you miss a dose of captopril, take the missed dose as soon as possible, unless it is almost time for the next dose. In that case, do not take the missed dose at all; just wait until the next scheduled dose. Do not double the dose.

Captopril does not cure high blood pressure, but it will help control the condition as long as you continue to take it.

SIDE EFFECTS

Minor. Abdominal pain, constipation, cough, diarrhea, dizziness, dry mouth, fatigue, flushing, headache, insomnia, loss of appetite, loss of taste, nausea, or vomiting. These side effects should disappear over time as your body adjusts to the medication.

This medication can increase your sensitivity to sunlight. It is, therefore, important to avoid prolonged exposure to sunlight and sunlamps. Always wear protective clothing and sunglasses when out of doors, and use an effective sunscreen.

To relieve constipation, increase the amount of fiber in your diet (fresh fruits and vegetables, salads, bran, and whole-grain breads). You can also increase your level of exercise and drink more water (unless your doctor directs you to do otherwise).

To relieve mouth dryness, suck on ice chips or a piece of hard candy or chew sugarless gum.

To avoid dizziness or light-headedness when you stand, contract and relax the muscles of your legs for a few moments before rising. Do this by pushing one foot against the floor while raising the other foot slightly, alternating feet so that you are "pumping" your legs.

Major. Tell your doctor about any side effects that are persistent or particularly bothersome. IT IS ESPECIALLY IMPORTANT TO TELL YOUR DOCTOR about chest pain; chills; difficult or painful urination; fever; itching; mouth sores; palpitations; prolonged vomiting or diarrhea; rash; sore throat; swelling of the face, hands, or feet; tingling in the fingers or toes; unusual bleeding or bruising; or yellowing of the eyes or skin.

INTERACTIONS

Captopril interacts with several other types of medications:

1. Diuretics (water pills) and other antihypertensive medications can cause an excessive drop in blood pressure when combined with captopril (especially with the first dose).

2. The combination of captopril with spironolactone, triamterene, amiloride, potassium supplements, or salt substitutes can lead to hyperkalemia (dangerously high levels of potassium in the bloodstream).

3. Antineoplastic agents (anticancer drugs) or chloramphenicol can increase the bone marrow side effects of captopril.

4. Concurrent use of captopril and allopurinol can increase the risk of developing an allergic reaction to the medication.

5. Indomethacin and other nonsteroidal anti-inflammatory drugs can decrease the blood-pressure-lowering effects of captopril.

6. Captopril can delay the body's elimination of lithium. Concurrent use of captopril and lithium may cause lithium toxicity.

Before starting captopril, BE SURE TO TELL YOUR DOCTOR about any drugs you are taking, especially any of those listed above.

WARNINGS

• Tell your doctor about any reactions you have or have had to medications, especially to benazepril, captopril, enalapril lisinopril, quinapril, or ramipril.

• Tell your doctor if you now have or if you have ever had aortic stenosis, blood disorders, kidney disease, kidney transplant, liver disease, systemic lupus erythematosus, or a heart attack or stroke.

• Be careful—excessive perspiration, dehydration, or prolonged vomiting or diarrhea can lead to an excessive drop in blood pressure while you are taking this medication. Contact your doctor if you have any of these symptoms.

• Before having surgery or other medical or dental treatment, tell your doctor you are taking this drug.

• The first few doses of this drug may cause dizziness. Try to avoid any sudden changes in posture.

• If you have high blood pressure, do not take any over-the-counter (nonprescription) medications for weight control, or for allergy, asthma, sinus, cough, or cold problems unless you first check with your doctor.
• Do not stop taking this medication unless you first consult your doctor. Stopping this drug abruptly may lead to a rise in blood pressure.
• Be sure to tell your doctor if you are pregnant. Captopril has been found to cause birth defects in the fetus if taken during the second or third trimester of pregnancy. Also tell your doctor if you are breast-feeding an infant. Captopril passes into breast milk. The effects of this drug on the infant have not been determined.

---

captopril and hydrochlorothiazide combination

BRAND NAME (Manufacturer)
Capozide (Squibb)
TYPE OF DRUG
Antihypertensive and diuretic
INGREDIENTS
captopril and hydrochlorothiazide
DOSAGE FORM
Tablets (25 mg captopril and 15 mg hydrochlorothiazide; 25 mg captopril and 25 mg hydrochlorothiazide; 50 mg captopril and 15 mg hydrochlorothiazide; 50 mg captopril and 25 mg hydrochlorothiazide)
STORAGE
Tablets should be stored at room temperature in a tightly closed container. This medication should be stored away from moisture and high heat (greater than 86°F).

USES

Captopril and hydrochlorothiazide combination is used to treat high blood pressure. Captopril is a vasodilator (it widens the blood vessels) that acts by blocking the production of chemicals that may be responsible for constricting blood vessels. Hydrochlorothiazide is a diuretic (water pill) that reduces body fluid accumulation by increasing the elimination of salt and water through the kidneys.

TREATMENT

To obtain the maximum benefit from this medication, take it on an empty stomach one hour before meals. In order to become accustomed to taking this medication, take it at the same time(s) every day. Allow several weeks to notice its full effects.

Avoid taking a dose of this medication after 6:00 P.M.; otherwise, you may have to get up during the night to urinate.

If you miss a dose of this medication, take the missed dose as soon as possible, unless it is almost time for the next dose. In that case, do not take the missed dose at all; just wait until the next scheduled dose. Do not double the dose.

Captopril and hydrochlorothiazide combination does not cure high blood pressure, but it will help to control the condition as long as you continue to take it.

SIDE EFFECTS

Minor. Abdominal pain, blurred vision, constipation, cough, cramping, diarrhea, dizziness, fatigue, flushing, headache, insomnia, loss of appetite, or loss of taste. These side effects should disappear as your body adjusts to this medication.

Hydrochlorothiazide and captopril can increase your sensitivity to sunlight. It is, therefore, important to avoid prolonged exposure to sunlight and sunlamps. Wear protective clothing and sunglasses, and use an effective sunscreen.

To relieve constipation, increase the amount of fiber in your diet (fresh fruits and vegetables, salads, bran, and whole-grain breads) and exercise (unless your doctor directs you to do otherwise).

To relieve mouth dryness, suck on ice chips or hard candy or chew sugarless gum.

To avoid dizziness or light-headedness when you stand, contract and relax the muscles of your legs for a few moments before rising. Do this by alternately pushing one foot against the floor while raising the other foot slightly, so that you are "pumping" your legs in a pedaling motion.

Major. Tell your doctor about any side effects you experience that are persistent or particularly bothersome. IT IS ESPECIALLY IMPORTANT TO TELL YOUR DOCTOR about chest pain;

chills; cough; difficult or painful urination; dry mouth; fever; hair loss; itching; mouth sores; muscle pain or cramps; nausea; palpitations; rash; shortness of breath; sore throat; swelling of the face, hands, or feet; thirst; tingling in the fingers or toes; unusual bleeding or bruising; vomiting; weakness; or yellowing of the eyes or skin.

INTERACTIONS

Captopril and hydrochlorothiazide combination can interact with several other types of medications:

1. The combination of captopril with spironolactone, triamterene, amiloride, potassium supplements, or salt substitutes can lead to hyperkalemia (dangerously high levels of potassium in the bloodstream).

2. Antineoplastic agents (anticancer drugs) and chloramphenicol can increase the bone marrow side effects of captopril.

3. Concurrent use of captopril and allopurinol can increase the risk of developing an allergic reaction.

4. Diuretics (water pills) and other antihypertensive medications can cause an excessive drop in blood pressure when combined with captopril (especially with the first dose).

5. Hydrochlorothiazide can decrease the effectiveness of oral anticoagulants, antigout medications, insulin, oral antidiabetic medicines, and methenamine.

6. Captopril can delay the body's elimination of lithium. Concurrent use of captopril and lithium may cause lithium toxicity.

7. Fenfluramine can increase the blood-pressure-lowering effects of hydrochlorothiazide (which can be dangerous).

8. Indomethacin and other nonsteroidal anti-inflammatory drugs can decrease the blood-pressure-lowering effects of captopril and hydrochlorothiazide, thereby counteracting the desired effects.

9. Cholestyramine and colestipol decrease the absorption of hydrochlorothiazide from the gastrointestinal tract. Hydrochlorothiazide should, therefore, be taken one hour before or four hours after a dose of cholestyramine or colestipol (if you have also been prescribed one of these drugs).

10. Hydrochlorothiazide may increase the side effects of amphotericin B, calcium supplements, cortisone and cortisone-like steroids (such as dexamethasone, hydrocortisone, prednisone, and prednisolone), digoxin, digitalis, lithium, quinidine, sulfonamide antibiotics, and vitamin D.

Before starting captopril and hydrochlorothiazide combination, BE SURE TO TELL YOUR DOCTOR about any medications you are currently taking.

WARNINGS

• Tell your doctor about unusual or allergic reactions you have had to any medications, especially to captopril or to hydrochlorothiazide or other diuretics (such as bendroflumethiazide, benzthiazide, chlorothiazide, chlorthalidone, cyclothiazide, hydroflumethiazide, methyclothiazide, metolazone, polythiazide, quinethazone, trichlormethiazide, and furosemide) or to sulfa medications (oral antidiabetic medications or sulfonamide antibiotics).

• Tell your doctor if you have ever had aortic stenosis, blood disorders, diabetes mellitus, gout, kidney disease or problems with urination, kidney transplant, liver disease, pancreatic disease, a heart attack, or systemic lupus erythematosus.

• Hydrochlorothiazide can cause potassium loss. Signs of potassium loss include dry mouth, thirst, weakness, muscle pain or cramps, nausea, and vomiting. If you experience any of these symptoms, call your doctor. To help prevent this problem, your doctor may have blood tests performed periodically to monitor your potassium levels. To help avoid potassium loss, take this medication with a glass of fresh or frozen orange juice or cranberry juice, or eat a banana every day. The use of a salt substitute also helps to prevent potassium loss. Do not change your diet or use a salt substitute, however, until you discuss it with your doctor. Too much potassium may also be dangerous.

• Limit your intake of alcoholic beverages while taking this medication in order to prevent dizziness and light-headedness.

• If you have high blood pressure, do not take any over-the-counter (nonprescription) medications for weight control or for allergy, asthma, cough, cold, or sinus problems, unless your doctor directs you to do so.

• To prevent dehydration (severe water loss) while taking this medication, check with your doctor if you have any illness that causes severe or continuing diarrhea, nausea, or vomiting.

• This medication can raise blood-sugar levels in diabetic patients. Therefore, sugar levels should be carefully monitored with blood or urine tests when this medication is started.

• Before having surgery or any other medical or dental treatment, be sure to tell your doctor or dentist that you are taking this medication.

• This drug may cause dizziness. Use caution while driving or operating potentially dangerous machinery.

• A "fixed-dose" drug like this is not generally the first choice in the treatment of high blood pressure. Usually, the patient first receives each ingredient singly. If there is an adequate response to the fixed dose contained in this product, it can then be substituted. The advantage of a combination product is increased convenience and (often) decreased cost.

• Do not stop taking this medication unless you first consult your doctor. Stopping this drug abruptly may lead to a rise in blood pressure.

• Be sure to tell your doctor if you are pregnant. Captopril has been found to cause birth defects in the fetus if taken during the second or third trimester of pregnancy. Hydrochlorothiazide can cause adverse effects in the newborn infant if it is given to the mother close to term. Also tell your doctor if you are breast-feeding an infant. Although problems in humans have not been reported, small amounts of this drug can pass into breast milk, so caution is warranted.

---

carbamazepine

BRAND NAMES (Manufacturers)
carbamazepine (various manufacturers)
Epitol (Lemmon)
Tegretol (Geigy)
Tegretol Chewable (Geigy)
TYPE OF DRUG
Anticonvulsant
INGREDIENT
carbamazepine
DOSAGE FORMS
Tablets (200 mg)
Chewable tablets (100 mg)
Oral suspension (100 mg per 5-mL spoonful)

STORAGE
Carbamazepine tablets and oral suspension should be stored at room temperature in tightly closed containers.

USES
This medication is used for the treatment of seizure disorders, for relief of neuralgia (nerve pain), for alcohol withdrawal, and for a wide variety of mental disorders. The mechanism of carbamazepine's antiseizure activity is unknown, but it is not related to other anticonvulsants. Carbamazepine is not an ordinary pain reliever—it should not be used for minor aches or pains.

TREATMENT
Carbamazepine can be taken with food if stomach upset occurs unless your doctor directs otherwise.

Carbamazepine works best when the level of medicine in your bloodstream is kept constant. It is best, therefore, to take it at evenly spaced intervals day and night. For example, if you are to take four doses a day, the doses should be spaced six hours apart.

Try not to miss any doses of this medication. If you do miss a dose, take the missed dose as soon as possible, unless it is almost time for the next dose. In that case, do not take the missed dose at all; just return to your regular dosing schedule. Do not double the next dose unless your doctor directs you to do so. If you are taking carbamazepine for a seizure disorder and you miss two or more doses, be sure to contact your doctor.

SIDE EFFECTS
Minor. Agitation; blurred vision; confusion; constipation; diarrhea; dizziness; drowsiness; dry mouth; headache; loss of appetite; muscle or joint pain; nausea; restlessness; sweating; vomiting; or weakness. These side effects should disappear over time and as your body adjusts to the medication.

This medication can increase your sensitivity to sunlight. It is, therefore, important to avoid prolonged exposure to sunlight and sunlamps. Always wear protective clothing and sunglasses when out of doors, and use an effective sunscreen.

To relieve constipation, increase the amount of fiber in your diet (fresh fruits and vegetables, salads, bran, and whole-grain breads), exercise, and drink more water (unless your doctor directs you to do otherwise).

To relieve mouth dryness, suck on ice chips or a piece of hard candy or chew sugarless gum.

If you feel dizzy or light-headed, sit or lie down for a while; get up slowly from a sitting or reclining position; and be careful on stairs.

Major. Be sure to tell your doctor about any side effects that are persistent or particularly bothersome. IT IS ESPECIALLY IMPORTANT FOR YOU TO TELL YOUR DOCTOR about abdominal pain, chills, depression, difficulty in breathing, difficulty in urinating, eye discomfort, fainting, fever, hair loss, hallucinations, impotence, loss of balance, mouth sores, nightmares, numbness or tingling sensations, palpitations, ringing in the ears, skin rash, sore throat, swelling of the hands and feet, twitching, unusual bleeding or bruising, or yellowing of the eyes or skin.

INTERACTIONS

Carbamazepine interacts with other types of medications:

1. Concurrent use of it with central nervous system depressants (such as alcohol, antihistamines, barbiturates, benzodiazepine tranquilizers, muscle relaxants, narcotics, pain medications, and phenothiazine tranquilizers) or with tricyclic antidepressants can cause extreme drowsiness.

2. Phenobarbital, phenytoin, and primidone can decrease blood levels and effectiveness of carbamazepine.

3. Isoniazid, propoxyphene, verapamil, cimetidine, troleandomycin, and erythromycin can increase the blood levels of carbamazepine, which can increase side effects.

4. The combination of lithium and carbamazepine can lead to central nervous system side effects.

5. Carbamazepine can decrease the effectiveness of phenytoin, oral anticoagulants (blood thinners, such as warfarin), doxycycline, oral contraceptives (birth control pills), ethosuximide, valproic acid, aminophylline, and theophylline.

6. The use of carbamazepine within 14 days of the use of a monoamine oxidase (MAO) inhibitor can lead to serious side effects.

Before you start to take carbamazepine, BE SURE TO TELL YOUR DOCTOR about any medications you are currently taking, especially any of those listed above.

WARNINGS

• Tell your doctor about unusual or allergic reactions you have had to any medications, especially to carbamazepine or to tricyclic antidepressants (such as amitriptyline, desipramine, doxepin, imipramine, protriptyline, or nortriptyline).

• Tell your doctor if you now have or if you have ever had bone marrow depression, blood disorders, difficulty urinating, glaucoma, heart or blood vessel disease, kidney disease, or liver disease.

• Before having surgery or any other medical or dental treatment, be sure to tell your doctor or dentist that you are taking this medication.

• If this medication makes you dizzy or drowsy, do not take part in any activity that requires alertness, such as driving a car or operating potentially dangerous equipment.

• If you are taking this medication to control a seizure disorder, do not stop taking it suddenly. If you stop abruptly, you may experience uncontrollable seizures.

• Be sure to tell your doctor if you are pregnant. Birth defects have been reported more often in infants whose mothers have seizure disorders. It is unclear if the increased risk of birth defects is associated with the disorder or with the anticonvulsant medications, such as carbamazepine, that are used to treat the condition. The risks and benefits of treatment should be discussed with your doctor. Also tell your doctor if you are breast-feeding an infant. Relatively large amounts of carbamazepine pass into breast milk. Therefore, this drug is not recommended for lactating women.

---

carisoprodol

BRAND NAMES (Manufacturers)
carisoprodol (various manufacturers)
Soma (Wallace)
TYPE OF DRUG
Muscle relaxant
INGREDIENT
carisoprodol
DOSAGE FORM
Tablets (350 mg)

STORAGE

Carisoprodol should be stored at room temperature in a tightly closed container.

USES

This medication is used to relieve painful muscle conditions. It should be used in conjunction with rest, physical therapy, and other measures to alleviate discomfort. It is not clear exactly how carisoprodol works, but it is thought to act as a central nervous system depressant. However, carisoprodol does not seem to act directly on the muscles of the body.

TREATMENT

In order to avoid stomach irritation, you can take carisoprodol with food or with a full glass of water or milk (unless your doctor directs you to do otherwise).

If you miss a dose of this medication and remember within an hour, take the missed dose immediately. If more than an hour has passed, do not take the missed dose at all; just return to your regular dosing schedule.

SIDE EFFECTS

Minor. Dizziness, drowsiness, headache, hiccups, insomnia, nausea, stomach pain, or vomiting. These side effects should disappear as your body adjusts to the medication.

If you feel dizzy, sit or lie down for a while; get up slowly from a sitting or reclining position; and be careful on stairs.

Major. Tell your doctor about any side effects that are persistent or particularly bothersome. IT IS ESPECIALLY IMPORTANT TO TELL YOUR DOCTOR about agitation, depression, fainting, irritability, loss of coordination, palpitations, or tremors.

INTERACTIONS

Carisoprodol can be expected to interact with several other types of medications: Concurrent use of it with other central nervous system depressants (such as alcohol, antihistamines, barbiturates, benzodiazepine tranquilizers, muscle relaxants, narcotics, pain medications, phenothiazine tranquilizers, and sleeping medications) or with tricyclic antidepressants can lead to extreme drowsiness.

BE SURE TO TELL YOUR DOCTOR about any medications you are currently taking, especially any listed above.

WARNINGS

• Tell your doctor about unusual or allergic reactions you have had to any medications, especially to carisoprodol or meprobamate.

• Before starting to take carisoprodol, tell your doctor if you now have or if you have ever had kidney disease, liver disease, or porphyria.

• If this drug makes you dizzy or drowsy, avoid taking part in any activity that requires alertness, such as driving a car or operating potentially dangerous equipment or machinery.

• Some of these products contain the color additive FD&C Yellow No. 5 (tartrazine), which can cause allergic-type reactions (rash, fainting, shortness of breath) in certain susceptible individuals.

• Carisoprodol has the potential for abuse and should be used with caution. Do not increase the dosage or stop taking the drug unless you first consult your doctor. If you have been taking carisoprodol for several months and you stop taking it abruptly, it is possible that you could experience a withdrawal reaction. Your doctor may, therefore, want to decrease your dosage of the prescribed medication gradually.

• Be sure to tell your doctor if you are pregnant. Although carisoprodol appears to be safe to use during pregnancy, extensive and conclusive studies have not been conducted in humans. Also tell your doctor if you are breast-feeding an infant. This medication passes into breast milk and can cause excessive drowsiness and stomach upset in nursing infants.

cefaclor

BRAND NAME (Manufacturer)
Ceclor (Lilly)
TYPE OF DRUG
Cephalosporin antibiotic
INGREDIENT
cefaclor
DOSAGE FORMS
Capsules (250 mg and 500 mg)

Oral suspension (125 mg, 187 mg, 250 mg, and 375 mg
per 5-mL spoonful)

STORAGE

Cefaclor capsules should be stored at room temperature in a
tightly closed container. The oral-suspension form of this drug
should be stored in the refrigerator in a tightly closed container. Any unused portion of the oral suspension should be
discarded after 14 days because the drug loses its potency
after that time. This medication should never be frozen.

USES

Cefaclor is used to treat a wide variety of bacterial infections,
including those of the middle ear, skin, upper and lower respiratory tract, and urinary tract. This drug acts by severely
injuring the cell walls of the infecting bacteria, thereby preventing them from growing and multiplying. Cefaclor kills
susceptible bacteria, but it is not effective against viruses, parasites, or fungi.

TREATMENT

Cefaclor can be taken on an empty stomach or with food or a
glass of milk (in order to avoid an upset stomach).

The contents of the suspension form of cefaclor tend to settle on the bottom of the bottle, so it is necessary to shake the
container well to distribute the ingredients evenly and equalize the doses. Each dose should then be measured carefully
with a specially designed 5-mL measuring spoon or with the
dropper provided. An ordinary kitchen teaspoon is not accurate enough.

Cephalosporin antibiotics work best when the level of medicine in your bloodstream is kept at a constant level. It is best,
therefore, to take the doses at evenly spaced intervals day and
night. For example, if you are to take three doses a day, the
doses should be spaced eight hours apart.

If you miss a dose of this medication, take the missed dose
immediately. If you do not remember to take the missed dose
until it is almost time for your next dose, take it; space the
following dose halfway through the regular interval between
doses; then return to your regular dosing schedule. Try not to
skip any doses.

It is important to continue to take this medication for the
entire time prescribed by your doctor (usually seven to

14 days), even if the symptoms disappear before the end of that period. If you stop taking this drug too soon, resistant bacteria are given a chance to continue growing, and the infection could recur.

SIDE EFFECTS

Minor. Abdominal pain, diarrhea, dizziness, fatigue, headache, heartburn, loss of appetite, nausea, or vomiting. These minor side effects can be expected to disappear in time as your body becomes accustomed to the medication.

If you feel dizzy, sit or lie down for a while; get up slowly from a sitting or reclining position; and be careful on stairs.

Major. Tell your doctor about any side effects that are persistent or particularly bothersome. IT IS ESPECIALLY IMPORTANT TO TELL YOUR DOCTOR about darkened tongue, difficulty in breathing, fever, itching, joint pain, rash, rectal or vaginal itching, severe diarrhea (which can be watery or can contain pus or blood), sore mouth, stomach cramps, tingling in the hands or feet, or unusual bleeding or bruising. If symptoms of infection seem to be getting worse rather than improving, contact your doctor.

INTERACTIONS

Cefaclor interacts with several other types of medications:

1. Probenecid can increase the blood concentrations and side effects of this medication.

2. The side effects, especially effects on the kidneys, of furosemide, bumetanide, ethacrynic acid, colistin, vancomycin, polymyxin B, and aminoglycoside antibiotics can be increased by cefaclor.

BE SURE TO TELL YOUR DOCTOR about any medications you are currently taking, especially any listed above.

WARNINGS

• Be sure to tell your doctor about any unusual or allergic reactions you have or have ever had to any medication, especially to cefaclor or other cephalosporin antibiotics (such as cefamandole, cephalexin, cephradine, cefadroxil, cefazolin, cefixime, cefoperazone, cefotaxime, cefpodoxime, cefprozil, ceftizoxime, cephalothin, cephapirin, cefuroxime, and moxalactam) or to penicillin antibiotics.

• Tell your doctor if you now have or if you have ever had kidney disease.

• This medication has been prescribed for your current infection only. Another infection later on, or one that someone else has, may require a different medicine. You should not give your medication to other people or use it for other infections, unless your doctor specifically directs you to do so.

• People with diabetes who are taking cefaclor should know that this medication can cause a false-positive sugar reaction with a Clinitest urine glucose test. To avoid this problem while taking cefaclor, they should switch to Clinistix or Tes-Tape to test their urine sugar content.

• Be sure to tell your doctor if you are pregnant. Although the cephalosporin antibiotics appear to be safe when administered during pregnancy, extensive and conclusive studies in human subjects have not been conducted. Also be sure that you tell your doctor if you are breast-feeding an infant. Small amounts of this medication can pass into breast milk and may temporarily alter the bacterial balance in the intestinal tract of the nursing infant, resulting in diarrhea or other gastrointestinal disturbance.

cefadroxil

BRAND NAMES (Manufacturers)
cefadroxil (various manufacturers)
Duricef (Mead Johnson)
Ultracef (Bristol Labs)
TYPE OF DRUG
Cephalosporin antibiotic
INGREDIENT
cefadroxil
DOSAGE FORMS
Tablets (1 g)
Capsules (500 mg)
Oral suspension (125 mg, 250 mg, and 500 mg per each
   5-mL spoonful)
STORAGE
Cefadroxil tablets and capsules should be stored at room temperature in tightly closed containers. The oral-suspension form of this drug should be stored in the refrigerator in a tightly

closed container. Any unused portion of the oral suspension should be discarded after 14 days because the drug loses its potency after that time. This medication should never be frozen.

USES

Cefadroxil is used to treat a wide variety of bacterial infections, including those of the middle ear, skin, upper and lower respiratory tract, and urinary tract. This drug acts by severely injuring the cell walls of the infecting bacteria, thereby preventing them from growing and multiplying. Cefadroxil kills susceptible bacteria, but it is not effective against viruses, parasites, or fungi.

TREATMENT

You can take cefadroxil either on an empty stomach or, in order to avoid getting an upset stomach, with food or a glass of milk.

The contents of the oral-suspension form of cefadroxil tend to settle on the bottom of the bottle, so it is necessary to shake the container well to distribute the ingredients evenly and equalize the doses. Each dose should then be measured carefully with a specially designed 5-mL measuring spoon or with the dropper provided. An ordinary kitchen teaspoon is not accurate enough for therapeutic purposes.

Cephalosporin antibiotics work best when the level of medicine in your bloodstream is kept constant. It is best, therefore, to take the doses at evenly spaced intervals day and night. For example, if you are supposed to take two doses a day, the doses should be spaced 12 hours apart.

If you miss a dose of this medication, take the missed dose immediately. However, if you do not remember to take the missed dose until it is almost time for your next dose, take it; space the following dose halfway through the regular interval between doses; then return to your regular schedule. Try not to skip any doses.

It is important to continue to take this medication for the entire time prescribed by your doctor (usually seven to 14 days), even if the symptoms disappear before the end of that period. If you stop taking this drug too soon, resistant bacteria could continue growing, and the infection could occur again.

SIDE EFFECTS

Minor. Abdominal pain, diarrhea, dizziness, fatigue, headache, heartburn, loss of appetite, nausea, or vomiting. These side effects should disappear as you adjust to the drug.

If you feel dizzy, sit or lie down for a while; get up slowly from a sitting or reclining position; and be careful on stairs.

Major. Tell your doctor about any side effects that are persistent or particularly bothersome. IT IS ESPECIALLY IMPORTANT TO TELL YOUR DOCTOR about darkened tongue, difficulty in breathing, fever, itching, joint pain, rash, rectal or vaginal itching, severe diarrhea (which can be watery, or contain pus or blood), sore mouth, stomach cramps, tingling in the hands or feet, or unusual bleeding or bruising. If your symptoms of infection seem to be getting worse rather than improving, contact your doctor.

INTERACTIONS

Cefadroxil interacts with several other types of medications:
1. Probenecid can increase the blood concentrations and side effects of this medication.
2. The side effects, especially effects on the kidneys, of furosemide, bumetanide, ethacrynic acid, colistin, vancomycin, polymyxin B, and aminoglycoside antibiotics can be increased by cefadroxil.

Before you start to take this medication, BE SURE TO TELL YOUR DOCTOR about any other medications you are currently taking, especially any of those that are listed above.

WARNINGS

• Tell your doctor about unusual or allergic reactions you have or have ever had to any medication, especially to cefadroxil or other cephalosporin antibiotics (such as cefamandole, cephalexin, cefaclor, cephradine, cefazolin, cefixime, cefoperazone, cefotaxime, cefpodoxime, cefprozil, ceftizoxime, cephalothin, cephapirin, cefoxitin, cefuroxime, and moxalactam) or to penicillin antibiotics.
• Tell your doctor if you now have or if you have ever had kidney disease.
• This medication has been prescribed for your current infection only. Another infection later on, or one that someone else has, may require a different medicine. You should not

give your medication to other people or use it for other infections, unless so directed by your doctor.

• People with diabetes who are taking cefadroxil should know that this drug can cause a false-positive sugar reaction with a Clinitest urine glucose test. They should switch to Clinistix or Tes-Tape to test their urine for sugar.

• Be sure to tell your doctor if you are pregnant. Although the cephalosporin antibiotics appear to be safe during pregnancy, extensive studies in humans have not been conducted. Also tell your doctor if you are breast-feeding an infant. Small amounts of this medication pass into breast milk and may temporarily alter the bacterial balance in the intestinal tract of the nursing infant, resulting in diarrhea.

cefixime

BRAND NAME (Manufacturer)
Suprax (Lederle)
TYPE OF DRUG
Cephalosporin antibiotic
INGREDIENT
cefixime
DOSAGE FORMS
Tablets (200 mg and 400 mg)
Oral suspension (100 mg per 5-mL spoonful)
STORAGE
Cefixime tablets should be stored at room temperature in a tightly closed container. The oral-suspension form of the drug should be stored in the refrigerator in a tightly closed container. Any unused portion of the oral suspension should be discarded after 14 days because the drug loses its potency after that time. This medication should never be frozen.

USES
Cefixime is used to treat a wide variety of bacterial infections, including those of the middle ear, skin, upper and lower respiratory tract, and urinary tract. This drug acts by severely injuring the cell walls of the infecting bacteria, thereby preventing them from growing and multiplying.

TREATMENT

Cefixime can be taken on an empty stomach or with food or milk (to avoid stomach upset).

The ingredients of the suspension form of cefixime tend to settle on the bottom of the bottle, therefore it is necessary to shake the bottle well to distribute the ingredients evenly and equalize the doses. Each dose should then be measured carefully with a specially designed 5-mL measuring spoon or with the provided dropper. An ordinary kitchen teaspoon is not accurate enough for medical purposes.

Cephalosporin antibiotics work best when the level of medicine in your bloodstream is kept constant. It is best to take the doses at evenly spaced intervals day and night. For example, if you are to take two doses a day, the doses should be spaced 12 hours apart.

If you miss a dose of this medication, take the missed dose immediately. If you do not remember to take the missed dose until it is almost time for your next dose, take it; space the following dose halfway through the regular interval between doses; then return to your regular schedule. Try not to skip any doses of this medication.

It is important to try to take this medication for the entire time prescribed by your doctor (usually seven to 14 days), even if the symptoms disappear before the end of that period. If you stop taking the drug too soon, resistant bacteria could continue growing, and infection could recur.

SIDE EFFECTS

Minor. Abdominal pain, diarrhea, dizziness, fatigue, headache, heartburn, loss of appetite, nausea, or vomiting. These side effects should disappear as you adjust to the drug.

If you feel dizzy while you are taking this medication, sit or lie down for a while; get up slowly from a sitting or reclining position; and be careful on stairs. Do not operate any potentially dangerous equipment or work with any hazardous materials.

Major. Tell your doctor about any side effects that are persistent or particularly bothersome. IT IS ESPECIALLY IMPORTANT TO TELL YOUR DOCTOR about darkened tongue, difficulty in breathing, fever, itching, joint pain, rash, rectal or vaginal itching, severe diarrhea (which can be watery or contain pus or blood), sore mouth, stomach cramps, tingling in the hands or feet, or unusual bleeding or bruising. If your symptoms of infection seem to be getting worse rather than improving, contact your doctor.

INTERACTIONS

Cefixime interacts with several other types of medications:

1. Probenecid can increase the blood concentrations and side effects of this medication.

2. Aspirin can increase the blood concentrations of this medication, although the significance of this interaction is questionable.

3. The side effects, especially on the kidneys, of furosemide, bumetanide, ethacrynic acid, colistin, vancomycin, polymyxin B, and aminoglycoside antibiotics can be increased by cefixime.

4. Chloramphenicol should be avoided in combination with cephalosporins due to the possibility of an antagonistic (opposing) effect.

BE SURE TO TELL YOUR DOCTOR about any medications you are currently taking, especially any listed above.

WARNINGS

• Tell your doctor about any unusual or allergic reactions you have had to any medication, especially to cefixime or other cephalosporin antibiotics (such as cefoperazone, cefotaxime, cefpodoxime, ceftazidime, ceftizoxime, ceftriaxone, moxalactam) or to penicillin antibiotics.

• Tell your doctor if you now have or have ever had kidney disease.

• Tell your doctor if you now have or have ever had any type of gastrointestinal disease, particularly colitis.

• This medication has been prescribed for your current infection only. Another infection later on, or one that someone else has, may require a different medicine. You should not give your medication to other people or use it for other infections, unless your doctor specifically directs you to do so.

• People with diabetes who are taking cefixime should know that this medication can cause a false-positive sugar reaction with a Clinitest urine glucose test. To avoid this problem while taking cefixime, they should switch to Clinistix or Tes-Tape to test their urine sugar content.

• Cefixime may also cause a false-positive result for urinary ketones when tests using nitroprusside are used.
• Cefixime may interfere with blood tests.
• Be sure to tell your doctor if you are pregnant. Although the cephalosporin antibiotics appear to be safe during pregnancy, extensive studies in humans have not been conducted. Also tell your doctor if you are breast-feeding an infant. Small amounts of this medication pass into breast milk and may temporarily alter the bacterial balance in the intestinal tract of the nursing infant, resulting in diarrhea.

cefpodoxime

BRAND NAME (Manufacturer)
Vantin (Upjohn)
TYPE OF DRUG
Cephalosporin antibiotic
INGREDIENT
cefpodoxime proxetil
DOSAGE FORMS
Tablets (100 mg and 200 mg)
Oral suspension (50 mg and 100 mg per 5-mL spoonful)
STORAGE
Cefpodoxime tablets should be stored in a tightly closed container at room temperature, away from heat and direct sunlight. The oral-suspension form of this drug should be stored in the refrigerator in a tightly closed container. Any unused portion of the oral suspension should be discarded after 14 days because the drug loses its potency after that time. This medication should never be frozen.

USES

This medication is used to treat a wide variety of bacterial infections, including those of the middle ear, upper and lower respiratory tract, and urinary tract. This drug acts by severely injuring the cell walls of the infecting bacteria, thereby preventing them from growing and multiplying. Cefpodoxime kills susceptible bacteria, but it is not effective against viruses, parasites, or fungi.

TREATMENT

You should take cefpodoxime with food to improve its absorption. The contents of the suspension form of cefpodoxime tend to settle on the bottom of the bottle, so it is necessary to shake the container well immediately before each dose to distribute the ingredients evenly and equalize the doses. Each dose should then be measured carefully with a specially designed 5-mL measuring spoon. An ordinary kitchen spoon is not accurate enough.

Cephalosporin antibiotics work best when the level of medicine in your bloodstream is kept constant. It is therefore desirable to take the doses at evenly spaced intervals day and night. For example, if you are to take two doses a day, the doses should be spaced twelve hours apart.

It is very important to continue this medication for the entire time prescribed by your doctor (usually seven to 14 days), even if your symptoms disappear before the end of that period. If you stop taking this drug too soon, resistant bacteria are given the chance to grow and the infection may recur.

If you miss a dose of cefpodoxime, take the missed dose as soon as you remember. If it is almost time for your next dose, take the missed dose and space the following dose halfway through the regular interval between doses, then return to your regular schedule. Try not to skip any doses.

SIDE EFFECTS

Minor. Abdominal pain, diarrhea, dizziness, fatigue, headache, heartburn, loss of appetite, nausea, or vomiting.

If you feel dizzy or light-headed, sit or lie down for a while; get up slowly from a sitting or reclining position; and be careful on stairs.

Major. Tell your doctor about any side effects that are persistent or particularly bothersome. IT IS ESPECIALLY IMPORTANT TO TELL YOUR DOCTOR about darkened tongue, difficulty in breathing, fever, itching, joint pain, rash, rectal or vaginal itching, severe diarrhea (which may be watery or contain blood or pus), sore mouth, stomach cramps, tingling in the hands or feet, or unusual bleeding or bruising. If your symptoms of infection seem to be getting worse rather than improving, contact your doctor.

INTERACTIONS

Cefpodoxime interacts with a number of other types of medications:

1. Probenecid can increase the blood concentrations of cefpodoxime.

2. The side effects, especially effects on the kidneys, of furosemide, bumetanide, ethacrynic acid, colistin, vancomycin, polymyxin B, and aminoglycoside antibiotics can be increased by cefpodoxime.

3. High dose antacids or H_2 Blockers (cimetidine, ranitidine, famotidine, nizatidine) can decrease the effectiveness of cefpodoxime.

WARNINGS

• Tell your doctor about any unusual or allergic reactions you have had to any medications, especially cefpodoxime or other cephalosporin antibiotics (such as cefamandole, cephalexin, cefaclor, cefadroxil, cefazolin, cefoperazone, cefotaxime, ceftizoxime, cephalothin, cephradine, cephapirin, cefoxitin, cefuroxime, or moxalactam) or to penicillin antibiotics.

• Tell your doctor if you now have or have ever had kidney disease.

• This medication was prescribed for your current infection only. Another infection later on or one that someone else has may require a different medication. You should not give your medicine to other people or use it for other infections unless your doctor specifically instructs you to do so.

• People with diabetes taking this medication should know that cefpodoxime may cause a false positive sugar reaction with a Clinitest urine glucose test. To avoid this problem while taking cefpodoxime, they should switch to Clinistix or Testape to test their urine for sugar.

• Be sure to tell your doctor if you are pregnant. Although the cephalosporin antibiotics appear to be safe during pregnancy, extensive studies in humans have not been conducted. Also tell your doctor if you are breast-feeding an infant. Small amounts of this medication pass into breast milk and may temporarily alter the bacterial balance of the intestinal tract of the nursing infant. This alteration could bring about a case of diarrhea.

cefprozil

BRAND NAME (Manufacturer)
Cefzil (Bristol)
TYPE OF DRUG
Cephalosporin antibiotic
INGREDIENT
cefprozil
DOSAGE FORMS
Tablets (250 mg and 500 mg)
Oral suspension (125 mg and 250 mg per 5-mL spoonful)
STORAGE
Cefprozil tablets should be stored at room temperature in a
tightly closed container. The oral-suspension form of this drug
should also be stored in the refrigerator in a tightly closed
container. Any unused portion of the oral suspension should be
discarded after 14 days because the drug loses potency after
that time. This medication should never be frozen.

USES
This medication is used to treat a wide variety of bacterial infections, including those of the middle ear, skin, and upper
and lower respiratory tract. This drug acts by severely injuring the cell walls of the infecting bacteria, thereby preventing them from growing and multiplying. Cefprozil kills susceptible bacteria, but it is not effective against viruses, parasites,
or fungi.

TREATMENT
Cefprozil can be taken either on an empty stomach or with
food or milk (in order to avoid an upset stomach).
    The ingredients in the suspension form of cefprozil tend to
settle on the bottom of the bottle, therefore it is necessary to
shake the bottle well to distribute the ingredients evenly and
equalize the doses. Each dose should then be measured carefully with a specially designed 5-mL measuring spoon or with
the dropper provided. An ordinary kitchen teaspoon is not
accurate enough for medical purposes.
    Cephalosporin antibiotics work best when the level of med-
icine in your bloodstream is kept constant. It is best to take
the doses at evenly spaced intervals day and night. For ex-

ample, if you are to take two doses a day, the doses should be spaced 12 hours apart.

If you miss a dose of this medication, take the missed dose immediately. If you do not remember to take the missed dose until it is almost time for your next dose, take it; space the following dose halfway through the regular interval between doses; then return to your regular schedule. Try not to skip any doses of this medication.

It is important to try to take this medication for the entire time prescribed by your doctor (usually seven to 14 days), even if the symptoms disappear before the end of that period. If you stop taking the drug too soon, resistant bacteria could continue growing, and infection could recur.

SIDE EFFECTS

Minor. Abdominal pain, diarrhea, dizziness, fatigue, headache, heartburn, loss of appetite, nausea, or vomiting. These side effects should disappear as you adjust to the drug.

If you feel dizzy while you are taking this medication, sit or lie down for a while; get up slowly from a sitting or reclining position; and be careful on stairs. Do not operate any potentially dangerous equipment or work with any hazardous materials.

Major. Tell your doctor about any side effects that are persistent or particularly bothersome. IT IS ESPECIALLY IMPORTANT TO TELL YOUR DOCTOR about darkened tongue, difficulty in breathing, fever, itching, joint pain, rash, rectal or vaginal itching, severe diarrhea (which can be watery or contain pus or blood), sore mouth, stomach cramps, tingling in the hands or feet, or unusual bleeding or bruising. If your symptoms of infection seem to be getting worse rather than improving, contact your doctor.

INTERACTIONS

Cefprozil interacts with several other types of medications:
1. Probenecid can increase the blood concentrations and side effects of this medication.
2. The side effects, especially on the kidneys, of furosemide, bumetanide, ethacrynic acid, colistin, vancomycin, polymyxin B, and aminoglycoside antibiotics can be increased by cefprozil.

3. Chloramphenicol should be avoided in combination with cephalosporins due to the possibility of an antagonistic (opposing) effect.

  BE SURE TO TELL YOUR DOCTOR about any medications you are currently taking, especially any listed above.

WARNINGS

• Tell your doctor about any unusual or allergic reactions you have had to any medication, especially to cefprozil or other cephalosporin antibiotics (such as cefoperazone, cefotaxime, cefpodoxime, ceftazidime, ceftizoxime, ceftriaxone, and moxalactam) or to penicillin antibiotics.

• Tell your doctor if you now have or have ever had kidney disease.

• Tell your doctor if you now have or have ever had any type of gastrointestinal disease, particularly colitis.

• This medication has been prescribed for your current infection only. Another infection later on, or one that someone else has, may require a different medicine. You should not give your medication to other people or use it for other infections unless your doctor specifically directs you to do so.

• People with diabetes who are taking cefprozil should know that this medication can cause a false-positive sugar reaction with a Clinitest urine glucose test. To avoid this problem while taking cefprozil, they should switch to Clinistix or Tes-Tape to test their urine sugar content.

• Cefprozil may also cause a false-positive result for urinary ketones when tests using nitroprusside are used.

• Cefprozil may interfere with blood tests.

• Be sure to tell your doctor if you are pregnant. Although the cephalosporin antibiotics appear to be safe during pregnancy, extensive studies in humans have not been conducted. Also tell your doctor if you are breast-feeding an infant. Small amounts of this medication pass into breast milk and may temporarily alter the bacterial balance in the intestinal tract of the nursing infant, resulting in diarrhea.

cefuroxime

BRAND NAME (Manufacturer)
Ceftin (Allen & Hanburys)

TYPE OF DRUG
Cephalosporin antibiotic
INGREDIENT
cefuroxime axetil
DOSAGE FORMS
Tablets (125 mg, 250 mg, and 500 mg)
Oral suspension (125 mg per 5-mL spoonful)
STORAGE
Cefuroxime tablets should be stored at room temperature in a tightly closed container. The tablets should be protected from moisture.

USES

This medication is used to treat a wide variety of bacterial infections, including those of the middle ear, lower respiratory tract, skin, and urinary tract. It is also effective in the treatment of pharyngitis and tonsillitis. This drug acts by severely injuring the cell walls of the infecting bacteria, thereby preventing them from growing and multiplying. Cefuroxime kills susceptible bacteria, but it is not effective against viruses, parasites, or fungi.

TREATMENT

Cefuroxime can be taken either on an empty stomach or with food or milk (in order to avoid an upset stomach). The tablets may be crushed and mixed with food (such as applesauce or ice cream); however, a strong, persistent, bitter taste may be noted.

Cephalosporin antibiotics work best when the level of medicine in your bloodstream is kept constant. It is best, therefore, to take the doses at evenly spaced intervals day and night. For example, if you are supposed to take two doses a day, the doses should be spaced 12 hours apart.

If you miss a dose of this medication, take the missed dose immediately. If you do not remember to take the missed dose until it is almost time for your next dose, take it; space the following dose halfway through the regular interval between doses; then return to your regular dosing schedule. Try not to skip any doses.

It is important to continue to take this medication for the entire time prescribed by your doctor (usually seven to 14 days), even if the symptoms disappear before the end of that period. If you stop taking this drug too soon, resistant bacteria are given a chance to continue growing, and the infection could recur.

SIDE EFFECTS

Minor. Abdominal pain, diarrhea, dizziness, fatigue, headache, heartburn, loss of appetite, nausea, or vomiting. These side effects should disappear over time as your body adjusts to the medication.

If you feel dizzy, sit or lie down for a while; get up slowly from a sitting or reclining position; and be careful on stairs.

Major. Tell your doctor about any side effects that are persistent or particularly bothersome. IT IS ESPECIALLY IMPORTANT TO TELL YOUR DOCTOR about darkened tongue, difficulty in breathing, fever, itching, joint pain, rash, rectal or vaginal itching, severe diarrhea, sore mouth, stomach cramps, tingling in the hands or feet, or unusual bleeding or bruising. If your symptoms of infection seem to be getting worse rather than improving, you should contact your doctor.

INTERACTIONS

Cefuroxime interacts with several other types of medications:

1. Probenecid can increase the blood concentrations and side effects of this medication.

2. The side effects, especially effects on the kidneys, of furosemide, bumetanide, ethacrynic acid, colistin, vancomycin, polymyxin B, and aminoglycoside antibiotics can be increased by cefuroxime.

3. Concurrent use of this product and chloramphenicol is not recommended.

BE SURE TO TELL YOUR DOCTOR about any medications you are currently taking, especially any listed above.

WARNINGS

• Tell your doctor about any unusual or allergic reactions you have had to any medication, especially to cefuroxime or other cephalosporin antibiotics (such as cefaclor, cefamandole, cephalexin, cephradine, cefadroxil, cefazolin, cefixime, cefoperazone, cefotaxime, cefpodoxime, cefprozil, ceftizoxime, cephalothin, cephapirin, and moxalactam) or to penicillin antibiotics.

• Cefuroxime may cause a false-positive result for urinary ketones when tests using nitroprusside are used.
• Cefuroxime may interfere with blood tests.
• Tell your doctor if you now have or if you have ever had kidney disease or gastrointestinal disease, especially colitis.
• This medication has been prescribed for your current infection only. Another infection later on, or one that someone else has, may require a different medicine. You should not give your medication to other people or use it for other infections, unless your doctor specifically directs you to do so.
• People with diabetes taking cefuroxime should know that this drug can cause a false-positive sugar reaction with a Clinitest urine glucose test. To avoid this problem while taking cefuroxime, they should switch to Clinistix or Tes-Tape.
• Be sure to tell your doctor if you are pregnant. Although the cephalosporin antibiotics appear to be safe during pregnancy, extensive studies in humans have not been conducted. Also tell your doctor if you are breast-feeding an infant. Small amounts of this medication pass into breast milk and may temporarily alter the bacterial balance in the intestinal tract of the nursing infant, resulting in diarrhea.

cephalexin

BRAND NAMES (Manufacturers)
cephalexin monohydrate (various manufacturers)
Keflet (Dista)
Keflex (Dista)
Keftab (Dista)
TYPE OF DRUG
Cephalosporin antibiotic
INGREDIENT
cephalexin
DOSAGE FORMS
Tablets (250 mg and 500 mg)
Capsules (250 mg and 500 mg)
Oral suspension (125 mg and 250 mg per 5-mL spoonful)
Pediatric oral suspension (100 mg per mL)
STORAGE
Cephalexin tablets and capsules should be stored at room temperature in tightly closed containers. The oral-suspension

forms of this drug should be stored in the refrigerator in tightly closed containers. Any unused portion of the oral suspension should be discarded after 14 days because the drug loses its potency after that time. This medication should never be frozen.

USES

This medication is used to treat a wide variety of bacterial infections, including those of the bones, middle ear, prostate, skin, upper and lower respiratory tract, and urinary tract. This drug acts by severely injuring the cell walls of the infecting bacteria, thereby preventing them from growing and multiplying. Cephalexin kills susceptible bacteria, but it is not effective against viruses, parasites, or fungi.

TREATMENT

You can take cephalexin either on an empty stomach or, to avoid stomach upset, with food or milk.

The contents of the suspension form of cephalexin tend to settle on the bottom of the bottle, so it is necessary to shake the container well to distribute the ingredients evenly and equalize the doses. Each dose should then be measured carefully with a specially designed 5-mL measuring spoon or with the dropper provided. An ordinary kitchen teaspoon is not accurate enough.

Cephalosporin antibiotics work best when the level of medicine in your bloodstream is kept constant. It is best, therefore, to take your doses of this medication at evenly spaced intervals throughout the day and night. For example, if you are to take four doses of the medication a day, the doses should be spaced six hours apart.

If you miss a dose, take the missed dose immediately. However, if you do not remember to take the missed dose until it is almost time for your next dose, take it; space the following dose halfway through the regular interval between doses; then return to your regular schedule. Do not skip any doses.

It is important to continue to take this medication for the entire time prescribed by your doctor (usually seven to 14 days), even if the symptoms disappear before the end of that period. If you stop taking this drug too soon, resistant bacteria are given a chance to continue growing, and the infection could recur.

SIDE EFFECTS

Minor. Abdominal pain, diarrhea, dizziness, fatigue, headache, heartburn, loss of appetite, nausea, or vomiting. These side effects should disappear over time as your body adjusts to the medication.

If you feel dizzy, sit or lie down for a while; get up slowly from a sitting or reclining position; and be careful on stairs.

Major. Tell your doctor about any side effects that are persistent or particularly bothersome. IT IS ESPECIALLY IMPORTANT TO TELL YOUR DOCTOR about darkened tongue, difficulty in breathing, fever, itching, joint pain, rash, rectal or vaginal itching, severe diarrhea (which can be watery or contain pus or blood), sore mouth, stomach cramps, tingling in the hands or feet, or unusual bleeding or bruising. If your symptoms of infection seem to be getting worse rather than improving, you should contact your doctor.

INTERACTIONS

Cephalexin interacts with several other types of drugs:

1. Probenecid can increase the blood concentrations of this medication.

2. The side effects, especially effects on the kidneys, of furosemide, bumetanide, ethacrynic acid, colistin, vancomycin, polymyxin B, and aminoglycoside antibiotics can be increased by cephalexin.

BE SURE TO TELL YOUR DOCTOR about any medications you are currently taking, especially any of those listed above.

WARNINGS

• Tell your doctor about unusual or allergic reactions you have had to any medication, especially to cephalexin or other cephalosporin antibiotics (such as cefamandole, cephradine, cefaclor, cefadroxil, cefazolin, cefixime, cefoperazone, cefotaxime, cefpodoxime, cefprozil, ceftizoxime, cephalothin, cephapirin, cefoxitin, cefuroxime, and moxalactam) or to penicillin antibiotics.

• Tell your doctor if you now have or if you have ever had kidney disease.

• This medication has been prescribed for your current infection only. Another infection later on, or one that someone else has, may require a different medicine. You should not give your medication to other people or use it for other infections, unless your doctor specifically directs you to do so.

• People with diabetes taking cephalexin should know that this drug can cause a false-positive sugar reaction with a Clinitest urine glucose test. To avoid this problem while taking cephalexin, they should switch to Clinistix or Tes-Tape to test their urine for sugar.

• Be sure to tell your doctor if you are pregnant. Although the cephalosporin antibiotics appear to be safe during pregnancy, extensive studies in humans have not been conducted and cautious use is warranted. Also tell your doctor if you are breast-feeding an infant. Small amounts of this medication pass into breast milk and may temporarily alter the bacterial balance in the intestinal tract of the nursing infant, resulting in diarrhea.

---

cephradine

BRAND NAMES (Manufacturers)
cephradine (various manufacturers)
Velosef (Bristol-Myers Squibb)
TYPE OF DRUG
Cephalosporin antibiotic
INGREDIENT
cephradine
DOSAGE FORMS
Capsules (250 mg and 500 mg)
Oral suspension (125 mg and 250 mg per 5-mL spoonful)
STORAGE
Cephradine capsules should be stored at room temperature in tightly closed containers and out of the reach of children. The oral-suspension form of this drug should be stored in the refrigerator in a tightly closed container. Any unused portion of the oral suspension should be discarded after 14 days because the drug loses its potency after that time. This medication should never be frozen.

USES

This medication is used to treat a wide variety of bacterial infections, including those of the middle ear, prostate, skin, upper and lower respiratory tract, and urinary tract. This drug acts by severely injuring the cell walls of the infecting bacteria, thereby preventing them from growing and multiplying. Cephradine kills susceptible bacteria, but it is not effective against viruses, parasites, or fungi.

TREATMENT

You can take cephradine either on an empty stomach or, in order to avoid an upset stomach, with food or milk.

The contents of the suspension form of cephradine tend to settle on the bottom of the bottle; it is important to shake the container well to distribute the ingredients evenly and equalize the doses. Each dose should then be measured carefully with a specially designed 5-mL measuring spoon or with the dropper provided. An ordinary kitchen teaspoon is not accurate enough, and often kitchen teaspoons vary in size.

Cephalosporin antibiotics work best when the level of medicine in your bloodstream is kept constant. It is best, therefore, to take the doses at evenly spaced intervals day and night. For example, if you are to take four doses a day, the doses should be spaced six hours apart.

If you miss a dose of this medication, take the missed dose immediately. However, if you do not remember to take the missed dose until it is almost time for your next dose, take it and space the following dose halfway through the regular interval between doses; then return to your regular dosing schedule. It is important that you try not to skip any doses of this medication.

It is important to continue to take cephradine for the entire time prescribed by your doctor (usually seven to 14 days), even if the symptoms disappear before the end of that period. If you stop taking this drug too soon, resistant bacteria are given a chance to continue growing, and the infection could recur.

SIDE EFFECTS

Minor. Abdominal pain, diarrhea, dizziness, fatigue, headache, heartburn, loss of appetite, nausea, or vomiting. These side effects should disappear as your body adjusts to the medication.

If you feel dizzy, sit or lie down for a while; get up slowly from a sitting or reclining position; and be careful on stairs.

Major. Tell your doctor about any side effects that are persistent or particularly bothersome. IT IS ESPECIALLY IMPORTANT TO TELL YOUR DOCTOR about darkened tongue, difficulty in breathing, fever, itching, joint pain, rash, rectal or vaginal itching, severe diarrhea (which can be watery, or contain pus or blood), sore mouth, stomach cramps, tingling in the hands or feet, or unusual bleeding or bruising. If your symptoms of infection seem to be getting worse rather than improving, you should contact your doctor immediately.

INTERACTIONS

Cephradine interacts with several other types of medications:

1. Probenecid can increase the blood concentrations and side effects of this medication.

2. The side effects—especially as they relate to the kidneys—of furosemide, bumetanide, ethacrynic acid, colistin, vancomycin, polymyxin B, and aminoglycoside antibiotics can be increased by cephradine.

BE SURE TO TELL YOUR DOCTOR about any medications you are currently taking, especially any of the medications that are listed above.

WARNINGS

• Tell your doctor about unusual or allergic reactions you have had to any medication, especially to cephradine or other cephalosporin antibiotics (such as cefamandole, cephalexin, cefaclor, cefadroxil, cefazolin, cefixime, cefoperazone, cefotaxime, cefpodoxime, cefprozil, ceftizoxime, cephalothin, cephapirin, cefoxitin, cefuroxime, and moxalactam) or to penicillin antibiotics.

• Tell your doctor if you now have or if you have ever had kidney disease.

• This medication has been prescribed for your current infection only. Another infection later on, or one that someone else has, may require a different medicine. You should not give your medication to other people or use it for other infections, unless your doctor specifically directs you to do so.

• People with diabetes who are taking cephradine need to know that this drug can cause a false-positive sugar reaction with a Clinitest urine glucose test. To avoid this problem while taking cephradine, they should switch to Clinistix or Tes-Tape in order to test their urine sugar content accurately.

• Be sure to tell your doctor if you are pregnant. Although the cephalosporin antibiotics appear to be safe during pregnancy, extensive studies in humans have not been conducted. Also tell your doctor if you are breast-feeding. Small amounts of this medication pass into breast milk and may alter the bacterial balance in the intestinal tract of the nursing infant, resulting in diarrhea.

---

cetirizine

BRAND NAME (Manufacturer)
Zyrtec (Pfizer)
TYPE OF DRUG
Antihistamine
INGREDIENT
cetirizine
DOSAGE FORM
Tablets (5 mg and 10 mg)
STORAGE
Store cetirizine at room temperature in a tightly closed container.

USES

Cetirizine belongs to a group of drugs known as antihistamines, which act by blocking the action of histamine, a chemical released by the body during an allergic reaction. This medication is used to treat or prevent symptoms of allergy. It is also used as part of the treatment of some patients with asthma.

TREATMENT

Cetirizine can be taken with or without food. If you experience stomach upset after taking cetirizine, you may take it with food or with a full glass of milk or water (unless your doctor directs you to do otherwise).

If you miss a dose of cetirizine, take the missed dose as soon as possible, unless it is almost time for the next dose. In that case, do not take the missed dose at all; just wait until the next scheduled dose. Do not double the dose.

SIDE EFFECTS

Minor. Dizziness, drowsiness, dry mouth, and sore throat. These side effects should disappear as your body adjusts to the medication. Dry mouth can be relieved by chewing sugarless gum or sucking on ice chips or a piece of hard candy.

Major. Tell your doctor about any side effects that are persistent or particularly bothersome. IT IS ESPECIALLY IMPORTANT TO TELL YOUR DOCTOR about blurred vision, convulsions, feeling faint, increased sweating, irritability, mental confusion, rash, shakiness, trembling, or weight gain.

INTERACTIONS

Cetirizine can interact with other types of drugs: Concurrent use of it with other central nervous system depressants (such as alcohol, barbiturates, benzodiazepines, muscle relaxants, narcotics, pain medications, and phenothiazine tranquilizers) or with tricyclic antidepressants can cause extreme drowsiness.

Before starting to take cetirizine, BE SURE TO TELL YOUR DOCTOR about any medications you are currently taking, especially any of those listed above.

WARNINGS

• Tell your doctor about any unusual allergic reactions you have had to any medications, especially to cetirizine or any other antihistamines.

• Cetirizine can cause drowsiness or dizziness. Your ability to performs tasks that require mental alertness, such as driving an automobile or operating potentially dangerous tools or machinery, may be decreased. Appropriate caution should therefore be taken.

• Elderly patients may be more sensitive to side effects, especially confusion, drowsiness, and irritability. Report any such effects to your doctor.

• Before having surgery or other medical or dental treatment, tell your doctor or dentist you are taking this drug.

• Be sure to tell your doctor if you are pregnant. The effects of this medication have not been thoroughly studied in humans. Also tell your doctor if you are breast-feeding an infant. It is not known if cetirizine is distributed into breast milk.

chlordiazepoxide

BRAND NAMES (Manufacturers)
chlordiazepoxide hydrochloride (various manufacturers)
Libritabs (Roche)
Librium (Roche)
TYPE OF DRUG
Benzodiazepine sedative/hypnotic
INGREDIENT
chlordiazepoxide
DOSAGE FORMS
Capsules (5 mg, 10 mg, and 25 mg)
Tablets (5 mg, 10 mg, and 25 mg)
STORAGE
This medication should be stored at room temperature in tightly closed, light-resistant containers.

USES
Chlordiazepoxide is prescribed to treat the symptoms of anxiety and alcohol withdrawal. It is not clear exactly how this medicine works, but it may relieve anxiety by acting as a depressant of the central nervous system. This drug is used to relieve nervousness. It is effective for this purpose, but it is important to remove the cause of the anxiety as well.

TREATMENT
This medication should be taken exactly as directed by your doctor. It can be taken with food or a full glass of water if stomach upset occurs. Do not take this medication with a dose of antacids, since they may retard its absorption.

If you are taking this medication regularly and you miss a dose, take the missed dose immediately. If more than an hour has passed, however, skip the dose you missed and wait for the next scheduled dose. Do not double the dose.

SIDE EFFECTS
Minor. Bitter taste in the mouth, constipation, depression, diarrhea, dizziness, drowsiness (after a night's sleep), dry mouth, excessive salivation, fatigue, flushing, headache, heartburn, loss of appetite, nausea, nervousness, sweating, or vomiting.

As your body adjusts to the medicine, these side effects should disappear.

To relieve constipation, increase the fiber in your diet (fresh fruits and vegetables, salads, bran, and whole-grain breads), exercise, and drink more water (unless your doctor instructs you to do otherwise).

Dry mouth can be relieved by chewing sugarless gum or by sucking on ice chips.

If you feel dizzy, sit or lie down for a while; get up slowly from a sitting or reclining position; and be careful on stairs.

Major. Tell your doctor about any side effects that are persistent or particularly bothersome. IT IS ESPECIALLY IMPORTANT TO TELL YOUR DOCTOR about blurred or double vision, chest pain, difficulty in urinating, fainting, falling, fever, hallucinations, joint pain, mouth sores, nightmares, palpitations, rash, severe depression, shortness of breath, slurred speech, sore throat, uncoordinated movements, unusual excitement, unusual tiredness, or yellowing of the eyes or skin.

INTERACTIONS

Chlordiazepoxide interacts with several other drugs:

1. To prevent oversedation, this drug should not be taken with alcohol, other sedative drugs, central nervous system depressants (such as antihistamines, barbiturates, muscle relaxants, pain medicines, narcotics, medicines for seizures, and phenothiazine tranquilizers), or with antidepressants.

2. This medication may decrease the effectiveness of carbamazepine, levodopa, and oral anticoagulants (blood thinners) and may increase the effects of phenytoin.

3. Disulfiram, oral contraceptives (birth control pills), isoniazid, and cimetidine can increase the blood levels of chlordiazepoxide, which can lead to toxic effects.

4. Concurrent use of rifampin may decrease the effectiveness of chlordiazepoxide.

BE SURE TO TELL YOUR DOCTOR about any medications you are currently taking, especially any of the medications listed above.

WARNINGS

• Tell your doctor about unusual or allergic reactions you have had to any medications, especially to chlordiazepoxide or other benzodiazepine tranquilizers (such as alprazolam,

clorazepate, diazepam, flurazepam, halazepam, lorazepam, oxazepam, prazepam, temazepam, and triazolam).
• Tell your doctor if you now have or if you have ever had liver disease, kidney disease, epilepsy, lung disease, myasthenia gravis, porphyria, sleep apnea, mental depression, or mental illness.
• This medicine can cause drowsiness. Avoid tasks that require alertness, such as driving a car.
• Before having surgery or any other medical or dental treatment, tell your doctor or dentist that you are taking this drug.
• This medication has the potential for abuse and must be used with caution. Tolerance may develop quickly; do not increase the dosage of the drug without first consulting your doctor. It is also important not to stop this drug suddenly if you have been taking it in large amounts or if you have used it for several weeks. Your doctor may want to reduce your dosage of this medication gradually to avoid complications.
• This is a safe drug when used properly. When it is combined with other sedative drugs or alcohol, however, serious side effects may develop.
• Be sure to tell your doctor if you are pregnant. This medicine may increase the chance of birth defects if it is taken during the first three months of pregnancy. In addition, too much use of this medicine during the last six months of pregnancy may lead to addiction of the fetus, resulting in withdrawal side effects in the newborn. Use of this medicine during the last weeks of pregnancy may also cause excessive drowsiness, slowed heartbeat, and breathing difficulties in the infant. Tell your doctor if you are breast-feeding an infant. This medicine can pass into breast milk and cause excessive drowsiness, slowed heartbeat, and breathing difficulties in the nursing infant.

chlordiazepoxide and amitriptyline combination

BRAND NAMES (Manufacturers)
chlordiazepoxide and amitriptyline (various manufacturers)
Limbitrol (Roche)
Limbitrol DS (Roche)

TYPE OF DRUG
Benzodiazepine antianxiety and antidepressant
INGREDIENTS
chlordiazepoxide and amitriptyline
DOSAGE FORM
Tablets (5 mg chlordiazepoxide and 12.5 mg amitriptyline;
   10 mg chlordiazepoxide and 25 mg amitriptyline)
STORAGE
Chlordiazepoxide and amitriptyline combination tablets should
be stored at room temperature in a tightly closed, light-resis-
tant container.

USES
Chlordiazepoxide and amitriptyline combination is used for the
treatment of depression associated with anxiety. Amitriptyline
belongs to a group of drugs referred to as tricyclic antidepressants. These medicines are thought to relieve depression by
increasing the concentration of certain chemicals necessary
for nerve transmission in the brain. It is not clear exactly how
chlordiazepoxide works, but it may relieve anxiety by acting
as a depressant of the central nervous system (brain and spinal
cord).

TREATMENT
This medication combination should be taken exactly as your
doctor prescribes. In order to avoid stomach upset, you can
take this medication with food or with a full glass of milk or
water (unless your doctor directs you to do otherwise). Do
not take chlordiazepoxide and amitriptyline tablets with a
dose of antacids—they retard absorption of this medication.
   If you are taking this medication regularly and you miss a
dose, take the missed dose as soon as possible, unless it is almost time for your next dose. In that case, do not take the
missed dose at all; just return to your regular dosing schedule. Do not double the dose.
   The benefits of therapy with this medication may not become apparent for two or three weeks.

SIDE EFFECTS
Minor. Agitation, anxiety, blurred vision, confusion, constipation, cramps, diarrhea, dizziness, drowsiness, dry mouth,

fatigue, headache, heartburn, insomnia, loss of appetite, nausea, peculiar tastes in the mouth, restlessness, sweating, vomiting, weakness, or weight gain or loss. These side effects should disappear as your body adjusts to the medication.

This drug may cause increased sensitivity to sunlight, so avoid prolonged exposure to sunlight and sunlamps. Wear protective clothing and sunglasses, and use an effective sunscreen.

Amitriptyline may cause the urine to turn blue-green. This is a harmless effect.

Dry mouth can be relieved by chewing sugarless gum or sucking on ice chips or hard candy.

To relieve constipation, increase the amount of fiber in your diet (fresh fruits and vegetables, salads, bran, whole-grain breads), exercise, and drink more water (unless your doctor directs you to do otherwise).

To avoid dizziness or light-headedness when you stand, contract and relax the muscles of your legs for a few moments before rising. Do this by pushing one foot against the floor while raising the other foot slightly, alternating feet so that you are "pumping" your legs in a pedaling motion.

Major. Tell your doctor about any side effects that are persistent or particularly bothersome. IT IS ESPECIALLY IMPORTANT TO TELL YOUR DOCTOR about chest tightness, convulsions, difficult or painful urination, enlarged or painful breasts (in both sexes), fainting, fever, fluid retention, hair loss, hallucinations, impotence, mood changes, mouth sores, nervousness, nightmares, numbness in the fingers or toes, palpitations, ringing in the ears, skin rash, sore throat, tremors, uncoordinated movements or balance problems, unusual bleeding or bruising, or yellowing of the eyes or skin.

INTERACTIONS

Chlordiazepoxide and amitriptyline combination interacts with several other types of medications:

1. Extreme drowsiness can occur when this medicine is taken with central nervous system depressants (such as alcohol, antihistamines, barbiturates, other benzodiazepine tranquilizers, muscle relaxants, narcotics, pain medications, phenothazine tranquilizers, and sleeping medications) or with other antidepressants.

2. Amitriptyline may decrease the effectiveness of antiseizure medications and may block the blood-pressure-lowering effects of clonidine and guanethidine.

3. Estrogen-containing drugs and oral contraceptives (birth control pills) can increase the side effects and reduce the effectiveness of amitriptyline.

4. Amitriptyline may increase the side effects of thyroid medication and over-the-counter (nonprescription) cough, cold, allergy, asthma, sinus, and diet medications.

5. The concurrent use of amitriptyline and monoamine oxidase (MAO) inhibitors should be avoided because the combination may result in fever, convulsions, or high blood pressure. At least 14 days should separate the use of this drug and the use of an MAO inhibitor.

6. Chlordiazepoxide may decrease the effectiveness of levodopa and oral anticoagulants (blood thinners) and may increase the effects of phenytoin.

7. Disulfiram, oral contraceptives (birth control pills), isoniazid, and cimetidine can increase the blood levels of chlordiazepoxide, which could possibly lead to toxic effects.

8. Concurrent use of rifampin may decrease the effectiveness of the combination of chlordiazepoxide and amitriptyline.

9. Cimetidine can decrease the elimination of amitriptyline from the body, which can increase the possibility of side effects.

BE SURE TO TELL YOUR DOCTOR about any medications you are currently taking, especially any of the medications that are listed above.

WARNINGS

• Tell your doctor about unusual or allergic reactions you have had to any medications, especially to chlordiazepoxide or other benzodiazepine tranquilizers (such as alprazolam, clorazepate, diazepam, flurazepam, halazepam, lorazepam, oxazepam, prazepam, temazepam, and triazolam), or to amitriptyline or other tricyclic antidepressants (such as desipramine, imipramine, nortriptyline, or doxepin).

• Tell your doctor if you have a history of alcoholism or if you have ever had asthma, high blood pressure, liver or kidney disease, lung disease, myasthenia gravis, heart disease, a heart attack, circulatory disease, stomach problems, intestinal problems, difficulty in urinating, enlarged prostate gland, epilepsy, glaucoma, thyroid disease, mental illness, or electroshock therapy.

• If this drug makes you dizzy or drowsy, do not take part in any activity that requires alertness, such as driving an automobile or operating potentially dangerous equipment or machinery.

• Before having surgery or any other medical or dental treatment, be sure to tell your doctor or dentist that you are taking this medication.

• The effects of this medication may last as long as seven days after you have stopped taking it. It is therefore important that you continue to observe all precautions during this period.

• This medication has the potential for abuse and must be used with caution. Tolerance develops quickly; do not increase the dosage of the drug unless you first consult your doctor. It is also important not to stop taking this drug suddenly, especially if it has been used in large amounts or has been used for longer than several weeks. Abruptly stopping this medication may cause nausea, headache, stomach upset, fatigue, or a worsening of your condition. Your doctor may want to reduce the dosage gradually.

• Be sure to tell your doctor if you are pregnant. Chlordiazepoxide may increase the chance of birth defects if it is taken during the first three months of pregnancy. In addition, too much use of this medication during the last six months of pregnancy may lead to addiction of the fetus, resulting in withdrawal symptoms in the newborn. Use of this medication during the last weeks of pregnancy may cause excessive drowsiness, slowed heartbeat, and breathing difficulties in the newborn infant. Also tell your doctor if you are breast-feeding an infant. This medicine may pass into breast milk and cause excessive drowsiness, slowed heartbeat, breathing difficulty, and irritability in the nursing infant.

---

chlordiazepoxide and clidinium combination

BRAND NAMES (Manufacturers)
chlordiazepoxide with clidinium bromide
   (various manufacturers)

Clindex (Rugby)
Clinoxide (Geneva Generics)
Clipoxide (Schein)
Librax (Roche)
Lidox (Major)
TYPE OF DRUG
Benzodiazepine antianxiety and anticholinergic
INGREDIENTS
Chlordiazepoxide and clidinium
DOSAGE FORM
Capsules (5 mg chlordiazepoxide and 2.5 mg clidinium)
STORAGE
Chlordiazepoxide and clidinium combination capsules should be stored at room temperature in a tightly closed, light-resistant container.

USES
Chlordiazepoxide and clidinium combination is used in conjunction with other drugs to treat peptic ulcer or irritable bowel syndrome. Clidinium is an anticholinergic agent that slows the activity of the gastrointestinal tract and reduces the production of stomach acid. Chlordiazepoxide belongs to a group of drugs known as benzodiazepine tranquilizers. It is not clear exactly how chlordiazepoxide works, but it may relieve anxiety by acting as a depressant of the central nervous system.

TREATMENT
You should take chlordiazepoxide and clidinium combination 30 to 60 minutes before meals. It can be taken with a glass of water or milk. Do not take this medication with antacids, since they may interfere with absorption of the drug.

If you miss a dose of this medication, take the missed dose as soon as possible, unless it is almost time for you to take your next dose. In that case, do not take the missed dose at all; just return to your regular dosing schedule. Do not double the next dose.

SIDE EFFECTS
Minor. Blurred vision, change in your sense of taste, confusion, constipation, decreased sweating, depression, diarrhea, dizziness, drowsiness, dry mouth, fatigue, headache, insom-

nia, nausea, or vomiting. These side effects should disappear as your body adjusts to the medication.

This medication can cause increased sensitivity to sunlight. You should, therefore, avoid prolonged exposure to sunlight and sunlamps. Wear protective clothing and sunglasses, and use an effective sunscreen.

Dry mouth can be relieved by chewing sugarless gum or by sucking on ice chips or a piece of hard candy.

To relieve constipation, increase the amount of fiber in your diet (fresh fruits and vegetables, salads, bran, and whole-grain breads), exercise, and drink more water (unless your doctor directs you to do otherwise).

To avoid dizziness or light-headedness when you stand, contract and relax the muscles of your legs for a few minutes before rising. Do this by pushing one foot against the floor while raising the other foot slightly, alternating feet so that you are "pumping" your legs in a pedaling motion.

Major. Tell your doctor about any side effects that are persistent or particularly bothersome. IT IS ESPECIALLY IMPORTANT TO TELL YOUR DOCTOR about decreased sexual ability, difficulty in breathing, difficult or painful urination, excitation, fluid retention, hallucinations, palpitations, rash, sore throat, uncoordinated movements, or yellowing of the eyes or skin.

INTERACTIONS

This medication interacts with several other types of drugs:

1. Extreme drowsiness can occur when this medicine is taken with other central nervous system depressants (such as alcohol, antihistamines, barbiturates, muscle relaxants, narcotics, pain medications, phenothiazine tranquilizers, and sleeping medications) or with tricyclic antidepressants.

2. Chlordiazepoxide can decrease the effectiveness of carbamazepine, levodopa, and oral anticoagulants (blood thinners) and may increase the effects of phenytoin.

3. Disulfiram, oral contraceptives (birth control pills), isoniazid, and cimetidine can increase the blood levels of chlordiazepoxide, and this in turn could possibly lead to toxic effects.

4. Concurrent use of rifampin may decrease the effectiveness of chlordiazepoxide and clidinium.

5. Amantadine, haloperidol, phenothiazine tranquilizers, procainamide, quinidine, and tricyclic antidepressants may increase the side effects of clidinium.

Before starting to take this medication, BE SURE TO TELL YOUR DOCTOR about any medications you are currently taking, especially any of those listed above.

WARNINGS

• Tell your doctor if you have ever had unusual or allergic reactions to any medications, especially to chlordiazepoxide or other benzodiazepine tranquilizers (such as alprazolam, clorazepate, diazepam, flurazepam, halazepam, lorazepam, oxazepam, prazepam, temazepam, and triazolam) or to clidinium.

• Tell your doctor if you now have or if you have ever had glaucoma, obstructed bladder or intestine, enlarged prostate gland, heart disease, lung disease, liver disease, kidney disease, ulcerative colitis, porphyria, high blood pressure, myasthenia gravis, epilepsy, thyroid disease, emotional instability, or hiatal hernia.

• This medication can decrease sweating and heat release from the body. You should, therefore, avoid becoming overheated by strenuous exercise in hot weather and should avoid taking hot baths, showers, and saunas.

• This medicine can cause drowsiness. Avoid tasks that require alertness, such as driving a car or operating potentially dangerous equipment.

• Before having surgery or any other medical or dental treatment, tell your doctor or dentist that you are taking this drug. This medication has the potential for abuse and must be used with caution. Tolerance develops quickly; do not increase the dosage unless you first consult your doctor. It is also important not to stop taking this drug suddenly if you have been using it in large amounts or for longer than several weeks. Your doctor may reduce the dosage gradually.

• This is a safe drug when used properly. When it is combined with other sedative drugs or alcohol, however, serious side effects may develop.

• Be sure to tell your doctor if you are pregnant. This medicine may increase the chance of birth defects if it is taken during the first three months of pregnancy. In addition, too much use of this medicine during the last six months of pregnancy may cause the baby to become dependent on it. This may result in withdrawal symptoms in the infant at birth. Use of this medicine during the last weeks of pregnancy may cause excessive drowsiness, slowed heartbeat, and breathing difficulties in the newborn infant. Also tell your doctor if you are breast-feeding an infant. This medicine may pass into breast milk and cause excessive drowsiness, slowed heartbeat, and breathing difficulties in the nursing infant.

chlorhexidine gluconate

BRAND NAME (Manufacturer)
Peridex (Procter & Gamble)
TYPE OF DRUG
Oral rinse
INGREDIENT
chlorhexidine as the gluconate salt
DOSAGE FORM
Mouthwash (11.6% alcohol)
STORAGE
This product should be stored at room temperature in a tightly closed, light-resistant container. Chlorhexidine gluconate solution should not be frozen.

USES
Chlorhexidine gluconate solution is prescribed by dentists for the treatment of gingivitis and mouth infections and for the reduction of dental plaque. *Gingivitis* is a medical term for inflammation of the gums characterized by redness, swelling, and bleeding upon probing. Although it is unknown exactly how the product works, it is believed to eliminate bacteria, which can cause dental plaque. Dental plaque is one of several causes of gingivitis.

TREATMENT
Treatment with chlorhexidine gluconate solution should begin following a thorough cleaning of your teeth by your dental practitioner.

Measure one-half fluid ounce (as marked in the cap given with the product) of chlorhexidine gluconate solution, and swish in the mouth for at least 30 seconds twice daily. Do not dilute it in water or other liquids. It should be used full strength. Chlorhexidine gluconate solution should be used after brushing and flossing.

Do not swallow chlorhexidine gluconate solution following use. It should be expectorated (spit out) after rinsing the mouth.

Do not rinse your mouth with water after using this medication; doing so may increase the bad taste of this medicine. And do not eat or drink for several hours after use

SIDE EFFECTS

Minor. Irritation of the inside of the mouth can occur following use of this product. In addition, some patients may experience temporary taste disturbances. However, there have been no permanent taste disturbances reported with continued use of chlorhexidine.

Major. Be sure to tell your dentist about any side effects that are persistent or particularly bothersome. IT IS ESPECIALLY IMPORTANT TO TELL YOUR DENTIST about any inflammation and swelling of the parotid salivary gland.

Chlorhexidine may cause staining of the teeth and tongue. This staining will be more noticeable in patients who have a heavy accumulation of plaque. Usually, this staining is temporary and can be easily removed from most tooth surfaces with dental cleaning. Rarely, some persons, especially those with plaque, will have permanent stains.

INTERACTIONS

There do not appear to be any significant drug interactions with this medication. However, you should make sure your dentist knows about all the medications you are taking.

WARNINGS

• Tell your doctor and dentist about any reactions you have had to any drugs, especially to chlorhexidine gluconate solution.

• Chlorhexidine gluconate solution has not been fully evaluated in children under the age of 18. Therefore, the product should not be used by children in this age group.

• To determine the effectiveness of chlorhexidine use, it is advisable to have dental checkups at least every six months.

• Be sure to tell your dentist if you are pregnant or breast-feeding an infant. Scientific studies have not yet determined the effects of the administration of chlorhexidine to pregnant or nursing women or their babies. Therefore, use of this product during this time should be carefully considered.

---

chlorpromazine

BRAND NAMES (Manufacturers)
chlorpromazine hydrochloride (various manufacturers)
Ormazine (Hauck)
Thorazine (SmithKline Beecham)
Thorazine Spansules (SmithKline Beecham)
Thor-Prom (Major)
TYPE OF DRUG
Phenothiazine tranquilizer
INGREDIENT
chlorpromazine hydrochloride
DOSAGE FORMS
Tablets (10 mg, 25 mg, 50 mg, 100 mg, and 200 mg)
Sustained-release capsules (30 mg, 75 mg, 150 mg, 200 mg, and 300 mg)
Oral concentrate (30 mg per mL and 100 mg per mL)
Oral syrup (10 mg per 5-mL spoonful)
Suppositories (25 mg and 100 mg)
STORAGE
The tablet and capsule forms of this drug should be stored at room temperature in tightly closed, light-resistant containers. The oral syrup and suppository forms of this drug should be stored in the refrigerator in tightly closed, light-resistant containers. If the oral concentrate or syrup turns to a slight yellow color, the medicine is still effective and can be used. However, if the oral concentrate or syrup changes color markedly or has particles floating in it, it should not be used; instead, it should be discarded down the sink. Chlorpromazine should never be frozen.

USES

Chlorpromazine is prescribed for pain relief and to treat the symptoms of certain types of mental illness, such as emotional symptoms of psychosis and the manic phase of manic-depressive illness. This medication is thought to relieve the symptoms of mental illness by blocking certain chemicals involved with nerve transmission in the brain.

Chlorpromazine may also be used to treat tetanus, porphyria, uncontrollable hiccups, anxiety before surgery, and nausea and vomiting.

TREATMENT

To avoid stomach irritation, take the tablet or capsule forms of this medication with a meal or with a glass of water or milk (unless your doctor directs you to do otherwise). The sustained-release capsules should be taken whole: Do not crush, break, or open them prior to swallowing. Breaking the capsule would result in releasing the medication all at once, defeating the purpose of the extended-release capsules.

Measure the oral syrup carefully with a specially designed 5-mL measuring spoon. An ordinary kitchen teaspoon is not accurate enough.

The oral-concentrate form of this medication should be measured carefully with the dropper provided, then added to four ounces (one-half cup) or more of water, milk, a carbonated beverage, applesauce, or pudding immediately prior to administration. Be careful that the serving size is not more than the patient is willing or able to drink or eat; otherwise, the full dose may not be consumed. To prevent possible loss of effectiveness, the medication should not be diluted in tea, coffee, or apple juice.

To use the suppository form of this medication, remove the foil wrapper and moisten the suppository with water (if the suppository is too soft to insert, refrigerate it for half an hour or run cold water over it before removing the wrapper). Lie on your left side with your right knee bent. Push the suppository into the rectum, pointed end first. Lie still for a few minutes. Try to avoid having a bowel movement for at least an hour.

If you miss a dose of this medication, take the missed dose as soon as possible, then return to your regular schedule. If it is almost time for the next dose, however, skip the one you missed and return to your regular schedule. Do not double the dose (unless your doctor directs you to do so).

Antacids and antidiarrheal medicines may decrease the absorption of this medication from the gastrointestinal tract.

Therefore, at least one hour should separate doses of one of these medicines and chlorpromazine.

The full effects of this medication for the control of emotional or mental symptoms may not become apparent for two weeks after you start to take it.

SIDE EFFECTS

Minor. Blurred vision, constipation, decreased sweating, diarrhea, dizziness, drooling, drowsiness, dry mouth, fatigue, jitteriness, menstrual irregularities, nasal congestion, restlessness, tremors, vomiting, or weight gain. As your body adjusts to the medication, these side effects should disappear.

This medication can cause increased sensitivity to sunlight. It is, therefore, important to avoid prolonged exposure to sunlight or sunlamps. Wear protective clothing and use an effective sunscreen.

Chlorpromazine can also cause discoloration of the urine to red, pink, or red-brown. This is a harmless effect.

If you are constipated, increase the amount of fiber in your diet (fresh fruits and vegetables, salads, bran, and whole-grain breads), exercise, and drink more water (unless your doctor directs you to do otherwise).

Chew sugarless gum or suck on ice chips or a piece of hard candy to reduce mouth dryness.

To avoid dizziness or light-headedness when you stand, contract and relax the muscles of your legs for a few moments before rising. Do this by pushing one foot against the floor while raising the other foot slightly, alternating feet so that you are "pumping" your legs in a pedaling motion.

Major. Tell your doctor about any side effects that are persistent or particularly bothersome. IT IS ESPECIALLY IMPORTANT TO TELL YOUR DOCTOR about breast enlargement (in both sexes); chest pain; convulsions; darkened skin; difficulty in swallowing or breathing; fainting; fever; impotence; involuntary movements of the face, mouth, jaw, or tongue; palpitations; rash; sleep disorders; sore throat; uncoordinated movements; unusual bleeding or bruising; visual disturbances; or yellowing of the eyes or skin.

INTERACTIONS

Chlorpromazine will interact with several types of medications:

1. It can cause extreme drowsiness when combined with alcohol or other central nervous system depressants (such as barbiturates, benzodiazepine tranquilizers, muscle relaxants, narcotics, and pain medications) or with tricyclic antidepressants.

2. Chlorpromazine can decrease the effectiveness of amphetamines, guanethidine, anticonvulsants, and levodopa.

3. The side effects of cyclophosphamide, epinephrine, monoamine oxidase (MAO) inhibitors, phenytoin, and tricyclic antidepressants may be increased by this medication.

4. Chlorpromazine can increase the absorption of propranolol, which can increase the risks of side effects.

5. Lithium may increase the side effects and decrease the effectiveness of this medication.

Before starting to take chlorpromazine, BE SURE TO TELL YOUR DOCTOR about any medications you are currently taking, especially any of those listed above.

WARNINGS

• Tell your doctor about unusual or allergic reactions you have had to any medications, especially to chlorpromazine or any other phenothiazine tranquilizers (such as fluphenazine, mesoridazine, perphenazine, prochlorperazine, promazine, thioridazine, and trifluoperazine) or to loxapine.

• Tell your doctor if you have a history of alcoholism, or if you now have or ever had blood disease, bone marrow disease, brain disease, breast cancer, blockage in the urinary or digestive tract, drug-induced depression, epilepsy, high or low blood pressure, diabetes mellitus, glaucoma, heart or circulatory disease, liver disease, lung disease, Parkinson's disease, peptic ulcers, or an enlarged prostate gland.

• Tell your doctor about any recent exposure to a pesticide or an insecticide. Chlorpromazine may increase the side effects from the exposure.

• To prevent oversedation, avoid drinking alcoholic beverages while taking this medication.

• If this drug makes you dizzy or drowsy, avoid any activity that requires alertness. Be careful on stairs, and avoid getting up suddenly from a lying or sitting position.

• Before having surgery or any other medical or dental treatment, be sure to tell your doctor or dentist that you are taking this medication.

• Some of the side effects caused by this drug can be prevented by taking an antiparkinsonism drug. Discuss this with your doctor.

• This medication can decrease sweating and heat release from the body. You should, therefore, avoid becoming overheated by strenuous exercise in hot weather and should avoid taking hot baths, showers, and saunas.

• Do not stop taking this medication suddenly. If the drug is stopped abruptly, you may experience nausea, vomiting, stomach upset, headache, increased heart rate, insomnia, tremors, or a worsening of your condition. Your doctor may want to reduce the dosage gradually.

• If you are planning to have a myelogram or any other procedure in which dye will be injected into your spinal cord, tell your doctor that you are taking this medication.

• Avoid spilling the oral concentrate or oral syrup forms of this medication on your skin or clothing: It may cause redness and irritation of the skin.

• While you are being treated with this medication, do not take any over-the-counter (nonprescription) medications for weight control or for cough, cold, allergy, asthma, or sinus problems without first checking with your doctor. The combination of these medications with chlorpromazine may cause high blood pressure.

• Be sure to tell your doctor if you are pregnant. Small amounts of this medication cross the placenta. Although there are reports of safe use of this drug during pregnancy, there are also reports of liver disease and tremors in newborn infants whose mothers received this medication close to term. Also tell your doctor if you are breast-feeding an infant. Small amounts of this medication pass into breast milk and may affect the nursing infant.

chlorpropamide

BRAND NAMES (Manufacturers)
chlorpropamide (various manufacturers)
Diabinese (Pfizer)
TYPE OF DRUG
Oral antidiabetic

INGREDIENT
chlorpropamide
DOSAGE FORM
Tablets (100 mg and 250 mg)
STORAGE
Store at room temperature in a tightly closed container. This medication should not be refrigerated.

USES

Chlorpropamide is used for the treatment of diabetes mellitus that appears in adulthood and cannot be managed by control of diet alone. This type of diabetes is known as non–insulin-dependent diabetes (sometimes called type II diabetes). Chlorpropamide lowers blood sugar by increasing the release of insulin from the pancreas.

TREATMENT

In order for this medication to work correctly, it must be taken as your doctor has directed. It is best to take this medicine at the same time each day in order to maintain a constant blood-sugar level. It is important, therefore, to try not to miss any doses of this medication. If you do miss a dose, take it as soon as possible, unless it is almost time for the next dose. In that case, do not take the missed dose at all; just return to your regular dosing schedule. Do not double the next dose. Tell your doctor if you feel any side effects from missing a dose of this drug.

People with diabetes who are taking oral antidiabetic medication may need to be switched to insulin if they develop diabetic coma, have a severe infection, are scheduled for major surgery, or become pregnant.

SIDE EFFECTS

Minor. Diarrhea, headache, heartburn, loss of appetite, nausea, stomach discomfort, stomach pain, or vomiting. These side effects usually disappear during treatment, as your body adjusts to the medication.

Chlorpropamide may increase your sensitivity to sunlight. Use caution during exposure to the sun. You may want to wear protective clothing and sunglasses. Use an effective sunscreen and avoid exposure to sunlamps.

Major. If any side effects are persistent or particularly bothersome, it is important to notify your doctor. IT IS ESPECIALLY IMPORTANT TO TELL YOUR DOCTOR about dark urine, fatigue, itching of the skin, light-colored stools, sore throat and fever, unusual bleeding or bruising, or yellowish discoloration of the eyes or skin.

Chlorpropamide can also cause retention of body water, which in turn can lead to drowsiness; muscle cramps; seizures; swelling or puffiness of the face, hands, or ankles; and tiredness or weakness. IT IS IMPORTANT TO TELL YOUR DOCTOR if you notice the appearance of any of these side effects.

INTERACTIONS

Chlorpropamide will interact with several other types of medications:

1. Chloramphenicol, fenfluramine, guanethidine, insulin, miconazole, monoamine oxidase (MAO) inhibitors, oxyphenbutazone, oxytetracycline, phenylbutazone, probenecid, aspirin or other salicylates, sulfinpyrazone, or sulfonamide antibiotics, when combined with chlorpropamide, can lower blood-sugar levels—sometimes to dangerously low levels.

2. Thyroid hormones, dextrothyroxine, epinephrine, phenytoin, thiazide diuretics (water pills), or cortisonelike medications (such as dexamethasone, hydrocortisone, and prednisone), when combined with chlorpropamide, can actually increase blood-sugar levels.

3. Rifampin can decrease the blood levels of chlorpropamide, which can lead to a decrease in its effectiveness.

4. Antidiabetic medications can increase the effects of anticoagulants (blood thinners, such as warfarin), which can lead to bleeding complications.

5. Beta-blocking medications (acebutolol, atenolol, betaxolol, bisoprolol, carteolol, esmolol, labetalol, metoprolol, nadolol, penbutolol, pindolol, propranolol, and timolol), combined with chlorpropamide, can result in either high or low blood-sugar levels. Beta blockers can also mask the symptoms of low blood sugar, which can be dangerous.

6. Avoid drinking alcoholic beverages while taking this medication (unless otherwise directed by your doctor). Some patients who take this medicine suffer nausea, vomiting, dizziness, stomach pain, pounding headache, sweating, or redness of the face and skin when they drink alcohol. Also, large amounts of alcohol can lower blood sugar to dangerously low levels.

BE SURE TO TELL YOUR DOCTOR about any medications you are currently taking, especially any of those listed above.

WARNINGS

• It is important to tell your doctor if you have ever had unusual or allergic reactions to this medicine or to any sulfa medication (sulfonamide antibiotics, acetazolamide, diuretics [water pills], or other oral antidiabetics).

• Tell your doctor if you now have or if you have ever had kidney disease, liver disease, thyroid disease, or a severe infection.

• Be sure to follow the special diet that your doctor gave you. This is an essential part of controlling your blood sugar and is necessary in order for this medicine to work properly.

• Before having surgery or any other medical or dental treatment, be sure to tell your doctor or dentist that you are taking this medicine.

• Have tests conducted for sugar in your blood or urine, as directed by your doctor. Such a test is a convenient way to determine whether or not your diabetes is being controlled by this medicine.

• Eat or drink something containing sugar right away if you experience any symptoms of low blood sugar (such as anxiety, chills, cold sweats, cool or pale skin, drowsiness, excessive hunger, headache, nausea, nervousness, rapid heartbeat, shakiness, or unusual tiredness or weakness). It is important that your family and friends recognize the symptoms of low blood sugar and understand what to do if they observe any of these symptoms in you.

• Even if the symptoms of low blood sugar are corrected by eating or drinking sugar, it is important to contact your doctor as soon as possible after experiencing them. The blood-sugar-lowering effects of this medicine can last for hours, and the symptoms may return during this period. Good sources of sugar are orange juice, corn syrup, honey, sugar cubes, and table sugar. You are at greatest risk of developing low blood sugar if you skip or delay meals, exercise more than usual, cannot eat because of nausea or vomiting, or drink large amounts of alcoholic beverages.

• Be sure to tell your doctor if you are pregnant. Since extensive studies have not yet been conducted, it is not known whether this medication can cause problems when administered to a pregnant woman. Cautious use of this medication is thus warranted. It is also important to tell your doctor if you are currently breast-feeding an infant. It has been determined that this medicine can pass into breast milk. For this reason this medication is not recommended for use by any woman who is breast-feeding.

cholestyramine

BRAND NAMES (Manufacturers)
Cholybar (Parke-Davis)
Questran (Bristol Labs)
Questran Light (Bristol Labs)
TYPE OF DRUG
Antihyperlipidemic (lipid-lowering drug)
INGREDIENT
cholestyramine
DOSAGE FORMS
Oral powder (5 g of cholestyramine per packet or level
   scoop or 9 g of cholestyramine per packet or level scoop)
Bar (4 g of cholestyramine per bar)
STORAGE
Cholestyramine should be stored at room temperature in a tightly closed container. This medication should not be refrigerated.

USES
This medication is used to lower blood cholesterol and to treat itching associated with liver disease. Cholestyramine chemically binds to bile salts in the gastrointestinal tract and prevents the body from producing cholesterol.

TREATMENT
Cholestyramine is usually taken before meals. Each dose should be measured carefully and then added to two to six ounces of water, milk, fruit juice, or another noncarbonated drink. To avoid swallowing of air, this mixture should be taken slowly. The powder can also be mixed with applesauce, cereal,

crushed pineapple, or soup. You should never take cholestyramine dry because you might accidentally inhale the powder, and that could irritate your throat and lungs. For the bar form of the drug, chew thoroughly. As with the powder, this should be followed with plenty of fluids.

If you miss a dose of this medication, take it as soon as possible, unless it is almost time for the next dose. In that case, do not take the missed dose at all; just return to your regular dosing schedule. Do not double the next dose.

Cholestyramine does not cure hypercholesterolemia (high blood-cholesterol levels), but it will help to control the condition as long as you continue to take it.

SIDE EFFECTS

Minor. Anxiety, belching, constipation, diarrhea, dizziness, drowsiness, fatigue, gas, headache, hiccups, loss of appetite, nausea, stomach pain, vomiting, or weight loss or gain. These side effects should disappear as your body adjusts to the medication.

To relieve constipation, increase the amount of fiber in your diet (fresh fruits and vegetables, salads, bran, and whole-grain breads), exercise, and drink more water (unless your doctor directs you to do otherwise).

If you feel dizzy, sit or lie down for a while; get up slowly from a sitting or reclining position; and be careful on stairs.

Major. Tell your doctor about any side effects you experience that are persistent or particularly bothersome. IT IS ESPECIALLY IMPORTANT TO TELL YOUR DOCTOR about backaches; bloody or black, tarry stools; difficult or painful urination; fluid retention; muscle or joint pains; rash or irritation of the skin, tongue, or rectal area; ringing in the ears; swollen glands; tingling sensations; unusual bleeding or bruising; or unusual weakness.

INTERACTIONS

Cholestyramine interferes with the absorption of a number of other drugs, including phenylbutazone, warfarin (a blood thinner), thiazide diuretics (water pills), digoxin, penicillins, tetracycline, phenobarbital, folic acid, iron, thyroid hormones, cephalexin, clindamycin, trimethoprim, and fat-soluble vitamins (A, D, E, and K). The effectiveness of these medications will be decreased by cholestyramine. To avoid this interaction, take the other medications one hour before or four to six hours after a dose of cholestyramine.

BE SURE TO TELL YOUR DOCTOR about any medications you are currently taking, especially those listed above.

WARNINGS
• Tell your doctor about unusual or allergic reactions you have had to any medications, especially to cholestyramine.
• Tell your doctor if you now have or if you have ever had bleeding disorders, biliary obstruction, heart disease, hemorrhoids, gallstones or gallbladder disease, kidney disease, malabsorption, stomach ulcers, or an obstructed intestine.
• Cholestyramine should be used only in conjunction with diet, weight reduction, or correction of other conditions that could be causing elevated levels of blood cholesterol.
• This product contains the color additive FD&C Yellow No. 5 (tartrazine), which can cause allergic-type reactions (fainting, rash, shortness of breath) in certain susceptible individuals.
• The color of cholestyramine powder may vary from batch to batch. This does not change the effectiveness of the medication.
• Be sure to tell your doctor if you are pregnant. Although cholestyramine appears to be safe (because very little is absorbed into the bloodstream), extensive studies in humans during pregnancy have not been conducted. Also tell your doctor if you are breast-feeding an infant. It is not known whether cholestyramine passes into breast milk. However, cholestyramine can decrease the absorption of some vitamins in the mother, which could result in decreased availability of the vitamins to the nursing infant.

cimetidine

BRAND NAMES (Manufacturers)
cimetidine (various manufacturers)
Tagamet (SmithKline Beecham)
Tagamet HB* (SmithKline Beecham)
*Available over the counter (without a prescription)
TYPE OF DRUG
Gastric-acid-secretion inhibitor (decreases stomach acid)

INGREDIENT
cimetidine
DOSAGE FORMS
Tablets (100 mg, 200 mg, 300 mg, 400 mg, and 800 mg)
Oral liquid (300 mg per 5-mL spoonful, with 2.8% alcohol)
STORAGE
Cimetidine tablets and oral liquid should be stored at room temperature in tightly closed, light-resistant containers. This medication should never be frozen. If cimetidine is not properly stored (especially if it is exposed to light or heat) it may develop a strong, unpleasant odor.

USES
When obtained by prescription, cimetidine is used for the treatment of duodenal and gastric ulcers, for the long-term treatment of excessive stomach acid secretion, and for the prevention of recurrent ulcers. It is also used to treat gastro-esophagal reflux (backflow of stomach contents into the esophagus), which can cause heartburn. Cimetidine works by blocking the effects of histamine in the stomach, which reduces stomach acid secretion.

A lower-strength version of cimetidine is now available over the counter for heartburn (sour stomach).

TREATMENT
Take cimetidine with, or shortly after, meals and again at bedtime (unless your doctor directs otherwise).

The tablets should not be crushed or chewed because cimetidine has a bitter taste and an unpleasant odor.

The oral liquid should be measured carefully with a specially designed 5-mL measuring spoon. An ordinary kitchen teaspoon is not accurate enough.

Antacids can block the absorption of cimetidine. If you are taking antacids as well as cimetidine, at least one hour should separate doses of the two medications.

If you miss a dose of cimetidine, take the missed dose as soon as possible, unless it is almost time for the next dose. In that case, do not take the missed dose at all; just return to your regular dosing schedule. In no case should you double the next dose.

SIDE EFFECTS

Minor. Diarrhea, dizziness, drowsiness, headache, or muscle pain. These side effects should disappear as your body adjusts to the medication.

If you feel dizzy, sit or lie down for a while; stand up slowly; and be careful on stairs.

Major. Tell your doctor about any side effects that are persistent or particularly bothersome. IT IS ESPECIALLY IMPORTANT TO TELL YOUR DOCTOR about confusion, fever, hair loss, enlarged or painful breasts (in both sexes), hallucinations, impotence, palpitations, rash, sore throat, unusual bleeding or bruising, weakness, or yellowing of the eyes or skin.

INTERACTIONS

Cimetidine interacts with other types of medications:

1. It can decrease the elimination, and thus increase the side effects, of theophylline, aminophylline, oxtriphylline, phenytoin, carbamazepine, beta blockers, benzodiazepine tranquilizers (such as clorazepate, chlordiazepoxide, diazepam, flurazepam, halazepam, and prazepam), tricyclic antidepressants, oral anticoagulants (blood thinners, such as warfarin), lidocaine, verapamil, quinidine, nifedipine, metronidazole, codeine, and morphine.

2. The combination of cimetidine and antineoplastic agents (anticancer drugs) may increase the risk of blood disorders.

3. The absorption of ketoconazole is decreased by cimetidine; at least two hours should separate doses of these two medications.

4. Cimetidine may decrease the blood levels and effectiveness of digoxin.

BE SURE TO TELL YOUR DOCTOR about any medications you are currently taking, especially any of those listed above.

WARNINGS

• Cimetidine is now available over the counter. This does not mean that you should stop taking your prescription medicine and switch to the less expensive OTC version, however. The OTC version is only for the treatment of occasional heartburn. If you have stomach ulcer disease, your doctor will continue with the prescription version. If you have any questions about which version is best for you, discuss the matter with your doctor or pharmacist.

• Tell your doctor about any unusual or allergic reactions you have had to medications, especially to cimetidine, famotidine, nizatidine, or ranitidine.

• Tell your doctor if you now have or if you have ever had arthritis, kidney disease, liver disease, or organic brain syndrome.

• Cimetidine can decrease the elimination of alcohol from the body, which can prolong its intoxicating effects.

• Cimetidine should be taken continuously for as long as your doctor prescribes. Stopping therapy early may be a cause of ineffective treatment.

• Cigarette smoking may block the beneficial effects of therapy with cimetidine.

• If this drug makes you dizzy or drowsy, do not take part in any activity that requires alertness, such as driving a car or operating potentially dangerous equipment.

• Be sure to tell your doctor if you are pregnant. Cimetidine appears to be safe during pregnancy; however, extensive testing has not been conducted. Also tell your doctor if you are breast-feeding an infant. Small amounts of cimetidine pass into breast milk.

---

ciprofloxacin (systemic)

BRAND NAME (Manufacturer)
Cipro (Miles)
TYPE OF DRUG
Antibiotic
INGREDIENT
ciprofloxacin
DOSAGE FORM
Tablets (250 mg, 500 mg, and 750 mg)
STORAGE
Ciprofloxacin tablets should be stored at room temperature in a tightly closed container away from direct light.

USES

Ciprofloxacin is an antibiotic that is used to treat a wide variety of bacterial infections. It chemically attaches to the bacteria and prevents their growth and multiplication. Ciprofloxacin is not effective against viruses, parasites, or fungi.

TREATMENT

Ciprofloxacin is best taken two hours after a meal with a full glass (eight ounces) of water, however, it can be taken with or without meals. You should drink several additional glasses of water every day, unless your doctor directs you to do otherwise. Drinking extra water will help to prevent unwanted effects of ciprofloxacin.

Ciprofloxacin works best when the level of medicine in your bloodstream is kept constant. It is best, therefore, to take the doses at evenly spaced intervals day and night. For example, if you are to take two doses a day, the doses should be spaced 12 hours apart.

It is very important that you do not miss any doses of this medication. If you do miss a dose, take it as soon as you remember. However, if you do not remember to take the missed dose until it is almost time for your next dose, skip the missed dose and go back to your regular dosing schedule. Do not double the next dose.

Ciprofloxacin therapy may be required for four to six weeks or longer. It is important to continue to take this drug for the entire time prescribed, even if the symptoms of infection disappear before the end of that period. If you stop taking the drug too soon, resistant bacteria are given a chance to continue growing, and your infection could recur.

SIDE EFFECTS

Minor. Diarrhea, headache, light-headedness, nausea, stomach irritation, or vomiting. These side effects should disappear as your body adjusts to the medication.

Major. Tell your doctor about any side effects that are persistent or particularly bothersome. IT IS ESPECIALLY IMPORTANT TO TELL YOUR DOCTOR about blood in your urine, change in your vision, confusion, convulsions (seizures), agitation, dizziness, hallucinations, lower back pain, muscle or joint pain, pain or difficulty in urinating, restlessness, skin rash, tremor, unpleasant taste, unusual bleeding or bruising, or yellowing of the eyes or skin. If the symptoms of your infection do not improve in several days, contact your doctor.

INTERACTIONS

Ciprofloxacin interacts with several other drugs:

1. Use of antacids or iron-containing vitamins with ciprofloxacin can decrease the absorption of this medicine. Do not take antacids or iron products within four hours of taking this medicine.

2. Use of sucralfate with ciprofloxacin can decrease the absorption of ciprofloxacin. Do not take a dose of sucralfate within two hours of a dose of ciprofloxacin unless directed to do so by your doctor.

3. Use of medicine containing theophylline along with ciprofloxacin can lead to increased bloodstream levels of theophylline and therefore to an increased chance of theophylline-related side effects.

4. Regular consumption of large quantities of caffeine-containing products (coffee, tea, or caffeine-containing soft drinks) with ciprofloxacin may lead to exaggerated or prolonged effects of caffeine. Your doctor may wish for you to restrict intake of caffeine during treatment.

5. Use of probenecid with ciprofloxacin can increase the bloodstream levels of ciprofloxacin and thus increase the risk of ciprofloxacin-related side effects.

6. Do not use ciprofloxacin at the same time as didanosine, digoxin, or warfarin. Consult your doctor or pharmacist for advice on avoiding drug interactions if you are taking these medicines.

Before starting to take ciprofloxacin, BE SURE TO TELL YOUR DOCTOR about any other medications you are currently taking, especially any of those listed above.

WARNINGS

• Tell your doctor about unusual or allergic reactions you have had to any medications, especially to ciprofloxacin, enoxacin, ofloxacin, norfloxacin, cinoxacin, or nalidixic acid.

• Before starting to take this medication, be sure to tell your doctor if you now have or if you have ever had brain or spinal cord disease, epilepsy, kidney disease, or liver disease.

• To decrease the potential for harmful effects on your kidneys, you should increase your intake of fluids (nonalcoholic) unless your doctor directs you to do otherwise.

• Ciprofloxacin can cause dizziness or light-headedness, so patients taking this medicine should know how they react to this medicine before they operate an automobile or machinery, or engage in activities requiring alertness or coordination.

• This medicine can make your skin more sensitive to the sun. When you first begin taking this drug, avoid too much sun and do not use a sunlamp until you see how your skin responds to short periods of sun exposure. This is especially important if you tend to sunburn easily.

• Ciprofloxacin has been prescribed for your current infection only. Another infection later on, or one that someone else has, may require a different medicine. You should not give your medicine to other people or use it for other infections, unless your doctor specifically directs you to do so.

• Be sure to call your doctor if you experience a rash, swelling of the face, or difficulty breathing after taking ciprofloxacin.

• Be sure to tell your doctor if you are pregnant. This drug is not recommended for use in pregnant women because it can result in serious adverse effects in the developing fetus. And tell your doctor if you are breast-feeding an infant. Ciprofloxacin passes into breast milk; it is not recommended for use if you are currently breast-feeding.

---

clarithromycin

BRAND NAME (Manufacturer)
Biaxin (Abbott)
TYPE OF DRUG
Antibiotic
INGREDIENT
clarithromycin
DOSAGE FORMS
Oral suspension (125 mg and 250 mg per 5-mL spoonful)
Tablets (250 mg and 500 mg)
STORAGE
Clarithromycin tablets should be stored at room temperature in a tightly closed, light-resistant container. The suspension form should not be frozen or refrigerated. Any unused suspension medication should be discarded after 14 days because it will no longer be effective against infections.

USES
Clarithromycin is used to treat a wide variety of bacterial infections including infections of the upper and lower respiratory tracts and skin. It acts by preventing the bacteria from man-

ufacturing protein, which prevents their growth. Clarithromycin kills susceptible bacteria, but it is not effective against viruses, parasites, or fungi.

TREATMENT

Clarithromycin may be taken without regard to meals. If stomach upset should occur, clarithromycin may be taken with food or milk, unless your doctor tells you otherwise. The coated tablets should be swallowed whole; do not crush or chew these tablets.

Clarithromycin works best when the level of medicine in your bloodstream is kept constant. It is best, therefore, to take the doses at evenly spaced intervals, day and night. If you are to take two doses a day, the doses should be spaced 12 hours apart.

It is very important that you do not miss any doses of this medication. If you do miss a dose, take it as soon as you remember. However, if you do not remember to take the missed dose until it is almost time for your next dose, skip the missed dose and go back to you regular dosing schedule. Do not double the dose.

It is important to continue to take this medication for the entire time prescribed by your doctor (usually seven to 14 days), even if the symptoms disappear before the end of that period. If you stop taking the drug too soon, resistant bacteria are given a chance to continue growing and the infection could recur.

The contents of the oral-suspension form of clarithromycin tend to settle on the bottom of the bottle, so it is necessary to shake the container well to distribute the ingredients evenly and equalize the doses. Each dose should then be measured carefully with a specially designed 5-mL measuring spoon or with the dropper provided. An ordinary kitchen teaspoon is not accurate enough for therapeutic purposes.

SIDE EFFECTS

Minor. Abdominal pain/discomfort, abnormal taste, diarrhea, dyspepsia, headache, nausea. These side effects should disappear as your body adjusts to the medication.

Major. Tell your doctor about any side effects that are persistent or particularly bothersome. IT IS ESPECIALLY IMPOR-

TANT TO TELL YOUR DOCTOR about fever, hearing loss, rash, rectal or vaginal itching, yellowing of the eyes or skin, or persistent diarrhea. If your symptoms of infection seem to be getting worse rather than improving, you should contact your doctor.

INTERACTIONS

1. Clarithromycin can decrease the elimination of carbamazepine, aminophylline, theophylline, and oxtriphylline from the body, which can lead to serious side effects. Blood levels of digoxin and oral anticoagulants (blood thinners, such as warfarin) may also be increased by clarithromycin. Clarithromycin can increase the possibililty of irregular heart rate when taken with certain antihistamine drugs (terfenadine, loratidine, astemizole).

2. Clarithromycin can decrease the blood level and effectiveness of zidovudine. If you are taking both of these medications, you must take them at least four hours apart.

3. Clarithromycin can increase blood levels and may result in toxicity of carbamazepine (a seizure medicine). Your doctor may monitor you more closely to avoid this drug interaction if you are taking both clarithromycin and carbamazepine

BE SURE TO TELL YOUR DOCTOR about any medications you are currently taking, especially any of those listed above.

WARNINGS

• Tell your doctor about any unusual or allergic reactions you have had to any medications, especially to clarithromycin, erythromycin, or azithromycin.

• Tell your doctor if you have now or have ever had kidney disease or liver disease.

• This medication has been prescribed for your current infection only. Another infection later on, or one that someone else has, may require a different medication. You should not give your medicine to other people or use it for another infection, unless your doctor specifically directs you to do so.

• Before having surgery or any other medical or dental treatment, be sure to tell your doctor or dentist that you are taking clarithromycin.

• Be sure to tell your doctor if you are pregnant. The effects of this medication during pregnancy have not been thoroughly studied in humans. Also tell your doctor if you are breast-feeding an infant. Clarithromycin passes into breast milk in small amounts.

• Tell your doctor about any heart problems or irregular heart rate before taking clarithromycin.

---

clemastine

BRAND NAMES (Manufacturers)
Tavist (Sandoz)
Tavist–1 (Sandoz)
TYPE OF DRUG
Antihistamine
INGREDIENT
clemastine fumarate
DOSAGE FORMS
Tablets (1.34 mg and 2.68 mg)
Oral syrup (0.67 mg per 5-mL spoonful, with 5.5% alcohol)
STORAGE
Clemastine tablets and oral syrup should be stored at room temperature in tightly closed containers.

USES

This medication belongs to a group of drugs known as antihistamines (antihistamines block the action of histamine, a chemical that is released by the body during an allergic reaction). Clemastine is thus used to treat or prevent symptoms of allergy.

TREATMENT

To avoid stomach upset, you can take clemastine with food or with a full glass of milk or water (unless your doctor directs you to do otherwise).

Each dose of the oral syrup should be measured carefully with a specially designed 5-mL measuring spoon. An ordinary kitchen teaspoon is not accurate enough for therapeutic purposes.

If you miss a dose of this medication, take the missed dose as soon as possible, unless it is almost time for your next dose. In that case, do not take the missed dose at all; just return to your regular dosing schedule. Do not double the next dose.

SIDE EFFECTS

Minor. Blurred vision; confusion; constipation; diarrhea; difficult or painful urination; dizziness; drowsiness; dry mouth, throat, or nose; headache; irritability; loss of appetite; nausea; restlessness; ringing or buzzing in the ears; stomach upset; or unusual increase in sweating. These side effects should disappear as your body adjusts to the medication.

This medication can cause increased sensitivity to sunlight. It is, therefore, important to avoid prolonged exposure to sunlight and sunlamps. Wear protective clothing and use an effective sunscreen.

If you are constipated, increase the amount of fiber in your diet (fresh fruits and vegetables, salads, bran, and whole-grain breads), exercise, and drink more water (unless your doctor tells you not to do so).

Chew sugarless gum or suck on ice chips or a piece of hard candy to reduce mouth dryness.

If you feel dizzy or light-headed, sit or lie down for a while; get up from a sitting or lying position slowly; and be careful on stairs.

Major. Tell your doctor about any side effects that are persistent or particularly bothersome. IT IS ESPECIALLY IMPORTANT TO TELL YOUR DOCTOR about change in menstruation, clumsiness, feeling faint, flushing of the face, hallucinations, palpitations, rash, seizures, shortness of breath, sleeping disorders, sore throat or fever, tightness in the chest, unusual bleeding or bruising, or unusual tiredness or weakness.

INTERACTIONS

Clemastine interacts with other types of medications:

1. Concurrent use of it with central nervous system depressants (such as alcohol, barbiturates, benzodiazepine tranquilizers, muscle relaxants, narcotics, pain medications, and phenothiazine tranquilizers) or with tricyclic antidepressants can cause extreme drowsiness.

2. Monoamine oxidase (MAO) inhibitors (isocarboxazid, pargyline, phenelzine and tranylcypromine) can increase the side effects of this medication. At least 14 days should separate the use of this drug and the use of an MAO inhibitor.

3. Clemastine can also decrease the activity of oral anticoagulants (blood thinners, such as warfarin).

BE SURE TO TELL YOUR DOCTOR about any medications you are currently taking, especially any of the medications that are listed above.

WARNINGS

• Tell your doctor about unusual or allergic reactions you have had to any medications, especially to clemastine or to other antihistamines (such as astemizole, azatadine, brompheniramine, carbinoxamine, chlorpheniramine, cyproheptadine, dexchlorpheniramine, dimenhydrinate, dimethindene, diphenhydramine, diphenylpyraline, doxylamine, hydroxyzine, loratidine, phenidamine, promethazine, pyrilamine, terfenadine, trimeprazine, tripelennamine, and triprolidine).

• Tell your doctor if you now have or if you have ever had asthma, blood-vessel disease, glaucoma, high blood pressure, kidney disease, peptic ulcers, enlarged prostate gland, or thyroid disease.

• Clemastine can cause drowsiness or dizziness. Your ability to perform tasks that require alertness, such as driving a car or operating dangerous equipment, may be decreased. Appropriate caution should be taken.

• Drinking alcoholic beverages can increase the sedative effects of clemastine.

• Be sure to tell your doctor if you are pregnant. The effects of this medication during pregnancy have not been thoroughly studied in humans. Also tell your doctor if you are breast-feeding an infant. Small amounts of clemastine will pass into breast milk and may cause unusual excitement or irritability in nursing infants.

---

clindamycin (systemic)

BRAND NAMES (Manufacturers)
Cleocin HCl (Upjohn)
Cleocin Pediatric (Upjohn)
clindamycin (various manufacturers)
TYPE OF DRUG
Antibiotic
INGREDIENT
clindamycin palmitate hydrochloride

DOSAGE FORMS
Capsules (75 mg, 150 mg, and 300 mg)
Oral suspension (75 mg per 5-mL spoonful)
Vaginal cream (2%)

STORAGE
Clindamycin capsules and oral suspension should be stored at room temperature in tightly closed containers. The oral suspension should not be refrigerated or frozen; when chilled, it thickens and becomes difficult to pour. The suspension form of this medication should be discarded after 14 days because it loses potency.

USES
Clindamycin is an antibiotic that is used orally or vaginally to treat a wide variety of bacterial infections. It chemically attaches to the bacteria and prevents their growth and multiplication. Clindamycin kills susceptible bacteria, but it is not effective against viruses, parasites, or fungi.

TREATMENT
In order to prevent irritation to your esophagus (swallowing tube) or stomach, you should take clindamycin with food or a full glass of water or milk (unless your doctor directs you to do otherwise).

The suspension form of this medication should be shaken well just before measuring each dose. The contents tend to settle on the bottom of the bottle, so it is necessary to shake the container to distribute the ingredients evenly and equalize the doses. Each dose should then be measured carefully with a specially designed 5-mL measuring spoon. An ordinary kitchen teaspoon is not accurate enough to ensure that the proper dose will be taken.

Clindamycin works best when the level of medicine in your bloodstream is kept constant. It is best, therefore, to take the doses at evenly spaced intervals day and night. For example, if you are to take four doses a day, the doses should be spaced six hours apart.

Try not to miss any doses of this medication. If you do miss a dose, take it as soon as you remember. However, if you do not remember to take the missed dose until it is almost time for your next dose, take the missed dose immediately; space the following dose about halfway through the regular interval between doses; then continue with your regular dosing schedule.

It is important to continue to take this medication for the entire time prescribed by your doctor (usually seven to 14 days), even if your symptoms of infection disappear before the end of that period. If you stop taking the drug too soon, resistant bacteria are given a chance to continue growing, and your infection could recur.

SIDE EFFECTS

Minor. Diarrhea, loss of appetite, nausea, stomach or throat irritation, or vomiting. These side effects should disappear as your body adjusts to the medication. If the diarrhea becomes prolonged, CONTACT YOUR DOCTOR. Do not take antidiarrheal medicine.

Major. Tell your doctor about any side effects that are persistent or particularly bothersome. IT IS ESPECIALLY IMPORTANT TO TELL YOUR DOCTOR about bloody or pus-containing diarrhea, hives, itching, muscle or joint pain, skin rash, unusual bleeding or bruising, or yellowing of the eyes or skin. If the symptoms of your infection do not improve in several days, contact your doctor. This medication may not be effective for your particular infection.

INTERACTIONS

Clindamycin should not interact with other medications if it is used according to directions.

WARNINGS

• Tell your doctor about any unusual or allergic reactions you have had to any medications, especially to clindamycin or lincomycin.

• Before starting to take this medication, be sure to tell your doctor if you now have or if you have ever had colitis, kidney disease, or liver disease.

• Before having surgery or any other medical or dental treatment, be sure to tell your doctor or dentist that you are taking clindamycin.

• The 75 mg and 150 mg capsules of this medication contain the color additive FD&C Yellow No. 5 (tartrazine), which can cause allergic-type symptoms (fainting, shortness of breath, rash) in certain susceptible individuals.

• Clindamycin has been prescribed for your current infection only. Another infection later on may require a different medicine. You should not give your medicine to other people or use it for other infections unless your doctor specifically directs you to do so.

• Your doctor may tell you to avoid vaginal sexual intercourse when using the vaginal cream. This cream contains mineral oil, which will make condoms and vaginal diaphrams less effective and increase the likelihood of pregnancy. Appropriate steps should therefore be taken.

• Be sure to tell your doctor if you are pregnant. Although clindamycin appears to be safe during pregnancy, extensive studies in humans have not been conducted. Also tell your doctor if you are breast-feeding an infant. Small amounts of clindamycin pass into breast milk.

clindamycin (topical)

BRAND NAME (Manufacturer)
Cleocin T (Upjohn)
TYPE OF DRUG
Antibiotic
INGREDIENT
clindamycin phosphate
DOSAGE FORMS
Topical gel (1%)
Topical solution (1%)
Topical suspension (1%)
STORAGE
Clindamycin topical solution, gel, or lotion should be stored at room temperature in a tightly closed container. It should be kept away from flames and heat because the solution is flammable (it contains alcohol).

USES
Clindamycin topical solution is used to treat acne vulgaris. It is an antibiotic that is thought to act by suppressing the growth of certain bacteria that may be responsible for the formation of the acne sores.

TREATMENT

Before applying topical clindamycin, wash the affected area thoroughly with a mild soap and warm water. Then rinse well and pat dry. To avoid skin irritation from the alcohol, wait at least 30 minutes after washing or shaving before applying this medication.

The solution is packaged in a bottle with an applicator tip that can be used to apply the solution directly to the skin. Shake the container will before using the topical suspension form. Press the applicator tip firmly against your skin. The pressure applied determines the amount of medicine that will be released. Use the applicator with a dabbing motion rather than a rolling motion. A thin film of medication should be applied to the entire area of skin affected by acne.

Topical clindamycin does not cure acne, but it will help to control the condition as long as you continue to use it.

If you miss a dose of this medication, apply it as soon as possible, unless it is almost time for the next dose. In that case, do not apply the missed dose at all; just return to your regular dosing schedule.

It is important to continue to apply this medication for the entire time prescribed by your doctor (which may be several months), even if your symptoms disappear in several days. If you stop applying the medication too soon, the bacteria are given a chance to continue growing, and your infection could occur again.

If there is no improvement in your condition after six weeks of using this medication, check with your doctor. However, it may take up to 12 weeks before improvement in your acne is readily apparent.

SIDE EFFECTS

Minor. You may experience diarrhea, dry skin, fatigue, headache, nausea, oily skin, or stomach irritation. These minor side effects should disappear as your body adjusts to the medication.

If diarrhea becomes severe or prolonged, CONTACT YOUR DOCTOR. Do not take any antidiarrheal medicine.

Major. Tell your doctor about any side effects that are persistent or particularly bothersome. IT IS ESPECIALLY IMPORTANT TO TELL YOUR DOCTOR about diarrhea that is bloody or that contains pus, increased urination, itching, sore throat, or swelling of the face.

INTERACTIONS

If you are using another topical medication as well as clindamycin, it is best to apply them at different times to increase effectiveness and reduce the chance of skin irritation.

Use of abrasive or medicated cleansers, medicated cosmetics, or any topical, alcohol-containing preparations (such as after-shave lotions or perfume) in conjunction with topical clindamycin can result in excessive skin dryness and irritation.

WARNINGS

• Tell your doctor about unusual or allergic reactions you have had to any drugs, especially to clindamycin or lincomycin.
• Tell your doctor if you have ever had colitis.
• Because this medication contains alcohol, it can cause skin irritation in sensitive areas. In addition, it has an unpleasant taste if it gets on the mouth or lips. You should avoid getting this medication in your eyes, nose, or mouth, or in the areas surrounding scratches or burns.
• You may continue to use cosmetics while applying this medication (unless otherwise directed by your doctor), but it is best to use only water-based cosmetics rather than ones with an oil base.
• Be sure to tell your doctor if you are pregnant. Although topical clindamycin appears to be safe during pregnancy, extensive studies in humans have not been conducted. Also tell your doctor if you are breast-feeding an infant. It is not known whether topical clindamycin passes into breast milk.

clofibrate

BRAND NAMES (Manufacturers)
Atromid-S (Wyeth-Ayerst)
clofibrate (various manufacturers)
TYPE OF DRUG
Antihyperlipidemic (lipid-lowering drug)

INGREDIENT
clofibrate
DOSAGE FORM
Capsules (500 mg)
STORAGE
Clofibrate should be stored at room temperature in a tightly closed, light-resistant container. Avoid freezing and excessive heat.

USES
Clofibrate is used to reduce fat (lipid) or cholesterol in the blood in patients with atherosclerosis (hardening of the arteries) and in patients having certain kinds of skin lesions caused by excessive fat levels in the blood. It is not clearly understood how clofibrate works, but it appears to decrease the body's production of cholesterol and fats.

Before therapy with this drug is initiated, attempts are usually made to control serum-fat levels with diet, exercise, and weight loss, and to control diabetes and hypothyroidism.

TREATMENT
Clofibrate should be taken with food or immediately after a meal (unless your doctor directs you to do otherwise).

If you miss a dose of this medication, take the missed dose as soon as possible, unless it is almost time for the next dose. In that case, do not take the missed dose at all; just return to your regular dosing schedule. Do not double the next dose.

SIDE EFFECTS
Minor. Abdominal cramps, bloating, blurred vision, decreased sexual desire, diarrhea, dizziness, drowsiness, dry and brittle hair, dry skin, fatigue, gas, headache, increased sweating, itching, nausea, sore mouth, vomiting, weakness, or weight gain. These side effects should disappear as your body adjusts to the medication.

If you feel dizzy, sit or lie down for a while; get up slowly from a sitting or reclining position; and be careful on stairs.
Major. Tell your doctor about any side effects that are persistent or particularly bothersome. IT IS ESPECIALLY IMPORTANT TO TELL YOUR DOCTOR about bloody or black, tarry stools; chest pain; difficult or painful urination; impotence;

loss of hair; rash; palpitations; sore joints; tremors; or unusual bleeding, bruising, or muscle cramps.

INTERACTIONS

Clofibrate interacts with several other types of medications:
1. It can increase the side effects of oral anticoagulants (blood thinners, such as warfarin), lovastatin, pravastatin, simvastatin, oral antidiabetic agents, and phenytoin.
2. Rifampin can decrease the effectiveness of clofibrate.
3. Probenecid and furosemide can increase the side effects of clofibrate.

Before starting to take clofibrate, BE SURE TO TELL YOUR DOCTOR about any medications you are currently taking, especially any of those listed above.

WARNINGS

• Tell your doctor about unusual or allergic reactions you have had to any medications, especially to clofibrate.
• Before starting to take this medication, be sure to tell your doctor if you now have or if you have ever had diabetes mellitus, gallstones, heart disease, kidney disease, liver disease, stomach ulcers, or thyroid disease.
• Do not stop taking this medication without first checking with your doctor. Stopping this medication abruptly may lead to an increase in your blood-fat levels. Your doctor may want you to follow a special diet to prevent this.
• Be sure to tell your doctor if you are pregnant. Clofibrate crosses the placenta and can build up in the body of the developing fetus. Because clofibrate has long-term effects on the body, you should not become pregnant for at least two months after you stop taking this drug. Also tell your doctor if you are breast-feeding an infant. Clofibrate passes into breast milk; therefore breast-feeding is not recommended for lactating women using this medication.

clomiphene

BRAND NAMES (Manufacturers)
Clomid (Merrell Dow)
Milophene (Milex)
Serophene (Serono)

TYPE OF DRUG
Fertility drug
INGREDIENT
clomiphene
DOSAGE FORM
Tablets (50 mg)
STORAGE
Clomiphene should be stored at room temperature in a tightly closed, light-resistant container. Like all medications, clomiphene should be stored well out of the reach of children and pets.

USES

Clomiphene is used to treat infertility in women and men. This drug reverses some types of infertility in women by stimulating ovulation.

TREATMENT

Clomiphene can be taken either on an empty stomach or with food or milk, as directed by your doctor.

It is very important to follow your dosing schedule carefully. If you have any questions about taking this medication, BE SURE TO CHECK WITH YOUR DOCTOR.

If you miss one dose of this medication, take the missed dose as soon as possible. If you do not remember to take this medication until it is time for the next dose, it is all right to double the dose, and then return to your regular dosing schedule. If you miss more than one dose, CHECK WITH YOUR DOCTOR.

SIDE EFFECTS

Minor. Abdominal discomfort, bloating, dizziness, headache, insomnia, nausea, nervousness, or vomiting. These side effects should disappear over time as your body adjusts to the medication.

If you feel dizzy, sit or lie down for a while; get up slowly from a sitting or reclining position; and be careful on stairs.
Major. Tell your doctor about any side effects that are persistent or particularly bothersome. IT IS ESPECIALLY IMPORTANT TO TELL YOUR DOCTOR about breast tenderness, depression, fatigue, hair loss, hot flashes, pelvic pain, skin rash, or visual disturbances.

INTERACTIONS

Clomiphene should not interact with other medications if it is used according to directions.

WARNINGS

• Tell your doctor about unusual or allergic reactions you have had to any medications, especially to clomiphene.

• Before beginning to administer clomiphene, tell your doctor if you now have or if you have ever had any of the following symptoms: abnormal vaginal bleeding, clotting problems, tumors or cysts of the uterus or ovaries, liver disease, or mental depression.

• If clomiphene makes you dizzy, do not take part in any activity that requires alertness, such as driving a car or operating potentially dangerous equipment, and take care going up and down stairs.

• While taking this medication, it is important to carefully follow your doctor's directions for recording your body temperature and for the timing of sexual intercourse.

• The risk of a multiple pregnancy is increased when clomiphene is used. This medication should not be taken if you are already pregnant. If you should become pregnant during treatment with clomiphene, tell your doctor immediately and, unless directed to do otherwise, discontinue the medication at once. It has been reported to cause birth defects in the offspring of animals that received large doses of clomiphene during pregnancy. Also tell your doctor if you are breast-feeding an infant. It is not known whether clomiphene passes into breast milk.

clonazepam

BRAND NAME (Manufacturer)
Klonopin (Roche)
TYPE OF DRUG
Benzodiazepine anticonvulsant
INGREDIENT
clonazepam
DOSAGE FORM
Tablets (0.5 mg, 1 mg, and 2 mg)

STORAGE
Clonazepam should be stored at room temperature in a tightly closed, light-resistant container.

USES
This medication is used to treat certain seizure disorders and other mental disorders. It is unclear exactly how clonazepam works to treat convulsions, but it appears that this drug prevents the spread of seizures to all parts of the brain.

TREATMENT
This medication can be ingested either on an empty stomach or with food or milk. However, take it only as directed by your doctor.

Clonazepam works best when the level of medicine in your bloodstream is kept constant. It is best, therefore, to take the doses at evenly spaced intervals day and night. For example, if you are to take three doses a day, the doses should be spaced eight hours apart.

Try not to miss any doses of this medication. If you do miss a dose and remember within an hour, take the dose immediately. If more than an hour has passed, do not take the missed dose at all; just return to your regular dosing schedule. Do not double the next dose. If you miss two or more doses, be sure to CONTACT YOUR DOCTOR.

SIDE EFFECTS
Minor. Constipation, diarrhea, drowsiness, dry mouth, headache, increased appetite, insomnia, loss of appetite, nausea, runny nose, or weight loss or gain. These side effects should disappear as your body adjusts to the medication.

In order to relieve constipation, increase the amount of fiber in your diet (fresh fruits and vegetables, salads, bran, and whole-grain breads), exercise, and drink more water (unless your doctor directs you to do otherwise).

To relieve mouth dryness, chew sugarless gum or suck on ice chips or a piece of hard candy.

Major. Tell your doctor about any side effects that are persistent or particularly bothersome. IT IS ESPECIALLY IMPORTANT TO TELL YOUR DOCTOR about behavioral problems, confusion, depression, fever, fluid retention, hair loss, hallucinations, hysteria, increased or decreased urination, muscle weakness, palpitations, skin rash, slurred speech, sore gums, tremors, unusual bleeding or bruising, unusual body movements, or yellowing of the eyes or skin.

Clonazepam can also produce an increase in salivation, so it should be used cautiously by people who have swallowing difficulties. Contact your doctor if a change in the level of salivation becomes a problem.

INTERACTIONS

Clonazepam interacts with several other types of drugs:

1. Concurrent use of it with other central nervous system depressants (such as alcohol, antihistamines, barbiturates, benzodiazepine tranquilizers, muscle relaxants, narcotics, pain medications, phenothiazine tranquilizers, and sleeping medications) or with tricyclic antidepressants can cause extreme drowsiness.

2. Phenobarbital and phenytoin can decrease the blood levels and effectiveness of clonazepam.

3. Concurrent use of clonazepam and valproic acid can lead to increased seizure activity.

Before starting to take this medication, BE SURE TO TELL YOUR DOCTOR about any medications you are currently taking, especially any of those listed above.

WARNINGS

• Notify your doctor about any unusual or allergic reactions you have had to any medications, especially to clonazepam or to other benzodiazepine tranquilizers (such as alprazolam, chlordiazepoxide, clorazepate, diazepam, flurazepam, halazepam, lorazepam, oxazepam, prazepam, temazepam, or triazolam).

• Tell your doctor if you now have or if you have ever had glaucoma, kidney disease, liver disease, or lung disease.

• If this drug makes you dizzy or drowsy, do not take part in any activity that requires alertness, such as driving a car or operating potentially dangerous equipment. Children should be careful while playing.

• Do not stop taking this medication unless you first check with your doctor. If you have been taking this medication for several months or longer, stopping the drug abruptly could lead to a withdrawal reaction and a worsening of your condition. Your doctor may, therefore, want to reduce your dosage of this medication gradually.

• Be sure to tell your doctor if you are pregnant. Although no harmful effects have been reported during pregnancy, extensive studies have not been conducted. The risks and benefits of clonazepam therapy during pregnancy should be discussed with your doctor. Also tell your doctor if you are breast-feeding an infant. Small amounts of clonazepam pass into breast milk and may cause excessive drowsiness in nursing infants.

clonidine

BRAND NAMES (Manufacturers)
Catapres (Boehringer Ingelheim)
Catapres-TTS (Boehringer Ingelheim)
clonidine hydrochloride (various manufacturers)
TYPE OF DRUG
Antihypertensive
INGREDIENT
clonidine hydrochloride
DOSAGE FORMS
Tablets (0.1 mg, 0.2 mg, and 0.3 mg)
Transdermal patch (2.5 mg, 5 mg, and 7.5 mg per patch; release rate of clonidine is 0.1 mg, 0.2 mg, and 0.3 mg per 24 hours)
STORAGE
Clonidine tablets should be stored at room temperature in a tightly closed container. Do not remove a patch from its packaging until just before you apply it.

USES

This medication works on the central nervous system (brain and spinal cord) to prevent the release of chemicals responsible for maintaining high blood pressure. It has also been used to prevent hot flashes in women during menopause and to help patients during narcotic withdrawal.

TREATMENT

To avoid stomach irritation, you can take clonidine tablets with food or with a full glass of milk or water. In order to become accustomed to taking this medication, try to take it at the same time(s) every day.

Clonidine transdermal patches come with detailed patient instructions that should be carefully followed. Apply the patch to a hairless area of unbroken skin on the upper arm or chest. If the patch becomes loose before it is time to remove it (after seven days), apply adhesive tape over the patch to ensure good adhesion. To avoid skin irritation, apply each new patch to a different site. Do not cut the patch before applying, and be sure to keep the patch on your skin when showering, bathing, or swimming.

If you miss a dose of clonidine tablets, take the missed dose as soon as possible, unless it is almost time for your next dose. In that case, do not take the missed dose at all; just return to your regular dosing schedule. Do not double the next dose. If you miss more than two doses of this medication, contact your doctor.

If you forget to remove the clonidine transdermal patch after seven days, remove the old patch and apply a new one immediately to a different site.

Clonidine does not cure high blood pressure, but it will help control the condition as long as it is taken.

SIDE EFFECTS

Minor. Anxiety, constipation, decreased sexual desire, dizziness, drowsiness, dry eyes, dry mouth, fatigue, headache, insomnia, jaw pain, loss of appetite, nasal congestion, nausea, nervousness, or vomiting. These side effects should disappear as your body adjusts to the medication.

The patches can also cause burning, inflammation, itching, rash, or increased or decreased pigmentation of the skin at the site of application. Be sure to TELL YOUR DOCTOR if the skin reactions persist or become bothersome.

To prevent constipation, increase the amount of fiber in your diet (fresh fruits and vegetables, salads, bran, and whole-grain breads), unless your doctor tells you not to do so.

To relieve mouth dryness, suck on ice chips or a piece of hard candy or chew sugarless gum.

"Artificial tears" eye drops may help relieve eye dryness.

To avoid dizziness or light-headedness when you stand, contract and relax the muscles of your legs for a few moments before rising. Do this by pushing one foot against the floor while raising the other foot slightly, alternating feet so that you are "pumping" your legs in a pedaling motion.

Major. Tell your doctor about any side effects that are persistent or particularly bothersome. IT IS ESPECIALLY IMPORTANT TO TELL YOUR DOCTOR about chest pain; cold fingertips or toes; depression; difficulty in breathing; difficulty in urinating; enlarged, painful breasts (in both sexes); hair loss; hives; impotence; itching; nightmares; rash; swelling of the hands or feet; weight gain; or yellowing of the eyes or skin.

INTERACTIONS

Clonidine interacts with several other types of medications:

1. Concurrent use of clonidine with other central nervous system depressants (such as alcohol, antihistamines, barbiturates, benzodiazepine tranquilizers, muscle relaxants, narcotics, pain medications, phenothiazine tranquilizers, and sleeping medications) or with tricyclic antidepressants can cause extreme drowsiness.

2. Tricyclic antidepressants and anti-inflammatory agents (such as indomethacin) may block the blood-pressure-lowering effects of clonidine.

Before you start to take this medication, BE SURE TO TELL YOUR DOCTOR about any medications you are currently taking, especially any of those listed above.

WARNINGS

• Tell your doctor about any unusual or allergic reactions you have had to medications, especially to clonidine.

• Tell your doctor if you have ever had heart disease, kidney disease, depression, Raynaud's disease, or a heart attack or stroke.

• Before having surgery or any other medical or dental treatment, tell your doctor or dentist you are taking this drug.

• Do not take any over-the-counter (nonprescription) medications for weight control or for allergy, asthma, sinus, cough, or cold problems unless you first check with your doctor.

• If this drug makes you dizzy or drowsy, do not take part in any activity that requires alertness, such as driving a car or operating potentially dangerous equipment.

• Tolerance to this medication develops occasionally; consult your doctor if you feel that the drug is becoming less effective.

• Do not stop taking this medication without first consulting your doctor. If therapy with this drug is stopped abruptly, you may experience nervousness, agitation, headache, and a rise in blood pressure. Your doctor may therefore want to reduce your dosage of the drug gradually or start you on another medication.

• Make sure you have enough medication on hand to last through weekends, vacations, and holidays.

• Drinking alcoholic beverages, standing for prolonged periods, exercising, and hot weather can each increase the blood-pressure-lowering effects of clonidine and can cause fainting or dizziness.

• Be sure to tell your doctor if you are pregnant. Although clonidine appears to be safe in animals, extensive studies in humans during pregnancy have not been conducted. Also tell your doctor if you are breast-feeding an infant. Small amounts of clonidine pass into breast milk.

clorazepate

BRAND NAMES (Manufacturers)
clorazepate (various manufacturers)
Tranxene-SD (Abbott)
Tranxene T-Tabs (Abbott)
TYPE OF DRUG
Benzodiazepine sedative/hypnotic
INGREDIENT
clorazepate
DOSAGE FORMS
Capsules (3.75 mg, 7.5 mg, and 15 mg)
Tablets (3.75 mg, 7.5 mg, 11.25 mg, 15 mg, and 22.5 mg)
STORAGE
This medication should be stored at room temperature in tightly closed, light-resistant containers.

USES

Clorazepate is prescribed to treat the symptoms of anxiety and sometimes to treat seizures and alcohol-withdrawal symptoms. It is not clear exactly how this medicine works, but it may relieve anxiety by acting as a depressant of the central nervous system. Clorazepate is used to relieve nervousness.

It is effective for this purpose, but it is important to remove the cause of the anxiety as well.

TREATMENT

This medication should be taken exactly as directed by your doctor. It can be taken with food or a full glass of water if stomach upset occurs. Do not take this medication with a dose of antacids, since this may retard its absorption.

If you are taking this medication regularly and you miss a dose, take the missed dose immediately if you remember within an hour. If more than an hour has passed, skip the dose you missed and wait for the next scheduled dose. Do not double the next dose.

SIDE EFFECTS

Minor. Bitter taste in the mouth, constipation, depression, diarrhea, dizziness, drowsiness (after a night's sleep), dry mouth, excessive salivation, fatigue, flushing, headache, heartburn, loss of appetite, nausea, nervousness, sweating, or vomiting. As your body adjusts to the medicine, these side effects should disappear.

To relieve constipation, increase the amount of fiber in your diet (fresh fruits and vegetables, salads, bran, and whole-grain breads), exercise, and drink more water (unless your doctor directs you to do otherwise).

Dry mouth can be relieved by chewing sugarless gum or by sucking on ice chips.

If you feel dizzy, sit or lie down for a while; stand up slowly from a sitting or reclining position; and be careful on stairs.

Major. Tell your doctor about any side effects that are persistent or particularly bothersome. IT IS ESPECIALLY IMPORTANT TO TELL YOUR DOCTOR about blurred or double vision, chest pain, difficulty in urinating, fainting, falling, fever, joint pain, hallucinations, mouth sores, nightmares, palpitations, rash, severe depression, shortness of breath, slurred speech, sore throat, uncoordinated movements, unusual excitement, unusual tiredness, or yellowing of the eyes or skin.

INTERACTIONS

Clorazepate will interact with several other types of medication:
1. To prevent oversedation, this drug should not be taken with alcohol or other sedative drugs, central nervous system de-

pressants (such as antihistamines, barbiturates, muscle relaxants, pain medicines, narcotics, medicines for seizures, and phenothiazine tranquilizers), or with antidepressants.

2. This medication may decrease the effectiveness of carbamazepine, levodopa, and oral anticoagulants (blood thinners) and may increase the effects of phenytoin.

3. Disulfiram, oral contraceptives (birth control pills), isoniazid, and cimetidine can increase the blood levels of clorazepate, which can lead to increased sedation.

4. Concurrent use of rifampin may decrease the effectiveness of clorazepate.

BE SURE TO TELL YOUR DOCTOR about any medications you are currently taking, especially any of those listed above.

WARNINGS

• Tell your doctor about unusual or allergic reactions you have had to any medications, especially to clorazepate or other benzodiazepine tranquilizers (such as alprazolam, chlordiazepoxide, diazepam, flurazepam, halazepam, lorazepam, oxazepam, prazepam, temazepam, and triazolam).

• Tell your doctor if you now have or if you have ever had liver disease, kidney disease, epilepsy, lung disease, myasthenia gravis, porphyria, depression, or mental illness.

• This medicine can cause drowsiness. Avoid tasks that require alertness, such as driving an automobile or using potentially dangerous equipment. Take care in going up and down stairs.

• This medication has the potential for abuse and must be used with caution. Tolerance may develop quickly; do not increase the dosage without first consulting your doctor. It is also important not to stop taking this drug suddenly if you have been taking it in large amounts or if you have used it for several weeks. Your doctor may want to reduce the dosage gradually.

• This is a safe drug when used properly. When it is combined with other sedative drugs or alcohol, however, serious side effects may develop.

• Be sure to tell your doctor if you are pregnant. This medicine may increase the chance of birth defects if it is taken during the first three months of pregnancy. In addition, too much use of this medicine during the last six months of pregnancy may cause the baby to become dependent on it. This may result in withdrawal symptoms in the newborn. Use of this medicine during the last weeks of pregnancy may cause excessive drowsiness, slowed heartbeat, and breathing difficulties in the newborn. Tell your doctor if you are breast-feeding an infant. This medicine can pass into the breast milk and cause excessive drowsiness, slowed heartbeat, and breathing difficulties in the nursing infant.

clotrimazole (topical)

BRAND NAMES (Manufacturers)
Lotrimin (Schering)
Lotrimin AF* (Schering-Plough)
Mycelex (Miles)
Mycelex OTC* (Miles)
*Available without a prescription in 1% cream, lotion, and solution.
TYPE OF DRUG
Antifungal
INGREDIENT
clotrimazole
DOSAGE FORMS
Topical cream (1%)
Topical lotion (1%)
Topical solution (1%)
STORAGE
Store at room temperature in tightly closed containers. This medication should never be frozen.

USES
This medication is used to treat superficial fungal infections of the skin. Clotrimazole is an antifungal agent that is active against a broad range of fungi and yeasts. It acts by preventing the growth and multiplication of these organisms.

TREATMENT
Apply this medication in the morning and evening, unless your doctor directs you to do otherwise. Before applying clotrimazole, you should wash your hands. Then (unless otherwise directed) cleanse the affected area with soap and water. Pat the skin with a clean towel until it is almost dry. Gently mas-

sage a small amount of the cream, solution, or lotion over the entire area that is affected and the skin immediately surrounding this area. Do not bandage or cover the infection after applying the medication unless your doctor instructs you to do so. Wash your hands again after use.

Improvement in your condition may not become apparent for as much as a week after you begin treatment with this drug. However, you should be sure to complete the full course of therapy. If you stop using this drug too soon, resistant fungi are given a chance to continue growing, and the infection could recur. If your condition has not improved after four weeks of treatment with this medication, however, CONTACT YOUR DOCTOR. Clotrimazole may not be effective against the organism that is causing your infection.

If you miss a dose of this medication, apply the missed dose as soon as possible. If you do not remember until it is almost time for the next dose, however, do not apply the missed dose at all; just return to your regular dosing schedule. Do not use a double dose of the medication at the next application.

SIDE EFFECTS

Minor. You may experience some burning, itching, stinging, or redness when this drug is applied to the skin. These side effects should disappear as your body adjusts to the drug.
Major. Tell your doctor about any side effects that are persistent or particularly bothersome. IT IS ESPECIALLY IMPORTANT TO TELL YOUR DOCTOR about blistering, irritation, peeling of the skin, or swelling.

INTERACTIONS

Clotrimazole should not interact with other medications as long as it is used according to directions.

WARNINGS

• Tell your doctor about any unusual or allergic reactions you have had to any medications, especially to clotrimazole.
• Clotrimazole should not be used in or around the eyes.
• This medication has been prescribed for your current infection only. Another infection may require a different medication. Therefore, you should not give your medicine to other people or use it for other infections, unless your doctor specifically directs you to do so.

• In order to avoid reinfection, keep the affected area clean and dry, wear freshly laundered clothing, and try to avoid wearing tight-fitting clothing.
• Be sure to tell your doctor if you are pregnant. Small amounts of clotrimazole may be absorbed through the skin. It should, therefore, be used cautiously, especially during the first three months of pregnancy. Also tell your doctor if you are breast-feeding an infant. It is not known whether clotrimazole passes into breast milk.

---

clotrimazole (vaginal)

BRAND NAMES (Manufacturers)
Femcare (Schering)
Gyne-Lotrimin (Schering)*
Mycelex-G (Miles)
*Available OTC in 1% cream or 100-mg and 500 mg
    tablets.
TYPE OF DRUG
Antifungal
INGREDIENT
clotrimazole
DOSAGE FORMS
Vaginal cream (1%)
Vaginal tablets (100 mg and 500 mg)
STORAGE
Store at room temperature in a tightly closed container. This medication should never be frozen.

USES

This medication is used to treat fungal infections of the vagina. Clotrimazole is an antifungal agent that prevents the growth and multiplication of a wide range of fungi and yeast, including Candida.

TREATMENT

Clotrimazole vaginal cream and tablets are packaged with detailed directions for use. Be sure to follow these instructions carefully. An applicator will probably be provided for inserting the cream into the vagina. Use this medication at bedtime, unless otherwise directed by your doctor.

You should wash the area carefully prior to inserting the cream or tablet into the vagina.

If you begin to menstruate while being treated with clotrimazole, you should continue your regular dosing schedule.

If you miss a dose of this medication, insert the missed dose as soon as possible. However, if you do not remember until the following day, do not insert the missed dose at all; just return to your regular dosing schedule. Do not use a double dose of the medication at the next application.

It is important to continue to insert this medication for the entire time prescribed by your doctor—even if the symptoms disappear before the end of that period. If you stop using the drug too soon, resistant fungus could be given a chance to continue growing, and it is possible that your infection could recur.

Contact your doctor if symptoms do not improve within three days of treatment or if symptoms have not been relieved after seven days of treatment.

SIDE EFFECTS

Minor. You may experience vaginal burning, itching, or irritation when this drug is inserted. This sensation should disappear as your body adjusts to the medication. Your sexual partner may also experience some burning or irritation.

Do not treat any side effects that occur in the area of the infection unless you first consult your doctor.

Major. Tell your doctor about any side effects that are persistent or particularly bothersome. IT IS ESPECIALLY IMPORTANT TO TELL YOUR DOCTOR about abdominal cramps, blistering, bloating, excessive irritation, painful urination, or peeling of the skin.

INTERACTIONS

Clotrimazole should not interact with other medications if it is used according to directions.

WARNINGS

• Tell your doctor about unusual or allergic reactions you have had to any medications, especially to clotrimazole.

• Tell your doctor if you have had other vaginal infections, especially if they have been resistant to treatment.

• To prevent reinfection, avoid sexual intercourse or ask your partner to use a condom until treatment is completed.

• There may be some vaginal drainage while using this medication; therefore, you may want to use a sanitary napkin or panty liner to prevent the staining of clothing. However, the use of tampons is not recommended since they may soak up too much of the medicine.

• Whenever possible, wear cotton panties rather than those made of nylon or other nonporous materials while being treated for a vaginal fungus infection. In order to better prevent reinfection, remember to always wear freshly laundered underclothes.

• If there is no improvement in your condition, or if irritation in the area continues after several days of treatment, CONTACT YOUR DOCTOR. This medication may be causing an allergic reaction, or it may not be effective against the organism causing your infection.

• This medication has been prescribed for your current infection only. Another infection that develops later on, or one that someone else has, may require a different medication. Therefore, you should not give your medication to other women or use it for other infections unless your doctor specifically directs you to do so.

• Tell your doctor if you are pregnant. Clotrimazole appears to be safe during pregnancy. However, extensive studies have not been conducted. In addition, your doctor may want to change the instructions on how you are to use this drug if you are pregnant. Also tell your doctor if you are breast-feeding. It is not known whether this drug passes into breast milk.

clozapine

BRAND NAME (Manufacturer)
Clozaril (Sandoz)
TYPE OF DRUG
Antipsychotic
INGREDIENT
clozapine
DOSAGE FORM
Tablets (25 mg and 100 mg)
STORAGE
Clozapine tablets should be stored at room temperature in the unit-dose packages provided by the manufacturer.

USES

Clozapine is prescribed for the treatment of schizophrenia in patients who have not been helped by or could not tolerate other medications. The blood of patients taking this medication may be monitored weekly to prevent side effects that might affect their blood system.

TREATMENT

To avoid stomach irritation, you can take this medication with a meal or a glass of water or milk (unless your doctor directs you to do otherwise).

If you miss a dose of this medication, take the missed dose as soon as possible, then return to your regular dosing schedule. If it is almost time for the next dose, however, skip the one you missed and return to your regular schedule. Do not double the next dose (unless your doctor directs you to do otherwise).

The full effects of this medication for the control of emotional or mental symptoms may not become apparent for two weeks after you start to take it.

SIDE EFFECTS

Minor. Abdominal discomfort, constipation, dizziness, drowsiness, dry mouth, headache, heartburn, increased saliva production, light-headedness, nausea, vomiting, or weight gain. As your body adjusts to the medication, these side effects should disappear.

If you are constipated, increase the amount of fiber in your diet (fresh fruits and vegetables, salads, bran, and whole-grain breads). You can also increase your exercise and drink more water (unless your doctor directs you to do otherwise).

Chew sugarless gum or suck on ice chips or a piece of hard candy to reduce mouth dryness.

To avoid dizziness or light-headedness when you stand, contract and relax the muscles of your legs for a few moments before rising. Do this by pushing one foot against the floor while raising the other foot slightly, alternating feet so that you are "pumping" your legs in a pedaling motion.

Major. Tell your doctor about any side effects that are persistent or particularly bothersome. IT IS ESPECIALLY IMPORTANT TO TELL YOUR DOCTOR about anxiety, blurred vision, chest pain, chills, confusion, convulsions, difficulty in urinating, fainting, fever, increased sweating, loss of bladder control, mouth sores, muscle stiffness, nightmares, rapid heart rate, rash, restlessness, severe headache, sore throat, tremor, trouble sleeping, or unusual bleeding or bruising.

INTERACTIONS

Clozapine antipsychotic medication interacts with several other types of medications:

1. It can cause extreme drowsiness when combined with alcohol or other central nervous system (brain and spinal cord) depressants, such as barbiturates, benzodiazepine tranquilizers, muscle relaxants, phenothiazine tranquilizers, narcotics, and pain medications, or with tricyclic antidepressants.

2. Lithium may increase the side effects of this drug.

3. The effect of clozapine on blood cells may be increased by other drugs, such as antineoplastics (cancer medicine), antithyroid drugs, azathioprine, chloramphenicol, colchicine, flucytosine, interferon, and zidovudine.

4. The side effects of digoxin, phenytoin, and warfarin may be increased by this medication.

Before starting to take clozapine, BE SURE TO TELL YOUR DOCTOR about any other medications you are currently taking, especially if they are any of those listed above.

WARNINGS

• Be sure to tell your doctor about unusual or allergic reactions to medications, especially clozapine.

• Tell your doctor if you have a history of alcoholism or if you now have or have ever had blood disease, depression, enlarged prostate, gastrointestinal problems, glaucoma, heart or circulatory disease, liver disease, or seizures.

• To avoid oversedation, avoid drinking alcoholic beverages while taking this medication.

• If this drug makes you dizzy or drowsy, do not take part in any activity that requires alertness, such as driving a car or operating potentially dangerous equipment. Be careful on stairs, and avoid getting up suddenly from a lying or sitting position.

• Do not stop taking this medication suddenly. Your doctor may want to gradually reduce the amount you are taking before stopping the drug. Be sure to consult your doctor before stopping this medication.

• It is very important that you have your blood tested weekly and that you have your doctor check your progress regularly. The results of your blood tests will assist your doctor in making safe dosage adjustments for you.

• Be sure to tell your doctor if you are pregnant. Although clozapine appears to be safe in animals, extensive studies in humans have not been conducted. It is also very important that you tell your doctor if you are breast-feeding an infant. Small amounts of this medication pass into breast milk and may cause problems in the nursing infant.

---

codeine

BRAND NAMES (Manufacturers)
Codeine Phosphate (various manufacturers)
Codeine Sulfate (various manufacturers)
TYPE OF DRUG
Analgesic and cough suppressant
INGREDIENT
codeine
DOSAGE FORMS
Tablets (15 mg, 30 mg, and 60 mg)
Oral solution (15 mg per 5-mL measuring spoon)
STORAGE
Codine tablets and oral solution should be stored at room temperature in a tightly closed, light-resistant container.

USES
Codeine is a narcotic analgesic that acts directly on the central nervous system (brain and spinal cord). It is used to relieve mild to moderate pain or in order to suppress coughing. It is also used to stop diarrhea.

TREATMENT
In order to avoid stomach upset, you can take codeine with food or milk.

This drug works best if you take it at the onset of pain, rather than waiting until the pain has already become intense.

If you are taking this medication on a regular schedule and you miss a dose, take the missed dose as soon as possible, unless it is almost time for your next dose. In that case, do not take the missed dose at all; just return to your regular dosing schedule. Do not double the next dose.

SIDE EFFECTS

Minor. Constipation, dizziness, drowsiness, dry mouth, false sense of well-being, flushing, light-headedness, loss of appetite, nausea, painful or difficult urination, or sweating. These side effects should disappear as your body adjusts to the medication.

If you are constipated, increase the amount of fiber in your diet (fresh fruits and vegetables, salads, bran, and whole-grain breads), exercise, and drink more water (unless your doctor directs you to do otherwise).

Chew sugarless gum or suck on ice chips or a piece of hard candy to reduce mouth dryness.

If you feel dizzy, light-headed, or nauseated, sit or lie down for a while; get up from a sitting or lying position slowly; and be careful on stairs.

Major. Tell your doctor about any side effects that are persistent or particularly bothersome. IT IS ESPECIALLY IMPORTANT TO TELL YOUR DOCTOR about anxiety, breathing difficulties, excitation, fatigue, palpitations, rash, restlessness, sore throat and fever, tremors, or weakness.

INTERACTIONS

Codeine interacts with several other types of medications:

1. Concurrent use of this medication with other central nervous system depressants (such as alcohol, antihistamines, barbiturates, benzodiazepine tranquilizers, muscle relaxants, and phenothiazine tranquilizers) or with tricyclic antidepressants can cause extreme drowsiness.

2. A monoamine oxidase (MAO) inhibitor taken within 14 days of this medication can lead to unpredictable and severe side effects.

3. Cimetidine, combined with this medication, can cause confusion, disorientation, and shortness of breath.

BE SURE TO TELL YOUR DOCTOR about any medications you are currently taking.

WARNINGS

• Tell your doctor about unusual or allergic reactions you have had to medications, especially to codeine or to any other

narcotic analgesics (such as hydrocodone, hydromorphone, meperidine, methadone, morphine, oxycodone, and pro-poxyphene).
• Tell your doctor if you now have or if you have ever had acute abdominal conditions, asthma, brain disease, colitis, epilepsy, gallstones or gallbladder disease, head injuries, heart disease, kidney disease, liver disease, lung disease, mental illness, emotional disorders, prostate disease, thyroid disease, or urethral stricture.
• If this drug makes you dizzy or drowsy or blurs your vision, do not take part in any activity that requires mental alertness, such as driving an automobile, working with hazardous material, or operating potentially dangerous tools, equipment, or machinery.
• Before undergoing surgery or any other medical or dental treatment, tell your doctor or dentist you are taking this drug.
• Because this product contains codeine, it has the potential for abuse and must be used with caution. Usually, it should not be taken on a regular schedule for longer than ten days (unless your doctor directs you to do so). Tolerance develops quickly; do not increase the dosage or stop taking the drug abruptly unless you first consult your doctor. If you have been taking large amounts of this medication for long periods, you may experience a withdrawal reaction (muscle aches, diarrhea, gooseflesh, runny nose, nausea, vomiting, shivering, trembling, stomach cramps, sleep disorders, irritability, weakness, excessive yawning, or sweating) when you stop taking it. Your doctor may want to reduce the dosage gradually.
• Be sure to tell your doctor if you are pregnant. The effects of this medication during the early stages of pregnancy have not been thoroughly studied in humans. However, codeine, used regularly in large doses during the later stages of pregnancy, can result in addiction of the fetus, leading to withdrawal symptoms (irritability, excessive crying, tremors, fever, vomiting, diarrhea, sneezing, or excessive yawning) at birth. Also tell your doctor if you are breast-feeding an infant. Small amounts of this medication may pass into breast milk and cause excessive drowsiness in the nursing infant.

codeine and guaifenesin combination

BRAND NAMES (Manufacturers)
Cheracol (Upjohn)
Guiatuss A.C. (various manufacturers)
Guiatussin with Codeine (Rugby)
Mytussin AC (PBI)
Nortussin with Codeine (Vortech)
Robitussin A-C (Robins)
Tussi-Organidin NR (Wallace)
TYPE OF DRUG
Cough suppressant and expectorant combination
INGREDIENT
codeine and guaifenesin
DOSAGE FORM
Oral syrup (10 mg codeine and 100 mg guaifenesin per
5-mL spoonful, with 3.5% or 4.75% alcohol)
STORAGE
Codeine and guaifenesin combination should be stored at
room temperature in a tightly closed container.

USES
This medication is used to relieve coughs due to colds or infections or inflammation of the upper respiratory tract.
Guaifenesin is an expectorant that loosens bronchial secretions. Codeine is a narcotic cough suppressant that acts on
the cough center in the brain.

TREATMENT
You can take codeine and guaifenesin combination syrup either on an empty stomach or, to avoid stomach irritation, with
food or milk (as directed by your doctor).
  Each dose should be measured carefully with a specially
designed 5-mL measuring spoon. An ordinary kitchen teaspoon is not accurate enough.
  To help loosen the mucus in the bronchi, you should drink
a glass of water after each dose.
  If you miss a dose of this medication, take the missed one as
soon as possible, unless it is almost time for the next dose. In

that case, do not take the missed dose at all; just return to your regular dosing schedule. Do not double the next dose.

SIDE EFFECTS

Minor. Constipation, dizziness, drowsiness, nausea, restlessness, stomach upset, vomiting, or weakness. These side effects should disappear over time as your body adjusts to the medication.

To relieve constipation, increase the amount of fiber in your diet (fresh fruits and vegetables, salads, bran, and whole-grain breads), exercise, and drink more water (unless your doctor directs you to do otherwise).

If you feel dizzy, sit or lie down for a while; stand up slowly; and be careful on stairs.

Major. Be sure to notify your doctor about any side effects that are persistent or particularly bothersome. IT IS ESPECIALLY IMPORTANT TO TELL YOUR DOCTOR about blurred vision; cold or clammy skin; confusion; difficulty in breathing; or fainting.

INTERACTIONS

Codeine and guaifenesin combination can interact with several other types of medications:

1. Concurrent use with other central nervous system depressants (such as alcohol, barbiturates, benzodiazepine tranquilizers, muscle relaxants, other narcotics, pain medications, phenothiazine tranquilizers, and sleeping medications) or with tricyclic antidepressants can lead to extreme drowsiness.

2. Use of a monoamine oxidase (MAO) inhibitor within 14 days of use of codeine and guaifenesin combination can lead to serious side effects.

3. Cimetidine combined with this medication can cause confusion, disorientation, and shortness of breath.

Before starting to take codeine and guaifenesin combination, BE SURE TO TELL YOUR DOCTOR about any medications you are currently taking.

WARNINGS

• Tell your doctor about unusual or allergic reactions you have had to any medications, especially to guaifenesin or codeine, or to other narcotics (such as hydrocodone, hydro-

morphone, meperidine, methadone, opium, oxycodone, propoxyphene, and pentazocine).
• Before starting to take this medication, be sure to notify your doctor if you now have or if you have ever had any of the following: asthma, brain disease, enlarged prostate gland, gallstones or gallbladder disease, gastrointestinal diseases, heart disease, kidney disease, liver disease, lung disease, mental disorders, or thyroid disease.
• If this drug makes you dizzy or drowsy, do not take part in activities that require alertness, such as driving a car or operating potentially dangerous equipment. Be careful on stairs, and avoid getting up suddenly from a lying or sitting position.
• While you are taking this medication, drink several glasses of water a day to help loosen bronchial secretions, unless your doctor specifically directs you to do otherwise.
• Because this product contains codeine, it has the potential for abuse and must be used with caution. Tolerance may develop quickly; you should not use it in higher doses or for longer periods than recommended by your doctor. If you have been taking it for longer than several weeks, do not stop taking it until you first check with your doctor. Stopping the drug abruptly can lead to a withdrawal reaction (body aches, diarrhea, gooseflesh, vomiting, restlessness, runny nose, sneezing, sweating, trembling, or excessive yawning). Your doctor may, therefore, want to reduce your dosage gradually.
• Be sure to tell your doctor if you are pregnant. Large amounts of codeine taken during pregnancy can lead to addiction in the developing fetus, resulting in withdrawal reactions in the newborn infant. Also tell your doctor if you are breast-feeding an infant. Codeine may pass into breast milk and can cause extreme drowsiness in the nursing infant.

colchicine

BRAND NAMES (Manufacturers)
colchicine (various manufacturers)
Colchicine (Abbott)
TYPE OF DRUG
Antigout
INGREDIENT
colchicine

DOSAGE FORM
Tablets (0.5 mg and 0.6 mg)
STORAGE
Colchicine should be stored at room temperature in a tightly closed, light-resistant container.

USES

Colchicine is used to relieve the symptoms of a gout attack and to prevent further attacks. Colchicine prevents the movement of uric acid crystals, which are responsible for the pain in the joints that occurs during an attack of gout.

TREATMENT

Colchicine can be taken on an empty stomach or with food or a full glass of water or milk (as directed by your doctor).

If you are taking colchicine to control a gout attack, it is important that you understand how to take it and when it should be stopped. CHECK WITH YOUR DOCTOR.

If you miss a dose of this medication, take the missed dose as soon as possible, unless it is almost time for the next dose. In that case, do not take the missed dose at all; just return to your regular dosing schedule. Do not double the next dose.

SIDE EFFECTS

Minor. Abdominal pain, diarrhea, nausea, or vomiting. These side effects should disappear as your body adjusts to the medication.
Major. Tell your doctor about any side effects that are persistent or particularly bothersome. IT IS ESPECIALLY IMPORTANT TO TELL YOUR DOCTOR about difficult or painful urination, fever, loss of hair, muscle pain, persistent diarrhea, skin rash, sore throat, tingling in the hands or feet, or unusual bleeding or bruising.

INTERACTIONS

Colchicine interacts with several other types of medications:
1. It can decrease absorption of vitamin B_{12}.
2. The action of colchicine can be blocked by vitamin C and enhanced by sodium bicarbonate or ammonium chloride.
3. Colchicine can increase the drowsiness caused by central nervous system depressants.

BE SURE TO TELL YOUR DOCTOR about any medications you are currently taking.

WARNINGS
• Tell your doctor about unusual or allergic reactions you have had to any medications.
• Tell your doctor if you now have or if you have ever had blood disorders, gastrointestinal disorders, heart disease, kidney disease, or liver disease.
• Large amounts of alcohol can increase the blood levels of uric acid, which can decrease the effectiveness of colchicine. Alcohol ingestion should, therefore, be limited while you are taking this medication.
• Colchicine is not an analgesic (pain reliever) and does not relieve pain other than that of gout.
• Be sure to tell your doctor if you are pregnant. Colchicine is not recommended for use during pregnancy because it has been reported to cause birth defects in both animals and humans. Also tell your doctor if you are breast-feeding an infant. Colchicine passes into breast milk in small quantities.

---

colestipol

BRAND NAME (Manufacturer)
Colestid (Upjohn)
TYPE OF DRUG
Antihyperlipidemic (lipid-lowering drug)
INGREDIENT
colestipol
DOSAGE FORM
Oral granules (5 g per packet or level scoop)
STORAGE
Colestipol should be stored at room temperature in a tightly closed container.

USES
This medication is used to lower cholesterol levels. It chemically binds to bile salts in the gastrointestinal tract and prevents the body from producing cholesterol.

TREATMENT

Colestipol is usually taken before meals. Each dose should be measured carefully with a specially designed 5-mL measuring spoon. An ordinary kitchen teaspoon is not accurate enough. The dose should then be added to at least three ounces of fluid (water, milk, fruit juice, or other carbonated or noncarbonated beverage). The mixture should be stirred and completely mixed (the granules do not completely dissolve). After the solution has been drunk, the glass should be refilled with the same beverage and this solution swallowed as well. This ensures that the whole dose is taken. The granules can also be mixed with soup, applesauce, or crushed pineapple. You should never take colestipol dry; you might accidentally inhale the granules, which could irritate your throat and lungs.

If you miss a dose of this drug, take the missed dose as soon as possible, unless it is almost time for the next dose. In that case, do not take the missed dose at all; just return to your regular dosing schedule. Do not double the next dose.

Colestipol does not cure hypercholesterolemia (high blood-cholesterol levels), but it will help to control the condition as long as you continue to take it.

SIDE EFFECTS

Minor. Anxiety, belching, constipation, diarrhea, dizziness, drowsiness, fatigue, gas, headache, hiccups, loss of appetite, nausea, stomach pain, vomiting, or weight loss or gain. These side effects should disappear as your body adjusts to the medication.

To relieve constipation, increase the amount of fiber in your diet (fresh fruits and vegetables, salads, bran, and whole-grain breads), exercise, and drink more water (unless your doctor directs otherwise). A stool softener may also be helpful; ask your doctor or pharmacist to recommend one.

If you feel dizzy, sit or lie down for a while; get up slowly from a sitting or reclining position; and be careful on stairs.

Major. Tell your doctor about any side effects that are persistent or particularly bothersome. IT IS ESPECIALLY IMPORTANT TO TELL YOUR DOCTOR about backaches; bleeding gums; bloating; bloody or black, tarry stools; difficult or painful urination; muscle or joint pains; rash or irritation of the skin, tongue, or rectal area; ringing in the ears; swollen glands; tingling sensations; unusual bleeding or bruising; or unusual weakness.

INTERACTIONS

Colestipol interferes with the absorption of a number of other drugs, including phenylbutazone, warfarin, thiazide diuretics (water pills), digoxin, penicillins, tetracycline, phenobarbital, folic acid, iron, thyroid hormones, oral vancomycin, adrenocorticosteroids, and the fat-soluble vitamins A, D, E, and K. The effectiveness of these medications will be decreased by colestipol. To avoid this interaction, take the other medications one hour before or four to six hours after a dose of colestipol.

BE SURE TO TELL YOUR DOCTOR about any medications you are currently taking, especially any of those listed above.

WARNINGS

• Tell your doctor if you have ever had unusual or allergic reactions to any type of medication, especially to colestipol.
• Before starting to take this drug, be sure to tell your doctor if you now have or if you have ever had bleeding disorders, biliary obstruction, heart disease, hemorrhoids, gallstones or gallbladder disease, kidney disease, malabsorptive disorders, stomach ulcers, or an obstructed intestine.
• Colestipol should be used only in conjunction with a carefully regulated diet, weight reduction, or correction of other conditions that could be causing high blood cholesterol levels.
• Be sure to tell your doctor if you are pregnant. Although colestipol appears to be safe (because none is absorbed into the bloodstream), extensive studies in humans during pregnancy have not been conducted. Also be sure to tell your doctor if you are breast-feeding an infant. This medication can decrease absorption of some vitamins in the mother, which could result in decreased availability of the vitamins to the nursing infant.

cortisone (systemic)

BRAND NAMES (Manufacturers)
cortisone acetate (various manufacturers)
Cortone Acetate (Merck Sharp & Dohme)

TYPE OF DRUG
Adrenocorticosteroid hormone
INGREDIENT
cortisone
DOSAGE FORM
Tablets (5 mg, 10 mg, and 25 mg)
STORAGE
Cortisone tablets should be stored at room temperature in a tightly closed container.

USES

Your adrenal glands naturally produce certain cortisonelike chemicals. These chemicals are involved in various regulatory processes in the body (such as those involving fluid balance, temperature, and reaction to inflammation). Cortisone belongs to a group of drugs known as adrenocorticosteroids (or cortisonelike medications). It is used to treat a variety of disorders, including hormonal disorders; asthma; blood diseases; certain cancers; eye disorders; gastrointestinal disturbances, such as ulcerative colitis; respiratory diseases; and inflammations such as arthritis, dermatitis, and poison ivy. How this drug acts to relieve these disorders is not completely understood.

TREATMENT

In order to prevent stomach irritation, you can take cortisone with food or with milk.

If you are taking only one dose of this medication each day, try to take it before 9:00 A.M.

It is important to try not to miss any doses of cortisone. However, if you do miss a dose of this medication, follow these guidelines:
1. If you are taking it more than once a day, take the missed dose as soon as possible and return to your regular schedule. If it is already time for the next dose, double the dose.
2. If you are taking this medication once a day, take the dose you missed as soon as possible, unless you don't remember until the next day. In that case, do not take the missed dose at all; just follow your regular dosing schedule. Do not double the next dose.
3. If you are taking this drug every other day, take it as soon as you remember. If you missed the scheduled time by a whole

tiveness of vaccines and can lead to infection if a live-virus vaccine is administered.

• Before having surgery or any other medical or dental treatment, be sure to tell your doctor or dentist that you are taking this medication.

• If you are taking this medication for prolonged periods of time, you should wear or carry an identification card or notice indicating that you are taking an adrenocorticosteroid drug.

• Because this drug can cause glaucoma and cataracts with long-term use, your doctor may want you to have your eyes examined by an ophthalmologist from time to time during treatment.

• This medication can raise blood-sugar levels in people with diabetes, so blood sugar should be monitored carefully with blood or urine tests when this medication is being taken.

• Be sure to tell your doctor if you are pregnant. This drug crosses the placenta. Although studies in humans have not been conducted, birth defects have been observed in the offspring of animals that were given large doses of this type of drug during pregnancy. Also tell your doctor if you are breast-feeding an infant. Small amounts of this drug pass into breast milk and can cause growth suppression or a decrease in natural adrenocorticosteroid production in the nursing infant.

cromolyn sodium (inhalation)

BRAND NAME (Manufacturer)
Intal (Fisons)
TYPE OF DRUG
Antiallergic (antiasthmatic)
INGREDIENT
cromolyn
DOSAGE FORMS
Capsules for inhalation (20 mg)
Aerosol spray 8.1 g and 14.2 g (800 mcg per spray): for
    inhalation only
Solution (20 mg per 2-mL ampule): for inhalation only
STORAGE
Cromolyn sodium solution should be kept at room temperature in tightly closed, light-resistant storage containers. The container of the aerosol form is pressurized; it should, therefore,

never be punctured or broken. It should also be stored away from heat and direct sunlight.

USES

This medication is used to prevent asthma attacks. It is not effective in relieving asthma symptoms once an attack has begun. It works by preventing release of the body chemicals that are thought to be responsible for the symptoms of asthma or allergy.

TREATMENT

The solution form of this medication should be used only with a power-operated nebulizer equipped with a face mask. The solution form should never be used with a handheld nebulizer.

The aerosol form of this medication comes packaged with instructions for use. Read the instructions carefully; if you have any questions, check with your doctor or pharmacist. The aerosol can should be shaken well just before each dose is sprayed. The contents tend to settle on the bottom of the container, so it should be shaken to disperse the medication and equalize the doses. The 14.2 g container provides about 200 measured sprays, and the 8.1 g container provides about 112 measured sprays. The oral capsules for inhalation must not be swallowed.

Cromolyn sodium is most effective when therapy is started before contact with allergens (the suspected offending agents causing your allergy), so if you expect to be exposed to something to which you know you are allergic, it is a good idea to start taking your medication first.

This medication will work most effectively when the level of medicine in your bloodstream is kept constant. It is best, therefore, that you try to take the doses at evenly spaced intervals throughout the day and night. For example, if you are to take four doses of this medication a day, the doses should be evenly spaced at six hour intervals.

If you are using another inhaler to open up the lungs (a bronchodilator), it should be used 20 to 30 minutes before using cromolyn sodium.

The full benefits of this medication may not become apparent for up to four weeks after you start to take it.

If you miss a dose of this medication and remember within an hour or so, take the missed dose immediately. If more than an hour has passed, however, do not take the missed dose at all; just return to your regular dosing schedule. Do not double the next dose of this medication.

SIDE EFFECTS

Minor. Cough, dizziness, drowsiness, headache, increased urination, nasal congestion, nasal itching, nausea, sneezing, stomach irritation, or tearing. These side effects should disappear as your body adjusts to the medication.

If you feel dizzy, sit or lie down for a while; get up slowly from a sitting or reclining position; and be careful on stairs.

This medication can cause mouth dryness, throat irritation, and hoarseness. Gargling and rinsing your mouth after each dose helps to prevent these effects.

Major. Tell your doctor about any side effects that are persistent or particularly bothersome. IT IS ESPECIALLY IMPORTANT TO TELL YOUR DOCTOR about itching, joint swelling or pain, nosebleeds, nose burning, painful or increased urination, rash, swelling of the face or eyes, swollen glands, or wheezing.

INTERACTIONS

Cromolyn sodium should not interact with other medications if it is used according to directions.

WARNINGS

• Tell your doctor about unusual or allergic reactions you have had to any drugs.

• Before beginning treatment with this medication, tell your doctor if you now have or if you have ever had kidney or liver disease.

• Do not stop taking this medication unless you first check with your doctor. Stopping the drug abruptly may lead to a worsening of your condition.

• Be sure to tell your doctor if you are pregnant. Extensive safety studies in humans have not been conducted. Also tell your doctor if you are breast-feeding an infant. Cromolyn passes into breast milk in very small quantities.

cromolyn sodium (nasal)

BRAND NAME (Manufacturer)
Nasalcrom (Fisons)
TYPE OF DRUG
Antiallergic
INGREDIENT
cromolyn
DOSAGE FORM
Nasal solution (each spray delivers 5.2 mg)
STORAGE
Cromolyn sodium should be stored at room temperature in its original container.

USES

Cromolyn sodium nasal solution is used to prevent and treat allergic rhinitis (inflammation of the nasal passages resulting from allergies). Cromolyn sodium works by preventing the release of the body chemicals responsible for inflammation and swelling.

TREATMENT

This medication is for use within the nose only. The nasal passages should be cleared before administering the spray. You should inhale through the nose as you spray the solution. The container provides about 100 measured sprays.

This medication is most effective when therapy is started before contact with allergens (the suspected offending agents causing your allergy), so if you expect to be exposed to something to which you are certain you are allergic, it is always a good idea to start taking your medication first.

This medication works best when the level of medicine in your bloodstream is kept constant. It is best, therefore, to take the doses at evenly spaced intervals day and night. For example, if you are to take four doses a day, the doses should be spaced six hours apart.

The maximum benefits of this medication may not become fully apparent for as long as four weeks after you have started therapy.

If you miss a dose of this drug, take the missed dose as soon as possible, unless it is almost time for the next dose. In that case, do not take the missed dose at all; just return to your regular dosing schedule. Do not double the next dose.

SIDE EFFECTS

Minor. Bad taste in the mouth, headaches, irritation or stinging, nasal burning, postnasal drip, or sneezing. These side effects should stop as your body adjusts to the drug.

Major. Tell your doctor about any side effects that are persistent or particularly bothersome. IT IS ESPECIALLY IMPORTANT TO TELL YOUR DOCTOR if you experience nosebleeds or skin rash.

INTERACTIONS

Cromolyn sodium should not interact with other medications if it is used according to directions.

WARNINGS

• Tell your doctor about unusual or allergic reactions you have had to any medication, especially to cromolyn sodium.

• Be sure to tell your doctor if you now have or if you have ever had kidney or liver disease.

• Do not stop taking this medication unless you first check with your doctor, even if the symptoms of your disorder disappear. Stopping the drug abruptly can lead to a worsening of your condition. Cromolyn sodium should be continued as long as you have contact with the substance causing your allergic symptoms.

• Be sure to tell your doctor if you are pregnant. Extensive safety studies in humans have not been conducted. Also tell your doctor if you are breast-feeding an infant. Cromolyn passes into breast milk in very small quantities.

---

cyclobenzaprine

BRAND NAMES (Manufacturers)
cyclobenzaprine (various manufacturers)
Flexeril (Merck Sharp & Dohme)
TYPE OF DRUG
Muscle relaxant
INGREDIENT
cyclobenzaprine

DOSAGE FORM
Tablets (10 mg)
STORAGE
Cyclobenzaprine tablets should be stored at room temperature in a tightly closed container.

USES

Cyclobenzaprine is prescribed to relieve muscle pain and stiffness caused by injuries such as sprains or strains. It is not clear how this drug works, but it may block reflexes involved in producing and maintaining muscle spasms. It does not act directly on tense muscles.

TREATMENT

In order to avoid stomach irritation, you can take cyclobenzaprine with food or with a full glass of water or milk.

If you miss a dose of this medication and remember within an hour, take the missed dose; then return to your regular dosing schedule. If more than an hour has passed, do not take the missed dose at all; just return to your dosing schedule. Do not double the next dose.

SIDE EFFECTS

Minor. Abdominal pain, black tongue, blurred vision, constipation, diarrhea, dizziness, drowsiness, dry mouth, fatigue, indigestion, insomnia, loss of appetite, muscle pain, nausea, nervousness, sweating, unpleasant taste in the mouth, vomiting, or weakness. These side effects should disappear as your body adjusts to the medication.

If you are constipated, increase the amount of fiber in your diet (fresh fruits and vegetables, salads, bran, and whole-grain breads) and drink more water (unless your doctor directs you to do otherwise).

If you feel dizzy or light-headed, sit or lie down for a while; get up slowly from a sitting or reclining position; and be careful on stairs.

To relieve mouth dryness, chew sugarless gum, or suck on ice chips or hard candy.
Major. Tell your doctor about any side effects that are persistent or particularly bothersome. IT IS ESPECIALLY IMPORTANT TO TELL YOUR DOCTOR about confusion, depression, difficulty in urinating, disorientation, hallucinations, headache,

itching, numbness in the fingers or toes, palpitations, rash, swelling of the face or tongue, tremors, or yellowing of your skin or eyes.

INTERACTIONS

Cyclobenzaprine interacts with several other types of drugs:
1. Concurrent use of cyclobenzaprine with other central nervous system depressants (such as alcohol, antihistamines, barbiturates, antianxiety medications, narcotics, pain medications, tranquilizers, and sleeping medications) or with tricyclic antidepressants can cause extreme drowsiness.
2. Cyclobenzaprine can block the blood-pressure-lowering effects of clonidine and guanethidine.
3. Use of this drug within 14 days of a monoamine oxidase (MAO) inhibitor (tranylcypromine, phenelzine, isocarboxazid, and pargyline) can lead to severe reactions and high blood pressure.
  BE SURE TO TELL YOUR DOCTOR about any medications you are currently taking, especially those listed above.

WARNINGS

• Tell your doctor about unusual or allergic reactions you have had to medications, especially to cyclobenzaprine or to tricyclic antidepressants (such as amitriptyline, amoxapine, desipramine, doxepin, imipramine, nortriptyline, protriptyline, and trimipramine).
• Tell your doctor if you have ever had blood clots, epilepsy, heart disease, a heart attack, narrow-angle glaucoma, thyroid disease, or urinary retention.
• Use of cyclobenzaprine for periods longer than two to three weeks is not recommended because there is no evidence of benefit with prolonged use and because muscle spasm caused by sprain or strain is generally of short duration.
• This medication should not be taken as a substitute for rest, physical therapy, or other measures recommended by your doctor to treat your condition.
• If this medication makes you dizzy or drowsy or blurs your vision, do not take part in any activity that requires alertness, such as driving a car or operating potentially dangerous equipment.
• If you have been taking large doses of this medication for prolonged periods, you may experience nausea, headache,

or fatigue when you stop taking it until your body adjusts to the absence of the drug.

• Be sure to tell your doctor if you are pregnant. Although cyclobenzaprine appears to be safe during pregnancy, extensive studies in humans have not been conducted. Also tell your doctor if you are breast-feeding an infant. It is not known whether cyclobenzaprine passes into breast milk.

cyclosporine

BRAND NAME (Manufacturer)
Sandimmune (Sandoz)
TYPE OF DRUG
Immunosuppressant
INGREDIENT
cyclosporine
DOSAGE FORMS
Oral solution (100 mg per mL, with 12.5% alcohol)
Soft-gelatin capsules (25 mg and 100 mg)
STORAGE
Cyclosporine oral solution and capsules should be stored in the original container at room temperature. This medication should never be refrigerated or frozen. Once the solution has been opened, it should be used within two months.

USES

Cyclosporine is used to prevent organ rejection after kidney, liver, and heart transplants. It is not clearly understood how cyclosporine works, but it appears to prevent the body's rejection of foreign tissue. Cyclosporine is also used to treat severe psoriasis.

TREATMENT

To make it more palatable, the solution should be diluted with milk, chocolate milk, or orange juice (preferably at room temperature). The dose should be measured carefully with the dropper provided and placed in one of the fluids listed above. Use a glass container (cyclosporine chemically binds to wax-lined and plastic surfaces). Stir well and drink at once—do not allow the mixture to stand before drinking. Refill the glass with the same beverage and drink this solution to ensure that the whole dose is taken. The dropper should be wiped with a clean towel after use and stored in its container. If the dropper has been cleaned, make sure it is completely dry before using it again.

It is important not to miss any doses of this medication. If you do miss a dose, take the missed dose as soon as possible, unless it is almost time for the next dose. In that case, do not take the missed dose at all; just return to your regular dosing schedule. Do not double the next dose.

SIDE EFFECTS

Minor. Abdominal discomfort, diarrhea, flushing, headache, hiccups, leg cramps, loss of appetite, nausea, or vomiting. These side effects should disappear as your body adjusts to the medication.

Major. Tell your doctor about any side effects that are persistent or particularly bothersome. IT IS ESPECIALLY IMPORTANT TO TELL YOUR DOCTOR about acne; bleeding, tender, or enlarged gums; convulsions; difficult or painful urination; enlarged and painful breasts (in both sexes); fever; hair growth; hearing loss; muscle pain; rapid weight gain (three to five pounds within a week); sore throat; tingling of the hands or feet; tremors; unusual bleeding or bruising; or yellowing of the eyes or skin.

INTERACTIONS

Cyclosporine interacts with several other types of drugs:

1. Carbamazepine, isoniazid, rifampin, phenytoin, phenobarbital, and trimethoprim/sulfamethoxazole can decrease the blood levels of cyclosporine, decreasing its effectiveness.

2. Cimetidine, diltiazem, erythromycin, ketoconazole, oral contraceptives, danazol, and amphotericin B can increase the blood levels of cyclosporine, which can lead to an increase in side effects.

3. Tell your doctor if you are currently taking corticosteroids, verapamil, or nonsteroidal anti-inflammatory drugs.

BE SURE TO TELL YOUR DOCTOR about any medications you are currently taking.

WARNINGS

• Tell your doctor about unusual or allergic reactions you have had to any medications, especially to cyclosporine or to polyoxyethylated castor oil.

• Before starting to take this medication, be sure to tell your doctor if you now have or if you have ever had hypertension (high blood pressure) or gastrointestinal disorders.

• Repeated laboratory tests are necessary while you are taking cyclosporine to ensure that you are receiving the correct dosage and to avoid liver and kidney damage.

• Certain cancers have occurred in patients who received cyclosporine and other immunosuppressant drugs after transplantation. No direct causal effect has been established, however.

• Do not stop taking this medication without first consulting your doctor. If the drug is stopped abruptly, organ rejection may occur. Your doctor may, therefore, want to reduce your dosage gradually or start you on another drug if treatment with this drug is to be discontinued.

• Be sure to tell your doctor if you are pregnant. Although extensive studies in humans have not been conducted, cyclosporine has caused fetal damage when administered to animals. Also tell your doctor if you are breast-feeding, because cyclosporine passes into breast milk.

---

cyproheptadine

BRAND NAMES (Manufacturers)
cyproheptadine hydrochloride (various manufacturers)
Periactin (Merck Sharp & Dohme)
TYPE OF DRUG
Antihistamine
INGREDIENT
cyproheptadine
DOSAGE FORMS
Tablets (4 mg)
Oral syrup (2.5 mg per 5-mL spoonful with 5% alcohol)
STORAGE
Store at room temperature in a tightly closed container. Freezing of the oral syrup should be avoided.

USES

This medication belongs to a group of drugs known as antihistamines (antihistamines block the action of histamine, a chemical that is released by the body during an allergic reaction). It is used to treat or prevent symptoms of allergy. This has also been used to treat anorexia nervosa.

TREATMENT

To avoid stomach upset, you can take cyproheptadine with food or with a full glass of milk or water (unless your doctor directs you to do otherwise).

The oral syrup should be measured carefully with a specially designed 5-mL measuring spoon. An ordinary kitchen teaspoon is not accurate enough.

If you miss a dose of this medication, take the missed dose as soon as possible, unless it is almost time for your next dose. If it is almost time for the next dose, do not take the missed dose at all; just return to your regular dosing schedule. Do not double the next dose.

SIDE EFFECTS

Minor. Blurred vision; confusion; constipation; diarrhea; difficult or painful urination; dizziness; dry mouth, throat, or nose; headache; increased or decreased appetite; irritability; nausea; restlessness; ringing or buzzing in the ears; stomach upset; or unusual increase in sweating. These side effects should disappear as your body adjusts to the medication.

This medication can cause increased sensitivity to sunlight. It is, therefore, important to avoid prolonged exposure to sunlight and sunlamps. Wear protective clothing and use an effective sunscreen.

If you are constipated, increase the amount of fiber in your diet (fresh fruits and vegetables, salads, bran, and whole-grain breads), exercise, and drink more water (unless your doctor directs you not to do so).

Chew sugarless gum or suck on ice chips or a piece of hard candy to reduce mouth dryness.

If you feel dizzy or light-headed, sit or lie down for a while; get up slowly from a sitting or lying position; and be careful on stairs.

Major. Tell your doctor about any side effects that are persistent or particularly bothersome. IT IS ESPECIALLY IMPOR-

TANT TO TELL YOUR DOCTOR about change in menstruation, clumsiness, feeling faint, flushing of the face, hallucinations, palpitations, rash, seizures, shortness of breath, sleeping disorders, sore throat or fever, tightness in the chest, unusual bleeding or bruising, unusual tiredness or weakness, or yellowing of the eyes or skin.

INTERACTIONS

This drug will interact with several other types of medications:
1. Concurrent use of this medication with other central nervous system depressants (such as alcohol, barbiturates, benzodiazepine tranquilizers, muscle relaxants, narcotics, pain medications, and phenothiazine tranquilizers) or with tricyclic antidepressants can cause extreme drowsiness.
2. Monoamine oxidase (MAO) inhibitors (such as isocarboxazid, pargyline, phenelzine, and tranylcypromine) can increase the side effects of this medication.

BE SURE TO TELL YOUR DOCTOR about any medications you are currently taking.

WARNINGS

• Tell your doctor about unusual or allergic reactions you have had to any medications, especially to cyproheptadine or to other antihistamines (such as azatadine, astemizole, brompheniramine, carbinoxamine, chlorpheniramine, clemastine, cyproheptadine, dimenhydrinate, dimethindene, diphenhydramine, diphenylpyraline, doxylamine, hydroxyzine, phenidamine, promethazine, pyrilamine, terfenadine, trimeprazine, tripelennamine, and triprolidine).
• Tell your doctor if you now have or if you have ever had asthma, blood-vessel disease, glaucoma, high blood pressure, kidney disease, peptic ulcers, enlarged prostate gland, or thyroid disease.
• Cyproheptadine can cause drowsiness or dizziness. Your ability to perform tasks that require alertness, such as driving or operating potentially dangerous equipment, may be decreased.
• Be sure to tell your doctor if you are pregnant. The effects of this medication during pregnancy have not been thoroughly studied in humans. Also tell your doctor if you are breast-feeding an infant. Small amounts of cyproheptadine pass into breast milk. The drug may also inhibit lactation.

desipramine

BRAND NAMES (Manufacturers)
desipramine (various manufacturers)
Norpramin (Merrell Dow)
Pertofrane (Rorer)
TYPE OF DRUG
Tricyclic antidepressant
INGREDIENT
desipramine
DOSAGE FORM
Tablets (10 mg, 25 mg, 50 mg, 75 mg, 100 mg, and
   150 mg)
STORAGE
Desipramine capsules and tablets should be stored at room
temperature in tightly closed containers.

USES

Desipramine is used to relieve the symptoms of mental depression. This medication belongs to a group of drugs referred
to as the tricyclic antidepressants. These medicines are thought
to relieve depression by increasing the concentration of certain
chemicals necessary for nerve transmission in the brain.

TREATMENT

This drug should be taken exactly as your doctor prescribes.
You can take it with food to lessen stomach irritation, unless
your doctor tells you otherwise.

   If you miss a dose of this medication, take the missed dose
as soon as possible, then return to your regular dosing schedule. If, however, the dose you missed was a once-a-day bedtime dose, do not take that dose in the morning; check with
your doctor instead. If the dose is taken in the morning, it may
cause some unwanted side effects. Never double the dose.

   The effects of therapy with this medication may not become
apparent for several weeks.

SIDE EFFECTS

Minor. Agitation, anxiety, blurred vision, confusion, constipation, cramps, diarrhea, dizziness, drowsiness, dry mouth,
fatigue, heartburn, insomnia, loss of appetite, nausea, peculiar

tastes in the mouth, restlessness, sweating, vomiting, weakness, or weight gain or loss. As your body adjusts to the medication, these side effects should disappear.

This medication may increase your sensitivity to sunlight. You should therefore avoid prolonged exposure to sunlight and sunlamps. Wear protective clothing and sunglasses when out of doors, and use a sunscreen.

Dry mouth can be relieved by chewing sugarless gum or by sucking on ice chips or a piece of hard candy.

To relieve constipation, increase the amount of fiber in your diet (fresh fruits and vegetables, salads, bran, and whole-grain breads), exercise, and drink more water (unless your doctor directs you to do otherwise).

To avoid dizziness or light-headedness when you stand, contract and relax the muscles of your legs for a few moments before rising. Do this by pushing one foot against the floor while raising the other foot slightly, alternating feet so that you are "pumping" your legs in a pedaling motion.

Major. Tell your doctor about any side effects that are persistent or particularly bothersome. IT IS ESPECIALLY IMPORTANT TO TELL YOUR DOCTOR about chest pain, convulsions, difficulty in urinating, enlarged or painful breasts (in both sexes), fainting, fever, fluid retention, hair loss, hallucinations, headaches, impotence, mood changes, mouth sores, nervousness, nightmares, nosebleeds, numbness in the fingers or toes, palpitations, ringing in the ears, seizures, skin rash, sleep disorders, sore throat, tremors, uncoordinated movements or balance problems, unusual bleeding or bruising, or yellowing of the eyes or skin.

INTERACTIONS

Desipramine will interact with several other types of medications:

1. Extreme drowsiness can occur when this medicine is taken with central nervous system depressants (such as alcohol, antihistamines, barbiturates, benzodiazepine tranquilizers, muscle relaxants, narcotics, pain medications, phenothiazin tranquilizers, and medications to induce sleep) or with other antidepressants.

2. Desipramine may decrease the effectiveness of antiseizure medications.

3. It may block the blood-pressure-lowering effects of clonidine and guanethidine.

4. Cimetidine can decrease the elimination of desipramine from the body, increasing the possibility of side effects.

5. Birth control pills or estrogen-containing drugs can increase the side effects and reduce the effectiveness of the tricyclic antidepressants (including desipramine).

6. Tricyclic antidepressants may increase the side effects of thyroid medication and of over-the-counter (nonprescription) cough, cold, allergy, asthma, sinus, and diet drugs.

7. The concurrent use of tricyclic antidepressants and monoamine oxidase (MAO) inhibitors should be avoided because the combination may result in fever, convulsions, or high blood pressure. At least 14 days should separate the use of this drug and the use of an MAO inhibitor.

BE SURE TO TELL YOUR DOCTOR about any medications you are currently taking.

WARNINGS

• Tell your doctor if you have had unusual or allergic reactions to medications, especially to desipramine or any of the other tricyclic antidepressants (such as amitriptyline, imipramine, doxepin, trimipramine, amoxapine, protriptyline, maprotiline, and nortriptyline).

• Tell your doctor if you have a history of alcoholism or if you have had asthma, high blood pressure, liver disease, kidney disease, heart disease, a heart attack, circulatory disease, stomach problems, intestinal problems, difficulty in urinating, enlarged prostate gland, epilepsy, seizures, glaucoma, thyroid disease, mental illness, or electroshock therapy.

• If this drug makes you dizzy or drowsy, do not take part in any activity that requires alertness, such as driving a car or operating potentially dangerous equipment.

• Before having surgery or other medical or dental treatment, tell your doctor or dentist about this drug.

• Do not stop taking this drug suddenly. Stopping it abruptly can cause nausea, headache, stomach upset, fatigue, or a worsening of your condition. Your doctor may want to reduce the dosage gradually.

• The effects of this medication may last as long as seven days after you have stopped taking it, so continue to observe all precautions during that period.

• Be sure to tell your doctor if you are pregnant. Problems in humans have not been reported; however, studies in animals have shown that this medication can cause side effects in the fetus when given to the mother in large doses during pregnancy. Also tell your doctor if you are breast-feeding an infant. Small amounts of this drug can pass into breast milk, which may cause unwanted effects, such as irritability or sleeping problems, in the nursing infant.

dexamethasone (systemic)

BRAND NAMES (Manufacturers)
Decadron (Merck Sharp & Dohme)
Dexameth (Major)
dexamethasone (various manufacturers)
Dexone (Reid-Rowell)
Hexadrol (Organon)
TYPE OF DRUG
Adrenocorticosteroid hormone
INGREDIENT
dexamethasone
DOSAGE FORMS
Tablets (0.25 mg, 0.5 mg, 0.75 mg, 1 mg, 1.5 mg, 2 mg, 4 mg, and 6 mg)
Oral elixir (0.5 mg per 5-mL spoonful, with 5% alcohol)
Oral solution (0.5 mg per 5-mL spoonful)
Oral concentrate (0.5 mg per 0.5 mL, with 30% alcohol)
STORAGE
Dexamethasone should be stored at room temperature in a tightly closed container.

USES

Your adrenal glands naturally produce certain cortisonelike chemicals. These chemicals are involved in various regulatory processes in the body (such as those involving fluid balance, temperature, and the reaction to inflammation). Dexamethasone belongs to a group of drugs known as adrenocorticosteroids (or cortisonelike medications). It is used to treat a variety of disorders, including endocrine and rheumatic disorders; asthma; blood diseases; certain cancers; eye disorders; gastrointestinal disturbances, such as ulcerative colitis;

respiratory diseases; and inflammations such as arthritis, dermatitis, and poison ivy. How this drug acts to relieve these disorders is not completely understood.

TREATMENT

In order to prevent stomach irritation, you can take dexamethasone with food or milk.

If you are taking only one dose of this medication each day, try to take it before 9:00 A.M. This will mimic the body's normal production of this type of chemical.

The oral elixir and solution forms of this medication should be measured carefully with a specially designed 5-mL measuring spoon. An ordinary kitchen teaspoon is not accurate enough.

The oral concentrate may be diluted in juice, other liquids, or semi-solid foods like applesauce.

It is important to not miss any doses of dexamethasone. However, if you do miss a dose of this medication, follow these guidelines:

1. If you are taking this medication more than once a day, take the missed dose as soon as possible and return to your regular schedule. If it is already time for the next dose of medication, double the dose.

2. If you are taking this medication once a day, take the dose you missed as soon as possible, unless you don't remember until the next day. In that case, do not take the missed dose at all, just follow your regular dosing schedule. Do not double the next dose.

3. If you are taking this drug every other day, take it as soon as you remember. If you missed the scheduled time by a whole day, take it when you remember, then skip a day before you take the next dose. Do not double the next dose. If you miss more than one dose of dexamethasone, CONTACT YOUR DOCTOR.

SIDE EFFECTS

Minor. Dizziness, false sense of well-being, fatigue, increased appetite, increased sweating, indigestion, leg cramps, menstrual irregularities, muscle weakness, nausea, reddening of the skin on the face, restlessness, sleep disorders, thinning of the skin, or weight gain. These side effects should disappear as your body adjusts to the medication.

To help avoid potassium loss while using this drug, you can take your dose with a glass of fresh or frozen orange juice, or eat a banana each day. The use of a salt substitute also helps to prevent potassium loss. Check with your doctor before changing your diet or using a salt substitute.

Major. Tell your doctor about any side effects that are persistent or particularly bothersome. IT IS ESPECIALLY IMPORTANT TO TELL YOUR DOCTOR about abdominal enlargement or pain; acne or other skin problems; back or rib pain; bloody or black, tarry stools; blurred vision; convulsions; eye pain; fever and sore throat; growth impairment (in children); headaches; impaired healing of wounds; increased thirst and urination; mental depression; mood changes; muscle wasting; nightmares; peptic ulcers; rapid weight gain (three to five pounds within a week); rash; shortness of breath; unusual bleeding or bruising; or unusual weakness.

INTERACTIONS

This drug interacts with several other types of drugs:

1. Alcohol, aspirin, and anti-inflammatory medications (such as diclofenac, diflunisal, fenoprofen, flurbiprofen, ibuprofen, indomethacin, naproxen, piroxicam, sulindac, and tolmetin) aggravate the stomach problems that may occur with use of this medication.

2. The dosage of oral anticoagulants (blood thinners, such as warfarin), oral antidiabetic drugs, or insulin may need to be altered when this medication is started or stopped.

3. The loss of potassium caused by this medication can lead to serious side effects in individuals taking digoxin.

4. Thiazide diuretics (water pills) can increase the potassium loss caused by dexamethasone.

5. Phenobarbital, phenytoin, rifampin, and ephedrine can increase the elimination of dexamethasone from the body, thereby decreasing its effectiveness.

6. Oral contraceptives (birth control pills) and estrogen-containing drugs may decrease the elimination of this drug from the body, which can lead to an increase in side effects.

7. Dexamethasone can increase the elimination of aspirin and isoniazid from the body, thereby decreasing the effectiveness of these two medications.

8. Cholestyramine and colestipol can chemically bind this medication in the stomach and gastrointestinal tract, preventing its absorption.

BE SURE TO TELL YOUR DOCTOR about any medications you are currently taking, especially any of those listed above.

WARNINGS

• Tell your doctor about unusual or allergic reactions you have had to any medications, especially to dexamethasone or other adrenocorticosteroids (such as alcometasone, amcinonide, betamethasone, clobetasol, clocortolone, cortisone, desonide, desoximetasone, diflorasone, flumethasone, fluocinolone, fluocinonide, fluorometholone, flurandrenolide, halcinonide, hydrocortisone, methylprednisolone, paramethasone, prednisolone, prednisone, and triamcinolone).

• Tell your doctor if you now have or if you have ever had bone disease of any sort, diabetes mellitus, emotional instability, glaucoma, fungal infections, heart disease, high blood pressure, high cholesterol levels, myasthenia gravis, peptic ulcers, osteoporosis, thyroid disease, tuberculosis, ulcerative colitis, kidney disease, or liver disease.

• If you are using this medication for longer than a week, you may need to receive higher doses if you are subjected to stress, such as serious infections, injury, or surgery. Discuss this with your doctor.

• If you have been taking this drug for more than one or two weeks, do not stop taking it suddenly. If it is stopped abruptly, you may experience abdominal or back pain, dizziness, extreme weakness, fainting, fever, muscle or joint pain, nausea, vomiting, or shortness of breath. Your doctor may, therefore, want to reduce the dosage gradually. Never increase the dosage or take the drug for longer than the prescribed time unless you first consult your doctor.

• While you are taking this drug, you should not be vaccinated or immunized. This medication decreases the effectiveness of vaccines and can lead to infection if a live-virus vaccine is administered.

• Before having surgery or other medical or dental treatment, tell your doctor or dentist you are taking this drug.

• Because this drug can cause glaucoma and cataracts with long-term use, your doctor may want to have your eyes examined periodically by an ophthalmologist during treatment.

• If you are taking this medication for prolonged periods, you should wear or carry an identification card or notice stating that you are taking an adrenocorticosteroid.

• This drug can raise blood-sugar levels in patients with diabetes. Blood sugar should be monitored carefully with blood or urine tests when this drug is being taken.

• Be sure to tell your doctor if you are pregnant. This drug crosses the placenta and may cause adverse effects in the fetus. Birth defects have been observed in the offspring of animals that were given large doses of this type of drug during pregnancy. Also tell your doctor if you are breast-feeding an infant. Small amounts of this drug pass into breast milk and may cause growth suppression or a decrease in natural adrenocorticosteroid production in the nursing infant.

---

dexamethasone, neomycin, and polymyxin B combination (ophthalmic)

BRAND NAMES (Manufacturers)
AK-Trol (Akorn)
Dexacidin (Iolab Pharm)
Dexasporin (various manufacturers)
Maxitrol (Alcon)
TYPE OF DRUG
Ophthalmic adrenocorticosteroid and antibiotic
INGREDIENTS
dexamethasone, neomycin, and polymyxin B
DOSAGE FORMS
Ophthalmic suspension (0.1% dexamethasone, 3.5 mg
    neomycin, and 10,000 units polymyxin B per mL)
Ophthalmic ointment (0.1% dexamethasone, 3.5 mg
    neomycin, and 10,000 units polymyxin B per gram)
STORAGE
The ophthalmic suspension and ointment should be stored at room temperature (never frozen) in tightly closed containers. If the suspension or ointment changes color, don't use the medication. A change in color indicates a loss of effectiveness.

USES

This medication is used for the short-term treatment of bacterial infections and inflammation of the eyes.

Your adrenal glands naturally produce certain cortisonelike chemicals. These chemicals are involved in various regulatory processes in the body (such as those involving fluid balance, temperature, and the reaction to inflammation). Dexamethasone belongs to a group of drugs known as adrenocorticosteroids (or cortisonelike medications). It is used to relieve inflammation (redness, swelling, itching, and discomfort). How it does so is not completely understood.

Neomycin and polymyxin B are antibiotics, which act to prevent the growth and multiplication of infecting bacteria.

TREATMENT

Wash your hands with soap and water before using this medication. If you are using the suspension form, shake the bottle well before measuring out the drops. The contents tend to settle on the bottom of the bottle, so it is necessary to shake the container to distribute the ingredients evenly and to equalize the doses.

In order to prevent contamination of the medicine, be careful not to touch the tube portion of the dropper, and do not let the dropper touch the eye.

Note that the bottle of the eye drops is not completely full. This is to allow control of the number of drops used.

To apply the drops, tilt your head back and pull down the lower eyelid with one hand to make a pouch below the eyeball. Drop the medicine into the pouch and slowly close your eyes. Do not blink. Place one finger at the corner of the eye next to your nose, applying slight pressure (this is done to prevent loss of medication through the duct that drains fluid from the surface of the eye into the nose and throat), and keep your eyes closed for a minute or two. If you think that the medicine did not get into your eye, repeat the process once. If you are using a second medication in the form of eye drops, wait at least five minutes before administering the second type.

Follow the same general procedure for applying the ointment. Tilt your head back, pull down the lower eyelid, and squeeze the prescribed amount of ointment in a line along the pouch below the eyeball. Close your eyes, and place your finger at the corner of the eye near the nose for a minute or two. Do not rub your eyes. Wipe off excess ointment and the tip of the tube with clean tissues.

Since applying the medication is somewhat difficult to do, you may want someone else to apply it for you.

If you miss a dose of this drug, insert the drops or apply the ointment as soon as possible, unless it is almost time for the next application. In that case, do not use the missed dose; just return to the regular schedule.

Your doctor may advise you to reduce the number of times you are applying this medication when the inflammation and infection begin to improve. Continue to take this medication for the entire time prescribed by your doctor, even if the symptoms of infection disappear sooner. If you stop applying the drug too soon, bacteria are given a chance to continue growing, and the infection could recur.

SIDE EFFECTS

Minor. Blurred vision, burning, or stinging. These side effects should disappear as your body adjusts to the drug.

Major. Tell your doctor about any side effects that are persistent or particularly bothersome. IT IS ESPECIALLY IMPORTANT TO TELL YOUR DOCTOR about disturbed or reduced vision; eye pain, itching, or swelling; headache; rash; or severe irritation.

INTERACTIONS

This medication should not interact with any other medications as long as it is used according to directions.

WARNINGS

• Tell your doctor about any reactions you have had to medications, especially to dexamethasone or other adrenocorticosteroids (such as alcometasone, amcinonide, betamethasone, clobetasol, clocortolone, cortisone, desonide, desoximetasone, diflorasone, flumethasone, fluocinolone, fluorometholone, flurandrenolide, halcinonide, hydrocortisone, methylprednisolone, prednisolone, prednisone, and triamcinolone), to polymyxin B, to neomycin, or to any related antibiotic (amikacin, gentamicin, kanamycin, netilmicin, paromomycin, streptomycin, and tobramycin).

• Tell your doctor if you have ever had fungal or viral infections of the eye, inner-ear disease, kidney disease, or myasthenia gravis.

• If there is no change in your condition two or three days after starting to take this drug, contact your doctor. The drug may not be effective for your particular infection.

• Do not use this medication for longer than ten consecutive days unless your doctor directs you to do so. Prolonged use of this drug may result in glaucoma, secondary infection, cataracts, or eye damage. If you need to take this medication for several weeks, your doctor may want you to have an eye examination by an ophthalmologist.

• This medication has been prescribed for your current infection only. A subsequent infection may require a different medicine. Do not give this drug to other people or use it to treat other infections.

• Do not apply makeup to the affected eye.

• Be sure to tell your doctor if you are pregnant. When large amounts of dexamethasone are applied for prolonged periods, some of it is absorbed into the bloodstream. It may cross the placenta. Birth defects have been observed in the offspring of animals that were given large oral doses of this drug during pregnancy. Also tell your doctor if you are breast-feeding an infant. If absorbed through the eye, small amounts of dexamethasone can pass into breast milk and may cause growth suppression or a decrease in natural adrenocorticosteroid production in the nursing infant.

---

dexfenfluramine*

*This drug was recalled September 15, 1997, due to concern that it may cause heart damage.

BRAND NAME (Manufacturer)
Redux (Wyeth-Ayerst)
TYPE OF DRUG
Antiobesity
INGREDIENT
dexfenfluramine
DOSAGE FORM
Capsules (15 mg)

STORAGE
Store at room temperature in a tightly closed, light-resistant container. Do not refrigerate or freeze.

USES
Dexfenfluramine is used in the treatment of obesity. It is thought to relieve hunger by altering nerve impulses to the appetite control center in the brain. Other weight loss products (such as amphetamines) have been shown to be effective only for short periods (three to 12 weeks). Dexfenfluramine has been shown to maintain its effectiveness in certain patients for up to one year when used in conjunction with a reduced-calorie eating plan.

TREATMENT
Dexfenfluramine should be taken twice daily with meals (unless your doctor specifically instructs you to do otherwise).

To avoid difficulty in falling asleep, the last dose each day should be taken four to six hours before bedtime.

If you miss a dose, take it right away if you remember to take it within two hours of the correct time. Then take the next dose as scheduled. If more than two hours have elapsed since the missed dose, do not take the missed dose: Return to your regular schedule. Do not double the next dose.

SIDE EFFECTS
Minor. Blurred vision, constipation, diarrhea, dizziness, dry mouth, fatigue, insomnia, irritability, nausea, nervousness, restlessness, stomach pain, sweating, unpleasant taste in the mouth, or vomiting. These side effects should disappear as your body adjusts to the medication.

Dry mouth can be relieved by sucking on ice chips or a piece of hard candy. To prevent constipation, increase the fiber in your diet (fresh fruits and vegetables, whole-grain breads), exercise, and drink more water (unless your doctor tells you not to).
Major. Tell your doctor about any side effects that are persistent or particularly bothersome. IT IS ESPECIALLY IMPORTANT TO TELL YOUR DOCTOR about changes in sexual desire, chest pain, difficulty in urinating, fever, hair loss, headaches, menstrual irregularities, mental depression, mood changes, muscle pain, palpitations, rash, shortness of breath, swelling of the hands or feet, tremors, or unusual bleeding.

INTERACTIONS

Dexfenfluramine interacts with other types of medications:

1. Use of this medication within 14 days of a monoamine oxidase (MAO) inhibitor (such as isocarboxazid, pargyline, phenelzine, or tranylcypromine) can result in high blood pressure and other side effects.

2. Use of dexfenfluramine with agents for migraine (such as dihydroergotamine or sumatriptan) may result in a rare but serious effect termed serotonin syndrome. The syndrome requires IMMEDIATE MEDICAL ATTENTION and may include one or more of the following symptoms: agitation, anxiety, confusion, disorientation, hypomania, hypothermia, increased heart rate, loss of consciousness, restlessness, shivering, tremor, or weakness.

3. Dexfenfluramine may alter insulin and oral antidiabetic medication dosage requirements in diabetic patients.

4. This drug may increase the sedative effects of alcohol or other drugs that interact with central nervous system action.

WARNINGS

• The combination of the appetite suppressant fenfluramine and phentermine ("fen-phen") may cause heart problems by affecting the valves that help bring blood into and out of your heart. Since dexfenfluramine is chemically related to fenfluramine, dexfenfluramine may also cause this problem. It is very important, therefore, for to tell your doctor if you have any of the following symptoms: irregular heartbeat, difficulty breathing, puffiness of the feet or hands, or a decreased ability to exercise.

• It is very important to tell your doctor about any appetite suppressant you may have taken in the past. Tell your doctor about any unusual or allergic reactions you have had to any medications, especially to other appetite suppressants (such as diethylpropion, fenfluramine, or phentermine).

• Tell your doctor if you have a history of drug abuse or if you ever had angina, diabetes mellitus, heart or cardiovascular disease, high blood pressure, or pulmonary hypertension.

• Dexfenfluramine can cause drowsiness. Your ability to perform tasks that require alertness, such as driving a car or operating potentially dangerous machinery, may be decreased.

• Before having surgery or other medical or dental procedures, tell your doctor or dentist you are taking this drug.

• Be sure to tell your doctor if you are pregnant. Although extensive studies of dexfenfluramine in humans have not been conducted, it has been shown to cause side effects in the fetuses of animals that received large doses of the drug during pregnancy. Also tell your doctor if you are breast-feeding an infant. It is not known if this medication passes into human breast milk.

diazepam

BRAND NAMES (Manufacturers)
diazepam (various manufacturers)
Diazepam Intensol (Roxane)
Valium (Roche)
TYPE OF DRUG
Sedative/hypnotic
INGREDIENT
diazepam
DOSAGE FORMS
Oral solution (5 mg per 5-mL spoonful)
Oral intensol solution (5 mg per mL)
Tablets (2 mg, 5 mg, and 10 mg)
Sustained-release capsules (15 mg)
STORAGE
This medication should be stored at room temperature in a tightly closed, light-resistant container.

USES
Diazepam is prescribed to treat symptoms of anxiety and sometimes to treat muscle spasms, convulsions, seizures, or alcohol withdrawal. It is not clear exactly how this medicine works, but diazepam may relieve anxiety by acting as a depressant of the central nervous system (brain and spinal cord). It is currently used by many people to relieve nervousness. Diazepam is effective for this purpose for short periods, but it is also important to try to remove the cause of the anxiety.

TREATMENT
The oral intensol solution should be mixed with a nonalcoholic liquid or semisolid food such as water, juice, soda or sodalike beverages, applesauce, or pudding. Use only the cal-

ibrated dropper provided. Stir the liquid or food gently for a few seconds after adding the oral intensol solution. The entire amount of the mixture should be consumed immediately. Do not store prepared mixtures for future use. The tablet or capsule form of this medication should be taken exactly as directed by your doctor. It can be taken with food or a full glass of water if stomach upset occurs. Do not take this medication with a dose of antacids, since they may retard its absorption.

If you are taking this medication regularly and you miss a dose and remember within an hour, take the missed dose immediately. If more than an hour has passed, skip the dose you missed and wait for the next scheduled dose. Do not double the next dose.

SIDE EFFECTS

Minor. Bitter taste in the mouth, constipation, depression, diarrhea, dizziness, drowsiness (after a night's sleep), dry mouth, excessive salivation, fatigue, flushing, headache, heartburn, loss of appetite, nausea, nervousness, sweating, or vomiting. These side effects should disappear once your body gets accustomed to the medication.

To relieve constipation, increase the amount of fiber in your diet (fresh fruits and vegetables, salads, bran, and whole-grain breads), exercise, and drink more water (unless your doctor directs you to do otherwise).

Dry mouth can be relieved by chewing sugarless gum or by sucking on ice chips or hard candy.

If you feel dizzy, sit or lie down for a while; get up slowly from a sitting or reclining position; and be careful on stairs.

Major. Tell your doctor about any side effects that are persistent or particularly bothersome. IT IS ESPECIALLY IMPORTANT TO TELL YOUR DOCTOR about blurred or double vision, chest pain, difficulty in urinating, fainting, falling, fever, joint pain, hallucinations, mouth sores, nightmares, palpitations, rash, severe depression, shortness of breath, slurred speech, sore throat, uncoordinated movements, unusual excitement, unusual tiredness, or yellowing of the eyes or skin.

INTERACTIONS

This medication interacts with several other types of medications:

1. To prevent oversedation, this drug should not be taken with alcohol, other sedative drugs, or central nervous system depressants (such as antihistamines, barbiturates, muscle relaxants, pain medicines, narcotics, medicines for seizures, and tranquilizers), or with antidepressants.
2. This medication may decrease the effectiveness of carbamazepine, levodopa, and oral anticoagulants (blood thinners) and may increase the effects of phenytoin.
3. Disulfiram, oral contraceptives (birth control pills), isoniazid, fluoxetine, valproic acid, propranolol, metoprolol, ketoconazole, and cimetidine can increase the blood levels of diazepam, which can lead to toxic effects.
4. Concurrent use of rifampin may decrease the effectiveness of diazepam.

BE SURE TO TELL YOUR DOCTOR about any medications you are currently taking, especially any of those listed above.

WARNINGS

• Tell your doctor about unusual or allergic reactions you have had to any medications, especially to diazepam or other benzodiazepine tranquilizers (such as alprazolam, flurazepam, halazepam, lorazepam, oxazepam, prazepam, temazepam, and triazolam).
• Be sure to tell your doctor if you now have or if you have ever had liver disease, kidney disease, epilepsy, lung disease, myasthenia gravis, porphyria, mental depression, or mental illness.
• This medicine can cause drowsiness. Avoid tasks that require alertness, such as driving a car or operating potentially dangerous machinery.
• This medication has the potential for abuse and must be used with caution. Tolerance may develop quickly; do not increase your dosage of the drug without first consulting your doctor. It is also important not to stop taking this drug suddenly if you have been taking it in large amounts or if you have used it for several weeks. Your doctor may want to reduce your dosage gradually.
• This is a safe drug when used properly. When it is combined with other sedative drugs or alcohol, however, serious side effects can develop.
• Be sure to tell your doctor if you are pregnant. This medicine may increase the chance of birth defects if it is taken dur-

ing the first three months of pregnancy. In addition, too much use of this medicine during the last six months of pregnancy may cause the baby to become dependent on it, resulting in withdrawal side effects in the newborn. Use of diazepam during the last weeks of pregnancy may cause excessive drowsiness, slowed heartbeat, and breathing difficulties in the infant. Be sure to tell your doctor if you are breast-feeding an infant. This medication can pass into breast milk and cause excessive drowsiness, slowed heartbeat, and breathing difficulties in nursing infants.

diclofenac

BRAND NAME (Manufacturer)
Voltaren (Ciba-Geigy)
TYPE OF DRUG
Nonsteroidal anti-inflammatory analgesic
INGREDIENT
diclofenac
DOSAGE FORM
Enteric-coated tablets (25 mg, 50 mg, and 75 mg)
STORAGE
This medication should be stored in a tightly closed container at room temperature away from heat and direct sunlight.

USES
Diclofenac is used to treat the inflammation (pain, swelling, and stiffness) of arthritis and ankylosing spondylitis. Diclofenac has been shown to block the production of certain body chemicals, called prostaglandins, that may trigger pain. However, it is not yet fully understood how diclofenac works.

TREATMENT
You should take this medication on an empty stomach 30 to 60 minutes before meals or two hours after meals so it gets into your bloodstream quickly. To decrease stomach irritation, your doctor may want you to take this medication with food or antacids.

Do not break, crush, or chew the tablets before swallowing. They should be swallowed whole to lessen side effects.

It may take two weeks before you feel the full effects of this medication. Diclofenac does not cure arthritis or ankylosing spondylitis, but it will help to control the condition as long as you continue to take it.

It is important that you take diclofenac on schedule and do not miss any doses. If you do miss a dose, take it as soon as possible, unless it is almost time for your next dose. In that case, do not take the missed dose at all; just return to your regular dosing schedule. Do not double the next dose.

SIDE EFFECTS

Minor. Abdominal cramps, constipation, diarrhea, dizziness, headache, indigestion, or nausea. As your body adjusts to the drug, these side effects should disappear.

To relieve constipation, increase the amount of fiber in your diet (fresh fruits and vegetables, salads, bran, and whole-grain breads), exercise, and drink more water (unless your doctor directs you to do otherwise).

If you become dizzy, sit or lie down for a while; get up slowly from a sitting or reclining position; and be careful on stairs.

Major. Tell your doctor about any side effects that are persistent or particularly bothersome. IT IS ESPECIALLY IMPORTANT TO TELL YOUR DOCTOR about bloody or black, tarry stools; blurred vision; confusion; difficult or painful urination; palpitations; a problem with hearing, or ringing or buzzing in your ears; skin rash, hives, or itching; stomach pain; swelling of the feet or hands; tightness in the chest; unexplained sore throat and fever; soreness of the tongue or mouth; unusual fatigue or weakness; unusual weight gain; wheezing or difficulty in breathing; or yellowish discoloration of the eyes or skin.

INTERACTIONS

Diclofenac interacts with several other types of medications:
1. Anticoagulants (blood thinners, such as warfarin) can lead to an increase in bleeding complications.
2. Aspirin, other salicylates, and other anti-inflammatory medications can increase stomach irritation. Aspirin may also decrease the effectiveness of diclofenac. Therefore, aspirin should not be used concurrently with this medication.

3. Diclofenac can decrease the elimination of digoxin, methotrexate, and lithium from the body, which can lead to serious side effects.
4. The activity of diuretics (water pills) and drugs to lower blood pressure (propranolol, metoprolol) may be inhibited by diclofenac.
5. Diclofenac may alter a diabetic patient's response to insulin, oral hypoglycemic agents, or antiseizure medication (phenytoin).

Before starting to take diclofenac, BE SURE TO TELL YOUR DOCTOR about any medications you are taking, especially any of those listed above.

WARNINGS

• Before you start to take this medication, it is important to tell your doctor if you have ever had unusual or allergic reactions to diclofenac or to any of the other chemically related drugs (aspirin, other salicylates, diflunisal, fenoprofen, flurbiprofen, indomethacin, ketoprofen, meclofenamate, mefenamic acid, naproxen, oxyphenbutazone, phenylbutazone, piroxicam, sulindac, or tolmetin).
• Tell your doctor if you now have or if you have ever had asthma, bleeding problems, colitis, stomach ulcers or other stomach problems, epilepsy, heart disease, high blood pressure, kidney disease, liver disease, mental illness, or Parkinson's disease.
• If diclofenac makes you dizzy or drowsy, do not take part in any activity that requires alertness, such as driving a car or operating potentially dangerous machinery.
• Because this drug can prolong your bleeding time, it is important to tell your doctor or dentist that you are taking this drug before having surgery or any other medical or dental treatment.
• Stomach problems are more likely to occur if you take aspirin regularly or drink alcohol while being treated with this medication.
• Be sure to tell your doctor if you are pregnant or planning to become pregnant. This medication can cause unwanted effects on the heart or blood flow of the fetus. Studies in animals have also shown that this medicine, if taken late in pregnancy, may increase the length of pregnancy, prolong labor, or cause other problems during delivery. Also tell your doctor if

you are breast-feeding an infant. Small amounts of diclofenac can pass into breast milk.

dicloxacillin

BRAND NAMES (Manufacturers)
dicloxacillin sodium (various manufacturers)
Dycill (SmithKline Beecham)
Dynapen (Apothecon)
Pathocil (Wyeth-Ayerst)
TYPE OF DRUG
Penicillin antibiotic
INGREDIENT
dicloxacillin
DOSAGE FORMS
Capsules (125 mg, 250 mg, and 500 mg)
Oral suspension (62.5 mg per 5-mL spoonful)
STORAGE
Dicloxacillin capsules should be stored at room temperature in a tightly closed container. The oral suspension should be stored in the refrigerator in a tightly closed container. Any unused portion of the suspension should be discarded after 14 days because the drug loses its potency after that time. This medication should never be frozen.

USES
Dicloxacillin is used to treat a wide variety of bacterial infections, especially those caused by Staphylococcus bacteria. It acts by severely injuring the cell membranes of the infecting bacteria, thereby preventing them from growing and multiplying. Dicloxacillin kills susceptible bacteria, but it is not effective against viruses, parasites, or fungi.

TREATMENT
Dicloxacillin should be taken on an empty stomach or with a glass of water, one hour before or two hours after a meal. This medication should never be taken with fruit juices or carbonated beverages because the acidity of these drinks destroys the drug in the stomach.

The suspension form of this medication should be shaken well just before measuring each dose. The contents tend to settle at the bottom of the bottle, so it is necessary to shake the container to distribute the ingredients evenly and equalize the doses. Each dose should then be measured carefully with a specially designed 5-mL measuring spoon. An ordinary kitchen teaspoon is not accurate enough.

Dicloxacillin works best when the level of medicine in your bloodstream is kept constant. It is best, therefore, to take the doses at evenly spaced intervals day and night. For example, if you are taking four doses a day, the doses should be spaced six hours apart.

If you miss a dose of this medication, take the missed dose immediately. However, if you do not remember to take the missed dose until it is almost time for your next dose, take it; space the following dose about halfway through the regular interval between doses; then return to your regular schedule. Try not to skip any doses.

It is important for you to continue to take this medication for the entire time prescribed by your doctor (usually seven to 14 days), even if the symptoms of your infection disappear before the end of that period. If you stop taking the drug too soon, bacteria are given a chance to continue growing, and the infection could recur.

SIDE EFFECTS

Minor. Diarrhea, heartburn, nausea, or vomiting. These side effects should disappear over time as your body adjusts to this medication.

Major. Tell your doctor about any side effects that are persistent or particularly bothersome. IT IS ESPECIALLY IMPORTANT TO TELL YOUR DOCTOR about bloating, chills, cough, darkened tongue, difficulty in breathing, fever, irritation of the mouth, muscle aches, rash, rectal or vaginal itching, severe diarrhea, or sore throat. In addition, if the symptoms of your infection seem to be getting worse rather than improving, you should contact your doctor.

INTERACTIONS

Dicloxacillin interacts with other types of medications:
1. Probenecid can increase the blood concentrations and side effects of this medication.
2. Dicloxacillin may decrease the effectiveness of oral contraceptives (birth control pills), and pregnancy could result.

You should, therefore, use a different or additional form of birth control while taking this medication. Discuss this with your doctor.

BE SURE TO TELL YOUR DOCTOR about any medications you are currently taking, especially any of those listed above.

WARNINGS

• Tell your doctor about unusual or allergic reactions you have had to any medications, especially to dicloxacillin or penicillins, or to cephalosporin antibiotics, penicillamine, or griseofulvin.

• Tell your doctor if you now have or if you have ever had kidney disease, asthma, or allergies.

• This medication has been prescribed for your current infection only. Another infection later on, or one that someone else has, may require a different medicine. You should not give your medicine to other people or use it for other infections unless your doctor specifically directs you to do so.

• People with diabetes taking dicloxacillin should know that it can cause interference with a Clinitest urine glucose test. To avoid this problem, they should switch to Clinistix or Tes-Tape to test their urine for sugar.

• Be sure to tell your doctor if you are pregnant. Although dicloxacillin appears to be safe to take during pregnancy, extensive studies in humans have not been conducted. Also tell your doctor if you are breast-feeding an infant. Small amounts of this medication pass into breast milk and may temporarily alter the bacterial balance in the intestinal tract of the nursing infant, resulting in episodes of diarrhea.

dicyclomine

BRAND NAMES (Manufacturers)
Bentyl (Lakeside)
Byclomine (Major)
dicyclomine hydrochloride (various manufacturers)
Di-Spaz (Vortech)
TYPE OF DRUG
Antispasmodic
INGREDIENT
dicyclomine

DOSAGE FORMS
Tablets (20 mg)
Capsules (10 mg and 20 mg)
Oral liquid (10 mg per 5-mL spoonful)

STORAGE
Dicyclomine tablets, capsules, and oral liquid should be stored at room temperature in tightly closed containers. This medication should never be frozen.

USES
Dicyclomine is used to treat gastrointestinal tract disorders and irritable bowel syndrome. Dicyclomine acts directly on the muscles of the gastrointestinal tract to decrease tone and slow their activity.

TREATMENT
Dicyclomine can be taken before or after meals. Consult your doctor for specific recommendations.

Antacids and antidiarrheal medicines may prevent absorption of this drug; therefore, at least one hour should separate doses of dicyclomine and one of these medications.

Measure the liquid form of dicyclomine carefully with a specially designed 5-mL measuring spoon. An ordinary kitchen teaspoon is not accurate enough. You can then dilute the oral liquid in other liquids to mask its taste.

If you miss a dose of this medication, do not take the missed dose at all; just return to your regular dosing schedule. Do not double the next dose.

SIDE EFFECTS
Minor. Bloating; blurred vision; confusion; constipation; dizziness; drowsiness; dry mouth, throat, and nose; headache; increased sensitivity to light; insomnia; loss of taste; nausea; nervousness; decreased sweating; vomiting; or weakness. These side effects should disappear as your body adjusts to the medication.

If you are constipated, increase the amount of fiber in your diet (fresh fruits and vegetables, salads, bran, and whole-grain breads), exercise, and drink more water (unless your doctor directs you to do otherwise).

Chew sugarless gum or suck on ice chips or a piece of hard candy to reduce mouth dryness.

To avoid dizziness or light-headedness when you stand, contract and relax the muscles of your legs for a few moments before rising. Do this by pushing one foot against the floor while raising the other foot slightly, alternating feet so that you are "pumping" your legs in a pedaling motion.

Wear sunglasses if your eyes become sensitive to light.

Major. Be sure to tell your doctor about any side effects that are persistent or particularly bothersome. IT IS ESPECIALLY IMPORTANT TO TELL YOUR DOCTOR about difficulty in urinating, fever, hallucinations, impotence, palpitations, rash, short-term memory loss, or sore throat.

INTERACTIONS

Dicyclomine interacts with several other types of medications:
1. It can cause extreme drowsiness when combined with central nervous system depressants (such as alcohol, antihistamines, barbiturates, benzodiazepine tranquilizers, muscle relaxants, narcotics, pain medications, and phenothiazine tranquilizers) or with tricyclic antidepressants.
2. Amantadine, antihistamines, haloperidol, monoamine oxidase (MAO) inhibitors, phenothiazine tranquilizers, procainamide, quinidine, and tricyclic antidepressants can increase the side effects of dicyclomine.

BE SURE TO TELL YOUR DOCTOR about any medications you are currently taking.

WARNINGS

• Be sure to tell your doctor about unusual or allergic reactions you have had to any medications, especially to dicyclomine.
• Tell your doctor if you have ever had glaucoma; heart disease; hiatal hernia; high blood pressure; kidney, liver, or thyroid disease; myasthenia gravis; obstructed bladder; obstructed intestine; enlarged prostate gland; ulcerative colitis; or internal bleeding.
• If this medication makes you dizzy or drowsy or blurs your vision, do not take part in any activity that requires alertness, such as driving an automobile or operating potentially dangerous equipment or machinery. Be careful on stairs, and avoid getting up suddenly from a lying or sitting position.
• This drug can decrease sweating and heat release from the body. Avoid taking hot baths, showers, or saunas; to avoid getting overheated, do not exercise in hot weather.

• Before having surgery or other medical or dental treatment, be sure to tell your doctor or dentist you are taking this drug.
• Tell your doctor if you are pregnant. Although this drug appears to be safe during pregnancy, extensive studies in humans have not been conducted. Also tell your doctor if you are breast-feeding an infant. Small amounts of dicyclomine pass into breast milk.

---

diethylpropion

BRAND NAMES (Manufacturers)
diethylpropion hydrochloride (various manufacturers)
Tenuate (Lakeside)
Tenuate Dospan (Lakeside)
TYPE OF DRUG
Anorectic
INGREDIENT
diethylpropion
DOSAGE FORMS
Tablets (25 mg)
Sustained-release tablets (75 mg)
STORAGE
Diethylpropion tablets should be stored at room temperature in tightly closed, light-resistant containers.

USES

Diethylpropion is used as an appetite suppressant during the first few weeks of dieting to help establish new eating habits. This medication is thought to relieve hunger by altering nerve impulses to the appetite control center in the brain. Its effectiveness lasts only for short periods (three to 12 weeks), however.

TREATMENT

You can take diethylpropion with a full glass of water one hour before meals (unless your doctor directs you to do otherwise).

In order to avoid difficulty in falling asleep, the last dose of this medication each day should be taken four to six hours before bedtime (regular tablets) or ten to 14 hours before bedtime (sustained-release tablets).

The sustained-release form of this medication should be swallowed whole. Breaking, chewing, or crushing these tablets destroys their sustained-release activity and may increase the side effects.

If you miss a dose, take the missed dose as soon as possible, unless it is almost time for your next dose. In that case, do not take the missed dose; just return to your regular dosing schedule. Do not double the next dose.

SIDE EFFECTS

Minor. Blurred vision, constipation, diarrhea, dizziness, dry mouth, euphoria, fatigue, insomnia, irritability, nausea, nervousness, restlessness, stomach pain, sweating, tremors, unpleasant taste in the mouth, or vomiting. These side effects should disappear as your body adjusts to the medication.

Dry mouth can be relieved by sucking on ice chips or a piece of hard candy or by chewing sugarless gum.

In order to prevent constipation, increase the amount of fiber in your diet (fresh fruits and vegetables, salads, bran, and whole-grain breads), exercise, and drink more water (unless your doctor directs you to do otherwise).

Major. Tell your doctor about any side effects that are persistent or particularly bothersome. IT IS ESPECIALLY IMPORTANT TO TELL YOUR DOCTOR about changes in sexual desire, chest pain, difficulty in urinating, enlarged breasts (in both sexes), fever, hair loss, headaches, impotence, menstrual irregularities, mental depression, mood changes, mouth sores, muscle pains, nosebleeds, palpitations, rash, or sore throat.

INTERACTIONS

Diethylpropion interacts with several other types of drugs:

1. Use of diethylpropion within 14 days of use of a monoamine oxidase (MAO) inhibitor (such as isocarboxazid, pargyline, phenelzine, and tranylcypromine) can result in high blood pressure and other side effects.

2. Barbiturate medications and phenothiazine tranquilizers (especially chlorpromazine) can antagonize (act against) the appetite suppressant activity of this medication, decreasing its effectiveness.

3. Diethylpropion can decrease the blood-pressure-lowering effects of antihypertensive medications (especially guanethi-

dine) and may alter some insulin and oral antidiabetic medication dosages requirement in some diabetic patients.
4. The side effects of other central nervous system stimulants (such as caffeine and nonprescription appetite suppressants and cough, allergy, asthma, sinus, and cold preparations) may be increased by this medication.

   BE SURE TO TELL YOUR DOCTOR about any medications you are currently taking, especially any listed above.

WARNINGS

• Be sure to tell your doctor about unusual or allergic reactions you have had to any medications, especially to diethylpropion or other appetite suppressants (including benzphetamine, phendimetrazine, phenmetrazine, fenfluramine, mazindol, and phentermine), or to epinephrine, norepinephrine, ephedrine, amphetamine, dextroamphetamine, phenylephrine, phenylpropanolamine, pseudoephedrine, albuterol, metaproterenol, salmeterol, or terbutaline.

• Tell your doctor if you have a history of drug abuse, or if you have ever had angina, diabetes mellitus, emotional disturbances, glaucoma, heart or cardiovascular disease, high blood pressure, thyroid disease, or epilepsy.

• Diethylpropion can mask the symptoms of extreme fatigue and can cause dizziness or light-headedness. Your ability to perform tasks that require alertness, such as driving a car or operating potentially dangerous equipment, may be decreased. Appropriate caution should, therefore, be taken.

• Before surgery or other medical or dental treatment, tell your doctor or dentist you are taking diethylpropion.

• Diethylpropion is related to amphetamine and may be habit-forming when taken for long periods (both physical and psychological dependence can occur). Therefore, you should not increase the dosage of this drug or take it for longer than 12 weeks unless you first consult your doctor. Do not stop taking this drug abruptly if you have been taking large doses for a long time. Fatigue, sleep disorders, mental depression, nausea or vomiting, or stomach cramps or pain could occur. Your doctor may want to decrease your dosage gradually.

• Be sure to tell your doctor if you are pregnant. Although side effects in humans have not been thoroughly studied, some of the appetite suppressants, such as diethylpropion, have been shown to cause side effects in the fetuses of animals that received large doses during pregnancy. Also tell your doctor if you are breast-feeding an infant. It is not known whether this medication passes into breast milk.

---

diflunisal

BRAND NAMES (Manufacturers)
Dolobid (Merck Sharp & Dohme)
diflunisal (various manufacturers)
TYPE OF DRUG
Nonsteroidal anti-inflammatory analgesic
INGREDIENT
diflunisal
DOSAGE FORM
Tablets (250 mg and 500 mg)
STORAGE
This medication should be stored in a tightly closed container at room temperature, away from heat and direct sunlight.

USES
Diflunisal is used to treat the inflammation (pain, swelling, and stiffness) of osteoarthritis and muscle or skeletal injury. Diflunisal has been shown to block the production of certain body chemicals, called prostaglandins, that may trigger pain. However, it is not yet fully understood how diflunisal works.

TREATMENT
You should take this drug immediately after meals or with food in order to reduce stomach irritation. Do not break, crush, or chew the tablets before swallowing—they should be swallowed whole to lessen side effects and to maintain their benefits for a full 12 hours. Ask your doctor if you can take diflunisal with an antacid.

If you are taking diflunisal to relieve osteoarthritis, you must take it regularly, as directed by your doctor. It may take several days before you feel the full benefits of this medication. Diflunisal does not cure osteoarthritis, but it will help to control the condition as long as you continue to take it.

It is important to take diflunisal on schedule and not to miss any doses. If you do miss a dose of this medication, take the missed dose as soon as possible, unless more than six hours has passed. In that case, do not take the missed dose at all; just return to your regular dosing schedule. Do not double the next dose.

SIDE EFFECTS

Minor. Bloating, constipation, diarrhea, difficulty in sleeping, dizziness, drowsiness, headache, heartburn, indigestion, light-headedness, loss of appetite, nausea, nervousness, unusual sweating, or vomiting. As your body gets accustomed to the drug, these side effects should disappear.

To relieve constipation, increase the amount of fiber in your diet (fresh fruits and vegetables, salads, bran, and whole-grain breads). You can also increase your exercise and drink more water (unless your doctor directs you to do otherwise).

If you become dizzy, sit or lie down for a while; get up slowly from a sitting or reclining position; and be careful on stairs.

Major. Tell your doctor about any side effects that are persistent or particularly bothersome. IT IS ESPECIALLY IMPORTANT TO TELL YOUR DOCTOR about bloody or black, tarry stools; blurred vision; confusion; depression; difficult or painful urination; difficulty in breathing; palpitations; ringing or buzzing in the ears or difficulty in hearing; skin rash, hives, or itching; stomach pain; swelling of the feet; tightness in the chest; unexplained sore throat and fever; unusual bleeding or bruising; unusual fatigue or weakness; unusual weight gain; wheezing; or yellowing of the eyes or skin.

INTERACTIONS

Diflunisal interacts with several other types of medications:
1. Anticoagulants (blood thinners, such as warfarin), in combination with diflunisal, can lead to an increase in bleeding complications.
2. Aspirin, salicylates, or other anti-inflammatory medications may cause increased stomach irritation.
3. Antacids can lower blood diflunisal concentrations, decreasing its effectiveness.
4. Diflunisal can increase the blood concentrations and side effects of acetaminophen.

5. Diflunisal can increase or decrease some effects of hydrochlorothiazide and furosemide.

BE SURE TO TELL YOUR DOCTOR about any medications you are currently taking, especially those listed above.

WARNINGS

• Before you take this medication, it is important to tell your doctor if you have ever had unusual or allergic reactions to diflunisal or any chemically related drug (including aspirin or other salicylates, diclofenac, fenoprofen, flurbiprofen, ibuprofen, indomethacin, ketoprofen, meclofenamate, mefenamic acid, naproxen, oxyphenbutazone, phenylbutazone, piroxicam, sulindac, or tolmetin).

• Before you take this medication, tell your doctor if you now have or if you have ever had bleeding problems, colitis, stomach ulcers or other stomach problems, epilepsy, heart disease, high blood pressure, asthma, kidney disease, liver disease, mental illness, or Parkinson's disease.

• Be sure to tell your doctor if this drug makes you dizzy or drowsy, and do not take part in any activity that requires alertness, such as driving a car or operating potentially dangerous equipment.

• Because diflunisal can prolong your bleeding time, it is important to tell your doctor or dentist that you are taking this drug before having surgery or any other medical or dental treatment.

• Stomach problems are more likely to occur if you take aspirin regularly or drink alcohol while being treated with this medication. These should, therefore, be avoided (unless your doctor directs you to do otherwise).

• Be sure to tell your doctor if you are pregnant. Although studies in humans have not been conducted, unwanted side effects (defects in the spine and ribs) have been reported in the offspring of animals that received diflunisal during pregnancy. If taken during the last three months of pregnancy, this drug can cause heart problems in the fetus; it can also prolong labor. Also tell your doctor if you are breast-feeding an infant. Because diflunisal can pass into breast milk, breast-feeding while taking this drug is not recommended.

digoxin

BRAND NAMES (Manufacturers)
digoxin (various manufacturers)
Lanoxicaps (Burroughs Wellcome)
Lanoxin (Burroughs Wellcome)
TYPE OF DRUG
Cardiac glycoside
INGREDIENT
digoxin
DOSAGE FORMS
Tablets (0.125 mg, 0.25 mg, and 0.5 mg)
Capsules (0.05 mg, 0.1 mg, and 0.2 mg)
Pediatric elixir (0.05 mg per mL, with 10% alcohol)
STORAGE
Digoxin tablets, capsules, and pediatric elixir should be stored at room temperature in tightly closed, light-resistant containers. This medication should never be frozen.

USES

Digoxin is used to treat heart arrhythmias and congestive heart failure. It works directly on the muscle of the heart to strengthen the heartbeat and improve heart rhythm and contraction.

TREATMENT

To avoid stomach irritation, take digoxin with water or with food. Try to take it at the same time every day.

Measure the dose of the pediatric elixir carefully with the dropper provided. An ordinary kitchen teaspoon is not accurate enough.

Antacids decrease the absorption of digoxin from the gastrointestinal tract. Therefore, if you are taking both digoxin and an antacid, the dose of digoxin should be taken one hour before or two hours after a dose of antacids.

Try not to miss any doses of this medication. If you do miss a dose, take the missed dose as soon as possible, unless it is almost time for the next dose. In that case, do not take the missed dose at all; just return to your regular schedule.

Do not double the next dose. If you miss more than two doses of digoxin, contact your doctor.

Digoxin does not cure congestive heart failure, but it will help to control the condition as long as you continue to take the medication.

SIDE EFFECTS

Minor. Apathy, diarrhea, drowsiness, headache, muscle weakness, or tiredness. These side effects should disappear as your body adjusts to the medication.

Major. Tell your doctor about any side effects that are persistent or particularly bothersome. IT IS ESPECIALLY IMPORTANT TO TELL YOUR DOCTOR about disorientation, enlarged and painful breasts (in both sexes), hallucinations, loss of appetite, mental depression, nausea, palpitations, severe abdominal pain, slowed heart rate, visual disturbances (such as blurred or yellow vision), or vomiting.

INTERACTIONS

Digoxin interacts with several other types of medications (interactions may vary depending upon the dose of digoxin being used):

1. Penicillamine, antiseizure medications, rifampin, aminoglutethimide, and levodopa can decrease the blood levels and, therefore, the effectiveness of digoxin.

2. Erythromycin, amiodarone, captopril, benzodiazepine tranquilizers, flecainide, tetracycline, hydroxychloroquine, ibuprofen, indomethacin, verapamil, nifedipine, diltiazem, quinidine, quinine, and spironolactone can increase the blood levels of digoxin, which can lead to an increase in side effects.

3. Thyroid hormone, propylthiouracil, and methimazole can change the dosage requirements of digoxin.

4. Antacids, kaolinpectin, sulfasalazine, aminosalicylic acid, metoclopramide, antineoplastic agents (anticancer drugs), neomycin, colestipol, and cholestyramine can decrease the absorption of digoxin from the gastrointestinal tract, decreasing its effectiveness.

5. Calcium, tolbutamide, and reserpine can increase the side effects of digoxin.

6. Diuretics (water pills) and adrenocorticosteroids (cortisonelike medications) can cause hypokalemia (low blood levels of potassium), and hypokalemia can increase the side effects of digoxin.

BE SURE TO TELL YOUR DOCTOR about any medications you are currently taking—including over-the-counter products—especially any of those listed above.

WARNINGS

• Tell your doctor about unusual or allergic reactions you have had to any medications, especially to digoxin, digitoxin, or any other digitalis glycoside.

• Tell your doctor if you now have or if you have ever had kidney disease, lung disease, thyroid disease, hypokalemia (low blood levels of potassium), or hypercalcemia (high blood levels of calcium).

• The pharmacologic activity of the different brands of this drug varies widely—the tablets dissolve in the stomach and bowel at different rates and to varying degrees. Because of this variability, it is important not to change brands of the drug without consulting your doctor.

• Meals high in bran fiber may reduce the absorption of digoxin from the gastrointestinal tract. Avoid these types of meals when taking your dose of medication.

• Your doctor may want you to take your pulse daily while you are using digoxin. Contact your doctor if your pulse becomes slower than what your doctor tells you is normal, or if it drops below 50 beats per minute.

• Before having surgery or any other medical or dental treatment, be sure to tell your doctor or dentist that you are taking this medication.

• Before taking any over-the-counter (nonprescription) asthma, allergy, cough, cold, sinus, or diet product, be sure to check with your doctor or pharmacist. Some of these drugs can increase the side effects of digoxin.

• Be sure to tell your doctor if you are pregnant. Although this drug appears to be safe during pregnancy, extensive studies in humans have not been conducted. In addition, the dosage of digoxin required to control your symptoms may change during pregnancy. Also tell your doctor if you are breast-feeding an infant. Small amounts of digoxin pass into breast milk.

diltiazem

BRAND NAMES (Manufacturers)
Cardizem (Marion-Merrell Dow)
Cardizem CD (Marion-Merrell Dow)
Cardizem SR (Marion-Merrell Dow)
TYPE OF DRUG
Antianginal and antihypertensive
INGREDIENT
diltiazem
DOSAGE FORMS
Extended-release capsules (180 mg, 240 mg, and 300 mg)
Tablets (30 mg, 60 mg, 90 mg, and 120 mg)
Sustained-release capsules (60 mg, 90 mg, and 120 mg)
STORAGE
Diltiazem should be stored at room temperature in a tightly
closed container.

USES

This medication is used to prevent the symptoms of angina
(chest pain). It belongs to a group of drugs known as calcium
channel blockers. It is unclear exactly how it does so, but diltiazem dilates the blood vessels of the heart and increases the
amount of oxygen that reaches the heart muscle. This drug is
also prescribed to lower blood pressure in patients who have
a history of hypertension.

TREATMENT

If stomach irritation occurs, diltiazem can be taken either on
an empty stomach or with meals, as directed by your doctor.
The sustained-release and extended-release capsules should be
swallowed whole; chewing, crushing, or crumbling them destroys their controlled-release activity and possibly increases
the side effects.

In order to become accustomed to taking this medication, try
to take it at the same times each day.

Although diltiazem does not relieve chest pain once the
pain has begun, this medication can be used to prevent angina
attacks.

If you miss a dose of this medication, take the missed dose
as soon as possible, unless it is within four hours of the next

scheduled dose. In that case, do not take the missed dose at all; just return to your regular dosing schedule. Do not double the next dose.

This medication does not cure angina, but it will help to control the condition as long as you continue to take it.

SIDE EFFECTS

Minor. Constipation, diarrhea, dizziness, drowsiness, headache, insomnia, light-headedness, nausea, nervousness, stomach upset, or vomiting. These side effects should disappear as your body adjusts to the medication.

This drug can increase your sensitivity to sunlight. Therefore, avoid prolonged exposure to sunlight and sunlamps. Wear protective clothing and sunglasses, and use an effective sunscreen.

If you feel dizzy or light-headed, sit or lie down for a while; get up slowly from a sitting or reclining position; and be careful on stairs. To avoid dizziness when you stand, relax and contract the muscles of your legs for a few moments before rising. Do this by pushing one foot against the floor while raising the other foot slightly, alternating feet so that you are "pumping" your legs in a pedaling motion.

To relieve constipation, increase the amount of fiber in your diet (fresh fruits and vegetables, salads, bran, and whole-grain breads), exercise, and drink more water (unless your doctor directs you to do otherwise).

Major. Tell your doctor about any side effects that are persistent or particularly bothersome. IT IS ESPECIALLY IMPORTANT TO TELL YOUR DOCTOR about confusion, depression, fainting, fatigue, flushing, fluid retention, hallucinations, palpitations, skin rash, tingling in the fingers or toes, unusual weakness, or yellowing of the eyes or skin.

INTERACTIONS

Diltiazem can interact with several other medications:

1. Diltiazem should be used cautiously with beta blockers (acebutolol, atenolol, betaxolol, carteolol, esmolol, labetalol, metoprolol, nadolol, penbutolol, propranolol, pindolol, and timolol), digitoxin, digoxin, or disopyramide. Side effects on the heart may be increased by the concurrent use of these medications.

2. Cimetidine can reduce the elimination of diltiazem from the body, increasing the risk of side effects.

3. Diltiazem can increase the blood concentrations of carbamazepine and cyclosporine, which can increase the risk of side effects.

BE SURE TO TELL YOUR DOCTOR about any medications you are currently taking, especially any listed above.

WARNINGS

• Tell your doctor about unusual or allergic reactions you have had to any medications, especially to diltiazem.

• Be sure to tell your doctor if you now have or if you have ever had bradycardia (slow heartbeat), heart block, heart failure, kidney disease, liver disease, low blood pressure, or sick sinus syndrome.

• If this drug makes you dizzy or drowsy, avoid taking part in any activity that requires alertness, such as driving a car or operating potentially dangerous equipment.

• To prevent fainting while taking this drug, avoid drinking large amounts of alcohol. Also avoid prolonged standing and strenuous exercise in hot weather.

• Be sure to tell your doctor if you are pregnant. Extensive studies in pregnant women have not been conducted, but birth defects have been reported in the offspring of animals that received large doses of diltiazem during pregnancy. It is also known that diltiazem passes into breast milk. If you are breast-feeding an infant while being treated with this medication, tell your doctor. Unless directed to do otherwise, breast-feeding is not recommended at this time.

diphenhydramine

BRAND NAMES (Manufacturers)
AllerMax (Pfeiffer)
Belix* (Halsey)
Benadryl* (Parke-Davis)
Benadryl Kapseals (Parke-Davis)
Benylin Cough Syrup* (Parke-Davis)
Bydramine Cough Syrup* (Major)
Compoz* (Jeffrey Martin)
Diphen Cough Syrup* (My-K Lab)

diphenhydramine hydrochloride (various manufacturers)
Dormarex 2* (Republic)
Hydramine* (Goldline)
Nervine Nighttime Sleep Aid* (Miles)
Nordryl (Vortech)
Nytol* (Block)
Sleep-Eze 3* (Whitehall)
Sominex 2* (SmithKline Beecham)
Twilite* (Pfeiffer)
Unisom Nighttime Sleep Aid* (Leeming)
*Available over the counter (without a prescription)

TYPE OF DRUG
Antihistamine and sedative/hypnotic

INGREDIENT
diphenhydramine

DOSAGE FORMS
Tablets (50 mg)
Capsules (25 mg and 50 mg)
Elixir (12.5 mg per 5-mL spoonful, with 14% alcohol)
Oral syrup (12.5 mg per 5-mL spoonful, with 5% alcohol)

STORAGE
Store at room temperature in a tightly closed container, away
from heat and direct sunlight.

USES

Diphenhydramine belongs to a group of drugs known as antihistamines (antihistamines block the action of histamine, a
chemical that is released by the body during an allergic reaction). It is therefore used to treat or prevent symptoms of
allergy. It is also used to treat motion sickness and Parkinson's
disease, as a nighttime sleeping aid, and as a nonnarcotic
cough suppressant.

TREATMENT

To avoid stomach upset, take diphenhydramine with food,
milk, or water (unless your doctor directs you otherwise).

The elixir and oral syrup forms of this medication should
be measured carefully with a specially designed 5-mL measuring spoon. An ordinary teaspoon is not accurate enough
for medical purposes.

If you miss a dose of this medication, take the missed dose
as soon as possible, unless it is almost time for your next dose.

In that case, do not take the missed dose at all; just return to your regular dosing schedule. Do not double the next dose.

SIDE EFFECTS

Minor. Blurred vision; confusion; constipation; diarrhea; dizziness; dry mouth, throat, or nose; headache; irritability; loss of appetite; nausea; restlessness; stomach upset; or unusual increase in sweating. These side effects should disappear as your body adjusts to the medication.

This medication can cause increased sensitivity to sunlight. It is, therefore, important to avoid prolonged exposure to sunlight and sunlamps. Wear protective clothing and sunglasses, and use an effective sunscreen.

If you are constipated, increase the amount of fiber in your diet (fresh fruits and vegetables, salads, bran, and whole-grain breads), exercise, and drink more water (unless your doctor tells you not to do so).

To reduce mouth dryness, chew sugarless gum or suck on ice chips or a piece of hard candy.

If you feel dizzy or light-headed, sit or lie down for a while; get up slowly from a sitting or reclining position; and be careful on stairs.

Major. Tell your doctor about any side effects that are persistent or particularly bothersome. IT IS ESPECIALLY IMPORTANT TO TELL YOUR DOCTOR about changes in menstruation, clumsiness, difficult or painful urination, feeling faint, flushing of the face, hallucinations, palpitations, rash, ringing or buzzing in the ears, seizures, shortness of breath, sleeping disorders, sore throat or fever, tightness in the chest, unusual bleeding or bruising, or unusual tiredness or weakness.

INTERACTIONS

Diphenhydramine interacts with several other types of medications:

1. Concurrent use of diphenhydramine with other central nervous system depressants (for example, alcohol, barbiturates, benzodiazepine tranquilizers, muscle relaxants, narcotics, pain medications, and phenothiazine tranquilizers) or with tricyclic antidepressants can cause extreme fatigue or drowsiness.

2. Monoamine oxidase (MAO) inhibitors (isocarboxazid, pargyline, phenelzine, and tranylcypromine) can increase the side effects of this medication. At least 14 days should separate the use of this drug and the use of an MAO inhibitor.

3. Diphenhydramine can also interfere with the activity of oral anticoagulants (blood thinners, such as warfarin) and decrease their effectiveness.

BE SURE TO TELL YOUR DOCTOR about any medications you are currently taking, especially any of those listed above.

WARNINGS

• Be sure to tell your doctor about unusual or allergic reactions you have had to any medications, especially to diphenhydramine or to any other antihistamine (such as astemizole, azatadine, brompheniramine, carbinoxamine, chlorpheniramine, clemastine, cyproheptadine, dexchlorpheniramine, dimenhydrinate, dimethindene, diphenylpyraline, doxylamine, hydroxyzine, phenindamine, promethazine, pyrilamine, terfenadine, trimeprazine, tripelennamine, and triprolidine).

• Tell your doctor if you now have or if you have ever had asthma, blood vessel disease, glaucoma, high blood pressure, kidney disease, peptic ulcers, enlarged prostate gland, or thyroid disease.

• Diphenhydramine can cause drowsiness or dizziness. Your ability to perform tasks that require alertness, such as driving an automobile or operating potentially dangerous equipment or machinery, may be decreased. Appropriate caution should, therefore, be taken.

• Be sure to tell your doctor if you are pregnant. The effects of this medication during pregnancy have not been thoroughly studied in humans. Also be sure that you consult with your doctor if you are breast-feeding an infant. Small amounts of diphenhydramine pass into breast milk and may cause unusual excitement or irritability in nursing infants.

diphenoxylate and atropine combination

BRAND NAMES (Manufacturers)
Diphenatol (Rugby)
diphenoxylate hydrochloride with atropine sulfate
   (various manufacturers)

Lofene (Lannett)
Logen (Goldline)
Lomanate (Barre)
Lomotil (Searle)
Lonox (Geneva Generics)
Low-Quel (Halsey)

TYPE OF DRUG

Antidiarrheal (antispasmodic and anticholinergic)

INGREDIENTS

diphenoxylate and atropine

DOSAGE FORMS

Tablets (2.5 mg diphenoxylate and 0.025 mg atropine)
Oral liquid (2.5 mg diphenoxylate and 0.025 mg atropine
  per 5-mL spoonful, with 15% alcohol)

STORAGE

Diphenoxylate and atropine combination tablets and oral liquid should be stored at room temperature in tightly closed, light-resistant containers. Neither form should be frozen.

USES

Diphenoxylate and atropine combination is used to treat severe diarrhea. Diphenoxylate is related to the narcotic analgesics and acts by slowing the movement of the gastrointestinal tract. Small amounts of atropine are added to this medication in order to prevent abuse of the narcotic diphenoxylate.

TREATMENT

In order to avoid getting an upset stomach, you can take this medication with food or with a full glass of water or milk.

The oral liquid form of this medication should be measured carefully using a specially designed 5-mL measuring spoon. An ordinary kitchen teaspoon is not accurate enough.

If you miss a dose of this medication, do not take the missed dose at all; just return to your regular dosing schedule. Do not double the next dose.

SIDE EFFECTS

Minor. Blurred vision, constipation, dizziness, drowsiness, dry mouth, flushing, headache, loss of appetite, nervousness, sweating, or swollen gums. These side effects should disappear as your body adjusts to the medication.

To relieve mouth dryness, chew sugarless gum or suck on ice chips or a piece of hard candy.

If you feel dizzy or light-headed, sit or lie down for a while; get up slowly from a sitting or reclining position; and be careful on stairs.

Major. Tell your doctor about any side effects that are persistent or particularly bothersome. IT IS ESPECIALLY IMPORTANT TO TELL YOUR DOCTOR about abdominal pain, bloating, breathing difficulties, depression, difficult or painful urination, false sense of well-being, fever, hives, itching, numbness in the fingers or toes, palpitations, rash, severe nausea, vomiting, or weakness.

INTERACTIONS

This drug combination interacts with several other types of medications:

1. Concurrent use of this medication with central nervous system depressants (such as alcohol, antihistamines, barbiturates, benzodiazepine tranquilizers, muscle relaxants, narcotics, pain medications, and phenothiazine tranquilizers) or with tricyclic antidepressants can cause extreme drowsiness.

2. A monoamine oxidase (MAO) inhibitor (tranylcypromine, phenelzine, isocarboxazid, and pargyline) taken within 14 days of this medication can lead to unpredictable and severe side effects.

3. The side effects of the atropine component of this medication may be increased by amantadine, haloperidol, phenothiazine tranquilizers, procainamide, and quinidine.

BE SURE TO TELL YOUR DOCTOR about any medications you are currently taking, especially any of those listed above.

WARNINGS

• Tell your doctor about unusual or allergic reactions you have had to medications, especially to diphenoxylate or to atropine.

• Tell your doctor if you now have or if you have ever had drug-induced diarrhea, gallstones or gallbladder disease, glaucoma, heart disease, hiatal hernia, high blood pressure, kidney disease, liver disease, lung disease, myasthenia gravis, enlarged prostate gland, thyroid disease, or ulcerative colitis.

• If this medication makes you dizzy or drowsy, you should avoid taking part in any activity that requires alertness, such as driving a car or operating any potentially dangerous equipment.

• Before having surgery or any other medical or dental treatment, be sure to tell your doctor or dentist that you are taking this medication.

• Because this product contains diphenoxylate, it has the potential for abuse and must be used with caution. Tolerance develops quickly; do not increase the dosage or stop taking the drug unless you first consult your doctor. If you have been taking large amounts of this medication for long periods and then stop abruptly, you may experience a withdrawal reaction (muscle aches, diarrhea, gooseflesh, runny nose, nausea, vomiting, shivering, trembling, stomach cramps, sleep disorders, irritability, weakness, excessive yawning, or sweating). Your doctor may, therefore, want to reduce the dosage gradually.

• Check with your doctor if your diarrhea does not subside within two to three days. Unless your doctor specifically directs otherwise, you should not take this medication for more than five days.

• While taking this medication, drink lots of fluids to replace those lost with the diarrhea.

• Be sure to tell your doctor if you are pregnant. Although this medication has been shown to be safe in animals, its effects in humans during pregnancy have not been thoroughly studied. Also tell your doctor if you are breast-feeding an infant. Small amounts of this medication may pass into breast milk and cause excessive drowsiness in nursing infants.

dipyridamole

BRAND NAMES (Manufacturers)
dipyridamole (various manufacturers)
Persantine (Boehringer Ingelheim)
Pyridamole (Major)
TYPE OF DRUG
Antianginal
INGREDIENT
dipyridamole
DOSAGE FORM
Tablets (25 mg, 50 mg, and 75 mg)

STORAGE
Store at room temperature in a tightly closed container.

USES
Dipyridamole is primarily used to prevent blood clot formation, especially in patients who have artificial heart valves. Dipyridamole has also been used to prevent chronic chest pain (angina) due to heart disease. It relieves chest pain by dilating the blood vessels of the heart and providing more oxygen to the heart muscle.

TREATMENT
You should take this medication on an empty stomach with a full glass of water one hour before or two hours after a meal. If this drug upsets your stomach, check with your doctor to see if you can take it with food.

The full benefits of this medication may not become apparent for up to two to three months.

If you miss a dose of this medication, take the missed dose as soon as possible, unless it is within four hours of your next scheduled dose. In that case, do not take the missed dose at all; just return to your regular dosing schedule. Do not double the next dose.

SIDE EFFECTS
Minor. Dizziness, fatigue, flushing, headache, nausea, stomach cramps, or weakness. These side effects should disappear as your body adjusts to the medication.

To avoid dizziness or light-headedness when you stand, contract and relax the muscles of your legs for a few moments before rising. Do this by pushing one foot against the floor while raising the other foot slightly, alternating feet so that you are "pumping" your legs in a pedaling motion.

Major. Tell your doctor about any side effects that are persistent or particularly bothersome. IT IS ESPECIALLY IMPORTANT TO TELL YOUR DOCTOR about fainting, skin rash, or a worsening of your chest pain.

INTERACTIONS
Dipyridamole should not interact with other medications if it is used according to directions.

WARNINGS

• Tell your doctor about unusual or allergic reactions you have had to any medications, especially to dipyridamole.

• Tell your doctor if you have ever had low blood pressure.

• The effectiveness of dipyridamole in controlling chronic angina is controversial. At one time, dipyridamole was indicated as "possibly effective" for long-term therapy of chronic angina, but the Food and Drug Administration (FDA) withdrew its approval for this use. Today, this drug is more frequently prescribed to prevent blood-clot formation.

• This drug does not stop chest pain from angina that has already begun. It is used only to prevent such pain.

• If this drug makes you dizzy, do not take part in any activity that requires alertness, such as driving an automobile or operating potentially dangerous equipment or machinery.

• Before having any surgery or other medical or dental treatment, be sure to tell your doctor or dentist that you are taking this medication.

• Be sure to tell your doctor if you are pregnant. Although this drug appears to be safe, extensive studies in humans during pregnancy have not been conducted. Also consult with your doctor if you are breast-feeding an infant. Small amounts of dipyridamole have been known to pass into breast milk, so caution is warranted.

disulfiram

BRAND NAMES (Manufacturers)
Antabuse (Wyeth-Ayerst)
disulfiram (various manufacturers)
TYPE OF DRUG
Antialcoholic
INGREDIENT
disulfiram
DOSAGE FORM
Tablets (250 mg and 500 mg)
STORAGE
Disulfiram should be stored at room temperature in a tightly closed, light-resistant container.

USES

Disulfiram is used as an aid to treat alcoholics who are strongly motivated to remain sober. Disulfiram blocks the breakdown of alcohol by the body, leading to an accumulation of the chemical acetaldehyde in the bloodstream. Buildup of acetaldehyde in the body can lead to a severe and very unpleasant reaction after alcohol consumption. Alcohol must be avoided to prevent this reaction.

TREATMENT

Disulfiram can be taken either on an empty stomach or with food or milk (as directed by your doctor). The tablets can also be crushed and mixed with most beverages, but not with those that contain alcohol.

If you miss a dose of this medication, take the missed dose as soon as possible, unless it is almost time for the next dose. In that case, do not take the missed dose at all; just return to your regular dosing schedule. Do not double the next dose.

SIDE EFFECTS

Minor. Drowsiness, fatigue, headache, metallic or garliclike aftertaste, and restlessness. These side effects should disappear as your body adjusts to the medication.

Major. Tell your doctor about any side effects that are persistent or particularly bothersome. IT IS ESPECIALLY IMPORTANT TO TELL YOUR DOCTOR about blurred vision, impotence, joint pain, mental disorders, skin rash, tingling sensations, or yellowing of the eyes or skin.

INTERACTIONS

Disulfiram interacts with several other types of medications:
1. It can increase the blood levels and side effects of diazepam, chlordiazepoxide, phenytoin, and oral anticoagulants (blood thinners, such as warfarin).
2. Concurrent use of disulfiram with isoniazid, antidepressants, metronidazole, or marijuana can lead to severe reactions.

BE SURE TO TELL YOUR DOCTOR about any medications you are currently taking, especially any of those listed above. Also be sure to tell your doctor if you use marijuana.

WARNINGS

• Tell your doctor about unusual or allergic reactions you have had to rubber or to any medications, especially to disulfiram, pesticides, or fungicides.

• Before starting to take this medication, be sure to tell your doctor if you have ever had brain damage, dermatitis, diabetes mellitus, epilepsy, heart disease, kidney disease, liver disease, mental disorders, or thyroid disease.

• It is important not to drink or to use any alcohol-containing preparations, medications, or foods (including beer, elixirs, tonics, wine, liquor, vinegar, sauces, after-shave lotions, liniments, or colognes) while taking this medication. Be sure to check the labels on any over-the-counter (nonprescription) products for their alcohol content, especially cough syrups, mouthwashes, and gargles.

• It is important that you understand the serious nature of the disulfiram-alcohol reaction. If you take disulfiram within 12 hours after ingesting alcohol or drink alcohol within two weeks after your last dose of disulfiram, you may experience blurred vision, chest pain, confusion, dizziness, fainting, flushing, headache, nausea, pounding heartbeat, sweating, vomiting, or weakness. The reaction usually occurs within five to ten minutes of drinking alcohol and can last from half an hour to two hours, depending on the dose of disulfiram and the quantity of alcohol ingested.

• If this drug makes you drowsy, do not take part in any activity that requires alertness, such as driving an automobile or operating potentially dangerous machinery or equipment. Be careful when going up and down stairs.

• Be sure to tell your doctor if you are pregnant. Birth defects have been reported in both animals and humans whose mothers received disulfiram during pregnancy. It must also be kept in mind that alcohol, even in small amounts, can cause a variety of birth defects when ingested during pregnancy. Also tell your doctor if you are breast-feeding an infant. It is not known if disulfiram passes into breast milk.

dorzolamide

BRAND NAME (Manufacturer)
Trusopt (Merck)

TYPE OF DRUG
Carbonic anhydrase inhibitor
INGREDIENT
dorzolamide
DOSAGE FORM
Ophthalmic solution 2%
STORAGE
Dorzolamide should be stored at room temperature in tightly closed, light-resistant containers. Never freeze this medication. Be sure to discard any outdated or unneeded medication, and store all drugs out of the reach of children and pets.

USES
Dorzolamide is used in the treatment of glaucoma and ocular hypertension.

TREATMENT
Wash your hands with soap and water before applying this medication. In order to avoid contamination of the eye drops, be careful not to touch the tube portion of the dropper or let it touch your eye; and DO NOT wipe off or rinse the dropper after each use.

To apply the eye drops, tilt your head back and pull down your lower eyelid with one hand to make a pouch below the eye. Drop the prescribed amount of medicine into this pouch and slowly close your eyes. Try not to blink. Keep your eyes closed, and place one finger at the corner of the eye next to your nose for a minute or two, applying slight pressure (this is done to prevent loss of the medication through the duct that drains fluid from the surface of the eye into the nose and throat). Then wipe away any excess with a clean tissue. Since the drops are somewhat difficult to apply, you may want someone else to apply them for you.

If more than one type of eye drop has been prescribed for you, wait at least ten minutes before applying the second eye medication.

If you miss a dose of dorzolamide, apply the missed dose as soon as possible, unless it is almost time for the next dose. In that case, do not attempt to administer the missed dose at all; just return to your regular dosing schedule. Do not double the next dose.

SIDE EFFECTS

Minor. Blurred vision, burning sensation in the eyes, headache, stinging or bitter taste in the mouth immediately following application. These side effects should lessen as your body adjusts to the medication.

Major. Tell your doctor about any side effects that are persistent or particularly bothersome. IT IS ESPECIALLY IMPORTANT TO TELL YOUR DOCTOR about allergic reactions, blurred vision, eye pain, fatigue, fever, muscle cramps, severe itching of the eyes, skin rash, unusual bleeding or bruising, or yellowing of the eyes or skin.

INTERACTIONS

Although no significant interactions have been seen with dorzolamide, other drugs of this type interact with other medications. Specifically, high doses of salicylates (aspirin, methyl salicylate) may increase the side effects of carbonic anhydrase inhibitors.

BE SURE TO TELL YOUR DOCTOR about any medications you are taking, especially any of those listed above.

WARNINGS

• Tell your doctor about any unusual or allergic reactions you have had to any medications, especially to dorzolamide, acetazolamide, methazolamide, sulfonamide antibiotics, diuretics (water pills), oral antidiabetics, dapsone, sulfone, or sulfoxone.

• Before starting this medication, be sure to tell your doctor if you now have or if you have ever had Addison's disease (underactive adrenal gland), chronic lung disease, diabetes mellitus, electrolyte disorders, gout, kidney disease, or liver disease.

• If this medication blurs your vision, try to avoid activities that require visual acuity, such as driving a car or operating potentially dangerous equipment.

• The preservative in dorzolamide (benzalkonium chloride) may be absorbed by soft contact lenses. Therefore, this medication should not be used while wearing soft contact lenses.

• Be sure to tell your doctor if you are pregnant. Although extensive studies of dorzolamide in humans have not been conducted, dorzolamide has been shown to cause side effects in the fetuses of animals that received large doses of the drug during pregnancy. Also tell your doctor if you are breast-feeding an infant. It is not known if this medication passes into breast milk.

---

doxazosin

BRAND NAME (Manufacturer)
Cardura (Roerig)
TYPE OF DRUG
Antihypertensive
INGREDIENT
doxazosin
DOSAGE FORM
Tablets (1 mg, 2 mg, 4 mg, and 8 mg)
STORAGE
Store doxazoxin at room temperature in a tightly closed container.

USES

Doxazosin mesylate is used to treat high blood pressure. It relaxes the muscle tissue of the blood vessels, which in turn lowers blood pressure. Doxazosin is also used to reduce urinary obstruction and relieve associated symptoms of benign prostatic hypertrophy (BPH).

TREATMENT

The first dose of this medication may cause fainting, especially in the elderly.

If you miss a dose of this medication, take it as soon as possible, unless it is almost time for your next dose. In that case, do not take the missed dose at all; just wait until the next scheduled dose. Do not double the dose.

This medication does not cure high blood pressure, but it will help to control the condition as long as you continue to take it. In order to become accustomed to taking this medication, try to take it at the same time(s) each day.

SIDE EFFECTS

Minor. Breast pain, constipation, diarrhea, dizziness, drowsiness, edema, frequent urination, headache, itching, lack of energy, malaise, nasal congestion, nausea, nervousness, rash, sweating, or weight gain. These side effects should disappear as your body adjusts to the medication. TELL YOUR DOCTOR if skin reactions or other side effects persist or become bothersome.

To prevent constipation, increase the amount of fiber in your diet (fresh fruits and vegetables, salads, bran, and whole-grain breads), unless your doctor tells you otherwise.

To avoid dizziness or light-headedness when you stand, contract and relax the muscles of your legs for a few moments before rising. Do this by pushing one foot against the floor while raising the other foot slightly, alternating feet so that you are "pumping" your legs in a pedaling motion.

Major. Tell your doctor about any side effects that are persistent or particularly bothersome. IT IS ESPECIALLY IMPORTANT TO TELL YOUR DOCTOR about blurred vision; chest pain; difficulty breathing; difficulty urinating; edema; fever; flulike syndrome; heart rate disturbance; nose bleeds; palpitations; persistent malaise/fatigue; postural effects (dizziness, light-headedness, vertigo leading to reductions in blood pressure or fainting); or ringing in the ears.

INTERACTIONS

Doxazosin has been known to interact with other types of medications:

1. The combination of doxazosin and alcohol or verapamil can bring about a severe drop in blood pressure and cause fainting.

2. The severity and duration of the blood-pressure-lowering effects of the initial dose of doxazosin may be enhanced by a beta blocker.

BE SURE TO TELL YOUR DOCTOR about any medications you are currently taking, especially those listed above.

WARNINGS

• Tell your doctor about unusual or allergic reactions you have had to any medications, especially to doxazosin, prazosin, or terazosin.

• Before starting to take this medication, be sure to tell your doctor if you now have or if you have ever had angina (chest pain) or any kind of kidney disease or liver disease.

• Because initial therapy with this drug may cause dizziness or fainting, your doctor will probably start you on a low dosage and increase the dosage gradually.

• If this drug makes you dizzy or drowsy or blurs your vision, do not take part in any activity that requires alertness, such as driving an automobile or operating potentially dangerous machinery.

• In order to avoid dizziness or fainting while taking this drug, try not to stand for long periods of time, avoid drinking excess amounts of alcohol, and try not to get overheated (avoid exercising strenuously in hot weather and taking hot baths, showers, and saunas).

• Before taking any over-the-counter (nonprescription) sinus, allergy, asthma, cough, cold, or diet preparations, check with your doctor or pharmacist. Some of these products can cause an increase in blood pressure.

• Do not stop taking this medication unless you first check with your doctor. If you stop taking this drug, you may experience a rise in blood pressure. Your doctor may want to decrease your dose gradually.

• Be sure to tell your doctor if you are pregnant. Although the drug appears to be safe, only limited studies have been conducted with pregnant women. Also tell your doctor if you are breast-feeding an infant. Doxazosin should be used with caution in nursing women.

---

doxepin

BRAND NAMES (Manufacturers)
Adapin (Pennwalt)
doxepin (various manufacturers)
Sinequan (Fisons)
TYPE OF DRUG
Tricyclic antidepressant
INGREDIENT
doxepin
DOSAGE FORMS
Capsules (10 mg, 25 mg, 50 mg, 75 mg, 100 mg, and 150 mg)
Oral concentrate (10 mg per mL)

STORAGE

Doxepin capsules and oral concentrate should be stored at room temperature in tightly closed containers. This medication should never be frozen.

USES

Doxepin is used to relieve the symptoms of mental depression. This medication belongs to a group of drugs referred to as tricyclic antidepressants. These medicines are thought to relieve depression by increasing the concentration of certain chemicals necessary for nerve transmission in the brain.

TREATMENT

This medication should be taken exactly as your doctor prescribes. You can take it with food to lessen the chance of stomach irritation (unless your doctor tells you to do otherwise).

Each dose of the oral concentrate should be diluted in at least four ounces (half a glass) of water, milk, or fruit juice just prior to administration. Measure the correct amount carefully with the dropper provided. DO NOT mix the medication with grape juice or with carbonated beverages, since they may decrease the medicine's effectiveness.

If you miss a dose of this medication, take the missed dose as soon as possible, then return to your regular dosing schedule. If the dose you missed was a once-a-day bedtime dose, do not take that dose in the morning; check with your doctor instead. If the dose is taken in the morning, it may cause some unwanted side effects. Never double the dose.

The antidepressant effects of therapy with this medication may not become apparent for two or three weeks.

SIDE EFFECTS

Minor. Blurred vision, constipation, cramps, diarrhea, dizziness, drowsiness, dry mouth, fatigue, indigestion, insomnia, loss of appetite, nausea, peculiar tastes in the mouth, restlessness, sweating, vomiting, weakness, or weight gain or loss. As your body adjusts to the medication, these side effects should disappear.

This drug may cause increased sensitivity to sunlight. Therefore, avoid prolonged exposure to sunlight and sunlamps. Wear protective clothing and use an effective sunscreen.

Dry mouth can be relieved by chewing sugarless gum or by sucking on ice chips or a piece of hard candy.

To relieve constipation, increase the amount of fiber in your diet (fresh fruits and vegetables, salads, bran, and whole-grain breads), exercise, and drink more water (unless your doctor directs you to do otherwise).

To avoid dizziness or light-headedness when you stand, contract and relax the muscles of your legs for a few moments before rising. Do this by pushing one foot against the floor while raising the other foot slightly, alternating feet so that you are "pumping" your legs in a pedaling motion.

Major. Tell your doctor about any side effects that are persistent or particularly bothersome. IT IS ESPECIALLY IMPORTANT TO TELL YOUR DOCTOR about agitation, anxiety, chest pain, confusion, convulsions, difficulty in urinating, enlarged or painful breasts (in both sexes), fainting, fever, fluid retention, hair loss, hallucinations, headaches, impotence, mood changes, mouth sores, nervousness, nightmares, numbness in the fingers or toes, palpitations, ringing in the ears, seizures, skin rash, sleep disorders, sore throat, a tendency to bleed or bruise, tremors, uncoordinated movements or balance problems, or yellowing of the eyes or skin.

INTERACTIONS

Doxepin interacts with a number of other types of medications:

1. Extreme drowsiness can occur when this medicine is taken with central nervous system depressants (such as alcohol, antihistamines, barbiturates, benzodiazepine tranquilizers, muscle relaxants, narcotics, pain medications, phenothiazine tranquilizers, and medications to induce sleep) or with other antidepressants.

2. Doxepin may decrease the effectiveness of antiseizure medications and may block the blood-pressure-lowering effects of clonidine and guanethidine.

3. Oral contraceptives (birth control pills) and estrogen-containing drugs can increase the side effects and reduce the effectiveness of the tricyclic antidepressants (including doxepin).

4. Cimetidine can decrease the elimination of doxepin from the body, which can increase the possibility that side effects will occur.

5. Tricyclic antidepressants may increase the side effects of thyroid medications and over-the-counter (nonprescription) cough, cold, allergy, asthma, sinus, and diet medications.
6. The concurrent use of this drug and monoamine oxidase (MAO) inhibitors should be avoided, because the combination may result in fever, convulsions, or high blood pressure. At least 14 days should separate the use of this drug and the use of an MAO inhibitor.

BE SURE TO TELL YOUR DOCTOR about any medications you are currently taking, especially any of those listed above.

WARNINGS

• Tell your doctor if you have had unusual or allergic reactions to any medications, especially to doxepin or any of the other tricyclic antidepressants (amitriptyline, imipramine, trimipramine, amoxapine, protriptyline, desipramine, maprotiline, and nortriptyline).
• Be sure to tell your doctor if you have a history of alcoholism or if you have ever had asthma, high blood pressure, liver or kidney disease, heart disease, a heart attack, circulatory disease, stomach problems, intestinal problems, difficulty in urinating, enlarged prostate gland, epilepsy, glaucoma, thyroid disease, mental illness, or electroshock therapy.
• If this drug makes you dizzy or drowsy, do not take part in any activity that requires alertness, such as driving a car or operating potentially dangerous equipment.
• Before having surgery or any other medical or dental treatment, be sure to tell your doctor or dentist that you are taking this medication.
• Do not stop taking this drug suddenly. Abruptly stopping it can cause nausea, headache, stomach upset, fatigue, or a worsening of your condition. Your doctor may want to reduce the dosage gradually.
• The effects of this medication may last as long as seven days after you have stopped taking it, so continue to observe all precautions during that period.
• Be sure to tell your doctor if you are pregnant. The effects of this drug during pregnancy have not been thoroughly studied in humans. Studies in animals have shown that this medication can cause side effects to the fetus if given to the mother in large doses during pregnancy. Also tell your doctor if you are breast-feeding an infant. Small amounts of this drug can pass

into breast milk and may cause unwanted effects in the nursing infant.

---

doxycycline

BRAND NAMES (Manufacturers)
Doryx (Parke-Davis)
Doxy-Caps (Edwards)
Doxychel Hyclate (Rachelle)
doxycycline (various manufacturers)
Vibramycin Hyclate (Pfizer)
Vibra Tabs (Pfizer)
TYPE OF DRUG
Tetracycline antibiotic
INGREDIENT
doxycycline
DOSAGE FORMS
Tablets (50 mg and 100 mg)
Capsules (50 mg and 100 mg)
Capsules, coated pellets (100 mg)
Oral suspension (25 mg per 5-mL spoonful)
Oral syrup (50 mg per 5-mL spoonful)
STORAGE
Doxycycline tablets, capsules, oral suspension, and oral syrup should be stored at room temperature in tightly closed, light-resistant containers. Any unused portion of the suspension form should be discarded after 14 days because the drug loses its potency after that period. This medication should never be frozen.

USES

Doxycycline is used to treat a wide variety of bacterial infections and to prevent or treat traveler's diarrhea. It acts by inhibiting the growth of bacteria.

Doxycycline kills susceptible bacteria, but it is not effective against viruses or fungi.

TREATMENT

To avoid stomach upset, you can take this drug with food (unless your doctor directs you to do otherwise).

The suspension should be shaken well just before measuring each dose. The contents tend to settle on the bottom of the bottle, so it is necessary to shake the container to distribute the ingredients evenly and equalize the doses. Each dose of the oral suspension or oral syrup should be measured carefully with a specially designed 5-mL measuring spoon. An ordinary teaspoon is not accurate enough for this purpose.

Do not mix the oral syrup form of this drug with other substances unless so directed by your doctor.

Doxycycline works best when the level of medicine in your bloodstream is kept constant. It is best, therefore, to take the doses at evenly spaced intervals day and night. For example, if you are to take two doses a day, the doses should be spaced 12 hours apart.

If you miss a dose of this medication, take the missed dose immediately. However, if you do not remember to take the missed dose until it is almost time for your next dose, take it; space the following dose about halfway through the regular interval between doses; then return to your regular dosing schedule. Try not to skip any doses.

It is very important that you take this drug for the entire time prescribed, even if the symptoms disappear before the end of that period. If you stop taking the drug too soon, resistant bacteria can continue to grow, and the infection could recur.

SIDE EFFECTS

Minor. Diarrhea, discoloration of the nails, dizziness, loss of appetite, nausea, stomach cramps and upset, or vomiting. These side effects should disappear as your body adjusts to the medication.

Doxycycline can increase your sensitivity to sunlight. You should, therefore, try to avoid prolonged exposure to sunlight and sunlamps. Wear protective clothing and sunglasses, and use an effective sunscreen.

Major. Tell your doctor about any side effects that are persistent or particularly bothersome. IT IS ESPECIALLY IMPORTANT TO TELL YOUR DOCTOR about darkened tongue, difficulty in breathing, joint pain, mouth irritation, rash, rectal or vaginal itching, sore throat and fever, unusual bleeding or bruising, or yellowing of the eyes or skin. If your symptoms of infection seem to be getting worse rather than improving, you should contact your doctor.

INTERACTIONS
Doxycycline interacts with other types of medications:
1. It can increase the absorption of digoxin, which may lead to digoxin toxicity.
2. The gastrointestinal side effects (nausea, vomiting, stomach upset) of theophylline may be increased by doxycycline.
3. The dosage of oral anticoagulants (blood thinners, such as warfarin) may need to be adjusted when this medication is started.
4. Doxycycline may decrease the effectiveness of oral contraceptives (birth control pills), and pregnancy could result. You should, therefore, use a different or additional form of birth control while taking doxycycline. Discuss this with your doctor.
5. Barbiturates, carbamazepine, phenytoin, and antacids can lower the blood levels of doxycycline, decreasing its effectiveness.
6. Iron can bind to doxycycline in the gastrointestinal tract, which can decrease its absorption and, therefore, its effectiveness.
   BE SURE TO TELL YOUR DOCTOR about any medications you are currently taking, especially any of those listed above.

WARNINGS
• Tell your doctor about any unusual or allergic reactions you have or ever have had to any medications, especially to doxycycline, oxytetracycline, tetracycline, or minocycline.
• Tell your doctor if you now have or if you have ever had kidney or liver disease.
• Doxycycline can affect tests for syphilis; if you are also being treated for this disease, tell your doctor you are taking this medication.
• Make sure that your prescription for this medication is marked with the drug's expiration date. The drug should be discarded after the expiration date. If doxycycline is used after it has expired, serious side effects (especially to the kidneys) could result.
• This medication has been prescribed for your current infection only. Another infection later on, or one that someone

else has, may require a different medicine. You should not give your medicine to other people or use it for other infections, unless your doctor specifically directs you to do so.

• Be sure to tell your doctor if you are pregnant or if you are breast-feeding an infant. Doxycycline should not be used during pregnancy and breast-feeding. It crosses the placenta and passes into breast milk. This drug can cause permanent discoloration of the teeth and can inhibit tooth and bone growth if used during their development. This drug should not be used by children less than eight years of age.

---

enalapril

BRAND NAME (Manufacturer)
Vasotec (Merck Sharp & Dohme)
TYPE OF DRUG
Antihypertensive
INGREDIENT
enalapril
DOSAGE FORM
Tablets (2.5 mg, 5 mg, 10 mg, and 20 mg)
STORAGE
Store enalapril at room temperature in a tightly closed container.

USES

Enalapril is used to treat high blood pressure. It is a vasodilator (it widens the blood vessels) that acts by blocking the production of chemicals that may be responsible for constricting or narrowing the blood vessels.

TREATMENT

Enalapril can be taken either on an empty stomach or with food if it causes stomach irritation. To become accustomed to taking this medication, try to take it at the same time(s) every day.

It may be several weeks before you notice the full effects of this medication.

If you miss a dose of enalapril, take the missed dose as soon as possible, unless it is almost time for the next dose. In that case, do not take the missed dose at all; just wait until the next scheduled dose. Do not double the dose.

Enalapril does not cure high blood pressure, but it will help to control the condition as long as you continue to take it.

SIDE EFFECTS

Minor. Abdominal pain, cough, diarrhea, dizziness, drowsiness, fatigue, headache, heartburn, insomnia, nausea, nervousness, sweating, or vomiting. These side effects should disappear as your body adjusts to the medication.

To avoid dizziness when you stand, contract and relax the muscles of your legs for a few moments before rising. Do this by alternately pushing one foot against the floor while lifting the other foot slightly in a pedaling motion.

Major. Tell your doctor about any side effects that are persistent or particularly bothersome. IT IS ESPECIALLY IMPORTANT TO TELL YOUR DOCTOR about chest pain; difficulty in breathing; fainting; fever; itching; light-headedness (especially during the first few days); muscle cramps; palpitations; rash; sore throat; swelling of the face, eyes, lips, or tongue; tingling in the fingers or toes; or yellowing of the eyes or skin.

INTERACTIONS

Enalapril interacts with several other types of medications:
1. Diuretics (water pills) and other antihypertensive medications can cause an excessive drop in blood pressure when they are combined with enalapril (especially with the first dose).
2. The combination of enalapril with spironolactone, triamterene, amiloride, potassium supplements, or salt substitutes can lead to hyperkalemia (dangerously high levels of potassium in the bloodstream).

Before starting to take enalapril, BE SURE TO TELL YOUR DOCTOR about any medications you are currently taking, especially any of those listed above.

WARNINGS

• Tell your doctor about unusual or allergic reactions you have had to any medications, especially to enalapril.
• Tell your doctor if you now have or if you have ever had blood disorders, heart failure, renal disease, or systemic lupus erythematosus.

• Excessive perspiration, dehydration, or prolonged vomiting or diarrhea can lead to an excessive drop in blood pressure while you are taking this medication. Contact your doctor if you have any of these symptoms.
• Before having surgery or other medical or dental treatment, tell your doctor or dentist you are taking this drug.
• If this drug makes you dizzy or drowsy, do not take part in any activity that requires alertness, such as driving an automobile or operating potentially dangerous tools, machinery, or other equipment.
• If you have high blood pressure, do not take any over-the-counter (nonprescription) medications for weight control or for asthma, sinus, cough, cold, or allergy problems unless you first check with your doctor.
• Be sure to tell your doctor if you are pregnant. Drugs in the same class as enalapril have been shown to cause birth defects, including kidney damage, low blood pressure, improper skull development, and death, when taken in the second and third trimesters. Also tell your doctor if you are breast-feeding an infant. It is not yet known if enalapril passes into human breast milk.

epinephrine (ophthalmic)

BRAND NAMES (Manufacturers)
Epifrin (Allergan)
Epinal (Alcon)
Eppy/N (Sola/Barnes-Hind)
Glaucon (Alcon)
TYPE OF DRUG
Antiglaucoma ophthalmic solution
INGREDIENT
epinephrine (adrenaline)
DOSAGE FORM
Ophthalmic solution (0.1%, 0.25%, 0.5%, 1%, and 2%)
STORAGE
Store at room temperature in a tightly closed, light-resistant container. This medication should never be frozen. The solution should be discarded if it turns brown or cloudy because this indicates deterioration and loss of potency.

USES

Epinephrine (ophthalmic) is used to treat glaucoma. It lowers the pressure in the eye by decreasing the production of aqueous humor (a particular fluid in the eye) and increasing its drainage.

TREATMENT

Wash your hands with soap and water before applying this medication. In order to avoid contamination of the eye drops, be careful not to touch the tube portion of the dropper or let it touch your eye; and DO NOT wipe off or rinse the dropper after each use.

To apply the eye drops, tilt your head back and pull down your lower eyelid with one hand to make a pouch below the eye. Drop the prescribed amount of medicine into this pouch and slowly close your eyes. Try not to blink. Keep your eyes closed, and place one finger at the corner of the eye next to your nose for a minute or two, applying slight pressure (this is done to prevent loss of the medication through the duct that drains fluid from the surface of the eye into the nose and throat). Then wipe away any excess with a clean tissue. Since the drops are somewhat difficult to apply, you may want to have someone else apply them for you.

If more than one type of eye drop has been prescribed for you, wait at least five minutes after applying epinephrine before using the other eye medication (to give the epinephrine time to work). However, if you are also using an eye drop that constricts your pupils, check with your doctor to see which drug should be applied first.

If you miss a dose of epinephrine, apply the missed dose as soon as possible, unless it is almost time for the next dose. In that case, do not apply the missed dose at all; just return to your regular dosing schedule. Do not double the next dose.

SIDE EFFECTS

Minor. Headache or stinging on initial application. These side effects should disappear over time as your body adjusts to the medication.

Major. Tell your doctor about any side effects that are persistent or particularly bothersome. IT IS ESPECIALLY IMPORTANT TO TELL YOUR DOCTOR about blurred vision, eye pain, fainting, palpitations, sweating, or trembling.

INTERACTIONS

Epinephrine interacts with several other types of medications:
1. Concurrent use of epinephrine and monoamine oxidase (MAO) inhibitors or tricyclic antidepressants can lead to serious side effects. At least 21 days should separate doses of epinephrine and either of these types of medications.
2. Digoxin can increase the side effects of epinephrine.

BE SURE TO NOTIFY YOUR DOCTOR about any medications you are currently taking, especially any of those listed above.

WARNINGS

• Tell your doctor about unusual or allergic reactions you have had to any medications, especially to epinephrine.
• Tell your doctor if you are allergic to sulfites.
• Before starting to take this medication, be sure to tell your doctor if you now have or if you have ever had diabetes mellitus, heart or blood-vessel disease, high blood pressure, a stroke, or thyroid disease.
• If this medication blurs your vision, try to avoid activities that require visual acuity, such as driving a car or operating potentially dangerous equipment.
• Epinephrine may occasionally cause discoloration of soft contact lenses. If you currently wear soft contact lenses, you should discuss with your doctor whether your medication or your contact lenses should be changed.
• Be sure to tell your doctor if you are pregnant. Although epinephrine (ophthalmic) appears to be safe during pregnancy, studies in humans have not been conducted. Also tell your doctor if you are breast-feeding an infant. It is not known whether epinephrine passes into breast milk.

ergoloid mesylates

BRAND NAMES (Manufacturers)
ergoloid mesylates (various manufacturers)
Gerimal (Rugby)
Hydergine (Sandoz)
TYPE OF DRUG
Vasodilator

INGREDIENT
ergoloid mesylates
DOSAGE FORMS
Capsules, liquid (1 mg)
Oral tablets (0.5 mg and 1 mg)
Sublingual tablets (0.5 mg and 1 mg)
Oral liquid (1 mg per mL, with 30% alcohol)
STORAGE
Ergoloid mesylates capsules, tablets, and oral liquid should be stored at room temperature in tightly closed, light-resistant containers. Never freeze this medication.

USES

This medication is used to reduce the symptoms associated with senility. It is not clear how ergoloid mesylates work, but it is thought that they act by dilating (widening) the blood vessels, thus increasing blood flow to the brain.

TREATMENT

In order to avoid stomach irritation, you can take the capsules, tablets, or oral liquid with food or milk. Be sure to measure the dose of the liquid form of this medication carefully with the dropper provided.

The sublingual form of this medication must be placed under the tongue and allowed to dissolve completely. Try not to swallow for as long as possible, because the drug is more completely absorbed through the lining of the mouth than it is from the stomach. Do not drink any liquid, eat, or smoke for at least ten minutes after placing the tablet under the tongue.

If you miss a dose of this medication, take the missed dose as soon as possible, unless it is almost time for the next dose. In that case, do not take the missed dose at all; just return to your regular dosing schedule. Do not double the next dose.

It may take three or four weeks for the effects of this medication to become apparent.

SIDE EFFECTS

Minor. Blurred vision, dizziness, drowsiness, flushing, headache, irritation under the tongue (with the sublingual form only), light-headedness, loss of appetite, nasal congestion, nausea, stomach cramps, or vomiting. These side effects should disappear as your body adjusts to the medication.

If you feel dizzy or light-headed, sit or lie down for a while; get up slowly from a sitting or reclining position; and be careful on stairs.

Major. Tell your doctor about any side effects that are persistent or particularly bothersome. IT IS ESPECIALLY IMPORTANT TO TELL YOUR DOCTOR about a slowed heart rate.

INTERACTIONS

Ergoloid mesylates should not interact with other medications if they are used according to directions.

WARNINGS

• Tell your doctor about unusual or allergic reactions you have had to any medications, especially to ergoloid mesylates or ergot alkaloids (such as ergonovine, ergotamine, or bromocriptine).

• Before starting to take this medication, be sure to tell your doctor if you now have or if you have ever had liver disease, low blood pressure, porphyria, severe mental illness, or a slowed heart rate.

• Ergoloid mesylates may lessen your ability to adjust to the cold. Therefore, since you may experience increased sensitivity, do not expose your body to very cold temperatures for prolonged periods.

• Your doctor may want you to take your pulse daily while you are using this medication. Contact your doctor if your pulse becomes slower than normal or if it drops below 50 beats per minute.

• If this drug makes you dizzy or drowsy or blurs your vision, do not take part in any activity that requires alertness, such as driving a car or operating potentially dangerous equipment. Be carefull going up and down stairs.

ergotamine

BRAND NAMES (Manufacturers)
Ergostat (Parke-Davis)
Medihaler Ergotamine (3M Pharmaceutical)
TYPE OF DRUG
Antimigraine (vasoconstrictor)

INGREDIENT
ergotamine
DOSAGE FORMS
Sublingual tablets (2 mg)
Aerosol (0.36 mg per spray)
STORAGE
This medication should be stored at room temperature in tightly closed, light-resistant containers.

The container of the aerosol is pressurized; it should therefore never be punctured, burned, or broken. It should also be stored away from heat and direct sunlight.

USES

This medication is used to treat migraine and cluster headaches. These headaches are thought to be caused by an increase in the diameter of the blood vessels in the head, which results in more blood flow, greated pressure, and pain. Ergotamine is a vasoconstrictor; it acts by constricting (narrowing) the blood vessels.

TREATMENT

Take this medication as soon as you notice your migraine headache symptoms. If you wait until the headache is severe, the drug takes longer to work and may not be as effective.

After you take either of these forms of ergotamine, you should try to lie down in a quiet, dark room for at least two hours (in order to help the medication work). The drug usually takes effect in 30 to 60 minutes.

It is very important that you understand how often you can repeat a dose of this medication during an attack (usually every 30 to 60 minutes for the sublingual tablets, and every five minutes for the aerosol spray) and the maximum amount of medication you can take per day (usually three sublingual tablets or six inhalations). Five is generally the maximum number of sublingual tablets and 15 is about the maximum number of inhalations that can be taken in any one-week period. CHECK WITH YOUR DOCTOR if you have any questions.

The sublingual tablets should be placed under your tongue. DO NOT swallow these tablets—they are more efficiently absorbed through the lining of the mouth than from the gastrointestinal tract. Try not to eat, drink, chew, or smoke while the tablet is dissolving.

The aerosol form of this medication comes packaged with instructions for use. Read the directions carefully; if you have any questions, check with your doctor or pharmacist. The aerosol can should be shaken well just before each dose is sprayed. The contents tend to settle on the bottom of the container, so it should be shaken to disperse the medication and equalize the doses. The container provides about 60 measured sprays.

If you are on prolonged treatment with this drug and you miss a dose, take it as soon as you remember. Wait four hours to take the next dose. It is very important that you consult your doctor before you discontinue using this drug. Your doctor may want to reduce your dosage gradually.

SIDE EFFECTS

Minor. Diarrhea, dizziness, headache, nausea, sensation of cold hands and feet with MILD numbness or tingling, or vomiting. These side effects should disappear as your body adjusts to the medication.

The aerosol form of ergotamine can cause hoarseness or throat irritation. Gargling or rinsing your mouth out with water after taking the dose may help prevent this side effect.

Major. Tell your doctor about any side effects that are persistent or particularly bothersome. IT IS ESPECIALLY IMPORTANT TO TELL YOUR DOCTOR about chest pain; coldness, numbness, pain, tingling, or dark discoloration of the fingers or toes; confusion; fluid retention; itching; localized swelling; muscle pain; severe abdominal pain and swelling; or unusual weakness.

INTERACTIONS

Ergotamine interacts with several other types of medications:

1. Ergotamine interacts with amphetamines, ephedrine, epinephrine (adrenaline), pseudoephedrine, erythromycin, and troleandomycin. Such combinations can lead to increases in blood pressure or increased risk of adverse reaction to ergotamine.

2. Do not drink alcoholic beverages while you are taking this medication. Since alcohol dilates (widens) the blood vessels (which are already dilated during migraine headaches), drinking will only make your headache worse.

3. Nicotine and cocaine decrease the effectiveness of ergotamine and make the headache worse.
4. The caffeine in tea, coffee, and cola drinks also interacts with this medication. It may actually help to relieve your headache.

BE SURE TO TELL YOUR DOCTOR about any medications or substances you are currently taking or using, especially any of those listed above.

WARNINGS

• Tell your doctor about unusual or allergic reactions you have had to any medications, especially to ergotamine or other ergot alkaloids (such as ergonovine or bromocriptine).
• Before starting to take this medication, be sure to tell your doctor if you now have or if you have ever had heart or blood-vessel disease, high blood pressure, infections, kidney disease, liver disease, or thyroid disease.
• Avoid any foods to which you are allergic.
• If this drug makes you dizzy or drowsy, do not take part in any activity that requires alertness, such as driving an automobile or operating potentially dangerous tools, machinery, or other equipment.
• Try to avoid exposure to cold. Since this drug acts by constricting blood vessels throughout the body, your fingers and toes may become especially sensitive.
• Elderly patients are more sensitive to the effects of ergotamine. Consult your doctor if the side effects become bothersome.
• This medication should not be taken for longer periods or in higher doses than recommended by your doctor. Extended use of this drug can lead to serious side effects. In addition, tolerance can develop—higher doses would be required to obtain the same beneficial effects (at the same time increasing the risk of side effects).
• Be sure to tell your doctor if you are pregnant. Ergotamine can cause contractions of the uterus, which can harm the developing fetus. This drug should not be used during pregnancy. Also tell your doctor if you are breast-feeding an infant. Ergotamine passes into breast milk and may cause vomiting, diarrhea, or convulsions in the nursing infant.

Save the inhaler piece from the aerosol container. Refill units are available that are less expensive.

---

ergotamine and caffeine combination

BRAND NAMES (Manufacturers)
Cafergot (Sandoz)
Cafetrate (Schein)
Wigraine (Organon)

TYPE OF DRUG
Antimigraine (vasoconstrictor)

INGREDIENTS
ergotamine and caffeine

DOSAGE FORMS
Tablets (1 mg ergotamine, 100 mg caffeine)
Suppositories (2 mg ergotamine, 100 mg caffeine)

STORAGE
Ergotamine and caffeine combination tablets should be stored at room temperature in tightly closed, light-resistant containers. They should also be stored away from heat and direct sunlight.

The suppository form of this drug should be kept in the refrigerator in a closed container. This medication should never be frozen.

USES
This medication is used to treat migraine and cluster headaches. These headaches are thought to be caused by an increase in the diameter of the blood vessels in the head, which results in increased blood flow, increased pressure, and pain. Ergotamine is a vasoconstrictor: it acts by constricting (narrowing) the blood vessels. Caffeine helps in both the absorption of the drug from the gastrointestinal tract and in constricting blood vessels.

TREATMENT
It is best to take this medication as soon as you notice your migraine headache symptoms. If you wait until the headache

becomes severe, the drug takes longer to work and may not be as effective.

After you take either of these forms of ergotamine and caffeine combination, you should try to lie down in a quiet, dark room for at least two hours (in order to help the medication work). The drug usually takes effect within 30 to 60 minutes.

It is very important that you understand how often you can repeat a dose of this medication during an attack (usually every 30 to 60 minutes) and the maximum number of tablets you can take per day (usually six tablets). Ten is generally the maximum number of tablets that can be taken in any one-week period. CHECK WITH YOUR DOCTOR if you have any questions.

The tablets should be swallowed with liquid. Take one tablet when you first notice your migraine headache symptoms. If necessary, take a second dose 30 to 60 minutes later to relieve your headache.

To use the suppository form of this medication, first unwrap it and moisten it slightly with water (if the suppository is too soft to insert, run cold water over it or refrigerate it for 30 minutes before you unwrap it). Lie down on your left side, with your right knee bent. Push the suppository well into the rectum with your finger. Try to avoid having a bowel movement for at least an hour to give the medication time to be absorbed. Insert one suppository when you first notice your migraine symptoms. If necessary, insert a second suppository one hour later for full relief of your migraine headache. Five is generally the maximum number of suppositories that can be taken in a one-week period.

If you are on prolonged treatment with this drug and you miss a dose, take it as soon as you remember. Wait four hours to take the next dose. It is very important that you consult your doctor before you discontinue using ergotamine and caffeine combination. Your doctor may want to reduce your dosage gradually.

SIDE EFFECTS

Minor. Diarrhea, dizziness, headache, nausea, nervousness or jitters, vomiting, or sensation of cold hands and feet with MILD numbness or tingling. These side effects should disappear as your body gets accustomed to the medication.

Major. Tell your doctor about any side effects that are persistent or particularly bothersome. IT IS ESPECIALLY IMPORTANT TO TELL YOUR DOCTOR about chest pain; coldness, numbness, pain, tingling, or dark discoloration of the fingers or toes; confusion; fluid retention; itching; localized swelling; muscle pain; severe abdominal pain and swelling; severe nausea or vomiting; or unusual weakness.

INTERACTIONS

Ergotamine and caffeine combination interacts with several other types of medications:

1. Ergotamine interacts with amphetamines, ephedrine, epinephrine (adrenaline), pseudoephedrine, erythromycin, and troleandomycin. Such combinations can lead to increases in blood pressure or increased risk of adverse reaction to ergotamine.

2. Do not drink alcoholic beverages while you are taking this medication. Since alcohol dilates (widens) the blood vessels, drinking will only make your headache worse.

3. Tobacco and cocaine decrease the effectiveness of ergotamine and can make the headache worse.

4. The caffeine in tea, coffee, and cola drinks also interacts with this medication.

BE SURE TO TELL YOUR DOCTOR about any medications or substances you are currently taking or using, especially any of those listed above.

WARNINGS

• Tell your doctor about unusual or allergic reactions you have had to medications, especially to ergotamine, caffeine, or any ergot alkaloid (ergonovine, ergoloid mesylates, and bromocriptine).

• Before starting to take ergotamine and caffeine combination, be sure to tell your doctor if you now have or if you have ever had heart or blood-vessel disease, high blood pressure, infections, kidney disease, liver disease, or thyroid disease.

• Avoid any foods to which you are allergic—they may make your headache worse.

• If this drug makes you dizzy or drowsy, do not take part in any activity that requires alertness, such as driving a car or operating potentially dangerous equipment.

• Since this drug acts by constricting blood vessels throughout the body (not just in the head), your fingers and toes may become especially sensitive to the cold.

• Elderly patients are more sensitive to the effects of ergotamine.

• This medication should not be taken for longer periods or in higher doses than recommended by your doctor. Extended use of this drug can lead to serious side effects. In addition, your body can develop a tolerance to this medication—higher doses would be required to obtain the same beneficial effects and, at the same time, the risk of side effects would be increased.

• Be sure to tell your doctor if you are pregnant. This medication can cause contractions of the uterus, which can harm the developing fetus. This drug should not be used during pregnancy. Also tell your doctor if you are breast-feeding an infant. Ergotamine and caffeine combination passes into breast milk and may cause vomiting, diarrhea, irritability, or convulsions in the nursing infant.

---

erythromycin

BRAND NAMES (Manufacturers)
E.E.S. 200 Liquid (Abbott)
E.E.S. 400 Filmtab (Abbott)
E-Mycin (Boots)
Eramycin (Wesley)
Eryc (Parke-Davis)
EryPed (Abbott)
Ery-Tab (Abbott)
Erythrocin Stearate Filmtabs (Abbott)
Erythromycin Base (Abbott)
Ilosone (Dista)
Ilosone Pulvules (Dista)
PCE Dispertab (Abbott)
Robimycin (Robins)
TYPE OF DRUG
Antibiotic
INGREDIENT
erythromycin

DOSAGE FORMS
Tablets (250 mg, 333 mg, and 500 mg)
Chewable tablets (200 mg)
Enteric-coated tablets (250 mg, 333 mg, and 500 mg)
Film-coated tablets (250 mg, 400 mg, and 500 mg)
Polymer-coated tablets (333 mg)
Capsules (250 mg)
Oral drops (100 mg per 2.5 mL)
Oral suspension (125 mg, 200 mg, 250 mg, and 400 mg per 5-mL spoonful)

STORAGE
Erythromycin tablets and capsules should be stored at room temperature in tightly closed, light-resistant containers. Erythromycin oral drops and oral suspension should be stored in the refrigerator in tightly closed, light-resistant containers. Any unused portion of the liquid forms should be discarded after 14 days. Erythromycin ethylsuccinate liquid does not need to be refrigerated; however, refrigeration helps to preserve the taste. This medication should never be frozen.

USES
Erythromycin is used to treat a wide variety of bacterial infections, including infections of the middle ear and the respiratory tract. It is also used to treat infections in persons who are allergic to penicillin. It acts by preventing the bacteria from growing. It is not effective against viruses, parasites, or fungi.

TREATMENT
In order to prevent stomach upset, erythromycin coated tablets and erythromycin estolate or ethylsuccinate can be taken with food or milk. Other erythromycin products should be taken with a full glass of water, preferably on an empty stomach, one hour before or two hours after a meal.

The liquid forms should be taken undiluted.

Each dose of the oral drops should be measured carefully with the dropper provided.

The oral-suspension form of this medication should be shaken well just before measuring each dose. The contents tend to settle on the bottom of the bottle, so it is necessary to shake the container to distribute the ingredients evenly and equalize the doses. Each dose should then be measured carefully with a specially designed 5-mL measuring spoon. An ordinary kitchen teaspoon is not accurate enough.

In order to prevent gastrointestinal side effects, the coated tablets and capsules should be swallowed whole; do not break, chew, or crush these products.

Erythromycin works best when the level of medicine in your bloodstream is kept constant. It is best, therefore, to take the doses at evenly spaced intervals day and night. For example, if you are to take four doses a day, the doses should be spaced six hours apart.

If you miss a dose of this medication, take the missed dose immediately. However, if you do not remember to take the missed dose until it is almost time for your next dose, take it; space the following dose about halfway through the regular interval between doses; then return to your regular schedule. Try not to skip any doses.

It is important to continue to take this medication for the entire time prescribed by your doctor (usually seven to 14 days), even if the symptoms disappear before the end of that period. If you stop taking this drug too soon, resistant bacteria continue growing, and the infection could recur.

SIDE EFFECTS

Minor. Abdominal cramps, diarrhea, fatigue, irritation of the mouth, loss of appetite, nausea, sore tongue, or vomiting. These side effects should disappear as your body adjusts to the medication.

Major. Tell your doctor about any side effects that are persistent or particularly bothersome. IT IS ESPECIALLY IMPORTANT TO TELL YOUR DOCTOR about fever, hearing loss, hives, rash, rectal or vaginal itching, or yellowing of the eyes or skin. If your symptoms of infection seem to be getting worse rather than improving, you should contact your doctor.

INTERACTIONS

1. Erythromycin can decrease the elimination of aminophylline, oxtriphylline, theophylline, digoxin, oral anticoagulants (blood thinners, such as warfarin), and carbamazepine from the body, which can lead to serious side effects.

2. Therapy with erythromycin may increase the effects of methylprednisolone.

BE SURE TO TELL YOUR DOCTOR about any medications you are currently taking, especially any listed above.

WARNINGS

• Tell your doctor about unusual or allergic reactions you have had to any medications, especially to erythromycin.
• Be sure to tell your doctor if you have ever had liver disease.
• This drug has been prescribed for your current infection only. Another infection later on, or one that someone else has, may require a different medication altogether. Do not give your medicine to other people or use it for other infections unless your doctor specifically directs you to.
• Before having surgery or any other medical or dental treatment, be sure to tell your doctor or dentist that you are taking erythromycin.
• Not all erythromycin products are chemically equivalent. However, they all produce the same therapeutic effect. Discuss with your doctor or pharmacist which forms of erythromycin are appropriate for you, and then choose the least expensive product among those recommended.
• Some of these products contain the color additive FD&C Yellow No. 5 (tartrazine), which can cause allergic-type reactions (difficulty in breathing, rash, fainting) in certain susceptible individuals.
• Be sure to tell your doctor if you are pregnant. Although erythromycin appears to be safe during pregnancy, extensive studies in humans have not been conducted. Also tell your doctor if you are breast-feeding an infant. Small amounts of this medication pass into breast milk and may temporarily alter the bacterial balance in the intestinal tract of the nursing infant, resulting in diarrhea.

erythromycin and sulfisoxazole combination

BRAND NAMES (Manufacturers)
erythromycin and sulfisoxazole (various manufacturers)
Eryzole (Alra)
Pediazole (Ross)

TYPE OF DRUG
Antibiotic
INGREDIENTS
erythromycin and sulfisoxazole
DOSAGE FORM
Oral suspension (200 mg erythromycin and 600 mg
  sulfisoxazole per 5-mL spoonful)
STORAGE
Store in the refrigerator (never freeze) in a tightly closed container. Any unused portion of the erythromycin and sulfisoxazole combination should be discarded after the expiration date (usually after 14 days) because the drug loses its potency after that time.

USES

Erythromycin and sulfisoxazole combination is used to treat acute otitis media (middle ear infection) in children. Erythromycin acts by preventing the bacteria from manufacturing protein, thereby preventing their growth. Sulfisoxazole also acts by preventing production of nutrients that are required for growth of the infecting bacteria. Erythromycin and sulfisoxazole combination kills a wide range of susceptible bacteria, but it is not effective against viruses, parasites, or fungi.

TREATMENT

In order to avoid stomach upset, you can take this medication either with food or with a full glass of water or milk. You can also take it on an empty stomach.

The oral suspension should be shaken well just before measuring each dose. The contents tend to settle on the bottom of the bottle, so it is necessary to shake the container to distribute the ingredients evenly and equalize the doses. Each dose should then be measured carefully with a specially designed 5-mL measuring spoon. An ordinary kitchen teaspoon is not accurate enough.

This medication works best when the level of medicine in the bloodstream is kept constant. It is best, therefore, to take the doses at evenly spaced intervals day and night. For example, if you are to take four doses a day, the doses should be spaced six hours apart.

If you miss a dose of this medication, take the missed dose immediately. However, if you do not remember to take the missed dose until it is almost time for your next dose, take it; space the following dose about halfway through the regular interval between doses; then return to your regular schedule. Try not to skip any doses.

It is important to continue to take this medication for the entire time prescribed by your doctor (usually seven to 14 days), even if the symptoms disappear before the end of that period. If you stop taking the drug too soon, resistant bacteria are given a chance to continue growing, and the infection could recur.

SIDE EFFECTS

Minor. Diarrhea, dizziness, headache, loss of appetite, nausea, sleep disorders, sore mouth or tongue, or vomiting. These side effects should disappear over time as your body adjusts to the medication.

This medication can cause increased sensitivity to sunlight. It is therefore important to avoid prolonged exposure to sunlight and sunlamps. Wear protective clothing and sunglasses, and use an effective sunscreen. However, sunscreens containing para-aminobenzoic acid (PABA) interfere with the antibacterial activity of sulfisoxazole and should not be used.

If you feel dizzy, sit or lie down for a while; get up slowly from a sitting or reclining position; and be careful on stairs.
Major. Tell your doctor about any side effects that are persistent or particularly bothersome. IT IS ESPECIALLY IMPORTANT TO TELL YOUR DOCTOR about aching or joint and muscle pain; convulsions; difficult or painful urination; difficulty in swallowing; hallucinations; mental depression; loss of hearing; redness, blistering or peeling of the skin; itching; rash; sore throat and fever; uncoordinated movements; unusual bleeding or bruising; unusual tiredness; or yellowing of the eyes or skin. If the symptoms of infection seem to be getting worse, contact your doctor.

INTERACTIONS

This medication interacts with several other types of drugs:
1. Erythromycin can decrease the elimination of aminophylline, oxtriphylline, theophylline, digoxin, oral anticoag-

ulants (blood thinners, such as warfarin), and carbamazepine from the body, which can lead to serious side effects.

2. Sulfisoxazole can increase the active blood levels of oral anticoagulants (blood thinners, such as warfarin), oral antidiabetic agents, methotrexate, oxyphenbutazone, phenylbutazone, and phenytoin, which can lead to serious side effects.

3. Methenamine can increase the side effects to the kidneys caused by sulfisoxazole.

4. Probenecid and sulfinpyrazone can increase the blood levels of sulfisoxazole.

5. Erythromycin may increase the effects of methylprednisolone.

Before starting to take this medication, BE SURE TO TELL YOUR DOCTOR about any medications you are currently taking, especially any of those drugs that are listed above.

WARNINGS

• Tell your doctor about unusual or allergic reactions you have or have ever had to any medications, especially to erythromycin, sulfisoxazole, any other sulfa medications (sulfonamide antibiotics, diuretics, dapsone, sulfoxone, oral antidiabetic medicines) or acetazolamide.

• Tell your doctor if you now have or if you have ever had glucose–6-phosphate dehydrogenase (G6PD) deficiency, kidney disease, liver disease, or porphyria.

• This medication has been prescribed for your current infection only. Another infection later on, or one that someone else has, may require a different medicine. You should not give your medicine to other people, nor should you use it yourself for other infections, unless your doctor specifically directs you to do so.

• Be sure to tell your doctor if you are pregnant. Small amounts of erythromycin and sulfisoxazole cross the placenta. Although these antibiotics appear to be safe during pregnancy, extensive studies in humans have not been conducted. Also tell your doctor if you are breast-feeding an infant. Small amounts of this medication pass into breast milk and may temporarily alter the bacterial balance in the intestinal tract of the infant, resulting in diarrhea. This medication should not be used in an infant less than two months of age in order to avoid side effects involving the liver.

---

estradiol (topical)

BRAND NAME (Manufacturer)
Estraderm (Ciba)
TYPE OF DRUG
Estrogen
INGREDIENT
estradiol
DOSAGE FORM
Transdermal patch (delivers 0.05 mg or 0.1 mg per
  24 hours)
STORAGE
Estradiol transdermal patches should be stored at room tem-
perature in their original packages.

USES
Estradiol is a synthetic estrogen that is used to treat menopausal
symptoms or other conditions associated with estrogen deficiency.

TREATMENT
Your prescription of estradiol will come with patient instructions. It is important that you follow the directions carefully.

Wash and dry your hands before and after applying the
patch. Apply the patch to a clean, dry, hairless area of the skin
on the trunk of the body or on the abdomen. Do not apply
to the breasts. Avoid applying the patch over a cut or to any
area of the body where tight clothes might rub against the
patch and cause it to loosen. Apply the patch immediately
after opening the packet and removing the protective liner.
Press the patch firmly to the skin with the palm of your hand
for about ten seconds. Make sure there is good contact of the
patch to the skin, especially around the edges. Rotate the application sites on the skin, waiting at least one week before
applying to the same site.

If the patch becomes loose or falls off, the same one can
be reapplied. If necessary, however, a new patch can be applied. In either case, continue with your original treatment
schedule.

If you miss an application of this medication, apply a new
patch as soon as possible, unless it is almost time for the next

application. In that case, return to your regular schedule. Do not apply a double dose.

SIDE EFFECTS

Minor. Acne, abdominal cramping, abnormal vaginal bleeding, bloating, breast tenderness, change in sexual desire, darkening of the skin, diarrhea, dizziness, fluid retention, frequent or painful urination, hair loss, headache, nausea, nervousness, skin irritation at patch site, vomiting, or weight gain. These side effects should disappear as your body adjusts to the drug.

If you feel dizzy, sit or lie down for a while; get up slowly from a sitting or reclining position; and be careful on stairs.

Eating a full breakfast or having a midmorning snack may help to relieve the nausea and vomiting.

This medication can increase your sensitivity to sunlight. You should therefore try to avoid prolonged exposure to sunlight and sunlamps. Wear protective clothing and sunglasses, and use an effective sunscreen.

Major. Tell your doctor about any side effects that are persistent or particularly bothersome. IT IS ESPECIALLY IMPORTANT TO TELL YOUR DOCTOR about blurred vision, chest pain, convulsions, depression, itching, loss of coordination, pain or inflammation of the calves or thighs, shortness of breath, skin rash, slurred speech, or yellowish discoloration of the eyes or skin.

INTERACTIONS

Estradiol interacts with several other types of medications:
1. It can decrease the effectiveness of oral anticoagulants (blood thinners, such as warfarin).
2. Carbamazepine, phenobarbital, phenytoin, primidone, and rifampin can reduce the effectiveness of estradiol.
3. Estradiol can increase the side effects and decrease the effectiveness of tricyclic antidepressants.

BE SURE TO TELL YOUR DOCTOR about any medications you are currently taking.

WARNINGS

• Estrogens can change your blood's clotting ability, so be especially careful to avoid injuries.

• Tell your doctor about unusual or allergic reactions you have had to any medications, especially to estradiol, other estrogens, or oral contraceptives.

• Tell your doctor if you now have or if you have ever had asthma, blood clot disorders, breast disease, depression, diabetes mellitus, epilepsy, endometriosis, gallstones or gallbladder disease, heart disease, high blood pressure, kidney disease, liver disease, migraine headaches, porphyria, or uterine tumors.

• Estrogens may cause a change in glucose tolerance in diabetic patients. Be sure to tell your doctor if you notice any abnormalities in your urine or blood-glucose levels.

• Although it is not known if estrogens can increase the risk of breast cancer, it is important that you examine your breasts regularly for lumps or discharge.

• If you notice tenderness, swelling, or bleeding of your gums, consult your doctor or dentist.

• Your doctor may schedule regular office visits to be sure your medication is working properly.

• Before having surgery or any other medical or dental treatment, be sure to tell your doctor or dentist that you are taking this medication.

• A package insert titled "Information for the Patient" should be dispensed with your prescription. It is important that you understand the possible risks and benefits of this medication. If you have any questions, check with your doctor or pharmacist.

• Cigarette smoking can greatly increase the risk of developing heart or blood vessel disorders while taking this medication. The risks increase with the amount of smoking and the age of the smoker.

• Be sure to tell your doctor if you are pregnant. If you suspect you are pregnant, discontinue use of the medication immediately. Estrogens have been shown to cause birth defects in the offspring of women who received these medications during pregnancy. Also tell your doctor if you are breast-feeding an infant. Small amounts of estrogen pass into breast milk, so caution is warranted. Estradiol can also decrease milk production.

estrogens, conjugated

BRAND NAMES (Manufacturers)
conjugated estrogens (various manufacturers)
Premarin (Wyeth-Ayerst)
TYPE OF DRUG
Estrogen
INGREDIENTS
conjugated estrogens
DOSAGE FORM
Tablets (0.3 mg, 0.625 mg, 0.9 mg, 1.25 mg, and 2.5 mg)
STORAGE
These tablets should be stored at room temperature in a tightly closed container.

USES

Conjugated estrogens are a group of estrogenlike products obtained from natural sources (the urine of pregnant mares). They are used to treat menopausal symptoms, prostatic cancer, uterine bleeding, and some cases of breast cancer. They can also be used in replacement therapy for women who do not produce enough estrogen of their own.

TREATMENT

In order to avoid stomach irritation, you can take conjugated estrogens with food or immediately after a meal.

Follow your doctor's instructions carefully when you take this medication. Often, conjugated estrogens are prescribed to be taken for three-week periods, with one week off (in order to reduce potential side effects).

If you miss a scheduled dose of this medication, take the missed dose as soon as possible, unless it is almost time for the next dose. In that case, do not take the missed dose at all; just return to your regular dosing schedule. Do not double the next dose.

SIDE EFFECTS

Minor. Bloating, change in sexual desire, depression, diarrhea, dizziness, headache, loss of appetite, nausea, or vomiting. These side effects should disappear as your body adjusts to the medication.

This medication can increase your sensitivity to sunlight. You should, therefore, try to avoid prolonged exposure to sunlight and sunlamps. Wear protective clothing and sunglasses, and use an effective sunscreen.

If you feel dizzy or light-headed, sit or lie down for a while; get up slowly from a sitting or reclining position; and be careful on stairs.

Major. Tell your doctor about side effects that are persistent or particularly bothersome. IT IS ESPECIALLY IMPORTANT TO TELL YOUR DOCTOR about changes in menstrual patterns; chest pain; difficulty in breathing; eye pain; loss of coordination; lumps in the breast; painful urination; pain in the calves; skin color changes; slurred speech; sudden, severe headache; swelling of the feet or ankles; vision changes; weight gain or loss; or yellowing of eyes or skin.

INTERACTIONS

Conjugated estrogens will interact with several other medications:

1. Estrogens can decrease the effectiveness of oral anticoagulants (blood thinners, such as warfarin).

2. Carbamazepine, ampicillin, phenobarbital, phenytoin, primidone, and rifampin can increase the elimination of estrogen from the body, thus decreasing its effectiveness.

3. Estrogens can increase the side effects and decrease the effectiveness of the tricyclic antidepressants.

BE SURE TO TELL YOUR DOCTOR about any medications you are currently taking, especially those listed above.

WARNINGS

• Tell your doctor about unusual or allergic reactions you have had to any medications, especially to conjugated estrogens, to oral contraceptives (birth control pills), or to any other estrogen product.

• Before starting to take this drug, tell your doctor if you have ever had asthma, blood clot disorders, breast cancer, diabetes mellitus, endometriosis, epilepsy, gallbladder disease, heart disease, high blood pressure, hypercalcemia, kidney disease, liver disease, migraines, porphyria, uterine fibroid tumors, vaginal bleeding, or depression.

• Studies have shown that estrogens increase the risk of certain types of cancer. Ask your pharmacist for the brochure

"Information for the Patient." It is important that you understand the possible risks and benefits of this medication. If you
have any questions, check with your doctor or pharmacist.

• Although it is not known if estrogens can increase the risk of
breast cancer, it is important that you examine your breasts
regularly for lumps or discharge.

• If you notice tenderness, swelling, or bleeding of your gums,
consult your doctor or dentist.

• Estrogens can cause a change in glucose tolerance in diabetic patients. If you are diabetic, be sure to tell your doctor if
you notice any abnormalities in your urine or blood-glucose
levels.

• Do not change your brand of medication without the con-
sent of your doctor. If your refill does not look the same, consult your doctor or pharmacist.

• Cigarette smoking increases the risk of serious side effects
from estrogens. The risk increases with both age and the
amount of smoking.

• If this medication makes you dizzy or light-headed, you
should not take part in any activity that requires alertness,
such as driving an automobile or operating potentially dangerous equipment or machinery.

• Estrogens can change your blood's clotting ability, so be especially careful to avoid injuries.

• Before having surgery or any other medical or dental treatment, be sure to tell your doctor or dentist that you are taking this medication.

• Be sure to tell your doctor if you are pregnant. If you suspect that you are pregnant, discontinue the use of this medication immediately. Several studies have shown that estrogens taken during pregnancy can cause birth defects in the
developing child. Also notify your doctor if you are breast-
feeding an infant. Estrogens have been known to pass into
breast milk.

ethinyl estradiol

BRAND NAMES (Manufacturers)
Estinyl (Schering)
Feminone (Upjohn)

TYPE OF DRUG
Estrogen
INGREDIENT
ethinyl estradiol
DOSAGE FORM
Tablets (0.02 mg, 0.05 mg, and 0.5 mg)
STORAGE
Ethinyl estradiol should be stored at room temperature in a tightly closed container. This medication should not be refrigerated.

USES
Ethinyl estradiol is a synthetic estrogen that is used to treat symptoms of menopause, certain types of breast cancer, and prostate cancer.

TREATMENT
To avoid stomach irritation, take ethinyl estradiol with food, milk, or water (unless your doctor directs otherwise).

If you miss a dose of this medication, take the missed dose as soon as possible, unless it is almost time for the next scheduled dose. In that case, do not take the missed dose at all; instead, return to your regular dosing schedule. Do not double the next dose of this medication.

SIDE EFFECTS
Minor. Abdominal cramping, abnormal vaginal bleeding, bloating, breast tenderness, darkening of the skin, diarrhea, dizziness, fluid retention, frequent or painful urination, headache, nausea, vomiting, or weight gain. These side effects should disappear over time as your body adjusts to the medication.

This medication can increase your sensitivity to sunlight. You should, therefore, try to avoid prolonged exposure to sunlight and sunlamps. Wear protective clothing and sunglasses, and use an effective sunscreen.

If you feel dizzy, sit or lie down for a while; get up slowly from a sitting or reclining position; and be careful on stairs.

Eating a full breakfast or having a midmorning snack may help to relieve the nausea and vomiting.

Major. Tell your doctor about any side effects that are persistent or particularly bothersome. IT IS ESPECIALLY IMPOR-

TANT TO TELL YOUR DOCTOR about blurred vision, chest pain, convulsions, depression, hair loss, itching, pain or inflammation of the calves or thighs, shortness of breath, skin rash, or yellowing of the eyes or skin.

INTERACTIONS

Ethinyl estradiol interacts with other types of medications:

1. It can decrease the effectiveness of oral anticoagulants (blood thinners, such as warfarin).

2. Ampicillin, carbamazepine, phenobarbital, phenytoin, primidone, and rifampin can reduce the effectiveness of ethinyl estradiol.

3. Ethinyl estradiol can increase the side effects and decrease the effectiveness of tricyclic antidepressants.

BE SURE TO TELL YOUR DOCTOR about any medications you are currently taking, especially any listed above.

WARNINGS

• Tell your doctor about unusual or allergic reactions you have had to any medications, especially to ethinyl estradiol or other estrogens, or to oral contraceptives (birth control pills).

• Tell your doctor if you now have or if you have ever had asthma, blood-clot disorders, breast disease, depression, diabetes mellitus, epilepsy, endometriosis, gallstones or gallbladder disease, heart disease, high blood pressure, kidney disease, liver disease, migraine headaches, porphyria, or uterine tumors.

• Some of these products contain the color additive FD&C Yellow No. 5 (tartrazine), which can cause allergic-type reactions (shortness of breath, fainting, rash) in certain susceptible individuals.

• Estrogens can change your blood's clotting ability, so be especially careful to avoid injuries.

• Estrogens can cause a change in glucose tolerance in diabetic patients. Be sure to tell your doctor if you notice any abnormalities in your urine or blood glucose levels.

• Before having surgery or any other medical or dental treatment, be sure to tell your doctor or dentist that you are taking this medication.

• A package insert titled "Information for the Patient" should be dispensed with your prescription. It is important that you understand the possible risks and benefits of this medication. If you have any questions, check with your doctor or pharmacist.

• Although it is not known if estrogens increase the risk of breast cancer, it is important that you examine your breasts regularly for lumps or discharge.

• Cigarette smoking can greatly increase the risk of developing heart or blood vessel disorders while taking this medication. The risks increase with the amount of smoking and the age of the smoker.

• Be sure to tell your doctor if you are pregnant. If you suspect you are pregnant, discontinue use of this medication immediately. Estrogens have caused birth defects in the offspring of women who received these medications during pregnancy. Also tell your doctor if you are breast-feeding an infant. Small amounts of estrogen pass into breast milk. Ethinyl estradiol can also decrease milk production.

ethosuximide

BRAND NAME (Manufacturer)
Zarontin (Parke-Davis)
TYPE OF DRUG
Anticonvulsant
INGREDIENT
ethosuximide
DOSAGE FORMS
Capsules (250 mg)
Oral syrup (250 mg per 5-mL spoonful)
STORAGE
Ethosuximide capsules and oral syrup should be stored at room temperature in tightly closed, light-resistant containers. It should never be frozen. Discard any outdated medication.

USES
This medication is used to treat absence (petit mal) seizures. Although it is not exactly clear how it does so, ethosuximide seems to prevent seizure activity by decreasing the activity of certain chemicals (nerve transmitters) in the brain.

TREATMENT

To avoid stomach irritation, take ethosuximide with food, water, or milk (unless your doctor directs you otherwise).

Each dose of the oral syrup form of this medication should be measured carefully with a specially designed 5-mL measuring spoon. A kitchen teaspoon is not accurate enough.

Ethosuximide works best when the level of medicine in your bloodstream is kept constant. It is best, therefore, to take the doses at evenly spaced intervals day and night. For example, if you are to take three doses a day, the doses should be spaced eight hours apart.

It is important to try not to miss any doses of this medication. If you do miss a dose, and remember within four hours, take the missed dose immediately and then return to your normal schedule. If more than four hours have passed, do not take the missed dose at all; just return to your regular dosing schedule. Do not double the next dose.

SIDE EFFECTS

Minor. Constipation, diarrhea, dizziness, drowsiness, headache, hiccups, loss of appetite, nausea, stomach upset, or weight loss. These side effects should disappear as your body adjusts to the medication.

To relieve constipation, increase the amount of fiber in your diet (fresh fruits and vegetables, salads, bran, and whole-grain breads), exercise, and drink more water (unless your doctor directs you to do otherwise).

If you feel dizzy, sit or lie down for a while; get up slowly from a sitting or reclining position; and be careful on stairs.

Major. Tell your doctor about any side effects that are persistent or particularly bothersome. IT IS ESPECIALLY IMPORTANT TO TELL YOUR DOCTOR about blurred vision, confusion, depression, difficult or painful urination, false sense of well-being, fatigue, inflammation of the eyes or tongue, irritability, joint pains, loss of coordination, mental disorders, mood changes, nervousness, skin rash, unusual bleeding or bruising, or vaginal bleeding.

INTERACTIONS

This drug can be expected to interact with several other types of medications:

1. Tricyclic antidepressants, haloperidol, thiothixene, phenothiazine tranquilizers, and alcohol can increase the risk of seizures. Dosage adjustments of ethosuximide may be necessary when any of these medications are started.

2. Isoniazid can increase the side effects of ethosuximide.

BE SURE TO TELL YOUR DOCTOR about any medications you are currently taking, especially any listed above.

WARNINGS

• Tell your doctor about unusual or allergic reactions you have had to any medications, especially to ethosuximide, methsuximide, or phensuximide.

• Tell your doctor if you now have or if you have ever had blood disorders, kidney disease, or liver disease.

• If this drug makes you dizzy or drowsy, do not take part in any activity that requires alertness, such as driving a car or operating potentially dangerous equipment. Children should be careful while playing.

• Before having surgery or any other medical or dental treatment, be sure to tell your doctor or dentist that you are taking ethosuximide.

• Do not stop taking this medication unless you first check with your doctor. Stopping the drug abruptly may lead to a worsening of your condition. Your doctor may want to reduce your dosage gradually or start you on another drug when treatment with ethosuximide is discontinued.

• Your doctor may schedule regular office visits, especially during the first few months of therapy, to be sure the drug is working properly.

• Be sure to tell your doctor if you are pregnant. Birth defects have been reported more often in infants whose mothers have seizure disorders. It is unclear if the increased risk of birth defects is associated with the disorder or with anticonvulsant medications. Also tell your doctor if you are breast-feeding an infant. Ethosuximide passes into breast milk.

etodolac

BRAND NAME (Manufacturer)
Lodine (Wyeth-Ayerst)

TYPE OF DRUG
Nonsteroidal anti-inflammatory analgesic
INGREDIENT
etodolac
DOSAGE FORMS
Capsules (200 mg and 300 mg)
Tablets (400 mg)
STORAGE
Store in a tightly closed, light-resistant container at room temperature. This medication should never be frozen.

USES

Etodolac is used to treat the pain and inflammation (swelling, stiffness) of acute and chronic osteoarthritis. It is also used for the relief of pain. Etodolac is not recommended for treating the symptoms of rheumatoid arthritis.

TREATMENT

You should take this medication on an empty stomach 30 to 60 minutes before meals or two hours after meals, so that it reaches your bloodstream quickly. However, to decrease stomach irritation, your doctor may want you to take the medication with food or antacids.

If etodolac is being taken to relieve arthritis, you must take it regularly as directed by your doctor. Etodolac does not cure osteoarthritis, but it will help to control the condition as long as you continue to take it.

It is important to take etodolac on schedule and not to miss any doses. If you do miss a dose, take it as soon as possible, unless it is almost time for your next dose. In that case, don't take the missed dose at all; just return to your regular dosing schedule. Do not double the next dose.

SIDE EFFECTS

Minor. Constipation, diarrhea, dizziness, drowsiness, excessive thirst, feeling of fullness, flatulence, headache, heartburn, increased appetite, indigestion, nausea, or nervousness. As your body adjusts to the drug, these side effects should disappear.

To relieve constipation, increase the amount of fiber in your diet (fresh fruits and vegetables, salads, bran, and whole-grain breads), exercise, and drink more water, unless your doctor directs you to do otherwise.

If you become dizzy or light-headed, sit or lie down for a while; get up slowly from a sitting or reclining position; and be careful on stairs.

Major. If any side effects are persistent or particularly bothersome, you should report them to your doctor. IT IS ESPECIALLY IMPORTANT TO TELL YOUR DOCTOR about bloody or black tarry stools; blurred vision; confusion; depression; difficulty breathing; difficult or painful urination; fever; palpitations; problems with hearing; ringing or buzzing in your ears; seizures; skin rash, hives, or itching; stomach pain; swelling; tremors; unusual bleeding or bruising; unusual fatigue or weakness; unusual weight gain; or yellowing of the eyes or skin.

INTERACTIONS

Etodolac interacts with several other types of medications:
1. Concurrent use of etodolac and anticoagulants (blood thinners, such as warfarin) can lead to an increase in bleeding complications.
2. Concurrent use of etodolac and aspirin, other salicylates, or other anti-inflammatory medications can increase stomach irritation.
3. Etodolac can interact with diuretics (water pills).
4. Probenecid may increase the blood levels of etodolac, which may increase the risk of side effects.
5. The action of beta blockers may be decreased by this drug.
   BE SURE TO TELL YOUR DOCTOR about any medications you are currently taking, especially any listed above.

WARNINGS

• Before you start to take this medication, it is important to tell your doctor if you have ever had unusual or allergic reactions to etodolac or to any of the other chemically related drugs (aspirin, other salicylates, diclofenac, diflunisal, fenoprofen, flurbiprofen, ibuprofen, indomethacin, ketorolac, meclofenamate, mefenamic acid, naproxen, oxyphenbutazone, phenylbutazone, piroxicam, sulindac, or tolmetin).
• Tell your doctor if you now have or if you have ever had asthma, bleeding problems, colitis, epilepsy, heart disease, high blood pressure, kidney disease, liver disease, mental illness, stomach ulcers or other stomach problems, or Parkinson's disease.

• If etodolac makes you dizzy or drowsy, do not take part in any activity that requires alertness, such as driving or operating dangerous machinery.

• Because etodolac can prolong bleeding time, be certain to tell your doctor that you are taking this drug before having surgery or any other medical or dental treatment.

• Stomach problems are more likely to occur if you take aspirin regularly or if you drink alcohol while being treated with etodolac. These should be avoided (unless your doctor directs you to do otherwise).

• The elderly may be at increased risk for experiencing side effects from this drug.

• Be sure to tell your doctor if you are pregnant. This type of medication can cause unwanted effects to the heart or to the blood flow of the fetus. Studies in animals have shown that this type of medication, if taken late in pregnancy, can prolong labor or cause other problems during delivery. Also tell your doctor if you are breast-feeding an infant. Small amounts of etodolac can pass into the breast milk.

famotidine

BRAND NAME (Manufacturer)
Pepcid (Merck Sharp & Dohme)
TYPE OF DRUG
Gastric acid secretion inhibitor (decreases stomach acid)
INGREDIENT
famotidine
DOSAGE FORMS
Tablets (20 mg and 40 mg)
Oral suspension (40 mg per 5-mL spoonful)
STORAGE
Famotidine should be stored at room temperature (never frozen) in a tightly closed container. Avoid exposure of this medication to high temperatures during storage.

USES

Famotidine is used to treat active duodenal ulcers. It is also used in the long-term treatment of excessive stomach acid secretion (Zollinger-Ellison syndrome) and in the prevention of recurrent ulcers. Famotidine reduces stomach acid secretions by blocking the effects of histamine in the stomach.

TREATMENT

If you are taking a single daily dose of famotidine, it is best to take the dose at bedtime in order to obtain the maximum benefits from it. Antacids will not affect the activity of famotidine. Check with your doctor to see if you should be taking antacids as part of your ulcer treatment.

The oral liquid should be measured carefully with a specially designed 5-mL measuring spoon. An ordinary kitchen teaspoon is not accurate enough to ensure that the proper dose will be taken.

If you miss a dose of famotidine, take the missed dose as soon as possible, unless it is almost time for the next dose. In that case, do not take the missed dose at all; just return to your regular dosing schedule. Do not double the next dose.

SIDE EFFECTS

Minor. Abdominal pain, acne, change in taste, constipation, diarrhea, dizziness, dry mouth, dry skin, fatigue, flushing, headache, insomnia, loss of appetite, nausea, or vomiting. These side effects should disappear as your body adjusts to this drug.

If you are constipated, increase the amount of fiber in your diet (fresh fruits and vegetables, salads, bran, and whole-grain breads), exercise, and drink more water (unless your doctor tells you not to do so).

To reduce mouth dryness, chew sugarless gum or suck on ice chips or hard candy.

If you feel dizzy or light-headed, sit or lie down for a while; get up slowly from a sitting or reclining position; and be careful on stairs.

Major. Tell your doctor about any side effects you are experiencing that are persistent or particularly bothersome. IT IS ESPECIALLY IMPORTANT TO TELL YOUR DOCTOR about anxiety, confusion, depression, fever, hair loss, hallucinations, itching, muscle or joint pain, palpitations, ringing in the ear, seizures, shortness of breath, tingling in the fingers or toes, or yellowing of the eyes or skin.

INTERACTIONS

No drug interactions with famotidine have yet been confirmed. It is still very important, however, to tell your doctor about all of the medications you are taking before starting famotidine.

WARNINGS

• Tell your doctor about any unusual or allergic reactions you have had to any medications, especially to famotidine or to the other gastric-acid secretion inhibitors (cimetidine and ranitidine).

• Before starting famotidine, tell your doctor if you now have or if you have ever had kidney disease.

• Famotidine should be taken continuously for as long as your doctor prescribes. Stopping therapy early may be a cause of ineffective treatment.

• Cigarette smoking may interfere with the beneficial effects of famotidine.

• Aspirin, foods known to cause stomach upset, and certain drinks (such as those containing caffeine) may worsen your stomach irritation.

• If this drug makes you dizzy or drowsy, do not take part in any activity that requires alertness, such as driving a car or operating potentially dangerous equipment.

• Be sure to tell your doctor if you are pregnant. Extensive studies in pregnant women have not yet been conducted. Also tell your doctor if you are breast-feeding an infant. Small amounts of famotidine are known to pass into animal milk.

---

felbamate

BRAND NAME (Manufacturer)
Felbatol (Wallace)
TYPE OF DRUG
Anticonvulsant
INGREDIENT
felbamate
DOSAGE FORMS
Tablets (400 mg and 600 mg)
Oral suspension (600 mg per 5-ml spoonful)

STORAGE
Felbamate tablets and oral suspension should be stored at room temperature in tightly closed containers.

USES
Felbamate is used for the treatment of seizure disorders and Lennox-Gastaut syndrome. The mechanism of action of felbamate is not related to any of the other anticonvulsant agents and is poorly understood. Although felbamate is effective when taken alone for certain seizure disorders, it may be taken with certain other anticonvulsants. Felbamate must be taken only as recommended by your doctor.

TREATMENT
Felbamate may be taken with food if stomach upset occurs, unless your doctor directs you to do otherwise.

Routine monitoring of the level of felbamate in your blood may only be necessary when giving felbamate with other anticonvulsant drugs. The doses of felbamate should be given at evenly spaced intervals day or night, depending on the dosage recommended by your doctor. For example, if you take three doses a day, they should be eight hours apart.

Try not to miss any doses. If you do, take the missed dose as soon as possible, unless it is almost time for the next dose. In that case, do not take the missed dose; return to your regular dosing schedule. Do not double the next dose unless your doctor directs you to. If you are taking felbamate for a seizure disorder and you miss two or more doses, contact your doctor.

SIDE EFFECTS
Minor. Constipation, diarrhea, dizziness, drowsiness, headache, nausea, rash, or vomiting. These side effects should disappear over time as your body adjusts to the medication.

This medication can increase your sensitivity to sunlight and sunlamps. Wear protective clothing and sunglasses, and use an effective sunscreen.

To relieve constipation, increase the fiber in your diet (fresh fruits and vegetables, whole-grain breads), exercise, and drink more water (unless your doctor directs you otherwise).

If you feel dizzy or light-headed, sit or lie down for a while; get up slowly from a sitting or reclining position.

Major. Tell your doctor about any side effects that are persistent or bothersome. IT IS ESPECIALLY IMPORTANT TO TELL YOUR DOCTOR about abnormal gait, blurred vision, chest pain, depression, difficulty breathing, double vision, fever, numbness or tingling in the hands or feet, palpitations, severe rash, sleepiness, tremor, or urinary incontinence.

INTERACTIONS

Felbamate interacts with several other types of medications:
1. Concurrent use of felbamate with central nervous system depressants (such as alcohol, antihistamines, barbiturates, benzodiazepine tranquilizers, muscle relaxants, narcotics, pain medications, and phenothiazine tranquilizers) or with tricyclic antidepressants can cause extreme drowsiness.
2. Felbamate can cause an increase in the blood levels of phenytoin and valproic acid.
3. Phenytoin and carbamazepine can cause a decrease in the blood levels and effectiveness of felbamate.
4. Felbamate can decrease blood levels of carbamazepine.
   Before you start to take felbamate, BE SURE TO TELL YOUR DOCTOR about any medications you are currently taking, especially any of those listed above.

WARNINGS

• Tell your doctor about unusual or allergic reactions you have had to any medications, especially to felbamate or to any other anticonvulsant medications.
• If this medication makes you dizzy or drowsy, do not take part in any activity that requires alertness, such as driving a car or operating potentially dangerous equipment. Be especially careful going up and down stairs.
• Aplastic anemia, a severe form of bone-marrow failure, has been reported with felbamate. To monitor for this rare adverse reaction, your doctor will check the level of white blood cells and red blood cells in your blood at regularly scheduled intervals, particularly during your first six months of therapy.
• Tell your doctor if you now have or if you have ever had bone marrow depression, blood disorders, urinary tract infections, urinary incontinence, glaucoma, heart or blood-vessel disease, kidney disease, or liver disease.
• Before having surgery or any other medical or dental treatment, tell your doctor that you are taking this drug.

• If you are taking this medication to control a seizure disorder, do not stop taking it suddenly. If you do stop abruptly, you may experience uncontrollable seizures.

• Tell your doctor if you are pregnant. Birth defects have been reported more often in infants whose mothers have seizure disorders. It is unclear if the increased risk is associated with the disorder or with the anticonvulsant medications. The risks and benefits of treatment should be discussed with your doctor. Also tell your doctor if you are breast-feeding an infant. Small amounts of felbamate pass into breast milk.

---

fenfluramine*

*This drug was recalled September 15, 1997, due to concern that it may cause heart damage.

BRAND NAME (Manufacturer)
Pondimin (Robins)
TYPE OF DRUG
Anorectic
INGREDIENT
fenfluramine
DOSAGE FORM
Tablets (20 mg)
STORAGE
Fenfluramine should be stored at room temperature in a tightly closed, light-resistant container.

USES

Fenfluramine is used as an appetite suppressant during the first few weeks of dieting to help establish new eating habits. This medication is thought to relieve hunger by altering nerve impulses to the appetite control center in the brain. Its effectiveness lasts only for short periods (three to 12 weeks).

TREATMENT

You can take fenfluramine with a full glass of water, one hour before meals (unless your doctor directs you to do otherwise).

If you miss a dose of this medication, take the missed dose as soon as possible, unless it is almost time for your next dose. In that case, do not take the missed dose at all; just return to your regular dosing schedule. Do not double the next dose.

SIDE EFFECTS

Minor. Blurred vision, constipation, diarrhea, dizziness, dry mouth, euphoria, fatigue, frequent urination, headache, insomnia, irritability, nausea, nervousness, restlessness, stomach pain, sweating, unpleasant taste in the mouth, or vomiting. These side effects should disappear as your body adjusts to the medication.

Dry mouth can be relieved by sucking on ice chips or a piece of hard candy or by chewing sugarless gum.

In order to prevent constipation, increase the amount of fiber in your diet (fresh fruits and vegetables, bran, and whole-grain breads), exercise, and drink more water (unless your doctor tells you not to do so).

Major. Tell your doctor about any side effects that are persistent or particularly bothersome. IT IS ESPECIALLY IMPORTANT TO TELL YOUR DOCTOR about changes in sexual desire, chest pain, difficulty in urinating, enlarged breasts (in both sexes), fever, hair loss, headaches, impotence, increased blood pressure, menstrual irregularities, mental depression, mood changes, mouth sores, muscle pains, nosebleeds, palpitations, rash, shortness of breath, sore throat, swelling of the hands and feet, or tremors.

INTERACTIONS

Fenfluramine interacts with several other types of medications:
1. Concurrent use of it with central nervous system depressants (such as alcohol, antihistamines, barbiturates, muscle relaxants, narcotics, pain medications, and phenothiazine tranquilizers) or with tricyclic antidepressants can cause extreme drowsiness.
2. Fenfluramine may alter insulin and oral diabetic medication dosage requirements in diabetic patients.
3. The blood-pressure-lowering effects of antihypertensive medications, especially guanethidine, reserpine, methyldopa, and diuretics (water pills), may be increased by this medication.
4. Use of fenfluramine within 14 days of a monoamine oxidase (MAO) inhibitor (isocarboxazid, pargyline, phenelzine, tranylcypromine) can result in high blood pressure and other side effects.

BE SURE TO TELL YOUR DOCTOR about any medications you are currently taking, especially those listed above.

WARNINGS

• The combination of the appetite suppressants fenfluramine and phentermine ("fen-phen") may cause heart problems by affecting the valves that help bring blood into and out of your heart. It is very important to tell your doctor if you have any of the following symptoms: irregular heartbeat, difficulty breathing, puffiness of the hands or feet, or a decreased ability to exercise.

• Tell your doctor about any unusual or allergic reactions you have had to any medications, especially to fenfluramine or other appetite suppressants (such as benzphetamine, phendimetrazine, diethylpropion, phenmetrazine, mazindol, and phentermine), or to epinephrine, norepinephrine, ephedrine, amphetamines, dextroamphetamine, phenylephrine, phenylpropanolamine, pseudoephedrine, albuterol, metaproterenol, or terbutaline.

• Tell your doctor if you have a history of drug abuse or alcoholism or if you have ever had angina, diabetes mellitus, emotional disturbances, glaucoma, heart or cardiovascular disease, high blood pressure, thyroid disease, epilepsy, or mental depression.

• Fenfluramine can mask the symptoms of extreme fatigue and can cause dizziness and light-headedness. Your ability to perform tasks that require alertness, such as driving a car, may be decreased during therapy with this medication.

• Before having surgery or any other medical or dental treatment, tell the doctor you are taking this medication.

• Fenfluramine is related to amphetamine and may be habit-forming when taken for long periods of time (both physical and psychological dependence can occur). You should, therefore, not increase the dosage of this medication or take it longer than 12 weeks, unless you first consult your doctor. It is also important that you not stop taking this medication abruptly. Fatigue, sleep disorders, mental depression, nausea, vomiting, stomach cramps, or pain could occur. Your doctor may want to decrease your dosage gradually in order to prevent these side effects.

• Fenfluramine can alter blood sugar levels in diabetic patients. Therefore, it is important to note that if you are diabetic and starting to take this medication, you should carefully monitor your blood or urine glucose levels for the first several days.

• Be sure to tell your doctor if you are pregnant. Although side effects in humans have not been studied, some of the appetite suppressants have been shown to cause side effects in the fetuses of animals that received large doses during pregnancy. Also, tell your doctor if you are breast-feeding an infant. It is not known whether this medication passes into breast milk.

fluconazole

BRAND NAME (Manufacturer)
Diflucan (Roerig)
TYPE OF DRUG
Antifungal Agent
INGREDIENT
fluconazole
DOSAGE FORMS
Tablets (50 mg, 100 mg, and 200 mg)
Oral suspension (50 mg and 200 mg per 5-mL spoonful)
STORAGE
The tablet form of this medication should be stored in a tightly closed container at room temperature, away from heat and direct sunlight. The suspension form should be stored in the refrigerator. Any unused portion of the oral suspension should be discarded after 14 days because it loses its potency after that time. This medication should be protected from freezing.

USES

Fluconazole is used to treat fungal infections of the mouth, throat, urinary tract, kidney, and liver. It is also used to treat pneumonia or meningitis caused by fungus. This medication acts by severely injuring the cell walls of the infecting fungus, thereby preventing them from growing and multiplying. Fluconazole is effective against susceptible fungus but does not kill bacteria, viruses, or parasites.

TREATMENT

This medication should be taken exactly as prescribed by your doctor, even if your symptoms improve. If you stop taking this medication too soon, resistant fungi are given a chance to grow and the infection may recur. You may have to take fluconazole for an extended period of time to completely cure the infection.

The contents of the suspension form of fluconazole tend to settle on the bottom of the bottle. Thus it is necessary to shake the container well immediately before each dose in order to distribute the ingredients evenly and to equalize the doses. Each dose should be carefully measured using a specially designed 5-mL measuring spoon. An ordinary kitchen spoon is not accurate enough.

If you miss a dose and remember within a few hours, take the missed dose and resume your regular schedule. If many hours have passed, take the missed dose as soon as you remember. Space the following dose halfway through the regular interval between doses, then return to your regular schedule. Try not to skip any doses.

SIDE EFFECTS

Minor. Abdominal pain or cramps, diarrhea, nausea, vomiting, dizziness, headache, skin rash, or itching.

Major. Tell your doctor about any side effects that are persistent or particularly bothersome. IT IS ESPECIALLY IMPORTANT TO TELL YOUR DOCTOR if you notice any yellowing of the skin or eyes, dark urine, or pale stools.

INTERACTIONS

Fluconazole interacts with several other types of drugs:

1. Fluconazole may increase the effectiveness of oral anticoagulants (blood thinners, such as warfarin), phenytoin, cyclosporine, and oral antidiabetic agents.

2. The effectiveness of fluconazole may be decreased when given together with rifampin.

BE SURE TO TELL YOUR DOCTOR about any medications you are currently taking, especially any of those listed above.

WARNINGS

• Tell your doctor about any unusual or allergic reactions you have had to any medications, especially to fluconazole.

• Tell your doctor if you now have or if you have ever had liver disease.

• This drug should not be taken if you are pregnant or breast-feeding an infant. Be sure to tell your doctor if you are pregnant or breast-feeding.

flunisolide (nasal)

BRAND NAME (Manufacturer)
Nasalide (Syntex)
TYPE OF DRUG
Nasal adrenocorticosteroid hormone
INGREDIENT
flunisolide
DOSAGE FORM
Nasal solution (25 mcg flunisolide per spray)
STORAGE
Flunisolide nasal solution should be stored at room temperature in a tightly closed container. Opened containers of this medication should be discarded after three months.

USES

Flunisolide nasal solution is used to relieve symptoms of rhinitis (inflammation of the nasal passages). How this drug acts to relieve these symptoms is not completely understood. Your adrenal glands naturally produce certain cortisonelike chemicals. These chemicals are involved in various regulatory processes in the body (such as those involving fluid balance, temperature, and reaction to inflammation). Flunisolide belongs to a group of drugs known as adrenocorticosteroids (or cortisonelike medications).

TREATMENT

Just before applying flunisolide nasal solution, clear your nasal passages of all secretions. Then carefully follow the patient instructions, which you should receive when your prescription is dispensed. The instructions will explain how to properly apply this medication. Do not increase the dose of flunisolide or increase the number of applications per day without first checking with your doctor.

If your doctor recommends that you use a nasal decongestant to clear your nasal passages, use the decongestant just before you apply flunisolide.

Relief from the symptoms of inflammation may not become apparent for up to three weeks after starting flunisolide. This drug does not cure the cause of inflammation, but it may help relieve the symptoms as long as you continue to use it.

Therefore, its effectiveness depends on regular use while the condition is present. Your doctor may then recommend that you gradually decrease the number of daily doses as your condition improves.

If there is no improvement in your condition within three weeks after starting flunisolide, check with your doctor. He or she may want you to stop the medication. Try not to miss any doses of this medication.

If you do miss a dose, apply the dose as soon as possible, unless it is almost time for the next dose. In that case, do not apply the missed dose; just return to your regular dosing schedule. You should never double the next dose.

SIDE EFFECTS

Minor. Drying of nasal passages, headache, loss of smell or taste, nasal congestion, nasal irritation, nausea, nosebleeds, sneezing, sore throat, vomiting, or watery eyes. These side effects should disappear as your body adjusts to this medication. A mild, temporary burning or stinging sensation may occur after this medication is applied.

Major. Tell your doctor about any side effects that are persistent or particularly bothersome. IT IS ESPECIALLY IMPORTANT TO TELL YOUR DOCTOR about persistent burning or stinging after application.

INTERACTIONS

This medication should not interact with any other medications as long as it is used according to directions.

WARNINGS

• Tell your doctor about unusual or allergic reactions you have had to any medications, especially to flunisolide or other adrenocorticosteroids (such as amcinonide, beclomethasone, betamethasone, clocortolone, cortisone, desonide, desoximetasone, dexamethasone, diflorasone, flumethasone, fluocinolone, fluocinonide, fluorometholone, flurandrenolide, halcinonide, hydrocortisone, methylprednisolone, paramethasone, prednisolone, prednisone, and triamcinolone).

• Before starting flunisolide, tell your doctor if you now have or if you have ever had chicken pox, diabetes mellitus, or tuberculosis.

• Flunisolide can slow the healing of wounds. Therefore, tell your doctor about recent nasal surgery or injury, recurrent nosebleeds, or nasal ulcers.

• Tell your doctor if you are pregnant. Birth defects have been observed in the offspring of animals that were given large doses of this drug during pregnancy. Tell your doctor if you are breast-feeding. Small amounts of adrenocorticosteroids do pass into breast milk and may cause growth suppression or a decrease in natural adrenocorticosteroid production in the nursing infant.

fluocinolone (topical)

BRAND NAMES (Manufacturers)
fluocinolone acetonide (various manufacturers)
Fluonid (Herbert)
Flurosyn (Rugby)
Synalar (Syntex)
Synalar-HP (Syntex)
Synemol (Syntex)
TYPE OF DRUG
Adrenocorticosteroid hormone
INGREDIENT
fluocinolone
DOSAGE FORMS
Cream (0.01%, 0.025%, and 0.2%)
Ointment (0.025%)
Solution (0.01%)
STORAGE
Store at room temperature in a tightly closed container. This medication should never be frozen.

USES
Your adrenal glands naturally produce certain cortisonelike chemicals. These chemicals are involved in various regulatory processes in the body (such as those involving fluid balance, temperature, and reaction to inflammation). Fluocinolone belongs to a group of drugs known as adrenocorticosteroids (or cortisonelike medications). It is used to relieve the skin inflammation (redness, swelling, itching, and discomfort) asso-

ciated with conditions such as dermatitis, eczema, and poison ivy. How this drug works is not completely understood.

TREATMENT

Before applying this medication, wash your hands. Then, unless your doctor gives you different instructions, gently wash the area of the skin where the medication is to be applied. With a clean towel, pat the area until it is almost dry; it should be slightly damp when you put the medicine on.

Apply a small amount of fluocinolone to the affected area in a thin layer. Do not bandage the area unless your doctor tells you to do so. If you have been directed to apply an occlusive dressing (such as kitchen plastic wrap), be sure to ask for instructions. Wash your hands again after application.

If you miss a dose of this medication, apply the missed dose as soon as possible, unless it is almost time for the next application. In that case, do not apply the missed dose at all; just return to your regular schedule. Do not put twice as much of the medication on your skin at the next application.

SIDE EFFECTS

Minor. Acne, burning, itching, rash, or skin dryness.

If the affected area is extremely dry or scaling, the skin may be moistened before applying the medication by soaking in water or by applying water with a clean cloth. The ointment form is probably better for dry skin.

A mild, temporary stinging sensation may occur after this medication is applied. If this persists, contact your doctor.

Major. Tell your doctor about any side effects that are persistent or particularly bothersome. IT IS ESPECIALLY IMPORTANT TO TELL YOUR DOCTOR about blistering, increased hair growth, irritation of the affected area, loss of skin color, secondary infection in the area being treated, or thinning of the skin with easy bruising.

INTERACTIONS

This medication should not interact with other medications as long as it is used according to directions.

WARNINGS

• Tell your doctor about unusual or allergic reactions you have had to any medications, especially to fluocinolone or any other adrenocorticosteroid (such as amcinonide, beclomethasone, betamethasone, clocortolone, cortisone, desonide, desoximetasone, dexamethasone, diflorasone, flumethasone, fluocinonide, fluorometholone, flurandrenolide, halcinonide, hydrocortisone, methylprednisolone, paramethasone, prednisolone, prednisone, and triamcinolone).

• Tell your doctor if you now have or if you have ever had blood-vessel disease, chicken pox, diabetes mellitus, fungal infection, peptic ulcers, shingles, tuberculosis, tuberculosis of the skin, vaccinia, or any other type of infection, especially at the site currently being treated.

• If irritation develops while using this drug, immediately discontinue its use and notify your doctor.

• This product is not for use in the eyes, nose, or mouth; contact may result in side effects.

• Do not use this product with an occlusive wrap unless your doctor directs you to do so. Systemic absorption of this drug is increased if large areas of the body are treated, particularly if occlusive bandages are used. If it is necessary for you to use this drug under a wrap, follow your doctor's instructions exactly; do not leave the wrap in place longer than specified.

• If you are using fluocinolone on a child's diaper area, do not put tight-fitting diapers or plastic pants on the child. This could lead to increased systemic absorption of the drug and a possible increase in side effects.

• Be sure to tell your doctor if you are pregnant. If large amounts of this drug are applied for prolonged periods, some of it will be absorbed and may cross the placenta. Although studies in humans have not been conducted, birth defects have been observed in the offspring of animals that were given large oral doses of this type of drug during pregnancy. Also tell your doctor if you are breast-feeding an infant. If absorbed through the skin, small amounts of this medication pass into breast milk and may cause growth suppression or a decrease in natural adrenocorticosteroid hormone production in the nursing infant.

---

fluocinonide (topical)

BRAND NAMES (Manufacturers)
fluocinonide (various manufacturers)

Lidex (Syntex)
Lidex-E (Syntex)
TYPE OF DRUG
Adrenocorticosteroid hormone
INGREDIENT
fluocinonide
DOSAGE FORMS
Ointment (0.05%)
Cream (0.05%)
Gel (0.05%)
Solution (0.05%, with 35% alcohol)
STORAGE
Fluocinonide ointment, cream, gel, and solution should be stored at room temperature in tightly closed containers. This medication should not be refrigerated, and it should never be frozen.

USES
Your adrenal glands naturally produce certain cortisonelike chemicals. These chemicals are involved in various regulatory processes in the body (such as those involving fluid balance, temperature, and reaction to inflammation). Fluocinonide belongs to a group of drugs known as adrenocorticosteroids (or cortisonelike medications). It is used to relieve the skin inflammation (redness, swelling, itching, and discomfort) associated with conditions such as dermatitis, eczema, and poison ivy. Exactly how this medication works is not completely understood.

TREATMENT
Before applying this medication, wash your hands. Then, unless your doctor gives you different instructions, gently wash the area of the skin where the medication is to be applied. With a clean towel, pat the area almost dry; it should be slightly damp when you put the medicine on.

Apply a small amount of fluocinonide to the affected area in a thin layer. Do not bandage the area unless your doctor tells you to do so. If you are to apply an occlusive dressing (like kitchen plastic wrap), be sure you understand the instructions. Wash your hands again after application.

If you miss a dose of this medication, apply the missed dose as soon as possible, unless it is almost time for the next application. In that case, do not apply the missed dose at all; just return to your regular schedule. Do not double the next dose.

SIDE EFFECTS

Minor. Acne, burning sensation, itching, rash, or dry skin.

If the affected area is extremely dry or scaling, the skin may be moistened before applying the medication by soaking in water or by applying water with a clean cloth. The ointment form is probably better for dry skin.

A mild, temporary stinging sensation may occur after this medication is applied. If this sensation persists, contact your doctor.

Major. Tell your doctor about any side effects that are persistent or particularly bothersome. IT IS ESPECIALLY IMPORTANT TO TELL YOUR DOCTOR about blistering, increased hair growth, irritation of the affected area, loss of skin color, secondary infection in the area being treated, or thinning of the skin with easy bruising.

INTERACTIONS

This medication should not interact with any other medications as long as it is used according to directions.

WARNINGS

• Tell your doctor about unusual or allergic reactions you have had to any medications, especially to fluocinonide or any other adrenocorticosteroid (such as amcinonide, betamethasone, clocortolone, cortisone, desonide, desoximetasone, dexamethasone, diflorasone, flumethasone, fluocinolone, fluorometholone, flurandrenolide, halcinonide, hydrocortisone, methylprednisolone, paramethasone, prednisolone, prednisone, and triamcinolone).

• Tell your doctor if you now have or if you have ever had blood-vessel disease, chicken pox, diabetes mellitus, fungal infection, peptic ulcers, shingles, tuberculosis, tuberculosis of the skin, vaccinia, or any other type of infection, especially at the site currently being treated.

• If any type of irritation develops while using this drug, you should immediately discontinue use of the medication and notify your doctor.

• Fluocinonide is a topical medication. It is meant for use on the skin only. This product is not for use in the eyes, nose, or mouth; contact may result in side effects.

• Do not use this product with an occlusive wrap unless your doctor directs you to do so. Systemic absorption of this drug is increased if large areas of the body are treated, particularly if occlusive bandages are used. If it is necessary for you to use this drug under a wrap, follow your doctor's instructions exactly; do not leave the wrap in place longer than specified.

• If you are using fluocinonide on a child's diaper area, do not put tight-fitting diapers or plastic pants on the child. This may lead to increased systemic absorption of the drug and a possible increase in side effects.

• Be sure to tell your doctor if you are pregnant. If large amounts of this drug are applied for prolonged periods, some of it will be absorbed and may cross the placenta. Although studies in humans have not been conducted, birth defects have been observed in the offspring of animals that were given large oral doses of this type of drug during pregnancy. Also tell your doctor if you are breast-feeding an infant. If absorbed through the skin, small amounts of fluocinonide pass into breast milk and may cause growth suppression or a decrease in natural adrenocorticosteroid hormone production in the nursing infant.

fluoxetine

BRAND NAME (Manufacturer)
Prozac (Dista)
TYPE OF DRUG
Cyclic antidepressant
INGREDIENT
fluoxetine
DOSAGE FORMS
Capsules (20 mg)
Liquid (20 mg per 5 mL spoonful)
STORAGE
Store at room temperature in a tightly closed container. Do not store in the bathroom. Heat or moisture can cause this medicine to break down.

USES

Fluoxetine is used to treat the symptoms of mental depression. It increases the concentration of certain chemicals necessary for nerve transmission in the brain. Fluoxetine is also used in the management of obsessive-compulsive disorder.

TREATMENT

This medication should be taken exactly as prescribed by your doctor. In order to avoid stomach irritation, you can take fluoxetine with food or with a full glass of water (unless your doctor directs you to do otherwise).

The effects of therapy with this medication may not become apparent for one to three weeks.

If you miss a dose of this medicine, it is not necessary to make up the missed dose. Skip that dose and continue at the next scheduled time. You should never take a double dose to make up for one you missed.

SIDE EFFECTS

Minor. Agitation, change in vision, changes in taste, constipation, decreased appetite, decreased mental concentration, decreased sex drive, diarrhea, dizziness, drowsiness, dry mouth, rapid heartbeat, flushing, frequent urination, headache, increased sweating, nausea, stomach cramps, stuffy nose, vomiting, or weight gain or loss.

Dry mouth can be relieved by chewing sugarless gum or sucking on hard candy.

To relieve constipation, increase the amount of fiber in your diet (fresh fruits and vegetables, salads, bran, and whole-grain breads), exercise, and drink more water (unless your doctor directs you to do otherwise).

To avoid dizziness or light-headedness when you stand, contract and relax the muscles of your legs for a few moments before rising.

Major. Tell your doctor about any side effects that are persistent or particularly bothersome. IT IS ESPECIALLY IMPORTANT TO TELL YOUR DOCTOR about anxiety, chills or fever, convulsions (seizures), difficulty in breathing, enlarged lymph glands (swelling under the jaw, in armpits, or in the groin area), joint or muscle pain, skin rash or hives, or swelling of the feet or lower legs.

INTERACTIONS

Fluoxetine interacts with a number of other types of drugs:

1. Extreme drowsiness can occur when this medicine is taken with central nervous system depressants (such as alcohol, antihistamines, barbiturates, benzodiazepine tranquilizers, muscle relaxants, narcotics, pain medications, phenothiazine tranquilizers, and medications to induce sleep) or with other antidepressants.

2. Fluoxetine may increase the effects of anticoagulants (blood thinners, such as warfarin) and certain heart medications (such as digitoxin).

3. Serious side effects may occur if a monoamine oxidase (MAO) inhibitor (such as furazolidone, isocarboxazid, pargyline, phenelzine, procarbazine, or tranylcypromine) is taken with fluoxetine. At least 14 days should separate the use of fluoxetine and the use of an MAO inhibitor.

4. Fluoxetine can increase agitation, restlessness, and stomach irritation when taken along with tryptophan.

Before starting to take fluoxetine, BE SURE TO TELL YOUR DOCTOR about any medications you are currently taking, especially any of those listed above.

WARNINGS

• Tell your doctor immediately if you develop a skin rash or hives while taking this medication, or if you have ever had an allergic reaction to fluoxetine.

• Tell your doctor if you have allergies to any substance such as foods, sulfites, or other preservatives or dyes.

• Before starting to take this medication, be sure to tell your doctor if you have a history of alcoholism or if you have ever had a heart attack, asthma, circulatory disease, difficulty in urinating, electroshock therapy, enlarged prostate gland, epilepsy, glaucoma, high blood pressure, intestinal problems, liver or kidney disease, mental illness, stomach problems, or thyroid disease.

• If this drug makes you dizzy or drowsy, do not take part in any activity that requires alertness, such as driving a car or operating potentially dangerous equipment.

• Do not stop taking this drug suddenly. Abruptly stopping it can cause nausea, headache, stomach upset, or a worsening of your condition. Your doctor may want to reduce the dosage gradually.

• The elderly may be at increased risk for side effects. Use this drug cautiously, and report any mental status changes to your doctor immediately.
• The effects of this medication may persist for as long as five weeks after you stop taking it, so continue to observe all precautions during that period.
• Be sure to tell your doctor if you are pregnant. Although birth defects have not been documented in animal studies, it is not known if fluoxetine is safe during human pregnancy. It is also not known if fluoxetine passes into breast milk, so be sure to tell your doctor if you are breast-feeding an infant.

---

fluphenazine

BRAND NAMES (Manufacturers)
fluphenazine (various manufacturers)
Permitil (Schering)
Prolixin (Princeton)
TYPE OF DRUG
Phenothiazine tranquilizer
INGREDIENT
fluphenazine
DOSAGE FORMS
Tablets (1 mg, 2.5 mg, 5 mg, and 10 mg)
Oral concentrate (5 mg per mL, with 1% alcohol)
Oral elixir (2.5 mg per 5-mL spoonful, with 14% alcohol)
STORAGE
The tablet form should be stored at room temperature in a tightly closed, light-resistant container. The oral concentrate and the elixir forms should be stored in the refrigerator in tightly closed, light-resistant containers. If the concentrate or elixir turns slightly yellow, the medicine is still effective and can be used. However, if it changes color markedly or has particles floating in it, it should not be used; discard it down the sink. This drug should never be frozen.

USES

Fluphenazine is prescribed to treat the symptoms of certain types of mental illness, such as emotional symptoms of psychosis, the manic phase of manic-depressive illness, and severe behavioral problems in children and adults. This medication is thought to relieve the symptoms of mental illness by blocking certain chemicals involved with nerve transmission in the brain.

TREATMENT

To avoid stomach irritation, you can take the tablet or elixir form of this medication with a meal or with a glass of water or milk (unless your doctor directs you to do otherwise).

Measure the oral elixir form of this medication carefully with a specially designed 5-mL measuring spoon. An ordinary kitchen teaspoon is not accurate enough for medical purposes.

Immediately prior to administration, the oral-concentrate form of this medication should be measured carefully with the dropper provided, then added to four ounces (½ cup) or more of water, milk, applesauce, pudding, or a cola-free, caffeine-free carbonated beverage. To prevent possible loss of effectiveness, the medication should not be diluted in tea, coffee, or apple juice.

Antacids and antidiarrheal medicines may decrease the absorption of this medication from the gastrointestinal tract. Therefore, at least one hour should separate doses of one of these medicines and fluphenazine.

The full effects of this medication for the control of emotional or mental symptoms may not become apparent until two weeks after the date you begin taking the drug.

If you miss a dose of this medication, take the missed dose as soon as possible and return to your regular dosing schedule. If it is almost time for the next dose, however, skip the one you missed and return to your regular schedule. Do not double the dose (unless your doctor directs you to do so).

SIDE EFFECTS

Minor. Blurred vision, constipation, decreased sweating, diarrhea, dizziness, drooling, drowsiness, dry mouth, fatigue, jitteriness, menstrual irregularities, nasal congestion, restlessness, vomiting, or weight gain. As your body adjusts to the medication, these side effects should disappear.

Fluphenazine can also cause discoloration of the urine to red, pink, or red-brown. This is a harmless effect.

This drug can cause increased sensitivity to sunlight. Therefore, avoid prolonged exposure to sunlight and sunlamps. Wear protective clothing and use an effective sunscreen.

If you are constipated, increase the amount of fiber in your diet (fresh fruits and vegetables, salads, bran, and whole-grain breads) and drink more water (unless your doctor directs you to do otherwise).

Chew sugarless gum or suck on ice chips or a piece of hard candy to reduce mouth dryness.

To avoid dizziness or light-headedness when you stand, contract and relax the muscles of your legs for a few moments before rising. Do this by pushing one foot against the floor while raising the other foot slightly, alternating feet so that you are "pumping" your legs in a pedaling motion.

Major. Tell your doctor about any side effects that are persistent or particularly bothersome. IT IS ESPECIALLY IMPORTANT TO TELL YOUR DOCTOR about breast enlargement (in both sexes); chest pain; convulsions; darkened skin; difficulty in swallowing or breathing; fainting; fever; impotence; involuntary movements of the face, mouth, jaw, tongue, or limbs; palpitations; rash; sleep disorders; sore throat; tremors; uncoordinated movements; unusual bleeding or bruising; visual disturbances; or yellowing of the eyes or skin. Also tell your doctor if your original symptoms worsen or change after you begin taking fluphenazine.

INTERACTIONS

Fluphenazine interacts with several other types of drugs:

1. It can cause extreme drowsiness when combined with alcohol or other central nervous system depressants (such as barbiturates, benzodiazepine tranquilizers, muscle relaxants, narcotics, and pain medications) or with tricyclic antidepressants.

2. Fluphenazine can decrease the effectiveness of amphetamines, guanethidine, anticonvulsants, and levodopa.

3. The side effects of epinephrine, monoamine oxidase (MAO) inhibitors, propranolol, phenytoin, and tricyclic antidepressants may be increased by this medication. At least 14 days should separate the use of this drug and the use of an MAO inhibitor.

4. Lithium may increase the side effects and decrease the effectiveness of this medication.

Before starting to take fluphenazine, BE SURE TO TELL YOUR DOCTOR about any medications you are currently taking, especially any of those listed above.

WARNINGS

• Tell your doctor about unusual or allergic reactions you have had to medications, especially to fluphenazine or any other phenothiazine tranquilizers (such as chlorpromazine, mesoridazine, perphenazine, prochlorperazine, promazine, thioridazine, and triflupromazine) or to loxapine.

• Tell your doctor if you have a history of alcoholism, blood disease, bone marrow disease, brain disease, breast cancer, blockage of the urinary or digestive tract, drug-induced depression, epilepsy, high or low blood pressure, diabetes mellitus, glaucoma, heart or circulatory disease, liver disease, lung disease, Parkinson's disease, peptic ulcers, or an enlarged prostate gland.

• Tell your doctor about any recent exposure to a pesticide or an insecticide. Fluphenazine may increase the side effects from the exposure.

• To prevent oversedation, avoid drinking alcoholic beverages while taking this medication.

• If this drug makes you dizzy or drowsy, do not take part in any activity that requires alertness, such as driving a car. Be careful on stairs, and avoid getting up suddenly from a lying or sitting position.

• Prior to having surgery or any other medical or dental treatment, be sure to tell your doctor or dentist that you are taking this medication.

• Some of the side effects of this medication can be prevented by taking an antiparkinsonism drug. Discuss this with your physician.

• This medication can decrease sweating and heat release from the body. You should, therefore, avoid getting overheated by strenuous exercise in hot weather and should avoid hot baths, showers, and saunas.

• Do not stop taking this medication suddenly. If the drug is stopped abruptly, you may experience nausea, vomiting, stomach upset, headache, increased heart rate, insomnia, tremors, or a worsening of your condition. Your doctor may want to reduce the dosage gradually.

• If you are planning to have a myelogram, or any other procedure in which dye will be injected into your spinal cord, tell your doctor that you are taking this medication.
• Avoid spilling the oral concentrate or elixir form of this medication on your skin or clothing; it may cause redness and irritation of the skin.
• While taking this medication, do not take any over-the-counter (nonprescription) medications for weight control or for cough, cold, allergy, asthma, or sinus problems without first checking with your doctor. The combination of these medications may cause high blood pressure.
• Some of these products contain the color additive FD&C Yellow No. 5 (tartrazine), which can cause allergic-type reactions (shortness of breath, rash, fainting) in certain susceptible individuals.
• A potentially permanent movement disorder called tardive dyskinesia may develop with the use of this medication. It is important to discuss this with your doctor and to report any unusual or uncontrolled movements.
• The elderly may be at greater risk for adverse effects when using this drug.
• Be sure to tell your doctor if you are pregnant. Small amounts of this medication cross the placenta. Although there are reports of safe use of this drug during pregnancy, there are also reports of liver disease and tremors in newborn infants whose mothers received this type of medication close to term. Also tell your doctor if you are breast-feeding an infant. Small amounts of this medication pass into breast milk and may cause unwanted effects in the nursing infant.

flurazepam

BRAND NAMES (Manufacturers)
Dalmane (Roche)
flurazepam (various manufacturers)
TYPE OF DRUG
Benzodiazepine sedative/hypnotic
INGREDIENT
flurazepam
DOSAGE FORM
Capsules (15 mg and 30 mg)

STORAGE
This medication should be stored at room temperature in a tightly closed, light-resistant container.

USES
Flurazepam is prescribed to treat insomnia (including problems in falling asleep, waking during the night, and early morning wakefulness). It is not clear exactly how this medicine works, but it may relieve insomnia by acting as a depressant of the central nervous system (brain and spinal cord).

TREATMENT
Flurazepam should be taken 10 to 15 minutes before bedtime. It can be taken with food or a full glass of water if stomach upset occurs. Do not take this medication with antacids, since they may slow its absorption from the gastrointestinal tract.

Your sleeping problem may improve the first night you take this medication, but it may take two or three nights before the effectiveness of flurazepam is noticed.

SIDE EFFECTS
Minor. Bitter taste in the mouth, constipation, depression, diarrhea, dizziness, daytime drowsiness, dry mouth, excessive salivation, fatigue, flushing, headache, heartburn, loss of appetite, nausea, nervousness, sweating, or vomiting. As your body adjusts to the medicine, these side effects should disappear.

To relieve constipation, increase the amount of fiber in your diet (fresh fruits and vegetables, salads, bran, and whole-grain breads), exercise, and drink more water (unless your doctor directs you to do otherwise).

Dry mouth can be relieved by chewing sugarless gum or by sucking on ice chips.

If you feel dizzy while taking this medication, sit or lie down for a while; get up slowly from a sitting or reclining position; and be careful on stairs.

Major. Tell your doctor about any side effects that are persistent or particularly bothersome. IT IS ESPECIALLY IMPORTANT TO TELL YOUR DOCTOR about blurred or double vision, chest pain, fainting, falling, fever, hallucinations, joint pain, nightmares, palpitations, rash, severe depression, shortness of breath, slurred speech, sore throat, uncoordinated movements, unusual excitement, unusual tiredness, or yellowing of the eyes or skin.

INTERACTIONS

Flurazepam interacts with several other types of drugs:

1. To prevent oversedation, this drug should not be taken with alcohol, other sedative drugs, central nervous system depressants (such as antihistamines, barbiturates, muscle relaxants, pain medicines, narcotics, drugs for seizures, phenothiazine tranquilizers), or with antidepressants.

2. This medication may decrease the effectiveness of levodopa and oral anticoagulants (blood thinners) and may increase the effects of phenytoin.

3. Disulfiram, oral contraceptives (birth control pills), isoniazid, and cimetidine can increase the blood levels of flurazepam, which can lead to increased side effects.

4. Concurrent use of rifampin or carbamazepine may decrease the effectiveness of flurazepam.

BE SURE TO TELL YOUR DOCTOR about any medications you are currently taking, especially any listed above.

WARNINGS

• Tell your doctor about any unusual or allergic reactions you have had to any medications, especially to flurazepam or other benzodiazepine tranquilizers (such as alprazolam, chlordiazepoxide, clorazepate, diazepam, halazepam, lorazepam, oxazepam, prazepam, temazepam, and triazolam).

• Tell your doctor if you now have or if you have ever had liver disease, kidney disease, epilepsy, lung disease, myasthenia gravis, porphyria, mental depression, or mental illness.

• Flurazepam can cause drowsiness. Avoid tasks that require alertness, such as driving a car or using potentially dangerous equipment.

• This medication has the potential for abuse and must be used with caution. Tolerance may develop quickly; do not increase the dosage of the drug without first consulting your doctor. It is also important not to stop taking this drug suddenly if you have been taking it in large amounts or if you have used it for several weeks. Your doctor may want to reduce the dosage gradually.

• This is a safe drug when used properly. When it is combined with other sedative drugs or with alcohol, however, serious side effects may develop.

• The elderly may be at increased risk for side effects when using this medication, especially daytime drowsiness or confusion. Report any changes in mental status to your doctor immediately.

• Be sure to tell your doctor if you are pregnant. This type of medicine has been shown to increase the chance of birth defects if it is taken during the first three months of pregnancy. In addition, too much use of this medicine during the last six months of pregnancy may result in addiction of the fetus—leading to withdrawal side effects at birth. Use of this medicine during the last weeks of pregnancy may cause excessive drowsiness, slowed heartbeat, and breathing difficulties in the newborn. It is very important to tell your doctor if you are breast-feeding an infant. This medicine can pass into breast milk and cause excessive drowsiness, slowed heartbeat, and breathing difficulties in nursing infants, so caution is warranted.

---

flurbiprofen

BRAND NAME (Manufacturer)
Ansaid (Upjohn)
TYPE OF DRUG
Nonsteroidal anti-inflammatory agent
INGREDIENT
flurbiprofen
DOSAGE FORM
Tablets (50 mg and 100 mg)
STORAGE
This medication should be stored at room temperature in a container that is resistant to light.

USES
Flurbiprofen is used to treat the inflammation (pain, swelling, and stiffness) of arthritis and osteoarthritis. Flurbiprofen has been shown to block the production of certain body chemicals, called prostaglandins, that may trigger pain.

TREATMENT

You should take this medication on an empty stomach 30 to 60 minutes before meals or two hours after meals, so that it gets into your bloodstream quickly. However, to decrease stomach irritation, your doctor may want you to take this medication with food or antacids. Always follow your doctor's directions.

To relieve your arthritis symptoms, you must take flurbiprofen regulary as directed by your doctor. It may take up to two weeks before you feel the full effects of this medication. Flurbiprofen does not cure arthritis or osteoarthritis, but it will help to control the condition as long as you continue to take it.

It is important to take flurbiprofen on schedule and not to miss any doses. If you do miss a dose, take it as soon as possible, unless it is almost time for your next dose. In that case, do not take the missed dose at all; just return to your regular dosing schedule. Do not double the next dose.

SIDE EFFECTS

Minor. Bloating, constipation, diarrhea, difficulty in sleeping, dizziness, drowsiness, headache, heartburn, indigestion, light-headedness, loss of appetite, nausea, nervousness, soreness of the mouth, unusual sweating, or vomiting. As your body adjusts to the medication, these side effects should disappear.

To relieve constipation, increase the amount of fiber in your diet (fresh fruits and vegetables, salads, bran, and whole-grain breads). You can also increase your exercise and drink more water (unless your doctor directs you to do otherwise).

If you become dizzy or light-headed, sit or lie down for a while; get up slowly from a sitting or reclining position; and be careful on stairs.

Major. Tell your doctor about any side effects that are persistent or particularly bothersome. IT IS ESPECIALLY IMPORTANT TO TELL YOUR DOCTOR about bloody or black, tarry stools; blurred vision; confusion; depression; difficult or painful urination; palpitations; a problem with hearing, or ringing or buzzing in your ears; skin rash, hives, or itching; stomach pain; swelling of the feet or hands; tightness in the chest; unexplained sore throat and fever; unusual bleeding or bruising; unusual fatigue or weakness; unusual weight gain; wheezing or difficulty in breathing; or yellowing of the eyes or skin.

INTERACTIONS

Flurbiprofen interacts with several other medications:

1. Anticoagulants (blood thinners, such as warfarin) can lead to an increase in bleeding complications.

2. Aspirin, other salicylates, and other anti-inflammatory medications can increase stomach irritation. Aspirin may also decrease the effectiveness of flurbiprofen.

3. Flurbiprofen can interact with diuretics (water pills).

4. Probenecid can increase blood levels of flurbiprofen, which may increase the risk of side effects.

5. The action of beta blockers may be decreased by this drug.

Before starting to take flurbiprofen, BE SURE TO TELL YOUR DOCTOR about any medications you are currently taking, especially any of those listed above.

WARNINGS

• Before taking this medication, tell your doctor if you have ever had unusual or allergic reactions to flurbiprofen or to any of the other chemically related drugs (aspirin, other salicylates, diclofenac, diflunisal, fenoprofen, ibuprofen, indomethacin, ketoprofen, meclofenamate, mefenamic acid, naproxen, oxyphenbutazone, phenylbutazone, piroxicam, sulindac, or tolmetin).

• Tell your doctor if you now have or if you have ever had asthma, bleeding problems, colitis, epilepsy, heart disease, high blood pressure, kidney disease, liver disease, mental illness, Parkinson's disease, or stomach ulcers or other stomach problems.

• If flurbiprofen makes you dizzy or drowsy, do not take part in any activity that requires alertness, such as driving a car or operating potentially dangerous machinery.

• Because this drug can prolong your bleeding time, it is important to tell your doctor or dentist that you are taking this drug before having surgery or any other medical or dental treatment.

• Stomach problems are more likely to occur if you take aspirin regularly or drink alcohol while being treated with this medication. These should, therefore, be avoided (unless your doctor directs you to do otherwise).

• The elderly may experience more side effects.

• Be sure to tell your doctor if you are pregnant or if you are planning to become pregnant. This medication can cause unwanted effects on the heart or blood flow to the fetus. Studies in animals have also shown that this medication, if taken late in pregnancy, may increase the length of pregnancy, prolong labor, or cause other problems during delivery. Also tell your doctor if you are breast-feeding an infant. Small amounts of flurbiprofen can pass into breast milk.

---

fluvastatin

BRAND NAME (Manufacturer)
Lescol (Sandoz)
TYPE OF DRUG
Antihyperlipidemic (lipid-lowering drug)
INGREDIENT
fluvastatin
DOSAGE FORM
Capsules (20 mg and 40 mg)
STORAGE
This medication should be stored at room temperature in a tightly closed container away from heat and direct sunlight.

USES

Fluvastatin is used to treat hyperlipidemia (high blood-fat levels). It may be prescribed with nondrug therapies such as diet control and exercise in an attempt to regulate lipid and cholesterol levels. Fluvastatin chemically interferes with an enzyme in the body that is responsible for synthesizing cholesterol. This enzyme blockade decreases the LDL (low-density lipoprotein) type of cholesterol. This type of cholesterol has been associated with coronary artery disease and atherosclerosis.

TREATMENT

This medication should be taken exactly as prescribed by your doctor. If you are to take the drug once a day, it is best to take the drug in the evening. Fluvastatin can be taken with meals or a with a full glass of water if stomach upset occurs.

While taking this medication, try to develop a set schedule for taking it. If you miss a dose and remember within a few hours, take the missed dose and resume your regular schedule.

If many hours have passed, skip the dose you missed and then take your next dose as scheduled. Do not double the dose.

SIDE EFFECTS

Minor. You may experience abdominal pain or cramps, constipation, diarrhea, gas, nausea, or stomach pain. These effects may be relieved by taking fluvastatin with a meal, by adding fiber to your diet, or by using mild stool softeners.

Major. Tell your doctor about any side effects that are persistent or particularly bothersome. IT IS ESPECIALLY IMPORTANT TO TELL YOUR DOCTOR about blurred vision (or any other visual changes or difficulties), or muscle pain or tenderness, especially when accompanied by malaise or fever.

INTERACTIONS

Fluvastatin interacts with several other types of drugs:

1. Fluvastatin may increase the blood levels of oral anticoagulants (blood thinners, such as warfarin) and digoxin, increasing the risk of toxicity of these agents.

2. Because of the risk of severe myopathy (muscle weakness), the combined use of fluvastatin with gemfibrozil or clofibrate should generally be avoided.

3. Cyclosporine, erythromycin, nicotinic acid, or niacin may increase the side effects of fluvastatin and should be used with extreme caution.

Be sure to tell your doctor about any medications your are currently taking, especially any of those listed above.

WARNINGS

• Tell you doctor about unusual or allergic reactions you have had to any medications.

• Tell your doctor if you have ever had liver disease, heart disease, stroke, or disorders of the digestive tract.

• Patients taking another drug in this same class developed eye-related problems during treatment. It is, therefore, advisable to have regular checkups with your ophthalmologist, who should be informed about your use of this drug.

• This drug should not be taken if you are pregnant. Serious side effects have been reported in the offspring of animals that were given this drug during pregnancy. Also be sure to tell your doctor if you are breast-feeding an infant. This medication should not be used while breast-feeding.

fluvoxamine

BRAND NAME (Manufacturer)
Luvox (Solvay)
TYPE OF DRUG
Antidepressant
INGREDIENT
fluvoxamine
DOSAGE FORM
Tablets (50 mg and 100 mg)
STORAGE
This medication should be stored in a tightly closed container at room temperature, away from heat and direct sunlight. Do not store in the bathroom.

USES
Fluvoxamine is used to treat the symptoms of obsessive-compulsive disorder, a mental condition. It works by increasing the concentration of certain chemicals that are necessary for nerve transmission in the brain.

TREATMENT
This medication should be taken exactly as prescribed by your doctor. In order to avoid stomach irritation, you can take fluvoxamine with food or a full glass of water (unless your doctor directed you to do otherwise).

The effects of treatment with fluvoxamine may not become apparent for one to four weeks.

If you are taking this medication once a day and you miss a dose, take the missed dose as soon as possible and return to your regular dosing schedule. Do not double the dose. If you are taking this medication more than once a day and you miss a dose, do not take the missed dose at all; just return to your regular dosing schedule. Again, do not double the dose.

SIDE EFFECTS
Minor. Changes in taste, constipation, decreased appetite, decreased sex drive, dizziness, drowsiness, dry mouth, frequent urination, headache, heartburn, increased sweating, insomnia, nausea, nervousness, runny nose, twitching, unusual tiredness or weakness, or weight loss.

To relieve constipation, increase the amount of fiber in your diet (fresh fruits and vegetables, salads, bran, and whole-grain breads), exercise, and drink more water (unless your doctor directs you to do otherwise).

To avoid dizziness when you stand, contract and relax the muscles in your legs for a few moments before rising.

Dry mouth can be relieved by chewing sugarless gum or sucking on ice chips or hard candy.

Major. Tell your doctor about any side effects that are persistent or especially bothersome. IT IS ESPECIALLY IMPORTANT TO TELL YOUR DOCTOR about anxiety, chills or fever, difficulty in breathing, easy bruising, enlarged lymph glands (swelling under the jaw, in the armpits, or in the groin area), eye problems, joint or muscle pain, mood or mental changes, seizures (convulsions), skin rash or hives, swelling in the feet or lower legs, or unusual tiredness or weakness.

INTERACTIONS

Fluvoxamine interacts with several medications:

1. Fluvoxamine may interfere with the elimination of alprazolam, midazolam or triazolam from your body, increasing the toxicity of these drugs.

2. Fluvoxamine may cause increased amounts of astemizole or terfenadine in the body. Large amounts of astemizole or terfenadine or in the body may cause the heart to beat irregularly.

3. The toxicity of amitriptyline, carbamazepine, cisapride, clomipramine, clozapine, imipramine, lithium, methadone, metoprolol, propranolol, theophylline, or warfarin may be increased if taken with fluvoxamine.

4. The combination of fluvoxamine and MAO inhibitors (including selegiline, procarbazine, furazolidone, isocarboxazid, pargyline, phenelzine, and tranylcypromine) may result in serious toxicities. You should wait at least 14 days between stopping fluvoxamine and starting an MAO inhibitor.

WARNINGS

• Tell your doctor immediately if you develop a skin rash or have hives while taking this medication, or if you have ever had a reaction in the past to fluvoxamine or to any other medication.

• Be sure to tell your doctor if you have or have ever had a history of alcoholism or drug abuse, or if you have ever had a heart attack, asthma, circulatory disease, difficulty in urinating, electroshock therapy, enlarged prostate gland, seizures or epilepsy, glaucoma, high blood pressure, intestinal problems, liver or kidney disease, mental illness, or thyroid disease.

• If this medication makes you drowsy or dizzy, do not take part in any activity that requires mental alertness, such as driving a car or operating dangerous equipment.

• Do not stop taking this medication abruptly. Stopping it suddenly can cause nausea, headache, stomach upset, or worsening of your condition. Your doctor may want to reduce the dose gradually.

• Elderly individuals may be at greater risk of experiencing unwanted or otherwise bothersome side effects. Use this drug cautiously and report any changes in mental status to your doctor immediately.

• The effects of this medication may be present for several weeks after you stop taking it. It is especially important that you continue to observe all precautions during this period.

• Be sure to tell your doctor if you are pregnant or plan to become pregnant. It is not known if fluvoxamine is safe to take during pregnancy. Also be sure to tell your doctor if you are breast-feeding an infant. Small amounts of fluvoxamine pass into breast milk.

furosemide

BRAND NAMES (Manufacturers)
furosemide (various manufacturers)
Lasix (Hoechst-Roussel)
Luramide (Major)
TYPE OF DRUG
Diuretic (water pill) and antihypertensive
INGREDIENT
furosemide
DOSAGE FORMS
Tablets (20 mg, 40 mg, 80 mg, and 200 mg)
Oral solution (10 mg per mL, and 40 mg per 5 mL, with 0.02%, 0.2%, or 11.5% alcohol)

STORAGE
Furosemide tablets should be stored at room temperature in a tightly closed, light-resistant container. The oral solution should be stored in the refrigerator in a tightly closed, light-resistant container. While furosemide in the solution form should be kept cold, this medication should never be frozen.

USES
Furosemide is prescribed to treat high blood pressure. It is also used to reduce fluid accumulation in the body caused by conditions such as heart failure, cirrhosis of the liver, kidney disease, and the long-term use of some medications. Furosemide reduces fluid accumulation by increasing the elimination of sodium and water through the kidneys.

TREATMENT
To decrease stomach irritation, you can take furosemide with a glass of milk or with a meal (unless your doctor directs you to do otherwise). Try to take it at the same time every day. Avoid taking a dose after 6:00 P.M.—this will prevent you from having to get up during the night to urinate.

This medication does not cure high blood pressure, but it will help to control the condition for as long as you continue to take it.

If you miss a dose of furosemide, take it as soon as possible, unless it is almost time for the next dose. In that case, do not take the missed dose at all; just wait until the next scheduled dose. Do not double the dose.

SIDE EFFECTS
Minor. Blurred vision, constipation, cramping, diarrhea, dizziness, headache, itching, loss of appetite, muscle spasms, nausea, sore mouth, stomach upset, vomiting, and weakness. As your body adjusts to the medication, these side effects should disappear.

This medication will cause an increase in the amount of urine or in your frequency of urination when you first begin to take it. It may also cause you to have an unusual feeling of tiredness. These effects should subside after several days.

Furosemide can cause increased sensitivity to sunlight. It is therefore important to avoid prolonged exposure to sun-

light and sunlamps. Wear protective clothing and use an effective sunscreen.

To avoid dizziness and light-headedness when you stand, contract and relax the muscles of your legs for a few moments before rising. Do this by pushing one foot against the floor while raising the other foot slightly, alternating feet so that you are "pumping" your legs in a pedaling motion.

Major. Tell your doctor about any side effects that are persistent or bothersome. IT IS ESPECIALLY IMPORTANT TO TELL YOUR DOCTOR about confusion, difficulty in breathing, dry mouth, fainting, increased thirst, joint pains, loss of appetite, mood changes, muscle cramps, palpitations, rash, ringing in the ears, severe abdominal pain, sore throat, tingling in the fingers or toes, unusual bleeding or bruising, or yellowing of the eyes or skin.

INTERACTIONS

Furosemide interacts with several other drugs:

1. It can increase the side effects of alcohol, barbiturates, narcotics, cephalosporin antibiotics, chloral hydrate, cortisonelike steroids (such as cortisone, dexamethasone, hydrocortisone, prednisone, and prednisolone), digoxin, digitalis, lithium, amphotericin B, clofibrate, aspirin, and theophylline.

2. The effectiveness of antigout medications, insulin, and oral antidiabetic medications may be decreased by furosemide.

3. Phenytoin can decrease the absorption and effectiveness of furosemide.

4. Indomethacin can decrease the diuretic effects of furosemide.

Before taking furosemide, BE SURE TO TELL YOUR DOCTOR if you are taking any of the medicines listed above.

WARNINGS

• Tell your doctor about unusual or allergic reactions you have had to any medications, especially to diuretics, oral antidiabetic medicines, or sulfonamide antibiotics.

• Tell your doctor if you now have, or if you have ever had, kidney disease or problems with urination; diabetes mellitus; gout; liver disease; asthma; pancreatic disease; or systemic lupus erythematosus (SLE).

• Furosemide can cause potassium loss. Signs of potassium loss include dry mouth, thirst, weakness, muscle pain or cramps, nausea, and vomiting. If you experience any of these symptoms, call your doctor. Your doctor may want to have blood tests performed periodically in order to monitor your blood-potassium levels. To help avoid potassium loss, take this medication with a glass of fresh or frozen orange juice or cranberry juice, or eat a banana every day. The use of a salt substitute also helps to prevent potassium loss. Do not change your diet, however, before discussing it with your doctor. Too much potassium may also be dangerous.

• Before having any kind of surgery or other medical or dental treatment, be sure to tell your doctor or dentist that you are taking furosemide.

• To avoid dizziness, light-headedness, or fainting, get up from a sitting or lying position slowly; and avoid standing for long periods of time. You should also avoid strenuous exercise and prolonged exposure to hot weather.

• While taking this medication, limit your intake of alcoholic beverages in order to prevent dizziness and light-headedness.

• If you have high blood pressure, do not take any over-the-counter (nonprescription) medications for weight control; or for cough, cold, asthma, allergy, or sinus problems; unless you first check with your doctor.

• To prevent severe water loss (dehydration) while taking this drug, check with your doctor if you have any illness that causes severe nausea, vomiting, or diarrhea.

• This medication can raise blood-sugar levels in diabetic patients. Therefore, blood sugar should be monitored carefully with blood or urine tests when treatment with this medication is started.

• Be sure to tell your doctor if you are pregnant. This drug crosses the placenta. Although studies in humans have not been completed, adverse effects have been observed on the fetuses of animals who received large doses of this drug during pregnancy. Also tell your doctor if you are breast-feeding an infant. Small amounts of furosemide pass into breast milk.

gabapentin

BRAND NAME (Manufacturer)
Neurontin (Parke-Davis)

TYPE OF DRUG
Anticonvulsant
INGREDIENT
gabapentin
DOSAGE FORM
Capsules (100 mg, 300 mg, and 400 mg)
STORAGE
Gabapentin should be stored at room temperature in tightly closed, light-resistant containers. This medication should never be frozen.

USES

Gabapentin is used in conjunction with other anticonvulsants for the treatment of seizure disorders. The mechanism of action of gabapentin is not related to that of any other anticonvulsant and is not well understood.

TREATMENT

If stomach upset occurs, gabapentin may be taken with food, unless your doctor instructs you to do otherwise.

Routine monitoring of the level of gabapentin in your bloodstream is not necessary. Doses should be administered at evenly spaced intervals day or night, depending on the specific dosage recommended by your doctor. For example, if you take three doses a day, the doses should be spaced eight hours apart.

Try not to miss any doses of this medication. If you do miss a dose, take the missed dose as soon as possible, unless it is almost time for your next dose. In that case, do not take the missed dose at all; just return to your regular dosing schedule. Do not double the next dose unless your doctor directs you to do so. If you miss two or more doses in a row, be sure to contact your doctor.

SIDE EFFECTS

Minor. Constipation, dizziness, drowsiness, headache, nausea, rash or vomiting. These side effects should disappear over time as your body adjusts to the medication.

This medication can increase your sensitivity to sunlight. It is therefore important to avoid prolonged exposure to sunlight or sunlamps. Wear protective clothing and sunglasses, and use an effective sunscreen.

In order to prevent constipation, increase the amount of fiber in your diet (fresh fruits and vegetables, salads, bran, whole-grain breads), exercise, and drink more water (unless your doctor tells you not to do so).

If you feel dizzy or lightheaded, sit or lie down for a while; get up slowly from a sitting or reclining position; and be careful when climbing stairs.

Major. Tell your doctor about any side effects that are persistent or particularly bothersome. IT IS ESPECIALLY IMPORTANT TO TELL YOUR DOCTOR about abnormal balance, abnormal dreaming/hallucinations, blurred vision, chest pain, depression, difficulty breathing, difficulty walking, difficulty with urination, double vision, elevated blood pressure, fever, forgetfulness, numbness or tingling in the hands or feet, palpitations, severe rash, skin discoloration, or tremor.

INTERACTIONS

Gabapentin interacts with several other types of medications:

1. Concurrent use of gabapentin with central nervous system depressants (such as alcohol, antihistamines, barbiturates, benzodiazepine tranquilizers, muscle relaxants, narcotics, pain medications, and phenothiazine tranquilizers), or with tricyclic antidepressants can cause extreme drowsiness.

2. Use of antacids with gabapentin can reduce the level of gabapentin in the blood, which may decrease the effectiveness of gabapentin. It is recommended that gabapentin be taken at least two hours after a dose of antacid.

Before you start gabapentin, BE SURE TO TELL YOUR DOCTOR about any medications you are currently taking, especially any of those listed above.

WARNINGS

• Tell your doctor about any unusual or allergic reactions you have had to any medications, especially to gabapentin or any other anticonvulsant medication.

• Before having surgery or any other medical or dental procedure, be sure to tell your doctor or dentist that you are taking this medication.

• If this medication makes you dizzy or drowsy, do not take part in any activity that requires alertness, such as driving a car or operating potentially dangerous equipment.

• Do not stop taking this medication suddenly. If you stop abruptly, you may experience an uncontrollable seizure.
• Be sure to tell your doctor if you now have or if you have ever had blood disorders, urinary tract infections, urinary incontinence, glaucoma, heart disease, kidney disease, or liver disease.
• Be sure to tell your doctor if you are pregnant. Although extensive studies of gabapentin in humans have not been conducted, gabapentin has been shown to cause side effects in the fetuses of animals that received large doses during pregnancy. Also tell your doctor if you are breast-feeding an infant. It is not known if this medication passes into breast milk.
• This medication has not been shown to be safe and effective in children under 12 years of age.

---

gemfibrozil

BRAND NAMES (Manufacturers)
gemfibrozil (various manufacturers)
Lopid (Parke-Davis)
TYPE OF DRUG
Antihyperlipidemic (lipid-lowering drug)
INGREDIENT
gemfibrozil
DOSAGE FORM
Tablets (600 mg)
STORAGE
This medication should be stored at room temperature in a tightly closed container.

USES

Gemfibrozil is used to treat hyperlipidemia (high blood-fat levels) in patients who have not responded to diet, weight reduction, exercise, and control of blood sugar. It is not clear how gemfibrozil lowers blood-lipid levels, but it is thought to decrease the body's production of certain fats.

TREATMENT

In order to maximize its effectiveness, gemfibrozil should be taken 30 minutes before meals.

If you miss a dose of this medication, take the missed dose of gemfibrozil as soon as possible, unless it is almost time for the next dose. In that case, do not take the missed dose; just return to your regular dosing schedule. Do not double the dose.

SIDE EFFECTS

Minor. Constipation, diarrhea, dizziness, dry mouth, gas, headache, insomnia, loss of appetite, nausea, and stomach upset. These side effects should disappear in several days, as your body adjusts to the medication.

To relieve constipation, increase the amount of fiber in your diet (bran, salads, fresh fruits and vegetables, and whole-grain breads), exercise, and drink more water (unless your doctor directs you to do otherwise).

If you feel dizzy, sit or lie down a while; get up slowly from a sitting or lying position; and be careful on stairs.

To help relieve mouth dryness, chew sugarless gum or suck on ice chips.

Major. Tell your doctor about any side effects that are persistent or particularly bothersome. IT IS ESPECIALLY IMPORTANT TO TELL YOUR DOCTOR about back pain, blurred vision, fatigue, muscle cramps, rash, swollen or painful joints, tingling sensations, or yellowing of the eyes or skin.

INTERACTIONS

Gemfibrozil can increase the effects of oral anticoagulants (blood thinners, such as warfarin), which can lead to bleeding complications. BE SURE TO TELL YOUR DOCTOR if you are already taking a medication of this type.

WARNINGS

• Tell your doctor about unusual or allergic reactions you have had to any medications, especially to gemfibrozil.

• Before starting to take this medication, be sure to tell your doctor if you now have, or if you have ever had, biliary disorders; gallstones or gallbladder disease; kidney disease; or liver disease.

• If this drug makes you dizzy or otherwise interferes with your vision, do not take part in activities that require mental alertness, such as driving an automobile or operating any potentially dangerous machinery or equipment.

• Do not stop taking this medication unless you first check with your doctor. Stopping the drug abruptly may lead to a rapid increase in blood-lipid (fats) and cholesterol levels. Your doctor may therefore want to start you on a special diet or another medication when gemfibrozil is discontinued.

• Large doses of gemfibrozil administered to animals for prolonged periods of time have been associated with benign and malignant cancers. This association has not been observed in humans.

• Be sure to tell your doctor if you are pregnant. Although gemfibrozil appears to be safe during pregnancy, extensive studies in humans have not yet been completed. Also tell your doctor if you are breast-feeding an infant. It is not known whether or not gemfibrozil passes into breast milk.

glipizide

BRAND NAME (Manufacturer)
Glucotrol (Roerig)
TYPE OF DRUG
Oral antidiabetic
INGREDIENT
glipizide
DOSAGE FORM
Tablets (5 mg and 10 mg)
STORAGE
This medication should be stored at room temperature in a tightly closed container.

USES

Glipizide is used for the treatment of diabetes mellitus (sugar diabetes), which appears in adulthood and cannot be managed by control of diet alone. This type of diabetes is known as non–insulin-dependent diabetes (sometimes called maturity-onset or type II diabetes). Glipizide lowers blood-sugar levels by increasing the release of insulin from the pancreas.

TREATMENT

This medication should be taken on an empty stomach 30 minutes before a meal (unless your doctor directs you to do otherwise).

It is important to try not to miss any doses of this medication. If you do miss a dose, take it as soon as possible, unless it is almost time for the next dose. In that case, do not take the missed dose at all; just return to your regular dosing schedule. Do not double the next dose. Tell your doctor if you feel any side effects from missing a dose of this drug.

People with diabetes who are taking oral antidiabetic medication may need to be switched to insulin if they develop diabetic coma, have a severe infection, are scheduled for major surgery, or become pregnant.

SIDE EFFECTS

Minor. Diarrhea, headache, heartburn, loss of appetite, nausea, stomach pain, stomach discomfort, or vomiting. These side effects usually go away during treatment, as your body adjusts to the medicine.

Glipizide may increase your sensitivity to sunlight. It is therefore important to use caution during exposure to the sun. Use an effective sunscreen and avoid exposure to sunlamps.

Major. If any side effects are persistent or particularly bothersome, it is important to notify your doctor. IT IS ESPECIALLY IMPORTANT TO TELL YOUR DOCTOR about dark urine, fatigue, itching of the skin, light-colored stools, rash, sore throat and fever, unusual bleeding or bruising, or yellowing of the eyes or skin.

INTERACTIONS

Glipizide interacts with a number of other medications:

1. Chloramphenicol, guanethidine, insulin, monoamine oxidase (MAO) inhibitors, oxyphenbutazone, oxytetracycline, phenylbutazone, probenecid, aspirin or other salicylates, and sulfonamide antibiotics, when combined with glipizide, can lower blood-sugar levels: Sometimes the level can be dangerously low.

2. Thyroid hormones; dextrothyroxine; epinephrine; phenytoin; thiazide diuretics (water pills); and cortisonelike medications (such as dexamethasone, hydrocortisone, prednisone), combined with glipizide, can actually increase blood-sugar levels—just what you are trying to avoid.

3. Antidiabetic medications can increase the effects of warfarin, which can lead to bleeding complications.

4. Beta-blocking medications (atenolol, metoprolol, nadolol, pindolol, propranolol, and timolol), combined with glipizide, can result in either high or low blood-sugar levels. Beta blockers can also mask the symptoms of low blood sugar, which can be dangerous.

BE SURE TO TELL YOUR DOCTOR if you are already taking any of the medications listed above.

WARNINGS

• It is important to tell your doctor if you have ever had any unusual or allergic reaction to this medicine or to any sulfa medication, including sulfonamide antibiotics, diuretics (water pills), or other oral antidiabetics.

• It is also important to tell your doctor if you now have, or if you have ever had, kidney disease, liver disease, severe infection, or thyroid disease.

• Avoid drinking alcoholic beverages while taking this medication (unless directed otherwise by your doctor). Some patients who take this medicine suffer nausea, vomiting, dizziness, stomach pain, pounding headache, sweating, and redness of the face and skin when they drink alcohol, and large amounts of alcohol can lower blood sugar to dangerously low levels.

• Follow the special diet that your doctor gave you. This is an important part of controlling your blood sugar and is necessary in order for this medicine to work properly.

• Be sure to tell your doctor or dentist that you are taking this medicine before having any kind of surgery or other medical or dental treatment.

• Test for sugar in your urine as directed by your doctor. It is a convenient way to determine whether or not your diabetes is being controlled by this medicine.

• Eat or drink something containing sugar right away if you experience any symptoms of low blood sugar (such as anxiety, chills, cold sweats, cool or pale skin, drowsiness, excessive hunger, headache, nausea, nervousness, rapid heartbeat, shakiness, or unusual tiredness or weakness). It is important that your family and friends know the symptoms of low blood sugar and what to do if they recognize any of these symptoms in you.

• Check with your doctor as soon as possible—even if these symptoms are corrected by the sugar. The blood-sugar-lowering effects of this medicine can last for hours, and the symptoms may return during this period. Good sources of sugar are orange juice, corn syrup, honey, sugar cubes, and table sugar. You are at greatest risk of developing low blood sugar if you skip or delay meals, exercise more than usual, cannot eat because of nausea or vomiting, or drink large amounts of alcohol.

• Be sure to tell your doctor if you are pregnant. Studies have not yet been completed in humans, but studies in animals have shown that this medicine can cause birth defects. Also tell your doctor if you are breast-feeding an infant. Small amounts of glipizide pass into breast milk.

glyburide

BRAND NAMES (Manufacturers)
DiaBeta (Hoechst-Roussel)
Micronase (Upjohn)
TYPE OF DRUG
Oral antidiabetic
INGREDIENT
glyburide
DOSAGE FORM
Tablets (1.25 mg, 2.5 mg, and 5 mg)
STORAGE
This medication should be stored at room temperature in a tightly closed container.

USES

Glyburide is used for the treatment of diabetes mellitus (sugar diabetes) that appears in adulthood and cannot be managed by control of diet alone. This type of diabetes is referred to as non–insulin-dependent diabetes (sometimes called maturity-onset or type II diabetes). Glyburide lowers blood-sugar levels by increasing the release of insulin from the pancreas.

TREATMENT

In order for glyburide to work correctly, it must be taken as directed by your doctor. To maintain a constant blood-sugar level, it is best to take this medication at the same time(s) each day. It is therefore important to try not to miss any doses of this medication. If you do miss a dose, take it as soon as possible, unless it is almost time for the next dose. In that case, do not take the missed dose at all; just return to your regular dosing schedule. Do not double the next dose. Tell your doctor if you feel any side effects from missing a dose of this drug.

It is important to note that people with diabetes who are taking oral antidiabetic medication may need to be switched to insulin if they develop diabetic coma, have a severe infection, are scheduled for major surgery, or become pregnant.

SIDE EFFECTS

Minor. Diarrhea, headache, heartburn, loss of appetite, nausea, stomach discomfort, stomach pain, or vomiting. The side effects from glyburide will most likely disappear during treatment as your body adjusts to the medicine.

Glyburide may increase your sensitivity to sunlight. It is therefore important to use caution during exposure to the sun. You may want to wear protective clothing and sunglasses. Use an effective sunscreen, and avoid exposure to sunlamps.

Major. If any side effects are persistent or particularly bothersome, it is important to notify your doctor. IT IS ESPECIALLY IMPORTANT TO TELL YOUR DOCTOR about dark urine, fatigue, itching of the skin, light-colored stools, rash, sore throat and fever, unusual bleeding or bruising, or yellowing of the eyes or skin.

INTERACTIONS

Glyburide interacts with a number of other medications:

1. Chloramphenicol, guanethidine, insulin, monoamine oxidase (MAO) inhibitors, oxyphenbutazone, oxytetracycline, phenylbutazone, probenecid, aspirin or other salicylates, and sulfonamide antibiotics, when combined with glyburide, can lower blood-sugar levels—sometimes to levels that are dangerously low.

2. Thyroid hormones, dextrothyroxine, epinephrine, phenytoin, thiazide diuretics (water pills), and cortisonelike medications (such as dexamethasone, hydrocortisone, prednisone), combined with glyburide, can actually increase blood-sugar levels.

3. Antidiabetic medications can increase the effects of warfarin, which can lead to bleeding complications.

4. Beta-blocking medications (atenolol, metoprolol, nadolol, pindolol, propranolol, and timolol), combined with glyburide, can result in either high or low blood-sugar levels. Beta blockers can also mask the symptoms of low blood sugar, which can be dangerous.

BE SURE TO TELL YOUR DOCTOR if you are already taking any of the medications listed above.

WARNINGS

• Tell your doctor if you have ever had unusual or allergic reactions to medications, especially to glyburide or to any sulfa medication, including sulfonamide antibiotics, diuretics (water pills), or other oral antidiabetics.

• Tell your doctor if you now have, or if you have ever had, kidney disease, liver disease, thyroid disease, or a severe infection.

• Follow the special diet that your doctor gave you. This is an important part of controlling your blood sugar and is necessary in order for this medicine to work properly.

• Avoid drinking alcoholic beverages while taking this medication (unless otherwise directed by your doctor). Some patients who take this medicine suffer nausea, vomiting, dizziness, stomach pain, pounding headache, sweating, and redness of the face and skin when they drink alcohol, and large amounts of alcohol can lower blood sugar to dangerously low levels.

• Be sure to tell your doctor or dentist that you are taking this medication before having any kind of surgery or other medical or dental treatment.

• Test for sugar in your urine as directed by your doctor. It is a convenient way to determine whether or not your diabetes is being controlled by this medicine.

• Eat or drink something containing sugar right away if you experience any symptoms of low blood sugar (such as anxiety, chills, cold sweats, cool or pale skin, drowsiness, excessive hunger, headache, nausea, nervousness, rapid heartbeat, shakiness, or unusual tiredness or weakness). It is also important that your family and friends recognize the symptoms of low blood sugar and know what to do if they observe any of these symptoms in you.

• Check with your doctor as soon as possible—even if these symptoms are corrected by the sugar. The blood-sugar-lowering effects of this medicine can last for hours, and the symptoms may return during this period. Good sources of sugar are orange juice, corn syrup, honey, sugar cubes, and table sugar. You are at greatest risk of developing low blood sugar if you skip or delay meals, exercise more than usual, cannot eat because of nausea or vomiting, or drink large amounts of alcohol.

• Be sure to tell your doctor if you are pregnant. Studies have not yet been completed in humans, but studies in animals have shown that this medication can cause birth defects.

---

griseofulvin

BRAND NAMES (Manufacturers)
Fulvicin P/G (Schering)
Fulvicin U/F (Schering)
Grifulvin V (Ortho Derm)
Grisactin (Wyeth-Ayerst)
Grisactin Ultra (Wyeth-Ayerst)
griseofulvin (various manufacturers)
Gris-PEG (Herbert)
Grivate (Fujisawa)
TYPE OF DRUG
Antifungal
INGREDIENT
griseofulvin
DOSAGE FORMS
Tablets (125 mg, 165 mg, 250 mg, 330 mg, and 500 mg)
Capsules (125 mg and 250 mg)
Oral suspension (125 mg per 5-mL teaspoonful with 0.2% alcohol)
STORAGE
Griseofulvin tablets, capsules, and oral suspension should be stored at room temperature in tightly closed containers. This medication should never be frozen.

USES

This medication is used to treat certain fungal infections of the skin and nails. Griseofulvin prevents the multiplication of susceptible fungi. It also enters the cells of skin, hair, and nails, and protects them from fungal invasion.

TREATMENT

In order to avoid stomach irritation, you can take griseofulvin with food or milk.

The oral-suspension form of this medication should be shaken well, just before measuring each dose. The contents tend to settle on the bottom of the bottle, so it is necessary to shake the container to evenly distribute the ingredients and equalize the doses. Each dose should then be measured carefully with a specially designed, 5-mL measuring spoon. An ordinary kitchen teaspoon is not accurate enough.

If you miss a dose of this medication, take the missed dose as soon as possible, unless it is almost time for the next dose. In that case, do not take the missed dose at all; just return to your regular dosing schedule. Do not double the next dose.

It is important to continue to take this medication for the entire time prescribed by your doctor (perhaps six months or more), even if the symptoms disappear before the end of that period. If you stop taking this drug too soon, resistant fungi are given a chance to continue growing, and your infection could recur.

SIDE EFFECTS

Minor. Diarrhea, dizziness, fatigue, headache, insomnia, nausea, stomach upset, and vomiting. These side effects should disappear in several days, as your body adjusts to the medication.

If you feel dizzy, sit or lie down a while; get up slowly from a sitting or lying position; and be careful on stairs.

This medication can increase your sensitivity to sunlight. You should therefore avoid prolonged exposure to sunlight and sunlamps. Wear protective clothing and sunglasses, and use an effective sunscreen.

Major. Tell your doctor about any bothersome side effects. IT IS ESPECIALLY IMPORTANT TO TELL YOUR DOCTOR about confusion, itching, skin rash, sore throat, or a tingling of the hands or feet.

INTERACTIONS

Griseofulvin interacts with other types of medication:
1. It can increase the effects of alcohol, resulting in flushing and an increased heart rate.

2. Barbiturates can cause a decrease in the effectiveness of griseofulvin.

3. Griseofulvin can decrease the effectiveness of oral anticoagulants (blood thinners, such as warfarin).

Before starting to take griseofulvin, BE SURE TO TELL YOUR DOCTOR if you are already taking any of these medications.

WARNINGS

• Tell your doctor about unusual or allergic reactions you have had to any medications, especially to griseofulvin, penicillins, cephalosporin antibiotics, or penicillamine.

• Before starting to take griseofulvin, be sure to tell your doctor if you now have, or if you have ever had, liver disease, porphyria, or systemic lupus erythematosus.

• If this drug makes you dizzy, do not take part in any activity that requires alertness, such as driving a car or operating potentially dangerous equipment.

• Observe good hygiene to control the source of infection and to prevent reinfection.

• Concurrent use of an appropriate topical antifungal medication may be necessary to help clear the infection.

• Be sure to tell your doctor if you are pregnant. Extensive studies in pregnant women have not yet been completed, but birth defects have been reported in animals whose mothers received large doses of griseofulvin during pregnancy. Also tell your doctor if you are breast-feeding an infant. It is not known whether or not griseofulvin passes into breast milk.

halcinonide (topical)

BRAND NAMES (Manufacturers)
Halog (Westwood-Squibb)
Halog-E (Westwood-Squibb)
TYPE OF DRUG
Adrenocorticosteroid hormone
INGREDIENT
halcinonide
DOSAGE FORMS
Ointment (0.1%)
Cream (0.025% and 0.1%)
Solution (0.1%)

STORAGE
Halcinonide ointment, cream, and solution should be stored at room temperature in tightly closed containers. This medication should never be frozen.

USES
Your adrenal glands naturally produce certain cortisonelike chemicals. These chemicals are involved in various regulatory processes in the body (such as fluid balance, temperature, and reactions to inflammation). Halcinonide belongs to a group of drugs known as adrenocorticosteroids (or cortisonelike medications). It is used to relieve the skin inflammation (redness, swelling, itching, and discomfort) associated with conditions such as dermatitis, eczema, and poison ivy.

TREATMENT
Before applying this medication, wash your hands. Then, unless your doctor gives you different instructions, gently wash the area of the skin where the medication is to be applied. With a clean towel, pat the area almost dry; it should be slightly damp when you put the medicine on.

Apply a small amount of the medication to the affected area in a thin layer. Do not bandage the area unless your doctor tells you to do so. If you are to apply an occlusive dressing (like kitchen plastic wrap), be sure you understand the instructions.

If you miss a dose of this drug, apply the dose as soon as possible, unless it is time for the next application. In that case, do not apply the missed dose, just return to your regular schedule. Do not double the dose.

SIDE EFFECTS
Minor. Acne, burning sensation, irritation of the affected area, itching, rash, and skin dryness.

If the affected area is extremely dry or scaling, the skin may be moistened before applying the medication by soaking in water or by applying water with a clean cloth. The ointment form is probably better for dry skin.

A mild, temporary stinging sensation may occur after this medication is applied. If this persists, contact your doctor.

Major. Tell your doctor about any side effects that are persistent or particularly bothersome. IT IS ESPECIALLY IMPOR-

TANT TO TELL YOUR DOCTOR about blistering, increased hair growth, loss of skin color, secondary infection in the area being treated, or thinning of the skin with easy bruising.

INTERACTIONS
This medication does not interact with any other medications, as long as it is used according to directions.

WARNINGS
• Tell your doctor about unusual or allergic reactions you have had to medications, especially to halcinonide or any other adrenocorticosteroids (such as amcinonide, betamethasone, cortisone, desonide, desoximetasone, dexamethasone, flumethasone, fluocinolone, fluocinonide, fluorometholone, fluprednisolone, flurandrenolide, hydrocortisone, methylprednisolone, paramethasone, prednisolone, prednisone, or triamcinolone).
• Tell your doctor if you now have, or if you have ever had, blood-vessel disease, chicken pox, diabetes mellitus, fungal infection, peptic ulcers, shingles, tuberculosis, tuberculosis of the skin, vaccinia, or any other type of infection, especially at the site currently being treated.
• If irritation develops while using this drug, immediately discontinue its use, and notify your doctor.
• This product is not for use in the eyes or mucous membranes. Exposure of this medication to the eye may result in ocular (eye related) side effects.
• Do not use this product with an occlusive wrap unless your doctor directs you to do so. Systemic absorption of this drug is increased if occlusive bandages are used. If it is necessary for you to use this drug under a wrap, follow your doctors instructions exactly; do not leave the wrap in place longer than specified.
• If you are using this medication on a child's diaper area, do not put tight-fitting diapers or plastic pants on the child. This may lead to increased systemic absorption of the drug and could possibly cause an increase in side effects.
• Be sure to tell your doctor if you are pregnant. If large amounts of this drug are applied for prolonged periods, some of it will be absorbed and may cross the placenta. Although studies in humans have not yet been completed, birth defects have been observed in the offspring of animals who were

given large oral doses of this type of drug during pregnancy. Also tell your doctor if you are breast-feeding an infant. If absorbed through the skin, small amounts of halcinonide are known to pass into breast milk and may cause growth suppression or a decrease in natural adrenocorticosteroid production in the nursing infant.

---

haloperidol

BRAND NAMES (Manufacturers)
Haldol (McNeil CPC)
haloperidol (various manufacturers)
TYPE OF DRUG
Antipsychotic
INGREDIENT
haloperidol
DOSAGE FORMS
Tablets (0.5 mg, 1 mg, 2 mg, 5 mg, 10 mg, and 20 mg)
Oral concentrate (2 mg per mL)
STORAGE
Haloperidol tablets and oral concentrate should be stored at room temperature in a tightly closed, light-resistant container. This medication should not be refrigerated and should never be frozen.

USES
Haloperidol is prescribed to treat the symptoms of certain types of mental illness, such as the emotional symptoms of psychosis, the manic phase of manic-depressive illness, Tourette's syndrome, and severe behavioral problems in children. This drug is thought to relieve symptoms of mental illness by blocking certain chemicals involved with nerve transmission in the brain.

TREATMENT
To avoid stomach irritation, you can take haloperidol tablets with a meal or with a glass of water or milk (unless your doctor directs you to do otherwise).

Immediately prior to administration, the oral-concentrate form of this medication should be measured carefully with the dropper provided, then added to four ounces (½ cup) or more of water, milk, applesauce, pudding, or a cola-free, caffeine-free carbonated beverage. To prevent possible loss of effectiveness, the medication should not be diluted in tea, coffee, other caffeine-containing beverages, or apple juice.

If you miss a dose of this medication and remember within six hours, take the missed dose as soon as possible, then return to your regular schedule. If more than six hours have passed, however, skip the missed dose and return to your regular dosing schedule. Do not double the next dose unless your doctor directs you to do so.

The full effects of haloperidol may not become apparent for two weeks after you start to take it.

SIDE EFFECTS

Minor. Blurred vision, constipation, decreased or increased sweating, diarrhea, dizziness, drooling, drowsiness, dry mouth, fatigue, headache, heartburn, jitteriness, loss of appetite, menstrual irregularities, nausea, restlessness, sleep disorders, vomiting, or weakness. As your body adjusts to the medication, these side effects should disappear.

This medication can cause increased sensitivity to sunlight. It is, therefore, important to avoid prolonged exposure to sunlight and sunlamps. Wear protective clothing and use an effective sunscreen.

If you are constipated, increase the amount of fiber in your diet (fresh fruits and vegetables, salads, bran, and whole-grain breads), exercise, and drink more water (unless your doctor directs you to do otherwise).

To reduce mouth dryness, chew sugarless gum or suck on ice chips or a piece of hard candy.

To avoid dizziness or light-headedness when you stand, contract and relax the muscles of your legs for a few moments before rising. Do this by pushing one foot against the floor while raising the other foot slightly, alternating feet so that you are "pumping" your legs in a pedaling motion.

Major. Tell your doctor about any side effects that are persistent or particularly bothersome. IT IS ESPECIALLY IMPORTANT TO TELL YOUR DOCTOR about aching joints and muscles; breast enlargement (in both sexes); chest pain; confusion; convulsions; difficulty in breathing or swallowing; difficulty in urinating; fainting; fever; fluid retention; hair loss; hallucinations; impotence; involuntary movements of the mouth, face, neck, tongue, or limbs; mouth sores; palpitations; skin darkening; skin rash; sore throat; tremors; unusual bleeding or bruising; visual disturbances; or yellowish discoloration of the eyes or skin.

INTERACTIONS
Haloperidol interacts with several other drugs:
1. It can cause extreme drowsiness when combined with alcohol or other central nervous system depressants (such as antihistamines, barbiturates, benzodiazepine tranquilizers, muscle relaxants, narcotics, and pain medications) or with tricyclic antidepressants.
2. This drug can lessen the effectiveness of guanethidine and anticonvulsants (antiseizure medications).
3. Haloperidol may increase the side effects of epinephrine, lithium, and methyldopa.
   Before starting to take haloperidol, BE SURE TO TELL YOUR DOCTOR about any medications you are currently taking, especially any of those listed above.

WARNINGS
• Tell your doctor about unusual or allergic reactions you have had to any medications, especially to haloperidol or to any other drugs that are used to treat mental illness.
• Tell your doctor if you now have or if you have ever had any blood disorders, blockage of the urinary tract, depression induced by drugs, enlarged prostate gland, epilepsy, glaucoma, heart or circulatory disease, kidney disease, liver disease, lung disease, mental depression, Parkinson's disease, peptic ulcers, or thyroid disease.
• In order to prevent oversedation, avoid drinking alcoholic beverages while taking this medication.
• If this medication makes you dizzy or drowsy, do not take part in any activity that requires alertness, such as driving a car or operating potentially dangerous machinery. Be careful on stairs, and avoid getting up suddenly from a lying or sitting position.
• This medication can decrease sweating and heat release from the body. You should, therefore, avoid getting overheated by strenuous exercise in hot weather and should avoid taking hot baths, showers, and saunas.

• Prior to having surgery or any other medical or dental treatment, be sure to tell your doctor or dentist that you are taking this medication.

• Some of the side effects caused by this drug can be prevented by taking an antiparkinsonism drug. Discuss this with your doctor.

• Do not stop taking this medication suddenly. If the drug is stopped abruptly, you may experience nausea, vomiting, stomach upset, headache, increased heart rate, insomnia, tremors, or a worsening of your condition. Your doctor may want to reduce the dosage gradually.

• The elderly may be at increased risk for side effects. Watch closely for side effects and for any other changes—especially in mental status—after taking haloperidol, and report them to your doctor.

• If you are planning to have a myelogram or any other procedure in which dye is injected into the spinal cord, tell your doctor that you are taking this medication.

• Avoid spilling the oral-concentrate form of this medication on your skin or clothing; it can cause redness and irritation of the skin.

• While taking haloperidol, do not take any over-the-counter (nonprescription) medications for weight control or for cough, cold, allergy, asthma, or sinus problems unless you first check with your doctor. The combination of these medications may cause high blood pressure.

• Haloperidol has the potential to cause a permanent movement disorder called tardive dyskinesia. It is important to discuss this with your doctor and to report any unusual or uncontrolled body movements.

• Some haloperidol formulations contain the color additive FD&C Yellow No. 5 (tartrazine), which can cause allergic-type reactions (rash, shortness of breath, fainting) in certain susceptible individuals.

• Be sure to tell your doctor if you are pregnant. A few cases of limb malformations have occurred in infants whose mothers had received haloperidol in combination with several other drugs during the first three months of pregnancy. Whether haloperidol was the cause is still not known. Also tell your doctor if you are breast-feeding an infant. Small amounts of haloperidol pass into breast milk.

hydralazine

BRAND NAMES (Manufacturers)
Apresoline (Ciba)
hydralazine hydrochloride (various manufacturers)
TYPE OF DRUG
Antihypertensive
INGREDIENT
hydralazine
DOSAGE FORM
Tablets (10 mg, 25 mg, 50 mg, and 100 mg)
STORAGE
Hydralazine tablets should be stored at room temperature in a tightly closed, light-resistant container.

USES

This medication is used to treat high blood pressure or heart failure. Hydralazine is a vasodilator that directly relaxes the muscle of the blood vessels and allows the blood to flow at a lower force, which causes a lowering of blood pressure.

TREATMENT

In order to avoid stomach irritation while you are taking this medication, you can take your dose of hydralazine with food or with a glass of water or milk. To become accustomed to taking this medication, try to take it at the same time(s) each day. It may take up to two weeks before the full effects of this medication are observed.

Try not to miss any doses of this medication. If you do miss a dose, take the missed dose as soon as possible, unless it is almost time for the next dose. In that case, do not take the missed dose at all; just return to your regular dosing schedule. Do not double the next dose.

Hydralazine does not cure high blood pressure, but it will help to control the condition as long as you continue to take the medication.

SIDE EFFECTS

Minor. Constipation, diarrhea, dizziness, drowsiness, flushing, headache, light-headedness, loss of appetite, muscle cramps, nasal congestion, nausea, or vomiting. These minor side effects should disappear as your body adjusts to therapy with this medication.

To relieve constipation, increase the amount of fiber in your diet (fresh fruits and vegetables, salads, bran, and whole-grain breads), exercise, and drink more water (unless your doctor directs you to do otherwise).

If you feel dizzy or light-headed, sit or lie down for a while; get up slowly from a sitting or reclining position; and be careful on stairs. To avoid dizziness or light-headedness when you stand, contract and relax the muscles of your legs for a few moments before rising. Do this by pushing one foot against the floor while raising the other foot slightly, alternating feet so that you are "pumping" your legs in a pedaling motion.

Major. Tell your doctor about any side effects that are persistent or particularly bothersome. IT IS ESPECIALLY IMPORTANT TO TELL YOUR DOCTOR about anxiety, chest pain, confusion, cramping, depression, difficulty in urinating, fever, itching, numbness or tingling in the fingers or toes, palpitations, rapid weight gain (three to five pounds within a week), rash, shortness of breath, sore throat, tenderness in the joints and muscles, tiredness, unusual bleeding or bruising, or yellowing of the eyes or skin.

INTERACTIONS

Hydralazine interacts with several other types of drugs:

1. The combination of alcohol and hydralazine can lead to dizziness and fainting. You should, therefore, avoid drinking alcoholic beverages while on this drug.

2. Used within 14 days of a monoamine oxidase (MAO) inhibitor, hydralazine can cause severe reactions.

Before you start to take hydralazine, BE SURE TO TELL YOUR DOCTOR about any medications you are currently taking, especially an MAO inhibitor.

WARNINGS

• Tell your doctor about any unusual or allergic reactions you have had to any medications, especially to hydralazine.

• Tell your doctor if you have ever had angina, heart disease, stroke, a heart attack, or kidney disease.

• To avoid dizziness or fainting, try not to stand for long periods of time, and avoid drinking alcohol. You should also try not to get overheated (avoid hot baths, showers, saunas, and strenuous exercise in hot weather).

• If this drug makes you dizzy or drowsy, avoid taking part in any activities that require alertness, such as driving a car or operating potentially dangerous machinery.

• Before having surgery or any other medical or dental treatment, be sure to tell your doctor or dentist that you are taking this medication.

• Do not take any over-the-counter (nonprescription) allergy, asthma, sinus, cough, cold, or diet products unless you first consult your doctor or pharmacist. The combination of these medications with hydralazine may cause an increase in blood pressure.

• Some hydralazine formulations contain the color additive FD&C Yellow No. 5 (tartrazine), which can cause allergic-type reactions (rash, shortness of breath, fainting) in certain susceptible individuals.

• Do not stop taking this medication until you check with your doctor. If this drug is stopped abruptly, you could experience a sudden rise in blood pressure and other complications. Your doctor may, therefore, want to decrease your dosage gradually.

• Be sure to tell your doctor if you are pregnant. Although studies in humans have not been conducted, hydralazine crosses the placenta, and studies have shown that it causes birth defects in the offspring of animals that received large doses of it during pregnancy. Also tell your doctor if you are breast-feeding an infant. It is not known whether hydralazine passes into breast milk.

hydrochlorothiazide

BRAND NAMES (Manufacturers)
Diaqua (Mallard)
Esidrix (Ciba)
Hydro-Chlor (Vortech)
hydrochlorothiazide (various manufacturers)
Hydro-D (Halsey)
HydroDIURIL (Merck Sharp & Dohme)
Hydromal (Hauck)
Hydro-T (Major)

Mictrin (EconoMed)
Oretic (Abbott)
TYPE OF DRUG
Diuretic and antihypertensive
INGREDIENT
hydrochlorothiazide
DOSAGE FORMS
Tablets (25 mg, 50 mg, and 100 mg)
Oral solution (50 mg per 5-mL spoonful)
Intensol oral solution (100 mg per mL)
STORAGE
This medication should be stored at room temperature in a tightly closed container.

USES

Hydrochlorothiazide is prescribed to treat high blood pressure (hypertension). It is also used to reduce fluid accumulation in the body caused by conditions such as heart failure, cirrhosis of the liver, kidney disease, and the long-term use of some medications. This medication reduces body fluid accumulation by increasing the elimination of salt and water through the kidneys.

TREATMENT

To decrease stomach irritation, you can take this medication with a glass of milk or with a meal (unless your doctor directs you to do otherwise). Each dose of the oral solution should be measured carefully with the dropper provided (Intensol solution) or a specially designed 5-mL measuring spoon. An ordinary kitchen teaspoon is not accurate enough. Try to take it at the same time every day. Avoid taking a dose after 6:00 P.M.; otherwise, you may have to get up during the night to urinate.

If you miss a dose of this medication, take the missed dose as soon as possible, unless it is almost time for the next dose. In that case, do not take the missed dose at all; just wait until the next scheduled dose. Do not double the dose.

This drug does not cure high blood pressure.

SIDE EFFECTS

Minor. Constipation, cramps, diarrhea, dizziness, drowsiness, headache, heartburn, loss of appetite, restlessness, or upset stomach. As your body adjusts to the medication, these side effects should disappear.

This drug can cause increased sensitivity to sunlight. Therefore, avoid prolonged exposure to sunlight and sunlamps. Wear protective clothing and use an effective sunscreen.

To relieve constipation, increase the amount of fiber in your diet (fresh fruits and vegetables, salads, bran, and whole-grain breads) and exercise more (unless your doctor directs you to do otherwise).

To avoid dizziness or light-headedness when you stand, contract and relax the muscles of your legs for a few moments before rising. Do this by pushing one foot against the floor while raising the other foot slightly, alternating feet so that you are "pumping" your legs in a pedaling motion.

Major. Tell your doctor about any side effects you experience that are persistent or particularly bothersome. IT IS ESPECIALLY IMPORTANT TO TELL YOUR DOCTOR about blurred vision, confusion, difficulty in breathing, dry mouth, excessive thirst, excessive weakness, fever, itching, joint pain, mood changes, muscle pain or spasms, nausea, palpitations, skin rash, sore throat, tingling in the fingers or toes, vomiting, or yellowing of the eyes or skin.

INTERACTIONS

Hydrochlorothiazide interacts with certain other drugs:

1. It can decrease the effectiveness of oral anticoagulants, antigout medications, insulin, oral antidiabetic medicines, and methenamine.

2. Fenfluramine can increase the blood-pressure-lowering effects of hydrochlorothiazide (which can be dangerous).

3. Indomethacin can decrease the blood-pressure-lowering effects of hydrochlorothiazide, thereby counteracting the desired effects.

4. Cholestyramine and colestipol decrease the absorption of this medication from the gastrointestinal tract. Hydrochlorothiazide should, therefore, be taken one hour before or four hours after a dose of cholestyramine or colestipol (if you have also been prescribed one of these medications).

5. Hydrochlorothiazide may increase the side effects of amphotericin B, calcium, cortisone and cortisonelike steroids (such as dexamethasone, hydrocortisone, prednisone, or prednisolone), digoxin, digitalis, lithium, and vitamin D.

BE SURE TO TELL YOUR DOCTOR about any medications you are currently taking, especially any of those listed above.

WARNINGS

• Be sure to tell your doctor about unusual or allergic reactions you have had to any medications, especially to hydrochlorothiazide or other sulfa medications, including other diuretics, oral antidiabetic medications, and sulfonamide antibiotics.

• Be sure to tell your doctor if you now have or if you have ever had kidney disease or problems with urination, diabetes mellitus, gout, liver disease, asthma, pancreatic disease, or systemic lupus erythematosus.

• Hydrochlorothiazide can cause potassium loss. Signs of potassium loss include dry mouth, thirst, weakness, muscle pain or cramps, nausea, and vomiting. If you experience any of these symptoms, it is important that you call your doctor. To help avoid potassium loss, take this medication with a glass of fresh or frozen orange or cranberry juice, or eat a banana every day. The use of a salt substitute also helps to prevent potassium loss. Do not change your diet or use a salt substitute, however, before discussing it with your doctor. Too much potassium can also be dangerous. Your doctor may want you to have blood tests performed periodically in order to monitor your potassium levels while you are taking this drug.

• To prevent dizziness and light-headedness, limit your intake of alcoholic beverages while taking this medication.

• Becoming overheated can be hazardous while you are taking this medication. Avoid strenuous exercise in hot weather and do not take hot baths, showers, or saunas.

• If you have high blood pressure, do not take any over-the-counter (nonprescription) medications for weight control or for allergy, asthma, cough, cold, or sinus problems unless your doctor directs you to do so.

• To prevent dehydration (severe water loss) while taking this medication, check with your doctor if you have any illness that causes severe or continuous nausea, vomiting, or diarrhea.

• This medication can raise blood-sugar levels in diabetic patients. Therefore, blood sugar should be carefully monitored by blood or urine tests when this medication is being taken.

• Before having surgery or any other medical or dental treatment, be sure to tell your doctor or dentist that you are taking this medication.

• Be certain to inform your doctor if you are pregnant. Hydrochlorothiazide can cross the placenta and may cause adverse effects on the developing fetus. Also tell your doctor if you are breast-feeding an infant. Although problems in humans have not been reported, small amounts of this medication can pass into breast milk, so caution is warranted.

---

hydrocortisone (systemic)

BRAND NAMES (Manufacturers)
Cortef (Upjohn)
hydrocortisone (various manufacturers)
Hydrocortone (Merck Sharp & Dohme)
TYPE OF DRUG
Adrenocorticosteroid hormone
INGREDIENT
hydrocortisone (cortisol)
DOSAGE FORMS
Tablets (5 mg, 10 mg, and 20 mg)
Oral suspension (10 mg per 5-mL spoonful)
STORAGE
Store at room temperature in a tightly closed container. Systemic hydrocortisone should not be refrigerated and should never be frozen.

USES

Your adrenal glands naturally produce certain cortisonelike chemicals. These chemicals are involved in various regulatory processes in the body (such as balance, temperature, and reaction to inflammation). Hydrocortisone belongs to a group of drugs known as adrenocorticosteroids (or cortisonelike medications). It is used to treat a variety of disorders, including endocrine (hormonal) and rheumatic disorders; asthma; blood diseases; certain cancers; eye disorders; gastrointestinal disturbances, such as ulcerative colitis; respiratory diseases; and inflammations such as arthritis, dermatitis, poison ivy, and other allergic conditions. How this medication acts to relieve these disorders is not completely understood.

TREATMENT

In order to prevent stomach irritation, you can take hydrocortisone with food or milk.

If you are taking only one dose of this medication each day, try to take it before 9:00 A.M. This mimics the normal hormonal production in your body.

The oral-suspension form of this medication should be shaken well just before measuring each dose. The contents tend to settle on the bottom of the bottle, so it is necessary to shake the container to distribute the ingredients evenly and equalize the doses. Each dose should then be measured carefully with a specially designed 5-mL measuring spoon. An ordinary kitchen teaspoon is not accurate enough.

It is important to try not to miss any doses of hydrocortisone. However, if you do miss a dose of this medication, follow these guidelines:

1. If you are taking hydrocortisone more than once a day, take the missed dose as soon as possible, then return to your regular schedule. If it is already time for the next dose, double the dose.

2. If you are taking this medication once a day, take the dose you missed as soon as possible, unless you don't remember until the next day. In that case, do not take the missed dose at all; just follow your regular schedule. Do not double the next dose.

3. If you are taking this drug every other day, take the missed dose as soon as you remember. If you missed the scheduled dose by a whole day, take it when you remember and then skip a day before you take the next dose. Do not double the dose.

If you miss more than one dose of hydrocortisone, CONTACT YOUR DOCTOR.

SIDE EFFECTS

Minor. Dizziness, false sense of well-being, increased appetite, increased sweating, indigestion, menstrual irregularities, nausea, reddening and swelling of the skin on the face, restlessness, sleep disorders, or weight gain. These side effects should disappear as your body adjusts to the medication.

To help avoid potassium loss while using systemic hydrocortisone, take your dose of medication with a glass of fresh or frozen orange juice, or eat a banana each day. The use of a salt substitute also helps to prevent potassium loss. Check with your doctor before changing your diet or using a salt substitute.

Major. Tell your doctor about any side effects that are persistent or particularly bothersome. IT IS ESPECIALLY IMPORTANT TO TELL YOUR DOCTOR about abdominal (area around and above the waist) enlargement; acne or other skin problems; back or rib pain; bloody or black, tarry stools; blurred vision; convulsions; eye pain; fever and sore throat; growth impairment (in children); headaches; slow healing of wounds; increased thirst and urination; mental depression; mood changes; muscle wasting; muscle weakness; nightmares; rapid weight gain (three to five pounds within a week); rash; red lines across the abdomen; severe abdominal pain; shortness of breath; thinning of the skin; unusual bleeding or bruising; or unusual weakness.

INTERACTIONS

The systemic form of hydrocortisone adrenocorticosteroid hormone interacts with several other types of medications:

1. Alcohol, aspirin, and anti-inflammatory medications (such as diclofenac, diflunisal, flurbiprofen, ibuprofen, indomethacin, ketoprofen, mefenamic acid, meclofenamate, naproxen, piroxicam, sulindac, and tolmetin) aggravate the stomach problems that are common with use of this medication.

2. The dosage of oral anticoagulants (blood thinners, such as warfarin), oral antidiabetic drugs, or insulin may need to be adjusted when this medication is started or stopped.

3. The loss of potassium caused by hydrocortisone can lead to serious side effects in individuals taking digoxin. Thiazide diuretics (water pills) can also increase the potassium loss caused by hydrocortisone.

4. Phenobarbital, phenytoin, rifampin, and ephedrine can increase the elimination of hydrocortisone from the body, thereby decreasing its effectiveness.

5. Oral contraceptives (birth control pills) and drugs that contain estrogen may decrease the elimination of this drug from the body, which can lead to an increase in side effects.

6. Hydrocortisone can increase the elimination of aspirin and isoniazid from the body, thereby decreasing the effectiveness of these two medications.

7. Cholestyramine and colestipol can chemically bind with this medication in the stomach and gastrointestinal tract, preventing its absorption and decreasing its effectiveness.

BE SURE TO TELL YOUR DOCTOR about any medications you are currently taking, especially any of those listed above.

WARNINGS

• Tell your doctor about unusual or allergic reactions you have had to any medications, especially to hydrocortisone or other adrenocorticosteroids (such as betamethasone, cortisone, dexamethasone, fluocinolone, methylprednisolone, prednisolone, prednisone, and triamcinolone).

• Tell your doctor if you now have or if you have ever had bone disease, diabetes mellitus, emotional instability, glaucoma, fungal infections, heart disease, high blood pressure, high cholesterol levels, myasthenia gravis, peptic ulcers, osteoporosis, thyroid disease, tuberculosis, ulcerative colitis, kidney disease, or liver disease.

• If you are using this medication for longer than a week, you may need to receive higher dosages if you are subjected to stress, such as serious infections, injury, or surgery. Discuss this with your doctor.

• If you have been taking this drug for more than a week, do not stop taking it suddenly. If it is stopped suddenly, you may experience abdominal or back pain, dizziness, fainting, fever, muscle or joint pain, nausea, vomiting, shortness of breath, or extreme weakness. Your doctor may, therefore, want to reduce the dosage gradually. Never increase the dosage or take the drug for longer than the prescribed time, unless you first consult your doctor.

• While you are taking this drug, you should not be vaccinated or immunized. This medication decreases the effectiveness of vaccines and can lead to overwhelming infection if a live-virus vaccine is administered.

• Before having surgery or any other medical or dental treatment, be sure to tell your doctor or dentist that you are taking this medication.

• Because this drug can cause glaucoma and cataracts with long-term use, your doctor may want you to have your eyes examined by an ophthalmologist periodically during treatment.

• If you are taking this medication for prolonged periods, you should wear or carry an identification card or notice that clearly states that you are taking an adrenocorticosteroid medication.

• This medication can raise blood-sugar levels in diabetic patients. Blood-sugar levels should, therefore, be monitored carefully with blood or urine tests.

• Be sure to tell your doctor if you are pregnant. This drug crosses the placenta. Although studies in humans have not been conducted, birth defects have been observed in the offspring of animals that were given large doses of this drug during pregnancy. Also tell your doctor if you are breast-feeding an infant. Small amounts of this drug pass into breast milk and may cause growth suppression or a decrease in natural adrenocorticosteroid hormone production in the nursing infant.

---

hydrocortisone (topical)

BRAND NAMES (Manufacturers)
Acticort 100 (Baker/Cummins)
Aeroseb-HC (Herbert)
Ala-Cort (Del-Ray)
Ala-Scalp (Del-Ray)
Bactine Hydrocortisone* (Miles)
CaldeCort Anti-Itch* (Fisons)
CaldeCort Light with Aloe* (Fisons)
Cetacort (Owen/Galderma)
Cortaid* (Upjohn)
Cort-Dome (Miles)
Cortef Feminine Itch* (Upjohn)
Cortizone-5* (Thompson)
Cortril (Pfizer)
Delcort (Mallard)
Dermacort (Solvay)

DermiCort* (Republic Drug)
Dermolate Anti-Itch* (Schering)
Dermolate Scalp-Itch* (Schering)
Dermtex HC with aloe* (Pfeiffer)
FoilleCort* (Blistex)
Gynecort* (Combe)
Hi-Cor (C & M Pharmaceuticals)
hydrocortisone acetate (various manufacturers)
Hydro-Tex (Syosset)
Hytone (Dermik)
LactiCare-HC (Stiefel)
Lanacort* (Combe)
Locoid (Ferndale)
Nutracort (Owen/Galderma)
Penecort (Herbert Labs)
Synacort (Syntex)
Texacort (GenDerm)
Westcort (Westwood-Squibb)
*Available over the counter (without a prescription) in
   concentrations of 0.5% or less.
TYPE OF DRUG
Adrenocorticosteroid hormone
INGREDIENT
hydrocortisone
DOSAGE FORMS
Cream (0.1%, 0.2%, 0.25%, 0.5%, 1%, and 2.5%)
Ointment (0.1%, 0.2%, 0.5%, 1%, and 2.5%)
Lotion (0.25%, 0.5%, 1%, 2%, and 2.5%)
Gel (0.5% and 1%)
Pump spray (0.5% and 1%)
Aerosol (0.5%)
STORAGE
Hydrocortisone cream, ointment, lotion, gel, pump spray, and
aerosol should be stored at room temperature in tightly closed
containers. This medication should never be frozen.
   The aerosol form is packaged under pressure. It should not
be stored near heat or an open flame or in direct sunlight,
and the container should never be punctured.

USES
Your adrenal glands naturally produce certain cortisonelike
chemicals. These chemicals are involved in various regula-

tory processes in the body (such as fluid balance, temperature, and reaction to inflammation). Hydrocortisone belongs to a group of drugs known as adrenocorticosteroids (or cortisonelike medications). It is used to relieve the skin inflammation (redness, swelling, itching, and discomfort) that is associated with conditions such as dermatitis, eczema, and poison ivy.

TREATMENT

Before applying this medication, wash your hands. Then, unless your doctor gives you different instructions, gently wash the area of the skin where the medication is to be applied. With a clean towel, pat the area almost dry; it should be slightly damp when you put the medicine on.

Apply a small amount of the medication to the affected area in a thin layer. Do not bandage the area unless your doctor tells you to do so. If you are to apply an occlusive dressing (like kitchen plastic wrap), be sure you understand the instructions. Wash your hands again after application.

If you are using the aerosol form, shake the can in order to disperse the medication evenly. Hold the can upright six to eight inches from the area to be sprayed, and spray the area for one to three seconds. DO NOT SMOKE while you are using the aerosol; the contents are under pressure and may explode if exposed to heat or flames.

If you miss a dose of this medication, apply the dose as soon as possible, unless it is almost time for the next application. In that case, do not apply the missed dose at all; just return to your regular dosing schedule. Do not double the next dose.

SIDE EFFECTS

Minor. Acne, burning sensation, itching, skin dryness, or rash.

If the affected area is extremely dry or scaling, the skin may be moistened before applying the medication by soaking in water or by applying water with a clean cloth. The ointment form is probably most suitable for dry skin.

A mild stinging sensation may occur after this medication is applied. If this sensation persists, contact your doctor.

Major. Tell your doctor about any side effects that are persistent or particularly bothersome. IT IS ESPECIALLY IMPORTANT TO TELL YOUR DOCTOR about blistering, increased hair growth, irritation of the affected area, loss of skin color, secondary infection in the area being treated, or thinning of the skin with easy bruising.

INTERACTIONS

This medication should not interact with other medications as long as it is used according to the directions given to you by your doctor or pharmacist.

WARNINGS

• Tell your doctor about unusual or allergic reactions you have had to any medications, especially to hydrocortisone or other adrenocorticosteroids (such as amcinonide, betamethasone, clocortolone, cortisone, desonide, desoximetasone, dexamethasone, diflorasone, flumethasone, fluocinolone, fluocinonide, flurandrenolide, halcinonide, methylprednisolone, paramethasone, prednisolone, prednisone, and triamcinolone).

• Tell your doctor if you now have or if you have ever had blood-vessel disease, chicken pox, diabetes mellitus, fungal infections, peptic ulcers, shingles, tuberculosis, tuberculosis of the skin, vaccinia, or any other type of infection, especially at the site currently being treated.

• If any irritation develops while using hydrocortisone, immediately discontinue its use and notify your doctor.

• This product is not for use in the eyes, nose, or mouth; contact may result in side effects.

• Do not use this product with an occlusive wrap unless your doctor directs you to do so. Systemic absorption of hydrocortisone is increased if large areas of the body are treated, particularly if occlusive bandages are used. If it is necessary for you to use this drug under a wrap, follow your doctor's instructions exactly; do not leave the wrap in place longer than specified.

• If you are using this medication on a child's diaper area, do not put tight-fitting diapers or plastic pants on the child. This may lead to increased systemic absorption of the drug and a possible increase in side effects.

• In order to avoid freezing skin tissue when using the aerosol or pump spray form of hydrocortisone, make sure that you do not spray for more than three seconds; and hold the container at least six inches away from the skin.

• When using the aerosol or pump spray form of this medication on the face, cover your eyes, and do not inhale the spray (in order to avoid side effects).

• Be sure to tell your doctor if you are pregnant. If large amounts of this drug are applied for prolonged periods, some of it will be absorbed and may cross the placenta. Although studies in humans have not been conducted, birth defects have been observed in the offspring of animals that were given large oral doses of this drug during pregnancy. Also tell your doctor if you are breast-feeding an infant. If absorbed through the skin, small amounts of hydrocortisone are known to pass into breast milk and may cause growth suppression or a decrease in natural adrenocorticosteroid hormone production in the nursing infant.

---

hydrocortisone, benzyl benzoate, bismuth resorcin compound, bismuth subgallate, zinc oxide, and Peruvian balsam combination (topical)

BRAND NAMES (Manufacturers)
Anumed HC (Major)
Anusol HC (Parke-Davis)
Hemorrhoidal HC (various manufacturers)
TYPE OF DRUG
Adrenocorticosteroid-containing hemorrhoidal and
    anorectal product
INGREDIENTS
hydrocortisone, benzyl benzoate, bismuth resorcin
    compound, bismuth subgallate, zinc oxide, and Peruvian
    balsam

DOSAGE FORMS

Rectal cream (0.5% hydrocortisone, 1.2% benzyl benzoate, 1.75% bismuth resorcin compound, 2.25% bismuth subgallate, 11% zinc oxide, and 1.8% Peruvian balsam)

Rectal suppositories (10 mg hydrocortisone, 1.2% benzyl benzoate, 1.75% bismuth resorcin compound, 2.25% bismuth subgallate, 11% zinc oxide, and 1.8% Peruvian balsam per suppository)

STORAGE

The rectal cream should be stored at room temperature (never frozen) in a tightly closed container. The rectal suppositories should be stored in a cool, dry place or in the refrigerator.

USES

This combination medication is used to relieve the pain, itching, and discomfort arising from hemorrhoids and irritated anorectal tissues.

Your adrenal glands naturally produce certain cortisonelike chemicals. These chemicals are involved in various regulatory processes in the body (such as fluid balance, temperature, and reaction to inflammation). Hydrocortisone belongs to a group of drugs known as adrenocorticosteroids (or cortisonelike drugs). Hydrocortisone is used to relieve the effects of inflammation (redness, swelling, itching, and discomfort). Zinc oxide is an astringent that causes shrinking and provides relief of irritation. The other ingredients provide a drying and softening effect.

TREATMENT

Wash your hands before applying this medication. To apply the rectal cream, first wash and dry the rectal area and then gently rub in a small amount of the cream. If you must insert the cream inside the rectum, attach the applicator tip to the opened tube. It may be helpful to lubricate the applicator with a small amount of petroleum jelly to ease insertion. Insert the applicator tip into the rectum and squeeze the tube. Remove the applicator from the tube and wash it with hot water and soap; then dry thoroughly. Wash your hands afterward.

To insert the suppository, unwrap it and moisten it slightly with water (if the suppository is too soft to insert, run cold water over it or refrigerate it for up to 30 minutes before you unwrap it). Lie down on your left side with your right knee bent. Push the suppository well into the rectum with your finger. Wash your hands again, and try not to have a bowel movement for at least an hour.

If you miss a dose of this medication, apply the cream or insert the suppository as soon as possible, unless it is almost time for the next application. In that case, do not use the missed dose at all; just wait until the next scheduled dose.

SIDE EFFECTS

Minor. Burning sensation upon application. The burning should disappear as your body adjusts to the medication.

Major. Tell your doctor about any side effects that are persistent or particularly bothersome. IT IS ESPECIALLY IMPORTANT TO TELL YOUR DOCTOR about any additional inflammation or infection at the site of application, as well as rectal pain, bleeding, leakage, itching, or blistering.

INTERACTIONS

This medication should not interact with any other medications as long as it is used according to the directions given to you by the doctor or pharmacist.

WARNINGS

• Tell your doctor about unusual or allergic reactions you have had to medications, especially to benzyl benzoate, bismuth resorcin compound, bismuth subgallate, Peruvian balsam, or to hydrocortisone or any other adrenocorticosteroid (such as amcinonide, betamethasone, clocortolone, cortisone, desonide, desoximetasone, dexamethasone, diflorasone, flumethasone, fluocinolone, fluocinonide, fluorometholone, flurandrenolide, halcinonide, methylprednisolone, paramethasone, prednisolone, prednisone, and triamcinolone).

• If additional irritation develops while using this drug, you should immediately discontinue its use and notify your doctor.

• You should not use this medication for more than seven consecutive days unless your doctor specifically directs you to do so.

• If this drug stains your clothing, the stain may be removed by washing with laundry detergent.

• Wearing a sanitary napkin may help to protect clothing and to keep the medication in the area.
• Be sure to tell your doctor if you are pregnant. If large amounts of hydrocortisone are applied for prolonged periods of time, some of it will be absorbed and may cross the placenta. Studies in humans have not been conducted, but birth defects have been observed in the offspring of animals that were given large oral doses of hydrocortisone during the gestation period. Also tell your doctor if you are breast-feeding an infant. If absorbed through the skin, small amounts of hydrocortisone pass into breast milk and may cause growth suppression or a decrease in natural adrenocorticosteroid hormone production in the nursing infant.

hydrocortisone, polymyxin B, and neomycin combination (otic)

BRAND NAMES (Manufacturers)
AK-Spore H.C. Otic (Akorn)
Cortatrigen Modified Ear Drops (Goldline)
Cortisporin Otic (Burroughs Wellcome)
Drotic (Ascher)
Otocort (Lemmon)
Otomycin-HPN Otic (Misemer)
TYPE OF DRUG
Otic adrenocorticosteroid and antibiotic
INGREDIENTS
hydrocortisone, polymyxin B, and neomycin
DOSAGE FORMS
Otic solution (1% hydrocortisone, 10,000 units polymyxin B, and 5 mg neomycin sulfate per mL)
Otic suspension (1% hydrocortisone, 10,000 units polymyxin B, and 5 mg neomycin sulfate per mL)
STORAGE
The medication should be stored at room temperature in tightly closed, light-resistant containers. It should not be refrigerated, and it should never be frozen.

USES

This medication is used to treat superficial bacterial infections of the outer ear. Your adrenal glands naturally produce certain cortisonelike chemicals. These chemicals are involved in various regulatory processes in the body (such as those involving fluid balance, temperature, and reaction to inflammation). Hydrocortisone belongs to a group of drugs known as adrenocorticosteroids (or cortisonelike medications). It is used to relieve inflammation (redness, swelling, itching, pain). Polymyxin B and neomycin are antibiotics, which act to prevent the growth and multiplication of the infecting bacteria.

TREATMENT

For accuracy, and in order to avoid contamination, another person should insert the ear drops if possible.

To warm the drops before administration, roll the bottle back and forth between your hands. DO NOT place the bottle in boiling water; high temperatures destroy the medication.

Before application, the suspension form of this medication should be shaken well. The contents tend to settle on the bottom of the bottle, so it is necessary to shake the container to distribute the ingredients evenly and equalize the doses.

To administer the ear drops, tilt the head to one side with the affected ear turned upward. Grasp the earlobe and gently pull it upward and back to straighten the ear canal. (If administering ear drops to a child, gently pull the earlobe downward and back.) Fill the dropper and place the prescribed number of drops into the ear. Be careful not to touch the dropper to the ear canal, since the dropper can easily become contaminated. Keep the ear tilted upward for about five minutes. Your doctor may want you to put a piece of cotton soaked with the medication into your ear to keep the medicine from leaking out. To avoid contamination, DO NOT wash or wipe the dropper after you use it.

If you miss a dose, administer as soon as possible, unless it is almost time for the next dose. In that case, don't use the missed dose at all; return to your regular dosing schedule.

It is important to continue to take this medication for the entire time prescribed by your doctor, even if the symptoms of infection disappear before the end of that period. If you stop

using the drug too soon, resistant bacteria are given a chance
to continue growing, and the infection could recur.

SIDE EFFECTS

Minor. Burning sensation upon application. The burning should
disappear as your body adjusts to the medication.

Major. Tell your doctor about any side effects that are persistent or particularly bothersome. IT IS ESPECIALLY IMPOR-
TANT TO TELL YOUR DOCTOR about itching, rash, redness,
or swelling at the site of application.

INTERACTIONS

This medication should not interact with any other medications as long as it is used according to directions from your
doctor or pharmacist.

WARNINGS

• Tell your doctor about unusual or allergic reactions you
have had to medications, especially to hydrocortisone or any
other adrenocorticosteroids (such as amcinonide, betamethasone, clocortolone, cortisone, desonide, desoximetasone, dexamethasone, diflorasone, flumethasone, fluocinolone,
fluocinonide, fluorometholone, flurandrenolide, halcinonide,
methylprednisolone, prednisolone, prednisone, and triamcinolone), to polymyxin B, or to neomycin or any related antibiotic (such as amikacin, colistimethate, colistin, gentamicin, kanamycin, netilmicin, paromycin, streptomycin,
tobramycin, or viomycin).

• Tell your doctor if you now have or if you have ever had
viral or fungal infections of the ear, a punctured eardrum,
myasthenia gravis, or kidney disease.

• Do not use this medication for longer than ten consecutive
days, unless your doctor directs you to do so. If there is no
change in your condition within two or three days after starting to take this medication, contact your doctor. The medication may not be effective for the type of infection you have.

• This drug has been prescribed for your current infection
only. Another infection later on, or one that someone else has,
may require a different medicine. You should not give your
medicine to other people or use it for other infections, unless
your doctor directs you to do so.

• Be sure to tell your doctor if you are pregnant. If large amounts of hydrocortisone are applied for long periods, some will be absorbed and may cross the placenta. Studies in humans have not been conducted, but birth defects have been observed in the offspring of animals given large oral doses during pregnancy. Also tell your doctor if you are breast-feeding an infant. If absorbed through the skin, small amounts of the drug pass into breast milk and may cause growth suppression or a decrease in natural adrenocorticosteroid hormone production in the infant.

---

hydrocortisone, polymyxin B, neomycin, and bacitracin combination (ophthalmic)

BRAND NAMES (Manufacturers)
Coracin (Hauck)
Cortisporin Ophthalmic (Burroughs Wellcome)
Triple Antibiotic with HC (various manufacturers)
TYPE OF DRUG
Ophthalmic adrenocorticosteroid and antibiotic
INGREDIENTS
hydrocortisone, polymyxin B, neomycin, and bacitracin
    (ointment only)
DOSAGE FORMS
Ophthalmic drops (1% hydrocortisone; 10,000 units
    polymyxin B; 0.5% neomycin; and 0.001% thimerosal
    per mL)
Ophthalmic ointment (1% hydrocortisone; 10,000 units
    polymyxin B; 0.5% neomycin; 400 units bacitracin)
STORAGE
This medication should be stored at room temperature (never frozen) in tightly closed containers. If the drops or ointment change color, do not use the medication. A change in color signifies that the drug has lost its therapeutic effectiveness.

USES
This medication is used for the short-term treatment of bacterial infections of the eyes.

Your adrenal glands naturally produce certain cortisonelike chemicals. These chemicals are involved in various regulatory processes in the body (such as those involving fluid balance, temperature, and reaction to inflammation). Hydrocortisone belongs to a group of drugs known as adrenocorticosteroids (or cortisonelike medications). It is used to relieve inflammation (redness, swelling, itching, and discomfort). How it does so is not completely understood.

Polymyxin B, neomycin, and bacitracin are antibiotics, which act to prevent the growth and multiplication of infecting bacteria. Thimerosal is a preservative.

TREATMENT

Wash your hands with soap and water before using this medication. If you are using the drops, shake the bottle well before measuring out the drops. The contents tend to settle on the bottom of the bottle, so it is necessary to shake the container to distribute the ingredients evenly and equalize the doses.

To prevent contamination of the medicine, do not touch the tube portion of the dropper or let it touch the eye.

Note that the bottle of the eye drops is not completely full. This is to allow control of the number of drops used when administering the medication.

To apply the drops, tilt your head back and pull down the lower eyelid with one hand to make a pouch below the eye. Drop the prescribed amount of medicine into the pouch and slowly close your eyes. Try not to blink. Keep your eyes closed, and place one finger at the corner of the eye next to your nose for a minute or two, applying a slight pressure (this is done to prevent loss of medication through the duct that drains fluid from the surface of the eye into the nose and throat). Then wipe away any excess with a clean tissue. If you don't think the medicine got into your eye, repeat the process once. If you are using more than one type of eye drop, wait at least five minutes between doses of the two types of medication.

Follow the same general procedure for applying the ointment. Tilt your head back, pull down the lower eyelid, and squeeze the ointment in a line along the pouch below the eye. Close your eyes, and place your finger at the corner of the eye near the nose for a minute or two. Do not rub your eyes. Wipe off excess ointment and the tip of the tube.

Since applying the medication is somewhat difficult to do, you may want someone else to apply it for you.

If you miss a dose of this medication, insert the drops or apply the ointment as soon as possible, unless it is almost time for the next application. In that case, do not use the missed dose at all; just wait until the next scheduled dose.

It is important to continue to take this medication for the entire time prescribed by your doctor, even if the symptoms of infection disappear before the end of that period. If you stop applying the drug too soon, resistant bacteria are given a chance to continue growing, and the infection could recur.

SIDE EFFECTS

Minor. Blurred vision, burning, or stinging. These side effects should disappear as your body adjusts to the medication.

Major. Tell your doctor about any side effects that are persistent or particularly bothersome. IT IS ESPECIALLY IMPORTANT TO TELL YOUR DOCTOR about disturbed or reduced vision; eye pain, itching, or swelling; headache; rash; continued burning; or severe irritation.

INTERACTIONS

This medication should not interact with other medications as long as it is used according to the directions given to you by your doctor or pharmacist.

WARNINGS

• Tell your doctor about unusual or allergic reactions you have had to any medications, especially to hydrocortisone or other adrenocorticosteroids (such as amcinonide, betamethasone, clocortolone, cortisone, desonide, desoximetasone, dexamethasone, diflorasone, flumethasone, fluocinolone, fluorometholone, flurandrenolide, halcinonide, methylprednisolone, prednisolone, prednisone, and triamcinolone) or to polymyxin B, neomycin, bacitracin, or any related antibiotic (amikacin, colistimethate, colistin, gentamicin, kanamycin, neomycin, netilmicin, paromycin, streptomycin, tobramycin, or viomycin), or to thimerosal or other mercury compounds.

• Tell your doctor if you now have or if you have ever had fungal or viral infections of the eye, cataracts, glaucoma, inner ear disease, kidney disease, or myasthenia gravis.

• Tell your doctor if you wear contact lenses. Your doctor may suggest that you wear eyeglasses until the infection is gone.
• If there is no change in your condition two or three days after starting to take this medication, contact your doctor. The medication may not be effective for your particular infection.
• Do not use this drug for longer than ten consecutive days, unless your doctor directs you to. Prolonged use of this drug may result in glaucoma, secondary infection, cataracts, or eye damage. If you need to take this drug for as long as six weeks, your doctor may want you to have an eye examination by an ophthalmologist.
• This medication has been prescribed for your current infection only. Another infection later on, or one that a family member or friend has, may require a different medicine. You should not give your medicine to other people or use it for other infections, unless your doctor specifically directs you to do so.
• In order to allow your eye infection to clear, you should not apply makeup to the affected eye during treatment with this medication.
• Be sure to tell your doctor if you are pregnant. When large amounts of hydrocortisone are applied for prolonged periods, some of it is absorbed into the bloodstream. It may cross the placenta. Studies in humans have not been conducted, but birth defects have been observed in the offspring of animals that were given large oral doses of hydrocortisone during pregnancy. Also tell your doctor if you are breast-feeding. If absorbed through the skin, small amounts of hydrocortisone pass into breast milk and may cause growth suppression or a decrease in natural adrenocorticosteroid hormone production in the nursing infant.

hydromorphone

BRAND NAMES (Manufacturers)
Dilaudid (Knoll)
hydromorphone hydrochloride (various manufacturers)
HydroStat (Richwood)
TYPE OF DRUG
Analgesic

INGREDIENT
hydromorphone
DOSAGE FORMS
Tablets (1 mg, 2 mg, 3 mg, 4 mg, and 8 mg)
Suppositories (3 mg)
Oral solution (5 mg per 5 mL)
STORAGE
Hydromorphone tablets and oral solution should be stored at
room temperature in a tightly closed, light-resistant container.
The suppositories should be stored in the refrigerator.

USES
Hydromorphone is a narcotic analgesic that acts directly on the
central nervous system (brain and spinal cord). It is used to
relieve moderate to severe pain.

TREATMENT
In order to avoid stomach upset, you can take oral hydromorphone tablets with food or milk. Each dose of the oral solution should be measured carefully with a specially designed
5-mL measuring spoon. An ordinary kitchen teaspoon is not
accurate enough for medical purposes.

To use the suppository, remove the foil wrapper and moisten
the suppository with water (if the suppository is too soft to insert, refrigerate it for half an hour or run cold water over it
before removing the wrapper). Lie on your left side with your
right knee bent. Push the suppository into the rectum, pointed
end first. Lie still for a few minutes. Try to avoid having a bowel
movement for at least an hour.

Hydromorphone works best if you take it at the onset of
pain, rather than when the pain becomes intense.

If you are taking this medication on a regular schedule and
you miss a dose, take the missed dose as soon as possible,
unless it is almost time for your next dose. In that case, do
not take the missed dose at all; just return to your regular dosing schedule. Do not double the next dose.

SIDE EFFECTS
Minor. Constipation, dizziness, drowsiness, dry mouth, false
sense of well-being, flushing, light-headedness, loss of appetite, nausea, or sweating. These side effects should disappear as your body adjusts to the medication.

If you are constipated, increase the amount of fiber in your diet (fresh fruits and vegetables, salads, bran, and whole-grain breads), exercise, and drink more water (unless your doctor directs you to do otherwise).

Chew sugarless gum or suck on ice chips or a piece of hard candy to reduce mouth dryness.

If you feel dizzy or light-headed, sit or lie down for a while; get up from a sitting or lying position slowly; and be careful on stairs.

Major. Tell your doctor about any side effects that are persistent or particularly bothersome. IT IS ESPECIALLY IMPORTANT TO TELL YOUR DOCTOR about anxiety, confusion, continued constipation, difficult or painful urination, difficulty in breathing, excitability, fatigue, rash, restlessness, sore throat and fever, tremors, or weakness.

INTERACTIONS

Hydromorphone interacts with several other types of drugs:
1. Concurrent use of it with other central nervous system depressants (such as alcohol, antihistamines, barbiturates, benzodiazepine tranquilizers, muscle relaxants, and phenothiazine tranquilizers) or with tricyclic antidepressants can cause extreme drowsiness.
2. A monoamine oxidase (MAO) inhibitor taken within 14 days of this medication can lead to unpredictable and severe side effects.

BE SURE TO TELL YOUR DOCTOR about any medications you are currently taking.

WARNINGS

• Tell your doctor about unusual or allergic reactions you have had to any medications, especially to hydromorphone or to any other narcotic analgesics (such as codeine, hydrocodone, meperidine, methadone, morphine, oxycodone, and propoxyphene).

• Tell your doctor if you now have or if you have ever had acute abdominal conditions, asthma, brain disease, colitis, epilepsy, gallstones or gallbladder disease, head injuries, heart disease, kidney disease, liver disease, lung disease, mental illness, emotional disorders, prostate disease, thyroid disease, or urethral stricture.

• If this drug makes you dizzy or drowsy, do not take part in any activity that requires alertness, such as driving a car or operating potentially dangerous machinery.

• Before having surgery or any other medical or dental treatment, be sure to tell your doctor or dentist that you are taking this medication.

• Hydromorphone has the potential for abuse and must be used with caution. Usually, you should not take it on a regular schedule for longer than ten days (unless your doctor directs you to do so). Tolerance develops quickly; do not increase the dosage or stop taking the drug abruptly, unless you first consult your doctor. If you have been taking large amounts of this medication for long periods, you may experience a withdrawal reaction (muscle aches, diarrhea, gooseflesh, runny nose, nausea, vomiting, shivering, trembling, stomach cramps, sleep disorders, irritability, weakness, excessive yawning, or sweating). Your doctor may, therefore, want to reduce the dosage gradually.

• The elderly may be more sensitive to side effects, especially constipation, mental effects, or breathing problems. Report any such effects to your doctor.

• Some hydromorphone formulations contain the color additive FD & C Yellow No. 5 (tartrazine), which can cause allergic-type reactions (rash, shortness of breath, fainting) in certain susceptible individuals.

• Be sure to tell your doctor if you are pregnant. The effects of this medication during the early stages of pregnancy have not been thoroughly studied in humans. However, hydromorphone used regularly in large doses during the later stages of pregnancy can result in addiction of the fetus, leading to withdrawal symptoms (irritability, excessive crying, tremors, fever, vomiting, diarrhea, sneezing, or excessive yawning) at birth. Also be sure to tell your doctor if you are breast-feeding an infant. Small amounts of this medication have been known to pass into breast milk and cause excessive drowsiness in the nursing infant.

hydroxyzine

BRAND NAMES (Manufacturers)
Anxanil (EconoMed)

Atarax (Roerig)
hydroxyzine hydrochloride (various manufacturers)
hydroxyzine pamoate (various manufacturers)
Vistaril (Pfizer)
TYPE OF DRUG
Antihistamine and sedative/hypnotic
INGREDIENT
hydroxyzine
DOSAGE FORMS
Tablets (10 mg, 25 mg, 50 mg, and 100 mg)
Capsules (25 mg, 50 mg, and 100 mg)
Oral solution (10 mg per 5-mL spoonful, with 0.5%
   alcohol)
Oral suspension (25 mg per 5-mL spoonful)
STORAGE
Hydroxyzine tablets, capsules, oral solution, and oral sus-
pension should be stored at room temperature in tightly closed,
light-resistant containers. This medication should never be
frozen.

USES

Hydroxyzine belongs to a group of drugs known as antihistamines (antihistamines block the action of histamine, which is
a chemical that is released by the body during an allergic reaction). This medication is used to treat or prevent symptoms
of allergy. It is also used as a sleeping aid and to relieve the
symptoms of anxiety and tension.

TREATMENT

To avoid stomach upset, you can take hydroxyzine with food
or with a full glass of milk or water (unless your doctor directs you to do otherwise).

The oral-suspension form of this medication should be
shaken well just before measuring each dose. The contents
tend to settle on the bottom of the bottle, so it is necessary to
shake the container to distribute the ingredients evenly and
equalize the doses. Each dose of the oral solution or oral suspension should be measured carefully with a specially designed 5-mL measuring spoon. An ordinary kitchen teaspoon
is not accurate enough for medical purposes.

If you miss a dose of this medication, take the missed dose
as soon as possible, unless it is almost time for your next dose.

In that case, don't take the missed dose at all; just return to your regular dosing schedule. Do not double the next dose.

SIDE EFFECTS

Minor. Drowsiness or dry mouth. These side effects should disappear as your body gets accustomed to the medication.

Dry mouth can be relieved by chewing sugarless gum or by sucking on ice chips or a piece of hard candy.

Major. Tell your doctor about any side effects that are persistent or particularly bothersome. IT IS ESPECIALLY IMPORTANT TO TELL YOUR DOCTOR about convulsions, feeling faint, irritability, mental confusion, rash, or trembling or shakiness.

INTERACTIONS

Hydroxyzine can interact with other types of drugs: Concurrent use of it with other central nervous system depressants (such as alcohol, barbiturates, benzodiazepine tranquilizers, muscle relaxants, narcotics, pain medications, and phenothiazine tranquilizers) or with tricyclic antidepressants can cause extreme drowsiness.

BE SURE TO TELL YOUR DOCTOR about any medications you are currently taking, especially any listed above.

WARNINGS

• Tell your doctor about allergic or unusual reactions you have had to medications, especially to hydroxyzine or to any other antihistamines (such as azatadine, brompheniramine, carbinoxamine, chlorpheniramine, clemastine, cyproheptadine, dexchlorpheniramine, dimenhydrinate, dimethindene, diphenhydramine, diphenylpyraline, doxylamine, promethazine, pyrilamine, trimeprazine, tripelennamine, and triprolidine).

• Hydroxyzine can cause drowsiness or dizziness. Your ability to perform tasks that require alertness, such as driving a car or operating potentially dangerous machinery, may be decreased. Appropriate caution should, therefore, be taken.

• Elderly patients may be more sensitive to side effects, especially drowsiness, confusion, and irritability. Report any such effects to your doctor.

• Be sure to tell your doctor if you are pregnant. The effects of this medication during pregnancy have not been thoroughly studied in humans. Also tell your doctor if you are breast-feeding an infant. Small amounts of hydroxyzine pass into breast milk.

ibuprofen

BRAND NAMES (Manufacturers)
Aches-N-Pain* (Lederle)
Advil* (Whitehall)
Advil Children's (Wyeth-Ayerst)
Genpril* (Goldline)
Haltran* (Roberts)
Ibuprin* (Thompson Medical)
ibuprofen (various manufacturers)
Medipren* (McNeil CPC)
Midol 200* (Glenbrook)
Motrin (Upjohn)
Motrin IB* (Upjohn)
Nuprin* (Bristol-Myers)
PediaProfen (McNeil CPC)
Rufen (Boots)
*Available over the counter (without a prescription) as
   200-mg tablets.
TYPE OF DRUG
Nonsteroidal anti-inflammatory analgesic
INGREDIENT
ibuprofen
DOSAGE FORMS
Tablets (200 mg, 300 mg, 400 mg, 600 mg, and 800 mg)
Oral suspension (100 mg per 5-mL spoonful)
STORAGE
Store in a tightly closed, light-resistant container at room temperature. This medication should never be frozen.

USES
Ibuprofen is used to treat the inflammation (pain, swelling, stiffness) of certain types of arthritis, gout, bursitis, and tendinitis. It is also used to treat painful menstruation. Ibuprofen has been shown to block production of prostaglandins, which may trigger pain.

TREATMENT

You should take this medication on an empty stomach 30 to 60 minutes before meals or two hours after meals so it gets into your bloodstream quickly. However, to decrease stomach irritation, your doctor may want you to take the medication with food or antacids.

The oral-suspension form of this medication should be shaken well just before measuring each dose. The contents tend to settle on the bottom of the bottle, so it is necessary to shake the container to distribute the ingredients evenly and equalize the doses. Each dose of the oral syrup or oral suspension should be measured carefully with a specially designed 5-mL measuring spoon. An ordinary kitchen teaspoon is not accurate enough.

If you are taking ibuprofen to relieve arthritis, you must take it regularly as directed by your doctor. It may take up to two weeks before you feel the full effects of this medication. Ibuprofen does not cure arthritis, but it will help to control the condition as long as you continue to take it.

It is important to take ibuprofen on schedule and not to miss any doses. If you do miss a dose, take it as soon as possible, unless it is almost time for your next dose. In that case, don't take the missed dose at all; just return to your regular dosing schedule. Do not double the next dose.

SIDE EFFECTS

Minor. Bloating, constipation, diarrhea, difficulty in sleeping, dizziness, drowsiness, headache, heartburn, indigestion, light-headedness, loss of appetite, nausea, nervousness, soreness of the mouth, unusual sweating, or vomiting. As your body adjusts to the drug, these side effects should disappear.

To relieve constipation, increase the amount of fiber in your diet (fresh fruits and vegetables, salads, bran, and whole-grain breads), exercise, and drink more water (unless your doctor directs you to do otherwise).

If you become dizzy or light-headed, sit or lie down for a while; get up slowly from a sitting or reclining position; and be careful on stairs.

Major. If you experience any side effects that are persistent or particularly bothersome, you should report them to your doctor. IT IS ESPECIALLY IMPORTANT TO TELL YOUR DOC-

TOR about bloody or black, tarry stools; blurred vision; confusion; depression; difficult or painful urination; palpitations; a problem with hearing; ringing or buzzing in your ears; skin rash, hives, or itching; stomach pain; swelling of the feet; tightness in the chest; unexplained sore throat and fever; unusual bleeding or bruising; unusual fatigue or weakness; unusual weight gain; wheezing or difficulty in breathing; or yellowing of the eyes or skin.

INTERACTIONS
Ibuprofen interacts with several other types of medications:
1. Anticoagulants (blood thinners, such as warfarin) can lead to an increase in bleeding complications.
2. Aspirin, other salicylates, and other anti-inflammatory medications can increase stomach irritation. Aspirin may also decrease the effectiveness of ibuprofen.
3. Ibuprofen can interact with diuretics (water pills).
4. Probenecid may increase blood levels of ibuprofen, which may increase the risk of side effects.
5. The action of beta blockers may be decreased by this drug.
   BE SURE TO TELL YOUR DOCTOR about any medications you are currently taking, especially any listed above.

WARNINGS
• Before you start to take this medication, it is important to tell your doctor if you have ever had unusual or allergic reactions to ibuprofen, or to any of the other chemically related drugs (aspirin, other salicylates, diclofenac, diflunisal, fenoprofen, flurbiprofen, indomethacin, ketoprofen, meclofenamate, mefenamic acid, naproxen, oxyphenbutazone, phenylbutazone, piroxicam, sulindac, or tolmetin).
• Tell your doctor if you now have or if you have ever had bleeding problems, colitis, stomach ulcers or other stomach problems, epilepsy, heart disease, high blood pressure, asthma, kidney disease, liver disease, mental illness, or Parkinson's disease.
• If ibuprofen makes you dizzy or drowsy, do not take part in any activity that requires alertness.
• Because this drug can prolong bleeding time, tell your doctor or dentist you are taking this drug before having surgery or other medical or dental treatment.

• Stomach problems are more likely to occur if you take aspirin regularly or drink alcohol while being treated with this medication. These should, therefore, be avoided (unless your doctor directs you to do otherwise).

• The elderly may be at increased risk for experiencing side effects of this drug.

• Be sure to tell your doctor if you are pregnant. This type of medication can cause unwanted effects to the heart or blood flow of the fetus. Studies in animals have also shown that this type of medicine, if taken late in pregnancy, may increase the length of pregnancy, prolong labor, or cause other problems during delivery. Also tell your doctor if you are breast-feeding an infant. Small amounts of ibuprofen can pass into breast milk.

imipramine

BRAND NAMES (Manufacturers)
imipramine hydrochloride (various manufacturers)
Janimine (Abbott)
Tofranil (Geigy)
Tofranil-PM (Geigy)
TYPE OF DRUG
Tricyclic antidepressant
INGREDIENT
imipramine
DOSAGE FORMS
Tablets (10 mg, 25 mg, and 50 mg)
Capsules (75 mg, 100 mg, 125 mg, and 150 mg)
STORAGE
Store at room temperature in a tightly closed container.

USES

Imipramine is used to relieve the symptoms of mental depression. This medication belongs to a group of drugs referred to as tricyclic antidepressants. These medicines are thought to relieve depression by increasing the concentration of certain chemicals necessary for nerve transmission in the brain. This medication is also used to treat enuresis (bed-wetting) in children six to 12 years of age.

TREATMENT

Imipramine should be taken exactly as your doctor prescribes. It can be taken with water or with food to lessen the chance of stomach irritation, unless your doctor tells you to do otherwise.

If you miss a dose of this medication, take the missed dose as soon as possible, then return to your regular dosing schedule. If the dose you missed was a once-a-day bedtime dose, do not take that dose in the morning; check with your doctor instead. If the dose is taken in the morning, it may cause unwanted side effects.

The effects of therapy with this medication may not become apparent for two or three weeks.

SIDE EFFECTS

Minor. Agitation, anxiety, blurred vision, confusion, constipation, cramps, diarrhea, dizziness, drowsiness, dry mouth, fatigue, heartburn, insomnia, loss of appetite, nausea, peculiar tastes in the mouth, restlessness, sweating, vomiting, weakness, or weight gain or loss. As your body adjusts to the medication, these side effects should disappear.

This drug may cause increased sensitivity to sunlight. Therefore, avoid prolonged exposure to sunlight and sunlamps. Wear protective clothing, and use an effective sunscreen.

Dry mouth caused by therapy with this medication can be relieved by chewing sugarless gum or by sucking on ice chips or a piece of hard candy.

To relieve constipation, increase the amount of fiber in your diet (fresh fruits and vegetables, salads, bran, and whole-grain breads). You can also increase your exercise and drink more water (unless your doctor directs you to do otherwise).

To avoid dizziness or light-headedness when you stand, contract and relax the muscles of your legs for a few moments before rising. Do this by pushing one foot against the floor while raising the other foot slightly, alternating feet so that you are "pumping" your legs in a pedaling motion.

Major. Tell your doctor about any side effects that are persistent or particularly bothersome. IT IS ESPECIALLY IMPORTANT TO TELL YOUR DOCTOR about chest pains, convulsions, difficulty in urinating, enlarged or painful breasts (in both sexes), fainting, fever, fluid retention, hair loss, hallucinations, headaches, impotence, mood changes, mouth sores, nervousness, nightmares, numbness in the fingers or toes, palpitations, ringing in the ears, seizures, skin rash, sleep disorders, sore throat, tremors, uncoordinated movements or balance problems, unusual bleeding or bruising, or yellowing of the eyes or skin.

INTERACTIONS

Imipramine interacts with a number of other types of medications:

1. Extreme drowsiness can occur when this medicine is taken with central nervous system depressants (such as alcohol, antihistamines, barbiturates, benzodiazepine tranquilizers, muscle relaxants, narcotics, pain medications, phenothiazine tranquilizers, and sleeping medications) or with other tricyclic antidepressants.

2. Imipramine may decrease the effectiveness of antiseizure medications. Imipramine may also possibly block the blood-pressure-lowering effects of clonidine and guanethidine.

3. Oral contraceptives (birth control pills) and drugs that contain estrogen can increase the side effects and reduce the effectiveness of the tricyclic antidepressants (including imipramine).

4. Cimetidine can decrease the breakdown of imipramine in the body, thus increasing the possibility of side effects.

5. Tricyclic antidepressants may increase the side effects of thyroid medication and of over-the-counter (nonprescription) cough, cold, allergy, asthma, sinus, and diet medications.

6. The concurrent use of tricyclic antidepressants and monoamine oxidase (MAO) inhibitors should be avoided because the combination may result in fever, convulsions, or high blood pressure. At least 14 days should separate the use of this drug and the use of an MAO inhibitor.

BE SURE TO TELL YOUR DOCTOR about any medications you are currently taking.

WARNINGS

• Tell your doctor if you have had unusual or allergic reactions to any medications, especially to imipramine or any of the other tricyclic antidepressants (such as amitriptyline, doxepin, trimipramine, amoxapine, protriptyline, desipramine, maprotiline, and nortriptyline).

• Tell your doctor if you have a history of alcoholism or if you have ever had asthma, high blood pressure, liver or kidney disease, heart disease, a heart attack, circulatory disease, stomach problems, intestinal problems, difficulty in urinating, enlarged prostate gland, epilepsy, glaucoma, thyroid disease, mental illness, or electroshock therapy.

• If the use of imipramine makes you dizzy or drowsy, do not take part in any activity that requires alertness, such as driving a car or operating potentially dangerous machinery.

• Before having surgery or any other medical or dental treatment, tell your doctor or dentist you are taking this drug.

• Do not stop taking this drug suddenly. Stopping it abruptly can cause nausea, headache, stomach upset, fatigue, or a worsening of your condition. Your doctor may want to reduce the dosage gradually.

• The effects of this medication may last as long as seven days after you stop taking it, so continue to observe all precautions during that period.

• Some of these products contain the color additive FD&C Yellow No. 5 (tartrazine), which can cause allergic-type reactions (skin rash, fainting, difficulty in breathing) in certain susceptible individuals.

• The elderly may be at increased risk for experiencing side effects. Report any such effects, especially dizziness, drowsiness, dry mouth, difficulty urinating, or mental confusion to your doctor.

• Be sure to tell your doctor if you are pregnant. Adverse effects have been observed in the fetuses of animals that were given large doses of this drug during pregnancy. Also tell your doctor if you are breast-feeding an infant. Small amounts of this drug can pass into breast milk and may cause unwanted effects in nursing infants.

indapamide

BRAND NAME (Manufacturer)
Lozol (Rorer)
TYPE OF DRUG
Diuretic and antihypertensive
INGREDIENT
indapamide

DOSAGE FORM
Tablets (1.25 mg and 2.5 mg)
STORAGE
Store at room temperature in a tightly closed container.

USES

Indapamide is prescribed to treat high blood pressure. It is also used to reduce fluid accumulation in the body caused by conditions such as heart failure, cirrhosis of the liver, kidney disease, and the long-term use of some drugs. This drug reduces fluid accumulation by increasing the elimination of salt and water through the kidneys.

TREATMENT

To decrease stomach irritation, you can take indapamide with a glass of milk or with a meal (unless your doctor directs you to do otherwise). Try to take it at the same time every day. Avoid taking a dose after 6:00 P.M. or you may have to get up in the night to urinate.

If you miss a dose of this medication, take the missed dose as soon as possible, unless it is almost time for the next dose. In that case, do not take the missed dose at all; just wait until the next scheduled dose. Do not double the dose.

This medication does not cure high blood pressure, but it will help to control the condition as long as you continue to take it.

SIDE EFFECTS

Minor. Constipation, cramps, diarrhea, dizziness, drowsiness, headache, heartburn, loss of appetite, restlessness, or upset stomach. As your body adjusts to the medication, these side effects should disappear.

This drug can cause increased sensitivity to sunlight. Therefore, avoid prolonged exposure to sunlight and sunlamps. Wear protective clothing, and use an effective sunscreen.

To relieve constipation, increase the amount of fiber in your diet (fresh fruits and vegetables, salads, bran, and whole-grain breads) and exercise more (unless your doctor directs you to do otherwise).

To avoid dizziness or light-headedness when you stand, contract and relax the muscles of your legs for a few moments before rising. Do this by pushing one foot against the floor while raising the other foot slightly, alternating feet so that you are "pumping" your legs in a pedaling motion.

Major. Tell your doctor about any side effects that are persistent or particularly bothersome. IT IS ESPECIALLY IMPORTANT TO TELL YOUR DOCTOR about blurred vision, confusion, difficulty in breathing, dry mouth, excessive thirst, excessive weakness, fever, itching, joint pain, mood changes, muscle pain or spasms, nausea, palpitations, skin rash, sore throat, tingling in the fingers or toes, unusual bleeding or bruising, vomiting, or yellowing of the eyes or skin.

INTERACTIONS

Indapamide interacts with several other types of medications:

1. It may decrease the effectiveness of oral anticoagulants, antigout medications, insulin, oral antidiabetic medicines, and methenamine.

2. Fenfluramine can increase the blood-pressure-lowering effects of indapamide (which can be dangerous).

3. Indomethacin can decrease the blood-pressure-lowering effects of indapamide, thereby counteracting the desired effects.

4. Cholestyramine and colestipol can decrease the absorption of this medication from the gastrointestinal tract. Indapamide should, therefore, be taken one hour before or four hours after a dose of cholestyramine or colestipol (if you have also been prescribed one of these drugs).

5. Indapamide may increase the side effects of amphotericin B, calcium, cortisone and cortisonelike steroids (such as dexamethasone, hydrocortisone, prednisone, and prednisolone), digoxin, digitalis, lithium, and vitamin D.

BE SURE TO TELL YOUR DOCTOR about any medications you are currently taking, especially any of those listed above.

WARNINGS

• Tell your doctor about unusual or allergic reactions you have had to any medications, especially to indapamide or any other sulfa drugs, including other diuretics, oral antidiabetic medications, and sulfonamide antibiotics.

• Tell your doctor if you now have or if you have ever had kidney disease or problems with urination, diabetes mellitus, gout, liver disease, asthma, pancreatic disease, or systemic lupus erythematosus.

• Indapamide can cause potassium loss. Signs of potassium loss include dry mouth, thirst, weakness, muscle pain or cramps, nausea, and vomiting. If you experience any of these symptoms, call your doctor. To help avoid potassium loss, take this drug with a glass of fresh or frozen orange juice or cranberry juice, or eat a banana every day. The use of a salt substitute also helps to prevent potassium loss. Do not change your diet or use a salt substitute, however, before discussing it with your doctor. Too much potassium can also be dangerous. Your doctor may want to have blood tests performed periodically to monitor your potassium levels.

• In order to avoid dizziness or fainting while taking this medication, avoid standing for long periods of time; avoid drinking excessive amounts of alcohol; and avoid getting overheated (do not exert yourself or perform strenuous exercise in hot weather or take hot baths, showers, or saunas).

• If you have high blood pressure, do not take any over-the-counter (nonprescription) medications for weight control or for allergy, asthma, cough, cold, or sinus problems unless your doctor directs you to do so.

• To prevent dehydration (severe water loss) while taking this medication, check with your doctor if you have any illness that causes severe or continuous nausea, vomiting, or diarrhea.

• This medication can raise blood-sugar levels in diabetic patients. Therefore, blood-sugar levels should be carefully monitored by blood or urine tests when this medication is being taken.

• Be sure to tell your doctor if you are pregnant. Studies in humans have not been conducted, but adverse effects have been observed in the fetuses of animals that received large doses of this drug during pregnancy. Also tell your doctor if you are breast-feeding an infant. Although problems in humans have not been reported, small amounts of this medication can pass into breast milk, so caution is warranted.

indomethacin

BRAND NAMES (Manufacturers)
Indocin (Merck Sharp & Dohme)
Indocin SR (Merck Sharp & Dohme)
indomethacin (various manufacturers)
TYPE OF DRUG
Nonsteroidal anti-inflammatory analgesic
INGREDIENT
indomethacin
DOSAGE FORMS
Capsules (25 mg and 50 mg)
Extended-release capsules (75 mg)
Oral suspension (25 mg per 5-mL spoonful, with 1% alcohol)
Rectal suppositories (50 mg)
STORAGE
Indomethacin capsules, oral suspension, and rectal suppositories should be stored in closed containers at room temperature away from heat and direct sunlight. The rectal suppositories can also be stored safely in the refrigerator.

USES

Indomethacin is used to treat the inflammation (pain, swelling, and stiffness) of certain types of arthritis, gout, bursitis, and tendinitis. Indomethacin has been shown to block the production of certain body chemicals, called prostaglandins, that may trigger pain. However, it is not yet fully understood how indomethacin works.

TREATMENT

You should take this drug immediately after meals or with food, in order to reduce stomach irritation. Ask your doctor if you can take indomethacin with an antacid.

Do not chew or crush the extended-release capsules; they should be swallowed whole. Breaking the capsule would release the medication all at once—defeating the purpose of the extended-release dosage form.

The suspension form of this medication should be shaken well just before measuring each dose. The contents tend to settle on the bottom of the bottle, so it is necessary to shake the container to distribute the ingredients evenly and equalize the doses. Each dose should be measured carefully with a specially designed 5-mL measuring spoon. An ordinary kitchen teaspoon is not accurate enough.

To use the rectal suppository form of this medication, remove the foil wrapper, and moisten the suppository with water. If the suppository is too soft to insert, refrigerate it for 30 minutes or run cold water over it before removing the foil wrapper. Lie on your left side with your right knee bent. Push the suppository into the rectum, pointed end first. Lie still for a few minutes. Try to avoid having a bowel movement for at least one hour.

It is important to take indomethacin on schedule and not to miss any doses. If you do miss a dose, take the missed dose as soon as possible, unless more than an hour has passed. In that case, do not take the missed dose at all; just return to your regular dosing schedule. Do not double the next dose.

This drug does not cure arthritis, but will help to control the condition as long as you continue to take it. It may take up to four weeks before you feel the full benefits of this medication.

SIDE EFFECTS

Minor. Bloating, constipation, diarrhea, difficulty in sleeping, dizziness, drowsiness, headache, heartburn, indigestion, light-headedness, loss of appetite, nausea, nervousness, soreness of the mouth, unusual sweating, or vomiting. As you adjust to the drug, the side effects should disappear.

To relieve constipation, increase the amount of fiber in your diet (fresh fruits and vegetables, salads, bran, and whole-grain breads), exercise, and drink more water (unless your doctor directs you to do otherwise).

If you become dizzy, sit or lie down for a while; get up slowly from a sitting or reclining position; and be careful on stairs.

Major. Tell your doctor about any side effects that are persistent or particularly bothersome. IT IS ESPECIALLY IMPORTANT TO TELL YOUR DOCTOR about bloody or black, tarry stools; blurred vision; confusion; depression; difficult or painful urination; palpitations; a problem with hearing; ringing or buzzing in the ears; skin rash, hives, or itching; stomach pain; swelling of the feet; rectal irritation; tightness in the chest; un-

explained sore throat and fever; unusual bleeding or bruising; unusual fatigue or weakness; unusual weight gain; wheezing or difficulty in breathing; or yellowing of the eyes or skin.

INTERACTIONS

Indomethacin interacts with several other types of drugs:

1. Use of anticoagulants (blood thinners, such as warfarin)
can lead to an increase in bleeding complications.

2. Anti-inflammatory medications such as aspirin, salicylates,
and diflunisal can cause increased stomach irritation when
used while taking this drug.

3. Indomethacin can decrease the elimination of lithium from
the body, possibly resulting in lithium toxicity.

4. Indomethacin may interfere with the blood-pressure-lowering effects of captopril, enalapril, or beta-blocking medications (acebutolol, atenolol, betaxolol, carteolol, esmolol, labetalol, metoprolol, nadolol, penbutolol, pindolol, propranolol,
timolol).

5. Indomethacin can interfere with the diuretic effects of
furosemide and thiazide-type diuretics (water pills).

6. Indomethacin can influence the effects of the potassium-
sparing diuretics (such as amiloride, spironolactone, or triamterene).

7. The concurrent use of triamterene and indomethacin can
result in kidney problems.

8. Probenecid can increase the amount of indomethacin in
the bloodstream when both drugs are being taken.

BE SURE TO TELL YOUR DOCTOR about any medications
you are currently taking, especially those listed above.

WARNINGS

• Tell your doctor if you have ever had unusual or allergic reactions to any medications, especially to indomethacin or any
chemically related drugs.

• Before taking indomethacin, tell your doctor if you now
have or if you have ever had bleeding problems, colitis, stomach ulcers or other stomach problems, epilepsy, heart disease,
high blood pressure, asthma, kidney disease, liver disease,
mental illness, or Parkinson's disease.

• If indomethacin makes you dizzy or drowsy, do not take
part in any activity that requires alertness, such as driving a
car or operating potentially dangerous machinery.

• If you will be taking this medication for a long period of time, your doctor may want to have your eyes examined periodically by an ophthalmologist. Some visual problems have been known to occur with long-term indomethacin use. Your doctor might want to keep a careful watch for these.

• Stomach problems are more likely to occur if you take aspirin regularly or drink alcohol while being treated with this medication. These should therefore be avoided (unless your doctor directs you to do otherwise).

• The elderly may be at increased risk for experiencing side effects of this drug.

• Be sure to tell your doctor if you are pregnant. Studies in animals have shown that indomethacin can cause unwanted effects in offspring, including lower birth weights, slower development of bones, nerve damage, and heart damage. If taken late in pregnancy, the drug can also prolong labor. Studies in humans have not been conducted. Also tell your doctor if you are breast-feeding. Small amounts of indomethacin can pass into breast milk, so caution is warranted.

---

insulin

BRAND NAMES (Manufacturers)
Humulin L (Lilly)
Humulin N (Lilly)
Humulin R (Lilly)
Iletin I (Lilly)
Iletin II (Lilly)
Insulatard NPH (Novo Nordisk)
Mixtard (Novo Nordisk)
Novolin (Novo Nordisk)
Velosulin (Novo Nordisk)
TYPE OF DRUG
Antidiabetic
INGREDIENT
insulin
DOSAGE FORMS
Injectable (all types) (100 units/mL)
Injectable (regular) (100 units/mL, 500 units/mL)
This drug is available only as an injectable (if swallowed, it is destroyed by stomach acid). Various types of insulin pro-

vide different times of onset and durations of action (see below).

Insulin type	Onset of action (in hours)	Duration of action (in hours)
Regular insulin	$1/2$	6
Insulin zinc suspension, prompt (Semilente)	$1\,1/2$	14
Isophane insulin (NPH)	1	24
Insulin zinc suspension (Lente)	1	24
Protamine zinc insulin (PZI)	6	36
Insulin zinc suspension, extended (Ultralente)	6	36

STORAGE
After opening, keep most forms (except 500 units/mL strength) at room temperature if used in six months. Refrigerate unopened vials of insulin, but never freeze this medication.

USES
Insulin is a hormone that is normally produced by the pancreas; it functions in the regulation of blood-sugar levels. This medication is used to treat diabetes mellitus (sugar diabetes) a disorder that results from an inability of the pancreas to produce enough insulin. Injectable insulin is used only to treat those patients whose blood-sugar levels cannot be controlled by diet or by oral antidiabetic medications.

TREATMENT
Your doctor, nurse, dietitian, or pharmacist will show you how to inject insulin, using a specially marked hypodermic syringe. This medication is packaged with printed instructions that should be carefully followed.

You may prefer to use presterilized disposable needles and syringes, which are used once and then discarded. If you use a glass syringe and metal needle, you must sterilize them before reuse.

Make sure that the insulin you are using is exactly the kind your doctor ordered and that its expiration date has not passed.

Do not shake the bottle; tip it gently, end to end, to mix. ALWAYS CHECK THE DOSE in the syringe at least twice before injecting it.

Clean the site of the injection thoroughly with an antiseptic, such as rubbing alcohol.

Change the site of the injection daily, and avoid injecting cold insulin.

NEVER use a vial of insulin if there are lumps in it. Make your insulin injection a regular part of your schedule, so that you do not miss any doses. Ask your doctor what to do if you have to take a dose later than the scheduled time.

SIDE EFFECTS

Minor. Insulin can cause redness and rash at the site of injection. Try to rotate injection sites in order to avoid this reaction.

Major. Be sure to tell your doctor about any side effects that are persistent or particularly bothersome. IT IS ESPECIALLY IMPORTANT TO TELL YOUR DOCTOR about palpitations, fainting, shortness of breath, skin rash, or sweating.

Too much insulin can cause hypoglycemia (low blood sugar), which can lead to anxiety, chills, cold sweats, drowsiness, fast heart rate, headache, loss of consciousness, nausea, nervousness, tremors, unusual hunger, or unusual weakness. If you experience these symptoms, you should eat a quick source of sugar (such as table sugar, orange juice, honey, or a nondiet cola). You should also make it a point to tell your doctor that you have had this reaction.

Too little insulin can cause symptoms of hyperglycemia (high blood sugar), such as confusion, drowsiness, dry skin, fatigue, flushing, frequent urination, fruitlike breath odor, loss of appetite, or rapid breathing. If you experience any of these symptoms, contact your doctor; he or she may want to modify your dosing schedule or change your insulin dosage.

INTERACTIONS

Insulin can be expected to interact with several other types of medications:

1. Insulin can increase the side effects of digoxin on the heart.
2. Oral contraceptives (birth control pills), adrenocorticosteroids (cortisonelike medicines), danazol, dextrothyroxine, furosemide, ethacrynic acid, thyroid hormone, thiazide di-

uretics (water pills), phenytoin, or nicotine (from smoking) can increase insulin requirements.

3. Monoamine oxidase (MAO) inhibitors, phenylbutazone, fenfluramine, guanethidine, disopyramide, sulfinpyrazone, tetracycline, alcohol, anabolic steroids, or large doses of aspirin can increase the effects of insulin, leading to hypoglycemia.

4. Beta blockers (acebutolol, atenolol, betaxolol, carteolol, esmolol, labetalol, metoprolol, nadolol, penbutolol, pindolol, propranolol, timolol) may prolong the effects of insulin and mask the signs of hypoglycemia.

BE SURE TO TELL YOUR DOCTOR about any medications you are currently taking, especially any of those listed above.

WARNINGS

• Tell your doctor about unusual or allergic reactions you have had to any medications, especially to insulin.

• Before starting to take this medication, be sure to tell your doctor if you now have or if you have ever had high fevers, infections, kidney disease, liver disease, thyroid disease, or severe nausea and vomiting.

• If your doctor prescribes two types of insulin to achieve better glucose control and recommends mixing the insulin into one syringe, always draw the regular insulin (clear) into the syringe first.

• Some insulin mixtures won't interact with each other for some time. Others react quickly and require immediate injection. Consult your doctor or pharmacist.

• Make sure that your friends and family are aware of the symptoms of an insulin reaction and know what to do should they observe any of the symptoms in you.

• Carry a card or wear a bracelet that identifies you as someone who has diabetes.

• Always have insulin and syringes available.

• When traveling, always carry an ample supply of your diabetic needs and, if possible, a prescription for insulin and syringes. Carry insulin and syringes on your person; baggage can be lost, delayed, or stolen.

• Do not store insulin in your car's glove compartment.

• To avoid the possibility of hypoglycemia (low blood-sugar levels), you should eat on a regular schedule and avoid skipping meals.

• Before having surgery or other medical or dental treatment, tell your doctor or dentist you are taking insulin.
• Check with your doctor or pharmacist before taking any over-the-counter (nonprescription) cough, cold, diet, allergy, asthma, or sinus medications. Some of these products affect blood-sugar levels.
• If you become ill, it is possible your insulin requirements may change. Consult your doctor.
• Be sure to tell your doctor if you are pregnant. Insulin dosing requirements often change during pregnancy.

---

ipecac

BRAND NAME (Manufacturer)
ipecac* (various manufacturers)
*Available over the counter (without a prescription)
TYPE OF DRUG
Emetic
INGREDIENT
ipecac
DOSAGE FORM
Oral syrup (with 1.5% or 2% alcohol)
STORAGE
Store at room temperature in a tightly closed container. This medication should not be refrigerated or frozen.

USES
Ipecac is for emergency use to treat drug overdose or poisoning. Ipecac works on the stomach and on the vomiting center in the brain to produce vomiting.

TREATMENT
Before administering ipecac, call a poison control center, emergency room, or physician for advice. You must administer ipecac with adequate amounts of water (½ glass for infants less than 1 year old; 1 to 2 glasses for children and adults) for adequate fluid in the stomach. If vomiting does not occur within 20 minutes after a second dose has been given, call again IMMEDIATELY for instructions.

SIDE EFFECTS

Minor. Ipecac can cause diarrhea, drowsiness, nausea, or vomiting that continues for more than 30 minutes. These side effects should disappear within several hours.

Major. Be sure to tell your doctor about any side effects that are persistent or particularly bothersome. IT IS ESPECIALLY IMPORTANT TO TELL YOUR DOCTOR about aching or stiffness of the muscles, difficulty in breathing, palpitations, stomach cramps or pain, or weakness as soon as possible.

INTERACTIONS

Ipecac oral syrup should not be administered with milk or with carbonated beverages; these fluids may affect how quickly ipecac works. In addition, activated charcoal will absorb ipecac. If both activated charcoal and ipecac oral syrup are to be administered, give the activated charcoal only after successful vomiting has been produced by the ipecac.

WARNINGS

• Vomiting is not the proper treatment in all cases of possible poisoning: Ipecac should not be used if gasoline, oils, kerosene, acids, alkalies (lye), corrosives, or strychnine has been swallowed, since vomiting of these substances may cause seizures, additional throat burns, or pneumonia.

• Unless otherwise directed by a health professional, ipecac should probably not be used if the poisoned patient has heart disease; is in shock, losing consciousness, or having seizures; or lacks a gag reflex.

• Muscle and heart disorders and at least one death have been reported as a result of the chronic use of ipecac by young women who were using it to induce vomiting.

• Ipecac is available over-the-counter (without a prescription) and can be purchased from most pharmacies. Mothers should have a one-ounce bottle of ipecac for each child in the house. Always call a poison control center, emergency room, or physician for instructions BEFORE administering ipecac.

• Be sure to tell your doctor if the overdose or poisoning victim is pregnant. Although ipecac appears to be safe, studies in pregnant women have not been done.

isoniazid

BRAND NAMES (Manufacturers)
isoniazid (various manufacturers)
Izonid (Major)
Laniazid (Lannett)
TYPE OF DRUG
Antitubercular
INGREDIENT
isoniazid
DOSAGE FORMS
Tablets (100 mg and 300 mg)
Oral syrup (50 mg per 5-mL spoonful)
STORAGE
Store at room temperature in a tightly closed, light-resistant container. This medication should never be frozen.

USES

Isoniazid is used to prevent and treat tuberculosis. It acts by severely injuring the cell structure of tuberculosis bacteria, thereby preventing them from growing and multiplying.

TREATMENT

In order to avoid stomach irritation, you can take isoniazid with food or a full glass of water or milk (unless your doctor directs you to do otherwise).

Antacids prevent the absorption of isoniazid from the gastrointestinal tract, so they should not be taken within an hour of a dose of isoniazid.

Each dose of the oral syrup should be measured carefully with a specially designed 5-mL measuring spoon. An ordinary kitchen teaspoon is not accurate enough for medical purposes.

It is important to continue to take this medication for the entire time prescribed by your doctor, even if your symptoms disappear before the end of that period. If you stop taking the drug too soon, your infection could recur.

It is common for therapy to last for at least six months and, at times, for as long as two years.

Try not to miss any doses of this medication. If you do miss a dose, take the missed dose as soon as possible, unless it is al-

most time for the next dose. In that case, do not take the
missed dose at all; just return to your regular dosing schedule. Do not double the next dose.

SIDE EFFECTS

Minor. Abdominal pain, dizziness, heartburn, nausea, or vomiting. These side effects should disappear as your body adjusts
to the medication.

If you feel dizzy, sit or lie down for a while; get up slowly
from a sitting or reclining position; and be careful on stairs.

Major. Tell your doctor about any side effects that are persistent or particularly bothersome. IT IS ESPECIALLY IMPOR-
TANT TO TELL YOUR DOCTOR about blurred vision, breast
enlargement (in both sexes), chills, darkening of the urine,
eye pain, fever, malaise, memory impairment, numbness or
tingling in the fingers or toes, rash, unusual bleeding or bruising, vision changes, weakness, or yellowish discoloration of the
eyes or skin.

Your doctor may want to prescribe vitamin B_6 (pyridoxine)
to prevent the numbness and tingling. However, do not take vitamin B_6 without consulting your doctor.

INTERACTIONS

Isoniazid interacts with several other types of medications:

1. Concurrent use of isoniazid and alcohol can lead to decreased effectiveness of isoniazid and increased side effects
on the liver.

2. The combination of isoniazid and cycloserine can result in
dizziness or drowsiness.

3. The combination of isoniazid and disulfiram can lead to
dizziness, loss of coordination, irritable disposition, and insomnia.

4. Isoniazid can decrease the breakdown of phenytoin and
carbamazepine in the body, which can lead to an increase in
side effects from phenytoin and carbamazepine.

5. Isoniazid can decrease the effectiveness of ketoconazole.

6. In combination, rifampin and isoniazid can increase the
risk of liver damage. However, this is a commonly prescribed
combination.

7. The effectiveness of isoniazid may be decreased by adrenocorticosteroids (cortisonelike medicines).

8. The side effects of benzodiazepine tranquilizers or meperidine may be increased by isoniazid.

BE SURE TO TELL YOUR DOCTOR about any medications you are currently taking, especially those listed above.

WARNINGS

• Tell your doctor about unusual or allergic reactions you have had to any medications, especially to isoniazid, ethionamide, pyrazinamide, or niacin (vitamin B₃).

• Before starting to take this medication, be sure to tell your doctor if you have a history of alcoholism or if you now have or have ever had kidney disease, liver disease, or seizures.

• If this drug makes you dizzy, avoid tasks that require alertness, such as driving a car.

• Your doctor may want you to have periodic eye examinations while taking this medication, especially if you begin to have vision side effects.

• Isoniazid can interact with several foods (skipjack fish, tuna, yeast extracts, sauerkraut juice, sausages, and certain cheeses), leading to severe reactions. You should, therefore, avoid eating these foods while being treated with isoniazid.

• People with diabetes using Clinitest urine glucose tests may get erroneously high sugar readings while they are taking isoniazid. Temporarily changing to Clinistix or Tes-Tape urine tests avoids this problem.

• Be sure to tell your doctor if you are pregnant. Although isoniazid appears to be safe during pregnancy, it does cross the placenta. Extensive studies in pregnant women have not been conducted. Also tell your doctor if you are breast-feeding an infant. Small amounts of isoniazid pass into breast milk.

---

isosorbide dinitrate

BRAND NAMES (Manufacturers)
Dilatrate-SR (Reed & Carnrick)
Iso-Bid (Geriatric)
Isordil Tembids (Wyeth-Ayerst)
Isordil Titradose (Wyeth-Ayerst)
isosorbide dinitrate (various manufacturers)
Sorbitrate (Zeneca)
Sorbitrate SA (Zeneca)

TYPE OF DRUG
Antianginal
INGREDIENT
isosorbide dinitrate
DOSAGE FORMS
Tablets (5 mg, 10 mg, 20 mg, 30 mg, and 40 mg)
Chewable tablets (5 mg and 10 mg)
Sublingual (intrabuccal) tablets (2.5 mg, 5 mg, and 10 mg)
Sustained-release tablets (40 mg)
Sustained-release capsules (40 mg)
STORAGE
Isosorbide dinitrate tablets and capsules should be stored in a
cool, dry place. This medication loses potency when exposed
to heat or moisture.

USES
Isosorbide dinitrate is a vasodilator that relaxes the muscle of
the blood vessels, leading to an increase in the oxygen supply
to the heart. It is used to relieve (chewable and sublingual
tablets) or to prevent (oral tablets and capsules) angina (chest
pain). The chewable and sublingual tablets act quickly; they
can be used to relieve chest pain after it has begun. The oral
tablets and capsules do not act quickly; they are used only to
prevent angina attacks.

TREATMENT
Take the chewable or sublingual forms of this medication at the
first sign of an angina attack. DO NOT WAIT for the attack
to become severe. Then sit down. These tablets are absorbed
more completely through the lining of the mouth than from
the stomach. Your mouth should be empty when you take
these tablets. Do not eat, drink, or smoke with a tablet in your
mouth. If the pain of an attack continues, you can take another tablet after five minutes, and a third tablet after another
five minutes. If three tablets provide no relief within 15 minutes, CONTACT YOUR DOCTOR IMMEDIATELY or go to the
nearest hospital.

The chewable tablet should be chewed for at least two minutes before swallowing.

Place the sublingual tablet under the tongue or against the
cheek and allow it to dissolve—DO NOT CHEW OR SWAL-
LOW IT. Do not swallow until the drug is dissolved, and do not

rinse your mouth for several minutes (this gives a greater opportunity for the drug to be absorbed through the lining of the mouth).

The regular tablets and the sustained-release forms of this medication should be taken with a full glass of water on an empty stomach. The sustained-release forms should be swallowed whole. Breaking, crushing, or chewing these tablets or capsules destroys their sustained-release activity and possibly increases the side effects.

If you are taking this medication on a regular schedule, try not to miss any doses. If you do miss a dose, take the missed dose as soon as possible, unless it is within two hours of the next dose (or six hours for the sustained-release forms). In that case, do not take the missed dose at all; return to your regular dosing schedule. Do not double the next dose.

Some doctors may recommend using this medication to prevent an anginal attack before expected physical or emotional stress. Discuss this with your doctor.

SIDE EFFECTS

Minor. Dizziness, flushing, headache, light-headedness, nausea, or vomiting may be experienced. These side effects should disappear as your body gets accustomed to the medication.

If you feel dizzy or light-headed, sit or lie down for a while; get up slowly from a sitting or reclining position; and be careful on stairs. To avoid dizziness or light-headedness when you stand, contract and relax the muscles of your legs for a few moments before rising. Do this by pushing one foot against the floor while raising the other foot slightly, alternating feet so that you are "pumping" your legs in a pedaling motion.

Acetaminophen may help relieve headaches caused by this medication.

Major. Tell your doctor about any side effects that are persistent or particularly bothersome. IT IS ESPECIALLY IMPORTANT TO TELL YOUR DOCTOR about fainting spells, palpitations, rash, restlessness, sweating, or unusual weakness.

INTERACTIONS

Isosorbide dinitrate can interact with other types of medications:

1. Isosorbide dinitrate, in combination with alcohol, can lead to dizziness and fainting.

2. Over-the-counter (nonprescription) sinus, allergy, cough, cold, asthma, and diet products can block the antianginal effects of isosorbide dinitrate.

BE SURE TO TELL YOUR DOCTOR about any medications you are taking at the present time, especially any of those listed above.

WARNINGS

• Tell your doctor about unusual or allergic reactions you have had to any medications, especially to isosorbide dinitrate or to any other nitrate-containing drugs (such as nitroglycerin).

• Before starting to take this medication, tell your doctor if you have ever had severe anemia, glaucoma, a heart attack, or thyroid disease.

• Before using this medication to relieve chest pain, be certain that the pain arises from the heart and is not due to a muscle spasm or to indigestion. If your chest pain is not relieved by use of this drug or if pain arises from a different location or differs in severity, CONSULT YOUR DOCTOR IMMEDIATELY.

• If this drug makes you dizzy or light-headed, do not take part in any activity that requires alertness, such as driving a car or operating potentially dangerous machinery.

• Before having surgery or any other medical or dental treatment, be sure to tell your doctor or dentist that you are taking this medication.

• Tolerance to this medication may develop. If the drug begins to lose its effectiveness, contact your doctor.

• Isosorbide dinitrate should not be discontinued unless you first consult your doctor. Stopping the drug abruptly may lead to further chest pain. Your doctor may, therefore, want to decrease your dosage gradually.

• If you have frequent diarrhea, you may not be absorbing the sustained-release form of this medication. Discuss this with your doctor.

• Be sure to tell your doctor if you are pregnant. Although this drug appears to be safe to use during pregnancy, extensive studies in pregnant women have not been conducted. Also notify your doctor if you are breast-feeding an infant. It is not known whether or not isosorbide dinitrate passes into breast milk.

isotretinoin

BRAND NAME (Manufacturer)
Accutane (Roche)
TYPE OF DRUG
Acne preparation
INGREDIENT
isotretinoin
DOSAGE FORM
Capsules (10 mg, 20 mg, and 40 mg)
STORAGE
Isotretinoin should be stored at room temperature in a tightly closed, light-resistant container.

USES

This medication is used to treat severe cystic acne. It is not clearly understood how isotretinoin works, but it decreases the production of sebum (an oily skin secretion) and dries up the acne lesions.

TREATMENT

An information leaflet is packaged with this product. Be sure to read it carefully.

Isotretinoin should be taken with meals to obtain maximum benefit.

It may take one to two months before the maximum effects of this medication are observed.

If you miss a dose of this medication, take the missed dose as soon as possible, and then return to your regular dosing schedule. However, if you do not remember until it is time for your next dose, double the next dose, and then return to your regular dosing schedule.

SIDE EFFECTS

Minor. Changes in skin color, drowsiness, dry lips or mouth, fatigue, fluid retention, headache, indigestion, inflammation of the eyelids, inflammation of the lips, irritation of the eyes, or thinning of the hair. These side effects may disappear as your body adjusts to the drug.

You may notice a worsening of your acne for the first few days of treatment.

This medication can cause increased sensitivity to sunlight. Therefore, avoid prolonged exposure to sunlight and sunlamps. You should wear protective clothing and sunglasses, and also use an effective sunscreen.

To relieve mouth dryness, chew sugarless gum or suck on ice chips or a piece of hard candy. If there is no relief within two weeks, consult your doctor.

Major. Tell your doctor about any side effects that are persistent or particularly bothersome. IT IS ESPECIALLY IMPORTANT TO TELL YOUR DOCTOR about black, tarry stools; bruising; burning or tingling sensation of the skin; changes in the menstrual cycle; depression; dizziness; hives; muscle pain; peeling of the palms and soles; rash; visual disturbances; or weight loss.

INTERACTIONS

This medication interacts with the following substances:

1. The concurrent use of alcohol and isotretinoin can lead to an increase in blood-lipid (fat) levels, which can be dangerous.

2. Vitamin A and isotretinoin together can result in additive toxic effects.

BE SURE TO TELL YOUR DOCTOR about any medications you are currently taking, especially vitamin A.

WARNINGS

• Tell your doctor about unusual or allergic reactions you have had to any medications, especially to isotretinoin, vitamin A, or the preservative parabens.

• Before starting to take this medication, tell your doctor if you now have or if you have ever had diabetes mellitus (sugar diabetes) or hyperlipidemia (high blood-lipid levels).

• If this drug makes you drowsy, do not take part in any activity that requires alertness, such as driving a car or operating potentially dangerous machinery.

• Be sure to tell your doctor if you are pregnant. Isotretinoin has been shown to cause birth defects in humans. An effective form of birth control should be used by women of child-bearing age while they are taking this drug and for at least one month before and after they stop taking it. Within two weeks of starting this drug, women should have a blood pregnancy test. If the test is negative, the drug will be started on the second or third day of the next normal menstrual period. Women should have a pregnancy test each month while they take this medication. All women must also sign an informed-consent sheet. Also tell your doctor if you are breast-feeding an infant. It is not known whether this drug passes into breast milk.

---

isradipine

BRAND NAME (Manufacturer)
DynaCirc Capsules (Sandoz)
TYPE OF DRUG
Antianginal (calcium channel blocker) and antihypertensive
INGREDIENT
isradipine
DOSAGE FORM
Capsules (2.5 mg and 5 mg)
STORAGE
Isradipine should be stored at room temperature in a tightly closed container, out of the reach of children and away from moisture and direct light.

USES
Isradipine is used to treat high blood pressure. It belongs to a group of drugs known as calcium channel blockers, which are useful for several cardiovascular conditions. Calcium channel blockers are less likely than beta blockers or thiazide diuretics to have adverse effects on plasma lipids or blood glucose control in hypertensive patients with diabetes, asthma, or hardening of the arteries. It is not fully understood how isradipine works, but by blocking calcium, it relaxes and prevents spasms of the blood vessels of the heart and reduces the oxygen needs of the heart muscle. Isradipine is also a potent vasodilator that relaxes the muscle tissue of the blood vessels, thereby lowering blood pressure.

TREATMENT
If you miss a dose of this medication, take the missed dose as soon as possible, unless it is almost time for the next dose. In that case, do not take the missed dose at all; just return to your regular dosing schedule. Do not double the next dose. If you have a heart condition and have been taking isradip-

ine regularly, it should not be stopped suddenly, as this may worsen your symptoms of heart disease.

This medication does not cure high blood pressure, but it will help to control the condition as long as you continue to take it. It may take several weeks to develop its full effect.

SIDE EFFECTS
Minor. Constipation, dizziness, flushing of the face, headaches, increased heart rate, nervousness, painful extremeties, rash, stomach upset, and swollen ankles.

To relieve constipation, increase the amount of fiber in your diet (fresh fruits and vegetables, salads, bran, and whole-grain breads), exercise, and drink more water (unless your doctor directs you to do otherwise).

Major. Tell your doctor about any side effects that are persistent or particularly bothersome. IT IS ESPECIALLY IMPORTANT TO TELL YOUR DOCTOR about changes in menstruation, confusion, depression, fainting, fatigue, hair loss, itching, loss of balance, palpitations, rapid weight gain (three to five pounds within a week), recurrent infections, shortness of breath, swelling of the hands or feet, tremors, or unusual weakness.

INTERACTIONS
Isradipine may increase the blood-pressure-lowering effect of beta blockers, especially if there is a preexisting heart condition. Isradipine may also increase the blood levels of the beta blocker propranolol.

Other drugs that may interact with isradipine are adenosine, calcium supplements, chlorpromazine, cimetidine, digoxin, fentanyl used in conjunction with anesthesia, phenylbutazone, prazosin, and tolbutamide.

WARNINGS
• Tell your doctor about unusual or allergic reactions you have or have ever had to any medications, especially to isradipine.
• Before starting to take this medication, be sure to tell your doctor if you now have or if you have ever had any type of heart disease, kidney disease, liver disease, low blood pressure, or a slowed heartbeat.

• Your doctor may want you to check your pulse on a regular basis while you are taking this medication. If your heart rate drops below 50 beats per minute, contact your doctor.

• If you experience angina symptoms, stopping this medication abruptly may lead to a worsening of your chest pain. Your doctor may, therefore, want to reduce your dosage gradually or have you switch to another medication when isradipine is discontinued.

• In order to prevent dizziness or light-headedness while taking this medication, try not to stand for long periods of time, avoid drinking alcoholic beverages, and try not to become overheated. Avoid exercising strenuously in hot weather, and do not take hot baths, showers, and saunas.

• Be sure to tell your doctor if you are pregnant. There are some indications that israpidine may cause birth defects in animals, but conclusive studies in humans have not been conducted. Also tell your doctor if you are breast-feeding an infant. It is not known whether isradipine passes into breast milk.

---

ketoprofen

BRAND NAMES (Manufacturers)
Orudis (Wyeth-Ayerst)
Oruvail (Wyeth-Ayerst)
TYPE OF DRUG
Nonsteroidal anti-inflammatory analgesic
INGREDIENT
ketoprofen
DOSAGE FORMS
Capsules (25 mg, 50 mg, and 75 mg)
Sustained-action capsules (200 mg)
STORAGE
Store at room temperature in a tightly closed container.

USES

Ketoprofen is used to treat rheumatoid arthritis and osteoarthritis. Ketoprofen has been shown to block the production of certain body chemicals, called prostaglandins, that trigger pain and inflammation. However, it is not yet fully understood how ketoprofen works.

TREATMENT

Ketoprofen should be taken immediately after meals or with food in order to reduce stomach irritation. Check with your doctor about taking ketoprofen with an antacid.

Take ketoprofen on schedule and try not to miss any doses. If you do miss a dose, take the missed dose as soon as possible, unless it is almost time for the next dose. In that case, do not take the missed dose at all; just return to your regular dosing schedule. Do not double the next dose.

Ketoprofen does not cure arthritis, but it will help to control symptoms as long as you take it.

SIDE EFFECTS

Minor. Abdominal pain, changes in taste, constipation, decreased or increased appetite, diarrhea, dizziness, drowsiness, dry mouth, excessive salivation, fatigue, flushing, gas, headache, heartburn, increased heart rate, increased thirst, nausea, nosebleeds, sweating, vomiting, or weight change. These side effects should disappear as your body adjusts to this medication.

Ketoprofen may cause increased sensitivity to sunlight. Therefore, it is important to avoid prolonged exposure to sunlight and sunlamps. Wear protective clothing and sunglasses, and use an effective sunscreen.

To relieve constipation, increase the amount of fiber in your diet (fresh fruits and vegetables, salads, bran, and whole-grain breads). You can also increase your exercise and drink more water (unless your doctor directs you to do otherwise).

If you become dizzy, sit or lie down; get up slowly from a sitting or reclining position; and be careful on stairs.

Major. Tell your doctor about any side effects that are persistent or particularly bothersome. IT IS ESPECIALLY IMPORTANT TO TELL YOUR DOCTOR about black or tarry stools, chills, confusion, decreased or painful urination, hair loss, itching, memory loss, mouth sores, muscle pains, palpitations, rash, shortness of breath, swelling of the feet, tingling in the fingers or toes, unusual bleeding or bruising, unusual weight gain, visual disturbances, or yellowing of the eyes or skin.

INTERACTIONS

Ketoprofen interacts with several other types of medications:

1. Ketoprofen can increase the risk of bleeding complications with anticoagulants (blood thinners, such as warfarin).
2. Ketoprofen has been known to interfere with the diuretic effects of furosemide and thiazide-type diuretics (water pills).
3. Aspirin can alter the blood levels and elimination of ketoprofen from the body.
4. Probenecid can increase the blood levels of ketoprofen, which in turn can lead to an increased chance of experiencing side effects.
5. The action of beta blockers may be affected by this drug.

BE SURE TO TELL YOUR DOCTOR about any medications you are currently taking, especially those listed above.

WARNINGS

• Tell your doctor about any unusual or allergic reactions you have had to any medications, especially to ketoprofen or to any other chemically related drugs, including aspirin, other salicylates, diclofenac, diflunisal, fenoprofen, flurbiprofen, ibuprofen, indomethacin, meclofenamate, mefenamic acid, naproxen, oxyphenbutazone, phenylbutazone, piroxicam, sulindac, or tolmetin.
• Before taking ketoprofen, tell your doctor if you now have or if you have ever had anemia, bleeding problems, gastrointestinal diseases, heart failure, hypertension, kidney disease, liver disease, or ulcers.
• If ketoprofen makes you dizzy or drowsy, do not take part in any activity that requires alertness, such as driving a car or operating potentially dangerous machinery.
• If vision problems develop while taking this medication, your doctor may refer you to an ophthalmologist.
• Stomach problems are more likely if you take aspirin regularly or drink alcohol while on this drug.
• Before having surgery or any other medical or dental treatment, be sure to tell your doctor or dentist that you are taking this medication. Your doctor or dentist may recommend stopping ketoprofen for several days prior to surgery, to decrease the risk of bleeding complications.
• The elderly may be at increased risk of experiencing some of the side effects of this medication.
• Be sure to tell your doctor if you are pregnant. Although ketoprofen appears to be safe in animals, studies in pregnant women have not been conducted. Ketoprofen should be

avoided late in pregnancy because it can alter fetal heart circulation. Also tell your doctor if you are breast-feeding an infant. It is not yet known whether ketoprofen passes into human breast milk.

---

ketorolac

BRAND NAME (Manufacturer)
Toradol (Syntex)
TYPE OF DRUG
Nonsteroidal anti-inflammatory analgesic
INGREDIENT
ketorolac
DOSAGE FORM
Tablets (10 mg)
STORAGE
Store in a tightly closed, light-resistant container at room temperature. This medication should never be frozen.

USES

Ketorolac is used orally for the short-term treatment (five to 14 days) of moderate to severe pain such as postpartum, postoperative (including that associated with oral, orthopedic, or gynecologic surgery), orthopedic (including musculoskeletal strains or sprains), or sciatic pain; and for visceral pain associated with cancer. Ketorolac is used for the pain, swelling, and stiffness that is often evident with certain types of arthritis, gout, bursitis, and tendinitis. Ketorolac has been shown to block the production of certain body chemicals, called prostaglandins, that may trigger pain.

TREATMENT

You should take this medication on an empty stomach 30 to 60 minutes before meals or two hours after meals, so that it reaches your bloodstream quickly. However, to decrease stomach irritation, your doctor may want you to take the medication with food or antacids.

If ketorolac is being taken to relieve arthritis, you must take it regularly as directed by your doctor. Ketorolac does not cure arthritis, but it will help to control the condition as long as you continue to take it.

It is important to take ketorolac on schedule and not to miss any doses. If you do miss a dose, take it as soon as possible, unless it is almost time for your next dose. In that case, don't take the missed dose at all; just return to your regular dosing schedule. Do not double the next dose.

SIDE EFFECTS

Minor. Constipation, diarrhea, dizziness, drowsiness, excessive thirst, feeling of fullness, flatulence, headache, heartburn, increased appetite, indigestion, nausea, or nervousness. As your body adjusts to the drug, these side effects should disappear.

To relieve constipation, increase the amount of fiber in your diet (fresh fruits and vegetables, salads, bran, and whole-grain breads), exercise, and drink more water (unless your doctor directs you to do otherwise).

If you become dizzy or light-headed, sit or lie down for a while; get up slowly from a sitting or reclining position; and be careful on stairs.

Major. If any side effects are persistent or particularly bothersome, you should report them to your doctor. IT IS ESPECIALLY IMPORTANT TO TELL YOUR DOCTOR about bloody or black, tarry stools; blurred vision; confusion; depression; difficult or painful urination; difficulty in breathing; fever; palpitations; problem with hearing; ringing or buzzing in your ears; seizures; skin rash, hives, or itching; stomach pain; swelling; tremors; unusual bleeding or bruising; unusual fatigue or weakness; unusual weight gain; or yellowing of the eyes or skin.

INTERACTIONS

Ketorolac interacts with several other types of medications:
1. Concurrent use of ketorolac and anticoagulants (blood thinners, such as warfarin) can lead to an increase in bleeding complications.
2. Concurrent use of ketorolac and aspirin, other salicylates, or other anti-inflammatory medications can increase stomach irritation.
3. Ketorolac can interact with diuretics (water pills).
4. Probenecid may increase the blood levels of ketorolac, which may increase the risk of side effects.

5. The action of beta blockers may be decreased by this drug.
6. Concurrent use of ketorolac and methotrexate may be associated with severe toxic levels of methotrexate.
7. Concurrent use of ketorolac and lithium may be associated with severe toxic levels of lithium.

BE SURE TO TELL YOUR DOCTOR about any medications you are currently taking, especially any listed above.

WARNINGS

• Before you start to take this medication, it is important to tell your doctor if you have ever had unusual or allergic reactions to ketorolac or to any of the other chemically related drugs (aspirin, other salicylates, diclofenac, diflunisal, fenoprofen, flurbiprofen, ibuprofen, indomethacin, meclofenamate, mefenamic acid, naproxen, oxyphenbutazone, phenylbutazone, piroxicam, sulindac, or tolmetin).
• Tell your doctor if you now have or if you have ever had bleeding problems, colitis, stomach ulcers, or other stomach problems, epilepsy, heart disease, high blood pressure, asthma, kidney disease, liver disease, mental illness, or Parkinson's disease.
• If ketorolac makes you dizzy or drowsy, do not take part in any activity that requires alertness, such as driving a car or operating hazardous machinery.
• Because ketorolac can prolong bleeding time, be certain to tell your doctor that you are taking this drug before having surgery or any other medical or dental treatment.
• Stomach problems are more likely to occur if you take aspirin regularly or if you drink alcohol while being treated with ketorolac. These should be avoided (unless your doctor directs you to do otherwise).
• The elderly may be at increased risk for experiencing side effects from this drug.
• Be sure to tell your doctor if you are pregnant. This type of medication can cause unwanted effects to the heart or to the blood flow of the fetus. Studies in animals have also shown that this type of medication, if taken late in pregnancy, can prolong labor or cause other problems during delivery. Also tell your doctor if you are breast-feeding an infant. Small amounts of ketorolac can pass into the breast milk.

labetalol

BRAND NAMES (Manufacturers)
Normodyne (Schering)
Trandate (Allen & Hanburys)
TYPE OF DRUG
Alpha/beta-adrenergic blocking agent
INGREDIENT
labetalol
DOSAGE FORM
Tablets (100 mg, 200 mg, and 300 mg)
STORAGE
Labetalol should be stored at room temperature in a tightly
closed container.

USES
Labetalol is used to treat high blood pressure. Labetalol belongs to a group of medicines known as beta-adrenergic blocking agents or, more commonly, beta blockers. These drugs
work by controlling impulses along certain nerve pathways.

TREATMENT
Labetalol can be taken either on an empty stomach or with
food or milk (as directed by your doctor). In order to become
accustomed to taking this medication, try to take it at the same
time(s) each day.
  If you miss a dose of this medication, take the missed dose
as soon as possible, unless it is almost time for your next dose.
In that case, do not take the missed dose at all; just wait until
the next scheduled dose. Do not double the dose.
  Labetalol does not cure high blood pressure, but it will help
control the condition.

SIDE EFFECTS
Minor. Abdominal pain; change in taste; diarrhea; dizziness;
drowsiness; dryness of the eyes, mouth, and skin; fainting; fatigue; headache; heartburn; light-headedness; nasal congestion;
nausea; numbness or tingling of the fingers or toes; scalp tingling; or vomiting. These side effects should disappear as your
body adjusts to this medication.

If you are extrasensitive to the cold, be sure to dress warmly during cold weather.

Plain, nonmedicated eye drops (artificial tears) may help to relieve eye dryness.

Sucking on ice chips or chewing sugarless gum helps to relieve mouth and throat dryness.

To avoid dizziness or light-headedness when you stand, contract and relax the muscles of your legs for a few moments before rising. Do this by alternately pushing one foot against the floor while raising the other foot slightly, so that you are "pumping" your legs in a pedaling motion.

Major. Tell your doctor about any side effects that are persistent or particularly bothersome. IT IS ESPECIALLY IMPORTANT TO TELL YOUR DOCTOR about cold hands or feet (due to decreased blood circulation to skin, fingers, and toes), confusion, depression, difficult or painful urination, impotence, itching, muscle cramps, rapid weight gain (three to five pounds within a week), rash, sore throat and fever, unusual bleeding or bruising, vision disturbances, wheezing or difficulty in breathing, or yellowing of the eyes or skin.

INTERACTIONS

This medication interacts with several other types of drugs:

1. Indomethacin, aspirin, and other salicylates may decrease the blood-pressure-lowering effects of beta blockers.

2. Concurrent use of beta-adrenergic blocking agents and calcium channel blockers (diltiazem, nifedipine, verapamil) or disopyramide can lead to heart failure or very low blood pressure. However, there may be times when your doctor may decide that multiple medications are necessary.

3. Cimetidine has been known to increase the blood concentrations of labetalol, which can result in measurably greater side effects.

4. Side effects may also be increased when beta blockers are taken with clonidine, digoxin, epinephrine, chlorpromazine, furosemide, hydralazine, phenylephrine, phenylpropanolamine, phenothiazine tranquilizers, prazosin, reserpine, or monoamine oxidase (MAO) inhibitors. At least 14 days should separate the use of a beta blocker and an MAO inhibitor.

5. Beta blockers may antagonize (work against) the effects of theophylline, aminophylline, albuterol, isoproterenol, metaproterenol, and terbutaline.

6. Beta blockers can also interact with insulin or oral antidiabetic agents, raising or lowering blood-sugar levels or masking the symptoms of low blood sugar.

7. Concurrent use of tricyclic antidepressants and labetalol can increase the risk of tremors.

8. Halothane anesthesia and nitroglycerin can increase the blood-pressure-lowering effects of labetalol.

BE SURE TO TELL YOUR DOCTOR about any drugs you are currently taking, especially any of those medications listed above.

WARNINGS

• Before you start taking this medication, it is important for you to tell your doctor about any unusual or allergic reaction you have had to any medications, especially to labetalol or to any other beta blocker (acebutolol, atenolol, betaxolol, carteolol, esmolol, metoprolol, nadolol, penbutolol, pindolol, propranolol, timolol).

• Tell your doctor if you now have or if you have ever had asthma, bronchitis, diabetes mellitus, heart block, heart failure, liver disease, pheochromocytoma, poor circulation in fingers and toes, or a slow heartbeat.

• You may want to check your pulse while taking this medication. If your pulse is much slower than your usual rate (or if it is less than 50 beats per minute), check with your doctor. A pulse rate that is too slow may cause circulation problems.

• This drug may affect your body's response to exercise. Ask your doctor how much exercise is appropriate given your state of health.

• Do not stop taking this medicine without first checking with your doctor. Some conditions may become worse when the medicine is stopped suddenly, and the danger of a heart attack is increased in some patients. Your doctor may want you to gradually reduce the amount of medicine you take before stopping completely. Have enough medicine on hand to last through vacations, holidays, and weekends.

• Before undergoing surgery or any other medical or dental treatment, tell your physician or dentist that you are taking this medicine. Often, this medication will be discontinued 48 hours prior to any major surgery.

• Labetalol can cause decreased alertness, dizziness, drowsiness, and light-headedness. Exercise caution while driving a car or using any potentially dangerous machinery.

• While taking this medicine, do not use any over-the-counter allergy, asthma, cough, cold, sinus, or diet preparation without first checking with your pharmacist or doctor. The combination of these medicines with a beta blocker can result in high blood pressure.

• Be sure to tell your doctor if you are pregnant. Although labetalol appears to be safe in animals, studies in pregnant women have not been conducted. Also tell your doctor if you are breast-feeding an infant. Small amounts of labetalol may pass into breast milk.

lamivudine

BRAND NAME (Manufacturer)
Epivir (Glaxo Wellcome)
TYPE OF DRUG
Antiviral
INGREDIENT
lamivudine
DOSAGE FORMS
Tablets (150 mg)
Oral solution (10 mg per mL)
STORAGE
Lamivudine tablets and solution should be stored at room temperature in tightly closed, light-resistant containers. This medication should never be frozen.

USES

Lamivudine is used in the treatment of human immunodeficiency virus (HIV) infection. HIV is the virus that causes AIDS. Lamivudine works by inhibiting the reproduction, or growth, of the virus, which slows down the progression of AIDS. Lamivudine does not cure AIDS, but this drug may delay the onset of other infections and diseases caused by AIDS. Lamivudine is used in combination with other anti-AIDS drugs, such as zidovudine.

TREATMENT

This medication works best when the level of medicine in your bloodstream is kept constant. It is best to take the drug at evenly spaced intervals throughout the day.

If you are taking lamivudine solution, use a special measuring spoon to measure the doses. If you miss a dose of this medication, take it as soon as possible. However, if it is almost time for your next dose, skip the missed dose and go back to your regular dosing schedule. Do not double the dose.

SIDE EFFECTS

Minor. Cough, dizziness, fatigue, headache, insomnia, nausea, or skin rash may occur with the use of this medication.
Major. You should tell your doctor about any side effects that are persistent or particularly bothersome. IT IS ESPECIALLY IMPORTANT TO TELL YOUR DOCTOR ABOUT tingling, burning, numbness, or pain in the hands, arms, feet, or legs; or nausea, vomiting, and severe abdominal pain.

INTERACTIONS

Lamivudine may interact with several other drugs:
1. Combined use of lamivudine with zidovudine may increase the amount of zidovudine in the body and may increase the toxicity of zidovudine.
2. Sulfamethoxazole and trimethoprim may interfere with your body's ability to eliminate lamivudine and increase the toxicity of lamivudine.

BE SURE TO TELL YOUR DOCTOR about any medications your are currently taking, especially any of those listed above.

WARNINGS

• Tell your doctor about any unusual or allergic reactions you have had to any medications, especially lamivudine or other medications used to treat HIV infection. Also tell your doctor about any allergic reaction you have had to any foods, preservatives, or dyes.
• You may require periodic blood sample checks at your physician's office to monitor the effects of lamivudine.
• Be sure to tell your doctor if you have anemia, liver disease, or vitamin deficiencies.
• Before having surgery or any other medical or dental treatment, tell your doctor or dentist that you are taking this drug.

• If you are infected with HIV, it is best to avoid any sexual activity involving an exchange of body fluids with other people. If you do have vaginal, anal, or oral sex, always use a latex condom.
• If you inject drugs, do not share needles with anyone.
• Be sure to tell your doctor if you are pregnant or plan to become pregnant. It is not known if lamivudine is safe to take during pregnancy. Tell your doctor if you are breast-feeding an infant. It is not known if lamivudine passes into breast milk, but the AIDS virus can be transmitted through breast milk.

lamotrigine

BRAND NAME (Manufacturer)
Lamictal (Glaxo Wellcome)
TYPE OF DRUG
Anticonvulsant
INGREDIENT
lamotrigine
DOSAGE FORM
Tablets (25 mg, 100 mg, 150 mg, and 200 mg)
STORAGE
Lamotrigine should be stored at room temperature in a tightly closed, light-resistant container. Never freeze this medication.

USES

This medication is used in conjunction with other anticonvulsants for the treatment of seizure disorders in adults. Lamotrigine is also useful in infants and children with Lennox-Gastaut syndrome. The mechanism of action of this drug is not related to any other anticonvulsant medication and is not well understood.

TREATMENT

If stomach upset occurs, lamotrigine may be taken with food—unless your doctor instructs you to do otherwise.

Routine monitoring of the level of lamotrigine in your bloodstream is not usually necessary. However, when beginning therapy it may be necessary to closely monitor the bloodstream levels of other anticonvulsants. The doses of lamotrigine should be administered at evenly spaced intervals day or night, depending on the specific dosage recommended by your doctor. For example, if you take two doses a day, the doses should be spaced 12 hours apart.

Try not to miss any doses of this medication. If you do miss a dose, take the missed dose as soon as possible, unless it is almost time for your next dose. In that case, do not take the missed dose at all; just return to your regular dosing schedule. Do not double the next dose unless your doctor directs you to do so. If you miss two or more doses in a row, be sure to contact your doctor.

SIDE EFFECTS

Minor. Blurred or double vision, constipation, difficulty with balance or walking, dizziness, drowsiness, headache, nausea, or vomiting. These side effects should disappear over time as your body adjusts to the medication.

Lamotrigine can increase your sensitivity to sunlight. It is therefore important to avoid prolonged exposure to sunlight or sunlamps. Wear protective clothing and sunglasses, and use an effective sunscreen.

In order to prevent constipation, increase the amount of fiber in your diet (fresh fruits and vegetables, salads, bran, whole-grain breads), exercise, and drink more water (unless your doctor tells you not to do so).

If you feel dizzy or lightheaded, sit or lie down for a while; get up slowly from a sitting or reclining position; and be careful when climbing stairs.

Major. Tell your doctor about any side effects that are persistent or particularly bothersome. IT IS ESPECIALLY IMPORTANT TO TELL YOUR DOCTOR about severe rash, abnormal balance, difficulty walking, depression, difficulty breathing, double vision, fever, numbness or tingling in the hands or feet, palpitations, skin discoloration, abnormal dreaming/hallucinations, tremor, or difficulty with urination.

INTERACTIONS

Lamotrigine interacts with several other types of medications:
1. Concurrent use of this medication with certain anticonvulsants (carbamazepine, phenobarbital, phenytoin, primidone) will result in a decrease in the level of lamotrigine in the bloodstream. The dose of lamotrigine may need to be increased.

2. Use of lamotrigine with valproic acid or carbamazepine may result in increased toxicity of these agents. The dose of these medications may need to be decreased.

Before you start lamotrigine, BE SURE TO TELL YOUR DOCTOR about any medications you are currently taking, especially any of those listed above.

WARNINGS

• Tell your doctor about any unusual or allergic reactions you have had to any medications, especially to lamotrigine or any other anticonvulsant medication.

• Before having surgery or any other medical or dental procedure, be sure to tell your doctor or dentist that you are taking this medication.

• If this medication makes you dizzy or drowsy, do not take part in any activity that requires alertness, such as driving a car or operating potentially dangerous equipment.

• Do not stop taking this medication suddenly. If you stop abruptly, you may experience an uncontrollable seizure.

• Be sure to contact your doctor immediately if you develop a skin rash while taking lamotrigine. It may indicate a serious medical event.

• Be sure to tell your doctor if you now have or have ever had blood disorders, urinary tract infections, urinary incontinence, glaucoma, heart disease, kidney disease, or liver disease.

• Be sure to tell your doctor if you are pregnant. Although extensive studies of lamotrigine in humans have not been conducted, lamotrigine has been shown to cause side effects in the fetuses of animals that received large doses of the drug during pregnancy. Also tell your doctor if you are breast-feeding an infant. Lamotrigine passes into breast milk, although its effects on the newborn are unknown.

---

levodopa

BRAND NAMES (Manufacturers)
Dopar (Roberts)
Larodopa (Roche)
TYPE OF DRUG
Antiparkinsonism agent

INGREDIENT
levodopa
DOSAGE FORMS
Tablets (100 mg, 250 mg, and 500 mg)
Capsules (100 mg, 250 mg, and 500 mg)
STORAGE
Levodopa tablets and capsules should be stored at room temperature in tightly closed, light-resistant containers.

USES
Levodopa is used to treat the symptoms of Parkinson's disease. It is converted in the body to dopamine, a chemical in the brain that is diminished in patients with Parkinson's disease.

TREATMENT
In order to avoid stomach irritation, you can take levodopa with food or with a full glass of milk or water (unless your doctor directs you to do otherwise).

You may not observe significant benefit from this drug for two to three weeks after starting to take it.

If you miss a dose, take the missed dose as soon as possible, unless it is within two hours of the next scheduled dose. In that case, do not take the missed dose at all; just return to your regular dosing schedule. Do not double the next dose.

SIDE EFFECTS
Minor. Abdominal pain, anxiety, bitter taste in the mouth, constipation, diarrhea, dizziness, dry mouth, fatigue, flushing, gas, headache, hiccups, hoarseness, increased hand tremors, increased sexual interest, increased sweating, insomnia, loss of appetite, nausea, offensive body odor, salivation, vision changes, vomiting, weakness, or weight gain. These side effects may disappear as your body adjusts to the medication.

Levodopa can cause a darkening of your urine or sweat. This is a harmless effect.

To relieve constipation, increase the amount of fiber in your diet (fresh fruits and vegetables, salads, bran, and whole-grain breads), drink more water, and exercise (unless your doctor directs you to do otherwise).

If you feel dizzy, sit or lie down for a while; get up slowly from a sitting or reclining position; and be careful on stairs.

To relieve mouth dryness, chew sugarless gum or suck on ice chips or a piece of hard candy.

Major. Tell your doctor about any side effects that are persistent or particularly bothersome. IT IS ESPECIALLY IMPORTANT TO TELL YOUR DOCTOR about bloody or black, tarry stools; confusion; convulsions; depression; fainting; false sense of well-being; loss of coordination; loss of hair; nightmares; painful erection; palpitations; rapid weight gain (three to five pounds within a week); skin rash; visual disturbances; uncontrolled movements; or unusual weakness.

INTERACTIONS

Levodopa interacts with several other types of medications:

1. The dosage of antihypertensive drugs may require adjustment when levodopa is started.

2. The effectiveness of levodopa may be decreased by the following: benzodiazepine tranquilizers, phenothiazine tranquilizers, haloperidol, thiothixene, phenytoin, papaverine, and reserpine.

3. Methyldopa can increase or decrease the side effects of therapy with levodopa.

4. Use of levodopa and a monoamine oxidase (MAO) inhibitor within 14 days of each other can lead to severe side effects.

5. Levodopa can increase the side effects of tricyclic antidepressants, ephedrine, and amphetamines.

6. Antacids may alter the absorption of levodopa from the gastrointestinal tract.

7. Pyridoxine (vitamin B$_6$) can decrease the effectiveness of levodopa.

BE SURE TO TELL YOUR DOCTOR about any medications you are taking, especially those listed above.

WARNINGS

• Tell your doctor about unusual or allergic reactions you have had to any medications, especially to levodopa.

• Before starting to take this medication, be sure to tell your doctor if you now have or if you have ever had asthma, diabetes mellitus, difficulty in urinating, epilepsy, glaucoma, heart disease, hormone disorders, kidney disease, liver disease, lung disease, melanoma (a type of skin cancer), mental disorders, or peptic ulcers.

• Some of these products contain the color additive FD&C Yellow No. 5 (tartrazine), which can cause allergic-type symptoms (difficulty in breathing, faintness, or rash) in certain susceptible individuals.

• If levodopa makes you dizzy or blurs your vision, avoid activities that require mental alertness, such as driving a car or operating potentially dangerous machinery.

• Notify your doctor if you start to experience any uncontrolled movements of the limbs or face while taking this medication.

• Before having surgery or any other medical or dental treatment, be sure to tell your doctor or dentist that you are taking this medication.

• Levodopa can cause erroneous readings of urine glucose and ketone tests. Patients with diabetes should not change their dosage unless they first check with their doctor.

• Pyridoxine (vitamin B6) can decrease the effectiveness of levodopa. Persons taking levodopa should avoid taking this vitamin and should avoid foods rich in pyridoxine (including beans, bacon, avocados, liver, dry skim milk, oatmeal, sweet potatoes, peas, and tuna).

• Be sure to tell your doctor if you are pregnant. Although levodopa appears to be safe in humans, birth defects have been reported in the offspring of animals that were administered large doses during pregnancy. Also tell your doctor if you are breast-feeding an infant. Levodopa passes into breast milk and can cause side effects in nursing infants.

levothyroxine

BRAND NAMES (Manufacturers)
Levothroid (Forest)
levothyroxine sodium (various manufacturers)
Levoxine (Daniels)
Synthroid (Flint)
TYPE OF DRUG
Thyroid hormone
INGREDIENT
levothyroxine

DOSAGE FORM
Tablets (0.025 mg, 0.05 mg, 0.075 mg, 0.088 mg, 0.1 mg,
0.112 mg, 0.125 mg, 0.137 mg, 0.15 mg, 0.175 mg,
0.2 mg, and 0.3 mg)

STORAGE
Levothyroxine tablets should be stored at room temperature
in a tightly closed, light-resistant container. This medication
should not be refrigerated.

USES
Levothyroxine is prescribed to replace natural thyroid hormones that are absent because of a disorder of the thyroid
gland. It is also used to help decrease the size of enlarged thyroid glands and to treat thyroid cancer. This product is prepared synthetically (artificially), but it is exactly like the natural
thyroid hormone that is produced by the human body.

TREATMENT
Levothyroxine tablets should be taken on an empty stomach
with a full glass of water. If the drug upsets your stomach, ask
your doctor if you can take it with food or a glass of milk.

In order to get accustomed to taking this drug, try to take
it at the same time each day. Try not to miss any doses. If you
do miss a dose of this drug, take it as soon as possible, unless it is almost time for the next dose. In that case, do not
take the missed dose at all; just return to your regular dosing
schedule. Do not double the next dose. If you miss more than
one or two doses, contact your doctor immediately.

SIDE EFFECTS
Minor. Constipation; dry, puffy skin; fatigue; headache; listlessness; or weight gain. These effects are symptoms of an underactive thyroid. They should disappear after your body adjusts to the medication. It could take several weeks for the
medication to take effect. Consult your doctor if these symptoms persist.

Major. Tell your doctor about any side effects that are persistent or particularly bothersome. Most of the major side effects
associated with this drug are the result of too large a dose.
The dosage of this medication may need to be adjusted if you
experience any of the following side effects: chest pain, diarrhea, fever, heat intolerance, insomnia, irritability, leg cramps,

menstrual irregularities, muscle aches, nervousness, palpitations, shortness of breath, sweating, trembling, or weight loss. CHECK WITH YOUR DOCTOR.

INTERACTIONS

Levothyroxine interacts with several other types of drugs:

1. Dosing requirements for digoxin, insulin, or oral antidiabetic agents may change when levothyroxine is used.

2. The effects of oral anticoagulants (blood thinners, such as warfarin) may be increased by levothyroxine, which could lead to bleeding complications.

3. Cholestyramine and colestipol prevent the body's absorbtion of levothyroxine. At least four hours should separate doses of levothyroxine and one of these drugs.

4. Oral contraceptives (birth control pills) and estrogen-containing drugs may change dosage requirements.

5. Phenobarbital may decrease the effects of levothyroxine; but tricyclic antidepressants and over-the-counter (nonprescription) allergy, asthma, cough, cold, sinus, and diet medications may increase its side effects.

BE SURE TO TELL YOUR DOCTOR about any medications you are currently taking.

WARNINGS

• Tell your doctor about unusual or allergic reactions you have had to any medications, especially to thyroid hormone, levothyroxine, or liothyronine or to any other substances such as foods, preservatives, or dyes.

• Tell your doctor if you now have or if you have ever had angina pectoris, diabetes mellitus, heart disease, high blood pressure, kidney disease, or an underactive adrenal or pituitary gland.

• If you have an underactive thyroid gland, you may need to take this medication for life. You should not stop taking it unless you first check with your doctor.

• Before having surgery or any other medical or dental treatment, be sure to tell your doctor or dentist that you are taking levothyroxine.

• Over-the-counter allergy, asthma, cough, cold, sinus, and diet medications can increase the side effects of levothyroxine. Therefore, check with your doctor or pharmacist before taking any of these products.

• Although many thyroid products are on the market, they are not all bioequivalent; that is, they may not all be absorbed into the bloodstream at the same rate or have the same over-all activity. DO NOT CHANGE BRANDS of this drug without first consulting your doctor or pharmacist to make sure you are receiving an equivalent product.

• Some of these products contain the color additive FD&C Yellow No. 5 (tartrazine), which can cause allergic-type reactions (fainting, rash, difficulty in breathing) in certain susceptible individuals.

• Tell your doctor if you are pregnant. Levothyroxine does not readily cross the placenta, and the drug appears to be safe during pregnancy. However, your dosing of levothyroxine may change during pregnancy. Also tell your doctor if you are breast-feeding an infant.

---

lindane

BRAND NAMES (Manufacturers)
G-well (Goldline)
Kwell (Reed & Carnrick)
lindane (various manufacturers)
Scabene (Stiefel)
TYPE OF DRUG
Pediculicide and scabicide
INGREDIENT
lindane (formerly known as gamma benzene hexachloride)
DOSAGE FORMS
Cream (1%)
Lotion (1%)
Shampoo (1%)
STORAGE
Lindane should be stored at room temperature in tightly closed containers and should never be frozen.

USES

This medication is used to eliminate crab lice, head lice, and scabies. Lindane is a central nervous system (brain and spinal cord) stimulant, which causes convulsions and death of the parasites (at the dosage generally used, it is not harmful to humans). Lindane cream and lotion are used to treat only scabies infestations. Lindane shampoo is used to treat only lice infestations.

TREATMENT

Complete directions for the use of these products are supplied by the manufacturers. Be sure to ask your doctor or pharmacist for these directions, and follow the instructions carefully.

If you are applying this medication to another person, you should wear plastic or rubber gloves on your hands in order to avoid absorption of this drug through your skin.

The lotion form of this medication should be shaken well before each dose is measured. The contents of the lotion tend to settle on the bottom of the bottle, so the bottle must be shaken in order to distribute the medication evenly and equalize the doses.

Be sure to rinse off this product according to the directions. If it is not rinsed off COMPLETELY, too much of the medication will be absorbed.

SIDE EFFECTS

Minor. A rash or skin irritation is likely to occur upon application.
Major. Tell your doctor about any side effects that are persistent or particularly bothersome. The serious side effects associated with this medication (clumsiness, convulsions, irritability, muscle cramps, palpitations, restlessness, unsteadiness, unusual nervousness, or vomiting) are due to absorption of this drug through the skin. This should not happen if the product is used according to directions. CONTACT YOUR DOCTOR if you experience any of these symptoms.

INTERACTIONS

Do not use other skin preparations (lotions, ointments, or oils). They increase the absorption of this product through the skin, which can lead to serious side effects.

WARNINGS

• Tell your doctor about unusual or allergic reactions you have had to any medications, especially to lindane.
• This product should NOT be used on the face. If you do get lindane in your eyes, it should be flushed out immediately. In order to decrease the amount of drug absorbed through the

skin, avoid using this product on any open wounds, cuts, or sores.

• Lice are easily transmitted from one person to another. All family members (and sexual partners) should be carefully examined. Personal items (such as clothing and towels) should be machine-washed using the "hot" temperature cycle and then dried. No unusual cleaning measures are required. Combs, brushes, and other washable items may be soaked in boiling water for one hour.

• After using the shampoo for head lice, you must remove the dead nits (eggs). Use a fine-tooth comb to remove them from your hair, or mix a solution of equal parts of water and vinegar and apply it to the affected area. Rub the solution in well. After several minutes, shampoo with your regular shampoo and then brush your hair. This process should remove all of the nits.

• Be sure to tell your doctor if you are pregnant. Lindane is absorbed through the skin and may cause central nervous system side effects in the mother and in the developing fetus. Also tell your doctor if you are breast-feeding an infant. Lindane probably passes into breast milk and may cause central nervous system side effects in nursing infants.

lisinopril

BRAND NAMES (Manufacturers)
Prinivil (Merck Sharp & Dohme)
Zestril (Stuart)
TYPE OF DRUG
Antihypertensive
INGREDIENT
lisinopril
DOSAGE FORM
Tablets (5 mg, 10 mg, 20 mg, and 40 mg)
STORAGE
Store this medication away from heat, direct light, or moisture.

USES
Lisinopril is currently approved for the treatment of hypertension (high blood pressure). It is also being investigated for

the treatment of heart failure. Lisinopril is a vasodilator (it widens the blood vessels) that acts by blocking the production of chemicals that may be responsible for constricting blood vessels.

TREATMENT

The duration of action of lisinopril permits once-a-day dosing. Lisinopril can be taken either on an empty stomach or with food if it causes stomach irritation.

If you miss a dose of this medication, take the missed dose as soon as possible, unless it is almost time for the next dose. In that case, do not take the missed dose at all; just wait until the next scheduled dose. Do not double the dose.

In some patients it may require two to four weeks of therapy to achieve maximum therapeutic benefit.

Lisinopril does not cure high blood pressure, but it will help to control the condition as long as you take it according to directions.

SIDE EFFECTS

Minor. Dizziness; headache; fatigue; diarrhea; nasal congestion; or dry, hacking cough.

To avoid dizziness or light-headedness when you stand, contract and relax the muscles of your legs for a few moments before rising. Do this by pushing one foot against the floor while raising the other foot slightly, alternating feet so that you are "pumping" your legs in a pedaling motion.

Major. Tell your physician about any effects that are persistent or bothersome. IT IS ESPECIALLY IMPORTANT TO TELL YOUR DOCTOR about chest pain; chills; difficult or painful urination; fever; itching; mouth sores; palpitations; prolonged vomiting or diarrhea; rash; shortness of breath; sore throat; swelling of the face, hands, or feet; tingling in the fingers or toes; unusual bleeding or bruising; or yellowing of the eyes or skin.

INTERACTIONS

1. Lisinopril tends to cause retention of potassium in the body. Many salt substitutes contain potassium chloride and should only be used with the advice of your physician. Caution should also be observed with low-salt foods, some of which may contain significant amounts of potassium. Other medications such as the diuretics (water pills), triamterene, spironolactone, or amiloride may cause potassium retention. Use of these medications together with lisinopril may lead to excessive levels of potassium in the blood.

2. The anti-inflammatory drug indomethacin may reduce the effectiveness of lisinopril.

3. Excessive hypotension (low blood pressure) may occur when starting lisinopril in patients on diuretics.

BE SURE TO TELL YOUR DOCTOR about any medications you are currently taking, especially those listed above.

WARNINGS

• Tell your doctor about unusual or allergic reactions you have had to any medications, especially to lisinopril, captopril, or enalapril.

• Tell your doctor if you have any other medical problems, such as diabetes, heart disease, kidney disease, liver disease, or systemic lupus erythematosus.

• Tell your doctor if you experience light-headedness, which may be a symptom of excessive hypotension (low blood pressure). This is especially likely to occur during the first few days of therapy. If fainting occurs, stop the drug and consult with your physician.

• Excessive perspiration or dehydration may cause an excessive fall in blood pressure.

• Report any evidence of infections (such as sore throat or fever) to your physician.

• If you have high blood pressure, do not take any over-the-counter (nonprescription) medication for weight control, or for allergy, asthma, sinus, cough, or cold problems unless you first check with your doctor.

• Because lisinopril is eliminated from the body through the kidneys, be sure to report to your physician any symptoms of kidney disease, such as difficulty in urinating.

• Before having surgery or any other medical or dental treatment, be sure to tell your doctor or dentist that you are taking this medication.

• Be sure to tell your doctor if you are pregnant or plan to become pregnant. Studies in animals, in which administered doses far exceeded those used in humans, have shown a decrease in the number of successful pregnancies. Also tell your doctor if you are breast-feeding an infant. It is not known whether lisinopril passes into breast milk.

---

lithium

BRAND NAMES (Manufacturers)
Cibalith-S (Ciba)
Eskalith (SmithKline Beecham)
Eskalith CR (SmithKline Beecham)
Lithane (Miles)
lithium carbonate (various manufacturers)
lithium citrate (various manufacturers)
Lithobid (Ciba)
Lithonate (Solvay)
Lithotabs (Solvay)
TYPE OF DRUG
Antimanic (mood stabilizer)
INGREDIENT
lithium
DOSAGE FORMS
Tablets (300 mg)
Extended-release tablets (300 mg and 450 mg)
Capsules (150 mg, 300 mg, and 600 mg)
Syrup (300 mg per 5-mL spoonful, with 0.3% alcohol)
STORAGE
Lithium tablets, capsules, and syrup should be stored at room temperature away from heat and direct sunlight. The medication should not be refrigerated, and the syrup form should not be frozen. Do not store the medication in the bathroom cabinet, because moisture may cause the breakdown of lithium. Do not keep these medications beyond the expiration date.

USES

Lithium is used to treat manic-depressive illness by controlling the manic (excited) phase of the illness and by reducing the frequency and severity of depression. Manic-depressive patients often experience unstable emotions ranging from excitement to hostility to depression. The mechanism of the mood-stabilizing effect of lithium is unknown, but it appears to work on the central nervous system to control emotions.

TREATMENT

Lithium should be taken exactly as directed by your doctor. The effectiveness of this medication depends upon the amount of lithium in your bloodstream. Therefore, the medication should be taken every day at regularly spaced intervals in order to keep a constant amount of lithium in your bloodstream.

The syrup form must be measured carefully with a specially designed 5-mL measuring spoon. An ordinary kitchen teaspoon is not accurate enough for theraputic purposes.

If you miss a dose of this medication, take it as soon as possible. However, if it is within two hours (six hours for extended-release tablets) of your next scheduled dose, skip the missed dose and return to your regular schedule. Do not take more than one dose at a time.

If you are taking the long-acting or slow-release form of lithium, swallow the tablet or capsule whole. Do not break, crush, or chew before swallowing.

An improvement in your condition may not be seen for several weeks after you start this drug.

SIDE EFFECTS

Minor. Acne, bloating, diarrhea, drowsiness, increased frequency of urination, increased thirst, nausea, trembling of the hands, weight gain, or weakness or tiredness. These side effects should disappear as your body makes an adjustment to this medication.

Major. Blurred vision, clumsiness, confusion, convulsions, difficulty in breathing, dizziness, fainting, palpitations, severe trembling, and slurred speech are possible effects of too much drug in the bloodstream. Dry, rough skin; hair loss; hoarseness; swelling of the feet or lower legs; swelling of the neck; unusual sensitivity to the cold; unusual tiredness; or unusual weight gain may be the result of low thyroid function caused by the medication. CHECK WITH YOUR DOCTOR IMMEDIATELY if any of these side effects appear.

INTERACTIONS

Lithium interacts with a number of other types of medications:
1. Aminophylline, caffeine, verapamil, acetazolamide, sodium bicarbonate, dyphylline, oxtriphylline, and theophylline can in-

crease the elimination of lithium from the body, thus decreasing its effectiveness.

2. Diuretics (water pills), especially hydrochlorothiazide, chlorothiazide, chlorthalidone, triamterene and hydrochlorothiazide combination, and furosemide may cause lithium toxicity by delaying the body's lithium elimination.

3. Captopril, chlorpromazine and other phenothiazine tranquilizers, ibuprofen, indomethacin, naproxen, and piroxicam can also slow lithium elimination.

4. Lithium can increase the side effects of haloperidol and other medications for mental illness.

5. Phenytoin, methyldopa, carbamazepine, and tetracycline can increase the side effects of lithium.

6. Drinking large amounts of caffeine-containing coffees, teas, or colas may reduce the effectiveness of lithium by increasing its elimination from the body through the urine.

BE SURE TO TELL YOUR DOCTOR about any medications you are currently taking, especially any of those listed above.

WARNINGS

• Tell your doctor about unusual or allergic reactions you have had to any medications, especially to lithium.

• Tell your doctor if you now have or if you have ever had diabetes mellitus, epilepsy, heart disease, kidney disease, Parkinson's disease, or thyroid disease.

• Elderly patients may be more sensitive to the side effects of lithium than younger patients.

• In order to maintain a constant level of lithium in your bloodstream, it is important to drink two to three quarts of water or other fluids each day and not to change the amount of salt in your diet, unless your doctor specifically directs you to do so.

• The loss of large amounts of body fluid (from prolonged vomiting or diarrhea or from heavy sweating due to hot weather, fever, exercise, saunas, or hot baths) can result in increased lithium levels in the blood, which can lead to an increase in side effects.

• The toxic dose of lithium is very close to the therapeutic dose, so it is extremely important to follow your correct dosing schedule. Diarrhea, drowsiness, lack of coordination, muscular weakness, and vomiting may be signs of toxicity. If these

symptoms occur for any length of time or begin shortly after taking a dose, be sure to inform your doctor.
• Lithium is not recommended for use during pregnancy, especially during the first three months, because of possible effects on the thyroid and heart of the developing fetus. Also tell your doctor if you are breast-feeding. Lithium also passes into breast milk and thus may cause side effects in the nursing infant.
• If this drug makes you drowsy or dizzy, do not take part in any activities that require alertness, such as driving a car or operating potentially dangerous machinery.

loperamide

BRAND NAME (Manufacturer)
Imodium (Janssen)
TYPE OF DRUG
Antidiarrheal
INGREDIENT
loperamide
DOSAGE FORMS
Capsules (2 mg)*
Oral liquid (1 mg per 5-mL spoonful)*
*Available over the counter (without a prescription)
STORAGE
Loperamide capsules and liquid should be stored at room temperature in tightly closed containers. This medication should never be frozen.

USES
Loperamide is used to treat acute and chronic diarrhea and to reduce the volume of discharge in patients who have ileostomies. It acts by slowing the movement of the gastrointestinal tract and decreasing the passage of water and other substances into the bowel.

TREATMENT
In order to avoid stomach upset, you can take loperamide with food or with a full glass of water or milk.

If you miss a dose of this medication, do not take the missed dose at all; just return to your regular dosing schedule. Do not double the next dose.

SIDE EFFECTS

Minor. Constipation, dizziness, drowsiness, dry mouth, fatigue, loss of appetite, nausea, or vomiting. These effects should disappear as your body adjusts to the drug.

To relieve constipation, exercise and drink more water (unless your doctor directs you to do otherwise).

To reduce mouth dryness, chew sugarless gum or suck on ice chips or a piece of hard candy.

If you feel dizzy or light-headed, sit or lie down for a while; get up from a sitting or lying position slowly; and be careful on stairs.

Major. Tell your doctor about any side effects that are persistent or particularly bothersome. IT IS ESPECIALLY IMPORTANT TO TELL YOUR DOCTOR about abdominal bloating or pain, fever, rash, or sore throat.

INTERACTIONS

Loperamide should not interact with any other drugs.

WARNINGS

• Tell your doctor about unusual or allergic reactions you have had to any medications.

• Tell your doctor if you now have or if you have ever had colitis, diarrhea caused by infectious organisms, drug-induced diarrhea, liver disease, dehydration, or conditions in which constipation must be avoided (such as hemorrhoids, diverticulitis, heart or blood vessel disorders, or blood clotting disorders).

• If this drug makes you dizzy or drowsy, do not take part in any activity that requires alertness.

• Before having surgery or any other medical or dental treatment, be sure to tell your doctor or dentist that you are taking this medication.

• Check with your doctor if your diarrhea does not subside within three days. Unless your doctor prescribes otherwise, do not take this drug for more than ten days at a time.

• While taking this medication, drink lots of fluids to replace those lost because of diarrhea.

• Be sure to tell your doctor if you are pregnant. The effects of this medication during pregnancy have not been thoroughly studied in humans. Also tell your doctor if you are breast-feeding an infant. It is not known whether loperamide passes into breast milk.

---

loracarbef

BRAND NAME (Manufacturer)
Lorabid (Lilly)
TYPE OF DRUG
Cephalosporin antibiotic
INGREDIENT
loracarbef
DOSAGE FORMS
Capsule (200 mg)
Oral suspension (100 mg and 200 mg per 5-mL spoonful)
STORAGE
Loracarbef capsules should be stored at room temperature in a tightly closed container. The oral-suspension form of the drug should be stored in the refrigerator in a tightly closed container. Any unused portion of the oral suspension should be discarded after 14 days because the drug loses potency after that time. This medication should never be frozen.

USES
Loracarbef is used to treat a wide variety of bacterial infections, including those of the middle ear, upper and lower respiratory tract, skin, and urinary tract. It is related to the antibiotic cephalosporin. Loracarbef acts by binding to essential proteins of the bacterial cell wall, thereby inhibiting the growth and multiplication of the infecting bacteria.

TREATMENT
Loracarbef should be taken on an empty stomach (one hour before or two hours after eating) to avoid a decrease in absorption of the drug.

The contents of the suspension form of loracarbef tend to settle on the bottom of the bottle; therefore, it is necessary to shake the bottle well to distribute the ingredients evenly and equalize the doses. Each dose should then be measured carefully with a specially designed 5-mL measuring spoon or with the dropper provided. An ordinary kitchen teaspoon is not accurate enough for medical purposes.

Cephalosporin antibiotics work best when the level of medicine in your bloodstream is kept constant. It is best to take the doses at evenly spaced intervals day and night. For example, if you are to take two doses a day, the doses should be spaced 12 hours apart. If you miss a dose of this medication, take the missed dose immediately. If you do not remember to take the missed dose until it is almost time for your next dose, take it; space the following dose halfway through the regular interval between doses, then return to your regular schedule. Try not to skip any doses of this medication.

It is important to try to take this medication for the entire time prescribed by your doctor (usually seven to 14 days), even if the symptoms disappear before the end of that period. If you stop taking the drug too soon, resistant bacteria could continue to grow, and infection could recur.

SIDE EFFECTS

Minor. Abdominal pain, diarrhea, dizziness, fatigue, headache, heartburn, loss of appetite, nausea, or vomiting. These side effects should disappear as you adjust to the drug.

If you feel dizzy while you are taking this medication, sit or lie down for a while; get up slowly from a sitting or reclining position; and be careful on stairs. Do not operate any potentially dangerous equipment or work with any hazardous materials.

Major. Tell your doctor about any side effects that are persistent or particularly bothersome. IT IS ESPECIALLY IMPORTANT TO TELL YOUR DOCTOR about chest pain, darkened tongue, difficulty in breathing, fever, itching, joint pain, rash, rectal or vaginal itching, severe diarrhea (which can be watery or contain pus or blood), sore mouth, stomach cramps, tingling in the hands or feet, or unusual bleeding or bruising. If your symptoms of infection seem to be getting worse rather than improving, contact your doctor.

INTERACTIONS

Loracarbef interacts with several other drugs:

1. Probenecid can increase the blood concentrations and side effects of this medication.
2. The side effects, especially on the kidneys, of diuretics (such as furosemide, bumetanide, or ethacrynic acid), colistin, vancomycin, polymyxin B, and aminoglycoside antibiotics can be increased by loracarbef.
3. Chloramphenicol should be avoided in combination with loracarbef due to the possibility of an antagonistic (opposing) effect.

BE SURE TO TELL YOUR DOCTOR about any medications you are currently taking, especially any listed above.

WARNINGS
• Tell your doctor about any unusual or allergic reactions you have had to any medications, especially to loracarbef or other cephalosporin antibiotics (such as cefoperazone, cefotaxime, cefpodoxime, ceftazidime, ceftizoxime, ceftriaxone, and moxalactam) or to penicillin antibiotics.
• Tell your doctor if you have ever had kidney disease.
• Tell your doctor if you have ever had any type of gastrointestinal disease, particularly colitis.
• This medication has been prescribed for your current infection only. Another infection later on, or one that someone else has, may require a different medicine. You should not give your medication to other people or use it for other infections, unless your doctor specifically directs you to do so.
• People with diabetes who are taking loracarbef should know that this medication may cause a false-positive sugar reaction with a Clinitest urine glucose test. To avoid this problem while taking loracarbef, they should switch to Clinistix or Tes-Tape to test their urine sugar content.
• Loracarbef may also cause a false-positive result for urinary ketones when tests using nitroprusside are used.
• Loracarbef may interfere with blood tests.
• Be sure to tell your doctor if you are pregnant. Although the cephalosporin-related antibiotics appear to be safe during pregnancy, extensive studies in humans have not been conducted. Also tell your doctor if you are breast-feeding an infant. Small amounts of this medication pass into breast milk and may temporarily alter the bacterial balance in the intestinal tract of the nursing infant, resulting in diarrhea.

loratadine

BRAND NAME (Manufacturer)
Claritin (Schering)
TYPE OF DRUG
Antihistamine
INGREDIENT
loratidine
DOSAGE FORM
Tablets (10 mg)
STORAGE
Store at room temperature in a tightly closed, light-resistant container.

USES

Loratadine is a long-acting antihistamine. Antihistamines block the action of histamine, a chemical released from the body during an allergic reaction. Loratadine is used to provide symptomatic relief of seasonal allergic rhinitis, such as hay fever.

TREATMENT

Loratadine should always be administered on an empty stomach in order to achieve effective blood levels of the drug.

If you miss a dose of this medication, take the missed dose as soon as possible, unless it is almost time for your next dose. If it is almost time for your next dose, do not take the missed dose at all; just return to your regular dosing schedule. Do not double the next dose.

Loratadine will not cure seasonal allergic rhinitis, but the medication will relieve the symptoms associated with the condition.

SIDE EFFECTS

Minor. Blurred vision; breast pain; confusion; constipation; diarrhea; difficult or painful urination; dizziness; dry mouth, throat, or nose; dry skin or hair; headache; increased or decreased appetite; irritability; itching; nausea; restlessness; ringing or buzzing in the ears; stomach upset; or sweating. These side effects should disappear as your body adjusts to the medication.

This medication can cause increased sensitivity to sunlight. It is very important to avoid prolonged exposure to sunlight and sunlamps. Wear protective clothing and use an effective sunscreen.

If you are constipated, increase the amount of fiber in your diet (fresh fruits and vegetables, salads, bran, and whole-grain breads). You can also increase your exercise and drink more water (unless your doctor directs you not to do so).

Chew sugarless gum or suck on ice chips or a piece of hard candy to reduce mouth dryness.

If you feel dizzy or light-headed, sit or lie down for a while; get up from a sitting or lying position slowly; and be careful on stairs.

Major. Tell your doctor about any side effects that are persistent or particularly bothersome. IT IS ESPECIALLY IMPORTANT TO TELL YOUR DOCTOR about anxiety, change in menstruation, clumsiness, depression, feeling faint, flushing of the face, hallucinations, migraines, palpitations, rash, seizures, shortness of breath, sleeping disorders, sore throat or fever, tightness in the chest or back, trouble breathing, unusual bleeding or bruising, unusual tiredness or weakness, urine discoloration, or yellowing of the eyes or skin.

INTERACTIONS

This drug interacts with several other types of drugs:

1. Concurrent use of this medication with other central nervous system depressants (such as alcohol, barbiturates, benzodiazepine tranquilizers, muscle relaxants, narcotics, pain medications, and phenothiazine tranquilizers) or with tricyclic antidepressants can cause extreme drowsiness.

2. Monoamine oxidase (MAO) inhibitors (such as isocarboxazid, pargyline, phenelzine, and tranylcypromine) can be expected to increase the side effects of this medication.

BE SURE TO TELL YOUR DOCTOR about any medications you are currently taking.

WARNINGS

• Tell your doctor about unusual or allergic reactions you have had to any medications, especially to loratadine, cyproheptadine, azatadine, or any other antihistamines (such as astemizole, brompheniramine, carbinoxamine, chlorpheniramine, clemastine, dimenhydrinate, dimethindene, diphen-

hydramine, diphenylpyraline, doxylamine, hydroxyzine, and terfenadine).
• Tell your doctor if you now have or if you have ever had asthma, blood-vessel disease, glaucoma, high blood pressure, kidney disease, liver disease, peptic ulcers, enlarged prostate gland, or thyroid disease.
• Because loratadine is primarily metabolized by the liver, patients with liver disease may require a lower dosage.
• Although loratadine causes less drowsiness than many of the other medications in its class, your ability to perform tasks that require alertness, such as driving a car or operating potentially dangerous machinery, may be impaired.
• Be sure to tell your doctor if you are pregnant. The effects of this medication during pregnancy have not been thoroughly studied in humans. Also tell your doctor if you are breast-feeding an infant. Loratadine should not be used by nursing mothers.

---

lorazepam

BRAND NAMES (Manufacturers)
Ativan (Wyeth)
lorazepam (various manufacturers)
TYPE OF DRUG
Benzodiazepine sedative/hypnotic
INGREDIENT
lorazepam
DOSAGE FORMS
Tablets (0.5 mg, 1 mg, and 2 mg)
Oral solution (2 mg/mL)
STORAGE
This medication should be stored at room temperature in a tightly closed, light-resistant container. It should not be refrigerated.

USES

Lorazepam is prescribed to treat symptoms of anxiety and anxiety associated with depression. It is not clear exactly how this medicine works, but it may relieve anxiety by acting as a depressant of the central nervous system (brain and spinal cord). This medication is currently used by many people to relieve nervousness. It is effective for this purpose for short periods, but it is important to try to remove the cause of the anxiety as well.

TREATMENT

Lorazepam should be taken exactly as your doctor directs. It can be taken with food or a full glass of water if stomach upset occurs. Do not take this medication with a dose of antacids, since they may slow its absorption from the gastrointestinal tract.

If you are taking this medication regularly and you miss a dose, take the missed dose immediately if you remember within an hour. If more than an hour has passed, skip the dose you missed and wait for the next scheduled dose. Do not double the dose.

SIDE EFFECTS

Minor. Bitter taste in the mouth, constipation, diarrhea, dizziness, drowsiness (after a night's sleep), dry mouth, fatigue, flushing, headache, heartburn, excessive salivation, loss of appetite, nausea, nervousness, sweating, or vomiting. As your body adjusts to the medication, these side effects should disappear.

To relieve constipation, increase the amount of fiber in your diet (fresh fruits and vegetables, salads, bran, and whole-grain breads), exercise, and drink more water (unless your doctor directs you to do otherwise).

Dry mouth can be relieved by chewing sugarless gum or by sucking on ice chips.

If you feel dizzy, sit or lie down for a while; get up slowly from a sitting or reclining position; and be careful on stairs.
Major. Tell your doctor about any side effects that are persistent or particularly bothersome. IT IS ESPECIALLY IMPORTANT TO TELL YOUR DOCTOR about blurred or double vision, chest pain, depression, difficulty in urinating, fainting, falling, fever, joint pain, hallucinations, memory problems, mouth sores, nightmares, palpitations, rash, shortness of breath, slurred speech, sore throat, uncoordinated movements, unusual excitement, unusual tiredness, or yellowing of the eyes or skin.

INTERACTIONS

Lorazepam interacts with several other types of medications:
1. To prevent oversedation, this drug should not be taken with alcohol, other sedative drugs, antidepressants, or central nervous system depressants (such as antihistamines, barbiturates, muscle relaxants, pain medicines, narcotics, medicines for seizures, and phenothiazine tranquilizers).
2. This medication may decrease the effectiveness of carbamazepine, levodopa, and oral anticoagulants (blood thinners) and may increase the effects of phenytoin.
3. Disulfiram, cimetidine, and isoniazid can increase the blood levels of lorazepam, which can lead to toxic effects.
4. Concurrent use of rifampin may decrease the effectiveness of lorazepam.

BE SURE TO TELL YOUR DOCTOR about any medications you are currently taking, especially any listed above.

WARNINGS

• Tell your doctor about unusual or allergic reactions you have had to any medications, especially to lorazepam or other benzodiazepine tranquilizers (such as alprazolam, chlordiazepoxide, clorazepate, diazepam, flurazepam, halazepam, midazolam, oxazepam, prazepam, temazepam, and triazolam).
• Tell your doctor if you now have or if you have ever had liver disease, kidney disease, epilepsy, lung disease, myasthenia gravis, porphyria, mental depression, or mental illness.
• This medicine can cause drowsiness. Avoid tasks that require alertness, such as driving a car or using potentially dangerous machinery.
• This medication has the potential for abuse and must be used with caution. Tolerance may develop quickly; do not increase the dosage without first consulting your doctor. It is also important not to stop this drug suddenly if you have been taking it in large amounts or if you have used it for several weeks. Your doctor may want to reduce the dosage gradually.
• This is a safe drug when used properly. When it is combined with other sedative drugs or alcohol, however, serious side effects can develop.
• Be sure to tell your doctor if you are pregnant. This medicine may increase the chance of birth defects if it is taken during the first three months of pregnancy. In addition, too much

use of this medicine during the last six months of pregnancy may cause the fetus to become dependent on it, resulting in withdrawal side effects in the newborn. Note that use of this drug during the last weeks of pregnancy may cause drowsiness, slowed heartbeat, and breathing difficulties in the newborn. Tell your doctor if you are breast-feeding. This drug can pass into the breast milk and cause drowsiness, slowed heartbeat, and breathing difficulties in the nursing infant.

losartan

BRAND NAME (Manufacturer)
Cozaar (Merck)
TYPE OF DRUG
Antihypertensive
INGREDIENT
losartan
DOSAGE FORM
Tablets (25 mg and 50 mg)
STORAGE
Store losartan at room temperature in a tightly closed container.

USES
Losartan is used to treat high blood pressure and potentially could be used for congestive heart failure. It is a vasodilator (it widens the blood vessels) that acts by blocking the production of chemicals that may be responsible for constricting or narrowing the blood vessels.

TREATMENT
Losartan can be taken on an empty stomach or, if it causes irritation, with food. To become accustomed to this medication, try to take it at the same time(s) every day.

It may be several weeks before you notice the full effects of losartan.

If you miss a dose, take the missed dose as soon as possible, unless it is almost time for the next dose. In that case, do not take the missed dose at all; just wait until the next scheduled dose. Do not double the dose.

Losartan does not cure high blood pressure, but it will help to control the condition as long as you continue to take it.

SIDE EFFECTS

Minor. Abdominal pain, cough, diarrhea, dizziness, drowsiness, fatigue, headache, insomnia, nausea, nervousness, sweating, or vomiting. These side effects should disappear as your body adjusts to the medication. To avoid dizziness when you stand, contract and relax the muscles of your legs for a few moments before rising. Do this by alternately pushing one foot against the floor while lifting the other foot slightly.

Major. Tell your doctor about any side effects that are persistent or particularly bothersome. IT IS ESPECIALLY IMPORTANT TO TELL YOUR DOCTOR about chest pain; difficulty breathing; fainting; fever; itching; light-headedness (especially during the first few days); muscle cramps; palpitations; rash; sore throat; swelling of the face, eyes, lips, or tongue; tingling in the fingers and toes; or yellowing of the eyes or skin.

INTERACTIONS

Losartan interacts with several other types of medications:
1. Diuretics and other antihypertensive medications can cause an excessive drop in blood pressure when they are combined with losartan (especially with the first dose).
2. The combination of losartan with amiloride, potassium supplements, salt substitutes, spironolactone, or triamterene can lead to hyperkalemia (dangerously high levels of potassium in the bloodstream).
3. Nonsteroidal anti-inflammatory agents (including ibuprofen, indomethacin, and naproxen) may reduce the effectiveness of this medication.

Before starting to take losartan, BE SURE TO TELL YOUR DOCTOR about any medications you are currently taking, especially any of those listed above.

WARNINGS

• Tell your doctor about any unusual allergic reactions you have had to any medications, especially to losartan.
• Tell your doctor if you now have or if you have ever had blood disorders, heart failure, renal disease, or systemic lupus erythematosus.

• Excessive perspiration, dehydration, or prolonged vomiting or diarrhea can lead to any excessive drop in blood pressure while you are taking this medication. Contact your doctor if you have any of these symptoms.

• Before having surgery or other medical or dental treatment, tell your doctor or dentist you are taking this drug.

• If this drug makes you dizzy or drowsy, do not take part in any activity that requires alertness, such as driving a car or operating potentially dangerous equipment.

• If you have high blood pressure, do not take any over-the-counter (nonprescription) medications for weight control or for asthma, sinus, cough, cold, or allergy problems unless you first check with your doctor.

• Be sure to tell your doctor if you are pregnant. Losartan is very similar to the class of drugs called ACE inhibitors (including captopril, enalapril and lisinopril), which have been shown to cause birth defects, including kidney damage, low blood pressure, improper skull development, and death when taken in the second and third trimesters. Also tell your doctor if you are breast-feeding an infant. It is not known if losartan is distributed into breast milk.

---

lovastatin

BRAND NAME (Manufacturer)
Mevacor (Merck Sharp & Dohme)
TYPE OF DRUG
Antihyperlipidemic (lipid-lowering drug)
INGREDIENT
lovastatin
DOSAGE FORM
Tablets (10 mg, 20 mg, and 40 mg)
STORAGE
This medication should be stored at room temperature in a tightly closed, light-resistant container. Exposure to heat or moisture may cause this drug to break down.

USES

Lovastatin is used to treat hyperlipidemia (high blood-fat levels). It is prescribed in conjunction with nondrug therapies, such as diet modification and regular exercise, in an attempt to regulate lipid and cholesterol levels. Lovastatin chemically interferes with an enzyme in the body that is responsible for synthesizing cholesterol. This decreases the LDL (low-density lipoprotein) type of cholesterol, which has been associated with coronary heart disease and atherosclerosis.

TREATMENT

This medication should be taken exactly as prescribed by your doctor. If you are to take the drug once a day, it is best to take the drug in the evening. Lovastatin can be taken with meals or a full glass of water if stomach upset occurs.

While using this medication, try to develop a set schedule for taking it. If you miss a dose and remember within a few hours, take the missed dose and resume your regular schedule. If many hours have passed, skip the dose you missed and then take your next dose as scheduled. Do not double the dose.

SIDE EFFECTS

Minor. Abdominal pain or cramps, constipation, diarrhea, gas, nausea, or stomach pain. These effects may be relieved by taking lovastatin with a meal, adding fiber to your diet, or using mild stool softeners.

Major. Tell your doctor about any side effects that are persistent or particularly bothersome. IT IS ESPECIALLY IMPORTANT TO TELL YOUR DOCTOR about blurred vision (or any other visual changes or difficulties) or muscle pain or tenderness, especially with malaise or fever.

INTERACTIONS

There do not appear to be any significant drug interactions with this medication. However, you should make sure your doctor knows all the medications you are currently taking.

WARNINGS

• Tell your doctor about unusual or allergic reactions you have had to any medications.

• Tell your doctor if you have ever had liver disease, heart disease, stroke, or disorders of the digestive tract.

• In preliminary studies with lovastatin, some patients were found to develop eye-related problems during treatment.

Although these findings are inconclusive, and it has not yet been determined whether lovastatin is involved in such occurrences, it is advisable to have regular checkups with your ophthalmologist and inform him or her of your use of this medication.

• This drug should not be taken if you are pregnant or breast-feeding an infant.

---

loxapine

BRAND NAMES (Manufacturers)
Loxitane (Lederle)
Loxitane C (Lederle)
TYPE OF DRUG
Antipsychotic
INGREDIENT
loxapine
DOSAGE FORMS
Capsules (5 mg, 10 mg, 25 mg, and 50 mg)
Oral concentrate (25 mg per mL)
STORAGE
Loxapine capsules and oral concentrate should be stored at room temperature (never frozen) in tightly closed containers. If the oral concentrate turns slightly yellowish, the drug is still effective and can be used. However, if the oral concentrate changes color markedly or has particles floating in it, it should not be used; it should be discarded down the sink.

USES

Loxapine is prescribed to treat the symptoms of mental illness, such as the emotional symptoms of psychosis. This medication is thought to relieve the symptoms of mental illness by blocking certain chemicals involved with nerve transmission in the brain.

TREATMENT

To avoid stomach irritation, you can take the tablet form of loxapine with a meal or with a glass of water or milk (unless your doctor directs you to do otherwise).

The oral-concentrate form of this medication should be measured carefully with the dropper provided and diluted in eight ounces (a full cup) or more of orange juice or grapefruit juice immediately prior to administration.

If you miss a dose of this medication, take the missed dose as soon as possible and return to your regular dosing schedule. If it is almost time for the next dose, however, skip the one you missed and then return to your regular schedule. Do not double the dose unless you are directed to do so by your physician.

Antacids and antidiarrheal medicines can decrease the absorption of this medication from the gastrointestinal tract. Therefore, at least one hour should separate doses of one of these medicines and loxapine.

The full effects of this medication for the control of emotional or mental symptoms may not become apparent for two weeks after you start to take it.

SIDE EFFECTS

Minor. Blurred vision, constipation, decreased sweating, diarrhea, dizziness, drooling, drowsiness, dry mouth, fatigue, jitteriness, menstrual irregularities, nasal congestion, restlessness, vomiting, or weight gain. As your body adjusts to the medication, these side effects should disappear.

This medication can cause increased sensitivity to sunlight. It is therefore important to avoid prolonged exposure to sunlight and sunlamps. Wear protective clothing and use an effective sunscreen.

If you are constipated, increase the amount of fiber in your diet (fresh fruits and vegetables, salads, bran, and whole-grain breads), exercise, and drink more water (unless your doctor directs you to do otherwise).

To reduce mouth dryness, chew sugarless gum or suck on ice chips or a piece of hard candy.

To avoid dizziness or light-headedness when you stand, contract and relax the muscles of your legs for a few moments before rising. Do this by pushing one foot against the floor while raising the other foot slightly, alternating feet so that you are "pumping" your legs in a pedaling motion.

Major. Tell your doctor about any side effects that are persistent or particularly bothersome. IT IS ESPECIALLY IMPORTANT TO TELL YOUR DOCTOR about breast enlargement (in both sexes); chest pain; convulsions; darkened skin; difficulty in swallowing or breathing; fainting; fever; impotence; involuntary movements of the face, mouth, jaw, or tongue; palpitations; rash; sleep disorders; sore throat; tremors; uncoordinated movements; unusual bleeding or bruising; visual disturbances; or yellowing of the eyes or skin.

INTERACTIONS

Loxapine can interact with a number of other types of medications:

1. It can cause extreme drowsiness when combined with alcohol or other central nervous system depressants (such as barbiturates, benzodiazepine tranquilizers, muscle relaxants, narcotics, and pain medications) or with tricyclic antidepressants.

2. This medication can cause a decrease in the effectiveness of amphetamines, guanethidine, anticonvulsants, and levodopa.

3. The side effects of epinephrine, monoamine oxidase (MAO) inhibitors, and tricyclic antidepressants may be increased when combined with this medication. At least 14 days should separate the use of this drug and the use of an MAO inhibitor.

BE SURE TO TELL YOUR DOCTOR about any medications you are currently taking, especially any of those listed above.

WARNINGS

• Tell your doctor about unusual or allergic reactions you have had to any medications, especially to loxapine or to any phenothiazine tranquilizer.

• Tell your doctor if you have a history of alcoholism or if you now have or ever had heart or circulatory disease, epilepsy, glaucoma, liver disease, Parkinson's disease, enlarged prostate gland, or blockage of the urinary tract.

• Avoid drinking alcoholic beverages while taking this medication, in order to prevent oversedation. If this medication makes you dizzy or drowsy, do not take part in any activity that requires alertness, such as driving a car or operating potentially dangerous machinery. Be careful on stairs, and avoid getting up suddenly from a lying or sitting position.

• Prior to having surgery or any other medical or dental treatment, be sure to tell your doctor or dentist that you are taking loxapine.

• Some of the side effects caused by this drug can be prevented by taking an antiparkinsonism drug. Discuss this with your doctor.

• This medication can decrease sweating and heat release from the body. Therefore, avoid getting overheated by strenuous exercise in hot weather, and avoid taking hot baths, showers, and saunas.

• This medication has the potential to cause a permanent movement disorder called tardive dyskinesia. Therefore, be sure to report any uncontrolled movements of the body to your doctor.

• Do not stop taking this medication suddenly. If the drug is stopped abruptly, you may experience nausea, vomiting, stomach upset, headache, increased heart rate, insomnia, tremors, or worsening of your condition. In taking you off this medication, your doctor may want to reduce the dosage in a gradual way.

• If you are planning to have a myelogram, or any other procedure in which dye is injected into the area surrounding the spinal cord, notify your doctor that this medication is being administered to you.

• Avoid getting the oral-concentrate form of this medication on your skin; it can cause redness and irritation.

• While you are taking this prescription medication, do not take any over-the-counter (nonprescription) medication or preparation for weight control or for cough, cold, asthma, allergy, or sinus problems unless you first check with your doctor. The combination of these two types of medications can cause high blood pressure.

• Elderly patients may be at increased risk of experiencing side effects of this medication.

• Be sure to tell your doctor if you are pregnant. Small amounts of this medication will cross the placenta. Although there are reports of safe use of this type of drug during pregnancy, there are also reports of liver disease and tremors in newborn infants whose mothers received this type of medication close to term. Also tell your doctor if you are breastfeeding an infant. Small amounts of this medication pass into breast milk and may cause unwanted effects in the nursing infant.

maprotiline

BRAND NAMES (Manufacturers)
Ludiomil (Ciba)
Maprotiline (Rugby)
Maprotiline HCl (various manufacturers)
TYPE OF DRUG
Tetracyclic antidepressant
INGREDIENT
maprotiline
DOSAGE FORM
Tablets (25 mg, 50 mg, and 75 mg)
STORAGE
Maprotiline tablets should be stored at room temperature in a
tightly closed container.

USES

Maprotiline is used to relieve the symptoms of mental depression. This medication is a tetracyclic antidepressant. It is related to a group of drugs referred to as the tricyclic antidepressants. These medicines are thought to relieve depression by
affecting nerve transmission in the brain.

TREATMENT

This medication should be taken exactly as your doctor prescribes. It can be taken with water or food to lessen the chance
of stomach irritation, unless your doctor tells you otherwise.

If you miss a dose of this medication, take the missed dose
as soon as possible, then return to your regular dosing schedule. However, if the dose you missed was a once-a-day bedtime dose, do not take that dose in the morning; check with
your doctor instead. If the dose is taken in the morning, it may
cause some unwanted side effects. Never double the dose.

The effects of therapy with this medication may not become
apparent for two or three weeks.

SIDE EFFECTS

Minor. Anxiety, blurred vision, confusion, constipation, diarrhea, dizziness, drowsiness, dry mouth, fatigue, heartburn,

insomnia, loss of appetite, nausea, peculiar tastes in the mouth, restlessness, sweating, vomiting, weakness, or weight gain or loss. As your body adjusts to the medication, these side effects should disappear.

This medication can cause increased sensitivity to sunlight. Avoid prolonged exposure to sunlight and sunlamps. Wear protective clothing, and use an effective sunscreen.

Mouth dryness can be relieved by chewing sugarless gum or by sucking on ice chips or a piece of hard candy.

To relieve constipation, increase the amount of fiber in your diet (fresh fruits and vegetables, salads, bran, and whole-grain breads), exercise, and drink more water (unless your doctor directs you to do otherwise).

To avoid dizziness or light-headedness when you stand, contract and relax the muscles of your legs for a few moments before rising. Do this by pushing one foot against the floor while raising the other foot slightly, alternating feet so that you are "pumping" your legs.

Major. Tell your doctor about any side effects that are persistent or particularly bothersome. IT IS ESPECIALLY IMPORTANT TO TELL YOUR DOCTOR about agitation, chest pain, convulsions, cramps, difficulty in urinating, enlarged or painful breasts (in both sexes), fainting, fever, fluid retention, hair loss, hallucinations, headaches, impotence, mood changes, mouth sores, nervousness, nightmares, numbness in the fingers or toes, palpitations, ringing in the ears, seizures, skin rash, sleep disorders, sore throat, tremors, uncoordinated movements or balance problems, unusual bleeding or bruising, or yellowing of the eyes or skin.

INTERACTIONS

Maprotiline has been known to interact with several other types of medications:

1. Extreme drowsiness can occur when this medicine is taken with central nervous system depressants (such as alcohol, antihistamines, barbiturates, benzodiazepine tranquilizers, muscle relaxants, narcotics, medications to relieve pain, phenothiazine tranquilizers, and sleeping medications) or with other antidepressants.

2. Maprotiline may decrease the effectiveness of antiseizure medications and may block the blood-pressure-lowering effects of clonidine and guanethidine.

3. Oral contraceptives (birth control pills) and estrogen-containing drugs can increase the side effects and reduce the effectiveness of tricyclic antidepressants and maprotiline.

4. Tetracyclic antidepressants may increase the side effects of thyroid medication and over-the-counter (nonprescription) allergy, cough, cold, asthma, sinus, and diet medications.

5. The concurrent use of tetracyclic antidepressants and monoamine oxidase (MAO) inhibitors should be avoided because the combination may result in fever, convulsions, or high blood pressure. At least 14 days should separate the use of this drug and the use of an MAO inhibitor.

Before starting to take maprotiline, BE SURE TO TELL YOUR DOCTOR about any medications you are currently taking, especially any of the drugs listed above.

WARNINGS

• Tell your doctor if you have had unusual or allergic reactions to any medications, especially to maprotiline or any of the tricyclic antidepressants (such as amitriptyline, imipramine, doxepin, trimipramine, amoxapine, protriptyline, desipramine, and nortriptyline).

• Tell your doctor if you have a history of alcoholism or if you have ever had asthma, high blood pressure, liver or kidney disease, heart disease, a heart attack, circulatory disease, stomach problems, intestinal problems, difficulty in urinating, enlarged prostate gland, epilepsy, glaucoma, thyroid disease, mental illness, or electroshock therapy.

• If this drug makes you dizzy or drowsy, do not take part in any activity that requires alertness, such as driving a car or operating potentially dangerous machinery.

• Before having surgery or other medical or dental treatment, tell your doctor or dentist about this drug.

• Do not stop taking this drug suddenly. Stopping it abruptly can cause nausea, headache, stomach upset, fatigue, or a worsening of your condition. Your doctor may want to reduce the dosage gradually.

• The effects of this medication may last as long as seven days after you have stopped taking it, so continue to observe all precautions during that period. Be sure to tell your doctor if the effects continue past that time.

• Elderly patients may be at increased risk of experiencing side effects from this medication.

• Be sure to tell your doctor if you are pregnant. Problems in humans have not been reported; however, studies in animals have shown that this type of medication can cause side effects in the fetus if given to the mother in large doses during pregnancy. Also be sure to tell your doctor if you are breast-feeding an infant. It is possible small amounts of this drug will pass into breast milk and cause unwanted side effects, such as irritability or sleeping problems, in the nursing infant.

mazindol

BRAND NAMES (Manufacturers)
Mazanor (Wyeth-Ayerst)
Sanorex (Sandoz)
TYPE OF DRUG
Antiobesity
INGREDIENT
mazindol
DOSAGE FORM
Tablets (1 mg and 2 mg)
STORAGE
Mazindol should be stored at room temperature in a tightly closed container.

USES

Mazindol is used as an appetite suppressant during the first few weeks of dieting, to help establish new eating habits. This medication is thought to relieve hunger by altering nerve impulses to the appetite control center in the brain. Its effectiveness lasts only for short periods of time (three to 12 weeks), however.

TREATMENT

Mazindol can be taken with a full glass of water one hour before meals (unless your doctor directs you to do otherwise).

If you miss a dose of this medication, take the missed dose as soon as possible, unless it is almost time for your next dose. In that case, do not take the missed dose at all; just return to your regular dosing schedule. Do not double the next dose.

In order to avoid difficulty in falling asleep, the last dose of this medication each day should be taken four to six hours before bedtime (for the 1-mg tablet) or ten to 14 hours before bedtime (for the 2-mg tablet).

SIDE EFFECTS

Minor. Constipation, diarrhea, dizziness, dry mouth, false sense of well-being, fatigue, insomnia, irritability, nausea, nervousness, restlessness, stomach pain, sweating, tremors, unpleasant taste in the mouth, or vomiting. These side effects should disappear as your body adjusts to the drug.

Dry mouth resulting from this medication can be relieved by sucking on ice chips or a piece of hard candy or by chewing sugarless gum.

In order to prevent constipation, increase the amount of fiber in your diet (fresh fruits and vegetables, salads, bran, and whole-grain breads). You can also increase your exercise and drink more water (unless your doctor directs you to do otherwise).

Major. Tell your doctor about any side effects that are persistent or particularly bothersome. IT IS ESPECIALLY IMPORTANT TO TELL YOUR DOCTOR about blurred vision, changes in sexual desire, chest pain, difficulty in urinating, enlarged breasts (in both sexes), fever, hair loss, headaches, impotence, increased blood pressure, menstrual irregularities, mental depression, mood changes, mouth sores, muscle pains, palpitations, rash, sore throat, or unusual bleeding or bruising.

INTERACTIONS

Mazindol interacts with several other types of medications:

1. Use of this medication within 14 days of a monoamine oxidase (MAO) inhibitor (such as isocarboxazid, pargyline, phenelzine, and tranylcypromine) can result in high blood pressure and other side effects.

2. Barbiturate medications and phenothiazine tranquilizers (especially chlorpromazine) can antagonize (act against) the appetite-suppressant activity of this medication.

3. Mazindol can decrease the blood-pressure-lowering effects of antihypertensive medications (especially guanethidine) and may alter insulin and oral antidiabetic medication dosage requirements in diabetic patients.

4. The side effects of other central nervous system stimulants, such as caffeine, over-the-counter (nonprescription) appetite suppressants or sinus, cough, cold, asthma, and allergy preparations, may be increased by the concurrent use of this medication.

Before starting to take mazindol, BE SURE TO TELL YOUR DOCTOR about any drugs you are taking.

WARNINGS

• Tell your doctor about unusual or allergic reactions you have had to any medications, especially to mazindol or other appetite suppressants (such as benzphetamine, phendimetrazine, diethylpropion, fenfluramine, phenmetrazine, and phentermine) or to epinephrine, norepinephrine, ephedrine, amphetamines, dextroamphetamine, phenylephrine, phenylpropanolamine, pseudoephedrine, albuterol, metaproterenol, or terbutaline.

• Tell your doctor if you have a history of drug abuse or if you have ever had angina, diabetes mellitus, emotional disturbances, glaucoma, heart or cardiovascular disease, high blood pressure, or thyroid disease.

• Mazindol can mask the symptoms of extreme fatigue and can cause dizziness or light-headedness. Your ability to perform tasks that require alertness, such as driving a car or operating potentially dangerous machinery, may be decreased. Appropriate caution should be taken.

• Before having surgery or any other medical or dental treatment, be sure to tell your doctor or dentist that you are taking this medication.

• Mazindol is related to amphetamine and may be habit-forming when taken for long periods of time (both physical and psychological dependence can occur). Therefore, you should not increase the dosage of this medication or take it for longer than 12 weeks unless you first consult your doctor. It is also important that you not stop taking this medication abruptly. Fatigue, sleep disorders, mental depression, nausea or vomiting, or stomach cramps or pain can occur while your body adjusts to discontinuation of this medication. Your doctor may want to decrease the dosage gradually.

• Mazindol should not be used in children less than 12 years of age.

• There is no specific information about the use of appetite suppressants such as this for the elderly.

• Be sure to tell your doctor if you are pregnant. Although studies in humans have not been conducted, it is known that some of the appetite suppressants cause side effects in the off-spring of animals that receive large doses of these drugs during pregnancy. Also tell your doctor if you are breast-feeding an infant. It is not known whether this medication passes into breast milk.

---

meclizine

BRAND NAMES (Manufacturers)
Antivert (Roerig)
Antivert/25 (Roerig)
Antivert/50 (Roerig)
Bonine* (Pfipharmecs)
Dizmiss* (Bowman)
meclizine hydrochloride (various manufacturers)
Nico-Vert (Edwards)
Wehvert* (Hauck)
*Available over the counter (without a prescription)
TYPE OF DRUG
Antihistamine/antiemetic/antivertigo
INGREDIENT
meclizine
DOSAGE FORMS
Tablets (12.5 mg, 25 mg, and 50 mg)
Capsules (30 mg)
Chewable tablets (25 mg)
STORAGE
Store at room temperature in a tightly closed container.

USES
Meclizine is used to provide symptomatic relief of dizziness and to prevent or relieve dizziness, nausea, and vomiting due to motion sickness. It is thought to relieve dizziness and vomiting by altering nerve transmission in the balance and vomiting centers in the brain.

TREATMENT
To avoid upsetting your stomach, you may take meclizine with food, milk, or water (unless your doctor directs you to do otherwise).

The chewable tablets should be chewed for at least two minutes in order to obtain the full therapeutic benefit of this medication.

If you are taking meclizine to prevent motion sickness, you should take it one hour before traveling.

If you miss a dose of this medication, take the missed dose as soon as possible, unless it is almost time for your next dose. In that case, do not take the missed dose at all; just return to your regular dosing schedule. Do not double the next dose.

SIDE EFFECTS

Minor. Confusion; constipation; diarrhea; dizziness; dry mouth, throat, or nose; headache; irritability; loss of appetite; nausea; restlessness; or stomach upset. These side effects should disappear as your body adjusts to the medication.

If you are constipated, increase the amount of fiber in your diet (fresh fruits and vegetables, salads, bran, and whole-grain breads), exercise, and drink more water (unless your doctor tells you not to do so).

Chew sugarless gum or suck on ice chips or a piece of hard candy to reduce mouth dryness.

Major. Tell your doctor about any side effects that are persistent or particularly bothersome. IT IS ESPECIALLY IMPORTANT TO TELL YOUR DOCTOR about blurred vision, change in menstruation, clumsiness, decreased blood pressure, difficult or painful urination, feeling faint, flushing of the face, hallucinations, palpitations, ringing or buzzing in the ears, rash, seizures, shortness of breath, sleeping disorders, sore throat or fever, tightness in the chest, unusual bleeding or bruising, unusual increase in sweating, or unusual tiredness or weakness.

INTERACTIONS

Meclizine interacts with several other types of medications:

1. Concurrent use with other central nervous system depressants (such as alcohol, barbiturates, benzodiazepine tranquilizers, muscle relaxants, narcotics, pain medications, and phenothiazine tranquilizers) or with tricyclic antidepressants can cause extreme drowsiness.

2. If you take meclizine on a regular basis and also take large amounts of aspirin (for example, for arthritis pain relief), tell your doctor. The effects of too much aspirin (tinnitus, or ringing in the ears) may be masked by meclizine.

BE SURE TO TELL YOUR DOCTOR about any medications you are currently taking, especially those listed above.

WARNINGS

• Tell your doctor about allergic or unusual reactions you have had to any medications, especially to meclizine, cyclizine, or buclizine.

• Tell your doctor if you now have or if you have ever had asthma, blood-vessel disease, glaucoma, high blood pressure, kidney disease, peptic ulcers, enlarged prostate gland, or thyroid disease.

• Meclizine can cause drowsiness or dizziness. Your ability to perform tasks that require alertness, such as driving a car or operating potentially dangerous machinery, may be decreased. Appropriate caution should be taken.

• Meclizine should be given to children under age 12 years only under the supervision of a doctor.

• The elderly may be especially sensitive to side effects, such as dry mouth.

• Be sure to tell your doctor if you are pregnant. The effects of this medication during pregnancy have not been thoroughly studied in humans. Also tell your doctor if you are breast-feeding an infant. Small amounts of meclizine pass into breast milk and may cause unusual excitement or irritability in nursing infants.

---

medroxyprogesterone

BRAND NAMES (Manufacturers)
Amen (Carnrick)
Curretab (Reid-Provident)
Cycrin (ESI Pharma)
medroxyprogesterone acetate (various manufacturers)
Provera (Upjohn)
TYPE OF DRUG
Progesterone
INGREDIENT
medroxyprogesterone

DOSAGE FORM
Tablets (2.5 mg, 5 mg, and 10 mg)
STORAGE
These tablets should be stored at room temperature in a tightly closed container. Medroxyprogesterone should not be refrigerated.

USES
Medroxyprogesterone is a synthetic progesterone (a female hormone naturally produced by the body) that is used to treat abnormal menstrual bleeding, difficult menstruation, or lack of menstruation. It can be used for other conditions as determined by your doctor.

TREATMENT
This medication may cause stomach irritation. To avoid or minimize this side effect, take medroxyprogesterone with food or immediately after a meal.

If you miss a dose of medroxyprogesterone, take the missed dose as soon as possible, unless it is almost time for the next dose of your medication. In that case, do not take the missed dose at all; just return to your regular dosing schedule. Do not double the next dose of this drug unless directed to do so by your doctor.

SIDE EFFECTS
Minor. Acne, dizziness, hair growth, headache, nausea, or vomiting. These side effects should disappear as your body adjusts to the medication.

This medication can increase your sensitivity to sunlight. Avoid prolonged exposure to sunlight and sunlamps. Wear protective clothing, and use an effective sunscreen.

This medication may cause tenderness, swelling, or bleeding of the gums. Brushing and flossing your teeth regularly may prevent this. You should also see your dentist regularly while you are taking this medicine.

If you feel dizzy or light-headed, sit or lie down for a while; get up slowly from a sitting or reclining position; and be careful on stairs.

Major. Tell your doctor about any side effects that are persistent or particularly bothersome. IT IS ESPECIALLY IMPORTANT TO TELL YOUR DOCTOR about breast tenderness;

change in menstrual patterns; chest pain; depression; fainting; hair loss; itching; pain in the calves; rapid weight gain (three to five pounds within a week); rash; slurred speech; sudden, severe headache; swelling of the feet or ankles; unusual vaginal bleeding; or yellowing of the eyes or skin.

INTERACTIONS
Medroxyprogesterone should not interact with other medications if it is used according to directions.

WARNINGS
• Tell your doctor about unusual or allergic reactions you have had to any medications, especially to medroxyprogesterone, progestin, or progesterone.
• Before starting this drug, tell your doctor if you have ever had cancer of the breast or genitals, clotting disorders, diabetes mellitus, depression, epilepsy, gallbladder disease, asthma, heart disease, kidney disease, liver disease, migraines, porphyria, stroke, or vaginal bleeding.
• A package insert should come with this drug. Read it carefully, and if you have any questions ask your doctor.
• If this drug makes you dizzy or drowsy, do not take part in any activities that require alertness, such as driving a car or operating potentially dangerous machinery.
• It is important to tell your doctor if you are pregnant. Medroxyprogesterone should not be used during the first four months of pregnancy because it has been shown to cause birth defects. Since hormones have long-term effects on the body, medroxyprogesterone should be stopped at least three months before you attempt to become pregnant. Also tell your doctor if you are breast-feeding an infant. Small amounts of medroxyprogesterone pass into breast milk.

mefenamic acid

BRAND NAME (Manufacturer)
Ponstel (Parke-Davis)
TYPE OF DRUG
Nonsteroidal anti-inflammatory analgesic
INGREDIENT
mefenamic acid

DOSAGE FORM
Capsules (250 mg)
STORAGE
This medication should be stored in a tightly closed container at room temperature away from heat and direct sunlight.

USES
Mefenamic acid is used to treat painful menstruation. This medication has been shown to block the production of certain body chemicals, called prostaglandins, that may trigger pain. However, it is not yet fully understood how it works.

TREATMENT
Mefenamic acid should be taken with food or antacids to lessen stomach irritation (unless your doctor recommends otherwise). Take this medication only as directed by your doctor. Do not take more of it or take it more often; and do not take it for longer than seven days at a time, unless your doctor tells you to do so. Taking too much of this medicine or using it for long periods of time may increase your chances of experiencing serious side effects.

It is important to take mefenamic acid on schedule and not to miss any doses. If you do miss a dose, take it as soon as possible, unless it is almost time for your next dose. In that case, do not take the missed dose at all; just return to your regular dosing schedule. Do not double the next dose.

SIDE EFFECTS
Minor. Bloating, constipation, diarrhea, difficulty in sleeping, dizziness, drowsiness, headache, heartburn, indigestion, lightheadedness, loss of appetite, nausea, nervousness, soreness of the mouth, unusual sweating, or vomiting. As your body adjusts to the drug, these side effects should disappear.

To relieve constipation, increase the amount of fiber in your diet (fresh fruits and vegetables, salads, bran, and whole-grain breads), exercise, and drink more water (unless your doctor directs you to do otherwise).

If you become dizzy, sit or lie down for a while; get up slowly from a sitting or reclining position; and be careful on stairs. Avoid operating a car or potentially dangerous equipment.

Major. If any side effects are persistent or particularly both-ersome, you should report them to your doctor. IT IS ESPE-CIALLY IMPORTANT TO TELL YOUR DOCTOR about bloody or black, tarry stools; blurred vision; confusion; depression; difficult or painful urination; palpitations; a problem with hearing; ringing or buzzing in the ears; severe diarrhea; skin rash, hives, or itching; stomach pain; swelling of the feet; tight-ness in the chest, shortness of breath, or wheezing; unex-plained sore throat and fever; unusual bleeding or bruising; unusual fatigue or weakness; unusual weight gain; or yel-lowing of the eyes or skin.

INTERACTIONS

Mefenamic acid interacts with several other medications:

1. Anticoagulants (blood thinners) such as warfarin can lead to an increase in bleeding complications if taken at the same time as mefenamic acid.

2. Concurrent use with aspirin, salicylates, or other anti-in-flammatory medications can increase stomach irritation. Aspirin may also decrease the effectiveness of mefenamic acid.

3. Probenecid may increase blood levels of mefenamic acid, which may increase the risk of side effects.

4. The action of beta blockers may be decreased by this med-ication.

5. The drug can interact with diuretics (water pills).

  BE SURE TO TELL YOUR DOCTOR about any medications you are currently taking, especially any listed above.

WARNINGS

• Tell your doctor if you have ever had unusual or allergic re-actions to any medications, especially to mefenamic acid or to any of the other chemically related drugs (aspirin, other sali-cylates, diclofenac, diflunisal, fenoprofen, flurbiprofen, ibupro-fen, meclofenamate, indomethacin, ketoprofen, naproxen, oxyphenbutazone, phenylbutazone, piroxicam, sulindac, or tolmetin).

• Before taking mefenamic acid, it is important to tell your doctor if you now have or if you have ever had any of the fol-lowing: asthma, bleeding problems, colitis, stomach ulcers or other stomach problems, epilepsy, heart disease, high blood pressure, kidney disease, liver disease, mental illness, or Parkinson's disease.

• If this drug makes you dizzy or drowsy, do not take part in any activity that requires mental alertness, such as driving an automobile or operating potentially dangerous machinery.

• Because mefenamic acid can prolong your bleeding time, it is important to tell your doctor or dentist that you are taking this drug before having surgery or any other medical or dental treatment.

• If you experience severe diarrhea while taking this medication, check with your doctor immediately. Do not take this medication again unless you first check with your doctor, because severe diarrhea can occur each time you take it.

• Stomach problems are more likely to occur if you take aspirin regularly or drink alcohol while being treated with this medication. These should, therefore, be avoided (unless your doctor directs you to do otherwise).

• If this drug is to be given to a child under 12 years of age, discuss the risks as well as the benefits with your doctor.

• Be sure to tell your doctor if you are pregnant. This type of medication may cause unwanted effects on the heart or blood flow in the fetus. And studies in animals have shown that this type of medicine, if taken late in pregnancy, can increase the length of pregnancy, prolong labor, and cause other problems during delivery. Mefenamic acid has not been shown to cause birth defects in animals; however, studies in humans have not been conducted. Also inform your doctor if you are breast-feeding. Small amounts of mefenamic acid pass into breast milk.

meperidine

BRAND NAMES (Manufacturers)
Demerol (Winthrop-Breon)
meperidine hydrochloride (various manufacturers)
TYPE OF DRUG
Analgesic
INGREDIENT
meperidine
DOSAGE FORMS
Tablets (50 mg and 100 mg)
Syrup (50 mg per 5-mL spoonful)

STORAGE
Store at room temperature in a tightly closed, light-resistant container. This medication should not be refrigerated and should never be frozen.

USES
Meperidine is a narcotic analgesic (pain reliever) that acts directly on the central nervous system (brain and spinal cord). It is used to relieve moderate to severe pain.

TREATMENT
In order to avoid stomach upset, you can take meperidine with food or milk. It works most effectively if you take it at the onset of pain, rather than waiting until the pain becomes intense.

Measure the syrup form of this medication carefully with a specially designed 5-mL measuring spoon. An ordinary kitchen teaspoon is not accurate enough. Each dose of the syrup should be diluted in four ounces (half a glass) of water in order to avoid the numbness of the mouth and throat that this medication can cause.

If you are taking this medication on a regular schedule and you miss a dose, take the missed dose as soon as possible, unless it is almost time for your next dose. In that case, do not take the missed dose at all; just return to your regular dosing schedule. Do not double the next dose.

SIDE EFFECTS
Minor. Constipation, dizziness, drowsiness, dry mouth, false sense of well-being, flushing, light-headedness, loss of appetite, nausea, rash, or sweating. These side effects should disappear as your body adjusts to the medication.

If you are constipated, increase the amount of fiber in your diet (fresh fruits and vegetables, salads, bran, and whole-grain breads). You can also increase your exercise and drink more water (unless your doctor directs you to do otherwise).

Chew sugarless gum or suck on ice chips or a piece of hard candy to reduce mouth dryness associated with the use of this medication.

If you feel dizzy or light-headed, sit or lie down for a while; get up from a sitting or lying position slowly; and be careful on stairs.

Major. Tell your doctor about any side effects that are persistent or particularly bothersome. IT IS ESPECIALLY IMPORTANT TO TELL YOUR DOCTOR about anxiety, breathing difficulties, excitability, fatigue, painful or difficult urination, restlessness, sore throat and fever, tremors, or weakness.

INTERACTIONS

Meperidine interacts with several other types of medications:
1. Concurrent use of this medication with other central nervous system depressants (such as alcohol, antihistamines, barbiturates, benzodiazepine tranquilizers, muscle relaxants, and phenothiazine tranquilizers) or with tricyclic antidepressants can cause extreme drowsiness.
2. A monoamine oxidase (MAO) inhibitor taken within 14 days of this medication can lead to unpredictable and severe side effects.
3. The combination of cimetidine and meperidine can cause confusion, disorientation, and shortness of breath.

  BE SURE TO TELL YOUR DOCTOR about any medications you are currently taking, especially any listed above.

WARNINGS

• Tell your doctor about unusual or allergic reactions you have had to any drugs, especially to meperidine or to any other narcotic analgesic (such as codeine, hydrocodone, hydromorphone, methadone, morphine, oxycodone, and propoxyphene).
• Tell your doctor if you now have or if you have ever had acute abdominal conditions, asthma, brain disease, colitis, epilepsy, gallstones or gallbladder disease, head injuries, heart disease, kidney disease, liver disease, lung disease, mental illness, emotional disorders, enlarged prostate gland, thyroid disease, or urethral stricture.
• If this drug makes you dizzy or drowsy, do not take part in any activity that requires alertness, such as driving a car or operating potentially dangerous machinery. Take special care going up and down stairs.
• Before having surgery or any other medical or dental treatment, tell your doctor or dentist about this drug.
• Meperidine has the potential for abuse and must be used with caution. Usually, it should not be taken on a regular schedule for longer than ten days (unless your doctor directs

you to do so). Tolerance develops quickly; do not increase the dosage or stop taking the drug abruptly unless you first consult your doctor. If you have been taking large amounts of this medication or have been taking it for a long period of time, you may experience withdrawal symptoms (muscle aches, diarrhea, gooseflesh, runny nose, nausea, vomiting, shivering, trembling, stomach cramps, sleep disorders, irritability, weakness, excessive yawning, or sweating) when you stop taking it. Your doctor may, therefore, want to reduce your dosage gradually.

• Tell your doctor if you are pregnant. The effects of this drug during the early stages of pregnancy have not been thoroughly studied in humans. However, the use of meperidine regularly in large doses during the later stages of pregnancy can result in addiction of the fetus. Also tell your doctor if you are breast-feeding. Small amounts of this drug may pass into breast milk and cause excessive drowsiness in the nursing infant.

meprobamate and aspirin combination

BRAND NAMES (Manufacturers)
aspirin and meprobamate combination (various manufacturers)
Epromate (Major)
Equagesic (Wyeth-Ayerst)
Equazine M (Rugby)
Mepro-analgesic (United Research)
Meprobamate Compound (Interstate)
Mepro Compound (Schein)
Meprogese (Geneva Generics)
Meprogesic Q (various manufacturers)
Micrainin (Wallace)
TYPE OF DRUG
Sedative and analgesic
INGREDIENTS
meprobamate and aspirin
DOSAGE FORM
Tablets (200 mg meprobamate and 325 mg aspirin)

STORAGE
Meprobamate and aspirin combination tablets should be stored at room temperature in a tightly closed, light-resistant container. Moisture can cause aspirin to decompose.

USES
Meprobamate and aspirin combination is used to relieve tension headaches and pain in muscles or joints associated with tension or anxiety. It is unclear exactly how meprobamate works to relieve anxiety and tension, but it appears to be a central nervous system (brain and spinal cord) depressant.

TREATMENT
In order to avoid stomach irritation, you can take meprobamate and aspirin combination with food or with a full glass of water or milk (unless your doctor directs otherwise).

If you are taking this medication on a regular schedule and you miss a dose, take the missed dose as soon as possible, unless it is almost time for the next dose. In that case, do not take the missed dose at all; just return to your regular dosing schedule. Do not double the next dose.

SIDE EFFECTS
Minor. Abdominal pain, diarrhea, dizziness, drowsiness, dry mouth, fatigue, headache, light-headedness, nausea, vomiting, or weakness. These side effects should disappear as your body adjusts to the medication.

If you feel dizzy or light-headed, sit or lie down for a while; get up slowly from a sitting or reclining position; and be careful on stairs.

Major. Tell your doctor about any side effects that are persistent or particularly bothersome. IT IS ESPECIALLY IMPORTANT TO TELL YOUR DOCTOR about blurred vision, buzzing in the ears, chest tightness, clumsiness, confusion, convulsions, difficult or painful urination, fainting, false sense of well-being, fever, headache, loss of coordination, mental depression, nightmares, numbness or tingling, palpitations, rapid weight gain, shortness of breath, skin rash, slurred speech, sore throat, unusual bleeding or bruising, or unusual weakness.

INTERACTIONS

This medicine interacts with several other types of medications:

1. Concurrent use of meprobamate with other central nervous system depressants (such as alcohol, antihistamines, barbiturates, benzodiazepine tranquilizers, muscle relaxants, narcotics, pain medications, phenothiazine tranquilizers, and sleeping medications) or with tricyclic antidepressants may cause extreme drowsiness.

2. Aspirin can increase the effects of blood thinners, such as warfarin, thereby leading to a possible increase in bleeding complications.

3. The antigout effects of probenecid and sulfinpyrazone may be blocked by aspirin.

4. Aspirin can increase the gastrointestinal side effects of anti-inflammatory medications, including nonsteroidal anti-inflammatory drugs, alcohol, phenylbutazone, and adrenocorticosteroids (cortisonelike medicines).

5. Ammonium chloride, methionine, and furosemide can increase the side effects of aspirin; and acetazolamide, methazolamide, antacids, and phenobarbital can decrease the effectiveness of aspirin.

6. Aspirin can increase the side effects of methotrexate, penicillin, thyroid hormone, phenytoin, sulfinpyrazone, naproxen, valproic acid, insulin, and oral antidiabetic medicines.

7. Aspirin can also decrease the therapeutic effects of spironolactone.

   BE SURE TO TELL YOUR DOCTOR about any medications you are currently taking, especially those listed above.

WARNINGS

• Tell your doctor about unusual or allergic reactions you have had to any medications, especially to meprobamate, carbromal, carisoprodol, mebutamate, tybamate, aspirin, methyl salicylate (oil of wintergreen), diclofenac, diflunisal, fenoprofen, flurbiprofen, ibuprofen, indomethacin, ketoprofen, meclofenamate, mefenamic acid, naproxen, piroxicam, sulindac, or tolmetin.

• Before starting to take meprobamate and aspirin combination, be sure to tell your doctor if you have a history of drug abuse or if you now have or have ever had asthma, bleeding disorders, congestive heart failure, diabetes, epilepsy, glucose-6-phosphate dehydrogenase (G6PD) deficiency, gout, hemophilia, high blood pressure, kidney disease, liver disease, nasal polyps, peptic ulcers, porphyria, or thyroid disease.

• Before having surgery or any other medical or dental treatment, be sure to tell your doctor or dentist that you are taking aspirin. Treatment with aspirin is usually discontinued five to seven days before surgery, to prevent bleeding complications.

• If this drug makes you dizzy or drowsy, avoid taking part in any activity that requires alertness, such as driving a car or operating potentially dangerous machinery.

• The use of aspirin in children (about 16 years of age or less) with the flu or chicken pox has been associated with a rare, life-threatening condition called Reye's syndrome. Aspirin-containing products should, therefore, not be given to children with signs of infection.

• Patients with diabetes should know that large doses of aspirin (greater than eight 325-mg tablets per day) can cause erroneous readings on urine glucose tests. They should check with their doctor before changing their insulin dosage while taking this medication.

• Meprobamate is a potentially habit-forming medication. It should be used with caution. If this drug is being used for several months, tolerance to it may develop. But do not stop taking the drug unless you first consult your doctor. A withdrawal reaction could result from stopping this medication abruptly. Your doctor may want to reduce your dosage of the medication gradually.

• Because this medication contains aspirin, additional medications with aspirin should not be administered without your doctor's approval. Check the labels on any over-the-counter (nonprescription) pain, sinus, allergy, asthma, cough, and cold products you might be taking to see if they contain aspirin.

• Be sure to tell your doctor if you are pregnant. Meprobamate can cause birth defects if taken during the first three months of pregnancy. In addition, large doses of aspirin taken close to term may prolong labor and may cause bleeding complications in the mother and heart problems in the infant. Also tell your doctor if you are breast-feeding an infant. Both meprobamate and aspirin pass into breast milk.

metaproterenol

BRAND NAMES (Manufacturers)
Alupent (Boehringer Ingelheim)
Metaprel (Sandoz)
TYPE OF DRUG
Bronchiodilator
INGREDIENT
metaproterenol
DOSAGE FORMS
Tablets (10 mg and 20 mg)
Oral syrup (10 mg per 5-mL spoonful)
Inhalation aerosol (each spray delivers 0.65 mg)
Solution for nebulization (0.4%, 0.6%, and 5%)
STORAGE
Metaproterenol tablets and oral syrup should be stored at room temperature in tightly closed, light-resistant containers. In contrast, the solution for nebulization should be stored in the refrigerator. The inhalation aerosol should be stored at room temperature away from excessive heat—the contents are pressurized, and the container can explode if heated. Metaproterenol syrup and solution should not be used if they turn brown or contain particles.

USES

Metaproterenol is used to relieve wheezing and shortness of breath caused by lung diseases such as asthma, bronchitis, and emphysema. This drug acts directly on the muscles of the bronchi (breathing tubes) to relieve bronchospasm (muscle contractions of the bronchi), thereby allowing air to move to and from the lungs.

TREATMENT

In order to lessen stomach upset, you can take metaproterenol tablets or oral syrup with food (unless your doctor directs you to do otherwise).

The oral syrup form of this medication should be measured carefully with a specially designed 5-mL measuring spoon. An ordinary kitchen teaspoon is not accurate enough.

The inhalation aerosol form of this medication is usually packaged along with an instruction sheet. Read the directions carefully before using this medication. The container should be shaken well just before each use. The contents tend to settle on the bottom, so it is necessary to shake the container in order to distribute the ingredients evenly and equalize the doses. If more than one inhalation is necessary, wait at least one full minute between doses, so that you receive the full therapeutic benefit of the first dose.

If you miss a dose of this medication and remember within an hour, take it; then follow your regular schedule for the next dose. If you miss the dose by more than an hour or so, just wait until the next scheduled dose. Do not double the dose.

If you are also using an aerosol corticosteroid (such as beclomethasone, dexamethasone, or triamcinolone), use the metaproterenol inhalation first and wait about five minutes before using the corticosteroid inhalation (unless otherwise directed by your doctor). This will allow the corticosteroid inhalation to more easily reach your lungs.

SIDE EFFECTS

Minor. Anxiety, dizziness, headache, flushing, irritability, insomnia, loss of appetite, muscle cramps, nausea, nervousness, restlessness, sweating, vomiting, weakness, or dryness or irritation of the mouth or throat (from the inhalation aerosol). These side effects should disappear as your body adjusts to the medication.

To help prevent dryness and irritation of the mouth or throat, rinse your mouth with water after each dose of the inhalation aerosol.

In order to avoid difficulty in falling asleep, check with your doctor to see if you can take the last dose of this medication several hours before bedtime each day.

If you feel dizzy, sit or lie down for a while; get up from a sitting or lying position slowly; and be careful on stairs.

Major. Tell your doctor about any side effects that are persistent or particularly bothersome. IT IS ESPECIALLY IMPORTANT TO TELL YOUR DOCTOR about chest pain, difficult breathing, difficult or painful urination, palpitations, rash, or tremors.

INTERACTIONS

Metaproterenol interacts with several other types of medications:

1. Beta blockers (acebutolol, atenolol, betaxolol, carteolol, esmolol, labetalol, metoprolol, nadolol, penbutolol, pindolol, propranolol, timolol) antagonize (act against) this medication, decreasing its effectiveness.

2. Monoamine oxidase (MAO) inhibitors, tricyclic antidepressants, antihistamines, levothyroxine, and over-the-counter (nonprescription) cough, cold, allergy, asthma, diet, and sinus medications may increase the side effects of metaproterenol. At least 14 days should separate the use of this drug and the use of an MAO inhibitor.

3. There may be a change in the dosage requirements of insulin or oral antidiabetic medications when metaproterenol is started.

4. The blood-pressure-lowering effects of guanethidine may be decreased by this medication.

5. The use of metaproterenol with other bronchodilator drugs (either oral or inhaled) can have additive side effects. Discuss this with your doctor.

BE SURE TO TELL YOUR DOCTOR about any medications you are currently taking, especially any of the medications listed above.

WARNINGS

• Tell your doctor about unusual or allergic reactions you have had, especially to metaproterenol or any related drug (such as albuterol, amphetamines, ephedrine, epinephrine, isoproterenol, norepinephrine, phenylephrine, phenylpropanolamine, pseudoephedrine, and terbutaline).

• Tell your doctor if you now have or if you have ever had diabetes, glaucoma, high blood pressure, epilepsy, heart disease, enlarged prostate gland, or thyroid disease.

• This medication can cause dizziness. Your ability to perform tasks that require alertness, such as driving a car or operating potentially dangerous machinery, may be decreased. Appropriate caution should therefore be taken.

• Before having surgery or any other medical or dental treatment, be sure to tell your doctor or dentist that you are taking this medication.

• Do not exceed the recommended dosage of this medication. Excessive use may lead to an increase in side effects or a loss of effectiveness.

• Try to avoid contact of the aerosol with your eyes.

• Do not puncture, break, or burn the aerosol container. The contents are under pressure and may explode.

• Contact your doctor if you do not respond to the usual dose of this medication. It may be a sign of worsening asthma, which may require additional therapy.

• Be sure to tell your doctor if you are pregnant. The effects of this medication during pregnancy have not been thoroughly studied in humans. Also tell your doctor if you are breast-feeding an infant. It is not known whether this drug passes into breast milk.

metformin

BRAND NAME (Manufacturer)
Glucophage (Bristol-Myers Squibb)
TYPE OF DRUG
Oral antidiabetic
INGREDIENT
metformin
DOSAGE FORMS
Tablets (500 mg and 850 mg)
STORAGE
This medication should be stored at room temperature in a tightly closed container. It should not be refrigerated or frozen. Discard any outdated medication.

USES

Metformin is used for the treatment of the form of diabetes mellitus that appears in adulthood and cannot be managed by exercise and control of diet alone. This kind of diabetes is known as type II or non–insulin-dependent diabetes. Metformin helps to control sugar in the blood by making the body more sensitive to insulin and by reducing the amount of sugar produced by the body. Metformin can be used alone or with other oral antidiabetic agents (such as sulfonylureas).

TREATMENT

In order for this medication to work correctly, it must be taken as directed by your doctor. It is best to take this medication at the same time each day in order to maintain constant blood sugar. And it is important to avoid missing any doses of metformin. If you do miss a dose, take it as soon as possible, unless it is almost time for your next regular dose. In that case, do not take the missed dose at all; just return to your regular dosing schedule. Do not double the dose. Tell your doctor if you feel any side effects from missing a dose of this drug. Metformin should be taken with a meal to lessen nausea and diarrhea.

SIDE EFFECTS

Minor. Headache, loss of appetite, metallic taste in mouth, nausea, stomach discomfort or gas. These side effects should lessen as your body adjusts to the drug.

Major. You should tell your doctor about any side effects that are persistent or particularly bothersome. IT IS ESPECIALLY IMPORTANT TO TELL YOUR DOCTOR about anxiousness; cold sweats; diarrhea; excessive hunger; fast, shallow breathing; headache; muscle cramps or pain; rapid pulse; shakiness; unusual sleepiness; or unusual tiredness or weakness.

INTERACTIONS

Metformin interacts with several other types of drugs:

1. Cimetidine, furosemide, and nifedipine may increase the blood concentration of metformin.

2. Alcohol and iodinated contrast material may increase the risk for some of the serious side effects of this medication.

3. Metformin may decrease the amount of glyburide or furosemide in the body.

4. Drugs such as amiloride, digoxin, morphine, procainamide, quinidine, quinine, ranitidine, triamterene, trimethoprim, and vancomycin may interfere with the body's ability to eliminate metformin.

BE SURE TO TELL YOUR DOCTOR about any medications your are currently taking, especially those listed above.

WARNINGS

• It is important to tell your doctor if you have ever had an unusual or allergic reaction to any medication, especially to metformin.

• It is also important to tell your doctor if you now have or have ever had kidney disease or liver disease.

• Avoid drinking alcohol while taking this medication. Alcohol may increase the risk of serious side effects with metformin.

• Before having surgery or any other medical or dental treatment, be sure to tell your doctor or dentist that your are taking this medication. IT IS ESPECIALLY IMPORTANT TO TELL YOUR DOCTOR that you are taking this medication if you are going to have any type of X ray or similar medical test. Your doctor may want you to stop taking this medication a few days before such testing is scheduled.

• Follow the special diet provided by your doctor. This is an important part of controlling your blood sugar and is necessary in order for this medication to work properly.

• Test for sugar in your urine as directed by your doctor. It is a convenient way to determine whether your diabetes is being controlled by this medication.

• Eat or drink something containing sugar right away if you experience any symptoms of hypoglycemia (low blood sugar), such as anxiety, chills, cold sweats, cool or pale skin, drowsiness, excessive hunger, headache, nausea, nervousness, rapid heartbeat, shakiness, or unusual tiredness or weakness. It is important for your family and friends to know the symptoms of low blood sugar. They should understand what to do if they observe any of these symptoms in you.

• Although it is very uncommon, metformin may cause a condition known as lactic acidosis. The symptoms of lactic acidosis are diarrhea, severe muscle pain or cramping, shallow and fast breathing, and unusual sleepiness, tiredness or weakness. IT IS IMPORTANT TO TELL YOUR DOCTOR IMMEDIATELY if your experience any of these symptoms.

• Be sure to tell your doctor if you are pregnant or plan to become pregnant. This drug has not been studied for use during pregnancy. Your doctor may switch you to insulin while you are pregnant or are planning to become pregnant. And be sure to tell your doctor if you are breast-feeding an infant. Small amounts of metformin may pass into breast milk.

methadone

BRAND NAMES (Manufacturers)
Dolophine (Lilly)
methadone hydrochloride (various manufacturers)
TYPE OF DRUG
Analgesic

INGREDIENT
methadone
DOSAGE FORMS
Tablets (5 mg, 10 mg, and 40 mg)
Oral solution (5 mg and 10 mg per 5-mL spoonful, with 8% alcohol; 10 mg per 10-mL spoonful; and 10 mg per 1-mL spoonful)
STORAGE
Methadone analgesic tablets and oral solution should be stored at room temperature in tightly closed, light-resistant containers, well out of the reach of children and pets.

USES
Methadone is a narcotic analgesic (pain reliever) that acts directly on the central nervous system (brain and spinal cord). It is used to relieve moderate to severe pain. It is also used to detoxify narcotic addicts and to provide temporary maintenance treatment for them.

TREATMENT
To avoid stomach upset, take methadone with food or milk. This medication is most effective if you take it at the onset of pain, rather than when the pain becomes intense.

Measure the dose of the solution form of this medication carefully with a specially designed 5-mL measuring spoon. An ordinary kitchen teaspoon is not accurate enough.

If you are taking this medication on a regular schedule and you miss a dose, take the missed dose as soon as possible, unless it is almost time for your next dose. In that case, do not take the missed dose at all; just return to your regular dosing schedule. Do not double the next dose.

SIDE EFFECTS
Minor. Constipation, dizziness, drowsiness, dry mouth, false sense of well-being, light-headedness, loss of appetite, nausea, or sweating. These side effects should disappear as your body adjusts to the medication.

If you are constipated, increase the amount of fiber in your diet (fresh fruits and vegetables, salads, bran, and whole-grain breads). You can also increase your exercise and drink more water (unless your doctor directs you to do otherwise).

Chew sugarless gum or suck on ice chips or a piece of hard candy to reduce mouth dryness.

If you feel dizzy or light-headed, sit or lie down for a while; get up from a sitting or lying position slowly; and be careful on stairs. Take special care when operating potentially dangerous equipment.

Major. Tell your doctor about any side effects that are persistent or particularly bothersome. IT IS ESPECIALLY IMPORTANT TO TELL YOUR DOCTOR about anxiety, breathing difficulties, excitability, fainting, fatigue, flushing, painful or difficult urination, palpitations, pinpoint pupils of eyes, rash, restlessness, sore throat, and fever, tremors, or weakness.

INTERACTIONS

Methadone interacts with several other types of medications:

1. Concurrent use of it with other central nervous system depressants (such as alcohol, antihistamines, barbiturates, benzodiazepine tranquilizers, muscle relaxants, and phenothiazine tranquilizers) or with tricyclic antidepressants can cause extreme drowsiness.

2. A monoamine oxidase (MAO) inhibitor taken within 14 days of this medication can lead to unpredictable and severe side effects.

3. Rifampin and phenytoin can decrease the blood levels and effectiveness of methadone.

4. The combination of cimetidine and this medication can cause confusion, disorientation, and shortness of breath.

BE SURE TO TELL YOUR DOCTOR about any medications you are currently taking, especially any listed above.

WARNINGS

• Tell your doctor about unusual or allergic reactions you have had to any medications, especially to methadone or to any other narcotic analgesic.

• Tell your doctor if you now have or if you have ever had acute abdominal conditions, asthma, brain disease, colitis, epilepsy, gallstones or gallbladder disease, head injuries, heart disease, kidney disease, liver disease, lung disease, mental illness, emotional disorders, enlarged prostate gland, thyroid disease, or urethral stricture.

• If this drug makes you dizzy or drowsy, do not take part in any activity that requires alertness, such as driving a car or operating potentially dangerous machinery.

• Before having surgery or any other medical or dental treatment, be sure to tell your doctor or dentist that you are taking this medication.

• Methadone has the potential for abuse and must be used with caution. Usually, it should not be taken on a regular schedule for longer than ten days (unless your doctor directs you to do so). Tolerance develops quickly; do not increase the dosage or stop taking the drug abruptly unless you first consult your doctor. If you have been taking large amounts of this medication or if you have been taking it for long periods of time, you may experience withdrawal symptoms (muscle aches, diarrhea, gooseflesh, runny nose, nausea, vomiting, shivering, trembling, stomach cramps, sleep disorders, irritability, weakness, excessive yawning, or sweating) when you stop taking it. Your doctor may, therefore, want to reduce the dosage gradually.

• Be sure to tell your doctor if you are pregnant. The effects of this medication during the early stages of pregnancy have not been thoroughly studied in humans. However, regular use of methadone in large doses during the later stages of pregnancy can result in addiction of the fetus, leading to the appearance of withdrawal symptoms (such as irritability, excessive crying, tremors, fever, vomiting, diarrhea, sneezing, or excessive yawning) at birth. Also tell your doctor if you are breast-feeding an infant. Small amounts of this medication may pass into breast milk and cause excessive drowsiness in the nursing infant.

methenamine

BRAND NAMES (Manufacturers)
Hiprex (Merrell Dow)
Mandameth (Major)
Mandelamine (Parke-Davis)
methenamine hippurate (various manufacturers)
methenamine mandelate (various manufacturers)
Urex (Riker)

TYPE OF DRUG
Antibiotic
INGREDIENT
methenamine
DOSAGE FORMS
Tablets (500 mg and 1 g)
Enteric-coated tablets (500 mg and 1 g)
Oral suspension (250 mg and 500 mg per 5-mL spoonful)
Oral granules (1-g packets)
STORAGE
Methenamine tablets, oral suspension, and granules should be stored at room temperature in tightly closed containers. This medication should not be refrigerated and should never be frozen.

USES
Methenamine is used to prevent and treat bacterial infections of the urinary tract.

TREATMENT
In order to avoid stomach irritation, you should take methenamine with food or with a full glass of water or milk (unless your doctor specifically directs you to do otherwise).

The oral-suspension form of this medication should be shaken well just before measuring each dose. The contents tend to settle on the bottom of the bottle, so it is necessary to shake the container to distribute the ingredients evenly and equalize the doses. Each dose should then be measured carefully with a specially designed 5-mL measuring spoon. An ordinary kitchen teaspoon is not accurate enough.

The enteric-coated tablets should be swallowed whole. breaking, crushing, or chewing these tablets increases their gastrointestinal side effects.

If you are taking the oral granules, the contents of the packet should be dissolved in two to four ounces of water just before you take the dose.

Try not to miss any doses of this medication. If you do miss a dose, take it immediately. However, if you do not remember to take the missed dose until it is almost time for your next dose, take the missed dose immediately; space the following dose about halfway through the regular interval between doses; then continue with your regular dosing schedule.

It is important to continue to take this medication for the entire time prescribed by your doctor (usually seven to 14 days), even if the symptoms disappear before the end of that period. If you stop taking the drug too soon, resistant bacteria are given a chance to continue growing, and the infection could recur.

This medication works best when your urine is acidic (pH 5.5 or below). You may want to talk to your doctor about testing the acidity of your urine before you begin treatment with methenamine.

SIDE EFFECTS

Minor. Abdominal cramps, diarrhea, headache, loss of appetite, nausea, or vomiting. These side effects should disappear as your body adjusts to the medication.

Major. Tell your doctor about any side effects that are persistent or particularly bothersome. IT IS ESPECIALLY IMPORTANT TO TELL YOUR DOCTOR about difficulty in breathing, difficult or painful urination, itching, mouth sores, rapid weight gain (three to five pounds within a week), shortness of breath, or skin rash.

INTERACTIONS

Methenamine interacts with several other types of medications:

1. Sodium bicarbonate, antacids, acetazolamide, and diuretics (water pills) can decrease the effectiveness of methenamine by preventing its conversion to formaldehyde.

2. Methenamine can increase the side effects (to the kidneys) of sulfonamide antibiotics.

Before starting to take methenamine, BE SURE TO TELL YOUR DOCTOR about any medications you are currently taking, especially any of the drugs listed above.

WARNINGS

• Tell your doctor about unusual or allergic reactions you have had to any medications, especially to methenamine.

• Before starting to take methenamine, be sure to tell your doctor if you now have or if you have ever had dehydration, kidney disease, or liver disease.

• Some of these products contain the color additive FD&C Yellow No. 5 (tartrazine), which can cause allergic-type re-

actions (fainting, rash, shortness of breath) in certain susceptible individuals.

• This medication has been prescribed for your current infection only. Another infection later on, or one that someone
else has, may require a different medicine. You should not
give your medicine to other people or use it for other infections, unless your doctor specifically directs you to do so.

• If the symptoms of your infection do not improve in several
days, CONTACT YOUR DOCTOR.

• In order for this medication to work properly, it is necessary that your urine remain acidic. You should, therefore, avoid
foods that cause the urine to become alkaline, such as milk
products. Your doctor may also want you to take vitamin C to
help keep the urine acidic.

• Be sure to tell your doctor if you are pregnant. Although
methenamine appears to be safe during pregnancy, it does
cross the placenta, and extensive studies have not been conducted. Also tell your doctor if you are breast-feeding an infant.
Small amounts of methenamine pass into breast milk.

methocarbamol

BRAND NAMES (Manufacturers)
Marbaxin (Vortech)
methocarbamol (various manufacturers)
Robaxin (Robins)
TYPE OF DRUG
Muscle relaxant
INGREDIENT
methocarbamol
DOSAGE FORM
Tablets (500 mg and 750 mg)
STORAGE
Methocarbamol should be stored at room temperature in a
tightly closed container. This medication should not be re-
frigerated.

USES

This medication is used to relieve the discomfort of painful
muscle aches and spasms. It should be used in conjunction
with rest, physical therapy, and other measures that your doc-

tor may prescribe. It is not clear exactly how methocarbamol works, but it is thought to relieve muscle spasms by acting as a central nervous system (brain and spinal cord) depressant.

TREATMENT

Methocarbamol can be taken either on an empty stomach or with food or a full glass of water or milk (as directed by your doctor). These tablets can be crushed and mixed with food or liquid if you have trouble swallowing them.

If you miss a dose of this medication and remember within an hour, take the missed dose immediately. If more than an hour has passed, do not take the missed dose; just return to your regular dosing schedule. Do not double the next dose.

SIDE EFFECTS

Minor. Dizziness, drowsiness, headache, light-headedness, metallic taste in the mouth, nausea, or stomach upset. These side effects should disappear as your body adjusts to the medication.

This medication can cause the urine to darken to brown, black, or green. This is a harmless effect.

If you feel dizzy or light-headed, sit or lie down for a while; get up slowly from a sitting or reclining position; and be careful on stairs. Be especially careful when driving an automobile or operating potentially dangerous equipment.

Major. Tell your doctor about any side effects you experience that are persistent or particularly bothersome. IT IS ESPECIALLY IMPORTANT TO TELL YOUR DOCTOR about fainting, fatigue, fever, flushing, nasal congestion, skin rash, uncoordinated movements, or visual disturbances.

INTERACTIONS

Methocarbamol interacts with several other types of medications:

1. Concurrent use of methocarbamol with other central nervous system depressants (such as alcohol, antihistamines, barbiturates, benzodiazepine tranquilizers, muscle relaxants, narcotics, pain medications, phenothiazine tranquilizers, and sleeping medications) or with tricyclic antidepressants can cause episodes of fatigue and extreme drowsiness.

2. Methocarbamol can decrease the effectiveness of pyridostigmine.

Before beginning to take methocarbamol, BE SURE TO NOTIFY YOUR DOCTOR regarding any medications you may be taking currently, especially any of the drugs referred to above.

WARNINGS

• Tell your doctor about unusual or allergic reactions you have had to any medications, especially to methocarbamol.
• Before starting to take this medication, be sure to tell your doctor if you now have or if you have ever had brain disease.
• If this drug makes you dizzy or drowsy, avoid taking part in any activity that requires mental alertness, such as driving a car or operating potentially dangerous machinery.
• Be sure to tell your doctor if you are pregnant. Although methocarbamol appears to be safe, extensive studies in humans have not been conducted. Also tell your doctor if you are breast-feeding an infant. Small amounts of methocarbamol pass into breast milk.

---

methotrexate

BRAND NAMES (Manufacturers)
Methotrexate (Lederle)
Rheumatrex Dose Pack (Lederle)
TYPE OF DRUG
Antineoplastic (anticancer drug), antipsoriatic
INGREDIENT
methotrexate
DOSAGE FORM
Tablets (2.5 mg)
STORAGE
Methotrexate should be stored at room temperature in a tightly closed container.

USES

Methotrexate is used to treat certain types of cancer and severe psoriasis. It works by slowing the growth rate of rapidly proliferating cells. Do not keep this or any other medication beyond the date written on the container.

TREATMENT

In order to avoid stomach irritation, you can take methotrexate with food or with a full glass of water or milk (unless your doctor directs you to do otherwise).

Try not to miss any doses of this medication. If you do miss a dose, take the missed dose as soon as possible, unless it is almost time for the next dose. In that case, do not take the missed dose at all; just return to your regular dosing schedule. Do not double the next dose. If you miss more than two doses in a row, CONTACT YOUR DOCTOR.

SIDE EFFECTS

Minor. Abdominal distress, fatigue, loss of appetite, nasal congestion, nausea, or vomiting. These side effects should disappear as your body adjusts to the medication. Methotrexate also causes hair loss, which is reversible when the medication is stopped.

This medication can increase your sensitivity to sunlight. You should therefore try to avoid prolonged exposure to sunlight and sunlamps. Wear protective clothing and sunglasses, and use an effective sunscreen.

Major. Tell your doctor about any side effects that are persistent or particularly bothersome. IT IS ESPECIALLY IMPORTANT TO TELL YOUR DOCTOR about back pain, blurred vision, convulsions, diarrhea, difficult or painful urination, drowsiness, fever, headache, itching, menstrual changes, mouth sores, rash, severe abdominal pain, skin color changes, unusual bleeding or bruising, or yellowing of the eyes or skin.

INTERACTIONS

Methotrexate interacts with several other types of medications:

1. Concurrent use of alcohol and methotrexate can lead to an increased risk of liver damage.

2. Methotrexate can block the effectiveness of antigout medications.

3. Phenylbutazone, probenecid, phenytoin, tetracycline, aspirin, chloramphenicol, salicylates, naproxen, ketoprofen, and sulfonamide antibiotics can increase the blood levels of methotrexate, which can lead to an increase in serious side effects.

4. Methotrexate has the capability of increasing the effects of the blood thinner warfarin, which can lead to bleeding complications.

5. Folic acid vitamins may decrease the effect of this medication.

Before starting to take methotrexate, BE SURE TO TELL YOUR DOCTOR about any medications you are currently taking, especially any of those listed above.

WARNINGS

• Tell your doctor about any unusual or allergic reactions you have ever had to any medications, especially any reaction to methotrexate.

• Before starting to take this medication, be sure to tell your doctor if you now have or if you have ever had blood disorders, gout, infection, kidney disease, liver disease, or inflammation of the gastrointestinal tract.

• If this drug makes you dizzy or drowsy, be careful going up and down stairs, and do not take part in any activity that requires alertness, such as driving an automobile or other vehicle or operating potentially dangerous tools, equipment, or machinery.

• While you are taking methotrexate, you should drink plenty of fluids so that you urinate often (unless your doctor directs you to do otherwise). This helps prevent kidney and bladder problems during therapy.

• You should not be immunized or vaccinated while taking methotrexate. The vaccination or immunization will not be effective and may lead to an infection if a live-virus vaccine is used.

• Methotrexate is a potent medication that can cause serious side effects. Your doctor will therefore want to monitor your therapy carefully with blood tests.

• It is important to tell your doctor if you are pregnant. Methotrexate has been shown to cause birth defects or death of the fetus. Effective contraception should be used during treatment and for at least eight weeks after treatment is stopped. Also tell your doctor if you are breast-feeding an infant. Methotrexate passes into breast milk and can cause side effects in nursing infants.

methyldopa

BRAND NAMES (Manufacturers)
Aldomet (Merck Sharp & Dohme)
methyldopa (various manufacturers)
TYPE OF DRUG
Antihypertensive
INGREDIENT
methyldopa
DOSAGE FORMS
Tablets (125 mg, 250 mg, and 500 mg)
Oral liquid (250 mg per 5-mL spoonful)
Oral suspension (250 mg per 5-mL spoonful, with 1%
  alcohol)
STORAGE
Store at room temperature in a tightly closed, light-resistant
container. This drug should never be frozen.

USES

Methyldopa is used to treat high blood pressure. It is not clear
exactly how methyldopa works, but it is thought to act on the
central nervous system (brain and spinal cord) to prevent the
release of chemicals responsible for maintaining high blood
pressure.

TREATMENT

In order to prevent stomach irritation, you can take methyldopa with food or a full glass of water or milk. Try to take it at
the same time(s) each day (unless your doctor directs you to do
otherwise).

The oral suspension should be shaken well before each
dose is measured. The contents tend to settle to the bottom
of the bottle, so the bottle should be shaken to distribute the
medication evenly and equalize the doses. Each dose should
then be measured carefully with a specially designed 5-mL
measuring spoon. An ordinary kitchen teaspoon is not accurate
enough.

Methyldopa does not cure high blood pressure, but it will
help to control the condition as long as you take it.

If you miss a dose of this medication, take the missed dose
as soon as possible, unless it is almost time for the next dose.

In that case, do not take the missed dose at all; just return to your regular dosing schedule. Do not double the next dose.

SIDE EFFECTS

Minor. Bloating, constipation, diarrhea, dizziness, drowsiness, dry mouth, gas, headache, light-headedness, loss of appetite, nasal congestion, nausea, vomiting, or weakness. These side effects should disappear as your body adjusts to the medication.

To relieve constipation, increase the amount of fiber in your diet (fresh fruits and vegetables, salads, bran, and whole-grain breads), exercise, and drink more water (unless your doctor directs you to do otherwise).

If you feel dizzy or light-headed, sit or lie down for a while; get up slowly from a sitting or reclining position; and be careful on stairs. To avoid dizziness or light-headedness when you stand, contract and relax the muscles of your legs for a few moments before rising. Do this by pushing one foot against the floor while raising the other foot slightly, alternating feet so that you are "pumping" your legs in a pedaling motion.

Major. Tell your doctor about any effects you experience that are persistant or particularly bothersome. IT IS ESPECIALLY IMPORTANT TO TELL YOUR DOCTOR about abdominal distention, blurred vision, breast enlargement (in both sexes), chest pain, confusion, decreased sexual ability, depression, difficulty in breathing, fainting, fatigue, fever, inflamed salivary glands, insomnia, nightmares, numbness or tingling, rapid weight gain (three to five pounds within a week), severe stomach cramps, sore joints, sore or "black" tongue, tremors, unusual bleeding or bruising, unusual body movements, or yellowing of the eyes or skin.

INTERACTIONS

Methyldopa will interact with several other types of medications:

1. It can increase or decrease the antiparkinsonism effects of levodopa.

2. The use of a monoamine oxidase (MAO) inhibitor within 14 days of methyldopa can cause headaches, severe hypertension, and hallucinations.

3. The combination of methyldopa and methotrimeprazine can cause a severe drop in blood pressure; methyldopa and haloperidol can cause irritability; methyldopa and phenoxy-benzamine can cause urinary retention; and methyldopa and alcohol can cause dizziness and fainting.

4. The effects of methyldopa may be increased by verapamil and fenfluramine.

5. Methyldopa can also increase the side effects of tolbutamide and lithium.

6. Methyldopa may increase the effects of norepinephrine and phenylpropanolamine, which may increase blood pressure.

Before starting to take methyldopa, BE SURE TO TELL YOUR DOCTOR about any medications you are currently taking, especially any of those drugs that are listed above.

WARNINGS

• Tell your doctor about unusual or allergic reactions you have had to any medications, especially to methyldopa.

• Before starting to take this medication, be sure to tell your doctor if you now have or if you have ever had anemia, angina, kidney disease, liver disease, mental depression, Parkinson's disease, or stroke.

• In order to avoid dizziness or fainting while you are taking this medication, try not to stand for long periods of time; avoid drinking excessive amounts of alcohol; and try not to get overheated (avoid strenuous exercise in hot weather and do not take hot baths, showers, or saunas).

• If this drug makes you dizzy or drowsy, avoid taking part in any activity that requires alertness, such as driving a car or operating potentially dangerous machinery.

• Before surgery or other medical or dental treatment, be sure that you tell your doctor or dentist you are taking this medication.

• Before taking any over-the-counter (nonprescription) allergy, asthma, sinus, cough, cold, or diet product, check with your doctor or pharmacist. Some of these products can cause an increase in blood pressure.

• Do not stop taking this medication unless you first check with your doctor. If this drug is stopped abruptly, you could experience a sudden rise in blood pressure. Your doctor may, therefore, want to decrease your dosage gradually.

• If you have an unexplained fever, especially during the first two or three weeks after starting to take this medication, CON-

TACT YOUR DOCTOR. Fever can be a sign of a serious reaction to methyldopa.

• Occasionally, during the second or third month of therapy,
drug tolerance may develop. If you notice a decrease in effectiveness of methyldopa, contact your doctor.

• Before donating blood or receiving a blood transfusion, be
sure that the doctor knows you are taking this medication. It
can cause changes in your blood cells.

• Aldomet suspension contains sodium bisulfite, which may
cause allergic-type reactions (hives, itching, wheezing) in certain susceptible persons.

• Be sure to tell your doctor if you are pregnant. Although
this drug appears to be safe, extensive studies in women during pregnancy have not been conducted. Also tell your doctor
if you are breast-feeding an infant. Small amounts of methyldopa pass into breast milk.

methyldopa and hydrochlorothiazide combination

BRAND NAMES (Manufacturers)
Aldoril (Merck Sharp & Dohme)
methyldopa and hydrochlorothiazide combination (various
  manufacturers)
TYPE OF DRUG
Antihypertensive and diuretic
INGREDIENTS
methyldopa and hydrochlorothiazide
DOSAGE FORM
Tablets (250 mg methyldopa and 15 mg hydrochlorothiazide;
  250 mg methyldopa and 25 mg hydrochlorothiazide;
  500 mg methyldopa and 30 mg hydrochlorothiazide;
  500 mg methyldopa and 50 mg hydrochlorothiazide)
STORAGE
These tablets should be stored at room temperature in a tightly
closed container.

USES

Methyldopa and hydrochlorothiazide combination is used to treat high blood pressure. It is not exactly clear how methyldopa works, but it is thought to act on the central nervous system (brain and spinal cord) to prevent the release of chemicals responsible for maintaining high blood pressure. Hydrochlorothiazide is a diuretic (water pill), which reduces fluid accumulation by increasing the elimination of salt and water through the kidneys.

TREATMENT

To avoid stomach irritation, you can take methyldopa and hydrochlorothiazide combination with food or with a full glass of water or milk (unless your doctor specifically directs you to do otherwise). In order to become accustomed to taking this medication, try to take it at the same time(s) each day. Avoid taking a dose after 6:00 P.M.; otherwise, you may have to get up during the night to urinate.

Methyldopa and hydrochlorothiazide combination is not intended as a cure for high blood pressure, but it will help to control the condition as long as you continue to take it according to directions.

If you miss a dose of this medication, take the missed dose as soon as possible, unless it is almost time for the next dose. In that case, do not take the missed dose at all; return to your regular dosing schedule. Do not double the dose.

SIDE EFFECTS

Minor. Bloating, constipation, diarrhea, dizziness, drowsiness, gas, headache, light-headedness, loss of appetite, nasal congestion, or increased urination. These effects should disappear as your body adjusts to the drug.

This medication can increase your sensitivity to sunlight. You should, therefore, avoid prolonged exposure to sunlight and sunlamps. Wear protective clothing and sunglasses, and use an effective sunscreen.

To relieve constipation, increase the amount of fiber in your diet (fresh fruits and vegetables, salads, bran, and whole-grain breads) and exercise (unless your doctor directs you to do otherwise).

If you feel dizzy or light-headed, sit or lie down for a while; get up slowly from a sitting or reclining position; and be careful on stairs. To avoid dizziness or light-headedness when you stand, contract and relax the muscles of your legs for a few moments before rising. Do this by pushing one foot against the floor while raising the other foot slightly, alternating feet, so you are "pumping" your legs in a pedaling motion.

Major. Tell your doctor about any side effects you experience that are persistent or particularly bothersome. IT IS ESPECIALLY IMPORTANT TO TELL YOUR DOCTOR about abdominal distention, blurred vision, breast enlargement (in both sexes), chest pain, confusion, decreased sexual ability, depression, difficulty in breathing, dry mouth, fainting, fatigue, fever, inflamed salivary glands, insomnia, joint pains, muscle pains or spasms, nausea, nightmares, numbness or tingling, rapid weight gain (three to five pounds within a week), severe stomach cramps, sore or "black" tongue, swelling of the feet or ankles, thirst, tremors, unusual bleeding or bruising, unusual body movements, vomiting, weakness, or yellowing of the eyes or skin.

INTERACTIONS

This medicine interacts with several other types of drugs:

1. Methyldopa can either increase or decrease the antiparkinsonism effects of levodopa.
2. The use of a monamine oxidase (MAO) inhibitor within 14 days of methyldopa can cause headaches, severe hypertension, and hallucinations.
3. The combination of methyldopa and methotrimeprazine can cause a severe drop in blood pressure; methyldopa and haloperidol can cause irritability; methyldopa and phenoxybenzamine can cause urinary retention; and methyldopa and alcohol can cause dizziness and fainting.
4. The effects of methyldopa may be increased by verapamil and fenfluramine, which may have a negative effect.
5. Methyldopa can increase the side effects of tolbutamide and lithium.
6. Methyldopa may increase the effects of norepinephrine and phenylpropanolamine, which may increase blood pressure.
7. Hydrochlorothiazide can decrease the effectiveness of oral anticoagulants (blood thinners, such as warfarin), antigout medications, insulin, oral antidiabetic medications, and methenamine.

8. Fenfluramine may increase the blood-pressure-lowering effects of hydrochlorothiazide, and indomethacin may decrease its blood-pressure-lowering effects.

9. Cholestyramine and colestipol can decrease the absorption of hydrochlorothiazide from the gastrointestinal tract. Therefore, this medication should be taken one hour before or four hours after a dose of either of these other drugs.

10. The side effects of amphotericin B, calcium, adrenocorticosteroids (cortisonelike medicines), digitalis, digoxin, lithium, quinidine, sulfonamide antibiotics, and vitamin D may be increased by hydrochlorothiazide.

BE SURE TO TELL YOUR DOCTOR about any medications you are currently taking.

WARNINGS

• Tell your doctor about unusual or allergic reactions you have had to medications, especially to methyldopa or hydrochlorothiazide or to any other sulfa medication (diuretics, oral antidiabetic medicines, sulfonamide antibiotics, dapsone, or sulfone).

• Before starting to take this medication, be sure to tell your doctor if you have ever had anemia, angina, diabetes mellitus, gout, kidney disease, liver disease, mental depression, Parkinson's disease, pancreatitis, or stroke.

• A doctor generally does not prescribe this drug or other "fixed-dose" products as the first choice in the treatment of high blood pressure. The patient should initially receive each ingredient singly. If the response is adequate to the dose contained in this product, it can then be substituted. The advantage of a combination product is its increased convenience.

• This medication can cause potassium loss. Signs of potassium loss include dry mouth, thirst, weakness, muscle pain or cramps, nausea, and vomiting. If you experience any of these symptoms, CONTACT YOUR DOCTOR. To help prevent this problem, your doctor may want to have blood tests performed periodically to monitor your potassium levels. To help avoid potassium loss, take this medication with a glass of fresh or frozen orange juice or cranberry juice or eat a banana every day. The use of a salt substitute also helps to prevent potassium loss. Do not change your diet or use a salt substitute, however, until you discuss it with your doctor. Too much potassium can also be dangerous.

• To prevent severe water loss (dehydration) while taking hydrochlorothiazide, check with your doctor if you have any illness that causes severe or continuous nausea, vomiting, or diarrhea.

• Hydrochlorothiazide can raise blood-sugar levels in diabetic patients. Blood sugar should therefore be monitored carefully when this medication is being taken.

• In order to avoid dizziness or fainting while taking this medication, try not to stand for long periods of time; avoid drinking excessive amounts of alcohol; and try not to get overheated (avoid strenuous exercise in hot weather and do not take hot baths, showers, or saunas).

• If this drug makes you dizzy or drowsy, avoid taking part in any activity that requires alertness. such as driving an automobile or operating potentially dangerous machinery.

• Before having surgery or any other medical or dental treatment, be sure to tell your doctor or dentist that you are taking this medication.

• Before taking any over-the-counter (nonprescription) allergy, asthma, sinus, cough, cold, or diet product, check with your doctor or pharmacist.

• Do not stop taking this medication unless you first check with your doctor. If this drug is stopped abruptly, you could experience a sudden rise in blood pressure. Your doctor may, therefore, want to decrease your dosage gradually.

• If you have an unexplained fever, especially during the first two to three weeks after starting to take this medication, CONTACT YOUR DOCTOR. Fever can be a sign of a serious reaction to methyldopa.

• Tolerance to this drug can develop, usually during the second or third month of therapy. If you notice a decrease in effectiveness of this drug, contact your doctor.

• Before donating blood or receiving a blood transfusion, be sure you let the doctor know that you are taking this medication. Methyldopa can cause a change in the blood cells.

• It is important to tell your doctor if you are pregnant. Methyldopa and hydrochlorothiazide cross the placenta and may cause adverse effects in the developing fetus. Also tell your doctor if you are breast-feeding an infant. Small amounts of both of these drugs pass into breast milk.

methylphenidate

BRAND NAMES (Manufacturers)
methylphenidate hydrochloride (various manufacturers)
Ritalin (Ciba)
Ritalin-SR (Ciba)
TYPE OF DRUG
Adrenergic
INGREDIENT
methylphenidate
DOSAGE FORMS
Tablets (5 mg, 10 mg, and 20 mg)
Sustained-release tablets (20 mg)
STORAGE
Methylphenidate should be stored at room temperature in tightly closed, light-resistant containers.

USES

Methylphenidate is a central nervous system (brain and spinal cord) stimulant that increases mental alertness and decreases fatigue. It is used in the treatment of narcolepsy (a disorder involving uncontrollable desires to sleep or actual sleep attacks that occur in a rapid and unpredictable manner), mild depression, and abnormal behavioral syndrome in children (hyperkinetic syndrome or attention deficit disorder). The way this medication works in abnormal behavioral syndrome in children is not clearly understood.

TREATMENT

In order to avoid stomach upset, you can take methylphenidate with food or with a full glass of water or milk (unless your doctor directs you to do otherwise).

If methylphenidate is being used to treat narcolepsy or abnormal behavioral syndrome in children, the first dose should be taken soon after awakening.

In order to avoid difficulty in falling asleep, the last dose of the regular tablets should be taken four to six hours before bedtime each day (the sustained-release tablets should be taken at least eight hours before bedtime).

The sustained-release tablets should be swallowed whole. Chewing, crushing, or breaking these tablets destroys their sustained-release activity and may increase the side effects.

If you miss a dose, take the missed dose as soon as possible, unless it is almost time for your next dose. In that case, do not take the missed dose; just return to your regular dosing schedule. Do not double the next dose of methylphenidate.

SIDE EFFECTS

Minor. Abdominal pain, dizziness, drowsiness, dry mouth, headache, insomnia, loss of appetite, nausea, nervousness, vomiting, or weakness. These side effects should disappear as your body adjusts to the medication.

Dry mouth can be relieved by sucking on ice chips or a piece of hard candy or by chewing sugarless gum.

If you feel dizzy, sit or lie down for a while; get up from a sitting or lying position slowly; and be careful on stairs.

Major. Tell your doctor about any side effects you experience that are persistent or particularly bothersome. IT IS ESPECIALLY IMPORTANT TO TELL YOUR DOCTOR about chest pain, fever, hair loss, hallucinations, hives, joint pain, mood changes, palpitations, rash, seizures, sore throat, uncoordinated movements, or bleeding or bruising.

INTERACTIONS

Methylphenidate interacts with several other types of medications:

1. Use of it within 14 days of using a monoamine oxidase (MAO) inhibitor (such as isocarboxazid, pargyline, phenelzine, tranylcypromine) can result in severe high blood pressure.

2. Methylphenidate can decrease the blood-pressure-lowering influence of antihypertensive medications (especially guanethidine).

3. Acetazolamide and sodium bicarbonate can decrease the elimination of methylphenidate from the body, thereby prolonging its action and increasing the risk of side effects.

4. Methylphenidate can decrease the elimination and increase the side effects of oral anticoagulants (blood thinners, such as warfarin), tricyclic antidepressants (such as amitriptyline, desipramine, imipramine, and nortriptyline), anticonvulsants (such as phenytoin, phenobarbital, and primidone), and phenylbutazone.

Before starting to take this medication, BE SURE TO TELL YOUR DOCTOR about any medications you are currently taking, especially any of those listed above.

WARNINGS

• Tell your doctor about unusual or allergic reactions you now have or have had to any medications, especially to methylphenidate.

• Tell your doctor if you have ever had epilepsy, glaucoma, high blood pressure, motor tics, Tourette's syndrome, anxiety, agitation, depression, or tension.

• Methylphenidate can mask the symptoms of extreme fatigue and can cause dizziness. Your ability to perform tasks that require alertness, such as driving a car or operating potentially dangerous machinery, may be decreased. Appropriate caution should, therefore, be taken. A child taking methylphenidate should be careful while engaging in physical activity.

• Before having surgery or any other medical or dental treatment, be sure to tell your doctor that you are taking this medication.

• Methylphenidate is related to amphetamine and may be habit-forming when taken for long periods of time (both physical and psychological dependence can occur). You should not increase the dosage of this medication or take it for longer than the prescribed time unless you first consult your doctor. It is also important that you not stop taking this medication abruptly; fatigue, sleep disorders, mental depression, nausea, vomiting, or stomach cramps or pain could occur. Your doctor may want to decrease the dosage gradually in order to prevent these side effects.

• Methylphenidate can slow growth in children. Therefore, if this medication is being taken by a child, your doctor may recommend drug-free periods during school holidays and summer vacations. Growth spurts often occur during these drug-free periods.

• Children may be more sensitive to certain side effects from this drug, such as loss of appetite, stomach pain, trouble sleeping, and weight loss.

• If cocaine is being used now or was used in the past, taking methylphenidate may cause severe nervousness, irritability, trouble sleeping, or possibly irregular heartbeat or seizures.

• Be sure to tell your doctor if you are pregnant. Effects of this drug during pregnancy have not been thoroughly studied in either humans or animals. Also tell your doctor if you are breast-feeding an infant. Small amounts of methylphenidate may pass into breast milk.

---

methylprednisolone (systemic)

BRAND NAMES (Manufacturers)
Medrol (Upjohn)
methylprednisolone (various manufacturers)
TYPE OF DRUG
Adrenocorticosteroid hormone
INGREDIENT
methylprednisolone
DOSAGE FORM
Tablets (2 mg, 4 mg, 8 mg, 16 mg, 24 mg, and 32 mg)
STORAGE
Store at room temperature in a tightly closed container.

USES

Your adrenal glands naturally produce certain cortisonelike chemicals. These chemicals are involved in various regulatory processes in the body (such as those involving fluid balance, temperature, and reactions to inflammation). Methylprednisolone belongs to a group of drugs known as adrenocorticosteroids (or cortisonelike medications). It is used to treat a variety of disorders, including endocrine and rheumatic disorders; asthma; blood diseases; certain cancers; eye disorders; gastrointestinal disturbances, such as ulcerative colitis; respiratory diseases; and inflammations, such as arthritis, dermatitis, and poison ivy. How this drug acts to relieve these disorders is not completely understood.

TREATMENT

In order to prevent stomach irritation, you can take methylprednisolone with food or milk.

If you are taking only one dose of this medication each day, try to take it before 9:00 A.M. This will mimic the body's normal production of this type of chemical.

It is important to try not to miss any doses of methylprednisolone. However, if you do miss a dose of this medication, follow these guidelines:

1. If you are taking this medication more than once a day, take the missed dose as soon as possible and return to your regular schedule. If it is already time for the next dose, double the dose.

2. If you are taking this medication once a day, take the dose you missed as soon as possible, unless you don't remember until the next day. In that case, do not take the missed dose at all; just follow your regular schedule. Do not double the next dose.

3. If you are taking this drug every other day, take it as soon as you remember. If you missed the scheduled time by a whole day, take it when you remember, and then skip a day before you take the next dose. Do not double the dose.

If you miss more than one dose, CONTACT YOUR DOCTOR IMMEDIATELY.

SIDE EFFECTS

Minor. Dizziness, false sense of well-being, increased appetite, increased susceptibility to infections, increased sweating, indigestion, menstrual irregularities, nausea, reddening of the skin on the face, restlessness, sleep disorders, or weight gain. These side effects should disappear as your body adjusts to the medication.

Major. Tell your doctor about any side effects that are persistent or particularly bothersome. IT IS ESPECIALLY IMPORTANT TO TELL YOUR DOCTOR about abdominal enlargement; abdominal pain; acne or other skin problems; back or rib pain; bloody or black, tarry stools; blurred vision; convulsions; eye pain; fever and sore throat; growth impairment (in children); headaches; impaired healing of wounds; increased thirst and urination; mental depression; mood changes; muscle wasting; muscle weakness; nightmares; rapid weight gain (three to five pounds within a week); rash; shortness of breath; thinning of the skin; unusual bleeding or bruising; and unusual weakness.

INTERACTIONS

Methylprednisolone interacts with several other types of medications:

1. Alcohol, aspirin, and anti-inflammatory medications (diclofenac, diflunisal, fenoprofen, flurbiprofen, ibuprofen, indomethacin, ketoprofen, mefenamic acid, meclofenamate, naproxen, piroxicam, sulindac, or tolmetin) aggravate the stomach problems that are common with use of methylprednisolone.

2. The dosage of oral anticoagulants (blood thinners, such as warfarin), oral antidiabetic medications, or insulin may need to be altered when this therapy with systemic methylprednisolone is started or stopped.

3. The loss of potassium caused by methylprednisolone can lead to serious side effects in individuals taking digoxin. Thiazide diuretics (water pills) can increase the potassium loss caused by methylprednisolone.

4. Phenobarbital, phenytoin, rifampin, and ephedrine can increase the elimination of methylprednisolone from the body, thereby decreasing its effectiveness.

5. Oral contraceptives (birth control pills) and estrogen-containing drugs may decrease the elimination of this medication from the body, which can lead to an increase in its side effects.

6. Methylprednisolone can increase the elimination of aspirin and isoniazid, thereby decreasing the effectiveness of these two medications.

7. Cholestyramine and colestipol can chemically bind this medication in the stomach and gastrointestinal tract and prevent its absorption.

BE SURE TO TELL YOUR DOCTOR about any medications you are currently taking, especially any of those listed above.

WARNINGS

• Tell your doctor about unusual or allergic reactions you have had to any medications, especially to methylprednisolone or other adrenocorticosteroids (such as betamethasone, cortisone, dexamethasone, hydrocortisone, paramethasone, prednisolone, prednisone, and triamcinolone).

• Tell your doctor if you now have or if you have ever had bone disease, diabetes mellitus, emotional instability, glaucoma, fungal infections, heart disease, high blood pressure, high cholesterol levels, myasthenia gravis, peptic ulcers, osteoporosis, thyroid disease, tuberculosis, ulcerative colitis, kidney disease, or liver disease.

• To help avoid potassium loss while using this drug, take your dose with a glass of fresh or frozen orange juice or eat a banana each day. The use of a salt substitute also helps to prevent potassium loss. Check with your doctor before using a salt substitute.

• If you are using this medication for longer than a week, you may need to have your dosage adjusted if you are subjected to stress, such as serious infections, injury, or surgery. Discuss this with your doctor.

• If you have been taking this drug for more than a week, do not stop taking it suddenly. If it is stopped suddenly, you may experience abdominal or back pain, dizziness, fainting, fever, muscle or joint pain, nausea, vomiting, shortness of breath, or extreme weakness. Your doctor may therefore want to reduce the dosage gradually. Never increase the dosage or take the drug for longer than the prescribed time, unless you first consult your doctor.

• While you are taking methylprednisolone, you should not be vaccinated or immunized. This medication decreases the effectiveness of vaccines and can lead to overwhelming infection if a live-virus vaccine is administered.

• Before having surgery or medical or dental treatment, be sure to tell your doctor or dentist about this drug.

• Because this drug can cause glaucoma and cataracts with long-term use, your doctor may want you to have your eyes examined by an ophthalmologist periodically while undergoing treatment.

• If you are taking this medication for prolonged periods, you should wear or carry a notice or identification card stating that you are taking an adrenocorticosteroid.

• This medication can raise blood-sugar levels in diabetic patients. Blood-sugar levels should therefore be monitored carefully with blood or urine tests when this medication is being taken.

• Some of these products contain the color additive FD&C Yellow No. 5 (tartrazine), which can cause allergic-type reactions in certain susceptible individuals.

• Be sure to tell your doctor if you are pregnant. This drug crosses the placenta. Although studies in humans have not been conducted, birth defects have been observed in the fetuses of animals that were given large doses of this type of drug during pregnancy. Also tell your doctor if you are breast-feeding an infant. Small amounts of methylprednisolone are known to pass into breast milk and may cause growth suppression or a decrease in natural adrenocorticosteroid production in the nursing infant.

metoclopramide

BRAND NAMES (Manufacturers)
Maxolon (SmithKline Beecham)
metoclopramide (various manufacturers)
Octamide (Adria)
Reglan (Robins)
TYPE OF DRUG
Dopamine antagonist and antiemetic
INGREDIENT
metoclopramide
DOSAGE FORMS
Tablets (5 mg and 10 mg)
Oral concentrate (10 mg per 5-mL spoonful)
Oral syrup (5 mg per 5-mL spoonful)
STORAGE
Metoclopramide tablets and oral syrup should be stored at room temperature in tightly closed containers. Do not freeze the syrup form of this medication.

USES

This medication is used to relieve the symptoms associated with diabetic gastric stasis or gastric reflux and to prevent nausea and vomiting. Metoclopramide acts directly on the vomiting center in the brain to prevent nausea and vomiting. It also increases the movement of the stomach and intestines.

TREATMENT

To obtain the best results from treatment, you should take metoclopramide tablets or syrup 30 minutes before a meal and at bedtime.

Each dose of the syrup should be measured carefully with a specially designed 5-mL measuring spoon. An ordinary kitchen teaspoon is not accurate enough.

If you miss a dose of this medication, take the missed dose as soon as possible, unless it is almost time for the next dose.

In that case, do not take the missed dose at all; just return to your regular dosing schedule. Do not double the next dose of this medication.

SIDE EFFECTS

Minor. Diarrhea, dizziness, drowsiness, dry mouth, fatigue, headache, insomnia, nausea, restlessness, or weakness. These side effects should disappear as your body adjusts to the medication.

If you feel dizzy or light-headed, sit or lie down for a while; stand up slowly; and be careful on stairs.

To relieve mouth dryness, chew sugarless gum or suck on ice chips or a piece of hard candy.

Major. Tell your doctor about any side effects that are persistent or particularly bothersome. IT IS ESPECIALLY IMPORTANT TO NOTIFY YOUR DOCTOR about anxiety; confusion; depression; disorientation; involuntary movements of the eyes, face, or limbs; muscle spasms; rash; or trembling of the hands.

INTERACTIONS

Metoclopramide interacts with several types of drugs:

1. Concurrent use of metoclopramide with other central nervous system depressants (such as alcohol, antihistamines, barbiturates, muscle relaxants, narcotics, pain medications, phenothiazine tranquilizers, benzodiazepine tranquilizers, and sleeping medications) or with tricyclic antidepressants can cause extreme drowsiness.

2. Narcotic analgesics may block the effectiveness of metoclopramide.

3. Metoclopramide can block the effectiveness of bromocriptine. It can also decrease the absorption of cimetidine and digoxin from the gastrointestinal tract, decreasing their effectiveness.

4. Metoclopramide can increase the absorption of acetaminophen, tetracycline, levodopa, and alcohol.

5. Diabetic patients should know that dosage requirements of insulin may change when metoclopramide is being taken.

Before starting to take metoclopramide, BE SURE TO NOTIFY YOUR DOCTOR about any medications you are currently taking, especially any of those drugs that are listed above.

WARNINGS

• Tell your doctor about unusual or allergic reactions you have had to any medications, especially to metoclopramide, procaine, or procainamide.

• Before starting to take metoclopramide, be sure to tell your doctor if you now have or if you have ever had epilepsy, kidney disease, liver disease, intestinal bleeding or blockage, Parkinson's disease, or pheochromocytoma.

• If this drug makes you dizzy or drowsy, do not take part in any activities that require mental alertness, such as driving an automobile or operating potentially dangerous machinery or equipment.

• Be sure to tell your doctor if you are pregnant. Extensive studies in women during pregnancy have not been conducted. Also tell your doctor if you are breast-feeding an infant. Metoclopramide passes into breast milk.

---

metoprolol

BRAND NAME (Manufacturer)
Lopressor (Geigy)
TYPE OF DRUG
Beta-adrenergic blocking agent
INGREDIENT
metoprolol
DOSAGE FORM
Tablets (50 mg and 100 mg)
STORAGE
Metoprolol should be stored at room temperature in a tightly closed, light-resistant container.

USES

Metoprolol is used to treat high blood pressure and angina (chest pain) and to prevent additional heart attacks in heart attack patients. Metoprolol belongs to a group of medicines known as beta-adrenergic blocking agents or, as they are more commonly known, beta blockers. This group of medications works by controlling the nerve impulses that travel along certain nerve pathways.

TREATMENT

Metoprolol can be taken with a glass of water, with meals, immediately following meals, or on an empty stomach, depending on your doctor's instructions. Try to take the medication at the same time(s) each day.

Try not to miss any doses of this medicine. If you do miss a dose of the medication, take the missed dose as soon as possible. However, if the next scheduled dose is within eight hours (if you are taking this medicine only once a day) or within four hours (if you are taking this medicine more than once a day), do not take the missed dose of the medication at all; just return to your regular dosing schedule. Do not double the next dose.

It is important to remember that metoprolol does not cure high blood pressure, but it will help to control the condition as long as you continue to take it.

SIDE EFFECTS

Minor. Anxiety; cold hands or feet (due to decreased blood circulation to the skin, fingers, and toes); constipation; decreased sexual ability; diarrhea; difficulty in sleeping; drowsiness; dryness of the eyes, mouth, and skin; headache; nausea; nervousness; stomach discomfort; tiredness; or weakness. These side effects should disappear during treatment, as your body adjusts to the medicine.

If you are extra-sensitive to the cold, be sure to dress warmly during cold weather.

To relieve constipation, increase the amount of fiber in your diet (fresh fruits and vegetables, salads, bran, and whole-grain breads) and exercise more (unless your doctor directs you to do otherwise).

Plain, nonmedicated eye drops (artificial tears) may help to relieve eye dryness.

Chew sugarless gum or suck on ice chips or a piece of hard candy to relieve mouth or throat dryness.

Major. Tell your doctor about any side effects that you are experiencing that are persistent or particularly bothersome. IT IS ESPECIALLY IMPORTANT TO TELL YOUR DOCTOR about breathing difficulty or wheezing, confusion, dizziness, fever and sore throat, hair loss, hallucinations, light-headedness, mental depression, nightmares, numbness or tingling of the fingers or toes, rapid weight gain (three to five pounds within a week), reduced alertness, skin rash, swelling, or any unusual bleeding or bruising.

INTERACTIONS

Metoprolol interacts with several other types of medications:
1. Indomethacin, aspirin, or other salicylates may decrease the blood-pressure-lowering effects of beta blockers.
2. Concurrent use of beta blockers and calcium channel blockers or disopyramide can lead to heart failure or very low blood pressure.
3. Cimetidine and oral contraceptives (birth control pills) can increase the blood concentrations of metoprolol, which can result in greater side effects.
4. Alcohol, barbiturates, and rifampin can decrease the effectiveness of metoprolol.
5. Side effects may be increased if beta blockers are taken with clonidine, digoxin, epinephrine, phenylephrine, phenylpropanolamine, phenothiazine tranquilizers, prazosin, or monoamine oxidase (MAO) inhibitors. At least 14 days should separate the use of a beta blocker and the use of an MAO inhibitor.
6. Beta blockers may antagonize (work against) the effects of theophylline, aminophylline, albuterol, isoproterenol, metaproterenol, and terbutaline.
7. Beta blockers can also interact with insulin or oral antidiabetic agents, raising or lowering blood-sugar levels and masking the symptoms of low blood sugar.
8. The action of beta blockers may be increased if they are used with chlorpromazine, furosemide, or hydralazine, which may have a negative effect.
   BE SURE TO TELL YOUR DOCTOR about any medications you are currently taking, especially any listed above.

WARNINGS

• Tell your doctor if you have ever had unusual or allergic reactions to any drugs, especially to metoprolol or any other beta blocker (acebutolol, atenolol, carteolol, esmolol, labetalol, nadolol, penbutolol, pindolol, propranolol, or timolol).
• Tell your doctor if you now have or have ever had allergies, asthma, hay fever, eczema, slow heartbeat, bronchitis, diabetes mellitus, emphysema, heart or blood-vessel disease, kid-

ney disease, liver disease, thyroid disease, or poor circulation in the fingers or toes.

• You may want to check your pulse while taking this medication. If your pulse is much slower than your usual rate (or if it is less than 50 beats per minute), get in touch with your doctor. A pulse rate that is too slow may cause circulation problems.

• This medicine may affect your body's response to exercise. Make sure you discuss with your doctor a safe amount of exercise for your medical condition.

• It is important that you do not stop taking this medicine without first checking with your doctor. Some conditions may become worse when the medicine is stopped suddenly, and the danger of a heart attack is increased in some patients. Your doctor may want you to reduce gradually the amount of medicine you take before stopping completely to minimize the potential risks. Make sure that you have enough medicine on hand to last through vacations, holidays, and weekends.

• Before having surgery or any other medical or dental treatment, tell your doctor or dentist that you are taking this medication.

• Metoprolol can cause dizziness, drowsiness, light-headedness, or decreased alertness. Exercise caution while driving a car or using any potentially dangerous machinery.

• While taking this medicine, do not use any over-the-counter (nonprescription) allergy, asthma, cough, cold, sinus, or diet preparation without first checking with your pharmacist or doctor. Some of these medicines can result in high blood pressure when taken at the same time as a beta blocker.

• Be sure to tell your doctor if you are pregnant. Animal studies have shown that some beta blockers, when used in very high doses, can cause problems in pregnancy. Adequate studies have not been conducted in humans, but there has been some association between beta blockers used during pregnancy and low birth weight, as well as breathing problems and slow heart rate in newborn infants. However, other reports have shown no effects on newborn infants. Also tell your doctor if you are breast-feeding an infant. Although this medicine has not been shown to cause problems in breast-fed infants, some of the medicine may pass into breast milk, so caution is warranted.

metronidazole

BRAND NAMES (Manufacturers)
Flagyl (Searle)
MetroGel (Curatek)
metronidazole (various manufacturers)
Protostat (Ortho)
TYPE OF DRUG
Antibiotic and antiparasitic
INGREDIENT
metronidazole
DOSAGE FORMS
Tablets (250 mg and 500 mg)
Topical gel (0.75%)
STORAGE
Metronidazole should be stored at room temperature in a tightly closed, light-resistant container. The topical gel form of this medication should never be frozen.

USES

Metronidazole is used to treat a wide variety of infections, including infections of the vagina, urinary tract, lower respiratory tract, bones, joints, intestinal tract, and skin. It is also used topically to treat acne rosacea. It acts by killing bacteria or parasites.

TREATMENT

In order to avoid stomach irritation, you should take metronidazole with food or with a full glass of water or milk (unless your doctor directs you to do otherwise).

Metronidazole works best when the level of medicine in your bloodstream is kept constant. It is best, therefore, to take the doses at evenly spaced intervals day and night. For example, if you are to take three doses a day, the doses should be spaced eight hours apart.

Try not to miss any doses of this medication. If you do miss a dose, take the missed dose as soon as possible, unless it is almost time for the next dose. In that case, do not take the missed dose at all; just return to your regular dosing schedule. Do not double the next dose.

It is important to continue to take this medication for the entire time prescribed by your doctor (usually seven to 14 days), even if the symptoms disappear before the end of that period. If you stop taking the drug too soon, resistant bacteria and parasites are given a chance to continue growing, and the infection could recur.

SIDE EFFECTS

Minor. Abdominal cramps, constipation, decreased sexual interest, diarrhea, dizziness, dry mouth, headache, insomnia, irritability, joint pain, loss of appetite, metallic taste in the mouth, nasal congestion, nausea, restlessness, or vomiting. These side effects should disappear as your body adjusts to the medication.

To relieve constipation, increase the amount of fiber in your diet (fresh fruits and vegetables, salads, bran, and whole-grain breads), exercise, and drink more water (unless your doctor directs you to do otherwise).

If you feel dizzy, sit or lie down for a while; get up slowly from a sitting or lying position; and be careful on stairs.

To relieve mouth dryness, chew sugarless gum or suck on ice chips or a piece of hard candy.

Major. Tell your doctor about any side effects that are persistent or particularly bothersome. IT IS ESPECIALLY IMPORTANT TO TELL YOUR DOCTOR about confusion, convulsions, flushing, hives, itching, joint pain, loss of bladder control, mouth sores, numbness or tingling in the fingers or toes, rash, sense of pressure inside your abdomen, unexplained sore throat and fever, or unusual weakness. If your symptoms of infection seem to be getting worse rather than improving, you should contact your doctor.

INTERACTIONS

Metronidazole interacts with several other types of medications:

1. Concurrent use of alcohol and metronidazole can lead to a severe reaction (abdominal cramps, nausea, vomiting, headache, and flushing), the severity of which is dependent upon the amount of alcohol ingested.

2. Concurrent use of disulfiram and metronidazole can lead to confusion.

3. The effects of oral anticoagulants (blood thinners, such as warfarin) may be increased by metronidazole, which can lead to bleeding complications.

4. Barbiturates can increase the breakdown of metronidazole, which can decrease its effectiveness.

5. Cimetidine can decrease the breakdown of metronidazole, which can increase the chance of side effects.

BE SURE TO TELL YOUR DOCTOR about any medications you are currently taking, especially any of those listed above.

WARNINGS

• Tell your doctor about unusual or allergic reactions you have had to any medications.

• Before starting to take this medication, be sure to tell your doctor if you now have or if you have ever had blood disorders, a central nervous system (brain or spinal cord) disease, or liver disease.

• When metronidazole is used to treat a vaginal infection, sexual partners should receive concurrent therapy in order to prevent reinfection. In addition, sexual intercourse should be avoided or condoms should be used until treatment is completed.

• This medication has been prescribed for your current infection only. Another infection later on, or one that someone else has, may require different drug therapy. Therefore, you should not give your medicine to other people or use it for other infections, unless your doctor specifically directs you to do so.

• If this drug makes you dizzy, avoid tasks that require alertness, such as driving a car or operating potentially dangerous machinery.

• Before having surgery or any other medical or dental treatment, be sure to tell your doctor or dentist that you are taking this medication.

• Be sure to tell your doctor if you are pregnant. Although metronidazole appears to be safe, it does cross the placenta, and extensive studies in pregnant women have not been conducted. Also tell your doctor if you are breast-feeding an infant. Metronidazole passes into breast milk.

mexiletine

BRAND NAME (Manufacturer)
Mexitil (Boehringer Ingelheim)
TYPE OF DRUG
Antiarrhythmic
INGREDIENT
mexiletine
DOSAGE FORM
Capsules (150 mg, 200 mg, and 250 mg)
STORAGE
Mexiletine should be stored at room temperature in a tightly closed container. It should not be exposed to high temperatures.

USES

Mexiletine is used to treat arrhythmias (irregular heart rhythms). This medication works through the suppression of irregular heartbeats and the establishment of a more normal rhythm.

TREATMENT

Mexiletine can be taken with meals or an antacid to decrease stomach irritation.

Try to take mexiletine at the same times each day. This medication is most effective when the amount of the drug in your bloodstream is kept at a constant level. Mexiletine should therefore be taken at evenly spaced intervals day and night. For example, if you are supposed to take mexiletine three times per day, the doses should be spaced eight hours apart. Your doctor can determine the best dose of mexiletine for you by measuring the amount in your blood. You may need periodic blood tests for this reason.

If you miss a dose of this medication and remember within four hours (if you are taking it three times per day) or within six hours (if you are taking it two times per day), take the missed dose and then return to your regular dosing schedule. If more time than that has passed, do not take the missed dose; just return to your regular dosing schedule. Do not double the next dose.

SIDE EFFECTS

Minor. Abdominal pain, altered taste, changes in appetite, constipation, diarrhea, dizziness, dry skin, fatigue, fluid accumulation, headaches, heartburn, hiccups, hot flashes, light-headedness, nausea, nervousness, sleeping problems, slowed heart rate, sweating, vomiting, or weakness. These side effects should disappear as your body adjusts to the medication.

You may experience constipation when taking this drug. To relieve constipation, increase the amount of fiber in your diet (fresh fruits and vegetables, salads, bran, and whole-grain breads), exercise, and drink more water (unless your doctor directs you to do otherwise).

If you become dizzy, sit or lie down for a while; get up slowly from a sitting or reclining position; and be careful on stairs.

Major. Tell your doctor about any side effects that are persistent or particularly bothersome. IT IS ESPECIALLY IMPORTANT TO TELL YOUR DOCTOR about black or tarry stools, chest pain, confusion, coordination difficulties, depression, difficult or painful urination, fainting, fever, hair loss, impotence, palpitations, psychological changes, rash, ringing in the ears, seizures, shortness of breath, speech difficulties, tingling or numbness in the hands or feet, trembling of the hands, or visual disturbances.

INTERACTIONS

Mexiletine interacts with several other types of medications:
1. Acetazolamide, sodium bicarbonate, or high doses of antacids can decrease the elimination of mexiletine from the body, which can increase the risks of side effects.
2. Cimetidine can increase the blood levels of mexiletine, which can increase the risks of side effects.
3. Phenytoin, rifampin, and phenobarbital can decrease the blood levels of mexiletine, which can decrease its effectiveness.

Before starting mexiletine, BE SURE TO TELL YOUR DOCTOR about any medications you are currently taking, especially any of those listed above.

WARNINGS

• Tell your doctor about any unusual or allergic reactions you have had to any medications, especially to mexiletine.

• Before taking mexiletine, tell your doctor if you now have or if you have ever had heart block, heart failure, liver disease, low blood pressure, or seizures.

• If this drug makes you dizzy or light-headed, do not take part in any activity that requires alertness, such as driving an automobile.

• Before having surgery or any other medical or dental treatment, be sure to tell your doctor or dentist that you are taking mexiletine.

• Do not take any over-the-counter (nonprescription) asthma, allergy, sinus, cough, cold, or diet preparation without first checking with your pharmacist or doctor.

• Do not stop taking this drug without first consulting your doctor. Stopping antiarrhythmics abruptly may cause a serious change in the activity of your heart. Your doctor may, therefore, want to reduce your dosage gradually.

• Be sure to tell your doctor if you are pregnant. Although mexiletine appears to be safe in animals, studies in pregnant women have not been conducted. Also tell your doctor if you are breast-feeding an infant. Small amounts of mexiletine pass into human breast milk.

---

miconazole (vaginal)

BRAND NAMES (Manufacturers)
Monistat 3* (Ortho)
Monistat 7* (Ortho)
Monistat Dual-Pak* (Ortho)
*Available without a prescription.
TYPE OF DRUG
Vaginal antifungal agent
INGREDIENT
miconazole
DOSAGE FORMS
Vaginal cream (2%)
Vaginal suppositories (100 mg and 200 mg)
STORAGE
Store at room temperature in a tightly closed container, out of reach of children and pets.

USES

Miconazole is used to treat fungal infections of the vagina. This medication is an antifungal agent that prevents the growth and multiplication of the yeastlike fungus, Candida.

TREATMENT

Miconazole vaginal cream and suppositories are packaged with detailed directions for use. Follow these instructions carefully. An applicator will probably be provided.

You should wash the vaginal area thoroughly prior to inserting the cream or suppository.

If you begin to menstruate while being treated with miconazole, continue with your regular dosing schedule.

If you miss a dose, insert the missed dose as soon as possible. However, if you do not remember until the following day, do not insert the missed dose at all; just return to your regular dosing schedule. Do not double the dose.

It is important to continue to insert this medication for the entire time prescribed by your doctor, even if the symptoms disappear before the end of that time. If you stop using the drug too soon, your infection could recur.

Usually, one three-day or one seven-day course of miconazole is sufficient. However, it may be repeated if your doctor determines that Candida is still causing your infection.

SIDE EFFECTS

Minor. You may experience vaginal burning, itching, or irritation when this drug is inserted. This sensation should disappear as your body adjusts to the medication.

Do not treat any side effects that occur in the area of the infection unless you first consult your doctor.

Major. Tell your doctor about any side effects that are persistent or particularly bothersome. IT IS ESPECIALLY IMPORTANT TO TELL YOUR DOCTOR about headache, hives, pelvic cramps, or skin rash.

INTERACTIONS

Miconazole (vaginal) does not interact with other medications if it is used according to directions.

WARNINGS

• Tell your doctor about unusual or allergic reactions you have had to any medications, especially to miconazole.

• Tell your doctor if you have had other vaginal infections, especially if they have been resistant to treatment.

• To prevent reinfection, avoid sexual intercourse or ask your partner to use a condom until treatment is complete.

• There may be some vaginal drainage while you are using this medication; therefore, you may want to use a sanitary napkin or panty liner to prevent the staining of clothing.

• Wear cotton underpants rather than those made of nylon or other nonporous materials while being treated for a fungal infection of the vagina. In order to prevent reinfection, always wear freshly laundered underclothes.

• If there is no improvement in your condition, or if irritation in the area continues after several days of treatment, CONTACT YOUR DOCTOR. This medication may possibly be causing an allergic reaction, or it may not be effective against the organism that is causing your infection.

• Miconazole has been prescribed for your current infection only. Another infection later on, or one that someone else has, may require a different medication. You should not give your medication to other women or use it for other infections you might have, unless your doctor specifically directs you to do so.

• Be sure to tell your doctor if you are pregnant. Small amounts of miconazole have been shown to be absorbed from the vagina, so caution should be used when using this medication. In addition, your doctor may want to change the instructions on how you are to insert this medication if you are pregnant. Also tell your doctor if you are breast-feeding an infant. It is not known whether or not miconazole passes into breast milk.

---

minocycline

BRAND NAMES (Manufacturers)
Dynacin (Medicis)
Minocin (Lederle)
TYPE OF DRUG
Antibiotic

INGREDIENT
minocycline
DOSAGE FORMS
Capsules (50 mg and 100 mg)
Tablets (50 mg and 100 mg)
Oral suspension (50 mg per 5-mL spoonful, with 5%
   alcohol)
STORAGE
Minocycline should be stored at room temperature in tightly
closed, light-resistant containers. This medication should not
be refrigerated.

USES
Minocycline is used to treat a wide range of bacterial infections
and to prevent meningococcal meningitis. It acts by preventing the growth of bacteria. This drug kills susceptible bacteria, but it is not effective against viruses or fungi.

TREATMENT
To avoid stomach upset, you can take this medication with
food (unless your doctor directs you to do otherwise).

The suspension form of this medication should be shaken
well just before measuring each dose. The contents tend to
settle on the bottom of the bottle, so it is necessary to shake the
container to distribute the ingredients evenly and equalize
the doses. Each dose should be measured carefully with a
specially designed 5-mL measuring spoon. An ordinary kitchen
teaspoon is not accurate enough.

Minocycline works best when the level of medicine in your
bloodstream is kept constant. It is best, therefore, to take the
doses at evenly spaced intervals day and night. For example,
if you are to take two doses a day, the doses should be spaced
12 hours apart.

If you miss a dose of this medication, take the missed dose
immediately. However, if you do not remember to take the
missed dose until it is almost time for your next dose, take it;
space the following dose about halfway through the regular
interval between doses; then return to your regular dosing
schedule. Try not to skip any doses.

It is important to continue to take this medication for the
entire time prescribed by your doctor, even if the symptoms
disappear before the end of that period. If you stop taking the

drug too soon, resistant bacteria are given a chance to continue growing, and the infection could recur.

SIDE EFFECTS

Minor. Diarrhea, dizziness, headache, light-headedness, loss of appetite, nausea, nail discoloration, stomach cramps and upset, or vomiting. These side effects should disappear as your body adjusts to the medication.

Minocycline can increase your sensitivity to sunlight. You should therefore try to avoid prolonged exposure to sunlight and sunlamps. Wear protective clothing and sunglasses, and use an effective sunscreen.

If you feel dizzy or light-headed, sit or lie down for a while; get up from a sitting or lying position slowly; and be careful on stairs.

Major. Tell your doctor about any side effects that are persistent or particularly bothersome. IT IS ESPECIALLY IMPORTANT TO TELL YOUR DOCTOR about darkened tongue, difficulty in breathing, joint pain, mouth irritation, rash, rectal or vaginal itching, sore throat and fever, unusual bleeding or bruising, or yellowing of the eyes or skin. And if your symptoms of infection seem to be getting worse rather than improving, you should contact your doctor.

INTERACTIONS

Minocycline interacts with several other types of medications:
1. It can increase the absorption of digoxin, which may lead to digoxin toxicity.
2. The gastrointestinal side effects (nausea, vomiting, and stomach upset) of theophylline may be increased by minocycline.
3. The dosage of oral anticoagulants (blood thinners, such as warfarin) may need to be adjusted when this medication is started.
4. Minocycline may decrease the effectiveness of oral contraceptives (birth control pills), and pregnancy could result. You should therefore use a different or additional form of birth control while taking minocycline. Discuss this matter with your doctor.
5. Antacids, calcium channel blockers, and iron may decrease the effects of this drug if they are taken at the same time. Two to three hours should separate doses of these medications and minocycline.

BE SURE TO TELL YOUR DOCTOR about any medications you are currently taking.

WARNINGS

• Tell your doctor about unusual or allergic reactions you have had to any medications, especially to minocycline or to oxytetracycline, doxycycline, or tetracycline.

• Tell your doctor if you now have or if you have ever had kidney or liver disease.

• Minocycline can cause dizziness or light-headedness. Your ability to perform tasks that require alertness, such as driving a car or operating potentially dangerous machinery, may be decreased. Appropriate caution should, therefore, be taken.

• Minocycline can affect tests for syphilis; tell your doctor you are taking this medication if you are also being treated for this disease.

• Make sure that your prescription for this medication is marked with the expiration date. The drug should be discarded after the expiration date. If the drug is used after this date, serious side effects (especially to the kidneys) could result.

• This medication has been prescribed for your current infection only. Another infection later on, or one that someone else has, may require a different medicine. You should not give your medicine to other people or use it for other infections, unless your doctor specifically directs you to do so.

• Be sure to tell your doctor if you are pregnant or if you are breast-feeding an infant. Minocycline crosses the placenta and passes into breast milk. In addition, it should not be used for infants or for children less than eight years of age. This drug can cause permanent discoloration of the teeth and can inhibit tooth and bone growth if used during their development.

---

minoxidil (topical)

BRAND NAME (Manufacturer)
Rogaine* (Upjohn)
*Available over the counter (without a prescription)
TYPE OF DRUG
Hair growth stimulant

INGREDIENT
minoxidil
DOSAGE FORM
2% solution (20 mg per mL); 60-mL and 180-mL bottle
STORAGE
Minoxidil topical solution should be stored at room temperature in a tightly closed container. It should be kept away from heat or flames because the solution is flammable (it contains alcohol).

USES
Minoxidil topical solution is used to stimulate hair growth in people who are balding. The drug seems to exert its maximum effect at the crown of the head. The exact way that it works is not known, but it may stimulate hair growth by improving the blood supply to the hair follicles.

TREATMENT
Before applying topical minoxidil, the hair and scalp should be dry. To avoid skin irritation from the alcohol contained in this product, wait at least 30 minutes after washing or shaving before applying this medication to the scalp. The evening dose of medication should be applied at least 30 minutes before bedtime for more complete absorption of the medication into the scalp. This will prevent the medication from rubbing onto the pillowcase.

Complete directions for the use of this product are supplied with the medication. Be sure to ask your doctor or pharmacist for these directions, and follow the instructions carefully. The solution is packaged with three applicators that can be used to apply the solution directly to the scalp. Apply 1 mL to the balding areas of the scalp twice daily (in the morning and evening), unless directed to do otherwise by your doctor. Six sprays with either of the spray applicators deliver a 1-mL dose. The rub-on applicator delivers a 1-mL dose when the bottle is squeezed to fill the top chamber to the black line. The full amount in the chamber should then be applied to the scalp. The total daily dosage should not exceed 2 mL. If fingertips are used to apply the solution, wash your hands afterward to avoid spreading the medication.

Two daily applications for up to four months may be required before evidence of hair regrowth is observed. The onset and degree of hair regrowth may be variable among different patients treated with this medicine. If hair regrowth occurs, two daily applications are necessary for additional and continued hair growth (unless your doctor directs otherwise).

First hair growth may be soft, downy, colorless hair that is barely visible. After further treatment, the new hair should be the same color and thickness as the other hair on the scalp.

If one or two applications are missed, restart twice daily applications and return to the usual schedule. Do not attempt to make up for missed doses.

It is important to continue to use this medication for the entire time prescribed by your doctor, even if hair growth does not appear within several months.

If there is no hair growth after at least four months or more, consult with your doctor, as this medication may not be effective for you.

SIDE EFFECTS

Minor. Diarrhea, dry skin/scalp, flaking, itching, local redness, nausea, or vomiting. These side effects should disappear as your body adjusts to the medication.

Major. Tell your doctor about any side effects that are persistent or particularly bothersome. IT IS ESPECIALLY IMPORTANT TO TELL YOUR DOCTOR about back pain, chest pain, cough, cold, dizziness, faintness, light-headedness, rapid heart beat, fluid retention, headache, weight gain, or worsening of hair loss.

INTERACTIONS

Use of abrasive or medicated cleansers, medicated cleaners, medicated cosmetics, or any topical, alcohol-containing preparations (such as after-shave lotions or cologne) along with topical minoxidil solution can result in excessive skin dryness and irritation.

WARNINGS

• Tell your doctor about unusual or allergic reactions you have had to any medications, especially to minoxidil.

• Before starting to use this medication, be sure to tell your doctor if you now have or if you have ever had heart disease, high blood pressure, or skin problems such as dermatitis or local abrasions.

• Because this medication contains alcohol, it can cause skin irritation to sensitive areas. You should therefore avoid getting this medication in your eyes, nose, or mouth, or in areas surrounding scratches or burns.
• Do not apply minoxidil to other areas of the body because absorption of the drug may be increased and the risk of side effects may become greater. Do not use along with other topical medication on your scalp, unless directed to do so by your doctor.
• Avoid inhaling the spray mist.
• If treatment is stopped, new hair growth will probably be shed within a few months.
• More frequent applications or use of larger doses (more than 1 mL twice daily) will not speed up the process of hair growth and may increase the possibility of side effects.

misoprostol

BRAND NAME (Manufacturer)
Cytotec (Searle)
TYPE OF DRUG
Prostaglandin E1 analog (gastrointestinal protective agent)
INGREDIENT
misoprostol
DOSAGE FORM
Tablets (100 mcg and 200 mcg)
STORAGE
Store at room temperature in a tightly closed container.

USES
Misoprostol is used to prevent stomach ulcers in people who are taking nonsteroidal anti-inflammatory drugs (NSAIDs). NSAIDs (such as aspirin, carprofen, diclofenac, diflunisal, fenoprofen, flurbiprofen, ibuprofen, indomethacin, ketoprofen, meclofenamate, mefenamic acid, naproxen, phenylbutazone, piroxicam, salsalate, sulindac, and tolmetin) are frequently prescribed to treat pain or arthritis. NSAIDs have been shown to cause ulcers in some patients. Misoprostol belongs to a group of chemicals called prostaglandins, which protect the stomach by decreasing the secretion of acid and increasing the secretion of mucus.

TREATMENT

This medication should be taken with meals and at bedtime, unless otherwise directed by your doctor.

If you miss a dose, take the missed dose as soon as possible, unless it is almost time for your next dose. If that is the case, do not take the missed dose at all; just return to your regular dosing schedule. Never take a double dose.

Misoprostol treatment should continue for as long as you take a NSAID. This medication should be taken exactly as prescribed by your doctor.

SIDE EFFECTS

Minor. Abdominal pain, change in appetite, constipation, diarrhea, flatulence, gas and bloating, heartburn, menstrual cramps and abnormal bleeding, nausea, or vomiting.

Major. Tell your doctor about any side effects that are persistent or particularly bothersome. IT IS ESPECIALLY IMPORTANT TO TELL YOUR DOCTOR ABOUT chest pain, difficulty in breathing, postmenopausal vaginal bleeding, or rash.

INTERACTIONS

Antacids decrease the absorption of misoprostol into the bloodstream. However, antacids do not appear to decrease the beneficial effects of misoprostol in preventing ulcers. Consult your doctor before using antacids with this product.

Before starting to take misoprostol, BE SURE TO TELL YOUR DOCTOR about any other medications you are currently taking.

WARNINGS

• Misoprostol should not be taken by anyone with a history of allergy to prostaglandins.
• Tell your doctor immediately if you develop a rash while taking this medication.
• Women should notify their doctors immediately if they experience any abnormal vaginal bleeding while taking this medication.
• Women of child-bearing age must use extreme caution not to become pregnant while taking misoprostol. This medication may cause miscarriage. Miscarriages caused by misoprostol may be incomplete, which could lead to potentially dangerous bleeding. ANY WOMAN WHO IS PREGNANT OR

PLANS TO BECOME PREGNANT SHOULD NOT TAKE MISO-
PROSTOL. If you are taking misoprostol and discover that you
are pregnant, stop taking the drug immediately and call your
doctor.
• Nursing mothers should not take misoprostol. The body con-
verts it to misoprostol acid, which can pass into breast milk
and cause diarrhea in the nursing infant.

mitotane

BRAND NAME (Manufacturer)
Lysodren (Bristol-Myers Oncology)
TYPE OF DRUG
Antineoplastic (anticancer drug)
INGREDIENT
mitotane
DOSAGE FORM
Tablets (500 mg)
STORAGE
Mitotane should be stored at room temperature in a tightly
closed, light-resistant container.

USES
This medication is used to treat cancer of the adrenal gland
and Cushing's syndrome (overactive adrenal gland) in patients
on whom surgery cannot be performed. Mitotane directly suppresses the activity of the adrenal gland.

TREATMENT
Initial therapy with mitotane often occurs in the hospital until
the dosage is stabilized. Mitotane is potent medication. The
dosage is usually adjusted to an individual's needs and tolerance. Be sure you understand your doctor's instructions on
how this medication should be taken.

Mitotane tablets can be taken either on an empty stomach
or, to reduce stomach irritation, with food or milk (unless your
doctor directs you to do otherwise).

Try not to miss any doses of this medication. If you do miss
a dose, take the missed dose as soon as possible, unless it is almost time for the next dose. In that case, do not take the

missed dose at all; just return to your regular dosing schedule. Do not double the next dose.

SIDE EFFECTS

Minor. Diarrhea, dizziness, drowsiness, loss of appetite, nausea, or vomiting. These side effects should disappear as your body adjusts to the medication. However, it is important to continue taking this medication despite the nausea and vomiting that may occur.

Mitotane can also cause hair loss (which is reversible when the medication is discontinued).

If you feel dizzy, sit or lie down for a while; get up slowly from a sitting or reclining position; and be careful on stairs.

Major. Tell your doctor about any side effects that are persistent or particularly bothersome. IT IS ESPECIALLY IMPORTANT TO TELL YOUR DOCTOR about blurred vision, depression, difficult or painful urination, fainting, flushing, lethargy, muscle aches, or skin rash.

INTERACTIONS

Mitotane interacts with several other types of medications:

1. Concurrent use of it with central nervous system depressants (such as alcohol, antihistamines, barbiturates, benzodiazepine tranquilizers, muscle relaxants, narcotics, pain medications, phenothiazine tranquilizers, and sleeping medications) or with tricyclic antidepressants can cause extreme drowsiness.

2. Mitotane can decrease the effectiveness of adrenocorticosteroids (cortisonelike medications).

BE SURE TO TELL YOUR DOCTOR about any medications you are currently taking, especially any of those listed above.

WARNINGS

• Tell your doctor about unusual or allergic reactions you have had to any medications, especially to mitotane.

• Before starting to take this medication, be sure to tell your doctor if you now have or if you have ever had chronic infections or liver disease.

• If this medication makes you dizzy, drowsy, or tired or blurs your vision, avoid any activity that requires alertness, such as driving a car or operating potentially dangerous machinery.

• Do not stop taking this medication unless you first check with your doctor. The effects of mitotane on the adrenal glands last several weeks after you stop taking this drug.

• Mitotane can impair your body's response to injury, stress, illness, and infection. If you experience injury, stress, illness, or infection while taking this medication or shortly after you stop taking it (within several weeks), check with your doctor. You may need to take supplemental adrenal hormone during this period.

• Before having surgery or any other medical or dental treatment, be sure to tell your doctor or dentist that you are taking this medication.

• Be sure to tell your doctor if you are pregnant. Extensive studies of mitotane in pregnant women have not been conducted. The risks should be discussed with your doctor. Also tell your doctor if you are breast-feeding an infant. It is not known whether mitotane passes into breast milk.

---

morphine

BRAND NAMES (Manufacturers)
morphine sulfate (various manufacturers)
MS Contin (Purdue-Frederick)
MSIR (Purdue-Frederick)
Oramorph SR (Roxane)
RMS (Upsher-Smith)
Roxanol (Roxane)
Roxanol SR (Roxane)
TYPE OF DRUG
Analgesic
INGREDIENT
morphine
DOSAGE FORMS
Capsules (15 mg and 30 mg)
Tablets (15 mg and 30 mg)
Sustained-release tablets (15 mg, 30 mg, 60 mg, and 100 mg)
Oral solution (10 mg and 20 mg per 5-mL spoonful, with 10% alcohol; 20 mg per mL; 100 mg per 5-mL spoonful)
Rectal suppositories (5 mg, 10 mg, 20 mg, and 30 mg)

STORAGE
Morphine tablets and oral solution should be stored at room
temperature in tightly closed, light-resistant containers. The
rectal suppositories should be stored in the refrigerator.

USES
Morphine is a narcotic analgesic that acts directly on the central nervous system (brain and spinal cord). It is used to relieve moderate to severe pain.

TREATMENT
In order to avoid stomach upset, you can take morphine with
food or milk. This medication works most effectively if you
take it at the onset of pain, rather than waiting until the pain
becomes intense.

The solution form of this medication can be mixed with
fruit juices to improve the taste. Measure each dose carefully
with a specially designed 5-mL measuring spoon or with the
dropper provided. An ordinary kitchen teaspoon is not accurate enough.

The sustained-release tablets should be swallowed whole.
Chewing, crushing, or crumbling the tablets destroys their
sustained-release activity and possibly increases the side effects.

To use the suppository form of this medication, remove the
foil wrapper and moisten the suppository with water (if the
suppository is too soft to insert, refrigerate it for half an hour or
run cold water over it before removing the wrapper). Lie on
your left side with your right knee bent. Push the suppository
into the rectum, pointed end first. Lie still for a few minutes. Try
to avoid having a bowel movement for at least an hour (to
give the medication time to be absorbed).

If you are taking this drug on a regular schedule and you
miss a dose, take the missed dose as soon as possible, unless
it is almost time for your next dose. In that case, do not take the
missed dose at all; just return to your regular dosing schedule. Do not double the next dose.

SIDE EFFECTS
Minor. Constipation, dizziness, drowsiness, dry mouth, false
sense of well-being, flushing, light-headedness, loss of ap-

petite, nausea, rash, or sweating. These side effects should disappear as your body adjusts to the medication.

If you are constipated, increase the amount of fiber in your diet (fresh fruits and vegetables, salads, bran, and whole-grain breads), exercise, and drink more water (unless your doctor directs you to do otherwise).

Chew sugarless gum or suck on ice chips to reduce mouth dryness.

If you feel dizzy or light-headed, sit or lie down for a while; get up from a sitting or lying position slowly; and be careful on stairs.

Major. Tell your doctor about any side effects that are persistent or particularly bothersome. IT IS ESPECIALLY IMPORTANT TO TELL YOUR DOCTOR about anxiety, difficulty in breathing, excitation, fainting, fatigue, painful or difficult urination, palpitations, restlessness, sore throat and fever, tremors, or weakness.

INTERACTIONS

Morphine will interact with several other types of medications:

1. Concurrent use of it with other central nervous system depressants (such as alcohol, antihistamines, barbiturates, benzodiazepine tranquilizers, muscle relaxants, and phenothiazine tranquilizers) or with tricyclic antidepressants can cause extreme drowsiness.

2. A monoamine oxidase (MAO) inhibitor taken within 14 days of this medication can lead to unpredictable and severe side effects.

3. The depressant effects of morphine can be dangerously increased by chloral hydrate, glutethimide, beta blockers, and furazolidone.

4. The combination of cimetidine and morphine can cause confusion, disorientation, and shortness of breath.

BE SURE TO TELL YOUR DOCTOR about any medications you are currently taking, especially any of those listed above.

WARNINGS

• Tell your doctor about unusual or allergic reactions you have had to any medications, especially to morphine or to other narcotic analgesics (such as codeine, hydrocodone, hydromorphone, meperidine, methadone, oxycodone, and propoxyphene).

• Tell your doctor if you now have or if you have ever had acute abdominal conditions, asthma, brain disease, colitis, epilepsy, gallstones or gallbladder disease, head injuries, heart disease, kidney disease, liver disease, lung disease, mental illness, emotional disorders, enlarged prostate gland, thyroid disease, or urethral stricture.

• If this drug makes you dizzy or drowsy, do not take part in any activity that requires alertness, such as driving a car or operating potentially dangerous machinery.

• Before having surgery or any other medical or dental treatment, be sure to tell your doctor or dentist that you are taking this medication.

• Morphine has the potential for abuse and must be used with caution. Usually, it should not be taken for longer than ten days (unless your doctor directs you otherwise). Tolerance develops quickly; do not increase the dosage or stop taking the drug abruptly, unless you first consult your doctor. If you have been taking large amounts of this drug, or if you have been taking it for long periods of time, you may experience a withdrawal reaction (muscle aches, diarrhea, gooseflesh, runny nose, nausea, vomiting, shivering, trembling, stomach cramps, sleep disorders, irritability, weakness, excessive yawning, or sweating) when you stop taking it. Your doctor may therefore want to reduce the dosage gradually.

• Be sure to tell your doctor if you are pregnant. The effects of this medication during the early stages of pregnancy have not been thoroughly studied in humans. However, regular use of morphine in large doses during the later stages of pregnancy can result in addiction of the fetus, leading to withdrawal symptoms (irritability, excessive crying, tremors, fever, vomiting, diarrhea, sneezing, or excessive yawning) at birth. Also tell your doctor if you are breast-feeding an infant. Small amounts of this medication may pass into breast milk and cause excessive drowsiness in the nursing infant.

---

nabumetone

BRAND NAME (Manufacturer)
Relafen (SmithKline Beecham)

TYPE OF DRUG
Nonsteroidal anti-inflammatory analgesic
INGREDIENT
nabumetone
DOSAGE FORM
Tablet (500 mg and 750 mg)
STORAGE
Store nabnumetone tablets in a tightly closed, light-resistant container at room temperature. This medication should not be refrigerated.

USES

Nabumetone is used to treat the inflammation (pain, swelling, stiffness) of rheumatoid arthritis and osteoarthritis. Nabumetone has been shown to block production of certain body chemicals, called prostaglandins, that may trigger pain.

TREATMENT

Nabumetone may be taken on an empty stomach or with food or milk. Your doctor may direct you to take the medication with food or antacids to decrease stomach upset.

To relieve your arthritis symptoms, you must take nabumetone regularly as directed by your doctor. It may take up to two weeks before you feel the full effects of this medication. Nabumetone does not cure arthritis, but it will help to control the condition as long as you continue to take it.

It is important to continue to take nabumetone on schedule and not to miss any doses. If you do miss a dose, take it as soon as possible, unless it is almost time for your next dose. In that case, don't take the missed dose at all; just return to your regular dosing schedule. Do not double the next dose.

SIDE EFFECTS

Minor. Bloating, constipation, diarrhea, difficulty in sleeping, dizziness, drowsiness, headache, heartburn, indigestion, light-headedness, loss of appetite, nausea, nervousness, soreness of the mouth, unusual sweating, or vomiting. As your body adjusts to the drug, these side effects should disappear.

To relieve constipation, increase the amount of fiber in your diet (fresh fruits and vegetables, salads, bran, and whole-grain breads), exercise, and drink more water (unless your doctor directs you to do otherwise).

If you become dizzy or light-headed, sit or lie down for a while; get up slowly from a sitting or reclining position; and be careful on stairs.

Major. If any side effects are persistent or particularly bothersome, you should report them to your doctor. IT IS ESPECIALLY IMPORTANT TO TELL YOUR DOCTOR about bloody or black, tarry stools; blurred vision; confusion; depression; difficult or painful urination; palpitations; a problem with hearing; ringing or buzzing in your ears; skin rash, hives, or itching; stomach pain; swelling of the feet; tightness in the chest; unexplained sore throat and fever; unusual bleeding or bruising; unusual fatigue or weakness; unusual weight gain; wheezing or difficulty in breathing; or yellowing of the eyes or skin.

INTERACTIONS

Nabumetone interacts with several other types of medications:

1. Anticoagulants (blood thinners, such as warfarin) can lead to an increase in bleeding complications.

2. Aspirin, other salicylates, and other anti-inflammatory medications can increase stomach irritation. Aspirin may also decrease the effectiveness of nabumetone.

3. Nabumetone can interact with diuretics (water pills).

4. Probenecid can increase blood levels of nabumetone, which may increase the risk of side effects.

5. The action of beta blockers may be decreased by this drug.

BE SURE TO TELL YOUR DOCTOR about any medications you are currently taking, especially any of those listed above.

WARNINGS

• Before you start to take this medication, it is important to tell your doctor if you have ever had any unusual or allergic reactions to nabumetone or any of the other chemically related drugs (aspirin, other salicylates, ibuprofen, diclofenac, diflunisal, fenoprofen, indomethacin, ketoprofen, meclofenamate, mefenamic acid, naproxen, oxyphenbutazone, phenylbutazone, piroxicam, sulindac, or tolmetin).

• Tell your doctor if you now have or if you have ever had bleeding problems, colitis, stomach ulcers or other stomach problems, epilepsy, heart disease, high blood pressure, asthma, kidney disease, liver disease, mental illness, or Parkinson's disease.

• If nabumetone makes you dizzy or drowsy, do not take part in any activity that requires alertness, such as driving a car or operating potentially dangerous equipment.

• Because nabumetone can prolong bleeding time, tell your doctor or dentist that you are taking this drug before having surgery or other medical or dental treatment.

• Stomach problems are more likely to occur if you take aspirin regularly or drink alcohol while being treated with this medication. This should be avoided (unless your doctor directs you to do otherwise).

• The elderly may be at increased risk for experiencing side effects from this drug.

• Be sure to tell your doctor if you are pregnant. This type of medication can cause unwanted effects on the heart of, or the blood flow to, the fetus. Studies in animals have shown that this type of medicine, if taken late in pregnancy, may increase the length of pregnancy, prolong labor, or cause other problems during delivery. Also tell your doctor if you are breast-feeding an infant. Small amounts of nabumetone have been known to pass into breast milk.

---

naproxen

BRAND NAMES (Manufacturers)
Aleve* (Procter & Gamble)
Anaprox (Syntex)
Anaprox DS (Syntex)
Naprosyn (Syntex)
* Available over the counter (without a prescription)
TYPE OF DRUG
Nonsteroidal anti-inflammatory analgesic
INGREDIENT
naproxen (Naprosyn)
naproxen as the sodium salt (Aleve and Anaprox)
DOSAGE FORMS
Tablets (225 mg [Aleve]; 250 mg, 375 mg, and 500 mg [Naprosyn]; 275 mg and 550 mg [Anaprox])
Oral suspension (125 mg per 5-mL spoonful [Naprosyn])

STORAGE
This medication should be stored in a tightly closed container at room temperature, away from heat and direct sunlight.

USES
Naproxen is used to treat the inflammation (pain, swelling, and stiffness) of certain types of arthritis, gout, bursitis, and tendinitis. Naproxen is also used to treat painful menstruation. Naproxen has been shown to block the production of certain body chemicals, called prostaglandins, that may trigger pain. However, it is not yet fully understood how naproxen works.

TREATMENT
You should take this medication on an empty stomach 30 to 60 minutes before meals or two hours after meals, so that it gets into your bloodstream quickly. However, to decrease stomach irritation, your doctor may want you to take the medicine with food or antacids.

It is important to take naproxen on schedule and not to miss any doses. If you do miss a dose, take it as soon as possible, unless it is almost time for your next dose. In that case, do not take the missed dose at all; just return to your regular dosing schedule. Do not double the next dose.

If you are taking naproxen to relieve arthritis, you must take it regularly, as directed by your doctor. It may take up to four weeks before you feel the full benefits of this medication. Naproxen does not cure arthritis, but it will help to relieve the condition as long as you continue to take it.

SIDE EFFECTS
Minor. Bloating, constipation, diarrhea, difficulty in sleeping, dizziness, drowsiness, headache, heartburn, indigestion, lightheadedness, loss of appetite, nausea, nervousness, soreness of the mouth, unusual sweating, and vomiting. As your body adjusts to the medication, these side effects should disappear.

To relieve constipation, increase the amount of fiber in your diet (fresh fruits and vegetables, salads, bran, and whole-grain breads), exercise, and drink more water (unless your doctor directs you to do otherwise).

If you become dizzy, sit or lie down for a while; get up slowly from a sitting or reclining position; and be careful on stairs.

Major. Tell your doctor about any side effects that are persistent or particularly bothersome. IT IS ESPECIALLY IMPORTANT TO TELL YOUR DOCTOR about bloody or black, tarry stools; blurred vision; confusion; depression; palpitations; ringing or buzzing in the ears or a problem with hearing; shortness of breath or wheezing; skin rash, hives, or itching; stomach pain; sudden decrease in amount of urine; swelling of the feet; tightness in the chest; unexplained sore throat and fever; unusual bleeding or bruising; unusual fatigue or weakness; unusual weight gain; or yellowing of the eyes or skin.

INTERACTIONS

Naproxen interacts with several other types of medications:
1. Concurrent use of anticoagulants (blood thinners, such as warfarin) can lead to an increase in bleeding complications.
2. Aspirin, salicylates, or other anti-inflammatory medications can cause increased stomach irritation when used concurrently with naproxen.
3. Naproxen can decrease the elimination of lithium and methotrexate from the body, resulting in possible toxicity from these medications.
4. Naproxen may interfere with the blood-pressure-lowering effects of beta-blocking medications (such as acebutolol, atenolol, betaxolol, carteolol, esmolol, labetalol, metoprolol, nadolol, penbutolol, pindolol, propranolol, and timolol).
5. This medication can also interfere with the diuretic effects of furosemide and thiazide-type diuretics.
6. Probenecid can increase the amount of naproxen in the bloodstream when both drugs are being taken.

Before starting to take this medication, BE SURE TO TELL YOUR DOCTOR about any medications you are currently taking, especially any of those listed above.

WARNINGS

• Before you take this medication, it is important to tell your doctor if you have ever had unusual or allergic reactions to any medications, especially to naproxen or any of the other chemically related drugs (including aspirin, other salicylates, carprofen, diclofenac, diflunisal, fenoprofen, flurbiprofen, indomethacin, ketoprofen, meclofenamate, mefenamic acid, oxyphenbutazone, phenylbutazone, piroxicam, sulindac, or tolmetin).

• Before taking this medication, it is important to tell your doctor if you now have or if you have ever had bleeding problems, colitis, stomach ulcers or other stomach problems, asthma, epilepsy, heart disease, high blood pressure, kidney disease, liver disease, mental illness, or Parkinson's disease.

• If naproxen makes you dizzy or drowsy, do not take part in any activity that requires alertness, such as driving a car or operating potentially dangerous machinery.

• Because naproxen can prolong your bleeding time, it is important to tell your doctor or dentist that you are taking this drug before having surgery or any other medical or dental treatment.

• Stomach problems are more likely to occur if you take aspirin regularly or drink alcohol while being treated with this medication. You should avoid taking frequent doses of aspirin or drinking alcohol while undergoing treatment with this medication (unless your doctor tells you otherwise).

• Be sure to tell your doctor if you are pregnant. Naproxen may cause unwanted effects on the heart or blood flow of the fetus. Studies in animals have shown that taking naproxen late in pregnancy may increase the length of pregnancy, prolong labor, or cause other problems during delivery. Also be sure to tell your doctor if you are currently breast-feeding an infant. Small amounts of this medication have been shown to pass into breast milk.

---

neomycin, polymyxin B, and bacitracin or gramicidin combination (ophthalmic)

BRAND NAMES (Manufacturers)
AK-Spore (Akorn)
neomycin, polymyxin B, and bacitracin or gramicidin combination (various manufacturers)
Neomycin-Polymyxin-Gramicidin (Iolab)
Neosporin (Burroughs Wellcome)
TYPE OF DRUG
Ophthalmic antibiotic

INGREDIENTS
neomycin, polymyxin B, and bacitracin (ointment only) or
  gramicidin (drops only)

DOSAGE FORMS
Ophthalmic drops (1.75 mg neomycin, 10,000 units
  polymyxin B, and 0.025 mg gramicidin per mL)
Ophthalmic ointment (3.5 mg neomycin, 10,000 units
  polymyxin B, and 400 units bacitracin per gram)

STORAGE
The ophthalmic drops and ointment should be stored at room
temperature in tightly closed containers. This medication
should never be frozen.

USES
This medication combination is used to treat bacterial infections of the eye. It is an antibiotic combination that is effective
against a wide range of bacteria. It acts by preventing the production of nutrients that are required for growth of the infecting bacteria. This medication is not effective against infections caused by viruses or fungi.

TREATMENT
Wash your hands with soap and water before using this medication. In order to prevent contamination of the medication,
be careful not to touch the tube portion of the dropper, and
do not let the dropper touch your eye.

Note that the bottle of eye drops is not completely full. This
is to allow control of the number of drops dispensed. To apply
the eye drops, tilt your head back and pull down the lower
eyelid with one hand to make a pouch below the eye. Drop
the prescribed amount of medicine into this pouch and slowly
close your eyes. Try not to blink. Keep your eyes closed, and
place one finger at the corner of the eye next to your nose for
a minute or two, applying slight pressure (this is done to prevent loss of medication through the duct that drains fluid from
the surface of the eye into the nose and throat). Then wipe
away any excess with a clean tissue. If you don't think the
medicine got into the eye, repeat the process once. If you are
using more than one kind of eye drop, wait at least five minutes before applying the other medication(s).

Follow the same general procedure for the ointment. Tilt your head back, pull down your lower eyelid, and squeeze the ointment in a line along the pouch below the eye. Close the eye and place your finger at the corner of the eye near the nose for a minute or two. Do not rub your eyes. Wipe off excess ointment and the tip of the tube with clean tissues.

Since this medication is somewhat difficult to apply, you may prefer to have someone else apply it for you.

If you miss a dose of this medication, insert the drops or apply the ointment as soon as possible, unless it is almost time for the next application. In that case, do not use the missed dose; just return to your regular dosing schedule.

Continue using this medicine for the entire time prescribed by your doctor, even if the symptoms disappear. If you stop too soon, the infection could recur.

SIDE EFFECTS

Minor. Blurred vision, burning, or stinging. These side effects should disappear as your body adjusts to the drug.

Major. Tell your doctor about any side effects that are persistent or particularly bothersome. IT IS ESPECIALLY IMPORTANT TO TELL YOUR DOCTOR about disturbed or reduced vision and about itching, rash, redness, or swelling in or around your eyes (other than the original symptoms of your infection). If the infection seems to be getting worse rather than improving, contact your doctor.

INTERACTIONS

This medication should not interact with other medications as long as it is used according to directions.

WARNINGS

• Tell your doctor about unusual or allergic reactions you have had to any medications, especially to neomycin, bacitracin, polymyxin B, gramicidin, or any related antibiotics (such as amikacin, colistimethate, colistin, gentamicin, kanamycin, netilmicin, paromomycin, streptomycin, tobramycin, and viomycin).

• Tell your doctor if you now have or if you have ever had kidney disease, an injured cornea, inner ear disease, or myasthenia gravis.

• Do not use this medication for longer than ten consecutive days unless your doctor directs you to do so. Prolonged use of this drug may result in eye damage. If you need to use this medication for six weeks or longer, your doctor may want you to have an eye examination.

• This medication has been prescribed for your current infection only. Another infection later on may require a different medicine. You should not give your medicine to other people or use it for other infections, unless your doctor specifically directs you to do so.

• In order to allow your eye infection to clear, do not apply makeup to the affected eye.

• Tell your doctor if you are pregnant. The effects of this drug during pregnancy have not been studied.

---

nicotine gum

BRAND NAME (Manufacturer)
Nicorette* (Merrell Dow)
*Available over the counter (without a prescription)
TYPE OF DRUG
Stop-smoking aid
INGREDIENT
nicotine
DOSAGE FORM
Chewing gum (2 mg and 4 mg)
STORAGE
This medication should be kept in its original, child-resistant packaging until it is ready to be chewed.

USES

Nicotine gum is used as a temporary aid for smoking-cessation programs. It helps control the symptoms of nicotine withdrawal (such as irritability, headache, fatigue, and insomnia) and thus helps you to concentrate on overcoming the psychological and social aspects of your smoking habit.

TREATMENT

Use nicotine gum when you feel the urge to smoke. Keep the gum with you at all times. Place it where you usually keep your cigarettes. Whenever you feel that you want to smoke, put one piece of gum into your mouth. Chew the gum very slowly, until you taste it or feel a slight tingling in your mouth. As soon as you get the taste of the gum, stop chewing. After the taste or tingling is almost gone (after about one minute), chew slowly again until you taste the gum. Then stop chewing again. The gum should be chewed slowly for 30 minutes to release most of the nicotine. You should not expect the gum to give you the same quick satisfaction that smoking does. Do not drink caffeine-containing beverages while chewing a piece of nicotine gum.

Most people find that ten to 12 pieces of gum per day are enough to control their urge to smoke. Depending on your needs, you can adjust the rate of chewing and the time between pieces. Do not chew more than 30 pieces per day (unless your doctor directs you to do so).

The risk of smoking again is highest in the first few months, so it is important that you follow your smoking cessation program and use nicotine gum as directed during this period.

SIDE EFFECTS

Minor. Because of its nicotine content, the gum does not taste like ordinary chewing gum. It has a peppery taste. During the first several days of chewing the nicotine gum, you may experience mouth sores, jaw muscle aches, headaches, and increased salivation. These side effects should disappear as you continue to use the gum.

If you chew the gum too fast, you may feel effects similar to those experienced when people inhale a cigarette for the first time or when they smoke too fast. These effects include constipation, coughing, dizziness, dry mouth, gas pains, hiccups, hoarseness, insomnia, light-headedness, nausea, redness of the face, sneezing, stomach pain, stomach upset, throat and mouth irritation, and vomiting. Most of these side effects can be controlled by chewing the gum more slowly.

Major. If any of the side effects are persistent or particularly bothersome, report them to your doctor. IT IS ESPECIALLY IMPORTANT TO TELL YOUR DOCTOR about signs of too much nicotine (cold sweats, confusion, difficulty in breathing, disturbed hearing or vision, faintness, marked weakness, palpitations, or seizures).

If you accidently swallow a piece of gum, you should not experience adverse effects. The nicotine is released by chewing and is absorbed primarily in the mouth.

INTERACTIONS

Smoking cessation, with or without nicotine gum, may affect blood levels of certain medications (including aminophylline, caffeine, glutethimide, imipramine, pentazocine, phenacetin, propoxyphene, and theophylline).

Nicotine can reduce the diuretic effects of furosemide and lessen the blood-pressure-lowering effects of beta blockers.

BE SURE TO TELL YOUR DOCTOR about any medications you are currently taking, especially any listed above.

WARNINGS

• Tell your doctor if you have recently had a heart attack or if you have ever had heart palpitations or arrhythmias, angina, active temporomandibular (jaw) joint disease, cardiovascular disease, endocrine (hormone) disease, thyroid problems, pheochromocytoma, diabetes mellitus, high blood pressure, peptic ulcers, mouth or throat inflammation, or dental problems.

• Be sure to tell your doctor if you are pregnant. Nicotine (from the gum or from cigarette smoke) can cause fetal harm. Also tell your doctor if you are breast-feeding an infant. Small amounts of nicotine can pass into breast milk.

---

nicotine transdermal patch

BRAND NAMES (Manufacturers)
Habitrol (Basel)
Nicoderm (Marion Merrell Dow)
Nicotrol (Parke-Davis)
ProStep (Lederle)
TYPE OF DRUG
Stop-smoking aid
INGREDIENT
nicotine
DOSAGE FORM
Transdermal patches (5 mg, 7 mg, 10 mg, 11 mg, 14 mg, 15 mg, 21 mg, 22 mg)

STORAGE

This medication should be kept in its original, child-resistant packaging until the patch is ready to be applied to the skin. After use, the patch should be disposed of carefully, as the nicotine patches contain a large quantity of residual nicotine that may be harmful to children or pets.

USES

Nicotine patches are used as a temporary aid to smoking cessation programs. They help to control the symptoms of nicotine withdrawal (irritability, headache, fatigue, insomnia) and thus help you to concentrate on overcoming the psychological and social aspects of your smoking habit. Over time, the dose of nicotine delivered from the patch is lowered until you are gradually weaned off nicotine.

TREATMENT

IT IS IMPORTANT TO STOP SMOKING when therapy with nicotine patches is started. If you continue to smoke and use the nicotine patches, you increase the amount of nicotine in your blood and may be more likely to experience side effects. The nicotine patch should be applied daily to a hairless, clean, dry skin site on the upper trunk (chest, back, stomach) or upper outer arm. After 24 hours, the used patch should be removed and a new patch applied to a different site on your body. Try to change the patch at the same time every day, as this may prevent you from forgetting to apply a new patch. Depending on the type of nicotine patch your doctor prescribes and the severity of your withdrawal symptoms, you may use the patches daily for six to 12 weeks in order to help you stop smoking.

The risk of smoking again is considered highest in the first few months after finishing treatment with nicotine patches. Follow your smoking cessation program to prevent smoking "relapse."

SIDE EFFECTS

Minor. Abnormal dreams, diarrhea, difficulty sleeping, dry mouth, mood changes, skin rash, swelling, hives, burning or itching at the patch site, and sweating. These side effects should disappear as your body adjusts to the medication.

Major. If any of the side effects are persistent or particularly bothersome, report them to your doctor or pharmacist. IT IS ESPECIALLY IMPORTANT TO TELL YOUR DOCTOR about signs of too much nicotine (cold sweats, confusion, diarrhea, difficulty in breathing, disturbed hearing or vision, nervousness, nightmares, marked weakness, muscle palpitations, severe itching, or rash and seizures).

INTERACTIONS

Smoking cessation, with or without nicotine patches, may affect blood levels of certain medications (including aminophylline, caffeine, furosemide, imipramine, insulin, labetalol, pentazocine, prazosin, propoxyphene, and theophylline). Nicotine can also lessen the blood-pressure-lowering effects of beta blockers, such as propranolol. BE SURE TO TELL YOUR DOCTOR about any medications you are currently taking, especially those listed above.

WARNINGS

• Tell your doctor if you have recently had a heart attack. It is also important to tell your doctor if you now have or if you have ever had heart palpitations or irregular heartbeat, angina, heart disease, hormone imbalances, kidney problems, thyroid problems, pheochromocytoma, diabetes mellitus, high blood pressure, or stomach ulcers.
• Be sure to tell your doctor if you are pregnant. Nicotine (from the patches or from cigarette smoke) can cause fetal harm. Also tell your doctor if you are breast-feeding an infant. Small amounts of nicotine have been known to pass into breast milk.

---

nifedipine

BRAND NAMES (Manufacturers)
Adalat (Miles)
Procardia (Pfizer)
Procardia XL (Pfizer)
TYPE OF DRUG
Antianginal
INGREDIENT
nifedipine

DOSAGE FORMS
Capsules (10 mg and 20 mg)
Sustained-release tablets (30 mg, 60 mg, and 90 mg)
STORAGE
Nifedipine capsules should be stored at room temperature in a tightly closed, light-resistant container.

USES
This medication is used to treat various types of angina (chest pain). Nifedipine belongs to a group of drugs known as calcium channel blockers. By blocking calcium, nifedipine relaxes and prevents spasms of the blood vessels of the heart and reduces the oxygen needs of the heart muscle.

TREATMENT
Nifedipine should be taken on an empty stomach with a full glass of water one hour before or two hours after a meal (unless your doctor directs you to do otherwise). These capsules should be swallowed whole to obtain maximum benefit.

If you miss a dose of this medication, take the missed dose as soon as possible, unless it is within two hours of your next scheduled dose. In that case, do not take the missed dose at all; just return to your regular dosing schedule. Do not double the next dose.

SIDE EFFECTS
Minor. Bloating, cough, dizziness, flushing, gas, giddiness, headache, heartburn, heat sensation, nasal congestion, nausea, nervousness, sleep disturbances, sweating, or weakness. These side effects should disappear as your body adjusts to the medication.

If you feel dizzy or light-headed, sit or lie down for a while; get up slowly from a sitting or reclining position; and be careful on stairs. To avoid dizziness or light-headedness when you stand, contract and relax the muscles of your legs for a few moments before rising. Do this by pushing one foot against the floor while raising the other foot slightly, alternating feet so that you are "pumping" your legs in a pedaling motion.

Major. Tell your doctor about any side effects that are persistent or particularly bothersome. IT IS ESPECIALLY IMPORTANT TO TELL YOUR DOCTOR about blurred vision, chills, confusion, difficulty in breathing, fainting, fever, fluid retention, impotence, mood changes, muscle cramps, palpitations, rash, sore throat, or tremors.

INTERACTIONS

Nifedipine interacts with several other types of medications:

1. Nifedipine can increase the active blood levels of digoxin, warfarin, phenytoin, and quinine, which can lead to an increase in side effects.

2. The combination of nifedipine and beta blockers (acebutolol, atenolol, betaxolol, carteolol, esmolol, labetalol, metoprolol, nadolol, penbutolol, pindolol, propranolol, or timolol) can lead to a severe drop in blood pressure.

3. Nifedipine can lower quinidine blood levels, which can decrease its effectiveness.

4. Cimetidine can decrease the breakdown of nifedipine in the body. This breakdown can increase the risk of side effects of nifedipine.

Before starting to take nifedipine, BE SURE TO TELL YOUR DOCTOR about any medications you are currently taking, especially any of those listed above.

WARNINGS

• Tell your doctor about unusual or allergic reactions you have had to any medications, especially to nifedipine.

• Tell your doctor if you have ever had heart disease, kidney disease, low blood pressure, or liver disease.

• If this drug makes you dizzy or drowsy, do not take part in any activity that requires alertness, such as driving a car or operating potentially dangerous machinery.

• Before having surgery or any other medical or dental treatment, tell your doctor or dentist you are taking this drug.

• Do not stop taking this medication unless you first consult your doctor. Stopping this medication abruptly may lead to severe chest pain. Your doctor may, therefore, want to decrease your dosage gradually.

• Be sure to tell your doctor if you are pregnant. Nifedipine has been shown to cause birth defects in the offspring of animals that received large doses of it during pregnancy. This medication has not been studied in pregnant women. Also tell your doctor if you are breast-feeding an infant. It is not known whether nifedipine passes into breast milk.

nitrofurantoin

BRAND NAMES (Manufacturers)
Furadantin (Procter & Gamble Pharm.)
Macrobid (Procter & Gamble Pharm.)
Macrodantin (Procter & Gamble Pharm.)
nitrofurantoin (various manufacturers)
TYPE OF DRUG
Antibiotic
INGREDIENT
nitrofurantoin
DOSAGE FORMS
Capsules (25 mg, 50 mg, and 100 mg)
Capsules, dual-release (equivalent to 100 mg)
Oral suspension (25 mg per 5-mL spoonful)
STORAGE
Nitrofurantoin tablets, capsules, and oral suspension should be stored at room temperature in tightly closed, light-resistant containers. Never freeze this medication.

USES

Nitrofurantoin is used to treat bacterial infections of the urinary tract (bladder and kidneys). It kills susceptible bacteria by breaking down their cell membranes and interfering with their production of vital nutrients.

TREATMENT

In order to avoid stomach irritation and to increase the effectiveness of this drug, you can take it with a meal or with a glass of water or milk.

The tablets and capsules should be swallowed whole to obtain maximum benefit.

The oral-suspension form of this medication should be shaken well just before measuring each dose. The contents tend to settle on the bottom of the bottle, so it is necessary to shake the container in order to distribute the ingredients evenly and equalize the doses. Each dose of the medication should then be measured carefully with a specially designed 5-mL measuring spoon. An ordinary kitchen teaspoon is not accurate enough to measure your dose of the medication. You can then dilute the dose with water, milk, fruit juice, or infant's formula to mask the unpleasant taste.

Nitrofurantoin works best when the level of medicine in your urine is kept constant. It is best, therefore, to take the doses at evenly spaced invervals day and night. For example, if you are to take three doses a day, the doses should be spaced eight hours apart.

If you miss a dose of this medication, take the missed dose immediately. However, if you do not remember to take the missed dose until it is almost time for your next dose, take it; space the following dose about halfway through the regular interval between doses; then return to your regular dosing schedule. Try not to skip any doses.

It is important to continue to take this medication for the entire time prescribed by your doctor (usually seven to 14 days), even if the symptoms disappear before the end of that period. If you stop taking the drug too soon, resistant bacteria are given a chance to continue growing, and the infection could recur.

SIDE EFFECTS

Minor. Abdominal cramps, diarrhea, dizziness, drowsiness, loss of appetite, nausea, or vomiting. These side effects should disappear as your body adjusts to the medication.

Nitrofurantoin can cause your urine to change color (to rust yellow or brown). This is a harmless effect, but it may stain your underclothing. The color change will disappear after you stop taking the drug.

If this drug makes you dizzy, sit or lie down; get up slowly; and be careful on stairs.

Major. Tell your doctor about any side effects that are persistent or particularly bothersome. IT IS ESPECIALLY IMPORTANT TO TELL YOUR DOCTOR about chest pain, chills, cough, difficulty in breathing, fainting, fever, hair loss, irritation of the mouth, muscle aches, numbness or tingling, rash, rectal or vaginal itching, unusual bleeding or bruising, weakness, or yellowing of the eyes or skin. If your symptoms or infection seem to be getting worse rather than improving, you should contact your doctor.

INTERACTIONS

Nitrofurantoin interacts with other types of medications:

1. Probenecid and sulfinpyrazone can decrease the effectiveness and increase the side effects of nitrofurantoin.
2. Certain antacids (magnesium trisilicate) can decrease the absorption of nitrofurantoin from the gastrointestinal tract.

Before starting to take nitrofurantoin, BE SURE TO TELL YOUR DOCTOR about any medications you are currently taking, especially any of those listed above.

WARNINGS

• Tell your doctor about unusual or allergic reactions you have had to any medications, especially to nitrofurantoin, nitrofurazone, or furazolidone.
• Be sure to tell your doctor if you now have or if you have ever had anemia, diabetes mellitus, electrolyte abnormalities, glucose–6-phosphate dehydrogenase (G6PD) deficiency, kidney disease, lung disease, nerve damage, or vitamin B deficiencies.
• If this drug makes you dizzy or drowsy, do not take part in any activity that requires alertness, such as driving a car.
• Before surgery or other medical or dental treatment, tell your doctor or dentist you are taking this drug.
• People with diabetes should know that nitrofurantoin can cause false-positive results with some urine sugar tests (for example, Clinitest). Be sure to check with your doctor before adjusting your insulin dose.
• This medication has been prescribed for your current infection only. Another infection later on, or one that someone else has, may require a different medicine. You should not give your medicine to other people or use it for other infections unless your doctor specifically directs you to do so.
• Be sure to tell your doctor if you are pregnant. Nitrofurantoin should not be used close to term. It may cause anemia in the newborn infant. Nitrofurantoin should not be used in an infant less than one month of age. Also tell your doctor if you are breast-feeding an infant. Nitrofurantoin passes into the breast milk.

nitroglycerin (systemic)

BRAND NAMES (Manufacturers)
Nitrogard (Forest)

nitroglycerin (various manufacturers)
Nitroglyn (Kenwood)
Nitrong (Winthrop)
Nitrostat (Parke-Davis)
Nitro-Time (Time-Caps Labs)

TYPE OF DRUG
Antianginal

INGREDIENT
nitroglycerin

DOSAGE FORMS
Sustained-release tablets (2.6 mg and 6.5 mg)
Sustained-release capsules (2.5 mg, 6.5 mg, 9 mg, and
    13 mg)
Sublingual tablets (0.15 mg, 0.3 mg, 0.4 mg, and 0.6 mg)
Buccal tablets, controlled release (1 mg, 2 mg, and 3 mg)
Oral spray (0.4 mg per dose)

STORAGE
Nitroglycerin tablets, capsules, and oral spray should be stored
in a tightly capped bottle in a cool, dry place.

The sublingual tablets should be kept in their original glass
container. A small, temporary supply of tablets can also be
stored in a stainless-steel container that is now available. The
pendant-type container, which can be worn around your neck,
is a convenient storage place for an emergency supply. Never
store them in the refrigerator or the bathroom medicine cabinet, because the drug may lose its potency.

USES

This medication is used to treat angina (chest pain).
Nitroglycerin is a vasodilator, which relaxes the muscles of
the blood vessels, causing an increase in the oxygen supply to
the heart.

The sublingual tablets and oral spray act quickly and can
be used to relieve chest pain after it has started. The oral tablets
and capsules do not act quickly; they are used to prevent chest
pain.

TREATMENT

You should take the sustained-release tablets or capsules with
a full glass of water on an empty stomach one hour before or
two hours after a meal. The tablets and capsules should be
swallowed whole. Chewing, crushing, or breaking them de-

stroys their sustained-release activity and possibly increases the side effects.

NEVER chew or swallow the sublingual or buccal tablets. The sublingual tablet and oral spray forms of the drug are absorbed directly through the lining of the mouth. The sublingual tablet should be allowed to dissolve under the tongue or against the cheek.

To use the spray, remove the plastic cover on the container. Then, without shaking the container, spray the medication onto or under the tongue. Try not to inhale the spray. Close your mouth after each spray, and try to avoid swallowing right away. Nitroglycerin spray loses its effectiveness if it is swallowed.

Take one tablet or one or two spray doses at the first sign of chest pain. Sit down while you are waiting for the medicine to take effect. Do not eat, drink, or smoke while nitroglycerin is in your mouth. Try not to swallow while nitroglycerin is dissolving, and do not rinse your mouth afterward. Sublingual nitroglycerin or nitroglycerin spray should start working in one to three minutes. If there is no relief, take another tablet in five minutes. IF YOU TAKE THREE TABLETS OR THREE SPRAY DOSES WITHOUT ANY SIGN OF IMPROVEMENT, CALL A DOCTOR IMMEDIATELY OR GO TO A HOSPITAL EMERGENCY ROOM. As a preventive measure, take a nitroglycerin sublingual tablet or a spray dose five or ten minutes before heavy exercise, exposure to high altitudes or extreme cold, or any other potentially stressful situation. Be sure to carry some nitroglycerin sublingual tablets or oral spray with you at ALL times.

The buccal tablet should be placed between the upper lip and the gum on either side of the front teeth or between the cheek and the gum. The tablet is held in place by a sticky gel seal that develops once the tablet is in contact with saliva. If you wear dentures, the tablet can be placed anywhere between the cheek and the gum. Avoid drinking hot liquids or touching the tablet with your tongue. This can cause the tablet to dissolve faster and could increase the risk of side effects. If the buccal tablet is swallowed by mistake, replace it with another tablet. Nitroglycerin buccal tablets lose their effectiveness when swallowed. Try not to take the buccal tablet at bedtime in order to avoid inadvertently swallowing and choking on the tablet while you are sleeping.

If you miss a dose of the sustained-release tablets or capsules, take the missed dose as soon as possible, unless it is more than halfway through the interval between doses. In that case, do not take the missed dose at all; just return to your regular dosing schedule. Do not double the next dose.

SIDE EFFECTS

Minor. Dizziness, flushing of the face, headache, light-headedness, nausea, vomiting, or weakness. These side effects should disappear as your body adjusts to the medication.

If you feel dizzy or light-headed, sit or lie down for a while; get up slowly from a sitting or reclining position; and be careful on stairs. To avoid dizziness or light-headedness when you stand, contract and relax the muscles of your legs for a few moments before rising. Do this by pushing one foot against the floor while raising the other foot slightly, alternating feet so that you are "pumping" your legs in a pedaling motion.

Acetaminophen may help to relieve headaches caused by this medication.

Major. Tell your doctor about any side effects that are persistent or particularly bothersome. IT IS ESPECIALLY IMPORTANT TO TELL YOUR DOCTOR about diarrhea, fainting, palpitations, rash, or sweating.

INTERACTIONS

Nitroglycerin can interact with other types of medications:

1. The combination of alcohol and nitroglycerin can lead to dizziness and fainting.

2. Nitroglycerin can increase the side effects of the tricyclic antidepressants.

Before starting to take nitroglycerin, BE SURE TO TELL YOUR DOCTOR about any medications you are currently taking, especially tricyclic antidepressants (such as imipramine, desipramine, amitriptyline, and doxepin).

WARNINGS

• Tell your doctor about unusual or allergic reactions you have had to any medications, especially to nitroglycerin or isosorbide dinitrate.

• Before starting to take this medication, be sure to tell your doctor if you now have or if you have ever had anemia, glaucoma, a head injury, low blood pressure, or thyroid disease or if you have recently had a heart attack.

• If this drug makes you dizzy or light-headed, do not take part in any activity that requires alertness, such as driving a car or operating potentially dangerous machinery.

• Before surgery or other medical or dental treatment, tell your doctor or dentist you are taking this drug.

• Tolerance may develop to this medication within one to three months. If it seems to lose its effectiveness, contact your doctor.

• You should not discontinue use of nitroglycerin (if you have been taking it on a regular basis) unless you first consult your doctor. Stopping the drug abruptly may lead to further chest pain. Your doctor may therefore want to decrease your dosage gradually.

• If you have frequent diarrhea, you may not be absorbing the sustained-release form of this medication. Discuss this with your doctor.

• While taking this medication, do not take any over-the-counter (nonprescription) asthma, allergy, sinus, cough, cold, or diet preparations unless you first check with your doctor or pharmacist. Some of these drugs decrease the effectiveness of nitroglycerin.

• The cotton plug should be removed when the bottle is first opened; it should not be replaced. The cotton plug absorbs some of the medication, decreasing its potency.

• Nitroglycerin is highly flammable. Do not use it in places where it might be ignited.

• Be sure to tell your doctor if you are pregnant. Although the systemic form of nitroglycerin appears to be safe, extensive studies in pregnant women have not been conducted. Also tell your doctor if you are breast-feeding an infant. It is not known whether nitroglycerin passes into breast milk.

nitroglycerin (topical)

BRAND NAMES (Manufacturers)
Deponit (Schwarz)
Nitro-Bid (Marion)
Nitrodisc (Searle)
Nitro-Dur (Key)

nitroglycerin (various manufacturers)
Nitroglycerin Transdermal System (Major)
Nitrol (Savage)
Nitrostat (Parke-Davis)
Transderm-Nitro (Summit)
TYPE OF DRUG
Antianginal
INGREDIENT
nitroglycerin
DOSAGE FORMS
Ointment (2%)
Transdermal system (the patch delivers 0.1 mg, 0.2 mg,
    0.3 mg, 0.4 mg, or 0.6 mg per hour)
STORAGE
Nitroglycerin ointment and patches should be stored at room
temperature in their original containers. The ointment con-
tainer should always be tightly capped.

USES

Nitroglycerin is used to prevent angina (chest pain). It is a vasodilator, which relaxes the muscles of the blood vessels, causing an increase in the oxygen supply to the heart. The ointment and patches do not act quickly—they should not be
used to treat chest pain that has already started.

TREATMENT

The ointment comes with an applicator with which the prescribed dosage can be easily measured and applied. Before
a new dose is applied, the previous dose should be thoroughly
removed. Each dose should be applied to a new site on the
skin. Do not rub or massage the ointment into the skin. Just
spread the ointment in a thin, even layer, covering an area of
about the same size each time. Avoid contact of the ointment
with other parts of the body, since it is absorbed wherever it
touches the skin. Either use plastic or rubber gloves to apply
the ointment, or wash your hands immediately after application. Cover the ointment only if you are directed to do so by
your doctor.

  The transdermal system (patches) allows controlled, continuous release of nitroglycerin. Patches are convenient and
easy to use. For best results, apply the patch to a hairless or
clean-shaven area of skin, avoiding scars and wounds. Choose

a site (such as the chest or upper arm) that is not subject to excessive movement. It is all right to bathe or shower with a patch in place. In the event that a patch becomes dislodged, discard and replace it. Replace a patch by applying a new one before removing the old one. This allows for uninterrupted drug therapy, and skin irritation is minimized since the site is changed each time. If redness or irritation develops at the application site, consult your physician. Do not trim or cut the patches. This alters the dose of the medication.

If you miss an application of this medication, apply the missed application as soon as possible, unless it is more than halfway through the interval between doses. In that case, do not apply the missed application at all; just return to your regular dosing schedule. Do not double the next dose.

SIDE EFFECTS

Minor. Dizziness, flushing of the face, headache, light-headedness, nausea, vomiting, or weakness. These side effects should disappear as your body adjusts to the drug.

If you feel dizzy or light-headed, sit or lie down for a while; get up slowly; and be careful on stairs. To avoid dizziness or light-headedness when you stand, contract and relax the muscles of your legs for a few moments before rising. Do this by pushing one foot against the floor while raising the other foot slightly, alternating feet so that you are "pumping" your legs in a pedaling motion.

If you are experiencing headaches, acetaminophen may help to relieve them slightly.

Major. Tell your doctor about any side effects that are persistent or particularly bothersome. IT IS ESPECIALLY IMPORTANT TO TELL YOUR DOCTOR about fainting, palpitations, rash, or sweating.

INTERACTIONS

Nitroglycerin can interact with other types of medications:

1. The combination of alcohol and nitroglycerin can lead to dizziness and fainting.

2. Nitroglycerin can increase the side effects of the tricyclic antidepressants.

Before starting to take nitroglycerin, BE SURE TO TELL YOUR DOCTOR about any medications you are currently taking, especially tricyclic antidepressants.

WARNINGS

• Tell your doctor about unusual or allergic reactions you have had to any medications, especially to nitroglycerin or isosorbide dinitrate.

• Before starting to take this medication, be sure to tell your doctor if you now have or if you have ever had anemia, glaucoma, a head injury, low blood pressure, or thyroid disease or if you have recently had a heart attack or have a heart condition.

• If this drug makes you dizzy or light-headed, do not take part in any activity that requires alertness, such as driving a car or operating potentially dangerous machinery. Be especially careful when going up and down stairs.

• Before having surgery or any other medical or dental treatment, be sure to tell your doctor or dentist that you are taking this medication.

• Tolerance to this medication may develop within one to three months. If it seems to lose its effectiveness, contact your doctor.

• You should not discontinue use of nitroglycerin unless you first consult your doctor. Stopping the drug abruptly may lead to further chest pain. Your doctor may therefore want to decrease your dosage gradually.

• While taking this medication, do not take any over-the-counter (nonprescription) asthma, allergy, sinus, cough, cold, or diet preparations unless you first check with your doctor or pharmacist. Some of these drugs decrease the effectiveness of nitroglycerin.

• Nitroglycerin is highly flammable. Do not use it in places where it might be ignited.

• Be sure to tell your doctor if you are pregnant. The safety of this drug during pregnancy has not been determined. Although this drug appears to be safe, extensive studies in pregnant women have not yet been conducted. Also tell your doctor if you are breast-feeding an infant. It is not known whether nitroglycerin passes into breast milk.

---

nizatidine

BRAND NAME (Manufacturer)
Axid (Lilly)

TYPE OF DRUG
Gastric-acid-secretion inhibitor
INGREDIENT
nizatidine
DOSAGE FORM
Capsules (150 mg and 300 mg)
STORAGE
Nizatidine capsules should be stored at room temperature in a tightly closed, light-resistant container.

USES
Nizatidine is used to treat duodenal and gastric ulcers. It is also used in the long-term treatment of excessive stomach-acid secretion and in the prevention of recurrent ulcers. In addition, nizatidine is used to treat gastroesophageal reflux (backflow of stomach contents into the esophagus), which can cause heartburn. Nizatidine works by blocking the effects of histamine in the stomach, which reduces stomach-acid secretion.

TREATMENT
You can take nizatidine either on an empty stomach or with food or milk.

Antacids can block the absorption of nizatidine. If you are taking antacids as well as nizatidine, separate the administration times by at least one hour.

The dosage of nizatidine depends on the specific condition you are treating.

If you miss a dose of the nizatidine, take the missed dose as soon as possible, unless it is almost time for the next dose. In that case, do not take the missed dose at all; just return to your regular dosing schedule. Do not double the next dose.

SIDE EFFECTS
Minor. Constipation, diarrhea, dizziness, excess uric acid in the blood, fatigue, headache, itching, nausea, stomach upset, or sweating. These side effects should disappear as your body adjusts to the medication.

If you are constipated, increase the amount of fiber in your diet (fresh fruits and vegetables, salads, bran, and whole-grain breads), exercise, and drink more water (unless your doctor directs you not to do so).

If you feel dizzy or light-headed, sit or lie down for a while; get up from a sitting or lying position slowly; and be careful on stairs.

Major. Tell your doctor about any side effects that are persistent or particularly bothersome. IT IS ESPECIALLY IMPORTANT TO TELL YOUR DOCTOR about confusion, decreased sexual ability, excessive fatigue, fever, increased heart rate, unusual bleeding or bruising, or weakness.

INTERACTIONS

Nizatidine can interact with other types of medications:

1. Avoid simultaneous administration of nizatidine with antacids.

2. When a high dose of aspirin is given with it, nizatidine can increase the blood level of aspirin in your body, causing harmful side effects.

3. The effectiveness of nizatidine may be decreased by cigarette smoking. Avoid smoking while taking this medication.

4. Nizatidine may lead to increased effects of alcohol; therefore, alcohol should be avoided during nizatidine therapy.

BE SURE TO TELL YOUR DOCTOR about any medication you are currently taking, especially any that may be listed above.

WARNINGS

• Tell your doctor about any unusual or allergic reactions you have had to nizatidine, ranitidine, cimetidine, famotidine, or any other medications.

• Tell your doctor about any kidney or liver disease. You may need a lower dosage of nizatidine.

• Nizatidine should be taken continuously for as long as your doctor prescribes. Doing otherwise may result in ineffective therapy.

• Notify or remind your doctor that you are taking this medication if you need to have urine or stool testing done.

• Cigarette smoking may block the beneficial effects of nizatidine.

• If nizatidine makes you light-headed or dizzy, avoid tasks that require mental alertness, such as driving an automobile or operating potentially dangerous machinery or equipment.

• It is important to tell your doctor if you are pregnant. Nizatidine has not been proven safe and should be avoided in pregnancy; additional studies in humans are necessary. Also tell your doctor if you are breast-feeding an infant. Harmful concentrations of nizatidine do pass into breast milk.

norfloxacin

BRAND NAME (Manufacturer)
Noroxin (Merck Sharp & Dohme)
TYPE OF DRUG
Antibiotic
INGREDIENT
norfloxacin
DOSAGE FORM
Tablets (400 mg)
STORAGE
Norfloxacin should be stored at room temperature in a tightly closed container.

USES

Norfloxacin is an antibiotic that is used to treat bacterial infections of the urinary tract. It works by interfering with the reproduction of the bacteria. Norfloxacin kills susceptible bacteria but is not effective against viruses, parasites, or fungi.

TREATMENT

In order to obtain the maximum benefit from norfloxacin, it is best to take this drug on an empty stomach (one hour before or two hours after a meal) with a full glass of water. Antacids can decrease the absorption of this medication. Therefore, antacids should not be taken within two hours (before or after) of a dose of norfloxacin, unless otherwise directed by your doctor.

Norfloxacin works best when the level of medicine in your urine is kept constant. It is best, therefore, to take the doses at evenly spaced intervals day and night. For example, if you are to take two doses a day, the doses should be spaced 12 hours apart.

Try not to miss any doses of this medication. If you do miss a dose, take it as soon as you remember. However, if you do not remember to take the missed dose until it is almost time for your next dose, take it; space the following dose about halfway through the regular interval between doses; then continue with your regular dosing schedule.

Take this medication for the entire time prescribed by your doctor (usually five to 14 days), even if the symptoms disappear before the end of that period. If you stop taking the drug too soon, your infection could recur.

SIDE EFFECTS

Minor. Abdominal pain, constipation, diarrhea, dizziness, dry mouth, fatigue, gas, headache, heartburn, nausea, sleeping problems, or vomiting. These side effects should disappear as your body adjusts to this medication.

If you are constipated, increase the amount of fiber in your diet (fresh fruits and vegetables, salads, bran, and whole-grain breads), exercise, and drink more water (unless your doctor directs you to do otherwise).

To reduce mouth dryness, chew sugarless gum or suck on ice chips or hard candy.

If you feel dizzy or light-headed, sit or lie down for a while; get up slowly from a sitting or reclining position; and be careful on stairs.

Major. Tell your doctor about any side effects that are persistent or particularly bothersome. IT IS ESPECIALLY IMPORTANT TO TELL YOUR DOCTOR about depression, difficult or painful urination, rash, visual disturbances, or a yellowish discoloration of the skin or eyes. If the symptoms of your infection seem to be getting worse rather than improving, contact your doctor.

INTERACTIONS

Norfloxacin can interact with several other types of drugs:

1. Probenecid can block the excretion of norfloxacin into the urinary tract, decreasing its effectiveness in treating infections located there.

2. Antacids can decrease the absorption of norfloxacin from the gastrointestinal tract.

3. Nitrofurantoin may antagonize (act against) the effectiveness of norfloxacin.

BE SURE TO TELL YOUR DOCTOR about any medications you are currently taking, especially any of those mentioned above.

WARNINGS

• Tell your doctor about unusual or allergic reactions you have had to any medications, especially to norfloxacin or to the related antibiotics cinoxacin and nalidixic acid.

• Before starting norfloxacin, tell your doctor if you now have or if you have ever had liver disease or seizures.

• If this drug makes you dizzy, do not take part in any activity that requires alertness, such as driving a car or operating potentially dangerous machinery. Be especially careful when going up and down stairs.

• In order to prevent the formation of crystals in the kidneys, try to drink plenty of fluids (at least eight glasses of water or fruit juice each day) while you are taking this medication (unless your doctor directs you to do otherwise).

• This medication has been prescribed for your current infection only. A subsequent infection, or one that someone else has, may require a different kind of antibiotic. Do not give your medicine to other people or use it to treat other infections, unless your doctor specifically directs you to do so.

• Be sure to tell your doctor if you are pregnant. Studies in pregnant women have not been conducted. However, lameness has occurred in the immature offspring of animals that received large doses of norfloxacin during pregnancy. Also tell your doctor if you are breast-feeding an infant. It is not yet known if norfloxacin passes into breast milk.

nortriptyline

BRAND NAMES (Manufacturers)
Aventyl (Lilly)
Pamelor (Sandoz)
TYPE OF DRUG
Tricyclic antidepressant
INGREDIENT
nortriptyline
DOSAGE FORMS
Capsules (10 mg, 25 mg, 50 mg, and 75 mg)
Oral solution (10 mg per 5-mL spoonful, with 4% alcohol)
STORAGE
Store at room temperature in a tightly closed container.

USES

Nortriptyline is used to relieve the symptoms of mental depression. It is thought to relieve depression by increasing the concentration of certain chemicals necessary for nerve transmission in the brain.

TREATMENT

This medication should be taken exactly as your doctor prescribes. It can be taken with water or with food to lessen the chance of stomach irritation, unless your doctor tells you to do otherwise.

If you miss a dose of this medication, take the missed dose as soon as possible, then return to your regular dosing schedule. However, if the dose you missed was a once-a-day bedtime dose, do not take that dose in the morning; check with your doctor instead. If the dose is taken in the morning, it may cause unwanted side effects. Never double the dose.

The effects of therapy with this medication may not become apparent for two or three weeks.

SIDE EFFECTS

Minor. Anxiety, blurred vision, confusion, constipation, cramps, diarrhea, dizziness, drowsiness, dry mouth, fatigue, heartburn, insomnia, loss of appetite, nausea, peculiar tastes in the mouth, restlessness, sweating, vomiting, weakness, or weight gain or loss. As your body adjusts to the medication, these side effects should disappear.

This medication may increase your sensitivity to sunlight. You should, therefore, avoid prolonged exposure to sunlight or sunlamps. Wear protective clothing and use sunscreen.

Dry mouth caused by therapy with this medication can be relieved by chewing sugarless gum or by sucking on ice chips or a piece of hard candy.

To relieve constipation, increase the amount of fiber in your diet (fresh fruits and vegetables, salads, bran, and whole-grain breads), exercise, and drink more water (unless your doctor directs you to do otherwise).

To avoid dizziness or light-headedness when you stand, contract and relax the muscles of your legs for a few moments before rising. Do this by pushing one foot against the floor while raising the other foot slightly, alternating feet so that you are "pumping" your legs in a pedaling motion.

Major. Tell your doctor about any side effects that are persistent or particularly bothersome. IT IS ESPECIALLY IMPORTANT TO TELL YOUR DOCTOR about agitation, chest pain, convulsions, difficulty in urinating, enlarged or painful breasts (in both sexes), fainting, fever, fluid retention, hair loss, hallucinations, headaches, impotence, mood changes, mouth sores, nervousness, nightmares, numbness in the fingers or toes, palpitations, ringing in the ears, seizures, skin rash, sleep disorders, sore throat, swelling, tremors, uncoordinated movements or balance problems, unusual bleeding or bruising, or yellowing of the eyes or skin.

INTERACTIONS

Nortriptyline interacts with a number of other types of medications:

1. Extreme drowsiness can occur when this drug is taken with central nervous system depressants (such as alcohol, antihistamines, barbiturates, benzodiazepine tranquilizers, muscle relaxants, narcotics, pain medications, phenothiazine tranquilizers, and sleeping medications) or other tricyclic antidepressants.

2. Nortriptyline may decrease the effectiveness of antiseizure medications and may block the blood-pressure-lowering effects of clonidine and guanethidine.

3. Birth control pills and estrogen-containing drugs can increase the side effects and reduce the effectiveness of the tricyclic antidepressants (including nortriptyline).

4. Tricyclic antidepressants may increase the side effects of thyroid medication and over-the-counter (nonprescription) cough, cold, asthma, allergy, sinus, and diet medications.

5. The concurrent use of tricyclic antidepressants and monoamine oxidase (MAO) inhibitors should be avoided because the combination may result in fever, convulsions, or high blood pressure. At least 14 days should separate the use of this drug and the use of an MAO inhibitor.

6. Cimetidine can decrease the elimination of nortriptyline from the body, increasing the possibility of side effects.

Before starting to take nortriptyline, BE SURE TO TELL YOUR DOCTOR about any medications you are currently taking, especially any of those listed above.

WARNINGS

• Tell your doctor if you have had unusual or allergic reactions to any medications, especially to nortriptyline or any of the other tricyclic antidepressants (amitriptyline, imipramine, doxepin, trimipramine, amoxapine, protriptyline, desipramine, or maprotiline).

• Tell your doctor if you have a history of alcoholism or if you have ever had asthma, high blood pressure, liver or kidney disease, heart disease, a heart attack, circulatory disease, stomach problems, intestinal problems, difficulty in urinating, enlarged prostate gland, epilepsy, glaucoma, thyroid disease, mental illness, or electroshock therapy.

• If this drug makes you dizzy or drowsy, do not take part in any activity that requires alertness, such as driving a car or operating potentially dangerous machinery.

• Before having surgery or other medical or dental treatment, be sure to tell your doctor or dentist about this drug.

• Do not stop taking this drug suddenly. Abruptly stopping it can cause nausea, headache, stomach upset, fatigue, or a worsening of your condition. Your doctor may want to reduce the dosage gradually.

• The effects of nortriptyline may last as long as seven days after you have stopped taking it, so continue to observe all precautions during that period.

• Be sure to tell your doctor if you are pregnant. Problems in humans have not been reported; however, studies in animals have shown that this type of medication can cause side effects in the fetus when given to the mother in large doses during pregnancy. Also tell your doctor if you are breast-feeding an infant. Small amounts of this drug can pass into breast milk and may cause unwanted effects, such as irritability or sleeping problems, in nursing infants.

---

nystatin

BRAND NAMES (Manufacturers)
Mycostatin (Squibb)
Nilstat (Lederle)
nystatin (various manufacturers)
Nystex (Savage)

TYPE OF DRUG
Antifungal
INGREDIENT
nystatin
DOSAGE FORMS
Oral tablets (500,000 units)
Oral suspension (100,000 units per mL with
  not more than 1% alcohol)
Oral lozenges (200,000 units)
Vaginal tablets (100,000 units)
Topical cream, ointment, and powder (100,000 units per
  gram)
STORAGE
Nystatin should be stored at room temperature in a tightly
closed, light-resistant container. The oral lozenges should be
refrigerated. Nystatin must never be frozen.

USES
Nystatin is used to treat fungal infections of the throat, gastrointestinal tract, skin, and vagina. By chemically binding to
the cell membranes of fungal organisms, this medication
causes the cell contents to leak out, which kills the fungi.

TREATMENT
You can take the oral tablet form of nystatin either on an empty
stomach or with food or milk (as directed by your doctor).

  The oral suspension should be shaken well just before using
each dose. The contents tend to settle, so it is necessary to
shake the container to distribute the ingredients evenly and
equalize the doses.

  Each dose of the oral suspension should then be measured
carefully with a specially designed 5-mL measuring spoon.
An ordinary kitchen teaspoon is not accurate enough. Place
half of the dose in each side of your mouth. Try to hold the
suspension in the mouth or swish it through the mouth for as
long as possible before swallowing it.

  The oral lozenge form should be allowed to dissolve slowly
in the mouth.

  The vaginal tablets are packaged with instructions and an applicator for inserting the tablets into the vagina. Read the instructions carefully before using this product.

Occasionally, the vaginal tablets are prescribed to be taken orally (to treat mouth or throat infections). The tablets are sucked on to increase contact time with the mouth and throat.

The region where you are to apply the topical cream, ointment, or powder should be washed carefully and patted dry. A sufficient amount of medication should then be applied to the affected area. An occlusive dressing (like kitchen plastic wrap) should NOT be applied over the medication (unless your doctor directs you to do so).

If you are using the powder form to treat a foot infection, sprinkle liberally into your shoes and socks.

Try not to miss any doses of this medication. If you do miss a dose, take (or apply) the missed dose as soon as possible, unless it is almost time for the next dose. In that case, do not take (or apply) the missed dose at all; just return to your regular dosing schedule. Do not double the next dose of this medication.

Take this drug for the entire time prescribed by your doctor (usually a period of seven to 14 days), even if the symptoms disappear before the end of that time. If you stop taking the drug too soon, resistant fungi may be given a chance to continue growing, and your infection could possibly recur.

SIDE EFFECTS

Minor. Oral forms: diarrhea, nausea, or vomiting. Topical and vaginal forms: itching. These side effects should disappear as your body adjusts to the drug.

Major. Tell your doctor about any side effects that are persistent or particularly bothersome. IT IS ESPECIALLY IMPORTANT TO TELL YOUR DOCTOR about a rash. If symptoms of your infection seem to be getting worse rather than improving, tell your doctor.

INTERACTIONS

Nystatin should not interact with other medications if it is used according to directions.

WARNINGS

• Tell your doctor about unusual or allergic reactions you have had to any medications, especially to nystatin.

• If you are using this drug to treat a vaginal infection, avoid sexual intercourse or ask your partner to wear a condom until treatment has been completed. These measures help prevent reinfection. Use the vaginal tablets continuously, even during a menstrual period. Unless instructed otherwise by your doctor, do not douche during treatment or until three weeks after you stop using the vaginal tablets. Wear cotton underpants, rather than nylon or other nonporous materials, when you are being treated for fungal infections of the vagina. There may be some vaginal drainage while using the vaginal tablets, so you may wish to use a sanitary napkin or panty liner.

• This medication has been prescribed for your current infection only. Another infection later on, or one that someone else has, may require a different medicine. You should not give your medicine to other people or use it for other infections unless your doctor specifically directs you to do so.

• If the symptoms of infection do not begin to improve within two or three days after starting nystatin, BE SURE TO CONTACT YOUR DOCTOR. This medication may not be effective against the organism that is causing your infection.

• Be sure to tell your doctor if you are pregnant. Although nystatin appears to be safe during pregnancy, extensive and conclusive studies in humans have not been conducted. Also tell your doctor if you are breast-feeding an infant. It is not known whether this medication passes into breast milk.

ofloxacin

BRAND NAME (Manufacturer)
Floxin (McNeil)
TYPE OF DRUG
Quinolone antibiotic
INGREDIENT
ofloxacin
DOSAGE FORM
Tablets (200 mg, 300 mg, and 400 mg)
STORAGE
This medication should be stored in a tightly closed container at room temperature, away from heat and direct sunlight.

USES

Ofloxacin is an antibiotic that is used to treat skin and bone infections as well as infections of the urinary tract and prostate.

It is also used to treat pneumonia. Ofloxacin acts by severely injuring the cell walls of the infecting bacteria, thereby preventing them from growing and multiplying. This medication kills susceptible bacteria, but it is not effective against viruses, parasites, or fungi.

TREATMENT

Ofloxacin should be taken exactly as prescribed by your doctor, even if your symptoms improve. If you stop taking this drug too soon, resistant bacteria are given the chance to grow and the infection may recur. Ofloxacin is usually taken twice a day for seven to 14 days, although it may be given for longer periods of time. This medication can be taken with meals or a full glass of water if stomach upset occurs.

If you miss a dose of ofloxacin, take the missed dose as soon as possible. If it is almost time for your next dose, take the missed dose and space the following dose halfway through the regular interval between doses, then return to your regular schedule. Try not to skip any doses.

SIDE EFFECTS

Minor. Abdominal pain, diarrhea, dizziness, insomnia, lightheadedness, nausea, or vomiting. These side effects should disappear as your body adjusts to the drug.

Major. Tell your doctor about any side effects that are persistent or particularly bothersome. IT IS ESPECIALLY IMPORTANT TO TELL YOUR DOCTOR about agitation, headache, restlessness, severe diarrhea (which may be watery or contain blood or pus), or skin rash. If your symptoms of infection seem to be getting worse rather than improving, contact your doctor.

INTERACTIONS

Ofloxacin interacts with several other types of medications:
1. Probenecid can increase the concentrations of this drug in the blood.
2. Ofloxacin may increase the effects of theophylline or oral anticoagulants.
3. Ofloxacin may make you more susceptible to the effects of caffeine (anxiety, insomnia, palpitations). The use of large amounts of coffee, tea, or other caffeine-containing products should be avoided when taking this medication.

4. Antacids, iron, sucralfate, and zinc may decrease the absorption of ofloxacin. Thus, ofloxacin should be taken at least two hours before or two hours after those medications.

BE SURE TO TELL YOUR DOCTOR about any medications you are currently taking, especially any that may be listed above.

WARNINGS
• Tell your doctor about any unusual or allergic reactions you have had to any medications, especially to ofloxacin or ciprofloxacin.
• Tell your doctor if you now have or if you have ever had liver disease, kidney disease, or epilepsy.
• Avoid taking antacids within four hours of taking a dose of this medication.
• Be sure to tell your doctor if you are pregnant. Studies in pregnant women have not been conducted. However, lameness has occurred in the mature offspring of animals that received large doses of ofloxacin during pregnancy. Also tell your doctor if you are breast-feeding an infant. It is not yet known if ofloxacin passes into breast milk.

---

omeprazole

BRAND NAME (Manufacturer)
Prilosec (MSD)
TYPE OF DRUG
Gastric-acid-secretion inhibitor
INGREDIENT
omeprazole
DOSAGE FORM
Delayed-release capsules (20 mg)
STORAGE
Omeprazole should be stored at room temperature in a tightly closed container.

USES
Omeprazole is prescribed to treat peptic ulcer disease, gastroesophageal reflux, and hypersecretory syndromes. This medication suppresses stomach-acid secretion.

TREATMENT

Omeprazole capsules should not be opened, chewed, or crushed. They should be taken with a glass of water on an empty stomach. It is best to take the dose one hour before meals or two hours after meals.

Try to take the medication at the same time(s) each day. If you miss a dose of the medication, take the missed dose as soon as possible, then return to your regular dosing schedule. If it is almost time for the next dose, however, skip the one you missed and return to your regular schedule. Do not double the next dose of the medication (unless your doctor directs you to do so).

It is important that you take this medication for as long as prescribed by your doctor.

SIDE EFFECTS

Minor. Abdominal pain, burning sensation in mouth, constipation, diarrhea, dizziness, dry mouth, fatigue, headache, or palpitations.

To relieve constipation while you are being treated with this medication, increase the amount of fiber in your diet (fresh fruits and vegetables, salads, bran, and whole-grain breads), exercise, and drink more water (unless your doctor directs you to do otherwise).

To avoid dizziness when you stand, contract and relax the muscles of your legs for a few moments before rising. Do this by pushing one foot against the floor while raising the other foot slightly, alternating feet so that you are "pumping" your legs in a pedaling motion.

To relieve dry mouth, chew sugarless gum or suck on ice chips or a piece of hard candy.

Major. Tell your doctor about any side effects that are persistent or particularly bothersome. IT IS ESPECIALLY IMPORTANT TO TELL YOUR DOCTOR about itching, numbness or tingling of fingers or toes, rash, or yellowish discoloration of the eyes and skin.

INTERACTIONS

Omeprazole may increase the effects of diazepam, warfarin, and phenytoin.

Be sure to tell your doctor about any medications you are currently taking, especially any of the ones listed above.

WARNINGS

• Be sure to tell your doctor about unusual reactions you have had to any drugs, especially to omeprazole.

• Tell your doctor if you now have or if you have ever had thyroid disease, liver disease, Addison's disease, or Cushing's disease.

• This medication may cause dizziness and light-headedness, so use caution while driving a car or operating potentially dangerous equipment.

• Long-term and high-dose treatment with omeprazole has been associated with higher incidences of gastric tumors. Consult your doctor if you need to take high doses of omeprazole for a long time.

• Be sure to tell your doctor if you are pregnant. Adequate human studies have not been conducted with omeprazole. Also be sure to tell your doctor if you are breast-feeding an infant.

ondansetron

BRAND NAME (Manufacturer)
Zofran (Glaxo)
TYPE OF DRUG
Antiemetic (to prevent nausea and vomiting)
INGREDIENT
ondansetron
DOSAGE FORM
Tablets (4 mg and 8 mg)
STORAGE
This medication should be stored in a tightly closed container at room temperature, away from heat and direct sunlight.

USES

Ondansetron is used to prevent the nausea, vomiting, and retching associated with cancer chemotherapy. It is also used to prevent the nausea and vomiting that may occur following surgery. Though it is unclear precisely how ondansetron acts, it appears to work by blocking the release of certain chemicals in the brain that stimulate the impulse to vomit.

TREATMENT

This medication should be taken exactly as prescribed by your doctor. Ondansetron can be taken with meals or a with a full glass of water if you are bothered by stomach upset.

The effectiveness of this treatment is thought to be related to a steady level of ondansetron in the bloodstream. It is very important not to skip any doses of this medication.

SIDE EFFECTS

Minor. Constipation, diarrhea, dizziness, drowsiness, dryness of the mouth, fever or chills, headache, light-headedness, or skin rash.

To relieve constipation, increase the amount of fiber in your diet (fresh fruits and vegetables, salads, bran, and whole-grain breads), exercise, and drink more water (unless your doctor directs you to do otherwise).

Major. Tell your doctor about any side effects that are persistent or particularly bothersome. IT IS ESPECIALLY IMPORTANT TO TELL YOUR DOCTOR about shortness of breath, tightness of the chest, troubled breathing, or wheezing.

INTERACTIONS

At this time, ondansetron does not appear to interact with other drugs when used according to directions.

WARNINGS

• Tell your doctor about unusual, unexpected, or allergic reactions you have had to any medications, especially ondansetron.

• Notify your physician if you have ever had liver or kidney disease.

• If this drug makes you drowsy or dizzy, avoid taking part in any activity that requires alertness, such as driving an automobile or operating potentially dangerous equipment, tools, or machinery.

• Be sure to tell your doctor if you are pregnant. Extensive studies in pregnant women have not been conducted. Be sure to tell your doctor if you are breast-feeding an infant. It is not known if ondansetron passes into breast milk.

oral contraceptives

BRAND NAMES (Manufacturers)
Brevicon (Syntex)
Demulen (Searle)
Desogen (Organon)
Genora (Rugby)
Jenest (Organon)
Levlen (Berlex)
Levora (Hamilton)
Loestrin (Parke-Davis)
Lo/Ovral (Wyeth-Ayerst)
Modicon (Ortho)
Nelova (Warner/Chilcott)
Nordette (Wyeth-Ayerst)
Norethin (Roberts)
Norinyl (Syntex)
Ortho-Cept (Ortho)
Ortho-Novum (Ortho)
Ortho-Tricyclen (Ortho)
Ovcon (Bristol-Myers)
Ovral (Wyeth-Ayerst)
Tri-Levlen (Berlex)
Tri-Norinyl (Syntex)
Triphasil (Wyeth-Ayerst)
TYPE OF DRUG
Oral contraceptive
INGREDIENTS
estrogens and progestins
DOSAGE FORM
Tablets (in packages of 21 or 28 tablets; when 28 tablets are
    present, seven of the tablets either are placebos or contain
    iron)
STORAGE
Oral contraceptives should be stored at room temperature.
They should be kept in their original container, which is de-
signed to help you keep track of your dosing schedule.

USES
Oral contraceptives change the hormone balance of the body
to prevent pregnancy.

TREATMENT

To avoid stomach irritation, you can take oral contraceptives with food or with a full glass of water or milk.

In order to become accustomed to taking this medication, try to take it at the same time every day.

Use a supplemental method of birth control for the first week after you start taking oral contraceptives (the medication takes time to become fully effective).

Even if you do not start to menstruate on schedule at the end of the pill cycle, begin the next cycle of pills at the prescribed time. Many women taking oral contraceptives have irregular menstruation.

If you miss a dose of this medication and you are on a 21-day schedule, take the missed dose as soon as you remember. If you don't remember until the next day, take the dose of that day plus the one you missed; then return to your regular dosing schedule. If you miss two days' doses, you should take two tablets a day for the next two days; then return to your regular dosing schedule. You should also use another form of birth control for at least seven days following the missed pills. If you miss your dose three days in a row, you should stop taking this drug and use a different method of birth control until you check with your doctor. Your doctor may want you to start a new package seven days after the last tablet was missed and use an additional method of birth control until the start of your next period.

If you are on the 28-day schedule and you miss taking any one of the first 21 tablets, you should follow the instructions for the 21-day schedule. If you missed taking any of the last seven tablets, there is no danger of pregnancy, but you should take the first pill of the next month's cycle on the regularly scheduled day.

SIDE EFFECTS

Minor. Abdominal cramps, acne, backache, bloating, change in appetite, changes in sexual desire, diarrhea, dizziness, fatigue, headache, nasal congestion, nausea, nervousness, vaginal irritation, or vomiting. These side effects should disappear as your body adjusts to the medication.

This medication can increase your sensitivity to sunlight. Avoid prolonged exposure to sunlight and sunlamps. Wear protective clothing and use a sunscreen.

If you feel dizzy or light-headed, sit or lie down for a while; get up slowly from a sitting or reclining position; and be careful on stairs.

Major. Tell your doctor about any side effects that are persistent or particularly bothersome. IT IS ESPECIALLY IMPORTANT TO TELL YOUR DOCTOR about abdominal pain; breakthrough vaginal bleeding (spotting); changes in menstrual flow; chest pain; depression; difficult or painful urination; enlarged or tender breasts; hearing changes; increase or decrease in hair growth; migraine headaches; numbness or tingling; pain in your calves; rash; skin color changes; swelling of the feet, ankles, or lower legs; unusual bleeding or bruising; vaginal itching; weight changes; or yellowing of the eyes or skin.

INTERACTIONS

These drugs interact with several other medications:

1. Pain relievers, antimigraine preparations, rifampin, barbiturates, phenytoin, primidone, carbamazepine, isoniazid, neomycin, griseofulvin, penicillins, tetracycline, chloramphenicol, sulfonamide antibiotics, nitrofurantoin, and ampicillin can reduce the effectiveness of oral contraceptives and increase the risk of pregnancy. Your doctor may advise using an extra form of contraception, such as a condom.

2. Oral contraceptives can reduce the effectiveness of oral anticoagulants (blood thinners, such as warfarin), anticonvulsants, tricyclic antidepressants, antihypertensive agents, oral antidiabetic agents, and vitamins.

3. Oral contraceptives can increase the blood levels of caffeine, diazepam, chlordiazepoxide, metoprolol, propranolol, adrenocorticosteroids, imipramine, clomipramine, and phenytoin, which can lead to an increase in side effects.

4. Oral contraceptives can decrease the blood levels and, therefore, the effectiveness of lorazepam and oxazepam.

BE SURE TO TELL YOUR DOCTOR about any medications you are currently taking, especially those listed above.

WARNINGS

• Tell your doctor about unusual or allergic reactions you have had to any medications, especially to estrogens, progestins, or progesterones.

• Before starting to take this medication, be sure to tell your doctor if you now have or if you have ever had asthma, bleeding problems, breast cancer, clotting disorders, diabetes mellitus, endometriosis, epilepsy, gallbladder disease, heart disease, high blood pressure, kidney disease, liver disease, mental depression, migraine headaches, porphyria, strokes, thyroid disease, uterine tumors, vaginal bleeding, or vitamin deficiencies.

• Some women who have used an oral contraceptive have had difficulty becoming pregnant after discontinuing use. Most of these women had had scanty or irregular periods before starting oral contraceptives. Possible subsequent difficulty in becoming pregnant is a matter you should discuss with your doctor before using an oral contraceptive.

• Every prescription comes with a booklet that explains birth control pills. Read this booklet carefully. It contains exact directions on how to use this medicine correctly and describes the risks involved.

• Women over 30 years of age and women who smoke while taking this medication have an increased risk of developing serious heart or blood-vessel side effects.

• If this drug makes you dizzy, avoid taking part in any activity that requires alertness, such as driving an automobile or operating potentially dangerous tools, equipment, or machinery. Be careful on stairs.

• Before surgery or other medical or dental treatment, tell your doctor or dentist you are taking this drug.

• This type of drug has been suspected of causing cancer. If you have a family history of cancer, you should consult your doctor before taking oral contraceptives.

• Be sure to tell your doctor if you are pregnant. Oral contraceptives have been associated with birth defects in animals and in humans. Because hormones have long-term effects on the body, oral contraceptives should be stopped at least three months prior to becoming pregnant. Another method of birth control should be used for those three months. Also tell your doctor if you are breast-feeding an infant. This medication passes into breast milk.

orphenadrine, aspirin, and caffeine combination

BRAND NAMES (Manufacturers)
Norgesic (3M Pharmaceutical)
Norgesic Forte (3M Pharmaceutical)
TYPE OF DRUG
Muscle relaxant and analgesic
INGREDIENTS
orphenadrine, aspirin, and caffeine
DOSAGE FORM
Tablets (25 mg orphenadrine, 385 mg aspirin, and 30 mg caffeine [Norgesic]; 50 mg orphenadrine, 770 mg aspirin, and 60 mg caffeine [Norgesic Forte])
STORAGE
This medication should be stored at room temperature in a tightly closed, light-resistant container.

USES

Orphenadrine, aspirin, and caffeine combination drug is used to relax muscles and to relieve the pain of sprains, strains, and other muscle injuries. Orphenadrine acts as a central nervous system (brain and spinal cord) depressant, which blocks reflexes involved in producing and maintaining muscle spasms. It does not act directly on tense muscles. Caffeine is a central nervous system stimulant that acts by constricting the blood vessels in the head. This may help relieve headaches.

TREATMENT

These tablets should be taken with a full glass of water. To avoid stomach irritation, you can also take this medication with food or milk (unless your doctor directs otherwise).

If you miss a dose of this medication and remember within an hour, take the missed dose and then return to your regular dosing schedule. If it has been longer than an hour, do not take the missed dose at all; just return to your regular dosing schedule. Do not double the next dose.

SIDE EFFECTS

Minor. Blurred vision, confusion, constipation, diarrhea, dizziness, drowsiness, dry mouth, headache, indigestion, insomnia, nausea, nervousness, vomiting, or weakness. These side effects should disappear as your body adjusts to the medication.

If you are constipated, increase the amount of fiber in your diet (fresh fruits and vegetables, salads, bran, and whole-grain breads), exercise, and drink more water (unless your doctor directs you to do otherwise).

If you feel dizzy or light-headed, sit or lie down for a while; get up slowly from a sitting or reclining position; and be careful on stairs.

To relieve mouth dryness, suck on ice chips or a piece of hard candy or chew sugarless gum.

Major. Tell your doctor about any side effects that are persistent or particularly bothersome. IT IS ESPECIALLY IMPORTANT TO TELL YOUR DOCTOR about bloody or black, tarry stools; chest tightness; difficulty in breathing; difficulty in urinating; hearing loss; palpitations; rash; ringing in the ears; or severe abdominal pain.

INTERACTIONS

This medication interacts with several other types of drugs:

1. Orphenadrine can cause extreme drowsiness when combined with other central nervous system depressants (such as alcohol, antihistamines, barbiturates, benzodiazepine tranquilizers, phenothiazine tranquilizers, narcotics, and sleeping medications) or with tricyclic antidepressants.

2. Orphenadrine can cause confusion, anxiety, and tremors when combined with propoxyphene.

3. Aspirin can increase the active blood levels of methotrexate, oral antidiabetic agents, and oral anticoagulants (blood thinners, such as warfarin), which can lead to an increase in side effects.

4. The antigout activity of probenecid and sulfinpyrazone are decreased by aspirin.

5. The gastrointestinal side effects of anti-inflammatory medications may be increased by aspirin.

BE SURE TO TELL YOUR DOCTOR about any medications you are currently taking.

WARNINGS

• Tell your doctor about unusual or allergic reactions you have had to any drugs, especially to orphenadrine, caffeine, aspirin, other salicylates, methyl salicylate, or nonsteroidal anti-inflammatory agents (such as diclofenac, diflunisal, fenoprofen, flurbiprofen, ibuprofen, indomethacin, ketoprofen, meclofenamate, naproxen, piroxicam, sulindac, and tolmetin).

• Tell your doctor if you have ever had anemia, bladder obstruction, glaucoma, gout, kidney disease, liver disease, myasthenia gravis, peptic ulcers, enlarged prostate gland, intestinal obstruction, or bleeding problems.

• This medication should not be taken as a substitute for rest, physical therapy, or other measures recommended by your doctor to treat your condition.

• If this medication makes you dizzy or drowsy or blurs your vision, do not take part in any activity that requires alertness, such as driving a car or operating potentially dangerous machinery.

• Before having surgery or other medical or dental treatment, tell your doctor or dentist about this drug. Treatment with aspirin-containing drugs is usually discontinued several days before any major surgery to prevent bleeding complications.

• Because this product contains aspirin, additional medications that contain aspirin should not be taken without first getting your doctor's approval. Check the labels on over-the-counter (nonprescription) pain, sinus, allergy, asthma, cough, and cold products to see if they contain aspirin.

• The use of aspirin in children (about 16 years of age or less) with the flu or chicken pox has been associated with a rare, life-threatening condition called Reye's syndrome. Aspirin-containing products should therefore not be given to children who are exhibiting signs of infection.

• Diabetic patients should be aware that large doses of aspirin (more than six 385-mg tablets or three 770-mg tablets per day) may interfere with urine-sugar testing. People with diabetes should therefore check with their doctor before changing their insulin dose.

• Be sure to tell your doctor if you are pregnant. Aspirin can prolong labor if it is taken by the mother close to term and can cause heart problems in newborn infants. Also tell your doctor if you are breast-feeding an infant. It is not known whether orphenadrine passes into breast milk, but small quantities of aspirin and caffeine are able to pass into breast milk.

---

oxybutynin

BRAND NAMES (Manufacturers)
Ditropan (Marion)
oxybutynin (various manufacturers)
TYPE OF DRUG
Antispasmodic
INGREDIENT
oxybutynin
DOSAGE FORMS
Tablets (5 mg)
Oral syrup (5 mg per 5-mL spoonful)
STORAGE
Oxybutynin tablets and syrup should be stored at room temperature in tightly closed containers.

USES
Oxybutynin is used to relieve the symptoms associated with urinary incontinence (inability to control the bladder) or urinary frequency.

TREATMENT
Oxybutynin can be taken either on an empty stomach with water only or, to reduce stomach irritation, with food or milk (as directed by your doctor).

Each dose of the oral syrup should be measured carefully with a specially designed 5-mL measuring spoon. An ordinary kitchen teaspoon is not accurate enough.

If you miss a dose of this medication, take the missed dose as soon as possible, unless it is almost time for the next dose. In that case, do not take the missed dose at all; return to your regular dosing schedule.

SIDE EFFECTS
Minor. Bloating, blurred vision, constipation, decreased sweating, dizziness, drowsiness, dry mouth, insomnia, nausea, vomiting, or weakness. These side effects should disappear as your body adjusts to the medication.

This medication can also cause increased sensitivity of your eyes to sunlight. Sunglasses may help relieve the discomfort caused by bright lights.

To relieve constipation, increase the amount of fiber in your diet (fresh fruits and vegetables, salads, bran, and whole-grain breads) and exercise (unless your doctor directs you to do otherwise).

If you feel dizzy, sit or lie down for a while; get up slowly from a sitting or reclining position; and be careful on stairs.

To help relieve mouth dryness, chew sugarless gum or suck on ice chips or a piece of hard candy.

Major. Tell your doctor about any side effects that are persistent or particularly bothersome. IT IS ESPECIALLY IMPORTANT TO TELL YOUR DOCTOR about decreased sexual ability, difficult or painful urination, eye pain, itching, palpitations, or skin rash.

INTERACTIONS

Oxybutynin should not interact with other medications if it is used according to directions.

WARNINGS

• Tell your doctor about unusual or allergic reactions you have had to any medications, especially to oxybutynin.
• Before starting to take this medication, be sure to tell your doctor if you now have or if you have ever had bleeding disorders, glaucoma, heart disease, hiatal hernia, high blood pressure, intestinal blockage, kidney disease, liver disease, myasthenia gravis, enlarged prostate gland, thyroid disease, toxemia of pregnancy, ulcerative colitis, or urinary retention.
• If this drug makes you dizzy or blurs your vision, avoid taking part in any activity that requires alertness, such as driving a car or operating potentially dangerous machinery.
• This medication can decrease sweating and heat release from the body. You should, therefore, try not to become overheated (avoid strenuous exercise in hot weather, and do not take hot baths, showers, and saunas).
• Be sure to tell your doctor if you are pregnant. Although oxybutynin appears to be safe during pregnancy, extensive studies in humans have not been conducted. Also tell your doctor if you are breast-feeding. This drug may decrease milk

production. It is not known whether oxybutynin passes into breast milk.

---

pancreatin

BRAND NAMES (Manufacturers)
4× Pancreatin 600 mg* (Vitaline)
8× Pancreatin 900 mg* (Vitaline)
Donnazyme (Robins)
Pancreatin 5× USP* (Vitaline)
Pancreatin 8× USP* (Vitaline)
*Available over the counter (without a prescription)
TYPE OF DRUG
Digestive enzymes
INGREDIENTS
pancreatin, lipase, protease, and amylase
DOSAGE FORMS
Donnazyme oral tablet (lipase 1,000 units; amylase 12,500 units; protease 12,500 units)
4× Pancreatin tablets (lipase 12,000 units; amylase 60,000 units; protease 60,000 units)
8× Pancreatin tablets (lipase 22,500 units; amylase 180,000 units; protease 180,000 units)
STORAGE
Store at room temperature in a tightly closed container.

USES

This medication is a combination of specific digestive (pancreatic) enzymes obtained from pigs or cows. These enzymes aid in the digestion and absorption of fats and starches. Pancreatin is given for the treatment of various pancreatic-enzyme deficiencies resulting from conditions such as pancreatitis, cystic fibrosis, or gastrointestinal bypass surgery.

TREATMENT

In order to obtain the maximum benefit from this medication, you should take pancreatin just before or with meals or snacks. The tablets can be mixed with food. If you miss a dose of this medication, do not take the missed dose at all; just return to your regular dosing schedule. Do not double the next dose.

SIDE EFFECTS

Minor. Diarrhea, nausea, or stomach cramps. These side effects should disappear as your body adjusts to pancreatin.
Major. Tell your doctor about any side effects that are persistent or particularly bothersome. IT IS ESPECIALLY IMPORTANT TO TELL YOUR DOCTOR about bloody urine, hives, joint pain, skin rash, or swelling of the feet or legs.

INTERACTIONS

Pancreatin can decrease the absorption of iron from the gastrointestinal tract, which may lead to nutritional deficiency. Your doctor may want to prescribe iron supplements if this becomes a problem. Cimetidine or antacids are often prescribed concurrently with pancreatin in order to maximize its effectiveness. However, calcium- or magnesium-containing antacids should be avoided—they decrease this medication's effectiveness. You should discuss these possible interactions with your doctor.

WARNINGS

• Tell your doctor about any unusual or allergic reactions you have had to any medications, especially to pancreatin, pancrelipase, or any other digestive enzymes.
• Patients who have allergies to pork or beef products may also be allergic to pancreatin.
• Be sure to tell your doctor if you are pregnant. Although pancreatin appears to be safe during pregnancy, extensive studies have not been conducted. Also tell your doctor if you are breast-feeding an infant. It is not known whether pancreatin passes into breast milk.

---

pancrelipase

BRAND NAMES (Manufacturers)
Cotazym-S (Organon)
Creon 5 (Solvay)
Creon 10 (Solvay)
Creon 20 (Solvay)
Ku-Zyme HP (Schwarz)
Pancrease (McNeil)
Pancrease MT (McNeil)

Ultrase (Scandipharm)
Ultrase MT (Scandipharm)
Viokase (Robins)
Zymase (Organon)
TYPE OF DRUG
Digestive enzymes
INGREDIENTS
lipase, protease, and amylase
DOSAGE FORMS
Tablets (in various strengths)
Capsules (in various strengths)
Powder packets (in various strengths)
STORAGE
Pancrelipase tablets, capsules, and powder should be stored at room temperature in tightly closed containers. In any form, pancrelipase should not be refrigerated.

USES
This medication is a combination of specific digestive (pancreatic) enzymes obtained from pigs. These enzymes aid in the digestion and absorption of starches and fats. Pancrelipase is used in the treatment of various pancreatic-enzyme deficiencies resulting from conditions such as pancreatitis, cystic fibrosis, or gastrointestinal bypass surgery.

TREATMENT
In order to obtain the maximum benefit, you should take pancrelipase just before or with meals or snacks. The powder can be added to food; the tablets can also be crushed and mixed with food.

If you are taking the capsules containing the enteric-coated microspheres, swallow the capsule whole. Chewing, crushing, or breaking the capsules decreases their effectiveness and increases the side effects. However, if you have difficulty swallowing the capsules, you can open them and sprinkle the contents on a small amount of liquid or soft food, which you should then swallow without chewing. Do not mix this medication with alkaline foods (such as dairy products); they can reduce its effectiveness.

If you miss a dose of this medication, do not take the missed dose at all; just return to your regular dosing schedule. Do not double the next dose.

SIDE EFFECTS

Minor. Diarrhea, nausea, or stomach cramps. These side effects should disappear over time as your body adjusts to the medication.

Major. Tell your doctor about any side effects you experience that are persistent or particularly bothersome. IT IS ESPECIALLY IMPORTANT TO TELL YOUR DOCTOR about bloody urine, hives, joint pain, skin rash, or swelling of the feet.

INTERACTIONS

Pancrelipase can decrease the absorption of iron from the gastrointestinal tract, which may lead to nutritional deficiency. Your doctor may want to prescribe iron supplements if this becomes a problem. Cimetidine or antacids are often prescribed concurrently with pancrelipase in order to maximize its effectiveness. However, antacids that contain calcium or magnesium should be avoided—they decrease this medication's effectiveness. You should discuss these effects with your doctor.

WARNINGS

• Tell your doctor about unusual or allergic reactions you have had to any medications, especially to pancrelipase, pancreatin, or any other digestive enzymes.

• Patients who have allergies to pork products may also be allergic to pancrelipase, since it is obtained from pigs.

• The powder form as well as the powder from opened capsules of this medication can be very irritating to the nose and throat. Avoid inhaling the particles.

• Be sure to tell your doctor if you are pregnant. Although pancrelipase appears to be safe during pregnancy, extensive studies have not been conducted. Also tell your doctor if you are breast-feeding an infant. It is not known whether pancrelipase passes into breast milk.

papaverine

BRAND NAMES (Manufacturers)

Cerespan (Rorer)
papaverine hydrochloride (various manufacturers)
Pavabid Plateau (Marion)

Pavagen (Rugby)
Pavarine Spancaps (Vortech)
Pavased (Hauck)
Paverolan Lanacaps (Lannett)
TYPE OF DRUG
Vasodilator
INGREDIENT
papaverine
DOSAGE FORMS
Capsules (150 mg)
Tablets (100 mg and 300 mg)
STORAGE
Papaverine should be stored at room temperature in a tightly
closed container.

USES

Papaverine is used to treat circulation disorders. It is a vasodilator that acts directly on the muscle tissues of blood vessels to increase blood supply.

TREATMENT

In order to avoid stomach irritation, you can take papaverine
with food or with a full glass of water or milk. Ask your doctor
if you can take it with an antacid.

The sustained-release capsules should be swallowed whole.
Breaking, crushing, or chewing these capsules destroys their
sustained-release activity and possibly increases the side effects.

If you miss a dose of this medication, take the missed dose
as soon as possible, unless it is almost time for the next dose.
In that case, do not take the missed dose at all; just return to
your regular dosing schedule. Do not double the next dose.

SIDE EFFECTS

Minor. Abdominal distress, blurred vision, constipation, diarrhea, dizziness, drowsiness, fatigue, flushing, headache,
loss of appetite, nausea, or sweating. These side effects should
disappear as your body adjusts to the medication.

If you feel dizzy, sit or lie down for a while; get up slowly
from a sitting or reclining position; and be careful on stairs.

To relieve constipation, increase the amount of fiber in your
diet (fresh fruits and vegetables, salads, bran, and whole-grain

breads), exercise, and drink more water (unless your doctor directs you to do otherwise).

Major. Tell your doctor about any side effects you experience that are persistent or particularly bothersome. IT IS ESPECIALLY IMPORTANT TO TELL YOUR DOCTOR about depression, difficulty in breathing, palpitations, rash, unusual bleeding or bruising, or yellowing of the eyes or skin.

INTERACTIONS

Concurrent use of papaverine and levodopa can lead to decreased effectiveness of levodopa.

Before starting to take papaverine, BE SURE TO TELL YOUR DOCTOR about any medications you are currently taking, especially levodopa.

WARNINGS

• Tell your doctor about unusual or allergic reactions you have had to any medications, especially to papaverine.

• Be sure to tell your doctor if you have or if you have ever had angina, glaucoma, heart block, liver disease, low or high blood pressure, a heart attack, or Parkinson's disease.

• A government panel has recently reviewed the effectiveness of this medication in the treatment of hardening of the arteries and leg cramps and in the prevention of stroke. This drug may not be as effective as once thought. Before taking any over-the-counter (nonprescription) cough, cold, allergy, asthma, sinus, or diet medication, check with your doctor or pharmacist. Some of these products can decrease the effectiveness of papaverine.

• If this drug makes you dizzy or drowsy, do not take part in any activity that requires alertness, such as driving a car or operating potentially dangerous machinery.

• The beneficial effects of this medication may be decreased by the nicotine in cigarettes.

• To prevent dizziness and fainting while taking this medication, avoid drinking large quantities of alcohol, and try not to get overheated (avoid strenuous exercise in hot weather and do not take hot baths, showers, or saunas).

• Be sure to tell your doctor if you are pregnant. Although papaverine appears to be safe, extensive studies in pregnant women have not been conducted. Also tell your doctor if you are breast-feeding. It is not known whether papaverine passes into breast milk.

---

paroxetine

BRAND NAME (Manufacturer)
Paxil (SmithKline Beecham)
TYPE OF DRUG
Antidepressant
INGREDIENT
paroxetine
DOSAGE FORM
Tablets (20 mg and 30 mg)
STORAGE
This medication should be stored in a tightly closed container at room temperature, away from heat and direct sunlight. Do not store in the bathroom. Heat or moisture can cause this medicine to break down.

USES

Paroxetine is used to treat the symptoms of mental depression. It increases the concentration of certain chemicals that are necessary for nerve transmission in the brain.

TREATMENT

This medication should be taken exactly as prescribed by your doctor. In order to avoid stomach irritation, take paroxetine with food or a full glass of water (unless your doctor directs you to do otherwise).

The effects of treatment with this medication may not become apparent for one to three weeks.

If you miss a dose of this medicine, it is not necessary to make up the missed dose. Skip that dose and continue at the next scheduled time. You should never take a double dose to make up for the one you missed.

SIDE EFFECTS

Minor. Agitation, changes in taste, constipation, decreased concentration, decreased sex drive, diarrhea, dizziness, drowsiness, dry mouth, fast heartbeat, flushing, frequent urination, headache, increased sweating, loss of appetite, nausea, stuffy nose, vision changes, weight gain or loss.

Dry mouth can be relieved by chewing sugarless gum or sucking on hard candy.

To relieve constipation, increase the amount of fiber in your diet (fresh fruits and vegetables, salads, bran, and whole-grain breads), exercise, and drink more water (unless your doctor directs you to do otherwise).

To avoid dizziness when you stand, contract and relax the muscles in your legs for a few moments before rising.

Major. Tell your doctor about any side effects you experience that are persistent or particularly bothersome. IT IS ESPECIALLY IMPORTANT TO TELL YOUR DOCTOR about anxiety, chills or fever, convulsions (seizures), enlarged lymph glands (swelling under the jaw, in the armpits, or in the groin area), difficulty in breathing, joint or muscle pain, skin rash or hives, or swelling of the feet or lower legs.

INTERACTIONS

Paroxetine will interact with several other types of medications:

1. Extreme drowsiness can occur when this medication is taken with other central nervous system depressants (such as alcohol, antihistamines, barbiturates, benzodiazepine tranquilizers, muscle relaxants, narcotics, pain medications, phenothiazine tranquilizers, and sleeping medications) or with other antidepressants.

2. Paroxetine may increase the effects of oral anticoagulants (blood thinners, such as warfarin) and certain heart medications (such as digoxin).

3. Serious side effects may occur if a monoamine oxidase (MAO) inhibitor (such as furazolidone, isocarboxazid, pargyline, phenelzine, procarbazine, selegiline, or tranylcypromine) is taken with paroxetine. At least 14 days should separate the use of paroxetine and the use of an MAO inhibitor.

4. Paroxetine can increase agitation, restlessness, and stomach irritation when taken with tryptophan.

Before taking paroxetine, BE SURE TO TELL YOUR DOCTOR about any medication you are taking, especially any of those listed above.

WARNINGS

• Tell your doctor immediately if you develop a skin rash or have hives while taking this medication or if you have ever had a reaction to paroxetine before.

• Tell your doctor if you have a history of alcoholism, if you ever had a heart attack, asthma, circulatory disease, difficulty in urinating, electroshock therapy, enlarged prostate gland, epilepsy, glaucoma, high blood pressure, intestinal problems, liver or kidney disease, mental illness, or thyroid disease.

• If this medication makes you drowsy or dizzy, do not take part in any activity that requires mental alertness, such as driving a car or operating dangerous equipment.

• Do not stop taking this medication suddenly. Abruptly stopping it can cause nausea, headache, stomach upset, or a worsening of your condition. Your doctor may want to reduce the dose gradually.

• Elderly individuals may be at greater risk for side effects. Use this drug cautiously and report any mental-status changes to your doctor immediately.

• The effects of this medication may be present for as long as five weeks after you stop taking it, so continue to observe all precautions during this period.

• Be sure to tell your doctor if you are pregnant. Although birth defects have not been documented in animal studies, it is not known if paroxetine is safe during pregnancy. It is not known if paroxetine passes into breast milk, so be sure to tell your doctor if you are breast-feeding an infant.

---

pemoline

BRAND NAME (Manufacturer)
Cylert (Abbott)
TYPE OF DRUG
Stimulant
INGREDIENT
pemoline
DOSAGE FORMS
Tablets (18.75 mg, 37.5 mg, and 75 mg)
Chewable tablets (37.5 mg)

STORAGE
Pemoline should be stored at room temperature in a tightly closed container.

USES
Pemoline is a central nervous system (brain and spinal cord) stimulant that is used to treat attention deficit disorders (hyperkinetic syndrome). It is not yet clear how pemoline works to improve behavioral disorders in children, but it seems to decrease hyperactivity and increase attention span.

TREATMENT
Pemoline can be taken either on an empty stomach or with food or milk (as directed by your doctor). The chewable tablet form of this medication can be either chewed or swallowed whole.

If you miss a dose of this medication, take the missed dose as soon as possible, unless it is almost time for the next dose. In that case, do not take the missed dose at all; just return to your regular dosing schedule. Do not double the next dose of this medication.

You may not observe the full therapeutic benefits of this medication for three to four weeks.

SIDE EFFECTS
Minor. Dizziness, drowsiness, headache, insomnia, irritability, loss of appetite, nausea, stomachache, or weight loss. These side effects should disappear as your body adjusts to the drug.

If you feel dizzy, sit or lie down for a while; get up slowly from a sitting or reclining position; and be careful on stairs.
Major. Tell your doctor about any side effects you are experiencing that seem to be persistent or particularly bothersome. IT IS ESPECIALLY IMPORTANT TO TELL YOUR DOCTOR about convulsions; depression; hallucinations; palpitations; skin rash; unusual movements of the tongue, lips, face, hands, or feet; or yellowing of the eyes or skin.

INTERACTIONS
Pemoline should not interact with other medications if it is used according to the directions given to you by your doctor or pharmacist.

WARNINGS

• Tell your doctor about unusual or allergic reactions you have had to any medications, especially to pemoline.
• Before starting to take this medication, be sure to tell your doctor if you now have or if you have ever had kidney disease, liver disease, or mental disorders.
• If this drug makes you feel dizzy or drowsy, do not take part in any activity that requires alertness, such as driving an automobile or operating potentially dangerous machinery. Children who are taking this drug should be cautious while playing.
• This medication has the potential for abuse and must be used with caution. It should therefore not be taken in larger doses or for longer periods than prescribed by your doctor. In addition, you should not stop taking pemoline unless you first check with your doctor. Stopping the drug abruptly can lead to a withdrawal reaction. Your doctor may want to have you reduce the dosage gradually.
• Your doctor may want to interrupt pemoline therapy occasionally for short periods ("drug holidays") to see if the symptoms of the attention deficit disorder have disappeared.
• Be sure to tell your doctor if you are pregnant. Although pemoline appears to be safe, extensive and conclusive studies in humans during pregnancy have not been conducted. Also tell your doctor if you are breast-feeding an infant. It is not known whether pemoline passes into breast milk.

---

penicillamine

BRAND NAMES (Manufacturers)
Cuprimine (Merck Sharp & Dohme)
Depen Titratable Tablets (Wallace)
TYPE OF DRUG
Chelator and antirheumatic
INGREDIENT
penicillamine
DOSAGE FORMS
Tablets (250 mg)
Capsules (125 mg and 250 mg)
STORAGE
Store at room temperature in a tightly closed container.

USES

This drug is used to treat Wilson's disease (high levels of blood copper), severe rheumatoid arthritis, and cystinuria (high urine levels of cystine). Penicillamine binds to copper and cystine, which prevents their harmful effects on the body. It is not clearly understood how penicillamine relieves rheumatoid arthritis.

TREATMENT

In order to obtain the maximum benefit from penicillamine, you should take it on an empty stomach one hour before or two hours after a meal. To ensure maximal absorption of this drug, each dose should be separated from doses of other medications and from food and milk by at least an hour.

If you miss a dose of this drug, take the dose as soon as possible, unless it is almost time for the next dose. In that case, do not take the dose at all; return to your regular dosing schedule. Do not double the dose.

The full benefits of this drug may not become apparent for as long as three months after therapy.

SIDE EFFECTS

Minor. Altered taste sensations, diarrhea, loss of appetite, nausea, stomach upset, or vomiting. These side effects should disappear as your body gets accustomed to the medication.

Major. Tell your doctor about any side effects that are persistent or particularly bothersome. IT IS ESPECIALLY IMPORTANT TO TELL YOUR DOCTOR about breast enlargement (in both sexes), difficult or painful urination, difficulty in breathing, joint pain, loss of hair, mouth sores, ringing in the ears, skin rash, sore throat, tingling sensations in the fingers or toes, unusual bleeding or bruising, or wheezing.

INTERACTIONS

Penicillamine interacts with several other types of medications:

1. The absorption of penicillamine from the gastrointestinal tract can be decreased by iron or antacids.

2. Penicillamine can decrease the blood levels and beneficial effects of digoxin.

3. Concurrent use of penicillamine and gold salts, hydroxychloroquine, phenylbutazone, oxyphenbutazone, or anti-

cancer drugs can lead to increased side effects to the blood and kidneys.

BE SURE TO TELL YOUR DOCTOR about any medications you are currently taking, especially any of those listed above.

WARNINGS

• Tell your doctor about unusual or allergic reactions you have or ever have had to any medications, especially to penicillamine, penicillin, or cephalosporin antibiotics.

• Before starting to take this medication, be sure to tell your doctor if you now have or if you have ever had blood disorders or kidney disease.

• Do not stop taking this drug unless you first check with your doctor.

• Penicillamine can decrease the body's ability to repair wounds, so try to avoid injuring yourself while you are taking this medication. This warning is especially important for patients with diabetes.

• Before having surgery or any other medical or dental treatment, be sure to tell your doctor or dentist that you are taking this drug.

• Your doctor may want you to take pyridoxine (vitamin B) to prevent some of the side effects (for example, tingling sensations) of penicillamine.

• Be sure to tell your doctor if you are pregnant. Penicillamine has been reported to cause birth defects in both animals and humans. Also tell your doctor if you are breast-feeding an infant.

---

penicillin VK

BRAND NAMES (Manufacturers)
Beepen-VK (SmithKline Beecham)
Betapen-VK (Apothecon)
Ledercillin VK (Lederle)
penicillin VK (various manufacturers)
Pen-Vee K (Wyeth-Ayerst)
Robicillin VK (Robins)
V-Cillin K (Lilly)
Veetids (Bristol-Myers Squibb)

TYPE OF DRUG
Penicillin antibiotic
INGREDIENT
penicillin potassium phenoxymethyl
DOSAGE FORMS
Tablets (125 mg, 250 mg, and 500 mg)
Oral solution (125 mg and 250 mg per 5-mL spoonful)
STORAGE
Penicillin VK tablets should be stored at room temperature in
a tightly closed container. The oral solution should be stored
in the refrigerator in a tightly closed container. Any unused
portion of the solution should be discarded after 14 days be-
cause the drug loses its potency after that time. This medication
should never be frozen.

USES

Penicillin VK is used to treat a wide variety of bacterial infections, including infections of the middle ear, the respiratory
tract, and the urinary tract. It acts by severely injuring the cell
membranes of infecting bacteria, thereby preventing them
from growing and multiplying. Penicillin VK kills susceptible
bacteria, but it is not effective against viruses, parasites, or
fungi.

TREATMENT

Penicillin VK should be taken on an empty stomach or with
a glass of water one hour before or two hours after a meal.
This medication should never be taken with fruit juices or carbonated beverages because the acidity of these drinks destroys the drug in the stomach.

The oral solution should be measured carefully with a specially designed 5-mL measuring spoon. An ordinary kitchen
teaspoon is not accurate enough.

Penicillin VK works best when the level of medicine in your
bloodstream is kept constant. It is best, therefore, to take the
doses at evenly spaced intervals day and night. For example,
if you are taking four doses a day, the doses should be spaced
six hours apart.

If you miss a dose of this medication, take the missed dose
immediately. However, if you do not remember to take the
missed dose until it is almost time for the next dose, take it;
space the following dose about halfway through the regular

interval between doses; then return to your regular dosing schedule. Try not to skip any doses.

It is important to continue to take this medication for the entire time prescribed by your doctor (usually a period of up to seven to 14 days), even if the symptoms of infection disappear before the end of that time. If you stop taking the drug too soon, resistant bacteria are given a chance to continue growing, and the infection could recur.

SIDE EFFECTS

Minor. Diarrhea, heartburn, nausea, or vomiting. These side effects should disappear as your body adjusts to the drug.

Major. Tell your doctor about any side effects that are persistent or particularly bothersome. IT IS ESPECIALLY IMPORTANT TO TELL YOUR DOCTOR about bloating, chills, cough, darkened tongue, difficulty in breathing, fever, irritation of the mouth, muscle aches, rash, rectal or vaginal itching, severe diarrhea, or sore throat. If the infection seems to be getting worse rather than getting better, you should contact your physician.

INTERACTIONS

Penicillin VK will interact with several other types of medications:

1. Probenecid can increase the blood concentrations of this medication.

2. Oral neomycin may decrease the absorption of penicillin from the gastrointestinal tract.

3. Penicillin VK may decrease the effectiveness of oral contraceptives (birth control pills), and pregnancy could result. You should therefore use a different or additional form of birth control while taking this medication. Discuss this with your doctor.

BE SURE TO TELL YOUR DOCTOR about any medications you are currently taking, especially any of those listed above.

WARNINGS

• Tell your doctor about unusual or allergic reactions you have had to any medications, especially to penicillin or other penicillin antibiotics (such as ampicillin and amoxicillin), cephalosporin antibiotics, penicillamine, or griseofulvin.

• Tell your doctor if you now have or if you have ever had kidney disease, asthma, or allergies.

• This medication has been prescribed for your current infection only. Another infection later on, or one that someone else has, may require a different medicine. You should not give your medicine to other people or use it for other infections, unless your doctor specifically directs you to do so.

• People with diabetes who are taking penicillin should know that this drug can cause a false-positive sugar reaction with a Clinitest urine glucose test. To avoid this problem while taking penicillin, they should switch to Clinistix or Tes-Tape to test their urine for sugar.

• Be sure to tell your doctor if you are pregnant. Although penicillin appears to be safe during pregnancy, extensive studies in humans have not been conducted. Also tell your doctor if you are breast-feeding an infant. Small amounts of this medication pass into breast milk and may temporarily alter the bacterial balance in the intestinal tract of a nursing infant, resulting in diarrhea.

---

pentazocine

BRAND NAME (Manufacturer)
Talwin NX (Winthrop)
TYPE OF DRUG
Analgesic
INGREDIENTS
pentazocine and naloxone
DOSAGE FORM
Tablets (50 mg pentazocine and 0.5 mg naloxone)
STORAGE
Pentazocine tablets should be stored at room temperature in a tightly closed, light-resistant container.

USES

Pentazocine is a narcotic analgesic that acts directly on the central nervous system (brain and spinal cord) to relieve moderate to severe pain. Naloxone is added to this compound to prevent abuse. It is not absorbed from the gastrointestinal tract, but it does block the action of pentazocine if the drug is injected into the body.

TREATMENT

In order to avoid getting an upset stomach, you can take pentazocine with food or with a full glass of milk or water.

This medication works most effectively if you take it at the onset of pain, rather than waiting until the pain becomes intense.

If you are taking this medication on a regular schedule and you miss a dose, take the missed dose as soon as possible, unless it is almost time for your next dose. In that case, do not take the missed dose at all; just return to your regular dosing schedule. Do not double the next dose.

SIDE EFFECTS

Minor. Constipation, dizziness, drowsiness, dry mouth, false sense of well-being, flushing, light-headedness, loss of appetite, nausea, rash, or sweating. These side effects should disappear as your body adjusts to the medication.

If you are constipated, increase the amount of fiber in your diet (fresh fruits and vegetables, salads, bran, and whole-grain breads), exercise, and drink more water (unless your doctor directs you to do otherwise).

Chew sugarless gum or suck on ice chips or a piece of hard candy to reduce mouth dryness.

If you feel dizzy or light-headed, sit or lie down for a while; get up slowly from a sitting or lying position; and be careful on stairs.

Major. Tell your doctor about any side effects that are persistent or particularly bothersome. IT IS ESPECIALLY IMPORTANT TO TELL YOUR DOCTOR about anxiety, difficulty in breathing, excitation, fatigue, painful or difficult urination, palpitations, rash, restlessness, sore throat and fever, tremors, or weakness.

INTERACTIONS

Pentazocine interacts with several other types of drugs:

1. Concurrent use of it with other central nervous system depressants (such as alcohol, antihistamines, barbiturates, benzodiazepine tranquilizers, muscle relaxants, and phenothiazine tranquilizers) or with tricyclic antidepressants can cause extreme drowsiness.

2. A monoamine oxidase (MAO) inhibitor taken within 14 days of this drug can lead to unpredictable side effects.

3. The combination of cimetidine and this medication may cause confusion, disorientation, and shortness of breath.

BE SURE TO TELL YOUR DOCTOR about any medications you are currently taking, especially those listed above.

WARNINGS

• Tell your doctor about unusual or allergic reactions you have had to any medications, especially to pentazocine or to other narcotic analgesics (such as codeine, hydrocodone, hydromorphone, meperidine, methadone, morphine, oxycodone, and propoxyphene).

• Tell your doctor if you now have or if you have ever had acute abdominal conditions, asthma, brain disease, colitis, epilepsy, gallstones or gallbladder disease, head injuries, heart disease, kidney disease, liver disease, lung disease, mental illness, emotional disorders, enlarged prostate gland, thyroid disease, or urethral stricture.

• If this drug makes you dizzy or drowsy, do not take part in any activity that requires alertness, such as driving a car or operating potentially dangerous machinery.

• Before having surgery or any other medical or dental treatment, be sure to tell your doctor or dentist that you are taking this medication.

• Because this product contains pentazocine, it has the potential for abuse and must be used with caution. It should not normally be taken on a regular schedule for longer than ten days unless your doctor directs you to do so. Tolerance develops quickly; do not increase the dosage or stop taking the drug abruptly unless you first consult your doctor. If you have been taking large amounts of this medication, or have been taking it for long periods, you may experience a withdrawal reaction (muscle aches, diarrhea, gooseflesh, runny nose, nausea, vomiting, shivering, trembling, stomach cramps, sleep disorders, irritability, weakness, excessive yawning, or sweating) when you stop taking it.

• Be sure to tell your doctor if you are pregnant. The effects of this medication during the early stages of pregnancy have not been thoroughly studied in humans. However, pentazocine, used regularly in large doses during the later stages of pregnancy, may result in addiction of the fetus—leading to withdrawal symptoms (irritability, excessive crying, tremors, fever, vomiting, diarrhea, sneezing, or excessive yawning) at birth.

Also tell your doctor if you are breast-feeding an infant. Small amounts of this medication may pass into breast milk and cause excessive drowsiness in the nursing infant.

---

pentoxifylline

BRAND NAME (Manufacturer)
Trental (Hoechst-Roussel)
TYPE OF DRUG
Hemorrheologic
INGREDIENT
pentoxifylline
DOSAGE FORM
Sustained-release tablets (400 mg)
STORAGE
Store at room temperature in a tightly closed container.

USES

Pentoxifylline is used to treat intermittent claudication (leg pain caused by poor blood circulation) or peripheral vascular disease.

TREATMENT

Pentoxifylline should be taken with meals. The tablets should be swallowed whole; chewing, crushing, or breaking them will destroy the controlled-release activity and increase the risk of side effects.

If you miss a dose of pentoxifylline, take the missed dose as soon as possible, unless it is almost time for the next dose. In that case, do not take the missed dose at all; just wait until the next scheduled dose. Do not double the dose.

The benefits from pentoxifylline may be seen within two to four weeks after starting the medication.

SIDE EFFECTS

Minor. Abdominal pain, altered taste, belching, bloating, constipation, diarrhea, dizziness, drowsiness, dry mouth, excessive salivation, flushing, gas, headache, heartburn, insomnia, nasal congestion, nausea, nosebleeds, trembling of the hands, vomiting, or weight change. As your body adjusts to pentoxifylline, these side effects should disappear.

If you are constipated, increase the amount of fiber in your diet (fresh fruits and vegetables, salads, bran, and whole-grain breads), exercise, and drink more water (unless your doctor directs you to do otherwise).

To reduce mouth dryness, chew sugarless gum or suck on ice chips or a piece of hard candy.

If you feel dizzy or light-headed, lie or sit down for a while; get up slowly from a sitting or reclining position; and be careful on stairs.

Major. Tell your doctor about any side effects that are persistent or particularly bothersome. IT IS ESPECIALLY IMPORTANT TO TELL YOUR DOCTOR about chest pain, confusion, earache, flulike symptoms, itching, palpitations, rash, shortness of breath, sore throat, unusual bleeding or bruising, unusual weight gain, visual disturbances, or yellowing of the eyes or skin.

INTERACTIONS

Pentoxifylline interacts with other types of medications:

1. Anticoagulants (blood thinners, such as warfarin) in combination with pentoxifylline can increase the risk of bleeding complications.

2. Pentoxifylline can add to the blood-pressure-lowering effects of antihypertensive medications.

BE SURE TO TELL YOUR DOCTOR about any medications you are currently taking, especially any of the drugs that are listed above.

WARNINGS

• Before you take this medication, it is important to tell your doctor if you have or have ever had unusual or allergic reactions to any medications, especially to pentoxifylline or chemically related compounds, such as caffeine, dyphylline, oxtriphylline, theophylline, and aminophylline.

• Tell your doctor if you now have or if you have ever had liver disease, kidney disease, or peptic ulcer disease.

• Before having surgery or any other medical or dental treatment, be sure to tell your doctor or dentist that you are taking this drug. Pentoxifylline can increase bleeding complications.

• If pentoxifylline makes you dizzy or drowsy, do not take part in any activity that requires alertness, such as driving a car or operating dangerous machinery.
• Be sure to tell your doctor if you are pregnant. Although pentoxifylline appears to be safe in animals, studies in pregnant women have not been conducted. Also tell your doctor if you are breast-feeding an infant. Small amounts of pentoxifylline pass into human breast milk.

---

perphenazine and amitriptyline combination

BRAND NAMES (Manufacturers)
perphenazine and amitriptyline (various manufacturers)
Etrafon (Schering)
Triavil (Merck Sharp & Dohme)
TYPE OF DRUG
Phenothiazine tranquilizer and tricyclic antidepressant
INGREDIENTS
perphenazine and amitriptyline
DOSAGE FORM
Tablets (2 mg perphenazine and 10 mg amitriptyline; 2 mg perphenazine and 25 mg amitriptyline; 4 mg perphenazine and 10 mg amitriptyline; 4 mg perphenazine and 25 mg amitriptyline; and 4 mg perphenazine and 50 mg amitriptyline)
STORAGE
Store this drug at room temperature in a tightly closed, light-resistant container.

USES
Perphenazine and amitriptyline combination is used to relieve anxiety or depression. Amitriptyline belongs to a group of drugs referred to as tricyclic antidepressants. These medicines are thought to relieve depression by increasing the concentration of certain chemicals in the brain. Perphenazine is a phenothiazine tranquilizer. It is thought to relieve the symptoms of mental illness by blocking certain chemicals involved with nerve transmission in the brain.

TREATMENT

This medication should be taken exactly as your doctor prescribes. In order to avoid stomach irritation, you can take the tablets with food or with a full glass of water or milk (unless your doctor specifically directs you to do otherwise).

Antacids and antidiarrheal medicines may decrease the absorption of this medication from the gastrointestinal tract. Therefore, at least one hour should separate doses of perphenazine and amitriptyline combination and one of these medicines.

If you miss a dose of this medication, take the missed dose as soon as possible, unless it is within two hours of your next scheduled dose. In that case, do not take the missed dose at all; just return to your regular dosing schedule. Do not double your next dose of this medication.

The full benefits of this medication for the control of emotional or mental symptoms may not become apparent for two weeks after you start to take it.

SIDE EFFECTS

Minor. Bloating, blurred vision, constipation, cramps, decreased or increased sweating, diarrhea, dizziness, drowsiness, dry mouth, fatigue, headache, heartburn, insomnia, loss of appetite, nasal congestion, nausea, peculiar tastes in the mouth, restlessness, stomach upset, vomiting, weakness, or weight gain or loss. These side effects should disappear as your body adjusts to the medication.

This medication can increase your sensitivity to sunlight. You should therefore avoid prolonged exposure to sunlight and sunlamps. Wear protective clothing and sunglasses, and use an effective sunscreen.

This drug combination may cause a discoloration of the urine. This is a harmless effect.

If you experience dry mouth, you might want to try chewing sugarless gum or sucking on ice chips or a piece of hard candy.

To relieve constipation, increase the amount of fiber in your diet (fresh fruits and vegetables, salads, bran, and whole-grain breads). You can also increase your exercise level and drink more water (unless your doctor directs you otherwise).

To avoid dizziness and light-headedness when you stand, contract and relax the muscles of your legs for a few moments before rising. Do this by pushing one foot against the floor while raising the other foot slightly, alternating feet so that you are "pumping" your legs in a pedaling motion.

Major. Tell your doctor about any side effects you experience that are persistent or particularly bothersome. IT IS ESPECIALLY IMPORTANT TO TELL YOUR DOCTOR about agitation, confusion, convulsions, difficult or painful urination, enlarged or painful breasts (in both sexes), fainting, fever, hair loss, hallucinations, chest tightness, impotence, menstrual irregularities, mood changes, mouth sores, nervousness, nightmares, numbness in fingers or toes, palpitations, rash, ringing in the ears, sore throat, tremors, uncoordinated movements or balance problems, unusual bleeding or bruising, or yellowing of the eyes or skin.

INTERACTIONS

This drug interacts with several other types of drugs:

1. Extreme drowsiness can occur if this medication is taken with central nervous system depressants (such as alcohol, antihistamines, barbiturates, benzodiazepine tranquilizers, muscle relaxants, narcotics, pain medications, and sleeping medications) or with other antidepressants.

2. Amitriptyline may decrease the effectiveness of antiseizure medications and block the blood-pressure-lowering effects of clonidine and guanethidine.

3. Estrogens and oral contraceptives (birth control pills) can increase the side effects and reduce the effectiveness of amitriptyline.

4. Amitriptyline may increase the side effects of thyroid medication and of over-the-counter (nonprescription) cough, cold, allergy, asthma, sinus, and diet medications.

5. The concurrent use of this medication with monoamine oxidase (MAO) inhibitors should be avoided because the combination may result in fever, convulsions, or high blood pressure. At least 14 days should separate the use of this drug and the use of an MAO inhibitor.

6. Perphenazine can decrease the effectiveness of amphetamines, guanethidine, anticonvulsants, and levodopa.

7. The side effects of epinephrine and propranolol may be increased by perphenazine.

Before starting to take this medication, BE SURE TO TELL YOUR DOCTOR about any medications you are currently taking, especially any of those listed above.

WARNINGS

• Tell your doctor about unusual or allergic reactions you have or have ever had to any medications, especially to perphenazine or other phenothiazine tranquilizers (such as chlorpromazine, mesoridazine, fluphenazine, promazine, thioridazine, and prochlorperazine), or to amitriptyline or other tricyclic antidepressants (such as desipramine, doxepin, imipramine, and nortriptyline).

• Tell your doctor if you have ever had asthma, breast cancer, brain disease, diabetes mellitus, electroshock therapy, epilepsy, glaucoma, heart disease, a heart attack, liver disease, lung disease, kidney disease, thyroid disease, intestinal or urinary tract blockage, low or high blood pressure, Parkinson's disease, peptic ulcers, or enlarged prostate.

• The effects of this medication may last as long as seven days after you stop taking it, so continue to observe all precautions during that period.

• To prevent oversedation, avoid drinking alcoholic beverages while taking this medication.

• If this medication makes you dizzy or drowsy, do not take part in any activity that requires alertness, such as driving a car or operating potentially dangerous machinery. Be careful on stairs, and avoid getting up suddenly from a lying or sitting position.

• Prior to having surgery or any other medical or dental treatment, be sure to tell your doctor or dentist that you are taking this medication.

• This medication can decrease sweating and heat release from the body. You should therefore try not to get overheated (avoid exercising strenuously in hot weather and taking hot baths, showers, or saunas).

• Do not stop taking this medication suddenly. If the drug is stopped abruptly, you may experience nausea, vomiting, stomach upset, headache, increased heart rate, insomnia, tremors, or a worsening of your condition. Your doctor may want to reduce the dosage gradually.

• If you are planning to have a myelogram, or any other procedure in which dye will be injected into your spinal cord, tell your doctor you are taking this medication.

• While taking this medication, do not take any over-the-counter (nonprescription) medications for weight control or for cough, cold, asthma, allergy, or sinus problems without

first checking with your doctor. The combination of these medications with perphenazine and amitriptyline may cause high blood pressure.
• Be sure to tell your doctor if you are pregnant. Small amounts of this medication cross the placenta. Although there are reports of safe use of this drug during pregnancy, there are also reports of liver disease and tremors in newborn infants whose mothers received this type of medication close to term. Also tell your doctor if you are breast-feeding an infant. Small amounts of this medication pass into breast milk and may cause unwanted effects in the nursing infant.

phenazopyridine

BRAND NAMES (Manufacturers)
Azo-Standard* (PolyMedical)
Geridium (Goldline)
phenazopyridine hydrochloride (various manufacturers)
Pyridiate (various manufacturers)
Pyridium (Parke-Davis)
Urodine (various manufacturers)
Urogesic (Edwards)
*Available over the counter (without a prescription)
TYPE OF DRUG
Urinary tract analgesic
INGREDIENT
phenazopyridine
DOSAGE FORM
Tablets (95 mg, 100 mg, and 200 mg)
STORAGE
Phenazopyridine tablets should be stored at room temperature in a tightly closed, light-resistant container, well out of the reach of children and pets.

USES
Phenazopyridine is used for the symptomatic relief of the burning, pain, and discomfort caused by urinary tract infections or irritations. It is excreted in the urine, where it exerts a topical analgesic effect on the urinary tract. This medication is not useful for other types of pain.

TREATMENT

Phenazopyridine tablets should be taken with a full glass of water, either with meals or immediately after a meal.

If you miss a dose of this medication, take the missed dose as soon as possible, unless it is almost time for the next dose. In that case, do not take the missed dose at all; return to your regular dosing schedule. Do not double the dose.

SIDE EFFECTS

Minor. Dizziness, headache, indigestion, nausea, stomach cramps, or vomiting. These side effects should disappear as your body adjusts to the medication.

This drug causes urine to become orange-red. This is not harmful, but it may stain your clothing. The color of the urine will return to normal soon after the drug is discontinued.

If you feel dizzy, sit or lie down for a while; stand up slowly; and be careful on stairs.

Major. Tell your doctor about any side effects that are persistent or particularly bothersome. IT IS ESPECIALLY IMPORTANT TO TELL YOUR DOCTOR about a bluish color of the skin or fingernails, rash, unusual fatigue, or yellowing of the eyes or skin.

INTERACTIONS

Phenazopyridine should not interact with other medications as long as it is used according to directions.

WARNINGS

• Tell your doctor about unusual or allergic reactions you have had to any medications, especially to phenazopyridine.
• Notify your doctor if you have ever had kidney disease or heatitis.
• If this drug makes you dizzy, do not take part in any activity that requires alertness, such as driving a car.
• Diabetic patients using this medication may get delayed reactions or false-positive readings for sugar or ketones with urine tests. Clinitest is not affected by this medication, but the other urine sugar tests are.
• Be sure to tell your doctor if you are pregnant. Although phenazopyridine appears to be safe in animals, extensive studies in humans have not been conducted. Also tell your doctor

if you are breast-feeding an infant. It is not known whether phenazopyridine passes into breast milk.

---

phendimetrazine

BRAND NAMES (Manufacturers)
Bontril PDM (Carnrick)
Bontril Slow-Release (Carnrick)
Dyrexan-OD (Trimen)
Melfiat-105 (Numark)
phendimetrazine tartrate (various manufacturers)
Prelu-2 (Boehringer Ingelheim)
TYPE OF DRUG
Anorectic
INGREDIENT
phendimetrazine
DOSAGE FORMS
Tablets (35 mg)
Capsules (35 mg)
Sustained-release capsules (105 mg)
STORAGE
Phendimetrazine should be stored at room temperature in a tightly closed, light-resistant container. This medication should not be refrigerated.

USES
Phendimetrazine is used as an appetite suppressant during the first few weeks of dieting to help establish new eating habits. This medication is thought to relieve hunger by altering nerve impulses to the appetite control center in the brain. Its effectiveness lasts only for short periods (three to 12 weeks), however.

TREATMENT
You can take phendimetrazine with a full glass of water one hour before meals (unless your doctor directs otherwise).

The sustained-release form of this medication should be swallowed whole. Breaking, chewing, or crushing these capsules destroys their sustained-release activity and may increase the side effects.

In order to avoid difficulty in falling asleep, the last dose of this medication each day should be taken four to six hours (regular tablets) or ten to 14 hours (sustained-release capsules) before bedtime.

If you miss a dose of this medication, take the missed dose as soon as possible, unless it is almost time for your next dose. In that case, do not take the missed dose at all; just return to your regular dosing schedule. Do not double the next dose.

SIDE EFFECTS

Minor. Blurred vision, constipation, diarrhea, dizziness, dry mouth, false sense of well-being, fatigue, insomnia, irritability, nausea, nervousness, restlessness, stomach pain, sweating, unpleasant taste in the mouth, or vomiting. These side effects should disappear as your body adjusts to the medication.

Dry mouth can be relieved by sucking on ice chips or a piece of hard candy or by chewing sugarless gum.

In order to prevent constipation, increase the amount of fiber in your diet (fresh fruits and vegetables, salads, bran, and whole-grain breads). You can also increase your exercise and drink more water (unless your doctor tells you not to do so).

Major. Tell your doctor about any side effects you experience that are persistent or particularly bothersome. IT IS ESPECIALLY IMPORTANT TO TELL YOUR DOCTOR about changes in sexual desire, chest pain, difficulty in urinating, enlarged breasts (in either sex), fever, hair loss, headaches, impotence, menstrual irregularities, mental depression, mood changes, mouth sores, muscle pains, palpitations, rash, sore throat, tremors, or unusual bleeding or bruising.

INTERACTIONS

Phendimetrazine interacts with several other types of drugs:

1. Use of it within 14 days of a monoamine oxidase (MAO) inhibitor (furazolidine, isocarboxazid, pargyline, phenelzine, procarbazine, selegiline, or tranylcypromine) can result in high blood pressure and other side effects.

2. Phenothiazine tranquilizers (especially chlorpromazine) can antagonize (act against) the appetite-suppressant activity of this medication.

3. Phendimetrazine can decrease the blood-pressure-lowering effects of antihypertensive medications (especially guanethidine) and may alter insulin and oral antidiabetic medication dosage requirements in diabetic patients.

4. The side effects of other central nervous system stimulants, such as caffeine and over-the-counter (nonprescription) cough, allergy, asthma, sinus, diet, or cold preparations, may be increased by this medication.

Before starting to take phendimetrazine, BE SURE TO TELL YOUR DOCTOR about any medications you are currently taking, especially any of those drugs that are listed above.

WARNINGS

• Tell your doctor about unusual or allergic reactions you have or ever have had to any medications, especially to phendimetrazine or other appetite suppressants (such as benzphetamine, phenmetrazine, diethylpropion, fenfluramine, mazindol, and phentermine) or to epinephrine, norepinephrine, ephedrine, amphetamines, dextroamphetamine, phenylephrine, phenylpropanolamine, pseudoephedrine, albuterol, metaproterenol, or terbutaline.

• Tell your doctor if you have a history of drug abuse or if you have ever had angina, diabetes mellitus, emotional disturbances, glaucoma, heart or cardiovascular disease, high blood pressure, or thyroid disease.

• Phendimetrazine can mask the symptoms of extreme fatigue and can cause dizziness or light-headedness. Your ability to perform tasks that require alertness, such as driving a car or operating potentially dangerous machinery, may be decreased.

• Before having surgery or other medical or dental treatment, be sure that you tell your doctor or dentist you are taking this drug.

• Phendimetrazine is related to amphetamine and may be habit-forming when taken for long periods of time (both physical and psychological dependence can occur). You should not increase the dosage of this medication or take it for longer than 12 weeks without first consulting your doctor. It is also important that you not stop taking this medication abruptly—fatigue, sleep disorders, mental depression, nausea, vomiting, or stomach cramps or pain could occur. Your doctor may want to decrease your dosage gradually.

• It is important to tell your doctor if you are pregnant. Although studies of phendimetrazine in humans have not been conducted, some of the appetite suppressants have been shown to cause side effects in the fetuses of animals that received large doses during pregnancy. Also tell your doctor if you are breast-feeding an infant. It is not known whether this medication passes into breast milk.

phenelzine

BRAND NAME (Manufacturer)
Nardil (Parke-Davis)
TYPE OF DRUG
Monoamine oxidase (MAO) inhibitor
INGREDIENT
phenelzine
DOSAGE FORM
Tablets (15 mg)
STORAGE
Phenelzine should be stored at room temperature in a tightly closed, light-resistant container.

USES
This medication is used to treat clinical depression. Phenelzine belongs to a group of drugs known as monoamine oxidase (MAO) inhibitors. It is not clearly understood how it works, but it is thought to increase the amounts of certain chemicals in the brain that act to relieve depression.

TREATMENT
You can take phenelzine either on an empty stomach or, to avoid stomach irritation, with food or milk (as directed by your doctor).

If you are taking a single daily dose, it is best to take the dose in the morning.

If you miss a dose of this medication and remember within two hours, take the missed dose immediately and then return to your regular dosing schedule. If more than two hours have passed, do not take the missed dose at all; just return to your regular dosing schedule. Do not double the next dose.

The full therapeutic benefits of this medication may not be observed for up to four weeks after you start to take it.

SIDE EFFECTS

Minor. Constipation, diarrhea, dizziness, drowsiness, dry mouth, fatigue, headache, insomnia, nausea, restlessness, stomach upset, sweating, or weakness. These side effects should disappear as your body gets accustomed to the medication.

Phenelzine can increase your sensitivity to sunlight. Avoid prolonged exposure to sunlight and sunlamps. Wear protective clothing and sunglasses, and use an effective sunscreen.

If you feel dizzy, sit or lie down for a while; get up slowly from a sitting or reclining position; and be careful on stairs.

To relieve constipation, increase the amount of fiber in your diet (fresh fruits and vegetables, salads, bran, and whole-grain breads) and drink more water (unless your doctor directs you to do otherwise).

To relieve mouth dryness, chew sugarless gum or suck on ice chips or a piece of hard candy.

Major. Tell your doctor about any side effects that are persistent or particularly bothersome. IT IS ESPECIALLY IMPORTANT TO TELL YOUR DOCTOR about anxiety, blurred vision, changes in sexual ability, chills, confusion, convulsions, darkened tongue, difficult or painful urination, fainting, false sense of well-being, hallucinations, jitteriness, mental disorders, rapid weight gain (three to five pounds within a week), uncoordinated movements, or yellowing of the eyes or skin.

If you experience a severe headache, stiff neck, chest pains, palpitations, or vomiting while taking this medication, CONTACT YOUR DOCTOR OR AN EMERGENCY ROOM IMMEDIATELY. These symptoms may be the result of a food or drug interaction.

INTERACTIONS

Phenelzine interacts with a number of drugs and foods:

1. Concurrent use of phenelzine with central nervous system depressants (such as alcohol, barbiturates, benzodiazepine tranquilizers, muscle relaxants, narcotics, pain medications, phenothiazine tranquilizers, and sleeping medications) or with tricyclic antidepressants can lead to extreme drowsiness.

2. The dosage of anticonvulsant medications may need to be adjusted when phenelzine is started.

3. The use of phenelzine within 14 days of either another monoamine oxidase inhibitor or carbamazepine, cyclobenzaprine, methyldopa, guanethidine, reserpine, levodopa, meperidine or another narcotic, amphetamines, ephedrine, methylphenidate, phenylpropanolamine, pseudoephedrine, or a tricyclic antidepressant can lead to serious (sometimes fatal) side effects.

4. Tyramine-containing foods and beverages (aged cheeses, sour cream, yogurt, pickled herring, chicken livers, canned figs, raisins, bananas, avocados, soy sauce, broad bean pods, yeast extracts, beer, and certain wines), excessive amounts of caffeine-containing beverages (coffee, tea, cocoa, and cola), or chocolate can also cause serious reactions in patients on phenelzine therapy.

5. Phenelzine can increase the blood-sugar-lowering effects of insulin and oral antidiabetic medications.

Before starting to take this medication, BE SURE TO TELL YOUR DOCTOR about any medications you are currently taking, especially any of those listed above.

Be sure you are aware of the foods that interact with phenelzine.

WARNINGS

• Tell your doctor about unusual or allergic reactions you have had to any medications, especially to phenelzine.

• Before starting to take this medication, be sure to tell your doctor if you now have or if you have ever had asthma, bronchitis, diabetes mellitus, epilepsy, glaucoma, severe headaches, heart disease, blood-vessel disease, kidney disease, liver disease, mental disorders, Parkinson's disease, pheochromocytoma, or thyroid disease.

• If this drug makes you dizzy or drowsy, do not take part in any activity that requires alertness, such as driving a car or operating potentially dangerous machinery.

• Before having surgery or any other medical or dental treatment, be sure to tell your doctor or dentist that you are taking this medication.

• Check with your doctor or pharmacist before taking any nonprescription asthma, allergy, cough, cold, diet, or sinus preparations. Using these products in combination with phenelzine may cause serious side effects.

• If you also have angina, do not increase your amount of physical activity unless you first check with your doctor.

Phenelzine can decrease the symptoms of angina without decreasing the risks of strenuous exercise.
• Be sure to tell your doctor if you are pregnant. Studies in animals have shown that phenelzine can cause birth defects if it is taken in high doses during pregnancy. Studies in humans have not been conducted. Also tell your doctor if you are breast-feeding an infant. Small amounts of phenelzine may pass into breast milk.

phenobarbital

BRAND NAMES (Manufacturers)
phenobarbital (various manufacturers)
Solfoton (ECR)
TYPE OF DRUG
Barbiturate sedative and anticonvulsant
INGREDIENT
phenobarbital
DOSAGE FORMS
Tablets (15 mg, 16 mg, 30 mg, 32 mg, 60 mg, 65 mg, and 100 mg)
Capsules (16 mg)
Oral liquid (15 mg and 20 mg per 5-mL spoonful, with 13.5% alcohol)
STORAGE
Phenobarbital tablets and capsules should be stored at room temperature in tightly closed containers. The oral liquid should be stored at room temperature in a tightly closed, light-resistant container. Phenobarbital liquid should not be used if the solution becomes cloudy—it is no longer effective. This medication should never be frozen.

USES
Phenobarbital is used to control convulsions, to relieve anxiety or tension, and to promote sleep. Phenobarbital belongs to a group of drugs known as barbiturates. The barbiturates are central nervous system (brain and spinal cord) depressants.

TREATMENT
In order to avoid stomach irritation, you should take phenobarbital with food or with a full glass of water or milk.

The oral-liquid form should be measured carefully with a specially designed 5-mL measuring spoon. An ordinary kitchen teaspoon is not accurate enough. The liquid dose can be taken by itself or diluted with water, milk, or fruit juice.

If phenobarbital is being taken as a sleeping aid, take it 30 to 60 minutes before you want to go to sleep.

If you are taking this medication for the treatment of seizures, phenobarbital works best when the level of medicine in your bloodstream is kept constant. Thus it is best to take the doses at evenly spaced intervals day and night. For example, if you are to take three doses a day, the doses should be spaced eight hours apart.

If you are taking this medication on a regular basis and you miss a dose, take the missed dose as soon as you remember. However, if it is almost time for your next dose, do not take the missed dose at all; just return to your regular dosing schedule. Do not double the next dose. If you are taking this medication to control seizures and you miss more than two doses, be sure to contact your doctor immediately.

SIDE EFFECTS

Minor. Constipation, diarrhea, dizziness, drowsiness, a "hangover" feeling, headache, nausea, stomach upset, or vomiting. These side effects should disappear as your body adjusts to the medication.

To relieve constipation, increase the amount of fiber in your diet (fresh fruits and vegetables, salads, bran, and whole-grain breads), exercise, and drink more water (unless your doctor directs you to do otherwise).

If you feel dizzy or light-headed, sit or lie down for a while; get up slowly from a sitting or reclining position; and be careful on stairs.

Major. Tell your doctor about any side effects that are persistent or particularly bothersome. IT IS ESPECIALLY IMPORTANT TO TELL YOUR DOCTOR about chest tightness, confusion, depression, difficulty in breathing, excitation, fatigue, feeling faint, hives or itching, loss of coordination, muscle or joint pain, skin rash, slurred speech, sore throat, unusual bleeding or bruising, unusual weakness, or yellowing of the eyes or skin.

INTERACTIONS

Phenobarbital interacts with other types of medications:

1. Concurrent use of it with other central nervous system depressants (such as alcohol, antihistamines, benzodiazepine tranquilizers, muscle relaxants, narcotics, pain medications, phenothiazine tranquilizers, and sleeping medications) or with tricyclic antidepressants can cause extreme drowsiness.

2. Valproic acid, chloramphenicol, and monoamine oxidase (MAO) inhibitors can prolong the effects of the barbiturates.

3. Phenobarbital can increase the elimination from the body (thereby decreasing the effectiveness) of oral anticoagulants (blood thinners, such as warfarin), digitoxin, tricyclic antidepressants, cortisonelike medications, doxycycline, metronidazole, quinidine, oral contraceptives (birth control pills), estrogen-containing drugs, phenytoin, acetaminophen, and carbamazepine.

4. Phenobarbital can decrease the absorption of griseofulvin from the gastrointestinal tract.

5. The combination of phenobarbital and furosemide can cause low blood pressure and fainting.

6. Phenobarbital can increase the side effects of cyclophosphamide or large doses of acetaminophen.

BE SURE TO TELL YOUR DOCTOR about any medications you are currently taking, especially any listed above.

WARNINGS

• Tell your doctor about unusual or allergic reactions you have had to any medications, especially to phenobarbital or other barbiturates (such as amobarbital, butabarbital, mephobarbital, pentobarbital, primidone, and secobarbital).

• Tell your doctor if you now have or if you have ever had acute or chronic (long-term) pain, Addison's disease (caused by an underactive adrenal gland), diabetes mellitus, kidney disease, liver disease, lung disease, mental depression, porphyria, or thyroid disease.

• Before having surgery or any other medical or dental treatment, tell your doctor or dentist you are taking this drug.

• If this medication makes you dizzy or drowsy, do not take part in any activity that requires alertness, such as driving a car or operating potentially dangerous machinery.

• This drug has the potential for abuse and must be used with caution. Tolerance to the medication develops quickly; do not increase the dosage or stop taking this drug unless you first consult your doctor. If you have been taking this drug for a long time or have been taking large doses of it, you may experience anxiety, muscle twitching, tremors, weakness, dizziness, nausea, vomiting, insomnia, or blurred vision when you stop taking it. Your doctor may want to reduce your dosage of this medication gradually.

• Some of these products contain the color additive FD&C Yellow No. 5 (tartrazine), which can cause allergic-type reactions (rash, fainting, difficulty in breathing) in certain susceptible individuals.

• Be sure to tell your doctor if you are pregnant. Phenobarbital crosses the placenta, and birth defects have been associated with the use of this medication during pregnancy. If phenobarbital is used during the last three months of pregnancy, there is a chance that the infant will be born addicted to the medication and will experience a withdrawal reaction (seizures or irritability) at birth. The infant could also be born with bleeding problems. The risks and benefits of treatment should be discussed with your doctor. Also tell your doctor if you are breast-feeding an infant. Small amounts of phenobarbital pass into breast milk.

---

phentermine

BRAND NAMES (Manufacturers)
Adipex-P (Gate)
Anoxine-AM (Hauck)
Fastin (Beecham)
Ionamin (Fisons)
Obe-Nix (Abana)
Obephen (Hauck)
Oby-Cap (Richwood)
phentermine hydrochloride (various manufacturers)
Zantryl (Ion)
TYPE OF DRUG
Anorectic
INGREDIENT
phentermine
DOSAGE FORMS
Tablets (8 mg, 30 mg, and 37.5 mg)

Capsules (15 mg, 18.75 mg, 30 mg, and 37.5 mg)
Sustained-release capsules (15 mg and 30 mg)
STORAGE
Phentermine should be stored at room temperature in tightly closed, light-resistant containers.

USES
Phentermine is used as an appetite suppressant during the first few weeks of dieting to help establish new eating habits. This medication is thought to relieve hunger by altering nerve impulses to the appetite control center in the brain. Its effectiveness lasts only for short periods of time (three to 12 weeks).

TREATMENT
You can take phentermine tablets, capsules, or timed-release capsules with a full glass of water one hour before meals (unless your doctor directs you to do otherwise).

The timed-release form should be swallowed whole.

In order to avoid difficulty in falling asleep, the last daily dose of this medication should be taken four to six hours (regular tablets and capsules) or ten to 14 hours (timed-release capsules) before bedtime.

If you miss a dose, take the missed dose as soon as possible, unless it is almost time for your next dose. In that case, do not take the missed dose at all; just return to your regular dosing schedule. Do not double the next dose.

SIDE EFFECTS
Minor. Blurred vision, constipation, diarrhea, dizziness, dry mouth, false sense of well-being, fatigue, insomnia, irritability, nausea, nervousness, restlessness, stomach pain, sweating, unpleasant taste in the mouth, or vomiting. These side effects should disappear as your body adjusts to the drug.

Dry mouth can be relieved by sucking on ice chips or a piece of hard candy or by chewing sugarless gum.

In order to prevent constipation, increase the amount of fiber in your diet (fresh fruits and vegetables, salads, bran, and whole-grain breads), exercise, and drink more water (unless your doctor tells you not to do so).
Major. Tell your doctor about any side effects that are persistent or particularly bothersome. IT IS ESPECIALLY IMPORTANT TO TELL YOUR DOCTOR about changes in sexual de-

sire, chest pain, difficulty in urinating, enlarged breasts (in both sexes), fever, hair loss, headaches, impotence, menstrual irregularities, mental depression, mood changes, mouth sores, muscle pains, palpitations, rash, sore throat, or tremors.

INTERACTIONS

Phentermine interacts with several other types of medications:

1. Use of it within 14 days of a monoamine oxidase (MAO) inhibitor (furazolidine, isocarboxazid, pargyline, phenelzine, procarbazine, selegiline, or tranylcypromine) can result in high blood pressure and other side effects.

2. Barbiturate medications and phenothiazine tranquilizers (especially chlorpromazine) can antagonize (act against) the appetite-suppressant activity of this medication.

3. Phentermine can decrease the blood-pressure-lowering effects of antihypertensive medications (especially guanethidine) and may alter insulin and oral antidiabetic medication dosage requirements in diabetic patients.

4. The side effects of other central nervous system stimulants—such as caffeine or over-the-counter (nonprescription) cough, cold, sinus, asthma, diet, or allergy preparations—may be increased by this medication.

BE SURE TO TELL YOUR DOCTOR about any medications you are currently taking, especially any of those listed above.

WARNINGS

• The combination of the appetite suppressants fenfluramine and phentermine ("fen-phen") may cause heart problems by affecting the valves that bring blood into and out of your heart. It is very important to tell your doctor if you have any of the following symptoms: irregular heartbeat, difficulty breathing, puffiness of the feet or hands, or a decreased ability to exercise.

• Tell your doctor about unusual or allergic reactions you have had to any medications, especially to phentermine or other appetite suppressants (such as benzphetamine, phendimetrazine, diethylpropion, fenfluramine, mazindol, and phenmetrazine), or to epinephrine, norepinephrine, ephedrine, amphetamines, dextroamphetamine, phenylephrine, phenylpropanolamine, pseudoephedrine, albuterol, metaproterenol, or terbutaline.

• Tell your doctor if you have a history of drug abuse or if you now have or have ever had angina, diabetes mellitus, emotional disturbances, glaucoma, heart or cardiovascular disease, high blood pressure, or thyroid disease.

• Phentermine can mask the symptoms of extreme fatigue and can cause dizziness or light-headedness. Your ability to perform tasks that require alertness, such as driving a car or operating potentially dangerous machinery, may be decreased. Appropriate caution should therefore be taken.

• Before having surgery or other medical or dental treatment, tell your doctor or dentist you are taking this drug.

• Phentermine is related to amphetamine and may be habit-forming when taken for long periods of time (both physical and psychological dependence can occur). Thus you should not increase the dosage of this medication or take it for longer than 12 weeks without first consulting your doctor. Do not stop taking this medication abruptly—fatigue, sleep disorders, mental depression, nausea, vomiting, or stomach cramps or pain could occur. Your doctor may want to decrease your dosage gradually.

• Be sure to tell your doctor if you are pregnant. Although studies of phentermine in humans have not been conducted, some of the appetite suppressants have been shown to cause side effects in the fetuses of animals that received large doses during pregnancy. Also tell your doctor if you are breast-feeding an infant. It is not known whether this medication passes into breast milk.

---

phenylephrine, promethazine, and codeine combination

BRAND NAMES (Manufacturers)
Phenergan VC with Codeine (Wyeth-Ayerst)
Pherazine VC with Codeine (Halsey)
Prometh VC with Codeine (various manufacturers)
TYPE OF DRUG
Adrenergic (decongestant), antihistamine, and cough-suppressant combination
INGREDIENTS
phenylephrine, promethazine, and codeine

DOSAGE FORM

Oral syrup (5 mg phenylephrine, 6.25 mg promethazine, and 10 mg codeine per 5-mL spoonful, with 7% alcohol)

STORAGE

Phenylephrine, promethazine, and codeine combination should be stored at room temperature in a tightly closed, light-resistant container. This medication should never be frozen.

USES

This combination medication is used to provide symptomatic relief of coughs due to colds, minor upper-respiratory-tract infections, and allergy.

Phenylephrine belongs to a group of drugs known as adrenergic agents (decongestants), which constrict blood vessels in the nasal passages to reduce swelling and congestion.

Promethazine belongs to a group of drugs known as antihistamines, which block the actions of histamine, a chemical released by the body during an allergic reaction. It is used to relieve or prevent symptoms of allergy.

Codeine is a narcotic cough suppressant that acts on the cough reflex center in the brain.

TREATMENT

To avoid stomach upset, take this medication with food, milk, or water (unless your doctor directs otherwise).

Each dose should be measured carefully with a specially designed 5-mL measuring spoon. An ordinary kitchen teaspoon is not accurate enough.

If you miss a dose of this medication, take the missed dose as soon as possible, unless it is almost time for your next dose. In that case, do not take the missed dose at all; just return to your regular dosing schedule. Do not double the next dose.

SIDE EFFECTS

Minor. Blurred vision, confusion, constipation, diarrhea, dizziness, dry mouth, heartburn, insomnia, loss of appetite, nasal congestion, nausea, nervousness, rash, restlessness, sweating, vomiting, or weakness. These side effects should disappear as your body adjusts to the medication.

This medication can cause increased sensitivity to sunlight. It is, therefore, important to avoid prolonged exposure to sun-

light and sunlamps. Wear protective clothing and use an effective sunscreen.

If you are constipated, increase the amount of fiber in your diet (fresh fruits and vegetables, salads, bran, and whole-grain breads), exercise, and drink more water (unless your doctor directs you to do otherwise).

Chew sugarless gum or suck on ice chips or a piece of hard candy to reduce mouth dryness.

If you feel dizzy or light-headed, sit or lie down for a while; get up slowly from a sitting or reclining position; and be careful on stairs.

In order to avoid difficulty in falling asleep, check with your doctor to see if you can take the last dose of this medication several hours before bedtime each day.

Major. Tell your doctor about any side effects you may be experiencing that are persistent or particularly bothersome. IT IS ESPECIALLY IMPORTANT TO TELL YOUR DOCTOR about convulsions, difficult or painful urination, difficulty in breathing, disturbed coordination, excitation, fainting, headaches, muscle spasms, nightmares, nosebleeds, severe abdominal pain, or sore throat or fever.

INTERACTIONS

This medication interacts with other types of drugs:

1. Concurrent use of this medication with central nervous system depressants (such as alcohol, barbiturates, benzodiazepine tranquilizers, muscle relaxants, narcotics, pain medications, and phenothiazine tranquilizers) or with tricyclic antidepressants can cause extreme drowsiness.

2. This medication can decrease the effectiveness of amphetamines, guanethidine, anticonvulsants, and levodopa.

3. The side effects of monoamine oxidase (MAO) inhibitors (isocarboxazid, pargyline, phenelzine, or tranylcypromine) and tricyclic antidepressants may also be increased. At least 14 days should separate the use of this drug and the use of an MAO inhibitor.

BE SURE TO TELL YOUR DOCTOR about any medications you are currently taking, especially those listed above.

WARNINGS

• Tell your doctor about unusual or allergic reactions you have had to any medications, especially to promethazine or other antihistamines (such as azatadine, brompheniramine, carbinoxamine, clemastine, cyproheptadine, chlorpheniramine, dexbrompheniramine, dimenhydrinate, diphenhydramine, diphenylpyraline, doxylamine, hydroxyzine, pyrilamine, trimeprazine, tripelennamine, and triprolidine); to phenothiazine tranquilizers, phenylephrine, or other adrenergic agents (such as albuterol, amphetamines, ephedrine, epinephrine, isoproterenol, metaproterenol, norepinephrine, pseudoephedrine, phenylpropanolamine, and terbutaline); or to codeine or any other narcotic cough suppressant or pain medication.

• Tell your doctor if you now have or if you have ever had asthma, brain disease, blockage of the urinary or digestive tract, diabetes mellitus, colitis, gallbladder disease, glaucoma, heart or blood-vessel disease, high blood pressure, kidney disease, liver disease, lung disease, peptic ulcers, enlarged prostate gland, or thyroid disease.

• This medication can cause drowsiness. Your ability to perform tasks that require alertness, such as driving an automobile or operating potentially dangerous tools, machinery, or other equipment, may be decreased. Appropriate caution should therefore be taken.

• Because this product contains codeine, there is a potential for abuse. Use it with caution. This medication usually should not be taken for longer than ten days at a time since a tolerance may develop quickly. Talk to your doctor before increasing the dosage.

• Before having surgery or any other medical or dental treatment, be sure to tell your doctor or dentist that you are taking this medication.

• Be sure to tell your doctor if you are pregnant. The effects of this medication during the early stages of pregnancy have not been thoroughly studied in humans. However, regular use of codeine during the later stages of pregnancy may lead to addiction of the fetus, resulting in withdrawal symptoms (irritability, excessive crying, tremors, fever, vomiting, diarrhea, sneezing, or excessive yawning) in the newborn infant. Also tell your doctor if you are breast-feeding an infant. Small amounts of this medication pass into breast milk and may cause unusual excitement or irritability in nursing infants.

phenylpropanolamine and chlorpheniramine combination

BRAND NAMES (Manufacturers)
Allerest 12-Hour* (Fisons)
Cold-Gest (Major)
Condrin-LA (Hauck)
Conex D.A.* (Forest)
Contac 12-Hour* (SmithKline Consumer)
Demazin* (Schering)
Drize (Ascher)
Dura-Vent/A (Dura)
Genamin* (Goldline)
Gencold* (Goldline)
Myminic* (My-K Labs)
Ornade (SmithKline Beecham)
phenylpropanolamine HCl and chlorpheniramine maleate (Cord)
Resaid S.R. (Geneva Generics)
Rhinolar-Ex 12 (McGregor)
Ru-Tuss (Boots)
Teldrin (SmithKline Beecham)
Triaminic* (Dorsey)
Triaminic-12* (Sandoz)
Triphenyl (Rugby)
*Available over the counter (without a prescription)
TYPE OF DRUG
Adrenergic (decongestant) and antihistamine
INGREDIENTS
phenylpropanolamine and chlorpheniramine
DOSAGE FORMS
Oral tablets (25 mg or 37.5 mg phenylpropanolamine and 4 mg chlorpheniramine)
Sustained-release tablets (25 mg phenylpropanolamine and 4 mg chlorpheniramine)
Sustained-release capsules (75 mg phenylpropanolamine and 4 mg, 8 mg, 10 mg, or 12 mg chlorpheniramine)
Oral syrup (12.5 mg phenylpropanolamine and 2 mg chlorpheniramine per 5-mL spoonful, with 5% or 7.5% alcohol)

STORAGE
Store this drug at room temperature in a tightly closed container.

USES
This drug combination is used to relieve the symptoms of upper respiratory tract infections, hay fever and other allergies, and sinusitis (inflammation of the sinuses).

Phenylpropanolamine belongs to a group of drugs known as adrenergic agents (decongestants). They act by constricting (narrowing) blood vessels in the nasal passages, thereby reducing swelling and congestion.

Chlorpheniramine belongs to a group of drugs known as antihistamines, which block the action of histamine, a chemical released by the body during an allergic reaction. It is used to relieve or prevent symptoms of allergy.

TREATMENT
In order to avoid stomach upset, you can take phenylpropanolamine and chlorpheniramine combination with food or with a full glass of milk or water (unless your doctor directs you to do otherwise).

The oral syrup form of this medication should be measured carefully with a specially designed 5-mL measuring spoon.

The sustained-release tablets and capsules should be swallowed whole. Breaking, chewing, or crushing these tablets or capsules destroys their sustained-release activity and may increase the side effects.

If you miss a dose of this medication, take the missed dose as soon as possible, unless it is almost time for your next dose. In that case, do not take the missed dose at all; just return to your regular dosing schedule. Do not double the next dose.

SIDE EFFECTS
Minor. Anxiety; blurred vision; constipation; diarrhea; dizziness; drowsiness; dry mouth, nose, and throat; heartburn; insomnia; irritability; loss of appetite; nasal congestion; nausea; restlessness; decreased sweating; vomiting; or weakness. These side effects should disappear over time as your body adjusts to the medication.

This medication can increase your sensitivity to sunlight. Avoid prolonged exposure to sunlight and sunlamps, wear protective clothing, and use a sunscreen.

If you are constipated, increase the amount of fiber in your diet (fresh fruits and vegetables, salads, bran, and whole-grain breads), exercise, and drink more water (unless your doctor directs you to do otherwise).

Chew sugarless gum or suck on ice chips or a piece of hard candy to reduce mouth dryness.

If you feel dizzy, sit or lie down for a while; get up slowly from a sitting or reclining position; and be careful on stairs.

In order to avoid difficulty in falling asleep, take the last dose of this medication several hours before bedtime.

Major. Tell your doctor about any side effects that are persistent or particularly bothersome. IT IS ESPECIALLY IMPORTANT TO TELL YOUR DOCTOR about chest pain, convulsions, difficult or painful urination, difficulty in breathing, fainting, hallucinations, headaches, loss of coordination, confusion, mood changes, nosebleeds, palpitations, rash, severe abdominal pain, sore throat, or unusual bleeding or bruising.

INTERACTIONS

This drug will interact with several other types of medications:

1. Concurrent use of it with central nervous system depressants (such as alcohol, barbiturates, benzodiazepine tranquilizers, muscle relaxants, narcotics, pain medications, and phenothiazine tranquilizers) or with tricyclic antidepressants can cause extreme drowsiness.

2. Monoamine oxidase (MAO) inhibitors (furazolidine, isocarboxazid, pargyline, phenelzine, procarbazine, selegiline, or tranylcypromine) and tricyclic antidepressants can increase the side effects of this medication. At least 14 days should separate the use of this drug and the use of an MAO inhibitor.

3. The side effects of the antihistamine part of this medication may be increased by quinidine, procainamide, haloperidol, and phenothiazine tranquilizers; and the side effects of the decongestant component may be increased by digoxin or over-the-counter (nonprescription) diet, allergy, asthma, cough, cold, or sinus preparations.

4. The blood-pressure-lowering effects of guanethidine may be decreased by this medication.

BE SURE TO TELL YOUR DOCTOR about any medications you are currently taking, especially any listed above.

WARNINGS

• Tell your doctor about unusual or allergic reactions you have had to any medications, especially to chlorpheniramine or other antihistamines (such as azatadine, brompheniramine, carbinoxamine, clemastine, cyproheptadine, dexchlorpheniramine, dimenhydrinate, diphenhydramine, diphenylpyraline, doxylamine, hydroxyzine, promethazine, pyrilamine, trimeprazine, tripelennamine, and triprolidine) or to phenylpropanolamine or other adrenergic agents (such as albuterol, amphetamines, ephedrine, epinephrine, isoproterenol, metaproterenol, norepinephrine, pseudoephedrine, and terbutaline).
• Tell your doctor if you now have or if you have ever had diabetes mellitus, epilepsy, glaucoma, heart or blood-vessel disease, hiatal hernia, high blood pressure, myasthenia gravis, obstructed bladder or intestinal tract, peptic ulcers, enlarged prostate gland, or thyroid disease.
• Because this drug can reduce sweating and heat release from the body, avoid excessive work or exercise in hot weather, and do not take hot baths, showers, or saunas.
• This medication can cause drowsiness. Exercise caution when performing tasks that require alertness, such as driving a car or operating potentially dangerous machinery. Be especially careful going up and down stairs.
• Be sure to tell your doctor if you are pregnant. The effects of this medication during pregnancy have not been thoroughly studied in humans. Also tell your doctor if you are breast-feeding an infant. Small amounts of this medication pass into breast milk.

---

phenylpropanolamine and guaifenesin combination

BRAND NAMES (Manufacturers)
Banex-LA (Luchem)
Dura-Vent (Dura)
Entex LA (Procter & Gamble Pharm.)

Guaipax (Eon Labs)
Nolex LA (Carnrick)
TYPE OF DRUG
Adrenergic (decongestant) and expectorant
INGREDIENTS
phenylpropanolamine and guaifenesin
DOSAGE FORM
Sustained-release tablets (75 mg phenylpropanolamine and
    400 mg or 600 mg guaifenesin)
STORAGE
Phenylpropanolamine and guaifenesin combination tablets
should be stored at room temperature in tightly closed con-
tainers.

USES

This drug combination is used to relieve the coughing and
congestion associated with colds, sinusitis (inflammation of
the sinuses), sore throat, bronchitis, and asthma.

Phenylpropanolamine belongs to a group of drugs known as
adrenergic agents (decongestants). They act by constricting
(narrowing) blood vessels in the nasal passages, thereby reducing any swelling and congestion. Guaifenesin is an expectorant, a drug that loosens bronchial secretions.

TREATMENT

In order to avoid stomach upset, you can take phenylpropanolamine and guaifenesin combination with food or
with a full glass of milk or water (unless your doctor directs
you to do otherwise).

These sustained-release tablets should be swallowed whole.
Breaking, chewing, or crushing them destroys their sustained-
release activity and may increase side effects.

If you miss a dose of this medication, take the missed dose
as soon as possible, unless it is almost time for your next dose.
In that case, do not take the missed dose at all; just return to
your regular dosing schedule. Do not double the next dose.

SIDE EFFECTS

Minor. Insomnia, nervousness, or restlessness. These side effects
should disappear as your body adjusts to the medication.

In order to help you avoid difficulty in falling asleep, take the
last dose of this medication several hours before bedtime.

Major. Tell your doctor about any side effects that are persistent or particularly bothersome. IT IS ESPECIALLY IMPORTANT TO TELL YOUR DOCTOR about fainting, headaches, nosebleeds, or palpitations.

INTERACTIONS

This drug will interact with several other types of medications:
1. Monoamine oxidase (MAO) inhibitors (furazolidine, isocarboxazid, pargyline, phenelzine, procarbazine, selegiline, or tranylcypromine) can increase the side effects of this medication. At least 14 days should separate the use of this drug and the use of an MAO inhibitor.
2. The blood-pressure-lowering effects of guanethidine may be decreased by this medication.
3. The side effects of the decongestant component of this medication can be increased by digoxin or by over-the-counter (nonprescription) allergy, asthma, cough, cold, diet, or sinus preparations.
   BE SURE TO TELL YOUR DOCTOR about any medications you are taking at the present time, especially any of the ones listed above.

WARNINGS

• Tell your doctor about unusual or allergic reactions you have had to any medications, especially to guaifenesin or phenylpropanolamine or to other adrenergic agents (such as albuterol, amphetamines, ephedrine, epinephrine, isoproterenol, metaproterenol, norepinephrine, pseudoephedrine, and terbutaline).
• Tell your doctor if you now have or if you have ever had one or more of the following: diabetes mellitus, glaucoma, heart or blood-vessel disease, high blood pressure, enlarged prostate, or thyroid disease.
• While you are taking this drug, drink at least eight glasses of water a day to loosen bronchial secretions.
• Be sure to tell your doctor if you are pregnant. Also tell your doctor if you are breast-feeding an infant. Small amounts of this medication pass into breast milk and may cause unusual excitement or irritability in nursing infants.

phenylpropanolamine, phenylephrine, and brompheniramine combination

BRAND NAMES (Manufacturers)
Bromophen T.D. (Rugby)
brompheniramine, phenylephrine, and phenylpropanolamine (Lederle)
Dimetapp Extentabs* (Robins)
Normatane Elixir (Vortech)
Tamine SR (Geneva Generics)
*Recently reformulated Dimetapp does not contain phenylephrine and is available without a prescription.

TYPE OF DRUG
Adrenergic (decongestant) and antihistamine

INGREDIENTS
phenylpropanolamine, phenylephrine, and brompheniramine

DOSAGE FORMS
Sustained-release tablets (15 mg phenylpropanolamine, 15 mg phenylephrine, and 12 mg brompheniramine; recently reformulated Dimetapp Extentabs contain 75 mg phenylpropanolamine and 12 mg brompheniramine, but no phenylephrine)
Oral elixir (5 mg phenylpropanolamine, 5 mg phenylephrine, 4 mg brompheniramine per 5-mL spoonful, with 2.3% or 3% alcohol)

STORAGE
The tablets and oral elixir should be stored at room temperature in tightly closed, light-resistant containers. This medication should never be frozen.

USES

The combination of drugs in this medication is used to relieve the symptoms of upper-respiratory-tract infections, hay fever and other allergies, and sinusitis (inflammation of the sinuses).

Phenylpropanolamine and phenylephrine belong to a group of drugs known as adrenergic agents (decongestants). They act by constricting (narrowing) blood vessels in the nasal passages, thereby reducing swelling.

BromPheniramine belongs to a group of drugs known as antihistamines, which block the actions of histamine, a chemical released during an allergic reaction.

TREATMENT

In order to avoid stomach upset, you can take phenylpropanolamine, phenylephrine, and bromPheniramine combination with food or with a full glass of milk or water (unless your doctor directs you to do otherwise).

The oral elixir form of this medication should be measured carefully with a specially designed 5-mL measuring spoon. An ordinary kitchen teaspoon is not accurate enough.

The sustained-release tablets should be swallowed whole. Breaking, chewing, or crushing these tablets destroys their sustained-release activity and may increase their side effects.

If you miss a dose of this medication, take it as soon as possible, unless it is almost time for your next dose. In that case, do not take the missed dose at all; just return to your regular dosing schedule. Do not double the next dose.

SIDE EFFECTS

Minor. Anxiety; blurred vision; constipation; diarrhea; dizziness; drowsiness; dry mouth, nose, and throat; heartburn; insomnia; irritability; loss of appetite; nasal congestion; nausea; restlessness; decreased sweating; vomiting; or weakness. These side effects should disappear as your body adjusts to the medication.

If you are constipated, increase the amount of fiber in your diet (fresh fruits and vegetables, salads, bran, and whole-grain breads), and drink more water (unless your doctor directs you to do otherwise).

This medication can increase your sensitivity to sunlight. Accordingly, you should avoid prolonged exposure to sunlight and sunlamps, wear protective clothing, and use an effective sunscreen.

If you feel dizzy or light-headed, sit or lie down for a while; get up slowly from a sitting or reclining position; and be careful on stairs.

In order to avoid difficulty in falling asleep, take the last dose of this medication several hours before bedtime.

Major. Tell your doctor about any side effects that are persistent or particularly bothersome. IT IS ESPECIALLY IMPORTANT TO TELL YOUR DOCTOR about chest pain, confusion, convulsions, difficult or painful urination, difficulty in breathing, fainting, hallucinations, headaches, loss of coordination, mood changes, nosebleeds, palpitations, rash, severe abdominal pain, sore throat, or unusual bleeding or bruising.

INTERACTIONS

This drug can be expected to interact with several other medications:

1. Concurrent use of it with central nervous system depressants (such as alcohol, barbiturates, benzodiazepine tranquilizers, muscle relaxants, narcotics, pain medications, and phenothiazine tranquilizers) or with tricyclic antidepressants can cause extreme drowsiness.

2. Monoamine oxidase (MAO) inhibitors (furazolidine, isocarboxazid, pargyline, phenelzine, procarbazine, selegiline, or tranylcypromine) and tricyclic antidepressants can increase the side effects of this medication. At least 14 days should separate the use of this drug and the use of an MAO inhibitor.

3. The side effects of the antihistamine part of this medication may be increased by quinidine, procainamide, haloperidol, and phenothiazine tranquilizers; and the side effects of the decongestant component may be increased by digoxin or by over-the-counter (nonprescription) allergy, asthma, cough, cold, diet, or sinus preparations.

4. The blood-pressure-lowering effects of guanethidine may be decreased by this medication.

  BE SURE TO TELL YOUR DOCTOR about any medications you are currently taking, especially those listed above.

WARNINGS

• Tell your doctor about unusual or allergic reactions you have had to any medications, especially to brompheniramine, to other antihistamines (such as azatadine, chlorpheniramine, carbinoxamine, clemastine, cyproheptadine, dexchlorpheniramine, dimenhydrinate, diphenhydramine, diphenylpyraline, doxylamine, hydroxyzine, promethazine, pyrilamine, trimeprazine, tripelennamine, and triprolidine), or to phenylpropanolamine, phenylephrine, or other adrenergic agents (such as albuterol, ampheta-

mines, ephedrine, epinephrine, isoproterenol, metaproterenol, norepinephrine, pseudoephedrine, and terbutaline).
• Tell your doctor if you now have or if you have ever had diabetes mellitus, epilepsy, glaucoma, heart or blood-vessel disease, hiatal hernia, high blood pressure, myasthenia gravis, obstructed bladder or intestinal tract, peptic ulcers, enlarged prostate gland, or thyroid disease.
• Because this drug can reduce sweating and heat release from the body, avoid excessive work and exercise in hot weather, and do not take hot baths, showers, or saunas.
• This medication can cause drowsiness. Your ability to perform tasks that require alertness, such as driving a car or operating potentially dangerous machinery, may be decreased. Appropriate caution should therefore be taken.
• Be sure to tell your doctor if you are pregnant. Also tell your doctor if you are breast-feeding an infant. Small amounts of this medication pass into breast milk and may cause unusual excitement or irritability in nursing infants.

---

phenytoin

BRAND NAMES (Manufacturers)
Dilantin (Parke-Davis)
Dilantin Infatab (Parke-Davis)
Dilantin Kapseals (Parke-Davis)
Diphenylan (Lannett)
phenytoin (various manufacturers)
TYPE OF DRUG
Anticonvulsant
INGREDIENT
phenytoin
DOSAGE FORMS
Capsules (30 mg and 100 mg)
Chewable tablets (50 mg)
Oral suspension (125 mg per 5-mL spoonful, with less than 0.6% alcohol)
STORAGE
Phenytoin capsules, tablets, and oral suspension should be stored at room temperature in tightly closed, light-resistant containers. This medication should not be refrigerated and should never be frozen.

USES

Phenytoin is used to control certain types of convulsions, or seizures. It is not clear exactly how phenytoin works to control convulsions, but it appears to prevent the spread of seizure activity in the brain. Phenytoin may also be used to treat other conditions as determined by your physician.

TREATMENT

To avoid stomach irritation and increase this drug's absorption, take phenytoin with food or with a full glass of water or milk (unless your doctor directs you to do otherwise).

The tablet form of this medication should be chewed before swallowing.

The suspension form of this medication should be shaken well just before measuring each dose. The contents tend to settle on the bottom of the bottle, so it is necessary to shake the container to distribute the ingredients evenly and equalize the doses. Each dose should be measured carefully with a specially designed 5-mL measuring spoon.

Phenytoin works best when the level of medicine in your bloodstream is kept constant. It is best, therefore, to take the doses at evenly spaced intervals day and night. For example, if you are taking three doses a day, the doses should be spaced eight hours apart.

If you miss a dose of this medication, take the missed dose as soon as possible, unless it is almost time for the next dose. In that case, do not take the missed dose at all; just return to your regular dosing schedule. Do not double the next dose. If you miss two or more doses in a row, contact your doctor.

SIDE EFFECTS

Minor. Constipation, drowsiness (mild), headache, insomnia, nausea, or vomiting. These side effects should begin to disappear as your body gets accustomed to the medication.

To relieve constipation, increase the amount of fiber in your diet (fresh fruits and vegetables, salads, bran, and whole-grain breads), exercise, and drink more water (unless your doctor directs you to do otherwise).

Major. Tell your doctor about any side effects that are persistent or particularly bothersome. IT IS ESPECIALLY IMPORTANT TO TELL YOUR DOCTOR about blurred vision, change in the color of your urine, chest pain, confusion, dizziness, change in facial features, gum enlargement, increased hair growth, joint pain, muscle twitching, nervousness, numbness, rash, slurred speech, sore throat, swollen glands, uncoordinated movements, unusual bleeding or bruising, or yellowing of the eyes or skin.

INTERACTIONS

Phenytoin can be expected to interact with a number of other types of medications:

1. The effectiveness of phenytoin can be decreased by concurrent use of alcohol, barbiturates, folic acid, tricyclic antidepressants, reserpine, molindone, benzodiazepine tranquilizers, chloral hydrate, rifampin, phenothiazine tranquilizers, and haloperidol.

2. Phenytoin can decrease the effectiveness of calcifediol, warfarin, quinidine, disopyramide, dexamethasone, doxycycline, lamotrigine, levodopa, and oral contraceptives.

3. The active blood levels and side effects of phenytoin can be increased by chloramphenicol, cimetidine, disulfiram, isoniazid, ibuprofen, amiodarone, trimethoprim, sulfonamide antibiotics, tolbutamide, chlordiazepoxide, chlorpromazine, diazepam, estrogens, warfarin, ethosuximide, methylphenidate, or prochlorperazine.

4. Valproic acid can either increase or decrease the effects of phenytoin.

5. The dosage of oral antidiabetic medications may need to be adjusted when phenytoin is started.

6. Phenytoin may decrease the absorption of furosemide from the gastrointestinal tract, decreasing its effectiveness.

7. Antacids, calcium, oxacillin, sucralfate, medicines for diarrhea, and antineoplastics (anticancer drugs) may decrease the gastrointestinal absorption and effectiveness of phenytoin. Do not take phenytoin within two to three hours of taking an antacid or antidiarrheal.

Before starting to take phenytoin, BE SURE TO TELL YOUR DOCTOR about any medications you are currently taking, especially any of those listed above.

WARNINGS

• Tell your doctor about unusual or allergic reactions you have had to any medications, especially to phenytoin, ethotoin, or mephenytoin.

• Before starting to take this medication, be sure to tell your doctor if you now have or if you have ever had blood disorders, diabetes mellitus, or liver disease.

• If this drug makes you dizzy or drowsy, do not take part in any activity that requires alertness, such as driving a car or operating potentially dangerous machinery. Children should be careful while playing.

• Before surgery or other medical or dental treatment, tell your doctor or dentist you are taking phenytoin.

• Do not stop taking this medication unless you first consult your doctor. If this drug is stopped abruptly, you may experience uncontrollable seizures. Your doctor may want to reduce your dosage gradually. Be sure you have enough on hand for holidays and vacations.

• Although several generic versions of this drug are available, you should not switch from one brand to another without your doctor's assessment and approval. If you have your medication refilled and it looks different, be sure to consult with your pharmacist.

• Therapy with phenytoin may cause your gums to enlarge enough to cover your teeth. This can be minimized, at least partially, by frequent brushing and massaging of the gums with the rubber tip of a good toothbrush.

• Be sure to tell your doctor if you are pregnant. Birth defects have been reported more often in infants whose mothers have seizure disorders. It is unclear if the increased risk of birth defects is associated with the seizure disorders or with anticonvulsant medications such as phenytoin that are used to treat them. Discuss this with your doctor. Also tell your doctor if you are breast-feeding an infant.

---

pilocarpine (ophthalmic)

BRAND NAMES (Manufacturers)
Adsorbocarpine (Alcon)
Akarpine (Akorn)
Isopto Carpine (Alcon)
Ocusert Pilo-20 (Alza)
Ocusert Pilo-40 (Alza)
Pilocar (Iolab)
pilocarpine hydrochloride (various manufacturers)

TYPE OF DRUG
Antiglaucoma ophthalmic solution
INGREDIENT
pilocarpine
DOSAGE FORMS
Ophthalmic drops (0.25%, 0.5%, 1%, 2%, 3%, 4%, 5%, 6%, 8%, and 10%)
Ocular therapeutic system (oval ring of plastic that contains pilocarpine. The ring is placed in the eye, and the drug is released gradually over a period of seven days).
(20 mcg/hr and 40 mcg/hr)
STORAGE
Pilocarpine eye drops should be stored at room temperature in a tightly closed container. This medication should never be frozen. If it discolors or turns brown, it should be discarded. A color change signifies a loss of potency.

The ocular-therapeutic-system form of this medication should be stored in the refrigerator in its original container.

USES

Pilocarpine (ophthalmic) is used to reduce the increased pressure in the eye caused by glaucoma or other eye conditions. When pilocarpine is applied to the eye, it constricts the pupil and increases the flow of fluid (aqueous humor) out of the eye, thereby reducing the pressure.

TREATMENT

Wash your hands with soap and water before applying this medication. In order to avoid contamination of the eye drops, be careful not to touch the tube portion of the dropper or let it touch your eye; do not wipe off or rinse the dropper after you use it.

To apply the eye drops, tilt your head back and pull down your lower eyelid with one hand to make a pouch below the eye. Drop the prescribed amount of medicine into this pouch and slowly close your eyes. Try not to blink. Keep your eyes closed and place one finger at the corner of the eye next to your nose for a minute or two, applying a slight pressure (to prevent loss of medication through the duct that drains fluid from the surface of the eye into the nose and throat). Wipe away any excess with a clean tissue. If you think the medicine did not get into the eye, repeat the process once. Since the drops are somewhat difficult to apply, you may want some-one else to apply them for you.

If more than one type of eye drop has been prescribed, wait at least five minutes after instilling pilocarpine before using any other eye medicine (this is done in order to give the pi-locarpine a chance to work).

The ocular therapeutic system comes packaged with de-tailed instructions for insertion and removal. Follow these di-rections carefully. Damaged or deformed ocular-therapeutic systems should not be placed or retained in the eye. Use a new system instead.

If you miss a dose of this medication, apply the missed dose as soon as possible, unless it is almost time for the next dose. In that case, do not apply the missed dose at all; just return to your regular dosing schedule. Do not double the next dose.

SIDE EFFECTS

Minor. Blurred vision, browache, headache, or twitching of the eyelids. These side effects should disappear as your body adjusts to the medication.

Major. Tell your doctor about any side effects that are persis-tent or particularly bothersome. IT IS ESPECIALLY IMPOR-TANT TO TELL YOUR DOCTOR about diarrhea, difficult or painful urination, flushing, muscle tremors, nausea, near-sightedness, palpitations, shortness of breath, stomach cramps, or sweating.

INTERACTIONS

This medication should not interact with other drugs as long as it is applied according to directions.

WARNINGS

• Tell your doctor about unusual or allergic reactions you have had to any medications, especially to pilocarpine.

• Tell your doctor if you now have or if you have ever had asthma, epilepsy, heart disease, peptic ulcers, thyroid disease, Parkinson's disease, or blockage of the urinary tract.

• This drug can cause difficulty in adjusting to low light levels. Caution should be exercised during night driving and while performing hazardous tasks in poor light.

• Be sure to tell your doctor if you are pregnant. The effects of this drug during pregnancy have not been thoroughly studied in humans, but small amounts of pilocarpine may be absorbed into the bloodstream. Also tell your doctor if you are breast-feeding an infant.

---

pindolol

BRAND NAME (Manufacturer)
pinodol (various manufacturers)
Visken (Sandoz)
TYPE OF DRUG
Beta-adrenergic blocking agent
INGREDIENT
pindolol
DOSAGE FORM
Tablets (5 mg and 10 mg)
STORAGE
Pindolol should be stored at room temperature in a tightly closed, light-resistant container.

USES

Pindolol is used to treat high blood pressure. It belongs to a group of medicines known as beta-adrenergic blocking agents or, more commonly, beta blockers. These drugs work by controlling nerve impulses along certain nerve pathways.

TREATMENT

This medication can be taken with a glass of water, with meals, immediately following meals, or on an empty stomach (depending on your doctor's instructions). Taking your dosing schedule into consideration, you should try to take the medication at the same time or times each day.

Try not to miss any doses of this medicine. If you do miss a dose, take the missed dose as soon as possible, unless it is within eight hours (if you are taking this medicine once a day) or within four hours (if you are taking this medicine more than once a day) of your next scheduled dose. In those cases, do not take the missed dose at all; just return to your regular dosing schedule. Do not double the next dose.

Pindolol does not cure high blood pressure, but it will help to control the condition as long as you take it.

SIDE EFFECTS

Minor. Anxiety; constipation; decreased sexual ability; diarrhea; difficulty in sleeping; drowsiness; dryness of the eyes, mouth, and skin; headache; nausea; tiredness; or weakness. These effects should disappear as you adjust to the drug.

To relieve constipation, increase the amount of fiber in your diet (fresh fruits and vegetables, salads, bran, and whole-grain breads), exercise, and drink more water (unless your doctor directs you to do otherwise).

If you are extra-sensitive to the cold, be sure to dress warmly during cold weather.

Plain, nonmedicated eye drops (artificial tears) may help to relieve eye dryness.

Sucking on ice chips or chewing sugarless gum helps to relieve mouth or throat dryness.

Major. Tell your doctor about any side effects that are persistent or bothersome. IT IS ESPECIALLY IMPORTANT TO TELL YOUR DOCTOR about cold hands or feet (due to decreased blood circulation to skin, fingers, and toes), confusion, dizziness, fever and sore throat, hair loss, hallucinations, lightheadedness, mental depression, nightmares, numbness or tingling of the fingers or toes, rapid weight gain (three to five pounds within a week), reduced alertness, skin rash, swelling, unusual bleeding or bruising, or wheezing or difficulty in breathing.

INTERACTIONS

Pindolol interacts with a number of other types of drugs:

1. Indomethacin, aspirin, or other salicylates may decrease the blood-pressure-lowering effects of the beta blockers.

2. Concurrent use of beta blockers and calcium channel blockers (diltiazem, nifedipine, or verapamil) or disopyramide can lead to heart failure or very low blood pressure.

3. Cimetidine and oral contraceptives (birth control pills) can increase the blood concentrations of pindolol, which can result in greater side effects.

4. Side effects may also be increased when beta blockers are taken with clonidine, digoxin, epinephrine, phenylephrine, phenylpropanolamine, phenothiazine tranquilizers, prazosin, or monoamine oxidase (MAO) inhibitors. At least 14 days should separate the use of a beta blocker and the use of an MAO inhibitor.

5. Beta blockers may antagonize (work against) the effects of theophylline, aminophylline, albuterol, isoproterenol, metaproterenol, and terbutaline.

6. Beta blockers can also interact with insulin or oral antidiabetic agents, raising or lowering blood-sugar levels or masking the symptoms of low blood sugar.

7. The concurrent use of pindolol and reserpine can have additive blood-pressure-lowering effects.

8. The action of beta blockers may be increased if they are used with chlorpromazine, furosemide, or hydralazine.

9. Alcohol, barbiturates, and rifampin can decrease the blood concentrations of pindolol, which can result in a decrease in effectiveness.

BE SURE TO TELL YOUR DOCTOR about any medications you are currently taking, especially any listed above.

WARNINGS

• Before starting to take this drug, it is important to tell your doctor if you have ever had unusual or allergic reactions to any beta-blocking medication (acebutolol, atenolol, betaxolol, carteolol, esmolol, labetalol, metoprolol, nadolol, penbutolol, propranolol, or timolol).

• Be sure that you tell your doctor if you now have or if you have ever had allergies, asthma, hay fever, eczema, slow heartbeat, bronchitis, diabetes mellitus, emphysema, heart or blood-vessel disease, kidney disease, liver disease, thyroid disease, or poor circulation in your fingers or toes.

• You may want to check your pulse while taking this medication. If your pulse is much slower than your usual rate (or if it is less than 50 beats per minute), check with your doctor. A pulse rate that is too slow may cause circulation problems.

• This medicine may affect your body's response to exercise. Make sure you discuss with your doctor a safe amount of exercise for your medical condition.

• It is important that you do not stop taking this medicine unless you first check with your doctor. Some conditions may become worse when the medicine is stopped suddenly, and the danger of a heart attack is increased in some patients. Your doctor may want you to gradually reduce the amount of medicine you take before stopping completely. Make sure that you have enough medicine on hand to last through vacations, holidays, and weekends.

• Before having surgery or any other medical or dental treatment, tell your physician or dentist that you are taking pindolol. This medication will often be discontinued 48 hours prior to any major surgery.

• Pindolol can cause dizziness, drowsiness, light-headedness, or decreased alertness. Exercise caution while driving a car or using potentially dangerous machinery.

• While taking this medicine, do not use any over-the-counter (nonprescription) allergy, asthma, cough, cold, sinus, or diet preparations unless you first check with your pharmacist or doctor. Some of these medicines can result in high blood pressure if taken in conjunction with a beta blocker.

• Be sure to tell your doctor if you are pregnant. Animal studies have shown that some beta blockers can cause problems in pregnancy when used at very high doses. Adequate studies have not been conducted in humans, but there has been some association between beta blockers used during pregnancy and low birth weight, as well as breathing problems and slow heart rate in newborn infants. However, other reports have shown no effects on newborn infants. Also tell your doctor if you are breast-feeding. Although pindolol has not been shown to cause problems in breast-fed infants, some of the medicine may pass into breast milk.

---

piroxicam

BRAND NAMES (Manufacturers)
piroxicam (various manufacturers)
Feldene (Pfizer)
TYPE OF DRUG
Nonsteroidal anti-inflammatory analgesic
INGREDIENT
piroxicam
DOSAGE FORM
Capsules (10 mg and 20 mg)
STORAGE
Store in a tightly closed container at room temperature away from heat and direct sunlight. Do not refrigerate this medication. Do not keep this or any other medication beyond the expiration date written on the container.

USES

Piroxicam is used to treat the inflammation (pain, swelling, and stiffness) of certain types of arthritis, gout, bursitis, and tendinitis. Piroxicam blocks the production of certain body chemicals, called prostaglandins, that may trigger pain. It is not fully understood how piroxicam works, however.

TREATMENT

Take this medicine with food or antacids (unless your doctor directs you to do otherwise).

It is important to take piroxicam on schedule and not to miss any doses. If you do miss a dose, take the missed dose as soon as possible. However, if you are taking this drug once a day and are six hours late or if you take this drug twice a day and are two hours late, do not take the missed dose at all; just return to your regular dosing schedule. Do not double the next dose.

If you are taking piroxicam to relieve arthritis, you must take it regularly, as directed by your doctor. It may take up to three months before you feel the full benefits of this medication. Piroxicam does not cure arthritis, but it will help to control the condition as long as you continue to take it.

SIDE EFFECTS

Minor. Abdominal bloating, constipation, difficulty in sleeping, dizziness, drowsiness, headache, heartburn, indigestion, light-headedness, loss of appetite, nausea, nervousness, soreness of the mouth, unusual sweating, or vomiting. As your body adjusts to the drug, these side effects should disappear.

To relieve constipation, increase the amount of fiber in your diet (fresh fruits and vegetables, salads, bran, and whole-grain breads), exercise, and drink more water (unless your doctor directs you to do otherwise).

If you become dizzy, sit or lie down; get up slowly from a sitting or reclining position; and be careful on stairs.

Major. Tell your doctor about any side effects that are persistent or particularly bothersome. IT IS ESPECIALLY IMPORTANT TO TELL YOUR DOCTOR about bloody or black, tarry stools; blurred vision; confusion; depression; difficult or painful urination; a problem with hearing; palpitations; ringing or buzzing in the ears; skin rash, hives, or itching; stomach pain; swelling of the feet; tightness in the chest; unexplained sore throat and fever; unusual bleeding or bruising; unusual fatigue or weakness; unusual weight gain; wheezing or difficulty in breathing; or yellowing of the eyes or skin.

INTERACTIONS

Piroxicam can be expected to interact with several types of medications:

1. Anticoagulants (blood thinners, such as warfarin) can lead to an increase in bleeding complications.

2. Aspirin, salicylates, or other anti-inflammatory medications can increase stomach irritation.

3. Probenecid may increase blood levels of piroxicam, which may increase the risks of side effects.

4. The action of beta blockers may be decreased by this drug.

5. Piroxicam may interact with diuretics (water pills).

BE SURE TO TELL YOUR DOCTOR about any medications you are currently taking, especially any listed above.

WARNINGS

• Before you take this drug, BE SURE TO TELL YOUR DOCTOR if you have ever had unusual or allergic reactions to piroxicam or any of the other chemically related drugs (including aspirin or other salicylates, diclofenac, diflunisal, fenoprofen, flurbiprofen, ibuprofen, indomethacin, ketoprofen, meclofenamate, mefenamic acid, naproxen, oxyphenbutazone, phenylbutazone, sulindac, and tolmetin).

• Tell your doctor if you have ever had asthma, bleeding problems, colitis, epilepsy, heart disease, high blood pressure, kidney disease, liver disease, mental illness, Parkinson's disease, or stomach ulcers or other stomach problems.

• If this drug makes you dizzy or drowsy, do not take part in any activity that requires mental alertness, such as driving a car or operating potentially dangerous machinery or equipment.

• This drug can prolong bleeding time. Therefore, before having surgery or any other medical or dental treatment, it is important for you to tell your doctor or dentist that you are taking this medication.

• Stomach problems are more likely to occur if you take aspirin regularly or drink alcohol while being treated with this medication. Aspirin and alcohol should therefore be avoided (unless your doctor directs you to do otherwise).

• Be sure to tell your doctor if you are pregnant. Although studies in humans have not been conducted, unwanted cardiac (heart) side effects have been observed in the offspring of animals that received this type of drug during pregnancy. If taken late in pregnancy, it can also prolong labor. Also tell your doctor if you are breast-feeding an infant. Small amounts of piroxicam can pass into breast milk.

---

potassium chloride

BRAND NAMES (Manufacturers)
Cena-K (Century)
Kaochlor (Adria)
Kaon (Adria)
Kay Ciel (Forest)
K-Dur (Key)
K-Lor (Abbott)
Klor-Con (Upsher-Smith)
Klorvess (Sandoz)
Klotrix (Mead Johnson)
K-Lyte/Cl (Mead Johnson)
K-Tab (Abbott)
Micro-K (Robins)
Micro-K Extencaps (Robins)
potassium chloride (various manufacturers)
Rum-K (Fleming)
Slow-K (Ciba)
Ten-K (Summit)
TYPE OF DRUG
Potassium replacement
INGREDIENT
potassium chloride
DOSAGE FORMS
Effervescent tablets (20 mEq, 25 mEq, and 50 mEq)
Sustained-release tablets (6.7 mEq, 8 mEq, 10 mEq, and 20 mEq)
Enteric-coated tablets (2.5 mEq)
Sustained-release capsules (8 mEq and 10 mEq)
Oral liquid (10 mEq, 15 mEq, 20 mEq, 30 mEq, and 40 mEq per 15-mL spoonful; alcohol varying from 0% to 5%)
Oral powder (15 mEq, 20 mEq, and 25 mEq per packet)

STORAGE
Store at room temperature in a tightly closed container. Do not refrigerate potassium chloride.

USES
This medication is used to prevent or treat potassium deficiency, especially potassium deficiency that is caused by the use of diuretics (water pills).

TREATMENT
To avoid stomach irritation, this drug should be administered with food or immediately after a meal. Take it at the same time(s) each day.

Each dose of the liquid form of this medication should be measured carefully with a specially designed measuring spoon. An ordinary teaspoon is not accurate enough.

If you are taking the liquid, powder, or effervescent tablet form, dilute each dose in at least four ounces (½ cup) of cold water or juice. Be sure the medication has dissolved completely and has stopped fizzing before you drink it. Then sip it slowly. DO NOT use tomato juice to dissolve this medication (unless your doctor specifically directs you to do so). Tomato juice contains a great deal of sodium.

The sustained-release tablets and capsules should be swallowed whole. Chewing, crushing, or breaking these tablets or capsules destroys their sustained-release activity and possibly increases the side effects.

If you miss a dose of this medication, take the missed dose as soon as possible, unless it is within two hours of the next scheduled dose. In that case, do not take the missed dose at all; just return to your regular dosing schedule. Do not double the next dose.

SIDE EFFECTS
Minor. Diarrhea, nausea, stomach pains, or vomiting. These should disappear over time as your body makes an adjustment to the medicine.

Major. Tell your doctor about any side effects that are persistent or particularly bothersome. IT IS ESPECIALLY IMPORTANT TO TELL YOUR DOCTOR about anxiety; bloody or black, tarry stools; confusion; difficulty in breathing; numb ness or tingling in the arms, legs, or feet; palpitations; severe abdominal pain; or unusual weakness.

INTERACTIONS

Potassium chloride can be expected to interact with several other types of medications:

1. The combination of potassium chloride with amiloride, spironolactone, or triamterene can lead to hyperkalemia (high levels of potassium in the bloodstream).

2. The combination of digoxin and high doses of potassium chloride can lead to heart problems.

Before starting to take potassium chloride, BE SURE TO TELL YOUR DOCTOR about any medications you are currently taking, especially any of those listed above.

WARNINGS

• Tell your doctor about unusual or allergic reactions you have had to any medications, especially to potassium.

• Before starting to take this medication, be sure to tell your doctor if you now have or if you have ever had Addison's disease, dehydration, heart disease, heat cramps, hyperkalemia, intestinal blockage, kidney disease, myotonia congenita, or peptic ulcers.

• Ask your doctor about using a salt substitute instead of potassium chloride; salt substitutes are similar, but less expensive and more convenient. However, salt substitutes should only be used with your doctor's approval. Too much potassium can be dangerous.

• If you are taking the sustained-release tablets and you find something that looks like a tablet in your stool, there is no reason for concern. The drug is contained in a wax core that is designed to release the medication slowly. This wax core is eliminated in the stool.

• Some of these products contain the color additive FD&C Yellow No. 5 (tartrazine), which can cause allergic-type reactions (rash, shortness of breath, or fainting) in certain susceptible individuals.

• Be sure to tell your doctor if you are pregnant. Although this drug appears to be safe, extensive studies in pregnant women have not been conducted. Also tell your doctor if you are breast-feeding an infant.

pravastatin

BRAND NAME (Manufacturer)
Pravachol (Bristol-Myers Squibb)
TYPE OF DRUG
Antihyperlipidemic (lipid-lowering drug)
INGREDIENT
pravastatin
DOSAGE FORM
Tablets (10 mg, 20 mg, and 40 mg)
STORAGE
This medication should be stored in a tightly closed container at room temperature, away from heat and direct sunlight.

USES
Pravastatin is used to treat hyperlipidemia (high blood-fat levels). It may be prescribed with nondrug therapies such as diet control and exercise in an attempt to regulate lipid and cholesterol levels. Pravastatin chemically interferes with an enzyme in the body that is responsible for synthesizing cholesterol. This enzyme blockade decreases the LDL (low-density lipoprotein) type of cholesterol, which has been associated with coronary artery disease and atherosclerosis.

TREATMENT
This medication should be taken exactly as prescribed by your doctor. If you are to take pravastatin once a day, it is best to take the drug in the evening. Pravastatin can be taken with meals or a with a full glass of water if stomach upset occurs.

While using this medication, try to develop a set schedule for taking it. If you miss a dose and remember within a few hours, take the missed dose and resume your regular schedule. If many hours have passed, skip the dose you missed and then take your next dose as scheduled. Do not double the dose.

SIDE EFFECTS
Minor. Abdominal pain or cramps, constipation, diarrhea, gas, nausea, or stomach pain. These effects may be relieved by taking pravastatin with a meal, adding fiber to your diet, or using mild stool softeners, unless your doctor directs otherwise.

Major. Tell your doctor about any side effects that are persistent or particularly bothersome. IT IS ESPECIALLY IMPORTANT TO TELL YOUR DOCTOR about blurred vision (or any other visual changes or difficulties); or about muscle pain or tenderness, especially with malaise or fever.

INTERACTIONS

1. Pravastatin may increase the effectiveness of oral anticoagulants (blood thinners, such as warfarin) and digoxin.

2. Because of the risk of severe myopathy (muscle weakness) the combined use of pravastatin with gemfibrozil or clofibrate should generally be avoided.

3. Cyclosporine, erythromycin, nicotinic acid, or niacin may increase the side effects of pravastatin and should be used with extreme caution.

BE SURE TO TELL YOUR DOCTOR about any medications you are currently taking, especially those listed above.

WARNINGS

• Tell you doctor about unusual or allergic reactions you have had to any medications.

• Tell your doctor if you have ever had liver disease, heart disease, stroke, or disorders of the digestive tract.

• Patients taking another drug in this same class developed eye-related problems during treatment. It is advisable to have regular check-ups with your ophthalmologist, who should be informed of your use of this drug.

• This drug should not be taken if you are pregnant. Serious side effects have been reported in the offspring of animals that received this drug during pregnancy. Also be sure to tell your doctor if you are breast-feeding an infant. This drug should not be used while breast-feeding.

prazosin

BRAND NAMES (Manufacturers)
Minipress (Pfizer)
prazosin (various manufacturers)
TYPE OF DRUG
Antihypertensive

INGREDIENT
prazosin
DOSAGE FORM
Capsules (1 mg, 2 mg, 5 mg, and 10 mg)
STORAGE
Prazosin capsules should be stored at room temperature in a tightly closed, light-resistant container. This medication should not be refrigerated.

USES

Prazosin is used to treat high blood pressure. It is a vasodilator that relaxes the muscle tissue of the blood vessels, which in turn lowers blood pressure.

TREATMENT

To avoid stomach irritation, you can take prazosin with food or with a full glass of water or milk. In order to become accustomed to taking this medication, try to take it at the same time(s) each day.

The first dose of this medication can cause fainting, so it is often recommended that this dose be taken at bedtime.

If you miss a dose of this medication, take the missed dose as soon as possible, unless it is almost time for the next dose. In that case, do not take the missed dose at all; just return to your regular dosing schedule. Do not double the next dose.

Prazosin does not cure high blood pressure, but it will help to control the condition as long as you continue to take the medication.

The effects of this medication may not become apparent for two weeks.

SIDE EFFECTS

Minor. Abdominal pain, constipation, diarrhea, dizziness, drowsiness, dry mouth, frequent urination, headache, impotence, nasal congestion, nausea, nervousness, sweating, tiredness, vomiting, or weakness. These side effects should disappear as your body adjusts to the medication.

To relieve constipation, increase the amount of fiber in your diet (fresh fruits and vegetables, salads, bran, and whole-grain breads), exercise, and drink more water (unless your doctor directs you to do otherwise).

To relieve mouth dryness, chew sugarless gum or suck on ice chips or a piece of hard candy.

If you feel dizzy or light-headed, sit or lie down for a while; get up slowly from a sitting or reclining position; and be careful on stairs. To avoid dizziness or light-headedness when you stand, contract and relax the muscles of your legs for a few moments before rising. Do this by pushing one foot against the floor while raising the other foot slightly, alternating feet so that you are "pumping" your legs in a pedaling motion.

Major. Tell your doctor about any side effects that are persistent or particularly bothersome. IT IS ESPECIALLY IMPORTANT TO TELL YOUR DOCTOR about blurred vision; chest pain; constant erection; depression; difficulty in breathing; difficulty in urinating; fainting; hallucinations; itching; loss of hair; nosebleeds; palpitations; rapid weight gain (three to five pounds within a week); rash; ringing in the ears; swelling of the feet, legs, or ankles; or tingling of the fingers or toes.

INTERACTIONS

Prazosin may possibly interact with other types of medications:

1. The combination of prazosin and alcohol or verapamil can lead to a severe drop in blood pressure and fainting.

2. The severity and duration of the blood-pressure-lowering effects of the first dose of prazosin may be enhanced by a beta blocker.

BE SURE TO TELL YOUR DOCTOR about any medications you are currently taking, especially those listed above.

WARNINGS

• Tell your doctor about unusual or allergic reactions you have had to any medications, especially to doxazosin, prazosin, or terazosin.

• Before starting to take this medication, be sure to tell your doctor if you now have or if you have ever had angina (chest pain) or kidney disease.

• Because initial therapy with this drug may cause dizziness or fainting, your doctor will probably start you on a low dosage and increase the dosage gradually.

• If this drug makes you dizzy or drowsy or blurs your vision, do not take part in any activity that requires alertness, such as driving an automobile or operating potentially dangerous machinery.

• In order to avoid dizziness or fainting while taking this drug, try not to stand for long periods of time, avoid drinking excessive amounts of alcohol, and try not to get overheated (avoid exercising strenuously in hot weather and taking hot baths, showers, or saunas).

• Before taking any over-the-counter (nonprescription) sinus, allergy, asthma, cough, cold, or diet preparations, check with your doctor or pharmacist. Some of these products can cause an increase in blood pressure.

• Do not stop taking this medication unless you first check with your doctor. If you stop taking this drug you may experience a rise in blood pressure. Your doctor may, therefore, want to decrease your dosage gradually.

• Be sure to tell your doctor if you are pregnant. Although this drug appears to be safe, there have been only limited studies in pregnant women. Also tell your doctor if you are breast-feeding an infant.

---

prednisolone (systemic)

BRAND NAMES (Manufacturers)
Delta-Cortef (Upjohn)
prednisolone (various manufacturers)
Prelone (Muro)
TYPE OF DRUG
Adrenocorticosteroid hormone
INGREDIENT
prednisolone
DOSAGE FORMS
Tablets (5 mg)
Oral syrup (15 mg per 5-mL spoonful, with 5% alcohol)
STORAGE
Prednisolone tablets and oral syrup should be stored at room temperature (never frozen) in a tightly closed container.

USES
Your adrenal glands naturally produce certain cortisonelike chemicals. These chemicals are involved in various regulatory processes in the body (such as those involving fluid bal-

ance, temperature, and reaction to inflammation). Prednisolone belongs to a group of drugs known as adrenocorticosteroids (or cortisonelike medications). It is used to treat a variety of disorders, including endocrine and rheumatic disorders; asthma; blood diseases; certain cancers; eye disorders; gastrointestinal disturbances, such as ulcerative colitis; respiratory diseases; and inflammations, such as arthritis, dermatitis, and poison ivy. How this drug acts to relieve these disorders is not completely understood.

TREATMENT

In order to prevent stomach irritation, you can take prednisolone with food or milk.

Each dose of the oral syrup form should be measured carefully with a specially designed 5-mL measuring spoon. An ordinary kitchen teaspoon is not accurate enough.

If you are taking only one dose of this medication each day, try to take it before 9:00 A.M. This will mimic the body's normal production of this type of chemical.

It is important to try not to miss any doses of prednisolone. However, if you do miss a dose, follow these guidelines:

1. If you are taking it more than once a day, take the missed dose as soon as possible and return to your regular dosing schedule. If it is already time for the next dose, double it.

2. If you are taking this medication once a day, take the dose you missed as soon as possible, unless you don't remember until the next day. In that case, do not take the missed dose at all; just follow your regular dosing schedule. Do not double the next dose.

3. If you are taking this drug every other day, take it as soon as you remember. If you missed the scheduled time by a whole day, take it when you remember, then skip a day before you take the next dose. Do not double the next dose.

If you miss more than one dose of prednisolone, CONTACT YOUR DOCTOR.

SIDE EFFECTS

Minor. Dizziness, false sense of well-being, increased appetite, indigestion, menstrual irregularities, nausea, reddening of the skin on the face, restlessness, sleep disorders, sweating, or weight gain. These effects should begin to disappear as your body adjusts to the medication.

Major. Tell your doctor about any side effects that are persistent or particularly bothersome. IT IS ESPECIALLY IMPORTANT TO TELL YOUR DOCTOR about abdominal enlargement; abdominal pain; acne or other skin problems; back or rib pain; bloody or black, tarry stools; blurred vision; convulsions; eye pain; fever and sore throat; growth impairment (in children); headaches; impaired healing of wounds; increased thirst and urination; mental depression; mood changes; muscle wasting or weakness; rapid weight gain (three to five pounds within a week); rash; shortness of breath; thinning of the skin; unusual bruising or bleeding; or unusual weakness.

INTERACTIONS

Prednisolone interacts with several other types of medications:

1. Alcohol, aspirin, and anti-inflammatory medications (such as diclofenac, diflunisal, fenoprofen, flurbiprofen, ibuprofen, indomethacin, ketoprofen, meclofenamate, mefenamic acid, naproxen, piroxicam, sulindac, and tolmetin) aggravate the stomach problems that commonly accompany use of this medication.

2. The dosage of oral anticoagulants (blood thinners, such as wafarin), oral antidiabetic drugs, or insulin may require adjustment when this medication is being taken.

3. The loss of potassium caused by prednisolone can lead to serious side effects in individuals taking digoxin.

4. Thiazide diuretics (water pills) can increase the potassium loss caused by this medication.

5. Phenobarbital, phenytoin, rifampin, or ephedrine can increase the elimination of prednisolone from the body, thereby decreasing its effectiveness.

6. Oral contraceptives (birth control pills) and estrogen-containing drugs may decrease the elimination of this drug from the body, which can lead to an increase in side effects.

7. Prednisolone can increase the elimination of aspirin and isoniazid, thereby decreasing the effectiveness of these two medications.

8. Cholestyramine and colestipol can chemically bind this medication in the stomach and gastrointestinal tract, preventing its absorption.

BE SURE TO TELL YOUR DOCTOR about any medications you are currently taking, especially any listed above.

WARNINGS

• Tell your doctor about unusual or allergic reactions you have had to any medications, especially to prednisolone or other adrenocorticosteroids (such as betamethasone, cortisone, dexamethasone, hydrocortisone, methylprednisolone, prednisone, and triamcinolone).

• Tell your doctor if you now have or if you have ever had bone disease, diabetes mellitus, emotional instability, glaucoma, fungal infections, heart disease, high blood pressure, high cholesterol levels, myasthenia gravis, peptic ulcers, osteoporosis, thyroid disease, tuberculosis, ulcerative colitis, kidney disease, or liver disease.

• To help avoid potassium loss while you are using this medication, you can take your dose of the drug with a glass of fresh or frozen orange juice, or eat a banana each day. The use of a salt substitute also helps prevent potassium loss. Check with your doctor, however, before making any dietary changes or using a salt substitute.

• If you are using this medication for longer than a week and if you are subjected to stress, which you might experience as a result of serious infections, injury, or surgery, you may need to have your dosage adjusted. Discuss this with your doctor.

• If you have been taking this drug for more than a week, do not stop taking it suddenly. If it is stopped abruptly, you may experience abdominal or back pain, dizziness, fainting, fever, muscle or joint pain, nausea, vomiting, shortness of breath, or extreme weakness. Your doctor may, therefore, want to reduce the dosage gradually. Never increase the dosage or take the drug for longer than the prescribed time unless you first consult your doctor.

• While you are taking this drug, you should not be vaccinated or immunized. Prednisolone decreases the effectiveness of vaccines and can lead to overwhelming infection if a live-virus vaccine is administered.

• Before having surgery or any other medical or dental treatment, be sure to tell your doctor or dentist that you are taking this medication.

• Because this drug can cause glaucoma and cataracts with long-term use, your doctor may want you to have your eyes examined by an ophthalmologist periodically during treatment.

• If you are taking prednisolone for prolonged periods, you should wear or carry an identification card or notice stating that you are taking an adrenocorticosteroid.

• This medication can raise blood-sugar levels in diabetic patients. Blood-sugar levels should therefore be monitored carefully with blood or urine tests when this medication is being taken.

• Some of these products contain the color additive FD&C Yellow No. 5 (tartrazine), which can cause allergic-type reactions (shortness of breath, wheezing, rash, fainting) in certain susceptible individuals.

• Be sure to tell your doctor if you are pregnant. This drug crosses the placenta, and its safety in humans is not established. Birth defects have been observed in the fetuses of animals who were given large doses of this type of drug during pregnancy. Also tell your doctor if you are breast-feeding an infant. Small amounts of this drug pass into breast milk and may cause growth suppression or a decrease in natural adrenocorticosteroid hormone production in the nursing infant.

prednisone (systemic)

BRAND NAMES (Manufacturers)
Deltasone (Upjohn)
Liquid Pred (Muro)
Meticorten (Schering)
Orasone (Solvay)
Panasol-S (Seatrace)
Prednicen-M (Central)
prednisone (various manufacturers)
TYPE OF DRUG
Adrenocorticosteroid hormone
INGREDIENT
prednisone
DOSAGE FORMS
Tablets (1 mg, 2.5 mg, 5 mg, 10 mg, 20 mg, 25 mg, and 50 mg)
Oral syrup (5 mg per 5-mL spoonful, with 5% alcohol)
Oral solution (5 mg per 5-mL spoonful, with 5% alcohol)
Oral intensol solution (5 mg per mL, with 30% alcohol)

STORAGE
Prednisone should be stored at room temperature (never frozen) in a tightly closed container.

USES
Your adrenal glands naturally produce certain cortisonelike chemicals. These chemicals are involved in various regulatory processes in the body (such as those involving fluid balance, temperature, and reaction to inflammation). Prednisone belongs to a group of drugs known as adrenocorticosteroids (or cortisonelike medications). It is used to treat a variety of disorders, including endocrine and rheumatic disorders; asthma; blood diseases; certain cancers; eye disorders; gastrointestinal disturbances, such as ulcerative colitis; respiratory diseases; and inflammations, such as arthritis, dermatitis, and poison ivy. How this drug acts to relieve these disorders is not completely understood.

TREATMENT
In order to prevent stomach irritation, you can take prednisone with food or milk.

If you are taking only one dose of this medication each day, try to take it before 9:00 A.M.

The oral syrup or solution form of this medication should be measured carefully with a specially designed dropper (intensol solution) or 5-mL measuring spoon. An ordinary kitchen teaspoon is not accurate enough for therapeutic purposes.

It is important to try not to miss any doses of prednisone. However, if you do miss a dose, follow these guidelines:

1. If you are taking it more than once a day, take the missed dose as soon as possible and return to your regular dosing schedule. If it is already time for the next dose, double it.

2. If you are taking this medication once a day, take the dose you missed as soon as possible, unless you don't remember until the next day. In that case, do not take the missed dose at all; just follow your regular dosing schedule. Do not double the next dose.

3. If you are taking this drug every other day, take it when you remember. If you missed the scheduled dose by a whole day, take it; then skip a day before you take the next dose. Do not double the dose.

If you miss more than one dose of prednisone, CONTACT YOUR DOCTOR.

SIDE EFFECTS

Minor. Dizziness, false sense of well-being, increased appetite, increased sweating, indigestion, menstrual irregularities, nausea, reddening of the skin on the face, restlessness, sleep disorders, or weight gain. These side effects should disappear as your body adjusts to the medication.

Major. Tell your doctor about any side effects that are persistent or particularly bothersome. IT IS ESPECIALLY IMPORTANT TO TELL YOUR DOCTOR about abdominal enlargement; abdominal pain; acne or other skin problems; back or rib pain; bloody or black, tarry stools; blurred vision; convulsions; eye pain; fever and sore throat; growth impairment (in children); headaches; impaired healing of wounds; increased thirst and urination; mental depression; mood changes; muscle wasting or weakness; rapid weight gain (three to five pounds within a week); rash; shortness of breath; thinning of the skin; unusual bruising or bleeding; or unusual weakness.

INTERACTIONS

Prednisone interacts with several other types of medications:
1. Alcohol, aspirin, and anti-inflammatory medications (such as diclofenac diflunisal, fenoprofen, flurbiprofen, ibuprofen, indomethacin, ketoprofen, meclofenamate, mefenamic acid, naproxen, piroxicam, sulindac, or tolmetin) aggravate the stomach problems that are common with this drug.
2. The dosage of oral anticoagulants (blood thinners, such as warfarin), oral antidiabetic drugs, or insulin may need to be adjusted when this medication is being taken.
3. The loss of potassium caused by prednisone can lead to serious side effects in individuals taking digoxin.
4. Thiazide diuretics (water pills) can increase the potassium loss caused by this medication.
5. Phenobarbital, phenytoin, rifampin, and ephedrine can increase the elimination of prednisone from the body, thereby decreasing its effectiveness.
6. Oral contraceptives (birth control pills) and estrogen-containing drugs may decrease the elimination of this drug from the body, which can lead to an increase in side effects.

7. Prednisone can increase the elimination of aspirin and iso-niazid, decreasing the effectiveness of these two drugs.
8. Cholestyramine and colestipol can chemically bind this medication in the stomach and gastrointestinal tract, preventing its absorption.

BE SURE TO TELL YOUR DOCTOR about any medications you are currently taking.

WARNINGS

• Tell your doctor about unusual or allergic reactions you have had to any medications, especially to prednisone or other adrenocorticosteroids (such as betamethasone, cortisone, dexamethasone, hydrocortisone, methylprednisolone, prednisolone, and triamcinolone).
• Tell your doctor if you now have or if you have ever had bone disease, diabetes mellitus, emotional instability, glaucoma, fungal infections, heart disease, high blood pressure, high cholesterol levels, kidney disease, liver disease, myasthenia gravis, peptic ulcers, osteoporosis, thyroid disease, tuberculosis, or ulcerative colitis.
• To help avoid potassium loss while using this drug, take your dose with a glass of fresh or frozen orange juice or eat a banana each day. The use of a salt substitute also helps prevent potassium loss. Check with your doctor before making any dietary changes.
• If you are using this medication for longer than a week, you may need to have your dosage adjusted if you are subjected to stress, such as serious infections, injury, or surgery.
• If you have been taking this drug for more than a week, do not stop taking it suddenly. If it is stopped abruptly, you may experience abdominal or back pain, dizziness, fainting, fever, muscle or joint pain, nausea, vomiting, shortness of breath, or extreme weakness. Your doctor may therefore want to reduce the dosage gradually. Never increase the dosage or take the drug for longer than the prescribed time unless you first consult your doctor.
• While you are taking this drug, you should not be vaccinated or immunized. This medication decreases the effectiveness of vaccines and can lead to overwhelming infection if a live-virus vaccine is administered.
• Before surgery or other medical or dental treatment, tell your doctor or dentist you are taking this drug.

• Because this drug can cause glaucoma and cataracts with long-term use, your doctor may want you to have your eyes examined by an ophthalmologist.

• If you are taking this medication for prolonged periods, you should wear or carry an identification card or notice stating that you are taking an adrenocorticosteroid.

• This drug can raise blood-sugar levels in diabetic patients. Blood sugar should therefore be monitored carefully with blood or urine tests when this drug is started.

• Be sure to tell your doctor if you are pregnant. Birth defects have been observed in the fetuses of animals that were given large doses of this drug during pregnancy. Also tell your doctor if you are breast-feeding an infant. It has been shown that small amounts of this drug pass into breast milk and may cause growth suppression or a decrease in natural adrenocorticosteroid production in the nursing infant.

---

primidone

BRAND NAMES (Manufacturers)
Mysoline (Wyeth-Ayerst)
primidone (various manufacturers)
TYPE OF DRUG
Anticonvulsant
INGREDIENT
primidone
DOSAGE FORMS
Tablets (50 mg and 250 mg)
Oral suspension (250 mg per 5-mL spoonful)
STORAGE
Primidone tablets and oral suspension should be stored at room temperature in tightly closed containers. This medication should never be frozen.

USES
Primidone is used to treat a variety of seizure disorders. This drug is converted in the body to phenobarbital. It is not understood exactly how primidone or phenobarbital acts to decrease the number of seizures, but both drugs are central nervous system (brain and spinal cord) depressants.

TREATMENT

In order to avoid stomach irritation, you can take primidone with food or with a full glass of water or milk (unless your doctor directs you to do otherwise).

The oral-suspension form of this medication should be shaken well just before measuring each dose. The contents tend to settle on the bottom of the bottle, so it is necessary to shake the container to distribute the ingredients evenly and equalize the doses. Each dose should then be measured carefully with a specially designed 5-mL measuring spoon.

Primidone works best when the level of medicine in your bloodstream is kept constant. It is best, therefore, to take the doses at evenly spaced intervals day and night.

It is important to try not to miss any doses of this medication. If you do miss a dose and remember within two hours, take the missed dose immediately. If more than two hours have passed, do not take the missed dose at all; just return to your regular dosing schedule. Do not double the next dose. If you miss two or more consecutive doses, it is important that you contact your doctor as soon as possible.

SIDE EFFECTS

Minor. Dizziness, drowsiness, fatigue, loss of appetite, nausea, or vomiting. These side effects should begin to disappear as your body gets accustomed to to the medication.

If you feel dizzy, sit or lie down for a while; get up slowly from a sitting or reclining position; and be careful on stairs.
Major. Tell your doctor about any side effects that are persistent or particularly bothersome. TELL YOUR DOCTOR about blurred vision, emotional disturbances, irritability, loss of coordination, or skin rash.

INTERACTIONS

Primidone interacts with several other types of medications:
1. Concurrent use of primidone with other central nervous system depressants (such as alcohol, antihistamines, barbiturates, benzodiazepine tranquilizers, muscle relaxants, narcotics, pain medications, phenothiazine tranquilizers, and sleeping medications) or with tricyclic antidepressants can lead to extreme drowsiness.
2. The blood levels and therapeutic effects of oral anticoagulants (blood thinners, such as warfarin), adrenocorticosteroids

(cortisonelike medications), digitoxin, phenytoin, doxycycline, and tricyclic antidepressants can be decreased by primidone.
3. Primidone can decrease the absorption of griseofulvin from the gastrointestinal tract, thereby decreasing its effectiveness.

Before starting to take primidone, BE SURE TO TELL YOUR DOCTOR about any medications you are currently taking.

WARNINGS

• Tell your doctor about unusual or allergic reactions you have had to any medications, especially to primidone, phenobarbital, or other barbiturates (such as amobarbital, butabarbital, mephobarbital, pentobarbital, and secobarbital).
• Before starting to take primidone, be sure to tell your doctor if you now have or if you have ever had asthma, kidney disease, liver disease, or porphyria.
• If this drug makes you dizzy or drowsy, do not take part in any activity that requires alertness, such as driving a car.
• Before having surgery or any other medical or dental treatment, be sure to tell your doctor or dentist that you are taking primidone.
• Do not stop taking this medication unless you first check with your doctor. Stopping the drug abruptly can lead to a worsening of your condition. Your doctor may therefore want to reduce your dosage gradually or start you on another drug when primidone is stopped.
• Be sure to tell your doctor if you are pregnant. An increased risk of birth defects in infants of mothers with seizure disorders has been reported. It is unclear whether this increased risk is associated with the disorders or with the anticonvulsant medications, such as primidone, that are used to treat them. Such drugs may also lead to bleeding complications in the newborn. The risks and benefits of treatment should be discussed with your doctor. Also tell your doctor if you are breast-feeding an infant. Primidone passes into breast milk and can cause extreme drowsiness in nursing infants.

probenecid

BRAND NAMES (Manufacturers)
Probalan (Lannett)
probenecid (various manufacturers)

TYPE OF DRUG
Uricosuric (antigout preparation)
INGREDIENT
probenecid
DOSAGE FORM
Tablets (500 mg)
STORAGE
Probenecid should be stored at room temperature in a tightly closed container. This medication should not be refrigerated.

USES

Probenecid is used to prevent gout attacks. It increases the elimination of uric acid (the chemical responsible for the symptoms of gout) through the kidneys. Probenecid is also occasionally used in combination with penicillin or ampicillin to increase the length of time that the antibiotics remain in the bloodstream.

TREATMENT

In order to avoid stomach irritation, you may take probenecid with a full glass of water or milk. You should also drink at least ten to 12 full eight-ounce glasses of liquids (not alcoholic beverages) each day to prevent formation of uric acid kidney stones.

If you miss a dose of this medication, take the missed dose as soon as possible, unless it is almost time for the next dose. In that case, do not take the missed dose at all; just return to your regular dosing schedule. Do not double the next dose.

SIDE EFFECTS

Minor. Dizziness, frequent urination, headache, loss of appetite, nausea, rash, sore gums, or vomiting. These side effects should disappear as your body adjusts to the medication.

If you feel dizzy, sit or lie down for a while; get up slowly from a sitting or reclining position; and be careful on stairs.
Major. Tell your doctor about any side effects that are persistent or particularly bothersome. TELL YOUR DOCTOR about fatigue, fever, flushing, lower back pain, painful or difficult urination, sore throat, unusual bleeding or bruising, or yellowing of the eyes or skin.

INTERACTIONS

Probenecid can be expected to interact with several other types of medications:

1. Aspirin and pyrazinamide antagonize (act against) the antigout effects of probenecid.

2. The blood levels of methotrexate, sulfonamide antibiotics, nitrofurantoin, oral antidiabetic medicines, ketoprofen, naproxen, indomethacin, rifampin, sulindac, dapsone, and clofibrate can be increased by probenecid, which can lead to an increase in side effects.

3. Alcohol, chlorthalidone, ethacrynic acid, furosemide, or thiazide diuretics (water pills) can increase blood uric acid levels, which can decrease the effectiveness of probenecid.

Before starting to take probenecid, BE SURE TO TELL YOUR DOCTOR about any medications you are taking, especially any of those listed above.

WARNINGS

• Tell your doctor about unusual or allergic reactions you have had to any medications, especially to probenecid.

• Before starting to take probenecid, be sure to tell your doctor if you now have or if you have ever had blood diseases, diabetes mellitus, glucose–6-phosphate dehydrogenase (G6PD) deficiency, kidney stones, peptic ulcers, or porphyria.

• People with diabetes using Clinitest urine glucose tests may get erroneously high readings of blood-sugar levels while they are taking this drug. Temporarily changing to Clinistix or Tes-Tape urine tests will avoid this problem.

• If probenecid makes you dizzy, do not take part in any activity that requires alertness, such as driving a car or operating potentially dangerous machinery.

• Avoid taking large amounts of vitamin C while on probenecid. Vitamin C can increase the risk of kidney stone formation.

• Probenecid is not effective during an attack of gout. It is used to prevent attacks.

• Tell your doctor if you are pregnant. Although probenecid appears to be safe, it does cross the placenta. Extensive studies in pregnant women have not been conducted. Also tell your doctor if you are breast-feeding an infant. It is not known whether probenecid passes into breast milk.

procainamide

BRAND NAMES (Manufacturers)
procainamide hydrochloride (various manufacturers)
Procan-SR (Parke-Davis)
Promine (Major)
Pronestyl (Princeton)
TYPE OF DRUG
Antiarrhythmic
INGREDIENT
procainamide
DOSAGE FORMS
Tablets (250 mg, 375 mg, and 500 mg)
Sustained-release tablets (250 mg, 500 mg, 750 mg, and
   1,000 mg)
Capsules (250 mg, 375 mg, and 500 mg)
STORAGE
Procainamide tablets and capsules should be stored in tightly
closed containers in a cool, dry place. Exposure to moisture
causes deterioration of this medication.

USES

Procainamide is used to treat heart arrhythmias. It corrects irregular heartbeats to achieve a more normal rhythm.

TREATMENT

To increase absorption, take procainamide with a full glass
of water on an empty stomach one hour before or two hours
after a meal. However, if this medication upsets your stomach, ask your doctor if you can take it with food or milk.

Try to take it at the same time(s) each day. Procainamide
works best when the amount of drug in your bloodstream is
kept at a constant level. This medication should therefore be
taken at evenly spaced intervals day and night. For example,
if you are to take this medication four times per day, the doses
should be spaced six hours apart.

The sustained-release tablets should be swallowed whole.
Breaking, chewing, or crushing these tablets destroys their
sustained-release activity and possibly increases the side effects.

If you miss a dose of this medication and remember within two hours, take the missed dose immediately. If more than two hours have passed (four hours for the sustained-release tablets), do not take the missed dose; just return to your regular dosing schedule. Do not double the next dose.

SIDE EFFECTS

Minor. Bitter taste in the mouth, diarrhea, dizziness, dry mouth, loss of appetite, nausea, stomach upset, or vomiting. These side effects should disappear as your body adjusts to the medication.

If you feel dizzy, sit or lie down for a while; get up slowly from a sitting or reclining position; and be careful on stairs.

To relieve mouth dryness, chew sugarless gum or suck on ice chips or a piece of hard candy.

Major. Tell your doctor about any side effects that are persistent or particularly bothersome. IT IS ESPECIALLY IMPORTANT TO TELL YOUR DOCTOR about chest pain, chills, confusion, depression, fainting, fatigue, fever, giddiness, hallucinations, itching, joint pain, palpitations, rash, sore throat, unusual bleeding or bruising, or weakness.

INTERACTIONS

Procainamide interacts with several other types of medications:

1. The combination of digoxin and procainamide can lead to an increase in side effects to the heart.

2. Procainamide can block the effectiveness of neostigmine, pyridostigmine, and prostigmine.

3. Cimetidine, ranitidine, and amiodarone can increase the blood levels of procainamide, which can lead to an increase in side effects.

Before starting to take procainamide, TELL YOUR DOCTOR about any medications you are currently taking.

WARNINGS

• Tell your doctor about unusual or allergic reactions you have had to any medications, especially to procainamide, procaine, lidocaine, benzocaine, or tetracaine.

• Before starting this medication, be sure to tell your doctor if you now have or if you have ever had asthma, heart block, kidney disease, liver disease, myasthenia gravis, or systemic lupus erythematosus.

• If this drug makes you dizzy, do not take part in any activity that requires alertness, such as driving a car or operating potentially dangerous machinery.

• Before having surgery or any other medical or dental treatment, be sure to tell your doctor or dentist that you are taking this medication.

• Do not stop taking this drug without first consulting your doctor. Stopping procainamide abruptly may cause a serious change in the activity of your heart. Your doctor may therefore want to reduce your dosage gradually.

• If you are taking Procan-SR and you occasionally notice something in your stool that looks like a tablet, it does not mean that the drug is not being absorbed. The drug is "held" in a wax core designed to release the medication slowly. The wax core is eliminated in the stool after the drug has been absorbed.

• Some of these products contain the color additive FD&C Yellow No. 5 (tartrazine), which can cause allergic-type symptoms (rash, shortness of breath, fainting) in certain susceptible individuals.

• Be sure to tell your doctor if you are pregnant. Although this drug appears to be safe, extensive studies in pregnant women have not been conducted. Also tell your doctor if you are breast-feeding an infant. It is not known whether procainamide passes into breast milk.

prochlorperazine

BRAND NAMES (Manufacturers)
Compazine (SmithKline Beecham)
Compazine Spansules (SmithKline Beecham)
prochlorperazine maleate (various manufacturers)
TYPE OF DRUG
Phenothiazine tranquilizer and antiemetic
INGREDIENT
prochlorperazine
DOSAGE FORMS
Tablets (5 mg, 10 mg, and 25 mg)
Sustained-release capsules (10 mg, 15 mg, and 30 mg)

Suppositories (2.5 mg, 5 mg, and 25 mg)
Oral syrup (5 mg per 5-mL spoonful)

STORAGE

The tablet and capsule forms of this medication should be stored at room temperature in tightly closed, light-resistant containers. The oral syrup and suppository forms may be stored in the refrigerator in tightly closed, light-resistant containers.

If the oral syrup turns slightly yellow, the medicine is still effective and can be used. However, if the syrup changes color markedly or has particles floating in it, it should not be used; rather, it should be discarded down the sink. Prochlorperazine should never be frozen.

USES

Prochlorperazine is prescribed to treat the symptoms of certain types of mental illness, such as the emotional symptoms of psychosis, the manic phase of manic-depressive illness, and severe behavioral problems in children. This medication is thought to relieve the symptoms of mental illness by blocking certain chemicals involved with nerve transmission in the brain. Prochlorperazine is also frequently used to treat nausea and vomiting (this medication works at the vomiting center in the brain to relieve nausea and vomiting).

TREATMENT

To avoid stomach irritation, you can take the tablet or capsule form of this medication with a meal or with a glass of water or milk (unless your doctor directs you to do otherwise).

Antacids and antidiarrheal medicines may decrease the absorption of this medication from the gastrointestinal tract. Therefore, at least one hour should separate doses of one of these medicines and prochlorperazine.

The sustained-release capsules should be swallowed whole; do not crush, break, or open them. Breaking the capsules releases the medication all at once, destroying their sustained-release activity.

Measure the oral syrup carefully with a specially designed 5-mL measuring spoon. An ordinary kitchen teaspoon is not accurate enough.

To use the suppository form, remove the foil wrapper (if the suppository is too soft to insert, refrigerate it for half an hour or run cold water over it before removing the wrapper), and moisten the suppository with water. Lie on your left side with your right knee bent. Push the suppository into the rectum, pointed end first. Lie still for a few minutes. Try to avoid having a bowel movement for at least an hour (to give the medication time to be absorbed).

If you miss a dose of this medication, take the missed dose as soon as possible, unless it is almost time for your next dose. In that case, do not take the missed dose at all; just return to your regular schedule. Do not double the dose (unless your doctor directs you to do so).

The full effects of this medication for the control of emotional or mental symptoms may not become apparent for two weeks after you start to take it.

SIDE EFFECTS

Minor. Blurred vision, constipation, decreased sweating, diarrhea, dizziness, drooling, drowsiness, dry mouth, fatigue, jitteriness, menstrual irregularities, nasal congestion, restlessness, vomiting, or weight gain. As your body adjusts to the medication, these side effects should disappear.

Prochlorperazine can also cause discoloration of the urine to red, pink, or red-brown. This is a harmless effect.

This medication can cause increased sensitivity to sunlight. It is therefore important to avoid prolonged exposure to sunlight and sunlamps. Wear protective clothing and sunglasses, and use an effective sunscreen.

If you are constipated, increase the amount of fiber in your diet (fresh fruits and vegetables, salads, bran, and whole-grain breads), exercise, and drink more water (unless your doctor directs you to do otherwise).

Chew sugarless gum or suck on ice chips or a piece of hard candy to reduce mouth dryness.

To avoid dizziness or light-headedness when you stand, contract and relax the muscles of your legs for a few moments before rising. Do this by pushing one foot against the floor while raising the other foot slightly, alternating feet so that you are "pumping" your legs in a pedaling motion.

Major. Tell your doctor about any side effects that are persistent or particularly bothersome. IT IS ESPECIALLY IMPORTANT TO TELL YOUR DOCTOR about unusual bleeding or bruising; breast enlargement (in both sexes); chest pain; convulsions; darkened skin; difficulty in swallowing or breathing; fainting; fever; impotence; involuntary movements of the face, mouth, jaw, or tongue; palpitations; rash; sleep disorders; sore throat; tremors; uncoordinated movements; visual disturbances; or yellowing of the eyes or skin.

INTERACTIONS

Prochlorperazine interacts with several other types of medications:

1. It can cause drowsiness when combined with alcohol or central nervous system depressants (drugs that slow the activity of the brain and spinal cord), such as barbiturates, benzodiazepine tranquilizers, muscle relaxants, narcotics, and pain medications, or with tricyclic antidepressants.

2. Prochlorperazine can decrease the effectiveness of amphetamines, guanethidine, anticonvulsants, and levodopa.

3. The side effects of epinephrine, monoamine oxidase (MAO) inhibitors, propranolol, phenytoin, and tricyclic antidepressants may be increased by this medication. At least 14 days should separate the use of this drug and the use of an MAO inhibitor.

4. Lithium may increase the side effects and decrease the effectiveness of this medication.

5. Thiazide diuretics can enhance the blood-pressure-lowering side effects of prochlorperazine.

Before starting to take prochlorperazine, BE SURE TO TELL YOUR DOCTOR about any medications you are currently taking.

WARNINGS

• Tell your doctor about unusual reactions you have had to any drugs, especially to prochlorperazine or other phenothiazine tranquilizers (such as chlorpromazine, fluphenazine, mesoridazine, perphenazine, promazine, thioridazine, trifluoperazine, and triflupromazine) or to loxapine.

• Tell your doctor if you have a history of alcoholism or if you now have or have ever had any blood disease, bone marrow disease, brain disease, breast cancer, blockage in the urinary or digestive tracts, drug-induced depression, epilepsy, high or low blood pressure, diabetes mellitus, glaucoma, heart or circulatory disease, liver disease, lung disease, Parkinson's disease, peptic ulcers, or an enlarged prostate gland.

• Tell your doctor about any recent exposure to a pesticide or an insecticide. Prochlorperazine may increase the side effects from the exposure.

• To prevent oversedation, avoid drinking alcoholic beverages while taking this medication.

• If this medication makes you dizzy or drowsy, do not take part in any activity that requires alertness, such as driving a car or operating potentially dangerous machinery. Be careful on stairs, and avoid getting up suddenly from a lying or sitting position.

• Prior to having surgery or any other medical or dental treatment, be sure to tell your doctor or dentist that you are taking this medication.

• Some of the side effects caused by this drug can be prevented by taking an antiparkinsonism drug. Discuss this with your doctor.

• This medication can decrease sweating and heat release from the body. You should therefore try not to get overheated (avoid exercising strenuously in hot weather, and avoid taking hot baths, showers, or saunas).

• Do not stop taking prochlorperazine suddenly if you have been taking it for a prolonged period. If the drug is stopped abruptly, you may experience nausea, vomiting, stomach upset, headache, increased heart rate, insomnia, tremors, or a worsening of your condition. Your doctor may therefore want to reduce the dosage gradually.

• If you are planning to have a myelogram, or any other procedure in which dye will be injected into your spinal cord, tell your doctor that you are taking this medication.

• Avoid spilling the oral syrup form on your skin; it may cause redness and irritation.

• While taking this medication, do not take any over-the-counter (nonprescription) medications for weight control or for cough, cold, allergy, asthma, or sinus problems unless you first check with your doctor. The combination of these medications with prochlorperazine may cause an increase in blood pressure.

• Be sure to tell your doctor if you are pregnant. Although there are reports of safe use of this drug during pregnancy, there are also reports of liver disease and tremors in newborn infants whose mothers received this type of medication close to term. Also notify your doctor if you are breast-feeding an infant.

promethazine

BRAND NAMES (Manufacturers)
Phenameth (Major)
Phenergan (Wyeth-Ayerst)
promethazine (various manufacturers)
TYPE OF DRUG
Antihistamine and antiemetic
INGREDIENT
promethazine
DOSAGE FORMS
Tablets (12.5 mg, 25 mg, and 50 mg)
Oral syrup (6.25 mg per 5-mL spoonful, with 7% alcohol;
    25 mg per 5-mL spoonful, with 1.5% alcohol)
Rectal suppositories (12.5 mg, 25 mg, and 50 mg)
STORAGE
Promethazine tablets and oral syrup should be stored at room temperature (never frozen) in tightly closed, light-resistant containers. The suppositories should be kept in the refrigerator in a tightly closed container.

USES
Promethazine is prescribed for a wide range of conditions. It belongs to a group of drugs known as antihistamines, which block the action of histamine, a chemical that is released by the body during an allergic reaction. It is therefore used to treat or prevent symptoms of allergy or hay fever. Promethazine also (1) works at the vomiting center in the brain and can be used for the prevention or treatment of nausea and vomiting; (2) is a central nervous system (brain and spinal cord) depressant, which produces light sleep or mild sedation; and (3) prevents motion sickness.

TREATMENT
To avoid stomach irritation, you can take the tablet or oral syrup form of this medication with a meal or with a glass of water or milk (unless your doctor directs otherwise).

Measure the oral syrup carefully with a specially designed 5-mL measuring spoon. An ordinary kitchen teaspoon is not accurate enough.

To use the suppository, remove the foil wrapper (if the suppository is too soft to insert, refrigerate it for half an hour or run cold water over it before removing the wrapper), and moisten the suppository with water. Lie on your left side with your right knee bent. Push the suppository into the rectum, pointed end first. Lie still for a few minutes. Try to avoid having a bowel movement for at least an hour (to give the medication time to be absorbed).

If you are taking this medication regularly and you miss a dose, take the missed dose as soon as possible, unless it is almost time for the next dose. In that case, do not take the missed dose at all; just return to your regular schedule. Do not double the next dose.

SIDE EFFECTS

Minor. Blurred vision, diarrhea, dizziness, drowsiness, dry mouth, light-headedness, nausea, or vomiting. These side effects should disappear as your body adjusts to this drug.

This medication can cause increased sensitivity to sunlight. It is therefore important to avoid prolonged exposure to sunlight and sunlamps. Wear protective clothing and sunglasses, and use an effective sunscreen.

To reduce mouth dryness, chew sugarless gum or suck on ice chips or hard candy.

To avoid dizziness or light-headedness when you stand, contract and relax the muscles of your legs for a few moments before rising. Do this by alternately pushing one foot against the floor while raising the other foot slightly, so that you are "pumping" your legs in a pedaling motion.

Major. Tell your doctor about any side effects that are persistent or particularly bothersome. IT IS ESPECIALLY IMPORTANT TO TELL YOUR DOCTOR about confusion; disorientation; involuntary movements of the face, mouth, jaw, or tongue; rash; uncoordinated movements; unusual bleeding or bruising; or yellowing of the eyes or skin.

INTERACTIONS

This medication will interact with several other types of medications:

1. Promethazine can cause extreme drowsiness when combined with alcohol or other central nervous system depressants (drugs that slow the activity of the brain and spinal cord), such as barbiturates, benzodiazepine tranquilizers, muscle relaxants, narcotics, and pain medications, or with tricyclic antidepressants.

2. Promethazine can decrease the effectiveness of amphetamines, guanethidine, anticonvulsants, and levodopa.

3. The side effects of epinephrine, monoamine oxidase (MAO) inhibitors, propranolol, and tricyclic antidepressants may be increased by this medication. At least 14 days should separate the use of this medication and the use of an MAO inhibitor.

BE SURE TO TELL YOUR DOCTOR about any medications you are currently taking, especially any of those listed above.

WARNINGS

• Tell your doctor about any unusual or allergic reactions you have had to any medications, especially to promethazine or any chemically related phenothiazine drug (chlorpromazine, fluphenazine, mesoridazine, perphenazine, prochlorperazine, promazine, thioridazine, trifluoperazine, triflupromazine).

• Before starting promethazine, tell your doctor if you now have or if you have ever had asthma, blockage of the urinary or digestive tract, diabetes mellitus, enlarged prostate gland, epilepsy, glaucoma, heart disease, liver disease, peptic ulcers, or sleep apnea.

• To prevent oversedation, avoid drinking alcoholic beverages while taking this medication.

• If this medication makes you dizzy or drowsy, do not take part in any activity that requires alertness, such as driving a car or operating potentially dangerous machinery. Be careful going up and down stairs.

• Prior to having surgery or any other medical or dental treatment, be sure to tell your doctor or dentist that you are taking this medication.

• Be sure to tell your doctor if you are pregnant. Small amounts of this medication cross the placenta. Although there are reports of safe use of this drug during pregnancy, there are also reports of liver disease and tremors in newborns whose mothers received this medication close to term. Also tell your doctor if you are breast-feeding. Small amounts of this medication pass into breast milk and may cause unwanted effects in nursing infants, such as sudden infant death syndrome (SIDS) or sleep apnea.

---

promethazine and codeine combination

BRAND NAMES (Manufacturers)
Phenergan with Codeine (Wyeth-Ayerst)
Pherazine with Codeine (Halsey)
Prometh with Codeine (Goldline)
TYPE OF DRUG
Antihistamine and cough suppressant
INGREDIENTS
promethazine and codeine
DOSAGE FORM
Oral syrup (6.25 mg promethazine and 10 mg codeine per 5-mL spoonful, with 7% alcohol)
STORAGE
This medication should be stored at room temperature in a tightly closed, light-resistant container. This combination medication should never be frozen.

USES

This drug combination is used to provide symptomatic relief of coughs due to colds, minor upper-respiratory tract infections, and allergies.

Promethazine belongs to a group of drugs known as antihistamines, which block the actions of histamine, a chemical released by the body during an allergic reaction. It is used to relieve or prevent symptoms of allergy.

Codeine is a narcotic cough suppressant that acts at the cough reflex center in the brain.

TREATMENT

To avoid stomach upset, you can take this medication with food or with a full glass of milk or water (unless your doctor directs you to do otherwise).

The oral syrup should be shaken well just before measuring each dose. The contents tend to settle on the bottom of the bottle, so it is necessary to shake the container to distribute the ingredients evenly and equalize the doses. Each dose should then be measured carefully with a specially designed 5-mL measuring spoon. An ordinary kitchen teaspoon is not accurate enough.

If you miss a dose of this medication, take the missed dose as soon as possible, unless it is almost time for your next dose. In that case, do not take the missed dose at all; just return to your regular dosing schedule. Do not double the next dose.

SIDE EFFECTS

Minor. Blurred vision; constipation; diarrhea; dizziness; dry mouth, throat, or nose; irritability; loss of appetite; confusion; nausea; restlessness; stomach upset; or unusual increase in sweating. These side effects should disappear as your body adjusts to the medication.

This medication can cause increased sensitivity to sunlight. Avoid prolonged exposure to sunlight, wear protective clothing and sunglasses, and use an effective sunscreen.

If you are constipated, increase the amount of fiber in your diet (fresh fruits and vegetables, salads, bran, and whole-grain breads), exercise, and drink more water (unless your doctor tells you not to do so).

Chew sugarless gum or suck on ice chips or a piece of hard candy to reduce mouth dryness.

If you feel dizzy or light-headed, sit or lie down for a while; get up slowly from a sitting or reclining position; and be careful on stairs.

Major. Tell your doctor about any side effects that are persistent or particularly bothersome. IT IS ESPECIALLY IMPORTANT TO TELL YOUR DOCTOR about convulsions, difficulty in breathing, difficult or painful urination, disturbed coordination, excitation, fainting, headaches, muscle spasms, nightmares, nosebleeds, palpitations, rash, ringing or buzzing in the ears, severe abdominal pain, sore throat or fever, or yellowing of the eyes or skin.

INTERACTIONS

This medicine interacts with other types of drugs:

1. Concurrent use of it with central nervous system depressants (drugs that slow the activity of the brain and spinal cord), such as alcohol, barbiturates, benzodiazepine tranquilizers, muscle relaxants, narcotics, pain medications, and phenothiazine tranquilizers, or with tricyclic antidepressants, can cause extreme drowsiness.

2. This medication can decrease the effectiveness of amphetamines, guanethidine, anticonvulsants, and levodopa.

3. This combination medication can increase the side effects of monoamine oxidase (MAO) inhibitors (furazolidine, isocarboxazid, pargyline, phenelzine, procarbazine, selegiline, or tranylcypromine) and tricyclic antidepressants. At least 14 days should separate the use of this drug and the use of an MAO inhibitor.

BE SURE TO TELL YOUR DOCTOR about any medications you are currently taking, especially any listed above.

WARNINGS

• Tell your doctor about unusual or allergic reactions you have had to any medications, especially to promethazine or other antihistamines; to phenothiazine tranquilizers; to codeine; or to any other narcotic cough suppressant or pain medication.

• Tell your doctor if you now have or if you have ever had asthma, brain disease, blockage of the urinary or digestive tract, diabetes mellitus, colitis, gallstones or gallbladder disease, glaucoma, heart or blood-vessel disease, high blood pressure, kidney disease, liver disease, lung disease, peptic ulcers, enlarged prostate gland, or thyroid disease.

• This medication can cause drowsiness. Your ability to perform tasks that require alertness, such as driving a car or operating potentially dangerous machinery, may be decreased. Appropriate caution should therefore be taken.

• Before having surgery or any other medical or dental treatment, be sure to tell your doctor or dentist that you are taking this medication.

• Because this product contains codeine, it has the potential for abuse and must be used with caution. Usually, it should not be taken on a regular schedule for longer than ten days at a time. Tolerance develops quickly; do not increase the dosage or stop taking the drug abruptly unless you first consult your doctor. If you have been taking large amounts of this medication or have been taking it for a long period of time, you may experience a withdrawal reaction (muscle aches, diarrhea, gooseflesh, runny nose, nausea, vomiting, shivering, trembling, stomach cramps, sleep disorders, irritability, weakness, excessive yawning, or sweating) when you stop taking it. Your doctor may therefore want to have you reduce the dosage.

• Be sure to tell your doctor if you are pregnant. The effects of this medication during the early stages of pregnancy have not been thoroughly studied in humans. However, regular use of codeine during the later stages of pregnancy may lead to addiction of the fetus, resulting in withdrawal symptoms (irritability, excessive crying, tremors, fever, vomiting, diarrhea, sneezing, yawning) in the newborn infant. There are also reports of liver disease and tremors in newborns whose mothers received this medication close to term. Also tell your doctor if you are breast-feeding an infant. Small amounts of this medication pass into breast milk and may cause unusual excitement or irritability in nursing infants as well as sudden infant death syndrome (SIDS) or sleep apnea.

propoxyphene

BRAND NAMES (Manufacturers)
Darvon (Lilly)
Darvon-N (Lilly)
Dolene (Lederle)
propoxyphene hydrochloride (various manufacturers)
TYPE OF DRUG
Analgesic
INGREDIENT
propoxyphene
DOSAGE FORMS
Capsules (65 mg)
Tablets (100 mg)
Oral suspension (10 mg per mL)
STORAGE
This medication should be stored at room temperature in tightly closed containers. This medication should not be refrigerated, and it should never be frozen.

USES

Propoxyphene is a narcotic analgesic that acts on the central nervous system (brain and spinal cord) to relieve mild to moderate pain.

TREATMENT

In order to avoid stomach upset, you can take propoxyphene with food or milk.

The suspension form of this medication should be shaken well just before measuring each dose. The contents tend to settle on the bottom of the bottle, so it is necessary to shake the container to distribute the ingredients evenly and equalize the doses. Each dose should be measured carefully with a specially designed 5-mL measuring spoon. An ordinary kitchen teaspoon is not accurate enough.

This medication works best if taken at the first sign of pain. Do not wait for the pain to become severe.

If your doctor has prescribed this medication to be taken on a regular schedule and you miss a dose, take the missed dose as soon as possible, unless it is almost time for your next dose. Do not take the missed dose at all; just return to your regular dosing schedule. Do not double the next dose.

SIDE EFFECTS

Minor. Blurred vision, constipation, dizziness, drowsiness, indigestion, light-headedness, nausea, nervousness, restlessness, vomiting, or weakness. As your body adjusts to the medication, these side effects should disappear.

If you are constipated, increase the amount of fiber in your diet (fresh fruits and vegetables, salads, bran, and whole-grain breads), exercise, and drink more water (unless your doctor directs you to do otherwise).

If you feel dizzy or light-headed, sit or lie down for a while; get up slowly; and be careful on stairs.

Major. Tell your doctor about any troublesome side effects. IT IS ESPECIALLY IMPORTANT TO TELL YOUR DOCTOR about confusion, convulsions, darkening of the urine, depression, difficulty in breathing, hallucinations, palpitations, ringing in the ears, skin rash, yellow stools, or yellowing of the eyes or skin.

INTERACTIONS

Propoxyphene can interact with several types of drugs:

1. Concurrent use of it with other central nervous system depressants (such as antihistamines, barbiturates, tranquilizers, sleeping medications, muscle relaxants, and other pain medications) or with tricyclic antidepressants can cause extreme drowsiness.

2. Propoxyphene can increase carbamazepine blood levels, which in turn can result in greater side effects.

3. A monoamine oxidase (MAO) inhibitor taken within 14 days of this medication can lead to unpredictable and severe side effects.

4. Propoxyphene also interacts with alcohol, increasing its intoxicating effects. You should therefore avoid drinking alcoholic beverages while taking this medicine.

TELL YOUR DOCTOR about any medications you are currently taking, especially any of those listed above.

WARNINGS

• Tell your doctor about unusual or allergic reactions you have had to any medications, especially to propoxyphene or to other narcotic analgesics (such as codeine, hydrocodone, hydromorphone, meperidine, methadone, morphine, or oxycodone).

• Tell your doctor if you now have or if you have ever had acute abdominal conditions, asthma, brain disease, colitis, epilepsy, gallstones or gallbladder disease, head injuries, heart disease, kidney disease, liver disease, lung disease, mental illness, emotional disorders, enlarged prostate gland, thyroid disease, or urethral stricture.

• If this drug makes you dizzy or drowsy, do not take part in any activity that requires alertness, such as driving a car or operating potentially dangerous machinery.

• Before having surgery or any other medical or dental treatment, be sure to tell your doctor or dentist that you are taking this medication.

• Propoxyphene has the potential for abuse and must be used with caution. Usually you should not take it on a regular schedule for longer than ten days (unless your doctor directs you to do so). Tolerance develops quickly; do not increase the dosage or stop taking the drug abruptly, unless you first consult your doctor. If you have been taking large amounts of this medication or have been taking it for long periods of time, you may experience a withdrawal reaction (muscle aches, diarrhea, gooseflesh, runny nose, nausea, vomiting, shivering, trembling, stomach cramps, sleep disorders, irritability, weakness, excessive yawning, or sweating) when you stop taking it. Your doctor may therefore want to reduce the dosage gradually.

• Be sure to tell your doctor if you are pregnant. The effects of this medication during the early stages of pregnancy have not been thoroughly studied in humans. However, regular use of propoxyphene in large doses during the later stages of pregnancy can result in addiction of the fetus, leading to withdrawal symptoms (irritability, excessive crying, tremors, fever, vomiting, diarrhea, sneezing, or excessive yawning) at birth. Also tell your doctor if you are breast-feeding an infant. Small amounts of this medication may pass into breast milk and cause excessive drowsiness in the nursing infant.

propranolol

BRAND NAMES (Manufacturers)
Inderal (Wyeth-Ayerst)
Inderal LA (Wyeth-Ayerst)
propranolol (various manufacturers)
TYPE OF DRUG
Beta-adrenergic blocking agent
INGREDIENT
propranolol
DOSAGE FORMS
Tablets (10 mg, 20 mg, 40 mg, 60 mg, 80 mg, and 90 mg)
Extended-release capsules (60 mg, 80 mg, 120 mg, and 160 mg)
Oral solution (20 mg and 40 mg per 5-mL spoonful)
Oral concentrated solution (80 mg per mL)
STORAGE
Store at room temperature in a tightly closed, light-resistant container. The solutions should never be frozen.

USES

Propranolol is used to treat high blood pressure, angina pectoris (chest pain), and irregular heartbeats. It is also useful in preventing migraine headaches and preventing additional heart attacks in heart attack patients. Propranolol belongs to a group of medicines known as beta-adrenergic blocking agents or, more commonly, beta blockers. These drugs work by controlling nerve impulses along certain nerve pathways.

TREATMENT

Propranolol can be taken with a glass of water, with meals, immediately following meals, or on an empty stomach (depending on your doctor's instructions). Try to take the medication at the same time(s) each day.

The extended-release capsules should be swallowed whole. Do not chew or crush them. Breaking the capsule releases the medication all at once—defeating the purpose of extended-release capsules.

The oral solution should be measured with a specially designed 5-mL measuring spoon.

The oral-concentrated solution must be mixed in four ounces (½ cup) of water, juice, or soda before drinking. The cup should be refilled with more of the liquid, which must be swallowed to ensure that the entire dose is taken. This form may also be mixed with applesauce or pudding.

It is important to remember that propranolol does not cure high blood pressure, but it will help control the condition as long as you continue to take it.

Try not to miss any doses of this medicine. If you do miss a dose, take the missed dose as soon as possible, unless it is within eight hours (if you are taking this medicine only once a day) or within four hours (if you are taking this medicine more than once a day) of your next scheduled dose. In that case, do not take the missed dose at all; just return to your regular dosing schedule. Do not double the next dose of the medication.

SIDE EFFECTS

Minor. Anxiety; constipation; decreased sexual ability; diarrhea; difficulty in sleeping; drowsiness; dryness of the eyes, mouth, and skin; headache; nausea; nervousness; stomach discomfort; tiredness; or weakness. These side effects should disappear with time.

To relieve constipation, increase the amount of fiber in your diet (fresh fruits and vegetables, salads, bran, and whole-grain breads) and drink more water (unless your doctor directs you to do otherwise).

If you are extra-sensitive to the cold, be sure to dress warmly during cold weather.

Plain, nonmedicated eye drops (artificial tears) may help to relieve eye dryness.

Sucking on ice chips or chewing sugarless gum helps to relieve mouth and throat dryness.

Major. Tell your doctor about any side effects you experience that are persistent or particularly bothersome. IT IS ESPECIALLY IMPORTANT TO TELL YOUR DOCTOR about breathing difficulty or wheezing, cold hands or feet (due to decreased blood circulation to skin, fingers, and toes), confusion, depression, dizziness, hair loss, hallucinations, light-headedness, nightmares, numbness or tingling of the fingers or toes, rapid weight gain (three to five pounds within a week), reduced alertness, swelling, sore throat and fever, skin rash, or unusual bleeding or bruising.

INTERACTIONS

Propranolol interacts with a number of other types of medications:

1. Indomethacin, aspirin, or other salicylates lessen the blood-pressure-lowering effects of beta blockers.

2. Concurrent use of beta blockers and calcium channel blockers (diltiazem, nifedipine, or verapamil) or disopyramide can lead to heart failure or very low blood pressure.

3. Cimetidine and oral contraceptives (birth control pills) can increase the blood concentrations of propranolol, which can result in greater side effects.

4. Side effects may also be increased when beta blockers are taken with clonidine, digoxin, epinephrine, phenylephrine, phenylpropanolamine, phenothiazine tranquilizers, prazosin, reserpine, or monoamine oxidase (MAO) inhibitors. At least 14 days should separate the use of a beta blocker and an MAO inhibitor.

5. Barbiturates, alcohol, and rifampin can increase the breakdown of propranolol in the body, which can lead to a decrease in its effectiveness.

6. Beta blockers may antagonize (work against) the effects of theophylline, aminophylline, albuterol, isoproterenol, metaproterenol, and terbutaline.

7. Beta blockers can also interact with insulin or oral antidiabetic agents, raising or lowering blood-sugar levels or masking the symptoms of low blood sugar.

8. The action of beta blockers may be excessively increased if they are used with chlorpromazine, furosemide, or hydralazine.

BE SURE TO TELL YOUR DOCTOR about any medications you are currently taking, especially any of those listed above.

WARNINGS

• Before starting to take this medication, it is important to tell your doctor if you have ever had unusual or allergic reactions to any beta blocker (acebutolol, atenolol, betaxolol, carteolol, esmolol, labetalol, metoprolol, nadolol, penbutolol, pindolol, propranolol, or timolol).

• Tell your doctor if you now have or if you have ever had allergies, asthma, hay fever, eczema, slow heartbeat, bronchitis, diabetes mellitus, emphysema, heart or blood-vessel disease, kidney disease, liver disease, thyroid disease, or poor circulation in the fingers or toes.

• You may want to check your pulse while taking this medication. If your pulse is much slower than your usual rate (or if it is less than 50 beats per minute), check with your doctor. A pulse rate that is too slow may cause circulation problems.

• This medicine may affect your body's response to exercise. Make sure you ask your doctor what an appropriate amount of exercise would be for you, taking into account your medical condition.

• It is important that you do not stop taking this medicine without first checking with your doctor. Some conditions may become worse when the medicine is stopped suddenly, and the danger of a heart attack is increased in some patients. Your doctor may want you to gradually reduce the amount of medicine you take before stopping completely. Make sure that you have enough medicine on hand to last through vacations, holidays, and weekends.

• Before having surgery or any other medical or dental treatment, tell your physician or dentist that you are taking this medicine. Often, this medication will be discontinued 48 hours prior to any major surgery.

• Propranolol can cause dizziness, drowsiness, light-headedness, and decreased alertness. Use caution while driving a car or operating dangerous machinery. Be especially careful when going up or down stairs.

• While taking this medicine, do not use any over-the-counter (nonprescription) allergy, asthma, cough, cold, sinus, or diet preparations without first checking with your pharmacist or doctor. The combination of these medicines with a beta blocker can result in high blood pressure.

• Be sure to tell your doctor if you are pregnant. Animal studies have shown that some beta blockers can cause problems in pregnancy when used at very high doses. Adequate studies have not been done in humans, but there has been some association between use of beta blockers during pregnancy and low birth weight, as well as breathing problems and slow heart rate in newborn infants. However, other reports have shown no effects in newborn infants. Also tell your doctor if you are breast-feeding an infant. Although this medicine has not been shown to cause problems in breast-fed infants, some of the medicine may pass into breast milk, so caution is warranted.

---

protease inhibitors

BRAND NAME (Manufacturer)
Crixivan (Merck & Co.)
Invirase (Roche)
Norvir (Abbott)
TYPE OF DRUG
Antiviral
INGREDIENT
indinavir (Crixivan)
ritonavir (Norvir)
saquinavir (Invirase)
DOSAGE FORMS
Capsules (100 mg [ritonavir], 200 mg [indinavir and saquinavir], and 400 mg [indinavir])
Oral solution (80 mg/mL [ritonavir])
STORAGE
Indinavir capsules should be stored at room temperature in a tightly closed, light-resistant container, away from heat and direct sunlight. Do not store in the bathroom. Moisture may cause indinavir to break down. This medication should never be frozen.

Ritonavir capsules and oral solution should be stored in the refrigerator in tightly closed, light-resistant containers. This medication should never be frozen.

Saquinavir capsules should be stored at room temperature in a tightly closed, light-resistant container, away from heat and direct sunlight.

USES

Protease inhibitors are used in the treatment of human immunodeficiency virus (HIV) infection. HIV is the virus that causes AIDS. Protease inhibitors work by inhibiting the reproduction, or growth, of the virus, which slows down the progression of AIDS. Protease inhibitors do not cure AIDS, but these drugs may delay the onset of other infections and diseases caused by AIDS. Protease inhibitors are usually not used alone, but rather in combination with other anti-AIDS drugs, such as zidovudine and/or lamivudine. A combination of a protease inhibitor with two other anti-AIDS drugs has been shown to make the AIDS virus undetectable in the body.

TREATMENT

These medications work best when the level of medicine in your bloodstream is kept constant. It is best to take the drug at evenly spaced intervals throughout the day. IT IS IMPORTANT NOT TO MISS ANY DOSES OF PROTEASE INHIBITORS. The chances of the AIDS virus becoming resistant to protease inhibitors increase if the level of medication in the bloodstream is low.

If you are using the oral solution, use a special measuring spoon to measure the doses. If you miss a dose of this medication, take it as soon as possible. However, if it is almost time for your next dose, skip the missed dose and go back to your regular dosing schedule. Do not double the doses.

Indinavir should be taken with a full glass of water, one hour before or two hours after a meal. Ritonavir is best taken with food. Saquinavir should be taken within two hours of a full meal.

SIDE EFFECTS

Minor. Abdominal pain, changes in taste, diarrhea, dizziness, headache, nausea, tingling around the mouth or in the arms or legs, tiredness or sleepiness, trouble sleeping, vomiting, or weakness.

Major. You should tell your doctor about any side effects that are persistent or particularly bothersome. IT IS ESPECIALLY

IMPORTANT TO TELL YOUR DOCTOR ABOUT blood in the urine; confusion; difficulty urinating; easy bruising; low back pain; nausea, vomiting, or severe abdominal pain; seizures; tingling, burning, numbness, or pain in the hands, arms, feet, or legs; unusual or excessive tiredness or weakness; or vision changes.

INTERACTIONS

The protease inhibitors interact with a large number of other medications.

1. The protease inhibitors may interfere with the body's ability to break down and eliminate a number of other drugs. These include amlodipine, carbamazepine, clarithromycin, clonazepam, cyclosporine, desipramine, diltiazem, erythromycin, felodipine, fluoxetine, isradipine, loratadine, lovastatin, metoprolol, midazolam, nefazodone, nicardipine, nifedipine, nimodipine, nisoldipine, paroxetine, pindolol, pravastatin, propranolol, quinine, rifampin, saquinavir, sertraline, timolol, tramadol, trazodone, triazolam, venlafaxine, and verapamil.

2. The protease inhibitors may also increase the amount of astemizole, cisapride, or terfenadine in the body by interfering with the breakdown and elimination of these drugs. High amounts of astemizole, cisapride, or terfenadine in the body may cause the heart to beat irregularly. These drugs should not be used together.

3. Ritonavir may reduce the amount of oral contraceptives, sulfamethoxazole, or theophylline in the blood, making these drugs less effective.

4. Drugs such as carbamazepine, fluconazole, phenobarbital, phenytoin, rifabutin, and rifampin may increase the elimination of protease inhibitors from the body, decreasing the amount of this medication in the blood. This may make the protease inhibitors less effective.

5. Ritonavir may increase the toxicity of amiodarone, bepridil, bupropion, clozapine, encainide, flecainide, meperidine, piroxicam, propafenone, propoxyphene, and quinidine. Ritonavir should not be taken with any of these other drugs.

6. Ketoconazole may increase the amount of protease inhibitors in the blood.

7. Ritonavir oral solution contains alcohol. Alcohol-containing medications or products may cause a severe reaction when used with metronidazole or disulfiram.

IT IS IMPORTANT THAT YOUR TELL YOUR DOCTOR about all the medications you are taking before starting any of the protease inhibitors.

WARNINGS

• Tell your doctor about any unusual or allergic reactions you have had to any medications, especially to protease inhibitors or other medications used to treat HIV infection. Also tell your doctor about any allergic reaction you have had to any foods, preservatives, or dyes.

• Indinavir may cause kidney stones in some patients. BE SURE TO TELL YOUR DOCTOR if you have or have had kidney stones or other kidney problems. It is important to drink plenty of fluids while on indinavir. You should discuss this with your physician or pharmacist.

• Saquinavir may increase your sensitivity to the sun. You should therefore avoid prolonged exposure to sunlight or sunlamps. Wear protective clothing and sunglasses, and use an effective sunblock.

• You may require blood sample checks on a periodic basis at your physician's office to monitor the effects of the protease inhibitors.

• Be sure to tell your doctor if you have anemia, heart disease, high cholesterol, kidney or liver disease, kidney stones, or vitamin deficiencies.

• Before having surgery or any other medical or dental treatment, notify your doctor or dentist that you are taking this drug.

• If you are infected with HIV, it is best to avoid any sexual activity involving an exchange of body fluids with other people. If you do have vaginal, anal, or oral sex, always use a latex condom.

• If you take any form of drug by injection, do not share your needles with anyone else.

• Be sure to tell your doctor if you are pregnant or plan to become pregnant. It is not known if protease inhibitors are safe to take during pregnancy. Tell your doctor if you are breastfeeding an infant. It is not known if protease inhibitors pass into breast milk, but HIV or the AIDS virus can be transmitted through breast milk.

pseudoephedrine and terfenadine combination

BRAND NAME (Manufacturer)
Seldane-D (Marion Merrell Dow)
TYPE OF DRUG
Decongestant and antihistamine combination
INGREDIENTS
pseudoephedrine and terfenadine
DOSAGE FORM
Sustained-release tablets (120 mg pseudoephedrine and
60 mg terfenadine)
STORAGE
Pseudoephedrine and terfenadine combination should be
stored at room temperature in a tightly closed, light-resistant
container.

USES

This drug is used to relieve the symptoms associated with seasonal allergic rhinitis (sneezing, runny nose, itching, tearing,
and nasal congestion). This medication has not been studied for
the treatment of the common cold.

Pseudoephedrine belongs to a group of drugs known as
adrenergic agents (decongestants). They act by constricting
(narrowing) blood vessels in the nasal passages to reduce
swelling and congestion.

Terfenadine belongs to a group of pharmacological agents
known as antihistamines, which block the action of histamine,
a chemical that is released by the body during an allergic reaction. It is used to relieve or prevent symptoms of allergy.

TREATMENT

You can take pseudoephedrine and terfenadine combination
on an empty stomach or, to avoid stomach irritation, with
food or milk (as directed by your doctor).

The sustained-release tablets should be swallowed whole.
Breaking, chewing, or crushing these tablets destroys their
sustained-release activity and may increase their side effects.

If you miss a dose of this medication, take the missed dose
as soon as possible, unless it is almost time for the next dose.

In that case, do not take the missed dose at all; just return to your regular dosing schedule. Do not double the next dose.

This medication should be taken only as specifically directed by your doctor. Your doctor should be aware of all other medications you are taking before you start taking this drug.

SIDE EFFECTS

Minor. Abdominal pain; cough; dizziness; drowsiness; dry mouth, nose, or throat; fatigue; headache; increased appetite; insomnia; nausea; nervousness; nosebleeds; sore throat; sweating; vomiting; or weakness. These side effects should disappear as your body adjusts to this medication.

To reduce mouth dryness, chew sugarless gum or suck on ice chips or hard candy.

If you feel dizzy or light-headed, sit or lie down for a while; get up slowly from a sitting or reclining position; and be careful on stairs. Be especially careful when operating potentially dangerous machinery, working with hazardous materials, or driving a car.

Major. Tell your doctor about any side effects you are experiencing that are persistent or particularly bothersome. IT IS ESPECIALLY IMPORTANT TO TELL YOUR DOCTOR about bronchospasm, change in bowel habits, confusion, depression, hair loss, itching, menstrual disorders, muscle or bone pain, nightmares, palpitations, shortness of breath, tingling of your fingers or toes, tremors, urinary frequency, visual disturbances, or yellowing of the skin or eyes.

INTERACTIONS

Pseudoephedrine and terfenadine combination can interact with several other types of medication:

1. Concurrent use of this medication with ketoconazole or itraconazole may result in severe heart problems (cardiac arrest, arrhythmias) and even death. Therefore, use of this product in combination with ketoconazole, itraconazole, or similar medications (fluconazole, metronidazole, and miconazole) is not recommended.

2. Concurrent use of this medication with erythromycin or any other macrolide antibiotic (including troleandomycin and clarithromycin) may result in heart problems and therefore is not recommended.

3. Monoamine oxidase inhibitors (furazolidine, isocarbox-azid, pargyline, phenelzine, procarbazine, selegiline, or tranyl-cypromine) may prolong and intensify the effects of this medication.

4. Pseudoephedrine may reduce the antihypertensive effects of methyldopa, and reserpine; this may result in an increase in blood pressure.

5. Beta blockers may increase the reaction to pseudoephedrine, which may in turn cause an increase in the side effects from this medication.

6. The side effects of the decongestant component may be increased by digoxin or over-the-counter (nonprescription) asthma, allergy, cough, cold, diet, or sinus preparations.

Before starting to take this combination product, BE SURE TO TELL YOUR DOCTOR about any medications you are currently taking, especially any of those listed above.

WARNINGS

• Tell your doctor about any unusual or allergic reactions you have had to any medications, especially to terfenadine or other antihistamines (such as brompheniramine, carbinox-amine, chlorpheniramine, clemastine, cyproheptadine, dex-chlorpheniramine, dimenhydrinate, dimethindene, diphen-hydramine, diphenylpyraline, doxylamine, hydroxyzine, promethazine, pyrilamine, trimeprazine, tripelennamine, and triprolidine) or to pseudoephedrine or other adrenergic agents (such as albuterol, amphetamines, ephedrine, epinephrine, isoproterenol, metaproterenol, norepinephrine, phenyl-propanolamine, and terbutaline).

• Be sure to tell your doctor if you now have or if you have ever had diabetes mellitus, epilepsy, glaucoma, heart or blood-vessel disease, hiatal hernia, high blood pressure, myasthe-nia gravis, obstructed bladder or intestinal tract, peptic ulcers, enlarged prostate gland, or thyroid disease.

• This drug can reduce sweating and heat release from the body. Be sure to avoid excessive work and exercise in hot weather, and do not take hot baths, showers, or saunas.

• This medication can cause drowsiness. Your ability to perform tasks that require mental alertness, such as driving an auto-mobile or operating potentially dangerous machinery, may be decreased. Appropriate caution should be taken.

• Be sure to tell your doctor if you are pregnant. The effects of this medication during pregnancy have not been thoroughly studied in humans. Also be sure to tell your doctor if you are currently breast-feeding an infant. Small amounts of this medication pass into the breast milk and may cause adverse effects in the fetus; this medication should not be taken while breast-feeding.

---

pseudoephedrine, carbinoxamine, and dextromethorphan combination

BRAND NAMES (Manufacturers)
Carbodec DM (Rugby)
Cardec DM (various manufacturers)
Pseudo-Car DM (Geneva Generics)
Rondec-DM (Abbott)
Tussafed (Everett)

TYPE OF DRUG
Adrenergic (decongestant), antihistamine, and cough
   suppressant

INGREDIENTS
pseudoephedrine, carbinoxamine, and dextromethorphan

DOSAGE FORMS
Oral syrup (60 mg pseudoephedrine, 4 mg carbinoxamine,
   and 15 mg dextromethorphan per 5-mL spoonful)
Oral drops (25 mg pseudoephedrine, 2 mg carbinoxamine,
   and 4 mg dextromethorphan per 1-mL dropperful)

STORAGE
Pseudoephedrine, carbinoxamine, and dextromethorphan combination oral syrup and oral drops should be stored at room temperature in a tightly closed, light-resistant glass container. Avoid exposing these medications to excessive heat.

USES
This drug combination is used to relieve coughs and the symptoms of upper-respiratory-tract infections, hay fever and other allergies, and inflammation of the sinuses.

Pseudoephedrine belongs to a group of drugs known as adrenergic agents (decongestants). They act by constricting (narrowing) blood vessels in the nasal passages to reduce swelling and congestion.

Carbinoxamine belongs to a group of drugs known as antihistamines, which block the actions of histamine, a chemical released by the body during an allergic reaction. It is used to relieve or prevent symptoms of allergy.

Dextromethorphan is a cough suppressant, which acts at the cough reflex center in the brain.

TREATMENT

In order to avoid stomach upset, you can take this medicine with food or with a full glass of water (unless your doctor directs you to do otherwise).

The oral drops should be measured carefully with the dropper provided. The oral syrup should be measured carefully with a specially designed 5-mL measuring spoon.

If you miss a dose of this medication, take the missed dose as soon as possible, unless it is almost time for your next dose. In that case, do not take the missed dose at all; just return to your regular dosing schedule. Do not double the next dose.

SIDE EFFECTS

Minor. Abdominal pain, blurred vision, decreased sweating, diarrhea, dizziness, drowsiness, dry mouth, headache, heartburn, loss of appetite, nausea, nervousness, sleeping problems, vomiting, or weakness. These side effects should disappear as your body adjusts to the medication.

Chew sugarless gum or suck on ice chips or hard candy to reduce mouth dryness.

If you feel dizzy or light-headed, sit or lie down for a while; get up slowly from a sitting or reclining position; and be careful on stairs.

This medication can increase your sensitivity to sunlight. Avoid prolonged exposure to sunlight and sunlamps. Wear protective clothing, and use an effective sunscreen.

In order to avoid difficulty in falling asleep, you should take the last dose of this medication several hours before bedtime.

Major. Tell your doctor about any side effects that are persistent or particularly bothersome, especially chest pain, difficult or painful urination, difficulty in breathing, hallucinations, pallor, palpitations, seizures, or tremors.

INTERACTIONS

This medication interacts with several types of drugs:

1. Concurrent use of it with central nervous system depressants (drugs that slow the activity of the brain and spinal cord), such as alcohol, barbiturates, benzodiazepine tranquilizers, muscle relaxants, narcotics, pain medications, and phenothiazine tranquilizers, or with tricyclic antidepressants can lead to extreme drowsiness and fatigue.

2. Monoamine oxidase (MAO) inhibitors (furazolidine, isocarboxazid, pargyline, phenelzine, procarbazine, selegiline, or tranylcypromine) beta blockers (acebutolol, atenolol, betaxolol, carteolol, esmolol, labetalol, metoprolol, nadolol, penbutolol, pindolol, propranolol, or timolol), and tricyclic antidepressants can increase the side effects of this drug. At least 14 days should separate the use of this drug and the use of an MAO inhibitor.

3. The side effects of the antihistamine portion of this medication may be increased noticeably by quinidine, procainamide, haloperidol, and the various phenothiazine tranquilizers.

4. The side effects of the decongestant component may be increased by digoxin or over-the-counter (nonprescription) asthma, allergy, cough, cold, diet, or sinus preparations.

5. The blood-pressure-lowering effects of guanethidine, methyldopa, and reserpine may be decreased by this drug.

Before starting pseudoephedrine, carbinoxamine, and dextromethorphan combination, BE SURE TO TELL YOUR DOCTOR about any medications you are currently taking.

WARNINGS

• Tell your doctor about unusual or allergic reactions you have had to any medications, especially to carbinoxamine or other antihistamines (such as azatadine, chlorpheniramine, clemastine, cyproheptadine, dexchlorpheniramine, dimenhydrinate, dimethindene, diphenhydramine, diphenylpyraline, doxylamine, hydroxyzine, promethazine, pyrilamine, trimeprazine, tripelennamine, and triprolidine), to pseudoephedrine or other adrenergic agents (such as albuterol, amphetamines, ephedrine, epinephrine, isoproterenol, metaproterenol, norepinephrine, phenylpropanolamine, and terbutaline), or to dextromethorphan.

• Tell your doctor if you have ever had diabetes mellitus, glaucoma, heart or blood-vessel disease, high blood pressure, myasthenia gravis, obstructed bladder or intestinal tract, peptic ulcers, enlarged prostate, or thyroid disease.

• Because this drug can reduce sweating and heat release from the body, avoid excessive work and exercise in hot weather, do not take hot baths or showers, and steer clear of saunas.

• This medication can cause drowsiness. Avoid tasks that require alertness, such as driving a car or operating potentially dangerous machinery.

• Tell your doctor if you are pregnant. The safe use of this drug in human pregnancy has not been established. Also tell your doctor if you are breast-feeding an infant. Small amounts of this medication pass into breast milk and may cause unusual excitement or irritability in nursing infants.

---

pseudoephedrine, triprolidine, and codeine combination

BRAND NAMES (Manufacturers)
Actagen-C Cough Syrup (Goldline)
Actifed with Codeine (Burroughs Wellcome)
Allerfrin with Codeine (Rugby)
Triacin-C (various manufacturers)
Trifed-C (Geneva Generics)
TYPE OF DRUG
Adrenergic (decongestant), antihistamine, and cough
   suppressant
INGREDIENTS
pseudoephedrine, triprolidine, and codeine
DOSAGE FORM
Oral syrup (30 mg pseudoephedrine, 1.25 mg triprolidine, and 10 mg codeine per 5-mL spoonful, with 4.3% alcohol)

STORAGE
This medication should be stored at room temperature in a tightly closed container. It should not be refrigerated and it should never be frozen.

USES
This medication is used to provide symptomatic relief of coughs due to colds, minor upper-respiratory infections, and allergy.

Pseudoephedrine belongs to a group of drugs known as adrenergic agents (decongestants). These medications act therapeutically by constricting (narrowing) blood vessels in the nasal passages, thereby reducing swelling and congestion.

Triprolidine belongs to a group of drugs known as antihistamines, which block the action of histamine, a chemical released by the body during an allergic reaction. It is used to relieve or prevent symptoms of allergy.

Codeine is a narcotic cough suppressant, which acts at the cough-reflex center in the brain.

TREATMENT
To avoid stomach upset, you can take this medication with food or with a full glass of milk or water (unless your doctor directs you to do otherwise).

The oral syrup should be measured carefully with a specially designed 5-mL measuring spoon. An ordinary kitchen teaspoon is not accurate enough.

If you miss a dose of this medication, take the missed dose as soon as possible, unless it is almost time for your next dose. In that case, do not take the missed dose at all; just return to your regular dosing schedule. Do not double the next dose.

SIDE EFFECTS
Minor. Blurred vision; constipation; diarrhea; dizziness; dry mouth, throat, or nose; irritability; loss of appetite; nausea; restlessness; stomach upset; unusual increase in sweating; or vomiting. These side effects should disappear as your body adjusts to the medication.

This medication can cause increased sensitivity to sunlight. It is therefore important to avoid prolonged exposure to sunlight and sunlamps.

If you are constipated, increase the amount of fiber in your diet (fresh fruits and vegetables, salads, bran, and whole-grain breads). You can also increase your level of exercise and drink more water (unless your doctor directs you to do otherwise).

Chew sugarless gum or suck on ice chips or a piece of hard candy to reduce mouth dryness.

If you feel dizzy or light-headed, sit or lie down for a while; get up slowly from a sitting or reclining position; and be careful on stairs.

Major. Tell your doctor about any side effects that are persistent or particularly bothersome. IT IS ESPECIALLY IMPORTANT TO TELL YOUR DOCTOR about chest pain, confusion, difficult or painful urination, feeling faint, headaches, palpitations, rash, ringing or buzzing in the ears, severe abdominal pain, sore throat, or unusual bleeding or bruising.

INTERACTIONS

This medicine can be expected to interact with several other types of medications:

1. Concurrent use of it with other central nervous system depressants (drugs that slow the activity of the brain and spinal cord, such as alcohol, barbiturates, benzodiazepine tranquilizers, muscle relaxants, narcotics, pain medications, and phenothiazine tranquilizers) or with tricyclic antidepressants can cause extreme drowsiness.

2. Monoamine oxidase (MAO) inhibitors (furazolidine, isocarboxazid, pargyline, phenelzine, selegiline, or tranylcypromine) and tricyclic antidepressants can increase the side effects of this medication. At least 14 days should separate the use of this drug and the use of an MAO inhibitor.

3. The action of oral anticoagulants may be decreased by the antihistamine component of this drug.

4. Procarbazine may interact with the antihistamine component of this drug.

5. The side effects of the antihistamine component of this medication may be increased by quinidine, procainamide, haloperidol, or phenothiazine tranquilizers.

6. The blood-pressure-lowering effects of guanethidine, methyldopa, and reserpine may be decreased by this medication.

7. The side effects of the decongestant component of this medication may be increased by digoxin or over-the-counter (nonprescription) allergy, asthma, cough, cold, diet, or sinus preparations.

BE SURE TO TELL YOUR DOCTOR about any medications you are currently taking, especially any of those listed above.

WARNINGS

• Tell your doctor about unusual or allergic reactions you have had to any medications, especially to triprolidine or other antihistamines (such as azatadine, brompheniramine, carbinoxamine, clemastine, cyproheptadine, chlorpheniramine, dexbrompheniramine, dimenhydrinate, dimethindene, diphenhydramine, diphenylpyraline, doxylamine, hydroxyzine, promethazine, pyrilamine, trimeprazine, and tripelennamine), to pseudoephedrine or other adrenergic agents (such as albuterol, amphetamines, ephedrine, epinephrine, isoproterenol, metaproterenol, norepinephrine, phenylephrine, phenylpropanolamine, and terbutaline), or to codeine or any other narcotic cough suppressant or pain medication.
• Tell your doctor if you now have or if you have ever had asthma, any form of brain disease, blockage of the urinary or digestive tract, diabetes mellitus, colitis, gallbladder disease, glaucoma, heart or blood-vessel disease, high blood pressure, kidney disease, liver disease, lung disease, peptic ulcers, enlarged prostate gland, or thyroid disease.
• This medicine can cause drowsiness. Exercise caution while performing tasks that require alertness, such as driving an automobile or operating potentially dangerous machinery or equipment.
• While you are taking this medication, drink at least eight glasses of water a day to help loosen bronchial secretions.
• Because this product contains codeine, it has the potential for abuse and must be used with caution. Usually, it should not be taken on a regular schedule for longer than ten days at a time. Tolerance develops quickly; do not increase the dosage or stop taking the drug abruptly unless you first consult your doctor. If you have been taking large amounts of this medication, or if you have been taking it for long periods of time, you may experience a withdrawal reaction (muscle aches, diarrhea, gooseflesh, runny nose, nausea, vomiting, shivering, trembling, stomach cramps, sleep disorders, irritability, weakness, excessive yawning, or sweating) when you

stop taking it. Your doctor may therefore want to reduce the dosage gradually.

• Before surgery or other medical or dental treatment, it is very important to tell your doctor or dentist you are taking this drug.

• Be sure that you tell your doctor if you are pregnant. The effects of this drug during the early stages of pregnancy have not been thoroughly studied in humans. However, the regular use of codeine during the later stages of pregnancy may lead to addiction of the fetus, resulting in withdrawal symptoms (irritability, excessive crying, tremors, fever, vomiting, diarrhea, sneezing, or excessive yawning) in the newborn. Also tell your doctor if you are breast-feeding. Small amounts of this drug pass into breast milk and may cause unusual excitement or irritability in nursing infants.

---

quinapril

BRAND NAME (Manufacturer)
Accupril (Parke-Davis)
TYPE OF DRUG
Antihypertensive
INGREDIENT
quinapril
DOSAGE FORM
Tablets (5 mg, 10 mg, 20 mg, and 40 mg)
STORAGE
Store this medication at room temperature in a tightly closed container. It should not be refrigerated.

USES

Quinapril is used to treat high blood pressure. It is a vasodilator (it widens the blood vessels) that acts by blocking the production of chemicals that may be responsible for constricting or narrowing the blood vessels.

TREATMENT

Quinapril can be taken either on an empty stomach or, if the drug causes stomach irritation, with food. To avoid a decrease in the absorption of quinapril, food that has a high fat content should be avoided. In order to become accustomed to taking this medication, quinapril should be taken at the same time(s) every day.

It may be several weeks before you notice the full effects of this medication.

If you miss a dose of quinapril, take the missed dose as soon as possible, unless it is almost time for the next dose. In that case, do not take the missed dose at all; just wait until the next scheduled dose. Do not double the dose.

Quinapril does not cure high blood pressure, but it will help to control the condition for as long as you continue to take it.

SIDE EFFECTS

Minor. Abdominal pain, constipation, cough, diarrhea, dizziness, dry mouth, fatigue, flushing, headache, insomnia, loss of taste, loss of appetite, nausea, or vomiting. These side effects should disappear over time as your body adjusts to the medication.

Quinapril can increase your sensitivity to sunlight. It is important to avoid prolonged exposure to sunlight and sunlamps. Wear protective clothing and sunglasses, and use an effective sunscreen.

To relieve constipation, increase the amount of fiber in your diet (fresh fruits and vegetables, salads, bran, and whole-grain breads), exercise, and drink more water (unless your doctor directs you to do otherwise).

To relieve mouth dryness, suck on ice chips or a piece of hard candy, or chew sugarless gum.

To avoid dizziness or light-headedness when you stand, contract and relax the muscles of your legs for a few moments before rising. Do this by pushing one foot against the floor while raising the other foot slightly, alternating feet so that you are "pumping" your legs. Be especially careful on stairs.

Major. Tell your doctor about any side effects that are persistent or especially bothersome. IT IS ESPECIALLY IMPORTANT TO TELL YOUR DOCTOR about chest pains; chills; difficult or painful urination; fever; itching; mouth sores; palpitations; prolonged vomiting or diarrhea; rash; sore throat; swelling of the face, hands, or feet; tingling in the fingers or toes; unusual bleeding or bruising; or yellowing of the eyes or skin.

INTERACTIONS

Quinapril interacts with several other types of medications:

1. Diuretics (water pills) and other antihypertensive medications can cause an excessive drop in blood pressure when combined with quinapril (especially with the first dose).

2. The combination of quinapril with spironolactone, triamterene, amiloride, potassium supplements, or salt substitutes can lead to hyperkalemia (dangerously high levels of potassium in the bloodstream).

3. Antineoplastic agents (anticancer drugs) or chloramphenicol can increase the bone-marrow side effects of quinapril.

4. Concurrent use of quinapril and the antigout medication allopurinol can increase the risk of developing an allergic reaction.

5. Indomethacin can decrease the blood-pressure-lowering effects of quinapril.

6. Quinapril can delay the body's elimination of lithium. Concurrent use of quinapril and lithium may cause lithium toxicity.

7. Quinipril may reduce the amount of tetracycline absorbed by the body.

Before starting quinapril, BE SURE TO TELL YOUR DOCTOR about any drugs you are taking, especially any of those listed above.

WARNINGS

• Tell your doctor about any unusual or allergic reactions you have had to medications, especially to benazepril, captopril, enalapril, fosinopril, lisinopril, moexipril, quinapril, or ramipril.

• Tell your doctor if you now have or if you have ever had aortic stenosis, blood disorders, kidney disease, a kidney transplant, liver disease, systemic lupus erythematosus, or a heart attack or stroke.

• Excessive perspiration, dehydration, or prolonged vomiting or diarrhea can lead to an excessive drop in blood pressure while you are taking this medication. Contact your doctor if you have any of these symptoms.

• Before having surgery or other medical or dental treatment, tell your doctor that you are taking this drug.

• The first few doses of this drug may cause dizziness. Try to avoid any sudden changes in posture.

• If you have high blood pressure, do not take any over-the-counter (nonprescription) medications for weight control or for allergy, asthma, sinus, cough, or cold problems unless you first check with your doctor.

• Do not stop taking this medication unless you first consult your doctor. Stopping this drug abruptly may lead to a rise in blood pressure.

• Be sure to tell your doctor if you are pregnant. Quinapril may cause birth defects in the fetus if taken during the second or third trimester of pregnancy. Also tell your doctor if you are breast-feeding an infant. Quinapril may pass into breast milk. The effects of this drug on the infant have not been determined.

---

quinidine

BRAND NAMES (Manufacturers)
Cardioquin (Purdue Frederick)
Quinaglute Dura-Tabs (Berlex)
Quinidex Extentabs (Robins)
quinidine gluconate (various manufacturers)
quinidine sulfate (various manufacturers)
Quinora (Key)

TYPE OF DRUG
Antiarrhythmic

INGREDIENT
quinidine

DOSAGE FORMS
Tablets (100 mg, 200 mg, 275 mg, and 300 mg)
Sustained-release tablets (300 mg and 324 mg)

STORAGE
Quinidine tablets and capsules should be stored at room temperature in tightly closed, light-resistant containers.

USES
Quinidine is used to treat heart arrhythmias. It corrects irregular heartbeats and helps to achieve a more normal rhythm.

TREATMENT
To increase absorption of the drug, take quinidine on an empty stomach with a full glass of water one hour before or two

hours after a meal. To lessen stomach upset, ask your doctor if you can take it with food or milk.

Take quinidine at the same time(s) each day. It works best when the amount in your bloodstream is kept constant. This medication should, therefore, be taken at evenly spaced intervals day and night. For example, if you take quinidine four times per day, the doses should be six hours apart.

The sustained-release tablets should be swallowed whole.

If you miss a dose of this medication and remember within two hours, take the missed dose immediately and then return to your regular dosing schedule. If more than two hours have passed (four hours for the sustained-release tablets), do not take the missed dose at all; just return to your regular dosing schedule. Do not double the next dose.

SIDE EFFECTS

Minor. Abdominal pain, bitter taste in mouth, confusion, cramping, diarrhea, flushing, headache, loss of appetite, nausea, restlessness, or vomiting. These side effects should disappear as your body adjusts to the medication.

Major. Tell your doctor about any side effects that are persistent or particularly bothersome. IT IS ESPECIALLY IMPORTANT TO TELL YOUR DOCTOR about blurred vision, difficulty in breathing, dizziness, fainting, fever, headache, light-headedness, palpitations, rash, ringing in the ears, sore throat, or unusual bleeding or bruising.

INTERACTIONS

Quinidine interacts with several foods and medications:

1. It can increase the effects of the blood-thinner warfarin, which can lead to bleeding complications.

2. Acetazolamide, cimetidine, thiazide diuretics (water pills), sodium bicarbonate, antacids, and citrus fruit juices can increase the blood levels and thus the possibility of side effects of quinidine.

3. Nifedipine, phenobarbital, phenytoin, and rifampin can decrease blood levels of quinidine.

4. The combination of quinidine and phenothiazine tranquilizers, reserpine, nifedipine, amiodarone, or other antiarrhythmic agents can lead to cardiac side effects that can be very harmful.

5. Quinidine can increase blood levels of digoxin, leading to serious side effects.

BE SURE TO TELL YOUR DOCTOR about any medications you are currently taking, especially any listed above.

WARNINGS

• Tell your doctor about unusual or allergic reactions you have had to any drugs, especially to quinidine or quinine.

• Before starting to take this medication, be sure to tell your doctor if you have ever had heart block, hypokalemia (low blood levels of potassium), kidney disease, liver disease, lung disease, myasthenia gravis, psoriasis, or thyroid disease.

• Although many quinidine products are on the market, they are not all bioequivalent; that is, they may not all be absorbed into the bloodstream at the same rate or have the same overall pharmacologic activity. Do not change brands of this drug without consulting your doctor or pharmacist.

• Do not take any over-the-counter (nonprescription) products for asthma, allergy, sinus, cough, cold, or weight reduction unless you first check with your doctor or pharmacist.

• If this drug makes you dizzy or light-headed, do not take part in any activity that requires alertness, such as driving a car or operating potentially dangerous machinery.

• Before having surgery or other medical or dental treatment, tell your doctor or dentist you are currently taking this drug.

• Do not stop taking this drug without first consulting your doctor. Stopping quinidine abruptly may cause a serious change in the activity of your heart. Your doctor may want to reduce your dosage gradually.

• Be sure to tell your doctor if you are pregnant. Although this drug appears to be safe, extensive studies in pregnant women have not been conducted. Also tell your doctor if you are breast-feeding an infant. Small amounts of quinidine pass into breast milk.

ranitidine

BRAND NAMES (Manufacturers)
Zantac (Glaxo)
Zantac EFFERdose (Glaxo)
Zantac GELdose (Glaxo)

TYPE OF DRUG
Gastric-acid-secretion inhibitor (decreases stomach acid)
INGREDIENT
ranitidine
DOSAGE FORMS
Capsules (150 mg and 300 mg)
Granules effervescent (150 mg)
Tablets (150 mg and 300 mg)
Tablets effervescent (150 mg)
Oral syrup (15 mg per mL)
STORAGE
Ranitidine should be stored at room temperature in a tightly closed, light-resistant container.

USES
Ranitidine is used to treat duodenal and gastric ulcers. It is also used in the long-term treatment of excessive stomach acid secretion, in the prevention of recurrent ulcers, and in the treatment of reflex esophagitis (inflammation of the esophagus). Ranitidine works by blocking the effects of histamine on the stomach, thereby reducing stomach-acid secretion.

TREATMENT
You can take ranitidine either on an empty stomach or with food or milk.

Antacids can block the absorption of ranitidine. If you are taking antacids as well as ranitidine, at least one hour should separate doses of the two medications.

If you miss a dose of this medication, take the missed dose as soon as possible, unless it is almost time for the next dose. In that case, do not take the missed dose at all; just return to your regular dosing schedule. Do not double the next dose.

SIDE EFFECTS
Minor. Constipation, diarrhea, dizziness, headache, nausea, or stomach upset. These side effects should disappear as your body adjusts to the medication.

To relieve constipation, exercise and drink more water (unless your doctor directs you to do otherwise).

If you feel dizzy while taking this medication, sit or lie down for a while.

Major. Tell your doctor about any side effects that are persistent or particularly bothersome. IT IS ESPECIALLY IMPORTANT TO TELL YOUR DOCTOR about confusion, decreased sexual ability, unusual bleeding or bruising, or weakness.

INTERACTIONS

Ranitidine can interact with other types of medications:

1. Ranitidine may increase the blood-sugar-lowering effects of glipizide or glyburide.

2. Ranitidine can decrease the elimination warfarin (a blood-thinner) from the body, which can increase the risk of bleeding complications.

3. Ranitidine can increase blood levels of procainamide.

4. Ranitidine may cause a false-positive result with the Multistix urine protein test.

   BE SURE TO TELL YOUR DOCTOR about any medications you are currently taking, especially any listed above.

WARNINGS

• Tell your doctor about unusual or allergic reactions you have had to any medications, especially to ranitidine.

• Tell your doctor if you now have or if you have ever had kidney or liver disease.

• Ranitidine should be taken continuously for as long as your doctor prescribes. To do otherwise may result in ineffective therapy.

• Cigarette smoking may block the beneficial effects of ranitidine.

• If this drug makes you dizzy, do not take part in any activity that requires alertness.

• Be sure to tell your doctor if you are pregnant. Ranitidine appears to be safe during pregnancy; however, extensive testing has not been conducted. Also tell your doctor if you are breast-feeding an infant. Small amounts of ranitidine pass into breast milk.

---

reserpine

BRAND NAMES (Manufacturers)
reserpine (various manufacturers)
Serpalan (Lannett)

TYPE OF DRUG
Antihypertensive
INGREDIENT
reserpine
DOSAGE FORM
Tablets (0.1 mg, 0.25 mg, and 1 mg)
STORAGE
Reserpine tablets should be stored at room temperature in tightly closed, light-resistant containers.

USES
Reserpine is used to treat high blood pressure. It works by depleting certain chemicals from the nervous system that are responsible for maintaining high blood pressure.

TREATMENT
To avoid stomach irritation, you can take reserpine with food or with a full glass of water or milk (unless your doctor directs otherwise). Try to take reserpine at the same time(s) each day to become accustomed to taking it.

Reserpine does not cure hypertension, but it will help to control the condition as long as you continue to take it.

If you miss a dose of this medication, take the missed dose as soon as possible, unless it is almost time for the next dose. Do not take the missed dose at all; just return to your regular dosing schedule. Do not double the next dose.

SIDE EFFECTS
Minor. Abdominal pain, constipation, diarrhea, dizziness, dry mouth, headache, impotence, loss of appetite, nasal congestion, nausea, nosebleeds, vomiting, or weight gain. These side effects should disappear over time as your body adjusts to the medication.

To relieve constipation, increase the amount of fiber in your diet (fresh fruits and vegetables, salads, bran, and whole-grain breads), exercise, and drink more water (unless your doctor directs you to do otherwise).

If you feel dizzy, sit or lie down for a while; get up slowly from a sitting or reclining position; and be careful on stairs.

To relieve mouth dryness, chew sugarless gum or suck on ice chips or a piece of hard candy.

Major. Tell your doctor about any side effects that are persistent or particularly bothersome. IT IS ESPECIALLY IMPORTANT TO TELL YOUR DOCTOR about anxiety; black, tarry stools; chest pain; decrease in sexual desire; depression; difficulty in urinating; drowsiness; enlarged breasts (in both sexes); fainting; fatigue; flushing of the skin; hearing loss; itching; muscle aches; nervousness; nightmares; palpitations; pinpoint pupils of eyes; rapid weight gain (three to five pounds within a week); rash; severe dizziness; shortness of breath; tremors; unusual bleeding or bruising; or weakness.

INTERACTIONS

Reserpine interacts with several other types of medications:

1. Concurrent use of reserpine with central nervous system depressants such as alcohol, antihistamines, barbiturates, benzodiazepine tranquilizers, muscle relaxants; narcotics, pain medications, phenothiazine tranquilizers, and sleeping medications, or with tricyclic antidepressants can cause extreme drowsiness.

2. Reserpine can increase the side effects of digoxin, beta blockers, and quinidine and can decrease the effectiveness of levodopa.

3. Tricyclic antidepressants can decrease the blood-pressure-lowering effects of reserpine.

4. Concurrent use of reserpine and monoamine oxidase (MAO) inhibitors can lead to severe side effects. At least 14 days should separate the use of this drug and the use of an MAO inhibitor.

Before starting reserpine, TELL YOUR DOCTOR about any drugs you are taking, especially those drugs that are listed above.

WARNINGS

• Tell your doctor about unusual or allergic reactions you have had to any medications, especially to reserpine or to any Rauwolfia alkaloids.

• Before starting to take this medication, be sure to tell your doctor if you now have or if you have ever had arrhythmias, epilepsy, gallstones or gallbladder disease, heart disease, kidney disease, lung disease, mental depression, Parkinson's disease, peptic ulcers, pheochromocytoma, or ulcerative colitis.

- Reserpine should not be used within two weeks of electroshock therapy.
- If this drug makes you dizzy or drowsy, do not take part in any activity that requires alertness, such as driving an automobile or operating potentially dangerous machinery, tools, or equipment.
- Before having surgery or any other medical or dental procedure, be sure to inform your doctor or dentist you are taking this drug.
- Before taking any over-the-counter (nonprescription) cough, cold, sinus, asthma, allergy, or diet medications, consult your doctor or pharmacist. Some of these products may increase your blood pressure.
- Be sure to tell your doctor if you are pregnant. Reserpine has been reported to cause birth defects in infants whose mothers received the drug during pregnancy. Also tell your doctor if you are breast-feeding. Reserpine can pass into breast milk and cause side effects in the nursing infant.

---

rifampin

BRAND NAMES (Manufacturers)
Rifadin (Marion Merrell Dow)
Rimactane (Ciba)
TYPE OF DRUG
Antibiotic
INGREDIENT
rifampin
DOSAGE FORM
Capsules (150 mg and 300 mg)
STORAGE
Rifampin should be stored at room temperature in a tightly closed, light-resistant container.

USES
Rifampin is an antibiotic that is used to treat tuberculosis and to prevent meningococcal meningitis. Rifampin works by preventing the growth and multiplication of susceptible bacteria. Rifampin is not effective against viruses, parasites, or fungi, however.

TREATMENT

Rifampin should be taken with a full glass of water on an empty stomach one hour before or two hours after a meal. If this medication causes stomach irritation, check with your doctor to see if you can take it with food.

Try not to miss any doses of this medication. If you do miss a dose, take the missed dose as soon as possible, unless it is almost time for your next dose. In that case, do not take the missed dose at all; just return to your regular dosing schedule. Do not double your next dose of rifampin.

Continue to take this medication for the entire time prescribed by your doctor (which may be months to years), even if the symptoms disappear before the end of that period. If you stop taking the drug too soon, resistant bacteria will continue to grow, and your infection could recur.

SIDE EFFECTS

Minor. Diarrhea, dizziness, drowsiness, gas, headache, heartburn, loss of appetite, nausea, stomach irritation, or vomiting. These side effects should disappear as your body adjusts to the medication.

If you feel dizzy, sit or lie down for a while; get up slowly from a sitting or reclining position; and be careful on stairs.

Major. Tell your doctor about any side effects that are persistent or particularly bothersome. IT IS ESPECIALLY IMPORTANT TO TELL YOUR DOCTOR about confusion, difficult or painful urination, fatigue, fever, flushing, itching, muscle weakness, numbness, skin rash, uncoordinated movements, visual disturbances, or yellowing of the eyes or skin. And if your symptoms of infection seem to be worsening rather than improving, tell your doctor.

INTERACTIONS

Rifampin interacts with several other types of medications:

1. Concurrent use with para-aminosalicylic acid may decrease the blood levels and effectiveness of rifampin.

2. Rifampin can decrease the blood levels and effectiveness of metoprolol, propranolol, verapamil, aminophylline, theophylline, oxtriphylline, quinidine, adrenocorticosteroids (cortisonelike medicines), progestins, clofibrate, methadone, oral anticoagulants (blood thinners, such as warfarin), oral antidiabetic medicines, barbiturates, benzodiazepine tranquilizers, dapsone, digitoxin, and trimethoprim.

3. Concurrent use of rifampin with alcohol or isoniazid can lead to an increased risk of liver damage.

4. Rifampin may decrease the effectiveness of oral contraceptives (birth control pills), and pregnancy could result. You should use a different or additional form of birth control while taking rifampin. Discuss available options with your doctor.

BE SURE TO TELL YOUR DOCTOR about any medications you are currently taking.

WARNINGS

• Tell your doctor about unusual or allergic reactions you have had to any medications, especially to rifampin.

• Before beginning a course of treatment with this medication, be sure to tell your doctor if you have a history of alcoholism or liver disease.

• Rifampin has been prescribed for your current infection only. Another infection later on, or one that someone else has, may require a different medicine. You should not give your medicine to other people or use it for other infections, unless your doctor specifically directs you to do so.

• If this drug makes you dizzy or drowsy, do not take part in any activity that requires alertness, such as driving an automobile or operating potentially dangerous tools, machinery, or other equipment.

• Rifampin can cause reddish-orange to reddish-brown discoloration of your urine, feces, saliva, sputum, sweat, and tears. This is a harmless effect. The drug may also permanently discolor soft contact lenses. You might want to stop wearing them while you are taking this medication. Discuss this with your ophthalmologist.

• Do not stop taking this medication unless you first check with your doctor. Stopping the drug and restarting it at a later time can lead to an increase in side effects.

• Be sure to tell your doctor if you are pregnant. Although rifampin appears to be safe in humans, birth defects have been reported in the offspring of animals that received large doses of the drug during pregnancy. Also tell your doctor if you are breast-feeding an infant. Small amounts of rifampin pass into breast milk.

risperidone

BRAND NAME (Manufacturer)
Risperdal (Janssen)
TYPE OF DRUG
Antipsychotic
INGREDIENT
risperidone
DOSAGE FORM
Tablets (1 mg, 2 mg, 3 mg, and 4 mg)
STORAGE
This medication should be stored in a tightly closed container at room temperature, away from heat and direct sunlight.

USES

Risperidone is prescribed to treat symptoms of mental illness, such as the emotional symptoms of psychosis. This medication is thought to relieve the symptoms of mental illness by blocking certain chemicals involved with nerve transmission in the brain.

TREATMENT

This medication should be taken exactly as prescribed by your doctor. In order to avoid stomach irritation, take risperidone with food or a full glass of water (unless your doctor directs you to do otherwise).

The full effects of this medication for the control of emotional or mental symptoms may not become apparent for two weeks after you begin treatment.

If you miss a dose of this medicine, take the missed dose as soon as possible, and return to your regular dosing schedule. If it is almost time for your next dose, however, skip the one you missed and then return to your regular schedule. You should never take a double dose to make up for the one you missed unless directed to do so by your doctor.

SIDE EFFECTS

Minor. Blurred vision, changes in blood pressure, constipation, decreased sweating, diarrhea, dizziness, drooling, drowsiness, dry mouth, fatigue, jitters, menstrual irregularities, restlessness, stuffy nose, vomiting, or weight gain.

This medication can cause increased sensitivity to sunlight. It is therefore important to avoid prolonged exposure to sunlight or sunlamps. Wear protective clothing and use an effective sunscreen.

Dry mouth can be relieved by chewing sugarless gum or sucking on hard candy.

To relieve constipation, increase the amount of fiber in your diet (fresh fruits and vegetables, salads, bran, and whole-grain breads), exercise, and drink more water (unless your doctor directs you to do otherwise).

To avoid dizziness or light-headedness when you stand, contract and relax the muscles in your legs for a few moments before rising. Do this by pushing one foot against the floor while raising the other foot slightly, alternating feet so that you are "pumping" your legs in a pedaling motion.

Major. Tell your doctor about any side effects that are persistent or particularly bothersome. IT IS ESPECIALLY IMPORTANT TO TELL YOUR DOCTOR about breast enlargement (in both sexes); chest pain; convulsions (seizures); darkened skin; difficulty in breathing or swallowing; fainting; fever; impotence; involuntary movements of the face, mouth, tongue, or jaw; palpitations; skin rash or hives; sleep disorders; sore throat; tremors; uncoordinated movements; unusual bleeding or bruising; visual disturbances; or yellowing of either the eyes or the skin.

INTERACTIONS

Risperidone interacts with several other types of drugs:

1. Extreme drowsiness can occur when this medication is taken with other central nervous system depressants (such as alcohol, antihistamines, antidepressants, barbiturates, benzodiazepine tranquilizers, muscle relaxants, narcotics, pain medications, and sleeping medications).

2. The effects of levodopa may be decreased by this drug.

3. Risperidone may increase the effects of some blood-pressure medicines.

4. The side effects of monoamine oxidase (MAO) inhibitors and tricyclic antidepressants may be increased when combined with this medication.

Before taking risperidone, BE SURE TO TELL YOUR DOCTOR about any medication you are taking, especially any of those listed above.

WARNINGS

• Tell your doctor about any unusual or allergic reactions you have had to any medications, especially to risperidone.

• Tell your doctor if you have a history of alcoholism, if you now have or have ever had heart or circulatory disease, difficulty in urinating, enlarged prostate gland, epilepsy, glaucoma, liver disease, or Parkinson's disease.

• To prevent oversedation, avoid drinking alcoholic beverages while taking this medication.

• If this medication makes you drowsy or dizzy, do not take part in any activity that requires alertness, such as driving a car or operating dangerous equipment.

• Do not stop taking this medication suddenly. Stopping it abruptly can cause nausea, vomiting, headache, stomach upset, increased heart rate, insomnia, trembling, or a worsening of your condition. Your doctor may want to reduce the dose gradually.

• Some of the side effects of this drug can be prevented by taking an antiparkinson drug. Discuss this matter with your doctor.

• This medication may decrease sweating and heat release from the body. Therefore avoid getting overheated by strenuous exercise in hot weather and avoid taking hot baths, showers, or saunas.

• While taking this medication, do not take any over-the-counter (nonprescription) medication for weight control, or for cough, cold, asthma, allergy, or sinus problems unless you first check with your doctor.

• Prior to having surgery or any other medical or dental treatment, be sure to tell your doctor or dentist that you are taking risperidone.

• Be sure to tell your doctor if you are pregnant. The effects of this medication during pregnancy have not been thoroughly studied in humans. It is also not known if risperidone passes into breast milk in humans, so be sure to tell your doctor if you are breast-feeding an infant.

---

salmeterol

BRAND NAME (Manufacturer)
Serevent (Glaxo)

TYPE OF DRUG
Bronchodilator
INGREDIENT
salmeterol
DOSAGE FORM
Inhalation aerosol (each spray delivers 21 mcg)
STORAGE
This medication should be stored at room temperature, away from excessive heat. The contents are pressurized and can explode if heated.

USES

Salmeterol is used to relieve the wheezing and shortness of breath caused by lung diseases such as asthma and emphysema. This drug acts directly on the muscles of the bronchi (breathing tubes) to relieve bronchospasm (muscle contractions of the bronchi). This action reduces airway resistance and allows air to move more freely to and from the lungs.

TREATMENT

This medication should be taken exactly as prescribed by your doctor. Salmeterol is usually packaged with an instruction sheet. Read the directions carefully before using. The container should be shaken well just before each use. The contents tend to settle on the bottom, so it is necessary to shake the bottle in order to distribute the ingredients evenly and equalize the doses. If more than one inhalation is prescribed, wait one full minute between inhalations in order to receive the full benefit from the first dose.

If you miss a dose of this medicine, take the missed dose as soon as possible, then follow your regular dosing schedule for the next dose. Do not double the dose.

Salmeterol should not be used for acute asthma symptoms. This drug has a slow onset of action and is not effective for acute symptom relief. You should use a short-acting bronchodilator (such as albuterol) for acute symptoms. Discuss this with your doctor.

Salmeterol can be used to prevent exercise-induced bronchospasm. It should be administered 30 to 60 minutes before exercise.

SIDE EFFECTS

Minor. Anxiety, dizziness, drowsiness, dryness or irritation of the mouth or throat, fast heartbeat, flushing, loss of appetite, muscle cramps, nausea, sweating, tremors, vomiting, or weakness.

To help prevent dryness or irritation of the mouth or throat, rinse your mouth with water after each dose of salmeterol.

If you feel dizzy, sit or lie down for a while; get up slowly from a sitting or reclining position; and be careful on stairs.

Major. Tell your doctor about any side effects that are persistent or particularly bothersome. IT IS ESPECIALLY IMPORTANT TO TELL YOUR DOCTOR about chest pain, increased blood pressure, itching or rash, or palpitations.

INTERACTIONS

Salmeterol interacts with several other types of medications:

1. The beta blockers (acebutolol, atenolol, labetolol, metoprolol, nadolol, pindolol, propranolol, timolol) antagonize (act against) this medication, decreasing its effectiveness.

2. Monoamine oxidase (MAO) inhibitors, tricyclic antidepressants, antihistamines, levothyroxine, and over-the-counter (nonprescription) cough, cold, asthma, allergy, diet, and sinus medications may increase the side effects of this medication.

3. There may be a change in the dosage requirements of insulin or oral antidiabetic medications when salmeterol is started.

4. The use of salmeterol with other bronchodilator drugs (oral or inhalation) may have additive side effects. Discuss this with your doctor.

Before taking salmeterol, BE SURE TO TELL YOUR DOCTOR about any medication you are taking, especially any of those listed above.

WARNINGS

• Tell your doctor about any unusual or allergic reactions you have had to medications, especially to salmeterol or any related drugs (albuterol, amphetamines, ephedrine, epinephrine, isoproterenol, metaproterenol, norepinephrine, phenylephrine, phenylpropanolamine, pseudoephedrine, or terbutaline).

• Tell your doctor if you have ever had heart disease, enlarged prostate gland, epilepsy, glaucoma, high blood pressure, thyroid disease, or diabetes mellitus.

• If this medication makes you drowsy or dizzy, do not take part in any activity that requires mental alertness, such as driving a car or operating dangerous equipment.

• DO NOT EXCEED THE RECOMMENDED DOSE OF THIS MEDICATION; excessive use of salmeterol may lead to serious side effects.

• Do not puncture, break, or burn the aerosol container. The contents are under pressure and may explode.

• Be sure to tell your doctor if you are pregnant. The effects of this drug during pregnancy have not been well studied in humans, but salmeterol has caused side effects in the offspring of animals that received large doses during pregnancy. Also be sure to tell your doctor if you are breast-feeding an infant. It is not known if salmeterol passes into breast milk.

---

scopolamine (transdermal)

BRAND NAME (Manufacturer)
Transderm-Scop (Ciba)
TYPE OF DRUG
Antiemetic and antivertigo
INGREDIENT
scopolamine
DOSAGE FORM
Transdermal system (the patch delivers 0.5 mg of
   scopolamine over three days)
STORAGE
The scopolamine (transermal) patches should be stored at room temperature in their original containers. Always try to keep these containers away from direct heat and light.

USES
Scopolamine is used to prevent nausea and vomiting associated with motion sickness. Transdermal scopolamine is a small patch that is applied to the skin. Transdermal application (i.e., application of medicine through the skin) delivers reduced doses of scopolamine, which decreases the risk of adverse side effects.

TREATMENT

The transdermal system (patches) allows controlled continuous release of scopolamine. Patches are easy to use and convenient. For best results, wash and dry hands thoroughly before handling. Apply the disc to the hairless area of the skin behind the ear at least four hours before the antiemetic effect is required. Do not place over any cuts or irritations. Wash hands thoroughly after handling the disc to prevent direct contact of the medication with the eyes. The medication should last up to three days. If treatment is needed for more than three days, discard the used disc, and replace with a new disc behind the other ear. It is all right to bathe or shower with a patch in place. If the disc becomes displaced at any time during treatment, it should be discarded and a fresh one placed on the hairless area behind the other ear. If redness or irritation develops at the application site, consult your physician. Do not trim or cut the patches.

SIDE EFFECTS

Minor. Blurred vision and enlargement of pupils; drowsiness; or dryness of mouth, nose, and throat.

To relieve mouth dryness, chew sugarless gum or suck on ice chips or hard candy.

If you feel dizzy or light-headed, sit or lie down for a while.
Major. Tell your doctor about any side effects that are persistent or particularly bothersome. IT IS ESPECIALLY IMPORTANT TO TELL YOUR DOCTOR ABOUT blurred vision (severe); confusion (severe); convulsions; difficulty in breathing; dizziness; drowsiness (severe); dry mouth, nose, or throat (severe); eye pain (severe); fast heart beat; fever; rash; slurred speech; unusual excitement or restlessness; unusual warmth; dryness; or flushing of the skin.

INTERACTIONS

Scopolamine can interact with other types of medications:
1. It can cause additive drowsiness when combined with alcohol or other central nervous system depressants (such as antihistamines, barbiturates, benzodiazepine tranquilizers, muscle relaxants, narcotics, and pain medications) or with tricyclic antidepressants.
2. It can cause additive anticholinergic effects (such as dryness of mouth, nose, and throat, or difficulty in urinating)

when combined with drugs such as belladonna alkaloids, antidepressants, and antihistamines.

Before starting to take scopolamine, BE SURE TO TELL YOUR DOCTOR about any medications you are currently taking, especially any of those listed above.

WARNINGS

• Tell your doctor about unusual or allergic reactions you have had to any medications, especially to scopolamine.

• Tell your doctor if you now have or if you have ever had blockage of the urinary tract, stomach, or intestinal tract.

• Tell your doctor if you now have or if you have ever had metabolic, liver, or kidney disease.

• Tell your doctor if you have glaucoma (increased pressure in the eyeball).

• This medication may cause drowsiness or blurred vision. Make sure you know how you react to this medication before you attempt activities such as driving a car or operating potentially dangerous equipment.

• Patients who use the patch for more than three days are more likely to experience dizziness, headache, nausea, or vomiting for a short period of time following discontinuation.

• Do not use the transdermal system on children.

• Elderly patients may be especially susceptible to the central nervous system effects (confusion, sedation, memory impairment, unusual excitement) of scopolamine.

• Be sure to tell your doctor if you are pregnant. Extensive studies in pregnant women have not been conducted. Also tell your doctor if you are breast-feeding. It is not known whether scopolamine passes into breast milk.

selegiline

BRAND NAME (Manufacturer)
Eldepryl (Somerset)
TYPE OF DRUG
Antiparkinson agent
INGREDIENT
selegiline
DOSAGE FORM
Tablets (5 mg)

STORAGE
Selegilene should be stored at room temperature in a tightly closed container.

USES
This medication is used either alone or in combination with levodopa or levodopa/carbidopa to treat the symptoms of Parkinson's disease. This drug helps to increase and extend the beneficial effects of levodopa. Recent studies suggest that selegiline may help to slow the progression of Parkinson's disease when taken early in the course of the disease. This drug has also been used to treat depression.

TREATMENT
Selegiline should be taken exactly as your doctor prescribes. You can take it with food to lessen the chance of irritation, unless your doctor tells you otherwise.

If you miss a dose of this medication, take the missed dose as soon as possible, then return to your regular dosing schedule. However, if you do not remember the missed dose until late afternoon or evening, skip the missed dose. If the drug is taken late in the afternoon, it may cause some unwanted side effects. Never double the dose.

The full effects of this medication may not be apparent for two to three days. At that time, your doctor may change your dose of levodopa or levodopa/carbidopa.

SIDE EFFECTS
Minor. Dizziness, drowsiness, dryness of mouth, headache, heartburn, light-headedness, nausea, nervousness, restlessness, stomach pain, trouble sleeping, or vomiting. These side effects should lessen or disappear as your body adjusts to the medication.

Dry mouth can be relieved by chewing sugarless gum or by sucking on ice chips or a piece of hard candy.

To avoid dizziness or light-headedness when you stand, contract and relax the muscles of your legs for a few moments before rising. Do this by pushing one foot against the floor while raising the other foot slightly, alternating feet so that you are "pumping" your legs in a pedaling motion.

Major. Tell your doctor about any side effects that are persistent or particularly bothersome. IT IS ESPECIALLY IMPOR-

TANT TO TELL YOUR DOCTOR about blood in your urine; chest pain; convulsions; dark or tarry stools; difficulty in breathing; difficulty in speaking; difficulty in urination; fast heartbeat; feelings of euphoria; hallucinations; mood changes; persistent restlessness; severe stomach pain; stiff neck; or uncontrolled movements of your arms, legs, or face.

INTERACTIONS

When taken in the recommended dose at the times directed by your doctor, selegiline should not interact with many types of medications or foods.

Tell your doctor if you have taken the drug meperidine in the two to three weeks before starting selegiline.

Concurrent use of this medication and fluoxetine, fluvoxamine, nefazodone, paroxetine, sertraline, venlafaxine, or tricyclic antidepressants may cause serious side effects, including severe agitation, delerium, restlessness, tremor, fever, diarrhea, and incoordination. You should wait at least 14 days after stopping selegiline before starting one of these other medications.

Be sure to tell your doctor about any medications, including over-the-counter products, you are currently taking.

WARNINGS

• Tell your doctor if you have had unusual or allergic reactions to any medications, especially to selegiline or to any monoamine oxidase (MAO) inhibitors (such as furazolidine, isocarboxazid, pargyline, phenelzine, procarbazine, or tranylcypromine).
• Tell your doctor if you have a history of stomach problems, intestinal problems, asthma, high blood pressure, or seizure disorders.
• If this drug makes you dizzy or drowsy, do not take part in any activity that requires alertness, such as driving a car or operating potentially dangerous equipment.
• Before having surgery or any other medical or dental treatment, tell your doctor or dentist you are taking this drug.
• Your doctor may give you a list of foods that you should either avoid or limit in your diet. These foods or beverages may include those containing caffeine (coffee, tea, cola, or chocolate) or those containing a substance called tyramine (found in certain cheeses and meats).

• Be sure to tell your doctor if you are pregnant. This drug has not caused adverse effects to the fetuses in animal studies, and problems in humans have not been reported. Also tell your doctor if you are breast-feeding an infant.

---

sertraline

BRAND NAME (Manufacturer)
Zoloft (Roerig)
TYPE OF DRUG
Antidepressant
INGREDIENT
sertraline
DOSAGE FORM
Tablets (50 mg and 100 mg)
STORAGE
This medication should be stored in a tightly closed container at room temperature, away from heat and direct sunlight. Do not store in the bathroom. Heat or moisture can cause this medicine to break down.

USES
Sertraline is used to treat the symptoms of mental depression. It increases the concentration of certain chemicals that are necessary for nerve transmission in the brain.

TREATMENT
This medication should be taken exactly as prescribed by your doctor. In order to avoid stomach irritation, you can take sertraline with food or a full glass of water (unless your doctor directs you to do otherwise).

The effects of treatment with this medication may not become apparent for one to three weeks.

If you miss a dose of this medicine, it is not necessary to make up the missed dose. Skip that dose and continue at the next scheduled time. You should never take a double dose to make up for the one you missed.

SIDE EFFECTS
Minor. Agitation, changes in taste, constipation, decreased concentration, decreased sex drive, diarrhea, dizziness,

drowsiness, dry mouth, fast heartbeat, flushing, frequent urination, headache, increased sweating, loss of appetite, nausea,
stuffy nose, vision changes, or weight gain or loss.

Dry mouth can be relieved by chewing sugarless gum or
sucking on hard candy.

To relieve constipation, increase the amount of fiber in your
diet (fresh fruits and vegetables, salads, bran, and whole-grain
breads), exercise, and drink more water (unless your doctor
directs you to do otherwise).

To avoid dizziness when you stand, contract and relax the
muscles in your legs for a few moments before rising.

Major. Tell your doctor about any side effects that are persistent or particularly bothersome. IT IS ESPECIALLY IMPOR-
TANT TO TELL YOUR DOCTOR about anxiety, chills or fever,
convulsions (seizures), enlarged lymph glands (swelling under
the jaw, in the armpits, or in the groin area), difficulty in breathing, joint or muscle pain, skin rash or hives, or swelling of the
feet or lower legs.

INTERACTIONS

Sertraline interacts with several other types of drugs:

1. Extreme drowsiness can occur when this medication is
taken with other central nervous system depressants (such as
alcohol, antihistamines, barbiturates, benzodiazepine tranquilizers, muscle relaxants, narcotics, pain medications, phenothiazine tranquilizers, or sleeping medications) or with
other antidepressants.

2. Sertraline may increase the effects of oral anticoagulants
(blood thinners, such as warfarin) and certain heart medications
(such as digoxin).

3. Serious side effects may occur if a monoamine oxidase
(MAO) inhibitor (such as furazolidone, isocarboxazid, pargyline, phenelzine, procarbazine, selegiline, or tranylcypromine)
is taken with sertraline. At least 14 days should separate the use
of sertraline and the use of an MAO inhibitor.

4. Sertraline can increase agitation, restlessness, and stomach
irritation when taken with tryptophan.

Before taking sertraline, BE SURE TO TELL YOUR DOCTOR
about any medication you are taking, especially any of those
listed above.

WARNINGS

• Tell your doctor immediately if you develop a skin rash or have hives while taking this medication, or if you have ever had a reaction to sertraline before.

• Be sure that you tell your doctor if you have or ever have had a history of alcoholism or if you ever had a heart attack, asthma, circulatory disease, difficulty in urinating, electroshock therapy, enlarged prostate gland, epilepsy, glaucoma, high blood pressure, intestinal problems, liver or kidney disease, mental illness, or thyroid disease.

• If this medication makes you drowsy or dizzy, do not take part in any activity that requires mental alertness, such as driving a car or operating dangerous equipment.

• Do not stop taking this medication suddenly. Stopping it abruptly can cause nausea, headache, stomach upset, or a worsening of your condition. Your doctor may want to reduce the dose gradually.

• Elderly individuals may be at greater risk of experiencing unwanted or otherwise bothersome side effects. Use this drug cautiously and report any mental status changes to your doctor immediately.

• The effects of this medication may be present for as long as five weeks after you stop taking it. It is important that you continue to observe all precautions during this period.

• Be sure to tell your doctor if you are pregnant. Although birth defects have not been documented in animal studies, it is not known if sertraline is safe during pregnancy. It is not known if sertraline passes into breast milk, so be sure to tell your doctor if you are breast-feeding an infant.

---

simvastatin

BRAND NAME (Manufacturer)
Zocor (Merck Sharp & Dohme)
TYPE OF DRUG
Antihyperlipidemic (lipid-lowering drug)
INGREDIENT
simvastatin
DOSAGE FORM
Tablets (5 mg, 10 mg, 20 mg, and 40 mg)

STORAGE
This medication should be stored in a tightly closed container at room temperature, away from heat and direct sunlight. Simvastatin tablets should not be refrigerated.

USES
Simvastatin is used to treat hyperlipidemia (high blood-fat levels). It may be prescribed with nondrug therapies such as diet control and exercise in an attempt to regulate lipid and cholesterol levels. Simvastatin chemically interferes with an enzyme in the body that is responsible for synthesizing cholesterol. This enzyme blockade decreases the LDL (low-density lipoprotein) type of cholesterol, which has been associated with coronary artery disease and atherosclerosis.

TREATMENT
This medication should be taken exactly as prescribed by your doctor. If you are to take simvastatin once a day, it is best to take the drug in the evening. Simvastatin can be taken with meals or a with a full glass of water if stomach upset occurs.

While using this medication, try to develop a set schedule for taking it. If you miss a dose and remember within a few hours, take the missed dose and resume your regular schedule. If many hours have passed, skip the dose you missed and then take your next dose as scheduled. Do not double the dose.

SIDE EFFECTS
Minor. Abdominal pain or cramps, constipation, diarrhea, gas, nausea, or stomach pain. These effects may be relieved by taking simvastatin with a meal, adding fiber to your diet, or using mild stool softeners.

Major. Tell your doctor about any side effects that are persistent or particularly bothersome. IT IS ESPECIALLY IMPORTANT TO TELL YOUR DOCTOR about blurred vision (or any other visual changes or difficulties), or muscle pain or tenderness, especially with malaise or fever.

INTERACTIONS
1. Simvastatin may increase the effectiveness of oral anticoagulants (blood thinners, such as warfarin) and digoxin.

2. Because of the risk of severe myopathy (muscle weakness), the combined use of simvastatin with gemfibrozil or clofibrate should generally be avoided.

3. Cyclosporine, erythromycin, nicotinic acid, or niacin may increase the side effects of simvastatin and should be used with extreme caution.

BE SURE TO TELL YOUR DOCTOR about any medications you are taking, especially any of those listed above.

WARNINGS

• Tell your doctor about unusual or allergic reactions you have had to any medications.

• Be sure that you tell your doctor if you have ever had liver disease, heart disease, stroke, or digestive-tract disorders.

• Patients taking another drug in this same class developed eye-related problems during treatment. It is advisable to have regular checkups with your ophthalmologist, who should be informed of your use of this drug.

• This drug should not be taken if you are pregnant. Serious side effects have been reported in the offspring of animals given this drug during pregnancy. Also be sure to tell your doctor if you are breast-feeding an infant. This drug should not be used while breast-feeding.

---

sodium sulfacetamide (ophthalmic)

BRAND NAMES (Manufacturers)
AK-Sulf (Akorn)
AK-Sulf Forte (Akorn)
Bleph-10 (Allergan)
Cetamide (Alcon)
Isopto Cetamide (Alcon)
Sodium Sulamyd (Schering)
sodium sulfacetamide (various manufacturers)
Sulf-10 (Iolab Pharm.)
Sulten-10 (Bausch & Lomb)
TYPE OF DRUG
Ophthalmic antibiotic

INGREDIENT
sodium sulfacetamide
DOSAGE FORMS
Ophthalmic drops (10%, 15%, and 30%)
Ophthalmic ointment (10%)
STORAGE
Sodium sulfacetamide drops and ointment should be stored at room temperature in tightly closed containers. This medication should never be frozen. If the eye drops discolor or turn brown, they should be discarded.

USES

Sodium sulfacetamide is used to treat bacterial eye infections and corneal ulcers. Sodium sulfacetamide is an antibiotic that is effective against a wide range of bacteria. It acts by preventing production of the nutrients that are required for growth of the infecting bacteria. This medication, however, is not effective against infections that are caused by viruses or fungi.

TREATMENT

Wash your hands with soap and water before applying this medication. To avoid contamination of the eye drops or ointment, be careful not to touch the tube of the dropper or the tip of the ointment tube or let them touch your eyes; do not wipe off or rinse the dropper after use.

To apply the drops, tilt your head back and pull down the lower eyelid with one hand to make a pouch below the eye. Drop the prescribed amount of medicine into this pouch and slowly close your eyes. Try not to blink. Keep your eyes closed, and place one finger at the corner of the eye next to your nose for a minute or two, applying a slight pressure (this is done to prevent loss of medication through the duct that drains fluid from the surface of the eye into the nose and throat). Then wipe away any excess with a clean tissue.

To apply the ointment, tilt the head back, pull down the lower lid to form a pouch below the eye, and squeeze a small amount of ointment (approximately $1/8$ to $1/4$ inch) in a line along the pouch. Close the eyes, and place your finger at the corner of the eye next to your nose for a minute or two, but do not rub your eyes. Then wipe off any excess ointment with a clean tissue.

Since this medication is somewhat difficult to apply, you may want to have someone else apply it for you.

It is important to continue to take this medication for the entire time prescribed by your doctor, even if the symptoms disappear before the end of that period. If you stop applying the drug too soon, resistant bacteria are given a chance to continue growing, and the infection could recur.

If you miss a dose of this medication, apply the missed dose as soon as possible, unless it is almost time for your next dose. In that case, do not apply the missed dose at all; just return to your regular dosing schedule. Do not use twice as much medication at the next dose.

SIDE EFFECTS

Minor. Sodium sulfacetamide may cause blurred vision or burning or stinging in the eyes immediately after it is applied (especially the 30% solution). This effect should last only a few minutes.

Major. Tell your doctor about any side effects that are persistent or particularly bothersome. IT IS ESPECIALLY IMPORTANT TO TELL YOUR DOCTOR about signs of irritation in the eyes (such as redness, swelling, or itching) that last more than several minutes, chills, fever, itching, or difficulty in breathing. If your symptoms of infection are getting worse rather than improving, contact your doctor.

INTERACTIONS

This drug should not be used concurrently with preparations containing silver, such as silver nitrate opthalmic.

Be sure to tell your doctor about any medications you are currently taking.

WARNINGS

• Tell your doctor about unusual or allergic reactions you have had to any medications, especially to sodium sulfacetamide or to any other sulfa medication (diuretics, oral antidiabetic medications, sulfonamide antibiotics).

• This medication may cause allergic-type symptoms, such as hives, itching, wheezing, or anaphylaxis, in patients sensitive to sulfite.

• Sodium sulfacetamide may cause eye sensitivity to bright light; wearing sunglasses may help to lessen this problem.

• This medication has been prescribed for your current infection only. Another infection later on or one that someone else has may require a different medicine. You should not give your medicine to other people or use it for other infections, unless your doctor specifically directs you to do so.

• In order to allow your eye infection to clear, do not apply makeup to the affected eye.

• If there is no change in your condition two or three days after starting to take this medication, contact your doctor.

• Be sure to tell your doctor if you are pregnant. The safe use of this medication in human pregnancy has not been established. Although an ophthalmic, if large amounts of this drug are applied for prolonged periods, some of it may be absorbed into the bloodstream. Also tell your doctor if you are breast-feeding an infant. If this drug is absorbed, small amounts may pass into the breast milk and may temporarily alter the bacterial balance in the intestinal tract of the nursing infant, resulting in diarrhea.

---

spironolactone

BRAND NAMES (Manufacturers)
Aldactone (Searle)
spironolactone (various manufacturers)
TYPE OF DRUG
Diuretic and antihypertensive
INGREDIENT
spironolactone
DOSAGE FORM
Tablets (25 mg, 50 mg, and 100 mg)
STORAGE
Spironolactone should be stored at room temperature in a tightly closed, light-resistant container.

USES

This drug is used to treat high blood pressure. It is also used to reduce fluid accumulation in the body caused by conditions such as heart failure, cirrhosis of the liver, kidney disease, and the long-term use of some drugs.

Spironolactone reduces fluid accumulation by increasing the elimination of salt and water through the kidneys. It may be used in combination with other diuretics to prevent potassium loss. Since spironolactone blocks the effects of a chemical (aldosterone) released from the adrenal gland, it can also be used to diagnose and treat an overactive adrenal gland.

TREATMENT

To decrease stomach irritation, you can take spironolactone with a glass of milk or with a meal (unless your doctor directs you to do otherwise). Try to take it at the same time every day. Avoid taking a dose after 6:00 P.M.; otherwise, you may have to get up during the night to urinate.

This medication does not cure high blood pressure, but it will help to control the condition as long as you continue to take it.

If you miss a dose of this medication, take the missed dose as soon as possible, unless it is almost time for the next dose. In that case, do not take the missed dose at all; just wait until the next scheduled dose. Do not double the dose.

SIDE EFFECTS

Minor. Cramping, diarrhea, dizziness, drowsiness, dry mouth, headache, increased urination, nausea, rash, restlessness, vomiting, or weakness. As your body adjusts to the medication, these side effects should disappear.

Dry mouth can be relieved by chewing sugarless gum or sucking on hard candy.

To avoid dizziness or light-headedness when you stand, contract and relax the muscles of your legs for a few moments before rising. Do this by pushing one foot against the floor while raising the other foot slightly, alternating feet so that you are "pumping" your legs in a pedaling motion.

Major. Tell your doctor about any side effects that are persistent or particularly bothersome. IT IS ESPECIALLY IMPORTANT TO TELL YOUR DOCTOR about anxiety; clumsiness; confusion; deepening of the voice (in women); enlarged breasts (in both sexes); fever; impotence; increased hair growth; menstrual disturbances; muscle cramps; numbness or tingling in the hands, feet, or lips; palpitations; postmenopausal bleeding; rapid weight gain (three to five pounds within a week); stomach cramps; uncoordinated movements; or unusual tiredness or weakness.

INTERACTIONS

Spironolactone interacts with several medications and with a few foods:

1. Concurrent use of spironolactone with amiloride, antihypertensive agents (such as benazepril, captopril, enalapril, fosinopril, lisinopril, quinipril, and ramipril) triamterene, potassium salts, low-salt milk, salt substitutes, or laxatives can cause serious side effects such as hyperkalemia (high blood levels of potassium).

2. Spironolactone may increase the side effects of lithium, digoxin, digitoxin, and ammonium chloride.

3. The effectiveness of oral anticoagulants (blood thinners) may be decreased by this medication.

4. Aspirin may decrease the diuretic effects of spironolactone.

Before starting to take spironolactone, BE SURE TO TELL YOUR DOCTOR about any medications you are currently taking, especially any of those listed above.

WARNINGS

• Tell your doctor about unusual or allergic reactions you have had to any medications, especially to spironolactone or to any other diuretic.

• Tell your doctor if you have ever had kidney or urination problems, heart disease, hyperkalemia (high blood levels of potassium), liver disease, menstrual abnormalities, breast enlargement, or diabetes mellitus.

• Spironolactone can cause hyperkalemia. Signs of hyperkalemia include palpitations; confusion; numbness or tingling in the hands, feet, or lips; anxiety; or unusual tiredness or weakness. However, do not alter your diet in an effort to avoid this problem, unless your doctor tells you to do so. Elderly patients may be more susceptible to hyperkalemia.

• There are several "generic brands" of this drug. Consult your pharmacist about these items; some of them are not equivalent to the brand-name medications.

• Limit your intake of alcoholic beverages to prevent dizziness and light-headedness while taking this drug.

• Do not take any over-the-counter (nonprescription) medications for weight control or for allergy, asthma, cough, cold, or sinus problems unless you first check with your doctor.

• To prevent severe water loss (dehydration) while taking this medication, check with your doctor if you have any illness that brings on severe or continuous nausea, vomiting, or diarrhea.

• Be sure to tell your doctor if you are pregnant. This drug crosses the placenta, and its safety in human pregnancy has not been established. Adverse effects have been observed in the fetuses of animals that were given large doses of this drug during pregnancy. Also tell your doctor if you are breast-feeding an infant.

---

spironolactone and hydrochlorothiazide combination

BRAND NAMES (Manufacturers)
Aldactazide (Searle)
spironolactone and hydrochlorothiazide (various
  manufacturers)
Spirozide (Rugby)
TYPE OF DRUG
Diuretic and antihypertensive
INGREDIENTS
spironolactone and hydrochlorothiazide
DOSAGE FORM
Tablets (25 mg spironolactone and 25 mg hydrochloro-
  thiazide; 50 mg spironolactone and 50 mg hydrochloro-
  thiazide)
STORAGE
Store this medication at room temperature in a tightly closed, light-resistant container. It should not be refrigerated.

USES
Spironolactone and hydrochlorothiazide combination is prescribed to treat high blood pressure. It is also used to reduce fluid acccumulation in the body caused by conditions such as heart failure, cirrhosis of the liver, kidney disease, and the long-term use of some medications. This medication reduces fluid accumulation by increasing the elimination of salt and water through the kidneys. Spironolactone is combined with hydrochlorothiazide to prevent potassium loss from the body.

TREATMENT

To decrease stomach irritation, you can take this medication with a glass of milk or with a meal (unless your doctor directs you to do otherwise). Try to take it at the same time every day. Avoid taking a dose of this drug after 6:00 P.M.

This medication does not cure high blood pressure, but it will help to control the condition as long as you continue to take it.

If you miss a dose of this medication, take the missed dose as soon as possible, unless it is almost time for the next dose. In that case, do not take the missed dose at all; just wait until the next scheduled dose. Do not double the dose.

SIDE EFFECTS

Minor. Constipation, cramping, diarrhea, dizziness, headache, increased urination, loss of appetite, lack of energy, light-headedness, restlessness, or unusual sweating. These side effects should disappear over time as your body adjusts to this medication.

This medication can increase your sensitivity to sunlight. You should therefore avoid prolonged exposure to sunlight and sunlamps. Wear protective clothing and use an effective sunscreen.

To relieve constipation, increase the amount of fiber in your diet (fresh fruits and vegetables, salads, bran, and whole-grain breads) and exercise more (unless your doctor directs you to do otherwise).

To avoid dizziness or light-headedness when you stand, contract and relax the muscles of your legs for a few moments before rising. Do this by pushing one foot against the floor while raising the other foot slightly, alternating feet so that you are "pumping" your legs in a pedaling motion.

Major. Tell your doctor about any side effects you may be experiencing that are persistent or particularly bothersome. IT IS ESPECIALLY IMPORTANT TO TELL YOUR DOCTOR about anxiety; blurred vision; breast tenderness or enlargement (in both sexes); clumsiness; confusion; deepening of the voice (in women); drowsiness; dry mouth; impotence; increased hair growth; irregular menstrual periods or vaginal bleeding; joint pain; mood changes; muscle cramps; nausea; numbness or tingling in the hands, feet, or lips; palpitations; rapid weight gain (three to five pounds within a week); rash; sore throat and fever; swelling; thirst; unusual bleeding or bruising; unusual tiredness or weakness; vomiting; or yellowing of the eyes or skin.

INTERACTIONS

Spironolactone and hydrochlorothiazide combination interacts with several foods and medications:

1. Concurrent use of it with amiloride, antihypertensive agents (such as benazepril, captopril, enalapril, fosinopril, lisinopril, quinipril, and ramipril) triamterene, potassium salts, low-salt milk, salt substitutes, or laxatives can cause serious side effects from hyperkalemia (high levels of potassium in the blood).

2. This drug may decrease the effectiveness of oral anticoagulants, antigout medications, insulin, oral antidiabetic medicines, and methenamine.

3. Fenfluramine may increase the blood-pressure-lowering effects of this drug.

4. Indomethacin and aspirin may decrease the blood-pressure-lowering effects of this drug.

5. Cholestyramine and colestipol can decrease the absorption of this medication from the gastrointestinal tract. Therefore, spironolactone and hydrochlorothiazide combination should be taken one hour before or four hours after a dose of cholestyramine or colestipol if either of these medications has also been prescribed for you.

6. Spironolactone and hydrochlorothiazide may increase the side effects of calcium, cortisone, and cortisonelike steroids (such as dexamethasone, hydrocortisone, and prednisolone), digoxin, digitoxin, digitalis, lithium, quinidine, sulfonamide antibiotics, and vitamin D.

BE SURE TO TELL YOUR DOCTOR about any medications you are currently taking, especially those listed above.

WARNINGS

• Tell your doctor about unusual or allergic reactions you have had to any medications, especially to spironolactone or hydrochlorothiazide or to any other sulfa drug, including other diuretics (water pills), oral antidiabetic medications, or sulfonamide antibiotics.

• Before you start taking this medication, tell your doctor if you now have or if you have ever had kidney disease or problems with urination, diabetes mellitus, gout, liver disease, asthma, pancreas disease, systemic lupus erythematosus, hyperkalemia, menstrual abnormalities, breast enlargement, acidosis, or hypercalcemia.

• The hydrochlorothiazide component of this drug can occasionally cause potassium loss from the body. Signs of potassium loss include dry mouth, muscle pain or cramps, nausea, thirst, vomiting, and weakness. If you experience any of these symptoms, call your doctor.

• The spironolactone component of this drug can cause hyperkalemia, or increased potassium levels in the body. Signs of hyperkalemia include anxiety; confusion; numbness or tingling in the hands, feet, or lips; palpitations; or unusual tiredness or weakness. Do not alter your diet in an attempt to avoid this problem unless you first consult your doctor. Elderly patients may be more susceptible to hyperkalemia.

• There are several "generic brands" of this drug. Products made by different companies may not work in exactly the same way. Before switching brands, consult your doctor or pharmacist.

• Limit your intake of alcoholic beverages to prevent dizziness and light-headedness while taking this drug.

• Do not take any over-the-counter (nonprescription) medications for weight control or for allergy, asthma, cough, cold, or sinus problems unless you check with your doctor.

• To prevent dehydration (severe water loss), check with your doctor if you develop any illness that causes severe or continuous nausea, vomiting, or diarrhea.

• This drug can raise blood-sugar levels in diabetic patients. Blood sugar should be monitored carefully with blood or urine tests when this drug is being taken.

• A doctor does not usually prescribe a "fixed-dose" drug like this as the first choice in the treatment of high blood pressure. Usually, the patient first receives each ingredient singly. If there is an adequate response to the fixed dose contained in this product, it can then be substituted. The advantages of a combination product are increased convenience and (often) decreased cost.

• Be sure to tell your doctor if you are pregnant. This drug crosses the placenta, and its safety in human pregnancy has not been established. Adverse effects have been observed in the fetuses of animals that were given large doses of this drug during pregnancy. Also tell your doctor if you are breast-feeding an infant.

---

succimer

BRAND NAME (Manufacturer)
Chemet (McNeil Consumer Products)
TYPE OF DRUG
Oral chelator (remover) for lead
INGREDIENT
succimer
DOSAGE FORM
Capsules (100 mg)
STORAGE
Succimer capsules should be stored at room temperature in a tightly closed, light-resistent container.

USES
Succimer is used to remove excess lead in the body. Although patients with excess lead levels may not look or act sick, the lead may cause learning difficulties if left untreated over time. Succimer binds to the excess lead in the bloodstream. The combination of lead and succimer is removed from the body when the patient urinates.

TREATMENT
In order to avoid stomach upset, succimer capsules can be taken whole with food or with a glass of milk (unless your doctor directs you to do otherwise).

If succimer is prescribed for a young child who cannot swallow capsules, you may open the capsule and sprinkle the contents on a spoonful of soft food such as applesauce, ice cream, or pudding.

SIDE EFFECTS
Minor. Bad or metallic taste in mouth, diarrhea, loss of appetite, or vomiting. These side effects should disappear as your body adjusts to the medication.
Major. Tell your doctor about any side effects that are persistent or particularly bothersome. IT IS ESPECIALLY IMPORTANT TO TELL YOUR DOCTOR about severe abdominal pain,

severe headaches, skin rash, tingling in the arms or legs, or yellowing of the skin or eyes.

INTERACTIONS
It is not known at this time whether or not succimer interacts with any other medication.

WARNINGS
• It is important to tell your doctor if you have ever had an unusual or allergic reaction to succimer or any other medication.

• It is important that you drink plenty of fluids while taking this medication.

• Succimer may cause your breath or urine to have a bad odor. This is a harmless effect.

• This medication has been prescribed for your current condition only. Do not give this medication to other people or use it for any purpose other than the one prescribed by your doctor.

• Your doctor may want you to have regular blood tests to make sure that this medication is working properly.

• Be sure to tell your doctor if you are pregnant or if you are breast-feeding an infant. The safe use of this medication during human pregnancy or breast-feeding has not been established.

---

sucralfate

BRAND NAME (Manufacturer)
Carafate (Marion Merrel Dow)
TYPE OF DRUG
Antiulcer
INGREDIENT
sucralfate
DOSAGE FORM
Tablets (1 g)
STORAGE
Sucralfate should be stored at room temperature in a tightly closed container. This medication should not be refrigerated.

USES

Sucralfate is used for the short-term treatment of ulcers. This medication binds to the surface of the ulcer, thereby protecting it from stomach acid and promoting healing.

TREATMENT

In order to obtain maximum benefit from this drug, you should swallow it whole with a full glass of water. Take it on an empty stomach one hour before or two hours after a meal and at bedtime. Do not take antacids in the period from 30 minutes before to one hour after taking sucralfate.

Continue to take sucralfate for the full length of time prescribed by your doctor, even if your symptoms disappear. Your ulcer may not yet be healed. However, do not take it for more than eight weeks without your doctor's authorization.

If you miss a dose of this medication, take the missed dose as soon as possible, unless it is almost time for the next dose. In that case, do not take the missed dose at all; just return to your regular dosing schedule. Do not double the next dose.

SIDE EFFECTS

Minor. Back pain, constipation, diarrhea, dizziness, drowsiness, dry mouth, indigestion, nausea, or stomach pain. These side effects should disappear as your body adjusts to the medication.

To relieve constipation, exercise and drink more water (unless your doctor directs you to do otherwise).

If you feel dizzy, sit or lie down for a while; get up slowly from a sitting or reclining position; and be careful on stairs.

To relieve mouth dryness, chew sugarless gum or suck on ice chips or a piece of hard candy.

Major. Tell your doctor about any side effects that are persistent or particularly bothersome. IT IS ESPECIALLY IMPORTANT TO TELL YOUR DOCTOR about itching or rash. If your condition does not improve or seems to be getting worse, you should contact your doctor.

INTERACTIONS

1. Sucralfate may prevent the absorption of tetracycline, digoxin, phenytoin, ranitidine, and fat-soluble vitamins (vitamins A, D, E, and K) from the gastrointestinal tract. At least

one hour should separate doses of any of these medications and sucralfate.

2. Sucralfate may decrease stomach absorption of ciprofloxacin, norfloxacin, and ofloxacin. At least two hours should separate doses of these medications and sucralfate.

BE SURE TO TELL YOUR DOCTOR about any medications you are taking, especially any listed above.

WARNINGS

• Tell your doctor about unusual or allergic reactions you have had to any medications, especially to sucralfate.

• Tell your doctor if you now have or if you have ever had kidney disease.

• If sucralfate makes you dizzy or drowsy, do not take part in any activity that requires mental alertness, such as driving an automobile or operating potentially dangerous machinery or equipment.

• Be sure to tell your doctor if you are pregnant. Although sucralfate appears to be safe to use during gestation, extensive studies in pregnant women have not been conducted. Also tell your doctor if you are breast-feeding an infant. It is not known whether sucralfate passes into breast milk.

---

sulfamethoxazole and trimethoprim combination

BRAND NAMES (Manufacturers)
Bactrim (Roche)
Bactrim DS (Roche)
Bethaprim DS (Major)
Cotrim (Lemmon)
Cotrim DS (Lemmon)
Cotrim Pediatric (Lemmon)
Septra (Burroughs Wellcome)
Septra DS (Burroughs Wellcome)
sulfamethoxazole and trimethoprim (various manufacturers)
Sulfatrim (various manufacturers)
Sulfatrim DS (various manufacturers)
TYPE OF DRUG
Antibiotic

INGREDIENTS
sulfamethoxazole and trimethoprim
DOSAGE FORMS
Tablets (400 mg sulfamethoxazole and 80 mg trimethoprim)
Double-strength (DS) tablets (800 mg sulfamethoxazole and 160 mg trimethoprim)
Oral suspension (200 mg sulfamethoxazole and 40 mg trimethoprim per 5-mL spoonful)
STORAGE
Sulfamethoxazole and trimethoprim combination tablets and oral suspension should be stored at room temperature in tightly closed, light-resistant containers. The oral suspension does not need to be refrigerated. This medication should never be frozen.

USES
Sulfamethoxazole and trimethoprim combination is used to treat a broad range of infections, including urinary tract infections, certain respiratory and gastrointestinal infections, and otitis media (middle-ear infection). Sulfamethoxazole and trimethoprim acts by preventing production of the nutrients that are required for growth of the infecting bacteria.

TREATMENT
It is best to take this medication with a full glass of water on an empty stomach, either one hour before or two hours after a meal. However, if this drug causes stomach upset, check with your doctor to see if you can take it with food or milk.

The oral-suspension form of this medication should be shaken well just before measuring each dose. The contents tend to settle on the bottom of the bottle, so it is necessary to shake the container to distribute the ingredients evenly and equalize the doses. Each dose should then be measured carefully with a specially designed 5-mL measuring spoon. An ordinary kitchen teaspoon is not accurate enough.

This medication works best when the level of medicine in your bloodstream (and urine) is kept constant. It is best, therefore, to take the doses at evenly spaced intervals day and night. For example, if you are to take two doses a day, the doses should be spaced 12 hours apart. Try not to skip any doses.

If you miss a dose of this medication, take the missed dose immediately. However, if you do not remember to take the missed dose until it is almost time for your next dose, take the missed dose immediately; space the following dose about halfway through the regular interval between doses (wait about six hours if you are taking two doses a day); and then return to your regular dosing schedule.

It is important to continue to take this medication for the entire time prescribed by your doctor (usually seven to 14 days), even if the symptoms disappear before the end of that period. If you stop taking the drug too soon, resistant bacteria are given a chance to continue growing, and the infection could recur.

SIDE EFFECTS

Minor. Abdominal pain, diarrhea, dizziness, headache, loss of appetite, nausea, sore mouth, or vomiting. These side effects should disappear as your body adjusts to the drug.

Sulfamethoxazole can cause increased sensitivity to sunlight. It is, therefore, important to avoid prolonged exposure to sunlight and sunlamps. Wear protective clothing and sunglasses, and use a sunscreen. However, a sunscreen containing para-aminobenzoic acid (PABA) interferes with the antibacterial activity of this medication and should not be used.

If you feel dizzy, sit or lie down for a while; get up slowly from a sitting or reclining position; and be careful on stairs.

Major. Tell your doctor about any side effects that are persistent or particularly bothersome. IT IS ESPECIALLY IMPORTANT TO TELL YOUR DOCTOR about bloody urine, convulsions, difficult or painful urination, difficulty in breathing, difficulty in swallowing, fever, hallucinations, itching, joint pain, lower back pain, pale skin, rash, ringing in the ears, sore throat, swelling of the front part of the neck, swollen or inflamed tongue, tingling in the hands or feet, unusual bleeding or bruising, unusual fatigue, or yellowing of the eyes or skin. If your infection seems to be getting worse rather than improving, contact your doctor.

INTERACTIONS

This medicine will interact with several other types of medications:

1. Sulfamethoxazole can increase the blood levels of oral anticoagulants (blood thinners, such as warfarin), oral antidiabetic agents, methotrexate, aspirin, and phenytoin, which can lead to serious side effects.

2. Methenamine can increase the side effects to the kidneys caused by sulfamethoxazole.

3. Probenecid and sulfinpyrazone can increase the blood levels of sulfamethoxazole, which can lead to an increase in side effects.

4. Rifampin can increase the elimination of trimethoprim from the body, decreasing its antibacterial effects.

5. Concurrent use of trimethoprim with antineoplastic agents (anticancer drugs) can increase the risk of developing blood disorders.

6. Trimethoprim can decrease the elimination of phenytoin from the body and increase the chance of side effects.

BE SURE TO TELL YOUR DOCTOR about any medications you are currently taking, especially any drugs that are listed above.

WARNINGS

• Tell your doctor about unusual or allergic reactions you have had to any medications, especially to trimethoprim, sulfamethoxazole, or other sulfa drugs (other sulfonamide antibiotics, diuretics, dapsone, sulfoxone, oral antidiabetic medications, oral antiglaucoma medication, or acetazolamide).

• Tell your doctor if you now have or if you have ever had glucose–6-phosphate dehydrogenase (G6PD) deficiency, kidney disease, liver disease, porphyria, or megaloblastic anemia (folate-deficiency anemia).

• This medication has been prescribed for your current infection only. Another infection later on or one that someone else has may require a different medicine. You should not give your medicine to other people or use it for other infections, unless your doctor specifically directs you to do so.

• This medication should be taken with plenty of water in order to avoid kidney-stone formation.

• If this medication tends to make you dizzy or drowsy, do not take part in any activity that requires mental alertness, such as driving an automobile or operating potentially hazardous machinery or equipment.

• If there is no improvement in your condition several days after starting to take this medication, check with your doctor.

This medication may not be effective against the bacteria causing your infection.

• Before having surgery or any other medical or dental treatment, tell your doctor or dentist you are taking this drug.

• Be sure to tell your doctor if you are pregnant. Small amounts of sulfamethoxazole and trimethoprim cross the placenta. Although these drugs appear to be safe during pregnancy, extensive studies in humans have not been conducted. Trimethoprim has been shown to cause birth defects in the offspring of animals that received very large doses during pregnancy. Tell your doctor if you are breast-feeding. Small amounts of sulfamethoxazole pass into breast milk and may temporarily alter the bacterial balance in the intestinal tract of the nursing infant, resulting in diarrhea. Small amounts of trimethoprim also pass into breast milk, and there is a chance that it may cause anemia in the nursing infant. This combination medication should not be used in an infant less than two months of age (to avoid side effects involving the liver).

---

sulfasalazine

BRAND NAMES (Manufacturers)
Azulfidine (Kabi Pharmacia)
Azulfidine EN-tabs (Kabi Pharmacia)
sulfasalazine (various manufacturers)
TYPE OF DRUG
Sulfonamide and anti-inflammatory
INGREDIENT
sulfasalazine
DOSAGE FORMS
Tablets (500 mg)
Enteric-coated tablets (500 mg)
STORAGE
Store at room temperature in a tightly closed, light-resistant container. This drug should not be refrigerated.

USES

This medication is used to treat inflammatory bowel disease (regional enteritis or ulcerative colitis). In the intestine, sulfasalazine is converted to 5-aminosalicylic acid, an aspirin-like drug, which acts to relieve inflammation.

TREATMENT

In order to avoid stomach irritation while you are being treated with this medication, you should take your doses with a full glass of water, with food, or after meals (unless your doctor directs you to do otherwise).

The enteric-coated tablets should be swallowed whole. The enteric coating is added to lessen stomach irritation. Chewing, breaking, or crushing these tablets destroys the coating.

If you miss a dose of this medication, take the missed dose as soon as possible, unless it is almost time for the next dose. In that case, do not take the missed dose at all; just return to your regular dosing schedule. Do not double the next dose.

SIDE EFFECTS

Minor. Diarrhea, dizziness, drowsiness, insomnia, loss of appetite, mild headache, nausea, stomach upset, or vomiting. These side effects should disappear as your body adjusts to the drug.

This medication can increase your sensitivity to sunlight. Avoid prolonged exposure to sunlight and sunlamps. Wear protective clothing and use a sunscreen. However, a sunscreen containing para-aminobenzoic acid (PABA) interferes with this drug and should not be used.

Sulfasalazine can discolor contact lenses. You may want to stop wearing them while taking this medication. Discuss this with your ophthalmologist.

Sulfasalazine can cause your urine to change to an orange-yellow color. This is a harmless effect.

If you feel dizzy, sit or lie down for a while; get up slowly if you have been in a sitting or reclining position; and be careful on stairs.

Major. Tell your doctor about any side effects that are persistent or particularly bothersome. IT IS ESPECIALLY IMPORTANT TO TELL YOUR DOCTOR about blood in the urine, convulsions, depression, difficulty in swallowing, difficult or painful urination, fatigue, fever, hallucinations, hearing loss, itching, joint pain, lower back pain, mouth sores, pale skin, rash or peeling skin, ringing in the ears, severe headache, sore throat, swelling of the front part of the neck, tingling sensations, unusual bleeding or bruising, or a yellowish discoloration of the eyes or skin.

INTERACTIONS

Sulfasalazine interacts with a number of other types of medications:

1. It can increase the side effects of oral anticoagulants (blood thinners, such as warfarin), oral antidiabetic agents, methotrexate, aspirin, and phenytoin.

2. The blood levels and effectiveness of digoxin and folic acid are decreased by concurrent use of sulfasalazine.

3. Probenecid, methenamine, and sulfinpyrazone can increase the blood levels and side effects of sulfasalazine.

BE SURE TO TELL YOUR DOCTOR about any medications you are currently taking, especially any listed above.

WARNINGS

• Tell your doctor about unusual or allergic reactions you have had to any medications, especially to sulfasalazine, aspirin or other salicylates, or any sulfa drug (diuretics, oral antidiabetic medications, sulfonamide antibiotics, oral antiglaucoma medication, acetazolamide, sulfoxone, dapsone).

• Before starting to take this medication, be sure to tell your doctor if you now have or if you have ever had blood disorders, blockage of the urinary tract or intestine, glucose–6-phosphate dehydrogenase (G6PD) deficiency, kidney disease, liver disease, or porphyria.

• To help prevent the formation of kidney stones, try to drink at least eight to 12 glasses of water or fruit juice each day while you are taking this medication (unless your doctor directs you to do otherwise).

• Before having surgery or other medical or dental treatment, tell your doctor or dentist you are taking this drug.

• If your condition does not improve within a month or two after starting to take sulfasalazine, check with your doctor. It may be necessary to change your medication.

• Be sure to tell your doctor if you are pregnant. Although sulfasalazine appears to be safe during most of pregnancy, extensive studies in humans have not been conducted. There is also concern that if this drug is taken during the ninth month of pregnancy, it may cause liver or brain disorders in the infant. In addition, notify your physician if you are breast-feeding an infant. Small amounts of sulfasalazine pass into breast milk, so caution is warranted.

sulfathiazole, sulfacetamide, and sulfabenzamide combination

BRAND NAMES (Manufacturers)
Sulfa-Gyn (Mayrand)
Sultrin Triple Sulfa (Ortho)
Triple Sulfa vaginal (various manufacturers)
Trysul (Savage)
TYPE OF DRUG
Antibiotic
INGREDIENTS
sulfathiazole, sulfacetamide, and sulfabenzamide
DOSAGE FORMS
Vaginal tablets (172.5 mg sulfathiazole, 143.75 mg
  sulfacetamide, and 184 mg sulfabenzamide)
Vaginal cream (3.42% sulfathiazole, 2.86% sulfacetamide,
  and 3.7% sulfabenzamide)
STORAGE
This medication should be stored at room temperature (never frozen) in tightly closed, light-resistant containers.

USES

Sulfathiazole, sulfacetamide, and sulfabenzamide are sulfonamide antibiotics used to treat vaginal infections. They work by blocking production of nutrients needed by the infecting bacteria, thus killing the bacteria.

TREATMENT

This product comes with instructions and an applicator. Read the instructions carefully before use. Wash the applicator with warm water and soap, and dry it thoroughly after each use.

It is important to continue to take this medication for the entire time prescribed by your doctor, even if your symptoms disappear before the end of that period. If you stop taking the medication too soon, your infection could recur.

If you miss a dose of this medication, insert the missed dose as soon as possible, unless it is almost time for the next dose.

In that case, do not insert the missed dose; return to the regular dosing schedule. Do not double the dose.

SIDE EFFECTS

Minor. This medication combination can cause a mild, temporary burning or stinging sensation after each of the first few applications. As your body adjusts to this medication combination, this side effect should disappear.

Major. Tell your doctor about any side effects that are persistent or particularly bothersome. IT IS ESPECIALLY IMPORTANT TO TELL YOUR DOCTOR about itching, rash, redness, swelling, or any other signs of irritation that were not present before you started taking this medication.

INTERACTIONS

Sulfathiazole, sulfacetamide, and sulfabenzamide combination should not interact with other medications if it is used according to your doctor's directions.

WARNINGS

• Tell your doctor about unusual or allergic reactions you have had to any medications, especially to sulfathiazole, sulfacetamide, sulfabenzamide, or any other sulfa drug, including sulfonamide antibiotics, diuretics, oral antidiabetic medicines, oral antiglaucoma medication, dapsone, sulfone, and sulfoxone.

• Before starting to take this medication, tell your doctor if you now have or if you have ever had kidney disease.

• You should not use tampons while using this medication.

• During intercourse, your partner should wear a condom to prevent reinfection. Ask your doctor if your partner needs to be treated at the same time you are treated.

• This medication combination has been prescribed for your current infection only. Another infection later on, or one that someone else has, may require a different medicine. You should not give your medicine to other people or use it for other infections, unless your doctor directs you to do so.

• If symptoms do not begin to improve within several days after starting this medication, CONTACT YOUR DOCTOR. This medication may not be effective against your infection.

• If you are pregnant or breast-feeding, ASK YOUR DOCTOR if you should continue to use this medication.

sulfisoxazole and phenazopyridine combination

BRAND NAMES (Manufacturers)
Azo-Sulfisoxazole (various manufacturers)
TYPE OF DRUG
Antibiotic and urinary-tract analgesic
INGREDIENTS
sulfisoxazole and phenazopyridine
DOSAGE FORM
Tablets (500 mg sulfisoxazole and 50 mg phenazopyridine)
STORAGE
Sulfisoxazole and phenazopyridine combination tablets should be stored at room temperature in a tightly closed, light-resistant container.

USES

Sulfisoxazole and phenazopyridine combination is used to treat painful infections of the urinary tract. Sulfisoxazole is a sulfonamide antibiotic, which acts by preventing production of nutrients that are required for growth of infecting bacteria. Phenazopyridine is excreted in the urine, where it exerts a topical analgesic (pain-relieving) effect on the urinary tract. This medication is not useful for any pain other than that of a urinary-tract infection and so should not be taken for other diseases or conditions.

TREATMENT

It is best to take this medication with a full glass of water on an empty stomach, either one hour before or two hours after a meal. However, if it causes stomach upset, check with your doctor to see if you can take it with food or milk.

This medication works best when the level of medication in your blood and urine is kept constant. It is best, therefore, to take the doses at evenly spaced intervals day and night. For example, if you are to take two doses a day, the doses should be spaced 12 hours apart.

If you miss a dose of this medication, take the missed dose immediately. However, if you do not remember to take the missed dose until it is almost time for your next dose, take the missed dose immediately; space the following dose about halfway through the regular interval between doses; and then return to your regular dosing schedule. Try not to skip any doses.

It is important to continue to take this medication for the entire time prescribed by your doctor (usually seven to 14 days), even if your symptoms disappear before the end of that period. If you stop taking the drug too soon, resistant bacteria are given a chance to continue growing, and the infection could recur.

SIDE EFFECTS

Minor. Abdominal pain, diarrhea, dizziness, headache, indigestion, insomnia, loss of appetite, nausea, or vomiting. These side effects should disappear as your body adjusts to the medication.

Sulfisoxazole can cause increased sensitivity to sunlight. It is therefore important to avoid prolonged exposure to sunlight and sunlamps. Wear protective clothing and sunglasses, and use an effective sunscreen. However, a sunscreen containing para-aminobenzoic acid (PABA) interferes with the antibacterial activity of this medication and thus should not be used.

Phenazopyridine causes your urine to become orange-red in color. This is not harmful; however, it may stain your clothing. The urine will return to its normal color soon after the drug is discontinued.

If you feel dizzy, sit or lie down for a while; get up slowly from a sitting or reclining position; and be careful on stairs.

Major. Tell your doctor about any side effects that are persistent or particularly bothersome. IT IS ESPECIALLY IMPORTANT TO TELL YOUR DOCTOR about aching joints and muscles, back pain, bloating, blood in the urine, chest pain, chills, confusion, convulsions, depression, difficulty in breathing, difficulty in swallowing, difficult or painful urination, fever, hallucinations, hives, itching, loss of coordination, pale skin, rash or peeling skin, ringing in the ears, sore throat, swelling of the front part of the neck, swollen ankles, unusual bleeding or bruising, unusual tiredness, or yellowing of the eyes or skin. If your symptoms of infection seem to be getting worse rather than improving, you should contact your doctor.

INTERACTIONS

This drug interacts with several types of drugs:

1. Sulfisoxazole can increase the blood levels of oral antico-agulants (blood thinners, such as warfarin), oral antidiabetic agents, methotrexate, aspirin, thiopental, and phenytoin, which can lead to serious side effects.

2. Methenamine can increase the side effects to the kidneys caused by sulfisoxazole.

3. Probenecid and sulfinpyrazone can increase the side effects of sulfisoxazole.

BE SURE TO TELL YOUR DOCTOR about any medications you are currently taking, especially those listed above.

WARNINGS

• Tell your doctor about any reactions you have or ever have had to drugs, especially to phenazopyridine, sulfisoxazole, or any other sulfa drug (other sulfonamide antibiotics, diuretics, dapsone, sulfoxone, oral antidiabetic medications, oral antiglaucoma medications, or acetazolamide).

• Tell your doctor if you now have or if you have ever had glucose–6-phosphate dehydrogenase (G6PD) deficiency, kidney disease, liver disease, or porphyria.

• This medication has been prescribed for your current infection only. Another infection later on or one that someone else has may require a different medicine. You should not give your medicine to other people or use it for other infections, unless your doctor specifically directs you to do so.

• This medication should be taken with plenty of water in order to prevent kidney stone formation.

• If this drug makes you dizzy or drowsy, it is especially important that you not take part in any activity that requires alertness, such as driving a car or operating potentially dangerous machinery.

• Diabetic patients using this medication, which contains phenazopyridine, may get delayed reactions or false-positive readings for sugar or ketones with urine tests. Clinitest is not affected by this medication, but the other urine sugar tests may be. Discuss this with your doctor or pharmacist.

• If there is no improvement in your condition several days after starting to take this medication, check with your doctor. This medication may not be effective against the bacteria causing your infection.

• Before having surgery or any other medical or dental treatment, be sure to tell your doctor or dentist that you are taking this medication.
• Be sure to tell your doctor if you are pregnant. Small amounts of sulfisoxazole cross the placenta. Although this medication appears to be safe during pregnancy, extensive studies in humans have not been conducted. Also tell your doctor if you are breast-feeding. Small amounts of this medication pass into breast milk and may temporarily alter the bacterial balance in the intestinal tract of a nursing infant, resulting in diarrhea. This medication should not be used in an infant less than two months of age (in order to avoid side effects involving the liver).

sulfonamide antibiotics (oral)

BRAND NAMES (Manufacturers)
Gantanol (Roche)
Gulfasin (Major)
sulfadiazine (various manufacturers)
sulfamethizole (various manufacturers)
sulfamethoxazole (various manufacturers)
sulfisoxazole (various manufacturers)
Thiosulfil Forte (Wyeth-Ayerst)
Urobak (Shionogi USA)
TYPE OF DRUG
Anti-infective
INGREDIENTS AND DOSAGE FORMS
sulfadiazine Tablets (500 mg)
sulfamethizole (Thiosulfil Forte) Tablets (500 mg)
sulfamethoxazole (Gantanol, Urobak) Tablets (500 mg)
sulfisoxazole Tablets (500 mg)
STORAGE
Store at room temperature in the original container. Do not refrigerate this medication.

USES
Sulfonamide antibiotics are a family of related drugs that have activity against many types of bacteria. This group of medications is often used to treat urinary-tract infections, as well as

other infections. These medications kill the bacteria responsible for the infection.

TREATMENT

Sulfonamide antibiotics should be taken with a full glass of water on an empty stomach (either one hour before or two hours after a meal). Several additional glasses of water should also be taken every day (unless your doctor directs you to do otherwise). Sulfonamide antibiotics work best when the level of the medicine in your bloodstream is kept constant. It is best, therefore, to take the doses at evenly spaced intervals day and night. For example, if you are to take four doses a day, the doses should be spaced about six hours apart.

If you miss a dose, take the missed dose as soon as possible, unless it is almost time for your next dose. In that case, if you are taking two doses a day, space the missed dose and the following dose five to six hours apart; if you are taking three or more doses a day, space the missed dose and the following dose two to four hours apart, or double the next dose. Then return to your regular dosing schedule.

It is very important to continue to take these medications for the entire time prescribed by your doctor (usually ten days), even if the symptoms disappear before the end of that period. If you stop taking the drug too soon your infection could recur.

SIDE EFFECTS

Minor. Diarrhea, dizziness, headache, loss of appetite, nausea, or vomiting. As your body adjusts to the medication, these side effects should disappear.

These drugs can increase your sensitivity to sunlight. You should, therefore, avoid prolonged exposure to sunlight and sunlamps. Wear protective clothing and sunglasses, and use an effective sunscreen, but not a sunscreen that contains para-aminobenzoic acid (PABA). PABA interferes with the antibacterial activity of this medication.

Major. Tell your doctor about any side effects that are persistent or particularly bothersome. IT IS ESPECIALLY IMPORTANT TO TELL YOUR DOCTOR about aching of joints and muscles; blood in the urine; difficulty in swallowing; itching; lower back pain; pain while urinating; pale skin; redness, blistering, or peeling of the skin; skin rash; sore throat and fever; swelling of the front part of the neck; unusual bleeding or bruising; unusual tiredness; or yellowing of the eyes or skin. If your symptoms of infection seem to be getting worse rather than improving, you should contact your doctor.

INTERACTIONS

Sulfonamides has been known to interact with several types of medications:

1. PABA products (sunscreens) can decrease the effectiveness of the sulfonamides.

2. The activity and side effects of anticoagulants (blood thinners, such as warfarin), oral antidiabetic medications, methotrexate, aspirin, phenytoin, and thiopental may be increased when sulfonamides are also taken.

3. Methenamine, probenecid, and sulfinpyrazone can increase the toxicity of the sulfonamides.

BE SURE TO TELL YOUR DOCTOR about any medications you are currently taking, especially any of those listed above.

WARNINGS

• Before starting to take this medication, tell your doctor about any unusual or allergic reactions you have had to any medications, especially to sulfonamide antibiotics or other sulfa drugs, including diuretics (water pills), dapsone, sulfoxone, oral antidiabetics, and oral antiglaucoma medication.

• Tell your doctor if you now have or if you have ever had glucose–6-phosphate dehydrogenase (G6PD) deficiency, liver disease, porphyria, or kidney disease.

• Before having surgery or any other medical or dental treatment, be sure to tell your doctor or dentist that you are taking a sulfonamide antibiotic.

• This medication has been prescribed for your current infection only. Another infection later on or one that someone else has may require a different medicine. You should not give your medicine to other people, and you should not use it for other infections, unless your doctor specifically directs you to do so.

• Be sure to tell your doctor if you are pregnant. These medications, if given to a woman late in pregnancy, can be toxic to the fetus. Also tell your doctor if you are breast-feeding an infant. Sulfonamides can pass into breast milk and may cause side effects in nursing infants who have G6PD deficiency. In addition, you should not give sulfonamides to an infant less than one month of age, unless your doctor specifically directs you to do so.

---

sulindac

BRAND NAME (Manufacturer)
Clinoril (Merck Sharp & Dohme)
sulindac (various manufacturers)
TYPE OF DRUG
Nonsteroidal anti-inflammatory analgesic
INGREDIENT
sulindac
DOSAGE FORM
Tablets (150 mg and 200 mg)
STORAGE
This medication should be stored in a closed container at room temperature away from heat and direct sunlight.

USES
Sulindac is used to treat the inflammation (pain, swelling, and stiffness) of certain types of arthritis, gout, bursitis, and tendinitis. Sulindac has been shown to block the production of certain body chemicals, called prostaglandins, that may trigger pain.

TREATMENT
To decrease stomach irritation, your doctor may want you to take this medication with food or antacids.

It is important to take sulindac on schedule and not to miss any doses. If you do miss a dose, take it as soon as possible, unless it is almost time for your next dose. In that case, do not take the missed dose at all; just return to your regular dosing schedule. Do not double the next dose.

If you are taking sulindac to relieve arthritis, you must take it regularly, as directed by your doctor. It may take up to three weeks for you to feel the full benefits of this medication. Sulindac does not cure arthritis, but it will help to control the condition as long as you continue to take it.

SIDE EFFECTS

Minor. Bloating, constipation, diarrhea, difficulty in sleeping, dizziness, drowsiness, headache, heartburn, indigestion, light-headedness, loss of appetite, nausea, nervousness, soreness of the mouth, unusual sweating, or vomiting. As you adjust to the medication, these side effects should stop.

To relieve constipation, increase the amount of fiber in your diet (fresh fruits and vegetables, salads, bran, and whole-grain breads), exercise, and drink more water (unless your doctor directs you to do otherwise).

If you become dizzy or light-headed while taking this drug, sit or lie down for a while; get up slowly from a sitting or reclining position; and be careful on stairs. Be especially careful when driving an automobile or operating potentially dangerous equipment.

Major. Tell your doctor about any side effects that are persistent or particularly bothersome. IT IS ESPECIALLY IMPORTANT TO TELL YOUR DOCTOR about bloody or black, tarry stools; blurred vision; chills; confusion; depression; difficulty in breathing; difficulty in hearing; difficult or painful urination; palpitations; ringing or buzzing in the ears; skin rash, hives, or itching; stomach pain; swelling; tightness in the chest; unexplained sore throat and fever; unusual bleeding or bruising; unusual fatigue or weakness; unusual weight gain; vaginal bleeding; wheezing; or yellowing of the eyes or skin.

INTERACTIONS

Sulindac interacts with several types of medications:

1. The combination of anticoagulants (blood thinners, such as warfarin) and sulindac can lead to an increase in bleeding complications.

2. Aspirin, salicylates, or other anti-inflammatory medications can cause an increase in stomach irritation.

3. Probenecid can increase the amount of sulindac in the bloodstream when the drugs are taken concurrently.

4. The blood-pressure-lowering effects of beta blockers may be decreased by this drug.

5. This medication may interact with diuretics (water pills) and cause an increase in the effects of the diuretic.

BE SURE TO TELL YOUR DOCTOR about any medications you are currently taking, especially any of those listed above.

WARNINGS

• Be sure to tell your doctor if you have ever had unusual or allergic reactions to sulindac or any of the other chemically related medications (including aspirin and other salicylates, diclofenac, diflunisal, etodoloc, fenoprofen, flurbiprofen, ibuprofen, indomethacin, ketoprofen, meclofenamate, mefenamic acid, nabumetone, naproxen, oxyphenbutazone, phenylbutazone, piroxicam, and tolmetin).

• Be sure to tell your doctor if you have ever had asthma, bleeding problems, colitis, stomach ulcers or other stomach problems, epilepsy, heart disease, high blood pressure, kidney disease, liver disease, mental illness, or Parkinson's disease.

• If sulindac tends to make you dizzy or drowsy, do not take part in any activity that requires mental alertness, such as driving an automobile or operating potentially dangerous machinery or equipment.

• Be sure to tell your doctor or dentist that you are taking this medication before having surgery or any other type of medical or dental treatment.

• Stomach problems are more likely to occur if you take aspirin or other salicylates regularly or drink alcoholic beverages while being treated with this medication. These should be avoided (unless your doctor directs you to do otherwise).

• Be sure to tell your doctor if you are pregnant. The safe use of this medication in human pregnancy has not been established. Side effects have been observed in the development of bones and organs in the offspring of animals that received sulindac during pregnancy. If taken late in pregnancy, this type of drug can prolong labor. Also tell your doctor if you are currently breast-feeding an infant. Small amounts of sulindac have been shown to pass into breast milk.

---

sumatriptin

BRAND NAME (Manufacturer)
Imitrex (Cerenex)
TYPE OF DRUG
Antimigraine agent
INGREDIENT
sumatriptin

DOSAGE FORM
Tablets (25 mg and 50 mg)
STORAGE
Store sumatriptin tablets at room temperature in a tightly closed container and protect from light and freezing.

USES
Although it is not completely known how sumatriptin works, this medicine helps to stop migraine headaches by altering the level of a chemical in the brain called serotonin. Sumatriptin is used for the treatment of migraine headaches for those patients who do not get relief from other anti-headache medicines, such as acetaminophen, aspirin, and nonsteroidal anti-inflammatory agents (NSAIDs). This drug will not be effective for preventing migraine headaches or for the treatment of cluster headaches.

TREATMENT
Sumatriptin may be taken with or without food. The tablet form must be swallowed whole (without crushing or chewing). This medication may work more effectively if you lie down in a quiet, darkened room after taking it.

If your migraine headache is less severe after your first sumatriptin tablet, your doctor may instruct you to take a second tablet two hours after the first tablet if the headache pain starts to come back. It is very important that you obtain specific instructions on the use of this medicine from your doctor. Never double the dose.

SIDE EFFECTS
Minor. Bad taste in your mouth; dizziness; ear, nose, or throat discomfort; flushing; muscle pain; nausea; skin rash; stiff neck; tingling; or weakness.
Major. Tell your doctor about any side effects that are persistent or particularly bothersome. IT IS ESPECIALLY IMPORTANT TO TELL YOUR DOCTOR about chest pain, irregular heartbeats, and tightness or heaviness in the chest.

INTERACTIONS
Sumatriptin can interact with a class of drugs called monoamine oxidase (MAO) inhibitors to produce dangerous

side effects. It very important that sumatriptin and MAO inhibitors not be taken together. If you were taking an MAO inhibitor, you must not take any doses of sumatriptin for at least two weeks in order to avoid this potentially dangerous drug interaction.

Sumatriptin may increase the side effects caused by ergot-containing or ergot-type drugs (such as methysergide and dihydroergotamine). Therefore, it is very important that the use of these ergot drugs and sumatriptin should be separated by at least 24 hours.

Before starting to take sumatriptin, BE SURE TO TELL YOUR DOCTOR about any medications you are currently taking, especially any of those listed above.

WARNINGS

• Tell your doctor about any unusual allergic reactions you have had to any medications, especially to sumatriptin.
• Tell your doctor if you have ever had a stroke, hardening of the arteries, high blood pressure, high blood cholesterol, or diabetes.
• Notify your doctor if you are a smoker or if you have a family history of heart disease.
• Be sure to tell your doctor if you are pregnant. The effects of this medication have not been thoroughly studied in humans.
• Inform your doctor if you are breast-feeding an infant. Small amounts of sumatriptin are distributed into breast milk.

---

tacrine

BRAND NAME (Manufacturer)
Cognex (Parke-Davis)
TYPE OF DRUG
Centrally acting cholinesterase inhibitor (Alzheimer's drug)
INGREDIENT
tacrine (THA)
DOSAGE FORM
Capsules (10 mg, 20 mg, 30 mg, and 40 mg)
STORAGE
This medication should be stored in a tightly closed container at room temperature, away from heat and direct sunlight.

USES

Tacrine is used to treat the symptoms of mild to moderate dementia associated with Alzheimer's disease. It is not clearly understood how this medication works therapeutically, but it is thought to act by balancing certain chemicals in the brain.

TREATMENT

This medication should be taken exactly as prescribed by your doctor. The effect of this treatment is thought to depend on its administration at regular intervals. Tacrine should be taken between meals whenever possible; however, this medication can be taken with meals to avoid stomach upset.

If you miss a dose of tacrine, take the missed dose as soon as possible, unless it is within three hours of your next dose. In that case, do not take the missed dose at all; just return to your regular dosing schedule. Do not double the next dose.

SIDE EFFECTS

Minor. Loose stools, diarrhea, nausea, or vomiting may occur during initiation of therapy or during an increase of the dose. Other effects include changes in blood pressure, chills, fever, headache, increased sweating, loss of appetite, muscle weakness, nervousness, and swelling of the hands or feet.

Major. Tell your doctor about any side effects that are persistent or particularly bothersome. IT IS ESPECIALLY IMPORTANT TO TELL YOUR DOCTOR about changes in the color of stool (black, very dark, or light), skin rash, unusual bleeding or bruising, or yellowing of the eyes or skin.

INTERACTIONS

Tacrine will interact with several other types of drugs:

1. This medication can increase the effects of theophylline or bethanechol.

2. Tacrine can decrease the effects of anticholinergics (such as benztropine).

3. Cimetidine can increase the effects of tacrine.

BE SURE TO TELL YOUR DOCTOR about any medications you are currently taking, especially those listed above.

WARNINGS

• Tell your doctor about any unusual or allergic reactions you have had to any medication, especially to tacrine.

• Tell your doctor if you now have or ever have had liver disease, epilepsy, asthma, sick sinus syndrome, or ulcers.
• Be sure to tell your doctor if you are pregnant or breast-feeding an infant. It is not known if tacrine is safe to use during pregnancy or while breast-feeding.

tamoxifen

BRAND NAME (Manufacturer)
Nolvadex (Zeneca)
TYPE OF DRUG
Antiestrogen and antineoplastic (anticancer drug)
INGREDIENT
tamoxifen
DOSAGE FORM
Tablets (10 mg)
STORAGE
Tamoxifen should be stored at room temperature in a tightly closed, light-resistant container.

USES
This medication is used in the treatment of advanced breast cancer. Tamoxifen is a nonsteroidal antiestrogen drug. It is not yet fully understood how tamoxifen works, but it is possible that the drug acts to block estrogen from binding to the breast tissue. This action would work to inhibit further tumor growth.

TREATMENT
Tamoxifen can be taken either on an empty stomach or with food or a glass of milk, unless your doctor directs you to do otherwise.
   If you miss a dose of this medication, take the missed dose as soon as possible, unless it is almost time for the next dose. In that case, do not take the missed dose at all; just return to your regular dosing schedule. Do not double the next dose.

SIDE EFFECTS
Minor. Distaste for food, dizziness, headache, hot flashes, light-headedness, nausea, vaginal itching, or vomiting. These side effects should disappear as your body adjusts to the medication.

It is extremely important that you continue to take this medication in spite of any nausea or vomiting that you may experience. If you do vomit immediately after taking a dose of tamoxifen, call your physician; it may be necessary for you to repeat the dose.

It is possible that you may experience an increase in bone and tumor pain when your treatment with tamoxifen is first started. The pain generally subsides rapidly but may require the temporary use of analgesics (pain relievers). Be sure to consult your doctor if you experience any unusual pain after starting therapy with tamoxifen.

If you feel dizzy or light-headed, sit or lie down for a while; get up slowly from a sitting or reclining position; and be careful on stairs.

Major. Tell your doctor about any side effects that are persistent or particularly bothersome. IT IS ESPECIALLY IMPORTANT TO TELL YOUR DOCTOR about blurred vision, chills, depression, fever, rapid weight gain (three to five pounds within a week), rash, sore throat, unusual weakness, or vaginal bleeding or discharge.

INTERACTIONS

The activity and anticoagulant (blood-thinning) effects of drugs such as warfarin can be increased when they are taken at the same time as tamoxifen. Be sure to tell your doctor if you are taking an anticoagulant.

WARNINGS

• Be sure to tell your doctor about any unusual or allergic reactions you have had to any medications, especially to tamoxifen.

• Before starting to take this medication, be sure to tell your doctor if you now have or if you have ever had blood disorders or visual disturbances.

• Before starting to take this medication, it is very important for you to tell your doctor if you are pregnant. Although there have been no studies done on the effects of this medication in pregnant women, isolated reports of problems have been documented when pregnant women have been using tamoxifen. Also be sure to notify your physician if you are breast-feeding.

temazepam

BRAND NAMES (Manufacturers)
Restoril (Sandoz)
temazepam (various manufacturers)
TYPE OF DRUG
Benzodiazepine sedative/hypnotic
INGREDIENT
temazepam
DOSAGE FORM
Capsules (7.5 mg, 15 mg, and 30 mg)
STORAGE
This medication should be stored at room temperature in a
tightly closed, light-resistant container. Temazepam should
not be refrigerated.

USES
Temazepam is prescribed to treat insomnia, including problems
with falling asleep, waking during the night, and early morning wakefulness. It is not clear exactly how this medicine
works, but it may relieve insomnia by acting as a depressant of
the central nervous system (brain and spinal cord).

TREATMENT
This medicine should be taken 30 to 60 minutes before bedtime. It can be taken with food or a full glass of water if stomach upset occurs. Do not take this medication with antacids,
since they may retard its absorption from the gastrointestinal
tract.
  If you are taking this medication regularly and you miss a
dose, take the missed dose immediately if you remember
within an hour. If more than an hour has passed, do not take
the missed dose at all; just wait for the next scheduled dose.
Do not double the dose.

SIDE EFFECTS
Minor. Bitter taste in the mouth, constipation, diarrhea, dizziness, drowsiness (after a night's sleep), dry mouth, excessive
salivation, fatigue, flushing, headache, heartburn, loss of appetite, nausea, nervousness, sweating, or vomiting. As your

body adjusts to the medication, these side effects should disappear.

To relieve constipation, increase the amount of fiber in your diet (fresh fruits and vegetables, salads, bran, and whole-grain breads). You can increase your exercise level and drink more water (unless your doctor directs you to do otherwise).

Dry mouth can be relieved by chewing sugarless gum or by sucking on ice chips.

If you feel dizzy, sit or lie down for a while; get up slowly from a sitting or reclining position; and be careful on stairs.

Major. Tell your doctor about any side effects that are persistent or particularly bothersome. IT IS ESPECIALLY IMPORTANT TO TELL YOUR DOCTOR about blurred or double vision, chest pain, depression, difficulty in urinating, fainting, falling, fever, joint pain, hallucinations, mouth sores, nightmares, palpitations, rash, severe depression, shortness of breath, slurred speech, sore throat, uncoordinated movements, unusual excitement, unusual tiredness, or yellowing of the eyes or skin.

INTERACTIONS

Temazepam interacts with several other types of drugs:

1. To prevent oversedation, this drug should not be taken with alcohol, other sedative drugs, or central nervous system depressants (such as antihistamines, barbiturates, muscle relaxants, pain medications, narcotics, antiseizure medications, and phenothiazine tranquilizers) or with antidepressants.

2. Temazepam may decrease the effectiveness of carbamazepine, levodopa, and oral anticoagulants (blood thinners, such as warfarin) and may increase the effects of phenytoin.

3. Disulfiram, cimetidine, oral contraceptives (birth control pills), and isoniazid may increase the blood levels of temazepam, which can lead to toxic effects.

4. Concurrent use of rifampin may decrease the effectiveness of temazepam.

BE SURE TO TELL YOUR DOCTOR about any medications you are currently taking, especially those listed above.

WARNINGS

• Tell your doctor about unusual or allergic reactions you have had to any medications, especially to temazepam or other benzodiazepine tranquilizers (such as alprazolam, chlordiazepoxide, clorazepate, diazepam, flurazepam, halazepam, lorazepam, oxazepam, prazepam, and triazolam).

• Tell your doctor if you now have or if you have ever had liver disease, kidney disease, epilepsy, lung disease, myasthenia gravis, porphyria, mental depression, or mental illness.

• This medicine is supposed to cause drowsiness. Avoid tasks that require alertness, such as driving a car.

• Temazepam has the potential for abuse and must be used with caution. Tolerance may develop quickly; do not increase the dosage without first consulting your doctor. It is also important not to stop taking this drug suddenly if you have been taking it in large amounts or if you have used it for several weeks. Your doctor may want to reduce the dosage gradually.

• This is a safe drug when used properly. When it is combined with other sedative drugs or alcohol, however, serious side effects may develop.

• Be sure to tell your doctor if you are pregnant. This type of medicine may increase the chance of birth defects if it is taken during the first three months of pregnancy. In addition, use of this medicine during the last six months of pregnancy may result in addiction of the fetus, leading to withdrawal side effects in the newborn. Use of this medicine during the last weeks of pregnancy may cause excessive drowsiness, slowed heartbeat, and breathing difficulties in the infant. Finally, tell your doctor if you are breast-feeding. This medicine can pass into breast milk and cause unwanted side effects in nursing infants.

terazosin

BRAND NAME (Manufacturer)
Hytrin (Abbott)
TYPE OF DRUG
Antihypertensive
INGREDIENT
terazosin
DOSAGE FORM
Tablets (1 mg, 2 mg, 5 mg, and 10 mg)
STORAGE
Terazosin tablets should be stored at room temperature in a tightly closed, light-resistant container.

USES

Terazosin is used to treat high blood pressure. It relaxes the muscle tissue of the blood vessels, which in turn lowers blood pressure.

Terazosin is also used to reduce urinary obstruction and relieve the symptoms associated with symptomatic benign prostatic hyperplasia (BPH). The drug can effectively relieve the hesitancy, terminal dribbling of urine, and sensation of incomplete bladder emptying often associated with BPH.

TREATMENT

The first dose of this medication may cause fainting, especially in the elderly.

If you miss a dose of this medication, take it as soon as possible, unless it is almost time for your next dose. In that case, do not take the missed dose at all; just wait until the next scheduled dose. Do not double the dose.

This medication does not cure high blood pressure, but it will help to control the condition as long as you continue to take it. In order to become accustomed to taking this medication, try to take it at the same time(s) each day.

A minimum of four to six weeks may be needed to see a response from the medication.

SIDE EFFECTS

Minor. Cold symptoms, constipation, diarrhea, dizziness, drowsiness, dry mouth, fluid retention, frequent urination, headache, itching, lack of energy, malaise, nasal congestion, nausea, nervousness, rash, sweating, or weight gain. These side effects should disappear as your body adjusts to the medication.

To prevent constipation, increase the amount of fiber in your diet (fresh fruits and vegetables, salads, bran, and whole-grain breads), unless your doctor tells you otherwise.

To avoid dizziness or light-headedness when you stand, contract and relax the muscles of your legs for a few moments before rising. Do this by pushing one foot against the floor while raising the other foot slightly, alternating feet so that you are "pumping" your legs.

Major. Tell your doctor about any side effects that are persistent or particularly bothersome. IT IS ESPECIALLY IMPOR

TANT TO TELL YOUR DOCTOR about blurred vision, chest pain, difficulty breathing, difficulty urinating, fever, flulike symptoms, heart-rate disturbance, impotence, nose bleeds, palpitations, persistent malaise or fatigue, postural effects (dizziness, light-headedness, vertigo leading to reductions in blood pressure or fainting), ringing in the ears, or swelling.

INTERACTIONS

Terazosin has been known to interact with certain other types of medications:

1. The combination of terazosin and alcohol or verapamil can lead to a severe drop in blood pressure and fainting.

2. The severity and duration of the blood-pressure-lowering effects of the initial dose of terazosin may be enhanced by a beta blocker.

BE SURE TO TELL YOUR DOCTOR about any medications you are currently taking, especially those listed above.

WARNINGS

• Tell your doctor about unusual or allergic reactions you have had to any medications, especially to terazosin, prazosin, or doxazosin.

• Before starting to take this medication, be sure to tell your doctor if you now have or if you have ever had angina (chest pain), kidney disease, or liver disease.

• Because initial therapy with this drug may cause dizziness or fainting, your doctor will probably start you on a low dosage and increase the dosage gradually.

• If this drug makes you dizzy or drowsy or blurs your vision, do not take part in any activity that requires alertness, such as driving a car or operating potentially dangerous tools or machinery.

• In order to avoid dizziness or fainting while taking this drug, try not to stand for long periods of time, avoid drinking excess amounts of alcohol, and try not to get overheated (avoid exercising strenuously in hot weather and taking hot baths, showers, or saunas).

• Before taking any over-the-counter (nonprescription) sinus, allergy, asthma, cough, cold, or diet preparations, check with your doctor or pharmacist. Some of these products can cause an increase in blood pressure.

• Terazosin is only indicated for hypertension and benign prostatic hyperplasia (BPH). This agent is not for symptoms or conditions that appear to be similar to BPH, such as cancer of the prostate.

• Do not stop taking this medication unless you first check with your doctor. If you stop taking this drug, you may experience a rise in blood pressure. Your doctor may want to decrease your dose gradually.

• Be sure to tell your doctor if you are pregnant. Although the drug appears to be safe, there have been only limited studies in pregnant women. Also tell your doctor if you are breastfeeding an infant; terazosin should be used with caution in nursing women.

---

terbutaline

BRAND NAMES (Manufacturers)
Brethaire (Geigy)
Brethine (Geigy)
Bricanyl (Marion Merrell Dow)
TYPE OF DRUG
Bronchodilator
INGREDIENT
terbutaline
DOSAGE FORMS
Tablets (2.5 mg and 5 mg)
Inhalation aerosol (each spray delivers 0.2 mg)
STORAGE
Terbutaline tablets should be stored at room temperature in a tightly closed, light-resistant container. They should not be refrigerated. The inhalation aerosol should be stored at room temperature away from excessive heat; the contents are pressurized and can explode if heated. Discard any outdated medication.

USES
Terbutaline is used to relieve wheezing and shortness of breath caused by lung diseases such as asthma, bronchitis, and emphysema. This drug acts directly on the muscles of the bronchi (breathing tubes) to relieve bronchospasm (muscle contractions of the bronchi), which in turn reduces airway resistance

and allows air to move more freely to and from the lungs—making breathing easier.

TREATMENT

In order to lessen stomach upset, you can take terbutaline with food (unless your doctor directs you to do otherwise).

The inhalation aerosol form of this medication is usually packaged with an instruction sheet. Read the directions carefully before using the medication. The contents should be shaken well just before each use. The contents tend to settle on the bottom, so it is necessary to shake the bottle to distribute the ingredients evenly and equalize the doses. If more than one inhalation is necessary, wait for at least one full minute between doses in order to receive the full benefit from the initial dose.

If you miss a dose of this medication and remember within an hour, take the missed dose immediately and then return to your regular schedule. If more than an hour has passed, do not take the missed dose at all; just return to your regular dosing schedule. Do not double the next dose.

SIDE EFFECTS

Minor. Anxiety, bad taste in the mouth, dizziness, headache, flushing, irritability, insomnia, loss of appetite, nausea, nervousness, restlessness, sweating, vomiting, or weakness. These side effects should disappear as your body adjusts to the medication.

To prevent dryness or irritation of the mouth or throat, rinse your mouth with water after each dose.

In order to avoid difficulty in falling asleep, check with your doctor to see if you can take the last dose of this medication several hours before bedtime each day.

If you feel dizzy or light-headed, sit or lie down for a while; get up from a sitting or lying position slowly; and be careful on stairs.

Major. Tell your doctor about any side effects that are persistent or particularly bothersome. IT IS ESPECIALLY IMPORTANT TO TELL YOUR DOCTOR about bluish coloration of the skin, chest pain, difficult or painful urination, increased wheezing or difficulty in breathing, muscle cramps, palpitations, or tremors.

INTERACTIONS

Terbutaline interacts with other types of medications:

1. The beta blockers (acebutolol, atenolol, betaxolol, carteolol, esmolol, labetalol, metoprolol, nadolol, penbutolol, pindolol, propranolol, or timolol) antagonize (act against) this medication, decreasing its effectiveness.

2. Monoamine oxidase (MAO) inhibitors; tricyclic antidepressants; antihistamines; levothyroxine; and over-the-counter (nonprescription) cough, cold, allergy, asthma, diet, and sinus medications may increase the side effects of terbutaline. At least 14 days should separate the use of this drug and the use of an MAO inhibitor.

3. There may be a change in the dosage requirements of insulin or oral antidiabetic medications when terbutaline is started.

4. The blood-pressure-lowering effects of guanethidine may be decreased by this medication.

5. The use of terbutaline with other bronchodilator drugs (either oral or inhalant drugs) can have additive side effects. Discuss this with your doctor.

BE SURE TO TELL YOUR DOCTOR about any medications you are currently taking, especially those listed above.

WARNINGS

• Tell your doctor about unusual or allergic reactions you have had to any medications, especially to terbutaline or any related drug (albuterol, amphetamines, ephedrine, epinephrine, isoproterenol, norepinephrine, phenylephrine, phenylpropanolamine, pseudoephedrine, or metaproterenol).

• BE SURE TO TELL YOUR DOCTOR if you now have or if you have ever had diabetes, glaucoma, high blood pressure, epilepsy, heart disease, enlarged prostate gland, or thyroid disease.

• This medication can cause dizziness. Your ability to perform tasks that require alertness, such as driving a car may be decreased. Appropriate caution should be taken.

• Before having surgery or any other medical or dental treatment, tell your doctor or dentist you are taking this drug.

• Avoid allowing the aerosol inhalation to come in contact with your eyes.

• Do not puncture, break, or burn the aerosol inhalation container. The contents are under pressure and may explode.

• Do not exceed the recommended dosage of this medication; excessive use may lead to an increase in side effects or a loss of effectiveness. Contact your doctor if you do not respond to the usual dose of this medication. It may be a sign of worsening asthma, and additional therapy may be needed.
• Tell your doctor if you are pregnant. Terbutaline should only be administered during pregnancy if the benefits to the mother clearly outweigh potential risks to the fetus. Also tell your doctor if you are breast-feeding. Small amounts of terbutaline pass into breast milk.

terfenadine

BRAND NAME (Manufacturer)
Seldane (Marion Merrell Dow)
TYPE OF DRUG
Antihistamine
INGREDIENT
terfenadine
DOSAGE FORM
Tablets (60 mg)
STORAGE
Terfenadine should be stored at room temperature in a tightly closed container. The tablets should not be exposed to high temperatures (above 104°F), direct sunlight, or moisture during storage.

USES
Terfenadine is used to treat the symptoms of allergic response, including sneezing, runny nose, itching, and tearing. This medication belongs to a group of drugs known as antihistamines, which act by blocking the action of histamine, a chemical that is released by the body during an allergic reaction.

TREATMENT
Terfenadine can be taken either on an empty stomach or with food or milk (unless your doctor directs otherwise).

Terfenadine should be taken only as needed to control the symptoms of allergy.

If you miss a dose of this medication and you are taking it on a regular schedule, take the missed dose as soon as possible, unless it is almost time for your next dose. In that case, do not take the missed dose at all; just return to your regular dosing schedule. Do not double the next dose.

SIDE EFFECTS

Minor. Abdominal pain; cough; dizziness; drowsiness; dry mouth, nose, or throat; fatigue; headache; increased appetite; insomnia; nausea; nervousness; nosebleeds; sore throat; sweating; vomiting; or weakness. These side effects should disappear as your body adjusts to this medication.

To reduce mouth dryness, chew sugarless gum or suck on ice chips or hard candy.

If you feel dizzy or light-headed, sit or lie down for a while; get up slowly from a sitting or reclining position; and be careful on stairs.

Major. Tell your doctor about any side effects that are persistent or particularly bothersome. IT IS ESPECIALLY IMPORTANT TO TELL YOUR DOCTOR about depression, hair loss, itching, menstrual disorders, muscle or bone pain, nightmares, palpitations, shortness of breath, tingling of your fingers or toes, tremors, urinary frequency, visual disturbances, or yellowing of the skin or eyes.

Hypotension (low blood pressure), palpitations, and dizziness could reflect undetected ventricular arrhythmias. In some patients, cardiac arrest and irregular heartbeat have been preceded by episodes of fainting.

INTERACTIONS

Terfenadine interacts with the following medications:
1. The combination of terfenadine and ketoconazole or itraconazole can result in serious adverse effects.
2. The combination of terfenadine and certain antibiotics, such as erythromycin, clarithromycin, and troleandomycin, can also result in serious adverse effects.

BE SURE TO TELL YOUR DOCTOR about any medications you are currently taking, especially any listed above.

WARNINGS

• Tell your doctor about unusual or allergic reactions you have had to any medications, especially to terfenadine.
• Before starting terfenadine, tell your doctor if you now have or if you have ever had asthma.

• Terfenadine causes less drowsiness than other antihistamines. However, until you see how it affects you, be cautious about performing tasks that require alertness, such as driving a car or operating potentially dangerous machinery.

• Be sure to tell your doctor if you are pregnant. This drug's safety in human pregnancy has not been established. Also tell your doctor if you are breast-feeding. The effects of terfenadine on nursing infants are not yet known.

• Be sure to take only the dose recommended by your doctor. DO NOT EXCEED THE PRESCRIBED DOSE.

• Before starting terfenadine, tell your doctor if you now have or if you have ever had high blood pressure, heart disease, or arrhythmias.

• Before starting terfenadine, tell you doctor if you now have or if you have ever had liver disease.

• Following high doses of terfenadine, serious cardiovascular adverse effects (QT interval prolongation, arrhythmias, cardiac arrest, and death) have been observed.

---

tetracycline

BRAND NAMES (Manufacturers)
Achromycin V (Lederle)
Panmycin (Upjohn)
Robitet Robicaps (Robins)
Sumycin (Bristol-Myers Squibb)
Tetracap (Circle)
tetracycline hydrochloride (various manufacturers)
Tetralan (Lannett)
TYPE OF DRUG
Tetracycline antibiotic
INGREDIENT
tetracycline
DOSAGE FORMS
Tablets (250 mg and 500 mg)
Capsules (100 mg, 250 mg, and 500 mg)
Oral suspension (125 mg per 5-mL spoonful)
STORAGE
Tetracycline tablets, capsules, and oral suspension should be stored at room temperature in tightly closed, light-resistant containers. Any unused portion of the suspension should be

discarded after 14 days because the drug loses its potency after that period. Discard any medication that is outdated or no longer needed. This medication should never be frozen.

USES
Tetracycline is used to treat acne (bacteria may be partly responsible for the development of acne lesions) and a wide variety of bacterial infections. It acts by inhibiting the growth of bacteria. Tetracycline kills susceptible bacteria, but it is not effective against viruses or fungi.

TREATMENT
Ideally, this medication should be taken on an empty stomach one hour before or two hours after a meal. It should be taken with a full glass of water in order to avoid irritating the throat or esophagus (swallowing tube). If this drug causes stomach upset, however, you can take it with food (unless your doctor directs you to do otherwise).

Avoid consuming dairy products (milk, cheese, etc.) within two hours of any dose of this drug. Avoid taking antacids and laxatives that contain aluminum, calcium, or magnesium within an hour or two of a dose. Avoid taking any medication containing iron within three hours of a dose. These products, including vitamins, chemically bind tetracycline in the stomach and gastrointestinal tract, preventing the drug from being absorbed into the body.

The oral-suspension form of this medication should be shaken well just before measuring each dose. The contents tend to settle on the bottom of the bottle, so it is necessary to shake the container to distribute the ingredients evenly and equalize the doses. Each dose should then be measured carefully with a specially designed 5-mL measuring spoon. An ordinary kitchen teaspoon is not accurate enough to ensure that the proper dose will be taken. The oral-suspension form of this medication should not be mixed with any other substance unless your doctor says so.

Tetracycline works best when the level of medicine in your bloodstream is kept constant. It is best, therefore, to take the doses at evenly spaced intervals day and night. For example, if you are to take four doses a day, the doses should be spaced six hours apart.

If you miss a dose of this medication, take the missed dose immediately. However, if you do not remember to take the missed dose until it is almost time for your next dose, take it; space the following dose about halfway through the regular interval between doses; and then return to your regular dosing schedule.

It is important to continue to take this medication for the entire time prescribed by your doctor, even if the symptoms disappear before the end of that period. If you stop taking the drug too soon, resistant bacteria are given a chance to continue growing, and the infection could recur.

SIDE EFFECTS

Minor. Diarrhea, discoloration of the nails, dizziness, loss of appetite, nausea, stomach cramps and upset, or vomiting. These side effects should disappear as your body adjusts to the medication.

Tetracycline can increase your sensitivity to sunlight. You should therefore avoid prolonged exposure to sunlight or sunlamps. Wear protective clothing and sunglasses, and use an effective sunscreen.

Major. Tell your doctor about any side effects that are persistent or particularly bothersome. IT IS ESPECIALLY IMPORTANT TO TELL YOUR DOCTOR about darkened tongue, difficulty in breathing, joint pain, mouth irritation, rash, rectal or vaginal itching, sore throat and fever, unusual bleeding or bruising, or yellowing of the eyes or skin. And if your symptoms of infection seem to be getting worse rather than improving, contact your doctor.

INTERACTIONS

Tetracycline interacts with other types of medications:

1. It can increase the absorption of digoxin, which may lead to digoxin toxicity.

2. The gastrointestinal side effects (nausea, vomiting, or stomach upset) of theophylline may be increased by tetracycline.

3. The dosage of oral anticoagulants (blood thinners, such as warfarin) may need to be adjusted when this medication is started.

4. Tetracycline may decrease the effectiveness of oral contraceptives (birth control pills), and pregnancy could result. You should, therefore, use a different or additional form of birth control while taking tetracycline. Discuss this matter with your doctor.

BE SURE TO TELL YOUR DOCTOR about any medications that you are currently taking, especially any of the medications that are listed above.

WARNINGS

• Tell your doctor about unusual or allergic reactions you have had to any medications, especially to tetracycline or to oxytetracycline, doxycycline, or minocycline.

• Tell your doctor if you now have or if you have ever had kidney or liver disease.

• Tetracycline can affect tests for syphilis; tell your doctor you are taking this drug if you are being treated for syphilis.

• Make sure that your prescription for this drug is marked with the expiration date. The drug should be discarded after the expiration date. If tetracycline is used after it has expired, serious side effects (especially to the kidneys) could result.

• This medication has been prescribed for your current infection only. Another infection later on, or one that someone else has, may require a different medicine. You should not give your medicine to other people or use it for other infections unless your doctor specifically directs you to do so.

• Be sure to tell your doctor if you are pregnant or if you are breast-feeding. Tetracycline crosses the placenta and passes into breast milk. If used during tooth development, this drug can cause permanent tooth discoloration. It can also inhibit tooth and bone growth in the fetus. It should not be used in pregnant or nursing women, or in children less than eight years of age.

---

theophylline

BRAND NAMES (Manufacturers)
Aquaphyllin (Ferndale)
Asmalix (Century)
Bronkodyl (Breon)
Elixomin (Cenci)
Elixophyllin (Berlex)
Lanophyllin (Lannett)

Quibron-T (Mead Johnson)
Slo-bid Gyrocaps (Rorer)
Slo-Phyllin (Rorer)
Somophyllin-T (Fisons)
Sustaire (Pfipharmics)
Theobid (Glaxo)
Theochron (Forest)
Theoclear (Central)
Theo-Dur (Key)
Theolair (Riker)
theophylline (various manufacturers)
Theospan (Laser)
Theo-24 (Searle)
Theovent (Schering)
Uniphyl (Purdue Frederick)
TYPE OF DRUG
Bronchodilator
INGREDIENT
theophylline
DOSAGE FORMS
Tablets (100 mg, 125 mg, 200 mg, 250 mg, and 300 mg)
Capsules (100 mg, 125 mg, 200 mg, 300 mg, and 400 mg)
Sustained-release tablets and capsules (50 mg, 60 mg,
   65 mg, 75 mg, 100 mg, 125 mg, 130 mg, 200 mg,
   250 mg, 260 mg, 300 mg, 400 mg, 450 mg, and 500 mg)
Oral liquid (80 mg per 15-mL spoonful, some with alcohol
   of varying amounts, including 1%, 7.5%, and 20%)
Oral suspension (300 mg per 15-mL spoonful)
STORAGE
Theophylline tablets, capsules, liquid, and suspension should
be stored at room temperature. It should also be kept in tightly
closed, light-resistant containers. This medication should never
be frozen. Discard any outdated medication.

USES
Theophylline is prescribed to treat breathing problems (wheezing and shortness of breath) caused by asthma, bronchitis, or
emphysema. It relaxes the smooth muscle of the bronchial
airways (breathing tubes), which opens the air passages to the
lungs and allows air to move in and out more easily.

TREATMENT

Theophylline should be taken on an empty stomach 30 to 60 minutes before a meal or two hours after a meal. If this medication causes stomach irritation, however, you can take it with food or with a full glass of water or milk (unless your doctor directs you to do otherwise).

Antidiarrheal medications and some antacids prevent the absorption of theophylline from the gastrointestinal tract. Therefore, at least one hour should separate doses of one of these medications and theophylline.

The sustained-release tablets and capsules should be swallowed whole. Chewing, crushing, or crumbling the tablets or capsules destroys their sustained-release activity and possibly increases the side effects. If the tablet is scored for breaking, you can break it along these lines. If the regular capsules are too large to swallow, they can be opened and the contents mixed with jam, jelly, or applesauce. The mixture should then be swallowed without chewing.

The theophylline sprinkle capsules can also be taken whole, or the capsule can be opened and the beads sprinkled on a spoonful of soft food, such as applesauce or pudding. The sprinkles should be swallowed immediately without chewing the beads. The contents of the capsule should not be subdivided in order to ensure equal doses.

If you are using the suspension form of this medication, the bottle should be shaken well just before measuring each dose. The contents tend to settle on the bottom of the bottle, so it is necessary to shake the container to distribute the medication evenly and equalize the doses. Each dose of the oral liquid or suspension should be measured carefully with a 5-mL measuring spoon or a dose cup designed for that purpose. Ordinary kitchen spoons are not accurate enough to ensure that you receive the proper dose.

Theophylline works best when the level of the medicine in your bloodstream is kept constant. It is best, therefore, to take it at evenly spaced intervals day and night. For example, if you are to take four doses a day, the doses should be spaced six hours apart. Try to take your medication at the same time(s) each day.

Try not to miss any doses of this medication. If you do miss a dose, take the missed dose as soon as possible, unless it is almost time for the next dose. In that case, do not take the missed dose at all; just return to your regular dosing schedule. Do not double the next dose.

SIDE EFFECTS

Minor. Diarrhea, dizziness, flushing, headache, heartburn, increased urination, insomnia, irritability, loss of appetite, nausea, nervousness, stomach pain, or vomiting. These side effects should disappear over time as your body adjusts to the medication.

If you feel dizzy or light-headed, sit or lie down for a while; get up slowly from a sitting or reclining position; and be careful on stairs.

Major. Tell your doctor about any side effects that are persistent or particularly bothersome. IT IS ESPECIALLY IMPORTANT TO TELL YOUR DOCTOR about black, tarry stools; confusion; convulsions; difficulty in breathing; fainting; muscle twitches; palpitations; rash; severe abdominal pain; or unusual weakness.

INTERACTIONS

Theophylline interacts with several other types of drugs:

1. It can increase the diuretic effect of furosemide.

2. Concurrent use of reserpine and theophylline can cause a rapid heart rate.

3. Beta blockers (acebutolol, atenolol, betaxolol, carteolol, esmolol, labetalol, metoprolol, nadolol, penbutolol, pindolol, propranolol, or timolol) can decrease the effectiveness of theophylline.

4. Theophylline can increase the side effects of over-the-counter (nonprescription) sinus, cough, cold, asthma, allergy, and diet products; digoxin; and oral anticoagulants (blood thinners, such as warfarin).

5. Theophylline can decrease the effectiveness of phenytoin and lithium.

6. Phenobarbital, carbamazepine, and rifampin can increase the elimination of theophylline from the body, decreasing its effectiveness.

7. Cimetidine, ciprofloxacin, clarithromycin, erythromycin, norfloxacin, troleandomycin, oral contraceptives (birth control pills), allopurinol, and thiabendazole can decrease the elimination of theophylline from the body and increase its side effects.

8. Verapamil can cause an increase in the effects of theophylline.

Before you start to take this medication, BE SURE TO TELL YOUR DOCTOR about any medications you are currently taking, especially any of those listed above.

WARNINGS

• Tell your doctor about unusual or allergic reactions you have had to any medications, especially to theophylline, aminophylline, caffeine, dyphylline, oxtriphylline, or theobromine.

• Tell your doctor if you now have or if you have ever had an enlarged prostate gland, fibrocystic breast disease, heart disease, kidney disease, low or high blood pressure, liver disease, stomach ulcers, or thyroid disease.

• Cigarette or marijuana smoking may affect this drug's action. BE SURE TO TELL YOUR DOCTOR if you smoke. However, do not quit smoking without first informing your doctor.

• High fever, diarrhea, flu, and influenza vaccinations can affect the action of this drug. Therefore, be sure to tell your doctor if you experience any episodes of high fever or prolonged diarrhea while taking this drug. Before having any vaccinations, especially those to prevent the flu, BE SURE TO TELL YOUR DOCTOR that you are taking this medication.

• Avoid drinking large amounts of caffeine-containing beverages (coffee, cocoa, tea, or cola drinks), and avoid eating large amounts of chocolate. These products may increase the side effects of theophylline.

• Do not change your diet without first consulting your doctor. A high-protein, low-carbohydrate diet or char-broiled foods may affect the action of this drug.

• Before having surgery or any other medical or dental treatment, be sure to tell your doctor or dentist that you are taking this medication.

• Before taking any over-the-counter (nonprescription) asthma, allergy, cough, cold, sinus, or diet products, ask your doctor or pharmacist. These products may add to the side effects of theophylline.

• Do not change brands or dosage forms of this medication without your doctor's permission. If your medication refill looks different, check with your doctor.

• The elderly and young children may be more sensitive to the effects of theophylline.

• Your doctor may require you to have periodic blood tests to be sure your medication is working properly.

• Be sure to tell your doctor if you are pregnant. Although theophylline appears to be safe during pregnancy, extensive studies in humans have not been conducted. Also tell your doctor if you are breast-feeding an infant. Small amounts of theophylline pass into breast milk and may cause irritability, fretfulness, or insomnia in nursing infants.

thioridazine

BRAND NAMES (Manufacturers)
Mellaril (Sandoz)
thioridazine hydrochloride (various manufacturers)
TYPE OF DRUG
Phenothiazine tranquilizer
INGREDIENT
thioridazine
DOSAGE FORMS
Tablets (10 mg, 15 mg, 25 mg, 50 mg, 100 mg, 150 mg, and 200 mg)
Oral concentrate (30 mg and 100 mg per mL, with 3% and 4.2% alcohol, respectively)
Oral suspension (25 mg and 100 mg per 5-mL spoonful)
STORAGE
The tablet form of this medication should be stored at room temperature in a tightly closed, light-resistant container. The oral concentrate and oral-suspension forms of this medication should be stored in the refrigerator in tightly closed, light-resistant containers. If the oral concentrate or suspension turns slightly yellowish, the medication is still effective and can be used. However, if it changes color markedly or has particles floating in it, it should not be used; rather, it should be discarded down the sink. This medication should never be frozen.

USES

Thioridazine is prescribed to treat the symptoms of certain types of mental illness, such as emotional symptoms of psychosis, the manic phase of manic-depressive illness, and severe behavioral problems in children. It may also be used for moderate to marked depression or sleep disturbances in adults. This medication is thought to relieve the symptoms of mental illness by blocking certain chemicals involved with nerve transmission in the brain. Thioridazine may also be used to treat anxiety.

TREATMENT

In order to avoid stomach irritation, you can take this medication with a meal or with a glass of water or milk (unless your doctor directs you to do otherwise).

Antacids and antidiarrheal medicines may decrease the absorption of this medication from the gastrointestinal tract. Therefore, at least one hour should separate doses of one of these medicines and thioridazine.

The oral-suspension form of this medication should be shaken well just before measuring each dose. The contents tend to settle on the bottom of the bottle, so it is necessary to shake the container to distribute the ingredients evenly and equalize the doses. Each dose should then be measured carefully with a specially designed 5-mL measuring spoon. An ordinary kitchen teaspoon is not accurate enough.

The oral-concentrate form of this medication should be measured carefully with the dropper provided, then added to four ounces ($\frac{1}{2}$ cup) or more of water, milk, or a carbonated beverage or to applesauce or pudding immediately prior to administration. To prevent possible loss of effectiveness, the medication should not be diluted in tea, coffee, or apple juice.

If you miss a dose of this medication, take the missed dose as soon as possible, unless it is almost time for your next dose. In that case, do not take the missed dose at all; just return to your regular dosing schedule. Do not double the next dose without your doctor's approval.

The full effects of this medication for the control of emotional or mental symptoms may not become apparent for at least two weeks after you start to take it.

SIDE EFFECTS

Minor. Blurred vision, constipation, decreased sweating, diarrhea, dizziness, drowsiness, dry mouth, fatigue, jitteriness, menstrual irregularities, nasal congestion, restlessness, vomiting, and weight gain. As your body adjusts to the medication, these side effects should disappear.

This medication can cause increased sensitivity to sunlight. It is, therefore, important to avoid prolonged exposure to sunlight and sunlamps. Wear protective clothing and sunglasses, and use an effective sunscreen.

Thioridazine can also cause discoloration of the urine to red, pink, or red-brown. This is a harmless effect.

If you are constipated, increase the amount of fiber in your diet (fresh fruits and vegetables, salads, bran, and whole-grain breads), exercise, and drink more water (unless your doctor directs you to do otherwise).

Chew sugarless gum or suck on ice chips or a piece of hard candy to reduce mouth dryness.

To avoid dizziness or light-headedness when you stand, contract and relax the muscles of your legs for a few moments before rising. Do this by pushing one foot against the floor while raising the other foot slightly, alternating feet so that you are "pumping" your legs in a pedaling motion.

Major. Tell your doctor about any side effects that are persistent or particularly bothersome. IT IS ESPECIALLY IMPORTANT TO TELL YOUR DOCTOR about breast enlargement (in both sexes); chest pain; convulsions; darkened skin; difficulty in swallowing or breathing; drooling; fainting; fever; impotence; involuntary movements of the face, mouth, jaw, or tongue; palpitations; rash; sleep disorders; sore throat; tremors; uncoordinated movements; unusual bleeding or bruising; visual disturbances; or yellowing of the eyes or skin.

INTERACTIONS

Thioridazine interacts with several other medications:
1. It can cause extreme drowsiness when combined with alcohol or other central nervous system depressants (drugs that slow the activity of the brain and spinal cord), such as barbiturates, benzodiazepine tranquilizers, muscle relaxants, narcotics, and pain medications, or with tricyclic antidepressants.
2. Thioridazine can decrease the effectiveness of amphetamines, guanethidine, anticonvulsants, and levodopa.
3. The side effects of epinephrine, monoamine oxidase (MAO) inhibitors, metoprolol, propranolol, phenytoin, and tricyclic antidepressants may be increased by this medication. At least

14 days should separate the use of this drug and the use of an MAO inhibitor.

4. Lithium may increase the side effects and decrease the effectiveness of this medication.

5. False-positive pregnancy tests may occur. If you think you may be pregnant, call your doctor.

BE SURE TO TELL YOUR DOCTOR about any medications you are currently taking, especially those listed above.

WARNINGS

• Tell your doctor about unusual or allergic reactions you have had to any medications, especially to thioridazine or any other phenothiazine tranquilizers (such as chlorpromazine, fluphenazine, mesoridazine, perphenazine, prochlorperazine, promazine, trifluoperazine, and triflupromazine) or to the antipsychotic drug loxapine.

• Tell your doctor if you have a history of alcoholism or if you now have or have ever had any blood disease, bone marrow disease, brain disease, breast cancer, blockage in the urinary or digestive tracts, drug-induced depression, epilepsy, high or low blood pressure, diabetes mellitus, glaucoma, heart or circulatory disease, liver disease, lung disease, Parkinson's disease, peptic ulcers, or enlarged prostate gland.

• Tell your doctor about any recent exposure to a pesticide or an insecticide. Thioridazine may increase the side effects from the exposure.

• To prevent oversedation, avoid drinking alcoholic beverages while taking this medication.

• If this medication makes you dizzy or drowsy, do not take part in any activity that requires alertness, such as driving a car or operating potentially dangerous machinery. Be careful on stairs, and avoid getting up suddenly from a lying or sitting position.

• Prior to having surgery or any other medical or dental treatment, be sure to tell your doctor or dentist that you are taking thioridazine.

• Some of the side effects caused by this drug can be prevented by taking an antiparkinsonism drug. Discuss this with your doctor.

• This medication can decrease sweating and heat release from the body. You should, therefore, try not to become overheated (avoid exercising strenuously in hot weather, and do not take hot baths, showers, or saunas).

• Do not stop taking this medication suddenly. If the drug is stopped abruptly, you may experience a number of withdrawal symptoms, such as nausea, vomiting, stomach upset, headache, increased heart rate, insomnia, and tremors, or a worsening of your condition. Your doctor may want to reduce the dosage gradually.

• If you are planning to have a myelogram or any other procedure in which dye will be injected into your spinal cord, tell your doctor that you are taking this medication.

• Avoid getting the oral concentrate or suspension form of this medication on your skin; either may cause redness and irritation.

• While taking this medication, do not take any over-the-counter (nonprescription) drugs for weight control or for cough, cold, allergy, asthma, or sinus problems unless you first check with your doctor. Concurrent use of any of these drugs and thioridazine may cause high blood pressure.

• Your doctor may schedule regular office visits for your first few months of therapy with this medication in order to monitor your progress and possibly adjust your dosage.

• Your doctor may want to schedule you for an eye examination if you take thioridazine for longer than a year. Prolonged use of this drug can cause visual disturbances.

• Be sure to tell your doctor if you are pregnant. Small amounts of this medication cross the placenta. Although there are reports of safe use of this drug during pregnancy, there are also reports of liver disease and tremors in newborn infants whose mothers received this type of medication close to term. Also tell your doctor if you are breast-feeding. Small amounts of this medication pass into breast milk and may cause unwanted effects in nursing infants.

thiothixene

BRAND NAMES (Manufacturers)
Navane (Roerig)
thiothixene (various manufacturers)
TYPE OF DRUG
Antipsychotic

INGREDIENT
thiothixene
DOSAGE FORMS
Capsules (1 mg, 2 mg, 5 mg, 10 mg, and 20 mg)
Oral solution (5 mg per mL)
Oral concentrate (5 mg per mL, with 7% alcohol)
STORAGE
Thiothixene capsules should be stored at room temperature
in a tightly closed, light-resistant container. The oral concentrate should be stored in the refrigerator in a tightly closed,
light-resistant container. This medication should never be
frozen. Discard any medication that is outdated or no longer
needed.

USES
Thiothixene is prescribed to treat the symptoms of certain
types of mental illness, such as emotional symptoms of psychosis.

TREATMENT
To avoid stomach irritation, you can take the capsule form of
thiothixene with a meal or with a glass of water or milk (unless
your doctor specifically directs you to do otherwise).

The oral-concentrate form of this medication should be
measured carefully with the dropper provided and then added
to eight ounces of water, milk, or a carbonated beverage, or to
applesauce or pudding immediately prior to administration.
To prevent possible loss of effectiveness, this medication should
not be diluted in tea, coffee, or apple juice.

Antacids and antidiarrheal medicines decrease the absorption of this medication from the gastrointestinal tract. Therefore,
at least one hour should separate doses of one of these medicines and thiothixene.

If you miss a dose of this medication, take the missed dose
as soon as possible and then return to your regular dosing
schedule. If it is almost time for the next dose, however, skip
the one you missed and return to your regular schedule. Do
not double the dose (unless so directed by your doctor).

The full effects of this medication for the control of emotional or mental symptoms may not become apparent for at
least two weeks after you start to take it.

SIDE EFFECTS

Minor. Blurred vision, constipation, decreased sweating, diarrhea, dizziness, drowsiness, dry mouth, fatigue, jitteriness, menstrual irregularities, nasal congestion, restlessness, vomiting, or weight gain. As your body adjusts to the medication, these side effects should disappear.

This medication can cause increased sensitivity to sunlight. It is therefore important to avoid prolonged exposure to sunlight and sunlamps. Wear protective clothing, and use an effective sunscreen.

Thiothixene can cause discoloration of the urine to red, pink, or red-brown. This is a harmless effect.

If you are constipated, increase the amount of fiber in your diet (fresh fruits and vegetables, salads, bran, and whole-grain breads), exercise, and drink more water (unless your doctor directs you to do otherwise).

To reduce mouth dryness, chew sugarless gum or suck on ice chips or a piece of hard candy.

To avoid dizziness or light-headedness when you stand, contract and relax the muscles of your legs for a few moments before rising. Do this by pushing one foot against the floor while raising the other foot slightly, alternating feet so that you are "pumping" your legs in a pedaling motion.

Major. Tell your doctor about any side effects that are persistent or particularly bothersome. IT IS ESPECIALLY IMPORTANT TO TELL YOUR DOCTOR about breast enlargement (in both sexes); chest pain; convulsions; darkened skin; difficulty in swallowing or breathing; drooling; fainting; fever; impotence; involuntary movements of the face, mouth, jaw, or tongue; palpitations; rash; sleep disorders; sore throat; tremors; uncoordinated movements; unusual bleeding or bruising; visual disturbances; or yellowing of the eyes or skin.

INTERACTIONS

Thiothixene interacts with other types of medications:

1. It can cause extreme drowsiness when combined with alcohol or other central nervous system depressants (drugs that slow the activity of the brain and spinal cord), such as barbiturates, benzodiazepine tranquilizers, muscle relaxants, narcotics, and pain medications, or with tricyclic antidepressants.

2. Thiothixene can decrease the effectiveness of amphetamines, anticonvulsants, guanethidine, and levodopa.

3. The side effects of epinephrine, monoamine oxidase (MAO) inhibitors, and tricyclic antidepressants may be increased by this medication. At least 14 days should separate the use of this drug and the use of an MAO inhibitor.
4. Lithium may increase the side effects and decrease the effectiveness of thiothixene.
5. False-positive pregnancy tests may occur. If you think you may be pregnant, call your doctor.

BE SURE TO TELL YOUR DOCTOR about any medications you are currently taking, especially any of those listed above.

WARNINGS
• Tell your doctor about unusual or allergic reactions you have had to any medications, especially to thiothixene, chlorprothixene, or any phenothiazine tranquilizer.
• Tell your doctor if you have a history of alcoholism or if you now have or have ever had blood disease, bone marrow disease, brain disease, breast cancer, blockage in the urinary or digestive tract, drug-induced depression, epilepsy, high or low blood pressure, diabetes mellitus, glaucoma, heart or circulatory disease, liver disease, lung disease, Parkinson's disease, peptic ulcers, or enlarged prostate gland.
• In order to prevent oversedation, avoid drinking alcoholic beverages while taking this medication.
• If this drug makes you dizzy or drowsy, do not take part in any activity that requires alertness, such as driving a car or operating potentially dangerous machinery.
• Prior to having surgery or any other medical or dental treatment, be sure to tell your doctor or dentist that you are taking this medication.
• Some of the side effects caused by this drug can be prevented by taking an antiparkinsonism drug. Discuss this with your doctor.
• This medication can decrease sweating and heat release from the body. You should, therefore, try not to become overheated (avoid exercising strenuously in hot weather, and do not take hot baths, showers, and saunas).
• Do not stop taking this medication suddenly. If the drug is stopped abruptly you may experience nausea, vomiting, stomach upset, headache, increased heart rate, insomnia, tremors, or worsening of your condition. Your doctor may want to reduce the dosage gradually.

• If you are planning to have a myelogram or any other procedure in which dye is injected into the space surrounding the spinal cord, tell your doctor that you are taking this medication.

• Avoid getting the oral-concentrate form of this medication on your skin; it can cause redness and irritation.

• While taking this medication, do not take any over-the-counter (nonprescription) medications for weight control or for cough, cold, allergy, asthma, or sinus problems unless you first check with your doctor. The combination of these medications may cause high blood pressure.

• Your doctor may schedule regular office visits during your first few months of therapy with this medication in order to monitor your progress.

• Be sure to tell your doctor if you are pregnant. Small amounts of this medication cross the placenta. Although there are reports of safe use of this drug during pregnancy, there are also reports of liver disease and tremors in newborn infants whose mothers received this type of medication close to term. Also tell your doctor if you are breast-feeding. Small amounts of this medication pass into breast milk and may cause unwanted effects in nursing infants.

---

thyroid hormone

BRAND NAMES (Manufacturers)
Armour Thyroid (USV)
S-P-T (Fleming)
Thyrar (USV)
Thyroid Strong (Marion Merrell Dow)
thyroid USP (various manufacturers)
TYPE OF DRUG
Thyroid hormone
INGREDIENT
thyroid hormone
DOSAGE FORMS
Tablets (15 mg, 30 mg, 60 mg, 65 mg, 90 mg, 120 mg, 130 mg, 180 mg, 200 mg, 240 mg, 250 mg, and 300 mg)
Sugar-coated tablets (30 mg, 60 mg, 120 mg, and 180 mg)
Capsules (60 mg, 120 mg, 180 mg, and 300 mg)

STORAGE
Store at room temperature in a tightly closed, light-resistant container. Discard outdated medication.

USES
This medication is prescribed to replace natural thyroid hormones that are absent because of a thyroid gland disorder. This product is obtained from animal thyroid glands.

TREATMENT
Thyroid hormone tablets should be taken on an empty stomach with a full glass of water. If this medication upsets your stomach, however, you can check with your doctor to see if you can take the medication with food or milk.

In order to get used to taking this medication, try to take it at the same time each day. Try not to miss any doses. If you do miss a dose of this medication, take it as soon as you remember, unless it is almost time for the next dose. In that case, do not take the missed dose at all; just return to your regular dosing schedule. Do not double the next dose. If you miss more than one or two doses of this medication, check with your doctor as soon as possible.

SIDE EFFECTS
Minor. Constipation, dry puffy skin, fatigue, headache, listlessness, muscle aches, or weight gain. These side effects should disappear over time as your body adjusts to the medication.

To relieve constipation, increase the amount of fiber in your diet (fresh fruits and vegetables, salads, bran, and whole-grain breads), exercise, and drink more water (unless your doctor directs you to do otherwise).

Major. Tell your doctor about any side effects that are persistent or particularly bothersome. Most of the major side effects associated with this drug are the result of too large a dose. The dosage of this medication may need to be adjusted if you experience any of the following side effects: chest pain, diarrhea, fever, heat intolerance, insomnia, irritability, leg cramps, menstrual irregularities, nervousness, palpitations, shortness of breath, sweating, trembling, or weight loss. If you experience any of these effects, CHECK WITH YOUR DOCTOR.

INTERACTIONS

Thyroid hormone interacts with other types of medications:

1. Dosing requirements for digoxin, insulin, or oral antidiabetic agents may change when this medication is used.

2. The effects of oral anticoagulants (blood thinners, such as warfarin) may be increased by thyroid hormone, which could lead to bleeding complications.

3. Cholestyramine and colestipol chemically bind thyroid hormone in the gastrointestinal tract, preventing its absorption. Therefore, at least four hours should separate doses of thyroid hormone and one of these drugs.

4. Oral contraceptives (birth control pills) and drugs that contain estrogen may change your dosing requirements for thyroid hormone.

5. Phenobarbital may decrease the effectiveness of thyroid hormone.

6. Phenytoin, tricyclic antidepressants, and over-the-counter (nonprescription) allergy, asthma, cough, cold, sinus, or diet medications may increase the side effects of thyroid hormone.

BE SURE TO TELL YOUR DOCTOR about any medications you are currently taking, especially any listed above.

WARNINGS

• Tell your doctor about unusual or allergic reactions you have had to any medications, especially to thyroid hormone, or to beef or pork products.

• Tell your doctor if you now have or if you have ever had angina pectoris, diabetes mellitus, heart disease, high blood pressure, kidney disease, or an underactive adrenal or pituitary gland.

• If you have an underactive thyroid gland, you may need to take this medication for life. You should not stop taking it unless you first check with your doctor.

• Patients with certain heart diseases may experience chest pain or shortness of breath while on this medication. Check with your doctor if you experience such effects. Do not overdo physical work or exercise.

• Before having surgery or any other medical or dental treatment, be sure to tell your doctor or dentist that you are taking thyroid hormone.

• Over-the-counter (nonprescription) allergy, asthma, cough, cold, sinus, and diet medications can increase the side effects

of thyroid hormone. Therefore, be sure to check with your doctor or pharmacist before taking any of these preparations.
• Although many thyroid products are on the market, they are not all bioequivalent—that is, they may not all be absorbed into the bloodstream at the same rate or have the same overall activity. Do not change brands of this drug without first consulting your doctor or pharmacist to make sure that you are receiving an equivalent product.
• Be sure to tell your doctor if you are pregnant. Thyroid hormone does not readily cross the placenta, and the drug appears to be safe during pregnancy. However, your dosing requirements of thyroid hormone may change during pregnancy. Also tell your doctor if you are breast-feeding. Small amounts of thyroid hormone pass into breast milk.

timolol (ophthalmic)

BRAND NAME (Manufacturer)
Timoptic (Merck & Co.)
Timoptic XE (Merck & Co.)
TYPE OF DRUG
Antiglaucoma ophthalmic solution
INGREDIENT
Timolol
DOSAGE FORM
Ophthalmic drops (0.25% and 0.5%)
Opthalmic gel (0.25% and 0.5%)
STORAGE
Timolol ophthalmic drops and gel should be stored at room temperature in a tightly closed container. This medication should never be frozen. If timolol (ophthalmic) discolors or turns brown, it should be discarded—a color change indicates a loss of potency.

USES
Timolol (ophthalmic) is used to reduce pressure in the eye caused by glaucoma or other eye conditions. This medication belongs to a group of drugs known as beta blockers. When applied to the eye, timolol reduces pressure within the eye by decreasing eye-fluid (aqueous humor) production and perhaps by increasing the outflow of fluid from the eye.

TREATMENT

Be sure to wash your hands with soap and water before applying this medication. In order to avoid contamination of the eye drops, be careful not to touch the tube portion of the dropper or let it touch your eye, and do not wipe off or rinse the dropper after you use it. The gel solution should be shaken once before using.

To apply the ophthalmic drops, tilt your head back and pull down your lower eyelid with one hand to make a pouch below the eye. Drop the prescribed amount of medicine into this pouch and slowly close your eyes. Try not to blink. Keep your eyes closed, and place one finger at the corner of the eye next to your nose for a minute or two, applying a slight pressure (this is done to prevent loss of medication through the duct that drains fluid from the surface of the eye into the nose and throat). Then wipe away any excess medication with a clean tissue. Since applying the medication is somewhat difficult to do, you may want to have someone else apply the ophthalmic drops for you.

If you miss a dose of this medication, apply the missed dose as soon as possible, unless it is almost time for your next dose. In that case, do not apply the missed dose at all; just return to your regular dosing schedule. If the medication is used only once a day, and you do not remember missing a dose until the following day, skip the missed dose. Do not double the next dose.

SIDE EFFECTS

Minor. When you apply this medication for the first time, you may have a stinging sensation in your eyes. This should stop in a few minutes.

Major. Be sure to tell your doctor about any side effects that are persistent or particularly bothersome. IT IS ESPECIALLY IMPORTANT TO TELL YOUR DOCTOR about itching, skin rash, hives, or irritation of the eye that lasts more than a few minutes after application. Major side effects are rare when this product is administered correctly. However, rare occurrences of anxiety, confusion, depression, dizziness, drowsiness, generalized rash, indigestion, loss of appetite, nausea, weakness, and a slight reduction of the resting heart rate have been observed in some users of this medication. If you have any of these symptoms, it is important that you contact your doctor as soon as possible.

INTERACTIONS

Timolol (ophthalmic) may increase the side effects of reserpine and oral beta blockers.

Before starting to take timolol (ophthalmic), BE SURE TO TELL YOUR DOCTOR about any medications you are currently taking.

WARNINGS

• Tell your doctor about unusual or allergic reactions you have had to any medications, especially to timolol or to any other beta blockers (acebutolol, atenolol, betaxolol, carteolol, esmolol, labetalol, metoprolol, nadolol, penbutolol, pindolol, or propranolol).
• Tell your doctor if you now have or if you have ever had asthma, diabetes mellitus, heart disease, or myasthenia gravis.
• Your doctor should check your eye pressure regularly to be sure the glaucoma is under control.
• Tell your doctor if you are pregnant. Small amounts of timolol may be absorbed into the bloodstream, and its safety in pregnancy has not been established. Birth defects have been observed in the fetuses of animals that were given large doses of this drug during pregnancy. Also tell your doctor if you are breast-feeding. If this drug reaches the bloodstream and passes into the breast milk, it can cause a slowed heart rate in the nursing infant.

---

timolol maleate (systemic)

BRAND NAMES (Manufacturers)
Blocadren (Merck & Co.)
timolol maleate (various manufacturers)
TYPE OF DRUG
Beta-adrenergic blocking agent
INGREDIENT
timolol
DOSAGE FORM
Tablets (5 mg, 10 mg, and 20 mg)

STORAGE
Timolol should be stored at room temperature in a tightly closed, light-resistant container.

USES
Timolol is used to treat high blood pressure and to prevent additional heart attacks in heart attack patients. This drug belongs to a group of medicines known as beta-adrenergic blocking agents or, more commonly, beta blockers. These drugs work by controlling nerve impulses along certain nerve pathways.

TREATMENT
Timolol tablets can be taken with a glass of water, with meals, immediately following meals, or on an empty stomach, depending on your doctor's instructions. You should try to take your dose(s) of the medication at the same time(s) each day.

Try not to miss any doses of this medication. If you do miss a dose, take the missed dose as soon as possible. However, if the next scheduled dose is within eight hours (if you are taking this medicine only once a day) or within four hours (if you are taking this medicine more than once a day), do not take the missed dose at all; just return to your regular dosing schedule. Do not double the next dose.

It is important to remember that timolol maleate does not cure high blood pressure, but it will help to control the condition as long as you continue to take it.

SIDE EFFECTS
Minor. Anxiety; constipation; decreased sexual ability; diarrhea; difficulty in sleeping; drowsiness; dryness of the eyes, mouth, and skin; headache; nausea; nervousness; stomach discomfort; tiredness; or weakness. These side effects should disappear during treatment as your body adjusts itself to the medicine.

If you are extra-sensitive to the cold, be sure to dress warmly during cold weather.

To relieve constipation, increase the fiber in your diet (fresh fruits and vegetables, salads, bran, and whole-grain breads) unless your doctor directs otherwise.

Plain, nonmedicated eye drops (artificial tears) may help to relieve eye dryness.

Sucking on ice chips or chewing sugarless gum helps to relieve mouth and throat dryness.

Major. Tell your doctor about any side effects that are persistent or particularly bothersome. IT IS ESPECIALLY IMPORTANT TO TELL YOUR DOCTOR about cold hands or feet (due to decreased blood circulation to skin, fingers, and toes), confusion, depression, dizziness, fever and sore throat, hair loss, hallucinations, light-headedness, nightmares, numbness or tingling of the fingers or toes, rapid weight gain (three to five pounds within a week), reduced level of alertness, skin rash, swelling, unusual bleeding or bruising, or wheezing or difficulty in breathing.

INTERACTIONS

Timolol may interact with several other types of drugs:

1. Indomethacin has been shown to decrease the effect of the beta blockers to lower blood pressure. This may also happen with aspirin or other salicylates.

2. Concurrent use of beta blockers and calcium channel blockers (diltiazem, nifedipine, or verapamil) or disopyramide can lead to heart failure or very low blood pressure.

3. Cimetidine and oral contraceptives (birth control pills) can increase the blood concentrations of timolol, which can result in greater side effects.

4. Side effects may also be increased when beta blockers are taken with clonidine, digoxin, epinephrine, phenylephrine, phenylpropanolamine, phenothiazine tranquilizers, prazosin, reserpine, or monoamine oxidase (MAO) inhibitors. At least 14 days should separate the use of a beta blocker and the use of an MAO inhibitor.

5. Alcohol, barbiturates, and rifampin can decrease the blood concentrations of beta blockers, which can result in a decrease in effectiveness.

6. Beta blockers may antagonize (work against) the effects of theophylline, aminophylline, albuterol, isoproterenol, metaproterenol, salmeterol, and terbutaline.

7. Beta blockers can also interact with insulin or oral antidiabetic agents, raising or lowering blood-sugar levels or masking the symptoms of low blood sugar.

8. The action of beta blockers may be increased if they are used with chlorpromazine, furosemide, or hydralazine.

BE SURE TO TELL YOUR DOCTOR about any medications you are currently taking, especially any of those listed above.

WARNINGS

• Before starting to take this medication, it is important to tell your doctor if you have ever had unusual or allergic reactions to timolol or to any beta blocker (acebutolol, atenolol, betaxolol, carteolol, esmolol, labetalol, metoprolol, nadolol, penbutolol, pindolol, or propranolol).

• Tell your doctor if you now have or if you have ever had allergies, asthma, hay fever, eczema, slow heartbeat, bronchitis, diabetes mellitus, emphysema, heart or blood-vessel disease, kidney disease, liver disease, thyroid disease, or poor circulation in the fingers or toes.

• You may want to check your pulse while taking this medication. If your pulse is much slower than your usual rate (or if it is less than 50 beats per minute), check with your doctor. A pulse rate that is too slow may cause circulation problems.

• This medicine may affect your body's response to exercise. Be sure you discuss with your doctor how much exercise is safe for you, taking into account your medical condition.

• It is important that you do not stop taking this medicine unless you first check with your doctor. Some conditions may become worse when the medicine is stopped suddenly, and the danger of a heart attack is increased in some patients. Your doctor may want you to gradually reduce the amount of medicine you take before stopping completely. Make sure that you have enough medicine on hand to last through weekends, vacations, and holidays.

• Before having surgery or any other medical or dental treatment, tell your doctor or dentist that you are taking this medication. Often, this medication will be discontinued 48 hours prior to major surgery.

• This medication can cause dizziness, drowsiness, light-headedness, or decreased alertness. Exercise caution while driving a car or using any potentially dangerous machinery.

• While taking this medicine, do not use any over-the-counter (nonprescription) allergy, asthma, cough, cold, sinus, or diet preparations unless you first check with your pharmacist or doctor. Some of these medications can bring about high blood pressure when combined with timolol.

• Be sure to tell your doctor if you are pregnant. Animal studies have shown that some beta blockers can cause problems during pregnancy when used at very high doses. There has been some association between use of beta blockers during pregnancy and low birth weight, as well as breathing problems and slow heart rate in newborn infants. However, other reports have shown no effects on newborn infants. Also tell your doctor if you are breast-feeding. Small amounts of timolol may pass into breast milk.

---

tobramycin (ophthalmic)

BRAND NAME (Manufacturer)
Tobrex (Alcon)
TYPE OF DRUG
Ophthalmic antibiotic
INGREDIENT
tobramycin
DOSAGE FORMS
Ophthalmic drops (0.3% tobramycin)
Ophthalmic ointment (0.3% tobramycin)
STORAGE
The ophthalmic solution and ointment should be stored at room temperature in tightly closed containers. Discard any medication that is outdated or no longer needed.

USES
Tobramycin ophthalmic is used for the short-term treatment of bacterial infections of the eyes. Tobramycin is an aminoglycoside antibiotic, which acts to prevent the growth and multiplication of infecting bacteria.

TREATMENT
Wash your hands with soap and water before using this medication. In order to prevent contamination of the medicine, be careful not to touch the tube portion of the dropper and do not let it touch the eye.

Note that the bottle of the eye drops is not completely full—this is to allow control of the number of drops used.

To apply the drops, tilt your head back and pull down the lower eyelid with one hand to make a pouch below the eye. Drop the prescribed amount of medicine into the pouch and slowly close your eyes. Try not to blink. Keep your eyes closed, and place one finger at the corner of the eye next to your nose for a minute or two, applying a slight pressure (this is done to prevent loss of medication through the duct that drains fluid from the surface of the eye into the nose and throat). Then wipe away any excess with a clean tissue. If you think that the medicine did not get into your eye, repeat the process once. If you are using more than one type of eye drop, wait at least five minutes between doses of the two types of medication.

Follow the same general procedure for applying the ointment. Tilt your head back, pull down the lower eyelid, and squeeze the prescribed amount of ointment in a line along the pouch below the eye. Close your eyes, and place your finger at the corner of the eye, near the nose, for a minute or two. Do not rub your eyes. Wipe off excess ointment and the tip of the tube with clean tissues.

Since applying the medication is somewhat difficult to do, you may want someone else to administer the drops or ointment for you.

If you miss a dose of this drug, insert the drops or apply the ointment as soon as possible, unless it is almost time for the next application. In that case, do not use the missed dose at all; just return to your regular dosing schedule.

It is important to continue to take this medication for the entire time prescribed by your doctor, even if the symptoms of infection disappear before the end of that period. If you stop applying the medication too soon, resistant bacteria are given a chance to continue growing, and the infection could occur again.

SIDE EFFECTS

Minor. Blurred vision, burning, or stinging. These side effects should disappear as your body gets accustomed to the drug. **Major.** Tell your doctor about any side effects that are persistent or particularly bothersome. IT IS ESPECIALLY IMPORTANT TO TELL YOUR DOCTOR about disturbed or reduced vision; eye pain, itching, or swelling; severe irritation; or rash.

INTERACTIONS

This medication should not interact with other medication as long as it is used according to directions.

WARNINGS

• Tell your doctor about any reactions you have had to drugs, especially to tobramycin or to any other aminoglycoside antibiotic (amikacin, gentamicin, kanamycin, neomycin, netilmicin, paromomycin, or streptomycin).

• Before starting tobramycin (ophthalmic), tell your doctor if you now have or if you have ever had fungal or viral infections of the eye, kidney disease, or myasthenia gravis.

• If there is no change in your condition two or three days after starting to take this drug, contact your doctor. The drug may not be effective for your infection.

• This medication has been prescribed for your current infection only. A subsequent infection or one that someone else has may require a different medicine. You should not give your medicine to other people or use it to treat other infections unless your doctor specifically directs you to do so.

• In order to allow your eye infection to clear, do not apply makeup to the affected eye.

• Be sure to tell your doctor if you are pregnant. Extensive studies in pregnant women have not been conducted. Also tell your doctor if you are breast-feeding an infant. Small amounts of tobramycin may pass into the breast milk.

tolazamide

BRAND NAMES (Manufacturers)
tolazamide (various manufacturers)
Tolinase (Upjohn)
TYPE OF DRUG
Oral antidiabetic
INGREDIENT
tolazamide
DOSAGE FORM
Tablets (100 mg, 250 mg, and 500 mg)
STORAGE
This medication should be stored at room temperature in a tightly closed container. Discard any outdated medication.

USES

Tolazamide is used for the treatment of diabetes mellitus (sugar diabetes) that appears in adulthood and cannot be managed by control of diet alone. This type of diabetes is referred to as non–insulin-dependent diabetes (also called maturity-onset or type II diabetes). Tolazamide lowers the blood-sugar level by increasing the release of insulin.

TREATMENT

In order for this medication to work correctly, it must be taken as directed by your doctor. It is best to take this medicine at the same time each day in order to maintain a constant blood-sugar level. It is therefore important to try not to miss any doses of tolazamide. If you do miss a dose, take it as soon as possible, unless it is almost time for the next dose. In that case, do not take the missed dose at all; just return to your regular dosing schedule. Do not double the next dose. Tell your doctor if you feel any side effects from missing a dose of this drug.

SIDE EFFECTS

Minor. Diarrhea, headache, heartburn, loss of appetite, nausea, stomach discomfort, stomach pain, or vomiting. These side effects usually disappear as your body adjusts to the drug.

Tolazamide may increase your sensitivity to sunlight. You should, therefore, avoid prolonged exposure to sunlight and sunlamps. Wear protective clothing and sunglasses, and use an effective sunscreen.

Major. Tell your doctor about any side effects that are persistent or particularly bothersome. IT IS ESPECIALLY IMPORTANT TO TELL YOUR DOCTOR about dark urine, fatigue, itching of the skin, light-colored stools, sore throat and fever, unusual bleeding or bruising, or yellowing of the eyes or skin.

INTERACTIONS

Tolazamide interacts with several other types of drugs:

1. Chloramphenicol, guanethidine, fenfluramine, sulfinpyrazone, insulin, monoamine oxidase (MAO) inhibitors, oxytetracycline, probenecid, aspirin or other salicylates, and sulfonamide antibiotics, when combined with tolazamide, can lower blood-sugar levels—sometimes to dangerously low levels. At least 14 days should separate the use of this drug and the use of an MAO inhibitor.

2. Thyroid hormones, dextrothyroxine, epinephrine, phenytoin, thiazide diuretics (water pills), and cortisonelike medications (such as dexamethasone, hydrocortisone, and prednisone), combined with tolazamide, can actually increase blood-sugar levels—just what you are trying to avoid.

3. Rifampin can decrease concentrations of tolazamide in the blood, which can lead to a decrease in its effectiveness.

4. Oral antidiabetic medications can increase the effects of the blood thinner warfarin, which can lead to bleeding complications.

5. Beta-blocking medications (acebutolol, atenolol, betaxolol, carteolol, esmolol, labetalol, metoprolol, nadolol, penbutolol, pindolol, propranolol, or timolol) combined with tolazamide can result in either high or low blood-sugar levels. Beta blockers can also mask the symptoms of low blood sugar, which can be dangerous.

BE SURE TO TELL YOUR DOCTOR about any medications you are currently taking, especially those listed above.

WARNINGS

• It is important to tell your doctor if you have ever had unusual or allergic reactions to tolazamide or to any other sulfa medication (sulfonamide antibiotics, diuretics [water pills], or other oral antidiabetics).

• It is also important to tell your doctor if you now have or if you have ever had kidney disease, liver disease, severe infections, or thyroid disease.

• Avoid drinking alcoholic beverages while taking this medication (unless otherwise directed by your doctor). Some patients who take this medicine suffer nausea, vomiting, dizziness, stomach pain, pounding headache, sweating, and redness of the face and skin when they drink alcohol. In addition, large amounts of alcohol can lower your blood-sugar concentration to a dangerously low level.

• Follow the special diet that your doctor gave you. This is an important part of controlling your blood sugar and is necessary for this medicine to work properly.

• Before having surgery or any other medical or dental treatment, be sure to tell your doctor or dentist that you are taking this medicine.

• Test for sugar in your urine as directed by your doctor. It is a convenient way to determine whether your diabetes is being controlled by this medicine.

• Eat or drink something containing sugar right away if you experience any symptoms of hypoglycemia (low blood sugar), such as anxiety, chills, cold sweats, cool or pale skin, drowsiness, excessive hunger, headache, nausea, nervousness, rapid heartbeat, shakiness, or unusual tiredness or weakness. It is important that your family and friends know the symptoms of low blood sugar and that they understand what to do if they observe any of these symptoms in you.

• Even if the hypoglycemic symptoms seem to disappear after you eat or drink a sugar-containing product, it is important to contact your doctor as soon as possible. The effects of tolazamide to lower blood sugar can last for hours, and your symptoms may return during this period. Good sources of sugar are orange juice, corn syrup, honey, sugar cubes, and table sugar. You are at greatest risk of developing low blood sugar if you skip or delay meals, exercise more than usual, are unable to eat because of nausea or vomiting, or drink large amounts of alcohol.

• You may need to be switched to insulin if you suffer diabetic coma, have a severe infection, are scheduled for major surgery, or become pregnant.

• Be sure to tell your doctor if you are pregnant. Your dosing requirements for tolazamide may change during pregnancy. Although extensive studies in humans have not been conducted, adverse effects have been observed in the fetuses of animals that received this type of medication during pregnancy. Also be sure to tell your doctor if you are breast-feeding an infant. Small amounts of tolazamide may pass into breast milk.

tolbutamide

BRAND NAMES (Manufacturers)
Orinase (Upjohn)
tolbutamide (various manufacturers)
TYPE OF DRUG
Oral antidiabetic
INGREDIENT
tolbutamide

DOSAGE FORM
Tablets (250 mg and 500 mg)
STORAGE
This medication should be stored at room temperature in a tightly closed container. Discard any outdated medication.

USES
Tolbutamide is used for the treatment of diabetes mellitus (sugar diabetes) that appears in adulthood and cannot be managed by control of diet alone. This type of diabetes is known as non–insulin-dependent diabetes (also called maturity-onset or type II diabetes). Tolbutamide lowers blood sugar by increasing the release of insulin from the pancreas.

TREATMENT
In order for this medication to work correctly, it must be taken as directed by your doctor. It is best to take this medicine at the same time(s) each day in order to maintain a constant blood-sugar level. It is therefore important to try not to miss any doses of tolbutamide. If you do miss a dose, take it as soon as possible, unless it is almost time for the next dose. In that case, do not take the missed dose at all; just return to your regular dosing schedule. Do not double the next dose. Tell your doctor if you feel any side effects from missing a dose of this drug.

SIDE EFFECTS
Minor. Diarrhea, headache, heartburn, loss of appetite, nausea, stomach discomfort, stomach pain, or vomiting. These side effects usually disappear during treatment as your body adjusts to the medication.

Tolbutamide may increase your sensitivity to sunlight. You should therefore avoid prolonged exposure to sunlight and sunlamps. Wear protective clothing and sunglasses, and use an effective sunscreen.

Major. Tell your doctor about any side effects that are persistent or particularly bothersome. IT IS ESPECIALLY IMPORTANT TO TELL YOUR DOCTOR about dark urine, fatigue, itching of the skin, light-colored stools, sore throat and fever, unusual bleeding or bruising, or yellowing of the eyes or skin.

INTERACTIONS

Tolbutamide interacts with a number of other types of drugs:

1. The combination of tolbutamide and chloramphenicol, guanethidine, insulin, fenfluramine, fluconazole, sulfinpyrazone, monoamine oxidase (MAO) inhibitors, oxytetracycline, probenecid, aspirin or other salicylates, or sulfonamide antibiotics can lower blood-sugar levels—sometimes to dangerously low levels. At least 14 days should separate the use of this drug and the use of an MAO inhibitor.

2. Thyroid hormones, dextrothyroxine, epinephrine, phenytoin, thiazide diuretics (water pills), and cortisonelike medications (such as dexamethasone, hydrocortisone, and prednisone), combined with tolbutamide, can actually increase blood-sugar levels—just what you are trying to avoid.

3. Rifampin can decrease the blood concentrations of tolbutamide, which can lead to a decrease in its effectiveness.

4. Oral antidiabetic medications can increase the effects of blood thinners, such as warfarin, which can lead to bleeding complications.

5. The combination of tolbutamide and beta-blocking medications (acebutolol, atenolol, betaxolol, carteolol, esmolol, labetalol, metoprolol, nadolol, penbutolol, pindolol, propranolol, or timolol) can result in either high or low blood-sugar levels. In addition, beta blockers can mask the symptoms of low blood sugar, which can be dangerous.

BE SURE TO TELL YOUR DOCTOR about any medications you are currently taking, especially those listed above.

WARNINGS

• It is important to tell your doctor if you now have or have ever had unusual or allergic reactions to tolbutamide or to any other sulfa medication (such as sulfonamide antibiotics), diuretics (water pills), or other oral antidiabetics.

• It is also important to tell your doctor if you now have or if you have ever had kidney disease, liver disease, severe infection, or thyroid disease.

• Be sure to avoid drinking alcoholic beverages while taking this medication (unless otherwise directed by your doctor). Some patients who take this medicine suffer nausea, vomiting, dizziness, stomach pain, pounding headache, sweating, and redness of the face and skin when they drink alcohol.

Large amounts of alcohol can also lower your blood-sugar concentration to a dangerously low level.
• Follow the special diet that your doctor gave you. This is an important part of controlling your blood-sugar levels and is necessary in order for this medicine to work properly.
• Before having surgery or any other medical or dental treatment, be sure to tell your doctor or dentist about this drug.
• It is very important to test for sugar in your urine as directed by your doctor. This is a convenient way to determine whether your diabetes is being controlled by this medicine.
• Eat or drink something containing sugar right away if you experience any symptoms of hypoglycemia (low blood sugar), such as anxiety, chills, cold sweats, cool or pale skin, drowsiness, excessive hunger, headache, nausea, nervousness, rapid heartbeat, shakiness, or unusual tiredness or weakness). It is important that your family and friends know the symptoms of low blood sugar and that they understand what to do if they observe any of these symptoms in you.
    Even if the hypoglycemic symptoms seem to disappear after you eat or drink a sugar-containing product, it is important to contact your doctor as soon as possible. The blood-sugar-lowering effects of tolbutamide can last for hours, and your symptoms may return during this period. Good sources of sugar are orange juice, corn syrup, honey, sugar cubes, and table sugar. You are at greatest risk of developing low blood sugar if you skip or delay meals, exercise more than usual, are unable to eat because of nausea or vomiting, or drink large amounts of alcohol.
• You may need to be switched to insulin if you have a severe infection, are scheduled for major surgery, suffer from diabetic coma, or become pregnant. Be sure to consult your doctor.
• Be sure to tell your doctor if you are pregnant. Your dosing requirements for tolbutamide may change during pregnancy, or you may be switched to insulin. Although extensive studies in humans have not been conducted, adverse effects have been observed in the fetuses of animals that received the drug tolbutamide during pregnancy. Also tell your doctor if you are breast-feeding an infant. Since small amounts of tolbutamide may pass into breast milk, caution is warranted.

tolmetin

BRAND NAMES (Manufacturers)
Tolectin (McNeil)
Tolectin DS (McNeil)
Tolectin-600 (McNeil)
tolmetin (various manufacturers)
TYPE OF DRUG
Nonsteroidal anti-inflammatory analgesic
INGREDIENT
tolmetin
DOSAGE FORMS
Tablets (200 mg and 600 mg)
Capsules (400 mg)
STORAGE
This medication should be stored in tightly closed containers at room temperature away from heat and direct sunlight. Tolmetin tablets and capsules should not be refrigerated.

USES

Tolmetin is used to treat the inflammation (pain, swelling, and stiffness) of certain types of arthritis, gout, bursitis, and tendinitis. Tolmetin has been shown to block the production of certain body chemicals that may trigger pain. However, it is not yet fully understood how tolmetin works.

TREATMENT

You should take this medication on an empty stomach 30 to 60 minutes before meals or two hours after meals, so it gets into your bloodstream quickly. However, to decrease stomach irritation, your doctor may want you to take the medicine with food or antacids.

If you are taking tolmetin to relieve arthritis, you must take it regularly, as directed by your doctor. It may take up to two weeks before you feel the full benefits of this medication.

Tolmetin does not cure arthritis, but it will help to control the condition as long as you continue treatment.

It is important to take tolmetin on schedule and not to miss any doses. If you do miss a dose, take it as soon as possible, unless it is almost time for your next dose. In that case, do not take the missed dose at all; just return to your regular dosing schedule. Do not double the next dose.

SIDE EFFECTS

Minor. Bloating, constipation, diarrhea, difficulty in sleeping, dizziness, drowsiness, headache, heartburn, indigestion, light-headedness, loss of appetite, nausea, nervousness, soreness of the mouth, unusual sweating, or vomiting. As your body adjusts to the drug, these side effects should disappear.

To relieve constipation, increase the amount of fiber in your diet (fresh fruits and vegetables, salads, bran, and whole-grain breads), exercise, and drink more water (unless your doctor directs you to do otherwise).

If you become dizzy or light-headed, sit or lie down for a while; get up slowly from a sitting or reclining position; and be careful on stairs.

Major. Tell your doctor about any side effects that are persistent or particularly bothersome. IT IS ESPECIALLY IMPORTANT TO TELL YOUR DOCTOR about bloody or black, tarry stools; blurred vision; confusion; depression; difficult or painful urination; difficulty in hearing; palpitations; ringing or buzzing in the ears; skin rash, hives, or itching; stomach pain; swelling of the feet; tightness in the chest; unexplained sore throat and fever; unusual bleeding or bruising; unusual fatigue or weakness; unusual weight gain; wheezing or difficulty in breathing; or yellowing of the eyes or skin.

INTERACTIONS

Tolmetin interacts with several types of medications:
1. Anticoagulants (blood thinners, such as warfarin) in combination with tolmetin can lead to an increase in bleeding complications.
2. Aspirin, salicylates, or other anti-inflammatory medications can increase the stomach irritation caused by tolmetin.
3. Probenecid may increase blood levels of tolmetin, which may increase the risk of side effects.
4. The action of beta blockers may be decreased by this drug.
5. This drug can interact with diuretics (water pills).
6. The side effects of methotrexate may be increased by tolmetin.

BE SURE TO TELL YOUR DOCTOR about any medications you are currently taking, especially any listed above.

WARNINGS

• Before you take this medication, it is important to tell your doctor if you have ever had unusual or allergic reactions to tolmetin or any of the other chemically related drugs (including aspirin, other salicylates, diclofenac, diflunisal, etodolac, fenoprofen, flurbiprofen, ibuprofen, ketoprofen, meclofenamate, mefenamic acid, nabumetone, naproxen, oxyphenbutazone, phenylbutazone, piroxicam, sulindac, and indomethacin).

• Tell your doctor if you have ever had asthma, bleeding problems, colitis, stomach ulcers or other stomach problems, epilepsy, heart disease, high blood pressure, kidney disease, liver disease, mental illness, or Parkinson's disease.

• If this drug makes you dizzy or drowsy, do not take part in any activity that requires alertness, such as driving a car or operating potentially dangerous machinery.

• Because tolmetin can prolong your bleeding time, it is important to tell your doctor or dentist that you are taking this drug before having surgery or any other medical or dental treatment.

• Stomach problems are more likely to occur if you take aspirin regularly or drink alcohol while being treated with this medication. These should therefore be avoided (unless your doctor directs you to do otherwise).

• Be sure to tell your doctor if you are pregnant. The safe use of this medicine in human pregnancy has not been established. Side effects have been observed in the offspring of animals that received this type of medication during pregnancy. If taken late in pregnancy, tolmetin can prolong labor. Also tell your doctor if you are breast-feeding an infant. Small amounts of tolmetin can pass into breast milk.

---

tramadol

BRAND NAME (Manufacturer)
Ultram (Ortho-McNeil)
TYPE OF DRUG
Analgesic
INGREDIENT
tramadol
DOSAGE FORM
Tablet (50 mg)

STORAGE
Tramadol should be stored at room temperature in a tightly closed, light-resistant container and should not be refrigerated. Never freeze this medication.

USES
Tramadol is used for the treatment of moderate to moderately severe pain. It acts on the central nervous system (brain and spinal cord) to relieve pain. The mechanism of action of tramadol is not related to any other analgesics, and the mechanism of action is poorly understood.

TREATMENT
Tramadol should be taken every four to six hours as needed for pain (unless your doctor specifically instructs you to do otherwise). It can be taken with food or on an empty stomach.

This medication works most effectively if you take it at the onset of pain, rather than waiting until the pain becomes intense.

If you are taking this medication on a schedule and you miss a scheduled dose, take the missed dose as soon as possible, unless it is almost time for your next dose. In that case, do not take the missed dose at all; just return to your regular schedule. Do not double the next dose unless your doctor directs you to do so.

SIDE EFFECTS
Minor. Constipation, diarrhea, dizziness, dry mouth, fatigue, itching, nausea or vomiting, nervousness, restlessness, sleep disorders, sweating, or upset stomach.

These side effects should disappear as your body adjusts to the medication.

Dry mouth can be relieved by sucking on ice chips or a piece of hard candy or by chewing sugarless gum.

If you feel dizzy or lightheaded, sit or lie down for a while; get up from a sitting or lying position slowly; and be careful when climbing stairs.

In order to prevent constipation, increase the amount of fiber in your diet (fresh fruits and vegetables, salads, bran, whole-grain breads), exercise, and drink more water (unless your doctor tells you not to do so).

Major. Tell your doctor about any side effects that are persistent or particularly bothersome. IT IS ESPECIALLY IMPORTANT TO TELL YOUR DOCTOR about black, tarry stools; chest tightness; difficulty in urinating; hallucinations; headaches; loss of coordination; mental depression; palpitations; rash; seizures; tremors; or trouble breathing.

INTERACTIONS
Tramadol interacts with several other types of medications:
1. Use of it within 14 days of a monoamine oxidase (MAO) inhibitor (isocarboxazid, pargyline, phenelzine, or tranylcypromine) can result in high blood pressure along with other side effects.
2. This medication may increase the sedative effects of alcohol or other drugs that interact with central nervous system action (such as anesthetic agents, opioids, phenothiazines, sedative hypnotics, or tranquilizers).
3. Tramadol may increase the risk of seizures in patients with epilepsy or in those patients that receive drugs that may increase the risk of seizure (such as MAO inhibitors and neuroleptics).
   BE SURE TO TELL YOUR DOCTOR about any medications you are currently taking, especially any listed above.

WARNINGS
• Tell your doctor about any unusual or allergic reactions you have had to any medications, especially to tramadol or to other analgesics.
• Before having surgery or other medical or dental procedures, tell your doctor or dentist that you are taking this drug.
• Tell your doctor if you have a history of drug abuse or if you ever had abdominal disease, peptic ulcers, epilepsy, head injuries, heart disease, kidney disease, or liver disease.
• Tramadol can cause drowsiness or dizziness. Your ability to perform tasks that require alertness, such as driving a car or operating potentially dangerous machinery, may be decreased.
• Be sure to tell your doctor if you are pregnant. Although extensive studies of tramadol in humans have not been conducted, tramadol has been shown to cause side effects in the fetuses of animals that received large doses of the drug during pregnancy. Tramadol is known to cross the placenta. Also

tell your doctor if you are breast-feeding an infant. It is not known if tramadol passes into breast milk.

---

trazodone

BRAND NAMES (Manufacturers)
Desyrel (Bristol-Myers Squibb)
Desyrel Dividose (Bristol-Myers Squibb)
trazodone (various manufacturers)
TYPE OF DRUG
Antidepressant
INGREDIENT
trazodone
DOSAGE FORM
Tablets (50 mg, 100 mg, 150 mg, and 300 mg)
STORAGE
Trazodone tablets should be stored at room temperature in a tightly closed, light-resistant container. Like all medications, trazodone should be stored well out of the reach of children and pets.

USES
Trazodone is used to relieve the symptoms of mental depression. It is thought to relieve depression by increasing the concentration of certain chemicals involved with nerve transmission in the brain.

TREATMENT
Trazodone should be taken exactly as your doctor prescribes. It can be taken with water, milk, or food to lessen stomach irritation (unless your doctor tells you to do otherwise).

If you miss a dose of this medication, take the missed dose as soon as possible, and then return to your regular dosing schedule. If, however, the dose you missed was a once-a-day bedtime dose, do not take that dose in the morning; check with your doctor instead. If the dose is taken in the morning, it may cause some unwanted side effects. Never double the next dose.

The benefits of therapy with this medication may not become apparent for two to four weeks.

SIDE EFFECTS

Minor. Blurred vision, constipation, diarrhea, dizziness, drowsiness, dry mouth, gas, headache, heartburn, light-headedness, nausea, sleep disorders, vomiting, or weight gain or loss. These side effects should disappear as your body adjusts to trazodone.

This medication can cause increased sensitivity to sunlight. It is therefore important to avoid prolonged exposure to sunlight and sunlamps. Wear protective clothing and sunglasses, and use an effective sunscreen.

Dry mouth can be relieved by chewing sugarless gum or by sucking on ice chips or a piece of hard candy.

To relieve constipation, increase the amount of fiber in your diet (fresh fruits and vegetables, salads, bran, and whole-grain breads), exercise, and drink more water (unless your doctor directs you to do otherwise).

To avoid dizziness and light-headedness when you stand, contract and relax the muscles of your legs for a few moments before rising. Do this by pushing one foot against the floor while raising the other foot slightly, alternating feet so you are "pumping" your legs in a pedaling motion.

Major. Tell your doctor about any side effects that are persistent or particularly bothersome. IT IS ESPECIALLY IMPORTANT TO TELL YOUR DOCTOR about chest tightness, confusion, difficult or painful urination, hallucinations, loss of coordination, mood changes, muscle aches or pains, palpitations, prolonged or inappropriate erection of the penis, rash, ringing in the ears, shortness of breath, tingling in the fingers or toes, tremors, unusual bleeding or bruising, or unusual tiredness or weakness.

INTERACTIONS

Trazodone interacts with several other types of medications:
1. Extreme drowsiness can occur when trazodone is taken with central nervous system depressants (drugs that slow the activity of the brain and spinal cord), including alcohol, antihistamines, barbiturates, benzodiazepine tranquilizers, muscle relaxants, narcotics, pain medications, phenothiazine tranquilizers, medications to promote sleep, or with tricyclic antidepressants.
2. The concurrent use of trazodone and monoamine oxidase (MAO) inhibitors should be avoided because the combina-

tion can result in fever, convulsions, or high blood pressure. At least 14 days should separate the use of this drug and the use of an MAO inhibitor.

3. Trazodone may increase the blood levels of digoxin and phenytoin, which may, in turn, lead to an increase in side effects.

4. The blood-pressure-lowering effects of antihypertensives may be increased by trazodone, which can be dangerous.

BE SURE TO TELL YOUR DOCTOR about any medications you are currently taking.

WARNINGS

• Tell your doctor if you have had unusual or allergic reactions to any medications, especially to trazodone.

• Tell your doctor if you have a history of alcoholism or if you ever had electroshock therapy, heart disease, a heart attack, kidney disease, or liver disease.

• If this drug makes you dizzy or drowsy, do not take part in any activity that requires alertness, such as driving a car or operating potentially dangerous tools, equipment, or machinery.

• Before having surgery or any other medical or dental treatment, be sure to tell your doctor or dentist that you are taking this medication.

• Do not stop taking this drug suddenly. Stopping this medication abruptly may cause nausea, headache, stomach upset, fatigue, or worsening of your condition. Your doctor may therefore want to reduce the dosage gradually.

• The effects of this medication may last as long as seven days after you stop taking it, so continue to observe all precautions during that period.

• Be sure to tell your doctor if you are pregnant. The safe use of this medication in pregnancy has not been established. Side effects have been observed in the offspring of animals that were given this medication in large doses during pregnancy. Also tell your doctor if you are breast-feeding an infant. Small amounts of this drug pass into breast milk and may cause unwanted effects, such as irritability or sleeping problems, in nursing infants.

tretinoin

BRAND NAME (Manufacturer)
Retin-A (Ortho)
TYPE OF DRUG
Acne preparation
INGREDIENT
tretinoin (retinoic acid; vitamin A acid)
DOSAGE FORMS
Cream (0.025%, 0.05%, and 0.1%)
Gel (0.025% and 0.01%, with 90% alcohol)
Liquid (0.05%, with 55% alcohol)
STORAGE
Tretinoin cream, gel, and liquid should be stored at room temperature in tightly closed, light-resistant containers.

USES

Tretinoin is used topically (on the skin) to treat acne vulgaris. It appears to work by increasing the turnover (death and replacement) of skin cells.

TREATMENT

Instructions for the patient are included with this product. They should be read carefully before application.

Wash your skin with a mild or hypoallergenic soap and warm water. Pat dry with a clean towel. Then wait about 30 minutes before applying tretinoin cream, gel, or liquid. The medication should be applied once a day just before going to bed. Apply it only to the skin where the acne lesions appear, unless you are directed to do otherwise by your doctor. Be sure to cover the entire affected area lightly. You may use a fingertip, gauze pad, or cotton swab to apply the liquid. To avoid applying too much medication, be careful not to oversaturate the gauze pad or cotton swab. To avoid contamination, use a gauze pad or cotton swab only once and then throw it away.

During the early weeks of treatment with this drug, there may be an apparent increase in skin lesions. This is usually not a reason to discontinue its use. However, your doctor may want to change the concentration of the drug. Benefits may be noted within two to three weeks, although more than six weeks may be required before definite benefits are observed.

If you miss a dose of this medication, apply the missed dose as soon as possible, then return to your regular dosing schedule. If you do not remember until the following day, do not apply the missed dose at all; just return to your regular dosing schedule.

SIDE EFFECTS

Minor. Immediately after applying tretinoin to your skin, you may experience a sensation of warmth or a mild stinging sensation, or your skin may become reddened. After a few days of treatment with this medication, some peeling of the skin is to be expected. You may also find that you have a heightened sensitivity to sunlight, wind, or cold.

If this drug does increase your sensitivity to sunlight, you should try to avoid prolonged exposure to sunlight and sunlamps. You should also wear protective clothing and use an effective sunscreen.

Major. Tell your doctor about any side effects that are persistent or particularly bothersome. IT IS ESPECIALLY IMPORTANT TO TELL YOUR DOCTOR about blistering, crusting, severe redness, severe burning, swelling, or marked darkening or lightening of the skin.

INTERACTIONS

Tretinoin interacts with several other products:
1. Abrasive or medicated soaps or cleaners.
2. Other acne preparations (particularly peeling agents containing sulfur, resorcinol, benzoyl peroxide, or salicylic acid).
3. Cosmetics that have a strong drying effect.
4. Locally applied products containing high amounts of alcohol, spices, or lime.

These products should be used with caution during treatment, since they can increase the extent of irritation

WARNINGS

• Tell your doctor about unusual or allergic reactions you have had to any drugs, especially to tretinoin or vitamin A.
• Before starting to take this medication, be sure to tell your doctor if you have eczema.

• This medication should not be used if you are sunburned; it may increase the irritation.

• Keep tretinoin away from the eyes, the mouth, the creases on either side of the nose, open cuts, and mucous membranes; it can severely irritate these sensitive areas.

• Avoid washing your face too often while using tretinoin. Be sure to use a mild or hypoallergenic soap.

• Normal use of nonmedicated cosmetics is permissible, but the skin should be cleaned thoroughly before tretinoin is applied.

• This medication has been prescribed for your current condition only. Do not give this medication to other people or use it for any purpose other than what was prescribed by your doctor.

• Be sure to tell your doctor if you are pregnant. The safe use of this medication in human pregnancy or during breast-feeding has not been established.

---

triamcinolone (topical)

BRAND NAMES (Manufacturers)
Aristocort (Fujisawa)
Aristocort A (Fujisawa)
Flutex (Syosset)
Kenalog (Westwood-Squibb)
Kenalog-H (Westwood-Squibb)
Triacet (various manufacturers)
triamcinolone acetonide (various manufacturers)
TYPE OF DRUG
Adrenocorticosteroid hormone
INGREDIENT
triamcinolone
DOSAGE FORMS
Ointment (0.025%, 0.1%, and 0.5%)
Cream (0.025%, 0.1%, and 0.5%)
Lotion (0.025% and 0.1%)
(Dental) Paste (0.1%)
Aerosol (two seconds of spray delivers approximately
    0.2 mg of drug, with 10.3% alcohol)

STORAGE

Triamcinolone ointment, cream, lotion, and paste should be stored at room temperature in tightly closed containers. This medication should never be frozen.

The spray (foam) form of this medication is packed under pressure. It should not be stored near heat or an open flame or in direct sunlight, and the container should never be punctured.

USES

Your adrenal glands naturally produce certain cortisonelike chemicals. These chemicals are involved in various processes in the body (such as maintenance of fluid balance, regulation of temperature, and reaction to inflammation). Triamcinolone belongs to a group of drugs known as adrenocorticosteroids (or cortisonelike medications). It is used to relieve the skin inflammation (redness, swelling, itching, and discomfort) associated with conditions such as dermatitis, eczema, and poison ivy. How this drug acts to relieve these disorders is not completely understood.

TREATMENT

Before applying this medication, wash your hands. Then, unless your doctor gives you different instructions, gently wash the area of the skin where the medication is to be applied. With a clean towel, pat the area almost dry; it should be slightly damp when you put the medicine on.

If you are using the lotion form of this medication, shake it well before pouring. The contents tend to settle on the bottom of the bottle, so it is necessary to shake the container to distribute the ingredients evenly and equalize the doses.

Apply a small amount of the medication to the affected area in a thin layer. Do not bandage the area unless your doctor tells you to do so. If you are to apply an occlusive dressing (like kitchen plastic wrap), be sure you understand the instructions. Wash your hands again after application.

If you are using the aerosol spray form of this medication, shake the can in order to disperse the medication evenly. Hold the can upright six to eight inches from the area to be sprayed, and spray the area for one to three seconds. DO NOT SMOKE while using the aerosol spray.

The dental paste should be applied with a cotton applicator, pressing (not rubbing) the paste onto the affected area. It is best applied after meals and at bedtime, unless directed otherwise by your doctor or dentist.

If you miss a dose of this medication, apply the dose as soon as possible, unless it is almost time for the next application. In that case, do not apply the missed dose; just return to your regular dosing schedule. Do not put twice as much of the medication on your skin at the next application.

SIDE EFFECTS

Minor. Acne, burning sensation, irritation of the affected area, or skin dryness.

If the affected area is extremely dry or scaling, the skin may be moistened by soaking in water or by applying water with a clean cloth before applying the medication. The ointment form is probably better for dry skin.

A mild, temporary stinging sensation may occur after this medication is applied. If this persists, contact your doctor.

Major. Tell your doctor about any side effects that are persistent or particularly bothersome. IT IS ESPECIALLY IMPORTANT TO TELL YOUR DOCTOR about blistering, increased hair growth, itching, loss of skin color, rash, secondary infection in the area being treated, or thinning of the skin with easy bruising.

INTERACTIONS

This medication should not interact with other medications as long as it is used according to the directions given to you by your doctor or pharmacist.

WARNINGS

• Tell your doctor about unusual or allergic reactions you have had to any medications, especially to triamcinolone or other adrenocorticosteroids (such as amcinonide, betamethasone, clocortolone, cortisone, desonide, desoximetasone, dexamethasone, diflorasone, flumethasone, fluocinolone, fluocinonide, fluorometholone, flurandrenolide, halcinonide, hydrocortisone, methylprednisolone, prednisolone, and prednisone).

• Tell your doctor if you now have or if you have ever had blood-vessel disease, chicken pox, diabetes mellitus, fungal infection, peptic ulcers, shingles, tuberculosis of the lungs or skin, vaccinia, or any other type of infection, especially at the site currently being treated.

• If any kind of irritation develops while you are using this drug, you should immediately discontinue its use and notify your doctor.

• This product is intended for topical use only. It is not for use in the eyes or on the mucous membranes; contact may result in side effects.

• Do not use this product with an occlusive wrap unless your doctor directs you to do so. Systemic absorption of this drug is increased if extensive areas of the body are treated, particularly if occlusive bandages are used. If it is necessary for you to use this drug under a wrap, follow your physician's instructions exactly. Do not leave the wrap in place longer than specified.

• If you are using this medication on a child's diaper area, it is important to not put tight-fitting diapers or plastic pants on the child. This may lead to increased systemic absorption of the medication and an increase in side effects.

• In order to avoid freezing skin tissue when using the aerosol form of triamcinolone, it is important that you are sure you do not spray for more than three seconds, and be sure to hold the container at least six inches away from the skin.

• To prevent side effects when using the aerosol form of this medication on the face, cover your eyes, and do not inhale the spray.

• Do not use this medication for longer than the time prescribed by your doctor.

• It is very important that you tell your doctor if you are pregnant. If large amounts of triamcinolone are applied for prolonged periods, some of it will be absorbed and may cross the placenta. Although extensive studies in humans have not yet been conducted, birth defects have been observed in the offspring of animals that were given large oral doses of this type of drug during pregnancy. Also notify your doctor if you are currently breast-feeding an infant. If absorbed through the skin, small amounts of triamcinolone pass into breast milk and may cause growth suppression or a decrease in the production of natural adrenocorticosteroid hormones in the nursing infant.

triamcinolone and nystatin combination (topical)

BRAND NAMES (Manufacturers)
Mycolog II (Bristol-Myers Squibb)
Myco-Triacet II (Lemmon)
triamcinolone and nystatin combination (topical) (various
    manufacturers)
TYPE OF DRUG
Adrenocorticosteroid and anti-infective
INGREDIENTS
triamcinolone and nystatin
DOSAGE FORMS
Cream (0.1% triamcinolone and 100,000 units nystatin
    per gram)
Ointment (0.1% triamcinolone and 100,000 units nystatin
    per gram)
STORAGE
The cream and ointment should be stored at room temperature
(never frozen) in tightly closed containers. Discard any out-
dated medicine or medicine no longer needed.

USES
Your adrenal glands naturally produce certain cortisonelike
chemicals. These chemicals are involved in various processes
in the body (such as maintenance of fluid balance, regulation
of temperature, and reaction to inflammation). Triamcinolone
belongs to a group of medications known as adrenocorticosteroids (or cortisonelike medications). It is used to relieve the
skin inflammation (redness, swelling, itching, and discomfort)
associated with conditions such as dermatitis, eczema, and
poison ivy. How this medication acts to relieve these disorders is not completely understood. Nystatin is an anti-infective
agent that is active against the fungus Candida.

TREATMENT
Before applying this medication, wash your hands. Then, unless your doctor gives you different instructions, gently wash
the area of skin where the medication is to be applied. With a

clean towel, pat the area almost dry; it should be slightly damp when you apply this particular medication.

Apply a small amount of this medication to the affected area in a thin layer. Do not bandage the area unless your doctor specifically tells you to do so. If you are to apply an occlusive dressing (like kitchen plastic wrap), be sure you understand the instructions. Wash your hands again afterward.

If you miss a dose of this medication, apply the dose as soon as possible, unless it is almost time for the next application. In that case, do not apply the missed dose at all; just return to your regular dosing schedule. Do not put twice as much of the medication on your skin at the next application.

Use this medication for the full length of time prescribed by your doctor; do not take the medication for longer than the prescribed period.

SIDE EFFECTS

Minor. Acne, burning sensation, irritation of the affected area, or skin dryness.

If the affected area is extremely dry or scaling, the skin may be moistened by soaking in water or by applying water with a clean cloth before applying the medication. The ointment form is probably most suitable for dry skin.

A mild, temporary stinging sensation may occur after this medication is applied. If this persists, contact your doctor.

Major. Tell your doctor about any side effects that are persistent or particularly bothersome. IT IS ESPECIALLY IMPORTANT TO TELL YOUR DOCTOR about blistering, increased hair growth, itching, loss of skin color, rash, secondary infection in the area being treated, or thinning of the skin with easy bruising. And if your symptoms of infection seem to be getting worse rather than improving, contact your doctor.

INTERACTIONS

This medication should not interact with other medications as long as it is used according to directions.

WARNINGS

• Tell your doctor about unusual or allergic reactions you have had to any medications, especially to triamcinolone or other adrenocorticosteroids (such as amcinonide, beta-methasone, clocortolone, cortisone, desonide, desoximeta-sone, dexamethasone, diflorasone, flumethasone, fluocinolone, fluocinonide, fluorometholone, flurandrenolide, halcinonide, hydrocortisone, methylprednisolone, prednisolone, and prednisone) or to nystatin.

• Tell your doctor if you now have or if you have ever had chicken pox, circulation problems, diabetes mellitus, peptic ulcers, shingles, tuberculosis of the lungs or skin, vaccinia, or viral or fungal infections of the skin in addition to a Candida infection.

• If any kind of irritation develops while you are using this drug, you should immediately discontinue its use and notify your doctor.

• Do not use in the eyes; contact may result in side effects.

• This medication should not be used in the external ear canal of people with perforated eardrums.

• Do not use this product with an occlusive wrap unless your doctor directs you to do so. Systemic absorption of this drug is increased when extensive areas of the body are treated, particularly if occlusive bandages are used. If it is necessary for you to use this drug under a wrap, follow your doctor's instructions exactly, and do not leave the wrap in place longer than specified.

• If you are using this medication on a child's diaper area, do not put tight-fitting diapers or plastic pants on the child. This may lead to increased systemic absorption of the drug and an increase in side effects.

• Be sure to tell your doctor if you are pregnant. If large amounts of this medication are applied for prolonged periods, some of it will be absorbed and may cross the placenta. Although studies in humans have not been conducted, birth defects have been observed in the offspring of animals that were given large oral doses of this type of medication during pregnancy. Also tell your doctor if you are breast-feeding an infant. If absorbed through the skin, small amounts of this medication pass into breast milk and may cause growth suppression or a decrease in natural adrenocorticosteroid hormone production in the nursing infant.

triamterene

BRAND NAME (Manufacturer)
Dyrenium (SmithKline Beecham)
TYPE OF DRUG
Diuretic and antihypertensive
INGREDIENT
triamterene
DOSAGE FORM
Capsules (50 mg and 100 mg)
STORAGE
Triamterene should be stored at room temperature in a tightly closed, light-resistant container.

USES

Triamterene is prescribed to treat high blood pressure. It is also used to reduce fluid accumulation in the body caused by conditions such as heart failure, cirrhosis of the liver, kidney disease, and the long-term use of some medications. Triamterene reduces fluid accumulation by increasing the elimination of salt and water through the kidneys. It may also be used in combination with other diuretics to prevent potassium loss.

TREATMENT

To decrease stomach irritation, you can take triamterene with a glass of milk or with a meal (unless your doctor directs you to do otherwise). Try to take it at the same time(s) every day. Avoid taking a dose after 6:00 P.M.; otherwise, you may have to get up during the night to urinate.

This medication does not cure high blood pressure, but it will help to control the condition as long as you take it.

If you miss a dose of this medication, take the missed dose as soon as possible, unless it is almost time for the next dose. In that case, do not take the missed dose at all; just wait until the next scheduled dose. Do not double the dose.

SIDE EFFECTS

Minor. Diarrhea, dizziness, drowsiness, dry mouth, headache, increased thirst, increased urination, nausea, tiredness, upset stomach, or vomiting. As your body adjusts to triamterene, these side effects from this medication should disappear.

Triamterene can cause increased sensitivity to sunlight. It is therefore important to avoid prolonged exposure to sunlight and sunlamps while you are taking this medication. Wear protective clothing and use a sunscreen.

Triamterene may cause the urine to turn bluish; this is a harmless side effect.

Dry mouth can be relieved by sucking on ice chips or a piece of hard candy or by chewing sugarless gum.

To avoid dizziness or light-headedness when you stand, contract and relax the muscles of your legs for a few moments before rising. Do this by pushing one foot against the floor while raising the other foot slightly, alternating feet so that you are "pumping" your legs in a pedaling motion. Be careful on stairs.

Major. Tell your doctor about any side effects that are persistent or particularly bothersome. IT IS ESPECIALLY IMPORTANT TO TELL YOUR DOCTOR about anxiety; back or flank (side) pain; confusion; cracking at the corners of the mouth; difficulty in breathing; extreme weakness; fever; mouth sores; numbness or tingling in the hands, feet, or lips; painful urination; palpitations; rash; a red or inflamed tongue; sore throat; unusual bleeding or bruising; or unusual tiredness.

INTERACTIONS

Triamterene will interact with several foods and other types of medications:

1. Concurrent use of it with antihypertensives, such as benazepril, captopril, enalapril, fusinopril, lisinopril, and ramipril, or with spironolactone, amiloride, potassium salts, low-salt milk, salt substitutes, or laxatives can cause serious side effects from hyperkalemia (high levels of potassium in the blood).

2. Triamterene may decrease the effectiveness of antigout medications, insulin, and oral antidiabetic medications.

3. Triamterene has been known to increase the side effects of lithium.

4. Indomethacin may decrease the diuretic effects of triamterene.

Before starting to take triamterene, BE SURE TO TELL YOUR DOCTOR about any medications you are currently taking, especially any of those listed above.

WARNINGS

• Before starting to take this medication, be sure to tell your doctor if you have ever had an unusual or allergic reaction to any medication, especially to triamterene or to any other diuretic.

• Be sure to tell your doctor if you now have or if you have ever had kidney disease, kidney stones, urination problems, hyperkalemia, diabetes mellitus, liver disease, acidosis, or gout.

• Triamterene can cause hyperkalemia (high blood levels of potassium). Signs of hyperkalemia include palpitations; confusion; numbness or tingling in the hands, feet, or lips; anxiety; or unusual tiredness or weakness. In order to avoid this problem, it is important that you not alter your diet, and do not use salt substitutes unless your doctor tells you to do so.

• You should limit your intake of alcoholic beverages while taking this drug in order to prevent dizziness and the feeling of light-headedness.

• Do not take any over-the-counter (nonprescription) medications for weight control or for allergy, asthma, cough, cold, or sinus problems unless you first check with your doctor. Some of these products can lead to an increase in blood pressure.

• It is possible that treatment with this medication can cause severe water loss (dehydration). In order to prevent this, be sure to check with your doctor if you have any illness that causes severe or continuous nausea, vomiting, or diarrhea.

• If you are taking quinidine (an antiarrhythmia heart medication), it is important to know that triamterene may interfere with the laboratory determination of your blood quinidine concentration. Before you undergo this type of test, be sure to tell your doctor that you are also taking the drug triamterene.

• Your doctor may schedule regular office visits to monitor your progress and possibly adjust your dosage.

• Be sure to tell your doctor if you are pregnant. This medication crosses the placenta, and its safety in human pregnancy has not been thoroughly investigated. However, effects have been reported in the fetuses of animals that received large doses of this medication during pregnancy. Also be sure to tell your doctor if you are breast-feeding an infant. It has been established that small amounts of triamterene pass into breast milk.

triamterene and hydrochlorothiazide combination

BRAND NAMES (Manufacturers)
Dyazide (SmithKline Beecham)
Maxzide (Lederle)
Maxzide-25MG (Lederle)
triamterene and hydrochlorothiazide (various
  manufacturers)
TYPE OF DRUG
Diuretic and antihypertensive
INGREDIENTS
triamterene and hydrochlorothiazide
DOSAGE FORMS
Capsules (37.5 mg triamterene and 25 mg hydrochloro-
  thiazide)
Tablets (37.5 mg triamterene and 25 mg hydrochloro-
  thiazide, and 75 mg triamterene and 50 mg
  hydrochlorothiazide)
STORAGE
This medication should be stored at room temperature in a
tightly closed, light-resistant container. It should not be refrigerated.

USES
Triamterene and hydrochlorothiazide combination is prescribed to treat high blood pressure. It is also used to reduce
fluid accumulation in the body caused by conditions such as
heart failure, cirrhosis of the liver, kidney disease, and the
long-term use of some medications. It reduces fluid accumulation by increasing the elimination of salt and water through
the kidneys. Triamterene is combined with hydrochlorothiazide to prevent potassium loss.

TREATMENT
To decrease stomach irritation, you can take this medication
with a glass of milk or with a meal (unless your doctor directs
you to do otherwise). Try to take it at the same time every day.

Avoid taking a dose after 6:00 P.M.; otherwise, you may have to get up during the night to urinate.

This drug does not cure high blood pressure but will help to control the condition as long as you continue to take it.

If you miss a dose of this medication, take the missed dose as soon as possible, unless it is almost time for the next dose. In that case, do not take the missed dose at all; just wait until the next scheduled dose. Do not double the dose.

SIDE EFFECTS

Minor. Constipation, cramps, diarrhea, dizziness, drowsiness, headache, increased urination, loss of appetite, restlessness, tiredness, or upset stomach. These side effects should disappear as your body gets accustomed to the medication.

This medication can cause increased sensitivity to sunlight. It is therefore important to avoid prolonged exposure to sunlight and sunlamps. Wear protective clothing and use an effective sunscreen.

Triamterene can cause the urine to turn bluish; this is a harmless side effect.

To relieve constipation, increase the amount of fiber in your diet (fresh fruits and vegetables, salads, bran, and whole-grain breads) and exercise more (unless your doctor directs you to do otherwise).

If you experience dryness of the mouth, you might want to try sucking on ice chips or a piece of hard candy or chewing sugarless gum.

To avoid dizziness or light-headedness when you stand, contract and relax the muscles of your legs for a few moments before rising. Do this by pushing one foot against the floor while raising the other foot slightly, alternating feet so that you are "pumping" your legs in a pedaling motion.

Major. Tell your doctor about any side effects that are persistent or particularly bothersome. IT IS ESPECIALLY IMPORTANT TO TELL YOUR DOCTOR about anxiety; back or flank (side) pain; confusion; cracking at the corners of the mouth; difficulty in breathing; difficulty in urinating; dry mouth; fever; itching; mood changes; mouth sores; muscle cramps or spasms; nausea; painful urination; palpitations; rash; red or inflamed tongue; sore throat; thirst; tingling or numbness in the hands, feet, or lips; unusual bleeding or bruising; unusual tiredness or weakness; vomiting; or yellowish discoloration of the eyes or skin.

INTERACTIONS

Triamterene and hydrochlorothiazide combination interacts with several foods and medications:

1. Concurrent use of it with antihypertensives, such as benazepril, captopril, enalapril, fusinopril, lisinopril, and ramipril, or with spironolactone, amiloride, potassium salts, low-salt milk, salt substitutes, or laxatives can cause serious side effects from hyperkalemia (high levels of potassium in the blood).

2. This drug may decrease the effectiveness of oral anticoagulants, antigout medications, insulin, oral antidiabetic medicines, and methenamine.

3. Fenfluramine may increase the blood-pressure-lowering effects of this drug (which can be dangerous).

4. Indomethacin may decrease the effectiveness of this medication.

5. Cholestyramine and colestipol can decrease the absorption of this medication from the gastrointestinal tract. Therefore, triamterene and hydrochlorothiazide combination should be taken one hour before or four hours after a dose of cholestyramine or colestipol if one of these medications has also been prescribed.

6. This medication may increase the side effects of amphotericin B, calcium, cortisone and cortisonelike steroids (such as dexamethasone, hydrocortisone, prednisone, and prednisolone), digoxin, digitalis, lithium, quinidine, sulfonamide antibiotics, and vitamin D.

BE SURE TO TELL YOUR DOCTOR about any medications you are currently taking.

WARNINGS

• Tell your doctor about unusual or allergic reactions you have had to any medications, especially to triamterene or hydrochlorothiazide or to any other sulfa drugs, including other diuretics, oral antidiabetic medications, and sulfonamide antibiotics.

• Before you start to take triamterene and hydrochlorothiazide combination, tell your doctor if you now have or if you have ever had kidney disease, kidney stones, problems with urination, diabetes mellitus, gout, liver disease, asthma, acidosis, pancreatic disease, systemic lupus erythematosus, anemia, blood disease, hypercalcemia, or hyperkalemia.

• This drug can occasionally cause potassium loss from the body. Signs of potassium loss include dry mouth, thirst, weakness, muscle pain or cramps, nausea, and vomiting. If you experience any of these symptoms, call your doctor.

• Triamterene can cause hyperkalemia (high levels of potassium in the blood). Signs of hyperkalemia include palpitations; confusion; numbness or tingling in the hands, feet, or lips; anxiety; or unusual tiredness or weakness. In order to avoid this problem, do not alter your diet, and do not use salt substitutes unless you first consult your doctor.

• If you are taking quinidine (an antiarrhythmia heart medication), it is important to know that triamterene may interfere with the laboratory determination of your blood-quinidine concentration. Before you undergo such a test, be sure to tell your doctor that you are also taking triamterene and hydrochlorothiazide combination.

• Limit your intake of beverages that contain alcohol while taking this medication in order to prevent dizziness and lightheadedness.

• Do not take any over-the-counter (nonprescription) medications for weight control or for allergy, asthma, cough, cold, or sinus problems unless you first check with your doctor. Some of these products can bring about an increase in blood pressure.

• Do not change brands of this medication without consulting your doctor.

• To prevent severe water loss (dehydration) while taking this medication, check with your physician if you have any illness that causes severe or continuing nausea, vomiting, or diarrhea.

• This medication can raise blood-sugar levels in diabetic patients. Therefore, blood sugar should be monitored carefully with blood or urine tests when this medication is being taken.

• A doctor does not usually prescribe a "fixed-dose" medication like triamterene and hydrochlorothiazide combination as the first choice in the treatment of high blood pressure. Usually, the patient will first receive each ingredient singly. If there is an adequate response to each drug individually, then the combination can be prescribed. The advantages of a combination product include increased convenience and (often) decreased cost to the consumer.

• Your doctor may schedule regular office visits in order to monitor your progress and possibly adjust the dosage of this medication.

• Be sure to tell your doctor if you are pregnant. This drug crosses the placenta, and its safety in human pregnancy has not been established. Adverse effects have been observed in the fetuses of animals that received large doses of this type of drug during pregnancy. And if you are breast-feeding an infant, tell your doctor. Small amounts of this drug pass into breast milk.

triazolam

BRAND NAME (Manufacturer)
Halcion (Upjohn)
triazolam (various manufacturers)
TYPE OF DRUG
Benzodiazepine sedative/hypnotic
INGREDIENT
triazolam
DOSAGE FORM
Tablets (0.125 mg and 0.25 mg)
STORAGE
This medication should be stored at room temperature in a tightly closed, light-resistant container.

USES

Triazolam is prescribed to treat insomnia, including problems with falling asleep, waking during the night, and early morning wakefulness. It is not clear exactly how this medicine works, but it may relieve insomnia by acting as a depressant of the central nervous system (brain and spinal cord).

TREATMENT

This medicine should be taken 30 to 60 minutes before bedtime. It can be taken with a full glass of water or with food if stomach upset occurs. But do not take this medication with a dose of antacid, which may slow its absorption.

If you are taking this medication regularly and you miss a dose, take the missed dose immediately if you remember

within an hour. If more than an hour has passed, skip the dose
you missed and wait for the next scheduled dose. Do not double the dose.

SIDE EFFECTS

Minor. Bitter taste in mouth, constipation, diarrhea, dizziness,
drowsiness (after a night's sleep), dry mouth, excessive salivation, fatigue, flushing, headache, heartburn, loss of appetite,
nausea, nervousness, sweating, or vomiting. As your body adjusts to the medication, these side effects should disappear.

To relieve constipation, increase the amount of fiber in your
diet (fresh fruits and vegetables, salads, bran, and whole-grain
breads), exercise, and drink more water (unless your doctor
directs you to do otherwise).

Dry mouth can be relieved by chewing sugarless gum or
by sucking on ice chips.

If you feel dizzy, sit or lie down for a while; get up slowly
from a sitting or reclining position; and be careful on stairs.

Major. Tell your doctor about any side effects that are persistent or particularly bothersome. IT IS ESPECIALLY IMPOR-
TANT TO TELL YOUR DOCTOR about blurred or double vision, chest pain, depression, difficulty in urinating, fainting,
falling, fever, hallucinations, joint pain, mouth sores, nightmares, palpitations, rash, shortness of breath, slurred speech,
sore throat, uncoordinated movements, unusual excitement,
unusual tiredness, or yellowing of the eyes or skin.

INTERACTIONS

Triazolam interacts with a number of other types of drugs:

1. To prevent oversedation, it should not be taken with alcohol, other sedative drugs, central nervous system depressants
(such as antihistamines, barbiturates, muscle relaxants, pain
medicines, narcotics, medicines for seizures, and phenothiazine tranquilizers), or with antidepressants.

2. Triazolam may decrease the effectiveness of carbamazepine,
levodopa, and oral anticoagulants (blood thinners, such as
warfarin) and may increase the side effects of phenytoin.

3. Disulfiram, oral contraceptives (birth control pills), isoniazid, and cimetidine can increase the blood levels of triazolam,
which can lead to toxic effects.

4. Concurrent use of rifampin may decrease the effectiveness
of triazolam.

BE SURE TO TELL YOUR DOCTOR about any medications you are currently taking, especially those listed above.

WARNINGS

• Tell your doctor about unusual or allergic reactions you have had to any medications, especially to triazolam or other benzodiazepine tranquilizers (such as alprazolam, chlordiazepoxide, clorazepate, diazepam, flurazepam, halazepam, lorazepam, prazepam, and temazepam).

• Tell your doctor if you now have or if you have ever had liver disease, kidney disease, epilepsy, lung disease, myasthenia gravis, porphyria, mental depression, or mental illness.

• This medicine can cause considerable drowsiness. Avoid tasks that require mental alertness, such as driving an automobile or operating potentially dangerous machinery or equipment.

• Triazolam has the potential for abuse and must be used with caution. Tolerance may develop quickly; do not increase the dosage unless you first consult your doctor. It is also important not to stop taking this drug suddenly if you have been taking it in large amounts or if you have used it for several weeks. Your doctor may want to reduce the dosage gradually.

• This is a safe drug when used properly. When it is combined with other sedative drugs or with alcohol, however, serious side effects can develop.

• Be sure to tell your doctor if you are pregnant. This type of medicine may increase the chance of birth defects if it is taken during the first three months of pregnancy. In addition, use of too much of this medicine during the last six months of pregnancy may lead to addiction of the fetus, resulting in withdrawal side effects in the newborn. Use of this medicine during the last weeks of pregnancy may cause excessive drowsiness, slowed heartbeat, and breathing difficulties in the infant. Tell your doctor if you are breast-feeding an infant. This medicine can pass into breast milk and cause unwanted side effects in nursing infants.

---

trichlormethiazide

BRAND NAMES (Manufacturers)
Diurese (American Urologicals)

Metahydrin (Merrell Dow)
Naqua (Schering)
trichlormethiazide (various manufacturers)
TYPE OF DRUG
Diuretic and antihypertensive
INGREDIENT
trichlormethiazide
DOSAGE FORM
Tablets (2 mg and 4 mg)
STORAGE
This medication should be stored at room temperature in a tightly closed container.

USES

Trichlormethiazide is prescribed to treat high blood pressure. It is also used to reduce fluid accumulation in the body caused by conditions such as heart failure, cirrhosis of the liver, and kidney disease and by the long-term use of some medications. This medication reduces fluid accumulation by increasing the elimination of sodium and water through the kidneys.

TREATMENT

To decrease stomach irritation, you can take this medication with a glass of milk or with a meal (unless your doctor directs you to do otherwise). Try to take it at the same time every day. Avoid taking a dose after 6:00 P.M.; otherwise, you may have to get up during the night to urinate.

If you miss a dose of this medication, take the missed dose as soon as possible, unless it is almost time for the next dose. In that case, do not take the missed dose at all; just wait until the next scheduled dose. Do not double the next dose.

This medication does not cure high blood pressure, but will help control the condition as long as you continue to take it.

SIDE EFFECTS

Minor. Constipation, cramps, diarrhea, dizziness, drowsiness, headache, heartburn, loss of appetite, nausea, restlessness, or upset stomach. As your body adjusts to the medication, these side effects should disappear.

This medication can cause increased sensitivity to sunlight. It is therefore important to avoid prolonged exposure to sun-

light and sunlamps. Wear protective clothing and use an effective sunscreen.

To avoid dizziness or light-headedness when you stand, contract and relax the muscles of your legs for a few moments before rising. Do this by pushing one foot against the floor while raising the other foot slightly, alternating feet so that you are "pumping" your legs in a pedaling motion.

Major. Tell your doctor about any side effects that are persistent or particularly bothersome. IT IS ESPECIALLY IMPORTANT TO TELL YOUR DOCTOR about blurred vision, confusion, difficulty in breathing, dry mouth, excessive thirst, excessive weakness, fever, itching, joint pain, mood changes, muscle pain or spasms, nausea, palpitations, skin rash, sore throat, tingling in the fingers or toes, vomiting, or yellowing of the eyes or skin.

INTERACTIONS

Trichlormethiazide interacts with several other types of medications:

1. It may decrease the effectiveness of oral anticoagulants, antigout medications, insulin, oral antidiabetic medicines, and methenamine.

2. Fenfluramine has been known to increase the blood-pressure-lowering effects of trichlormethiazide (which can be dangerous).

3. Indomethacin can decrease the blood-pressure-lowering effects of trichlormethiazide, thereby counteracting the desired effects.

4. Cholestyramine and colestipol decrease the absorption of this medication from the gastrointestinal tract. Trichlormethiazide should, therefore, be taken one hour before or four hours after a dose of cholestyramine or colestipol if one of these medications has also been prescribed.

5. Trichlormethiazide may increase the side effects of amphotericin B, calcium, cortisone and cortisonelike steroids (such as dexamethasone, hydrocortisone, prednisone, prednisolone), digoxin, digitalis, lithium, quinidine, sulfonamide antibiotics, and vitamin D.

BE SURE TO TELL YOUR DOCTOR about any medications you are currently taking, especially any of the ones mentioned above.

WARNINGS

• Tell your doctor about unusual or allergic reactions you have had to any medications, especially to trichlormethiazide or to other sulfa drugs, including other diuretics, oral antidiabetic medications, and sulfonamide antibiotics.

• Before you start taking trichlormethiazide, tell your doctor if you now have or if you have ever had kidney disease or problems with urination, diabetes mellitus, gout, liver disease, asthma, pancreatic disease, or systemic lupus erythematosus.

• Trichlormethiazide can cause potassium loss. Signs of potassium loss include dry mouth, thirst, weakness, muscle pain or cramps, nausea, and vomiting. If you experience any of these symptoms, call your doctor. To help avoid potassium loss, take this drug with a glass of fresh or frozen orange or cranberry juice, or eat a banana every day. The use of a salt substitute also helps to prevent potassium loss. Do not change your diet, however, before discussing it with your doctor: Too much potassium can also be dangerous. Your doctor may want to have blood tests performed periodically in order to monitor your potassium levels.

• In order to prevent dizziness and light-headedness, limit your intake of alcoholic beverages while taking this drug.

• Do not take any over-the-counter (nonprescription) medications for weight control or for allergy, asthma, cough, cold, or sinus problems unless directed to do so by your doctor.

• To prevent dehydration (severe water loss) while taking this medication, check with your doctor if you have any illness that causes severe or continuous nausea, vomiting, or diarrhea.

• This medication can raise blood-sugar levels in diabetic patients. Therefore, blood sugar should be carefully monitored with blood or urine tests when this medication is being taken.

• Some of these products contain the color additive FD&C Yellow No. 5 (tartrazine), which can cause allergic-type reactions (wheezing, rash, fainting, difficulty in breathing) in certain susceptible individuals.

• The elderly may be more likely to experience dizziness, light-headedness, and too much potassium loss as a result of therapy with this drug.

• Be sure to tell your doctor if you are pregnant. This drug is able to cross the placenta. Safety in human pregnancy has not been established. Adverse effects have been observed in the fetuses of animals that received large doses of this type of drug during pregnancy. Also tell your doctor if you are breast-feeding an infant. Although problems in humans have not been reported, small amounts of this drug can pass into breast milk, so caution is warranted.

---

trihexyphenidyl

BRAND NAMES (Manufacturers)
Artane (Lederle)
Trihexane (Rugby)
Trihexy (Geneva Generics)
trihexyphenidyl hydrochloride (various manufacturers)
TYPE OF DRUG
Antiparkinsonism agent
INGREDIENT
trihexyphenidyl
DOSAGE FORMS
Tablets (2 mg and 5 mg)
Oral elixir (2 mg per 5-mL spoonful, with 5% alcohol)
STORAGE
Store at room temperature in a tightly closed container. This medication should never be frozen.

USES
Trihexyphenidyl is used to treat the symptoms of Parkinson's disease or to control the side effects of phenothiazine tranquilizers. It is thought to act by balancing certain chemicals in the brain.

TREATMENT
In order to reduce stomach irritation, you should take tri-hexyphenidyl with food or just after a meal.

Antacids and antidiarrheal medications prevent the absorption of this medication from the gastrointestinal tract, so at least one hour should separate doses of trihexyphenidyl and one of these medicines.

The oral elixir form of this medication should be measured carefully with a specially designed 5-mL measuring spoon.

If you miss a dose of this medication, take the missed dose as soon as possible, unless it is within two hours of the next dose of the tablets or oral elixir. In that case, do not take the missed dose at all; just return to your regular dosing schedule. Do not double the next dose.

SIDE EFFECTS

Minor. Bloating; blurred vision; constipation; decreased sweating; dizziness; drowsiness; dry mouth, throat, and nose; false sense of well-being; headache; increased sensitivity of the eyes to light; muscle cramps; nausea; nervousness; and weakness. These side effects should disappear as your body adjusts to the medication.

If you are constipated, increase the amount of fiber in your diet (fresh fruits and vegetables, salads, bran, whole-grain breads), exercise, and drink more water (unless your doctor directs you to do otherwise).

Chew sugarless gum or suck on ice chips or a piece of hard candy to reduce mouth dryness.

Wear sunglasses if you find that your eyes have become sensitive to light.

If you feel dizzy, sit or lie down for a while; get up slowly from a sitting or reclining position; and be careful on stairs.

Major. Tell your doctor about any side effects that are persistent or particularly bothersome. IT IS ESPECIALLY IMPORTANT TO TELL YOUR DOCTOR about confusion, depression, difficulty in urinating, hallucinations, involuntary muscle movements, numbness or tingling of the fingers or toes, palpitations, or unusual excitement.

INTERACTIONS

Trihexyphenidyl interacts with other types of medications:
1. It can cause extreme drowsiness when combined with alcohol or other central nervous system depressants (drugs that slow the activity of the brain and spinal cord), such as antihistamines, barbiturates, benzodiazepine tranquilizers, muscle relaxants, narcotics, and pain medications, or with tricyclic antidepressants.
2. Amantadine, antihistamines, haloperidol, monoamine oxidase (MAO) inhibitors, phenothiazine tranquilizers, procainamide, quinidine, and tricyclic antidepressants can increase the side effects of trihexyphenidyl. At least 14 days should separate the use of this drug and the use of an MAO inhibitor.

3. Trihexyphenidyl can decrease the effectiveness of both chlorpromazine and levodopa.

BE SURE TO TELL YOUR DOCTOR about any medications you are currently taking.

WARNINGS
• Tell your doctor about unusual reactions you have had to any medications, especially to trihexyphenidyl.
• Tell your doctor if you now have or if you have ever had achalasia, glaucoma, heart disease, myasthenia gravis, blockage of the intestinal or urinary tract, enlarged prostate gland, stomach ulcers, or thyroid disease.
• If this drug makes you dizzy or drowsy, avoid any activity that requires alertness.
• This medication can decrease sweating and heat release from the body. You should therefore try not to get overheated (avoid exercising strenuously in hot weather, and do not take hot baths, showers, or saunas).
• Your doctor may recommend periodic eye exams to check pressure in your eyes.
• Be sure to tell your doctor if you are pregnant. Although trihexyphenidyl appears to be safe during pregnancy, extensive studies have not been conducted. Also tell your doctor if you are breast-feeding an infant. Small amounts of this medication may pass into breast milk.

trimethobenzamide

BRAND NAMES (Manufacturers)
Tebamide (G & W)
T-Gen (Goldline)
Tigan (Roberts)
trimethobenzamide (various manufacturers)
TYPE OF DRUG
Antiemetic (antinauseant)
INGREDIENT
trimethobenzamide
DOSAGE FORMS
Capsules (100 mg and 250 mg)
Suppositories (100 mg and 200 mg)

STORAGE
Trimethobenzamide should be stored at room temperature in a tightly closed container.

USES
Trimethobenzamide is used to control nausea and vomiting. It is thought to act directly on the vomiting center in the brain.

TREATMENT
Trimethobenzamide capsules can be taken with a full glass of water.

The suppository form of this medication should be inserted into the rectum (if the suppository is too soft to insert, run it under cold water or put it in the refrigerator for 30 minutes). To insert it, remove the foil wrapper, moisten the suppository with a little water, and then lie down on your left side with your right knee bent. Push the suppository into your rectum with your finger. Remain lying down for a few minutes. Try to avoid having a bowel movement for an hour or longer after inserting the suppository in order to allow time for the drug to be absorbed.

If you miss a dose of this medication, take the missed dose as soon as possible, unless it is almost time for the next dose. In that case, do not take the missed dose at all; return to your regular dosing schedule. Do not take a double dose to make up for the one you missed.

SIDE EFFECTS
Minor. Diarrhea, dizziness, drowsiness, headache, or muscle cramps. These side effects should disappear as your body adjusts to the medication.

If you feel dizzy or light-headed, sit or lie down for a while; get up slowly from a sitting or reclining position; and be careful on stairs.

Major. Tell your doctor about any side effects that are persistent or particularly bothersome. IT IS ESPECIALLY IMPORTANT TO TELL YOUR DOCTOR about back pain, blurred vision, convulsions, depression, disorientation, mouth sores, rash, tremors, unusual bleeding or bruising, unusual hand or face movements, or yellowish discoloration of the eyes or skin.

INTERACTIONS

Concurrent use of trimethobenzamide with central nervous system depressants (drugs that slow the activity of the brain and spinal cord), such as alcohol, antihistamines, barbiturates, benzodiazepine tranquilizers, muscle relaxants, narcotics, pain medications, phenothiazine tranquilizers, and sleeping medications, or with tricyclic antidepressants can cause extreme drowsiness.

BE SURE TO TELL YOUR DOCTOR about any medications you are currently taking, especially those listed above.

WARNINGS

• Tell your doctor about unusual or allergic reactions you have had to any medications, especially to trimethobenzamide (or to benzocaine or other local anesthetics if you are using the suppository form).
• Be sure to tell your doctor if you now have or if you have ever had acute fever, dehydration, electrolyte imbalance, intestinal infection, or viral infections.
• If this drug makes you dizzy or drowsy, do not take part in any activity that requires alertness, such as driving a car or operating potentially dangerous machinery.
• Be sure to tell your doctor if you are pregnant. Safe use in pregnancy has not been established. Extensive studies in pregnant women have not been conducted. Also tell your doctor if you are breast-feeding an infant. It is not known whether trimethobenzamide passes into breast milk.

---

valproic acid

BRAND NAMES (Manufacturers)
Depakene (Abbott)
Depakote* (Abbott)
valproic acid (various manufacturers)
*Note: Divalproex sodium, sold under the brand name Depakote, is chemically and therapeutically similar to valproic acid. It has been formulated as an enteric-coated tablet in order to prolong its effects and to decrease stomach irritation.
TYPE OF DRUG
Anticonvulsant

INGREDIENT
valproic acid
DOSAGE FORMS
Capsules (250 mg)
Enteric-coated tablets (125 mg, 250 mg, and 500 mg)
Oral syrup (250 mg per 5-mL spoonful)
Sprinkle capsule (125 mg)
STORAGE
Valproic acid should be stored at room temperature in a tightly closed container. This medication should never be frozen.

USES

Valproic acid is used to treat various seizure disorders. It prevents seizures or convulsions by increasing concentrations of a certain chemical (gamma-aminobutyric acid) in the brain.

TREATMENT

In order to avoid stomach irritation, you should take valproic acid with food or milk (unless your doctor directs you to do otherwise).

The capsules or enteric-coated tablets should be swallowed whole. Chewing or opening the capsules before swallowing releases their contents, which may cause irritation of the mouth and throat.

Each dose of valproic acid oral syrup should be measured carefully with a specially designed 5-mL measuring spoon. An ordinary kitchen teaspoon is not accurate enough to ensure that you receive the proper dose.

Only the specially designed sprinkle capsules should be opened before swallowing. The entire content of the sprinkle capsule should be placed on a teaspoonful of applesauce or pudding and swallowed immediately. Do not chew the food-drug mixture.

Valproic acid works best when the level of medication in the bloodstream is kept constant. It is best, therefore, to take the doses at evenly spaced intervals day and night. For example, if you are to take four doses a day, the doses should be spaced six hours apart.

It is important to try not to miss any doses of this medication. If you do miss a dose and remember within six hours, take the missed dose immediately. If more than six hours have passed, do not take the missed dose at all; just return to your regular dosing schedule. Do not double the next dose of this medication. If you miss two or more consecutive doses of valproic acid, contact your doctor as soon as possible for further instructions.

SIDE EFFECTS

Minor. Constipation, diarrhea, dizziness, drowsiness, hair loss, headache, increased or decreased appetite, insomnia, nausea, stomach upset, vomiting, or weight gain or loss. These side effects should disappear as your body adjusts to the medication.

To relieve constipation, increase the amount of fiber in your diet (fresh fruits and vegetables, salads, bran, and whole-grain breads), exercise, and drink more water (unless your doctor directs you to do otherwise).

If you feel dizzy, sit or lie down for a while; stand up slowly from a sitting or reclining position; and be careful when climbing or descending stairs.

Major. Tell your doctor about any side effects that are persistent or particularly bothersome. IT IS ESPECIALLY IMPORTANT TO TELL YOUR DOCTOR about blurred vision, cramps, depression, facial edema (swelling), loss of coordination, menstrual disorders, mental disorders, skin rash, tremors, unusual bleeding or bruising, weakness, or a yellowish discoloration of the eyes or skin.

INTERACTIONS

Valproic acid interacts with several other types of drugs:

1. Concurrent use of it with other central nervous system depressants (drugs that slow the activity of the brain and spinal cord) such as alcohol, antihistamines, barbiturates, muscle relaxants, narcotics, pain medications, phenothiazine tranquilizers, sleeping medications, or tricyclic antidepressants can lead to drowsiness.

2. Valproic acid can lead to bleeding complications when combined with oral anticoagulants (blood thinners, such as warfarin), aspirin, dipyridamole, or sulfinpyrazone.

3. Valproic acid can increase the blood levels and side effects of phenobarbital and primidone.

4. The combination of valproic acid and clonazepam or phenytoin can lead to an increase in seizure activity.

5. Aspirin may interfere with the metabolism of valproic acid, which in turn may result in increased toxicity and increased side effects.

Before beginning treatment with valproic acid, BE SURE TO TELL YOUR DOCTOR about any medications that you are currently taking, especially any of those medications listed above.

WARNINGS

• BE SURE TO TELL your doctor about unusual or allergic reactions you have had to any medications, especially to valproic acid, sodium valproate, or divalproex sodium.
• Be sure to tell your doctor if you now have or if you have ever had blood disorders, kidney disease, or liver disease.
• If this drug makes you dizzy or drowsy, do not take part in any activity that requires alertness, such as driving a car or operating potentially dangerous machinery.
• Before having surgery or any other medical or dental treatment, be sure to tell your doctor or dentist that you are taking this medication.
• Do not stop taking this medication unless you first check with your doctor. Stopping the drug abruptly may lead to a worsening of your condition. Your doctor may want to reduce your dosage gradually or start you on another medication when valproic acid is discontinued. Make sure you have enough medication on hand to last through weekends, holidays, and vacations.
• Diabetic patients should know that valproic acid can interfere with urine tests for ketones. You should therefore check with your doctor before adjusting your insulin dose to determine if any increase or decrease is necessary.
• Be sure to tell your doctor if you are pregnant. Valproic acid has been shown to cause birth defects in the offspring of animals that received large doses of the drug during pregnancy. It has also been associated with spinal cord birth defects in humans when used during the first three months of pregnancy. The risks and benefits of treatment should be discussed with your doctor. Also be sure to tell your doctor if you are breastfeeding an infant. Small amounts of valproic acid pass into breast milk.

venlafaxine

BRAND NAME (Manufacturer)
Effexor (Wyeth-Ayerst)
TYPE OF DRUG
Antidepressant
INGREDIENT
venlafaxine
DOSAGE FORM
Tablets (25 mg, 37.5 mg, 50 mg, 75 mg, and 100 mg)
STORAGE
This medication should be stored in a tightly closed container at room temperature, away from heat and direct sunlight. Do not store in the bathroom. Heat or moisture can cause this medicine to break down.

USES
Venlafaxine is used to treat the symptoms of clinical mental depression. It increases the concentration of certain chemicals that are necessary for nerve transmission in the brain.

TREATMENT
This medication should be taken exactly as prescribed by your doctor. In order to avoid stomach irritation, you should take venlafaxine with food (unless your doctor directs you to do otherwise).

The effects of treatment with this medication may not become apparent for one to three weeks.

If you miss a dose of this medicine, it is not necessary to make up the missed dose. Skip that dose and continue at the next scheduled time. You should never take a double dose to make up for the one you missed.

SIDE EFFECTS
Minor. Agitation, changes in taste, constipation, decreased concentration, decreased sex drive, diarrhea, dizziness, drowsiness, dry mouth, fast heartbeat, flushing, frequent urination, headache, increased sweating, loss of appetite, nausea, tremors, unusual dreams, vision changes, or weight gain or loss.

Dry mouth can be relieved by chewing sugarless gum or sucking on hard candy.

To relieve constipation, increase the amount of fiber in your diet (fresh fruits and vegetables, salads, bran, and whole-grain breads). You can also increase your level of exercise and drink more water (unless your doctor directs you to do otherwise).

To avoid dizziness when you stand, contract and relax your leg muscles for a few moments before rising.

Major. Tell your doctor about any side effects that are persistent or particularly bothersome. IT IS ESPECIALLY IMPORTANT TO TELL YOUR DOCTOR about anxiety, chills or fever, convulsions (seizures), difficulty in breathing, enlarged lymph glands (swelling under the jaw, in the armpits, or in the groin area), joint or muscle pain, skin rash or hives, or noticeable swelling of the feet or the lower legs.

INTERACTIONS

Venlafaxine interacts with several other types of drugs:

1. Extreme drowsiness can occur when this medication is taken with other central nervous system depressants (such as alcohol, antihistamines, barbiturates, benzodiazepine tranquilizers, muscle relaxants, narcotics, pain medications, phenothiazine tranquilizers, and sleeping medications) or with other antidepressants.

2. Serious side effects may occur if a monoamine oxidase (MAO) inhibitor (such as furazolidone, isocarboxazid, pargyline, phenelzine, procarbazine, selegiline, or tranylcypromine) is taken with venlafaxine. At least 14 days should separate the use of venlafaxine and the use of an MAO inhibitor.

3. When venlafaxine is combined with cimetidine and taken by the elderly or by individuals with high blood pressure or liver disease, there may be a higher risk of side effects.

Before taking venlafaxine, BE SURE TO TELL YOUR DOCTOR about any medications you are currently taking, especially any of those listed above.

WARNINGS

• Tell your doctor immediately if you develop a skin rash or have hives while taking this medication. Also let your doctor know you have ever had a reaction to venlafaxine before.

• Tell your doctor if you have a history of alcoholism; or if you ever had a heart attack, asthma, circulatory disease, difficulty in urinating, electroshock therapy, enlarged prostate gland, epilepsy, glaucoma, high blood pressure, intestinal problems, liver or kidney disease, mental illness, or thyroid disease.

• If this medication makes you dizzy or drowsy, do not take part in any activity that requires mental alertness, such as driving a car or operating potentially dangerous equipment.

• Do not stop taking this medication suddenly. Stopping it abruptly can cause nausea, headache, stomach upset, or a worsening of your condition. Your doctor may want to reduce the dose gradually.

• Elderly individuals may be at greater risk for side effects. Use this drug cautiously and report any changes in mental status to your doctor immediately.

• The effects of this medication may be present for as long as five weeks after you stop taking it, so continue to observe all precautions during this period.

• Be sure to tell your doctor if you are pregnant. Although birth defects have not been documented in animal studies, it is not known if venlafaxine is safe during pregnancy. Nor is it known if venlafaxine passes into breast milk, so be sure to tell your doctor if you are breast-feeding an infant.

---

verapamil

BRAND NAMES (Manufacturers)
Calan (Searle)
Calan SR (Searle)
Isoptin (Knoll)
Isoptin SR (Knoll)
verapamil (various manufacturers)
Verelan (Lederle)
TYPE OF DRUG
Antianginal (calcium channel blocker) and antihypertensive
INGREDIENT
verapamil
DOSAGE FORMS
Tablets (40 mg, 80 mg, and 120 mg)
Sustained-release tablets (120 mg, 180 mg, and 240 mg)
Sustained-release capsules (120 mg, 180 mg, and 240 mg)

STORAGE
Store this medication at room temperature in a tightly closed container. Do not refrigerate it.

USES
Verapamil is used to treat angina pectoris (chest pain) and high blood pressure. It belongs to a group of drugs known as calcium channel blockers. It is not clearly understood how verapamil works, but it is thought to increase the blood supply to the heart. It is also a vasodilator that relaxes the muscle tissue of the blood vessels, thereby lowering blood pressure.

TREATMENT
Verapamil can be taken either on an empty stomach or with meals, as directed by your doctor or pharmacist. The sustained-release tablets should not be crushed or chewed, but swallowed whole.

If you miss a dose of this medication, take the missed dose as soon as possible, unless it is almost time for the next dose. In that case, do not take the missed dose at all; just return to your regular dosing schedule. Do not double the next dose.

This medication does not cure high blood pressure, but it will help to control the condition as long as you continue to take it.

SIDE EFFECTS
Minor. Abdominal pain, blurred vision, constipation, dizziness, headache, muscle cramps, nausea, sleeplessness, or sweating. These side effects should disappear as your body adjusts to the medication.

To relieve constipation, increase the amount of fiber in your diet (fresh fruits and vegetables, salads, bran, and whole-grain breads), and drink more water (unless your doctor directs you to do otherwise).

Major. Tell your doctor about any side effects that are persistent or particularly bothersome. IT IS ESPECIALLY IMPORTANT TO TELL YOUR DOCTOR about changes in menstruation, confusion, depression, fainting, fatigue, hair loss, itching, loss of balance, palpitations, rapid weight gain (three to five pounds within a week), shortness of breath, swelling of the hands or feet, tremors, or unusual weakness.

INTERACTIONS

This drug will interact with a number of other types of medications:

1. The concurrent use of alcohol, quinidine, or prazosin and verapamil can cause a severe drop in blood pressure and result in fainting.

2. Beta blockers (acebutolol, atenolol, betaxolol, carteolol, esmolol, labetalol, metoprolol, nadolol, penbutolol, pindolol, propranolol, or timolol) and digoxin should be used cautiously with verapamil, because side effects to the heart may be increased.

3. Disopyramide should not be taken within 48 hours of verapamil; the combination of these medications could lead to heart failure.

4. Cimetidine can decrease the elimination of verapamil from the body, which can lead to an increased risk of side effects.

5. Sulfinpyrazone and rifampin can increase the elimination of verapamil from the body, which can lead to a decrease in its effectiveness.

6. Verapamil can cause an increase in the effects of the drugs carbamazepine or theophylline.

BE SURE TO TELL YOUR DOCTOR about any medications you are currently taking.

WARNINGS

• Tell your doctor about unusual or allergic reactions you have had to any medications, especially to verapamil.

• Before starting therapy with this medication, be sure that you inform your doctor if you have ever had any type of heart disease, kidney disease, liver disease, low blood pressure, or a slowed heartbeat.

• Your doctor may want you to check your pulse while you are taking this drug. If your heart rate drops below 50 beats per minute, contact your doctor.

• Verapamil is not effective for an attack of chest pain that has already started; this medication is only effective in preventing attacks from occurring.

• It is extremely important that you do not stop taking this medication without first consulting your doctor. Stopping abruptly may lead to a worsening of your chest pain. Your doctor may, therefore, want to reduce your dosage gradually

or have you switch to another similar medication when verapamil is discontinued.
• In order to prevent dizziness or fainting while taking this
medication, try not to stand for long periods of time, avoid
drinking alcoholic beverages, and try not to become overheated (avoid exerting yourself or exercising strenuously in
hot weather, and do not take hot baths, showers, or saunas).
• Be sure to tell your doctor if you are pregnant. Extensive
studies in pregnant women have not been conducted. Also
be sure to tell your doctor if you are breast-feeding an infant.
Small amounts of verapamil pass into breast milk and may
cause unwanted side effects in the nursing infant.

vitamins A, D, and C with fluoride

BRAND NAMES (Manufacturers)
Triple-Vita-Flor (P.B.I)
Tri-Vi-Flor (Bristol-Myers Squibb)
Tri-Vitamin with Fluoride Drops (Rugby)
Vi-Daylin F ADC Drops (Abbott)
TYPE OF DRUG
Multivitamin and fluoride supplement
INGREDIENTS
vitamin A, vitamin D, vitamin C, and fluoride
DOSAGE FORMS
Chewable tablets (2,500 IU [international units] vitamin A;
    400 IU vitamin D; 60 mg vitamin C; and 1 mg fluoride)
Oral drops (1,500 IU vitamin A; 400 IU vitamin D; 35 mg
    vitamin C; and 0.25 mg or 0.5 mg fluoride per mL)
STORAGE
The chewable tablets should be stored at room temperature
in a tightly closed, light-resistant container. The oral drops
should be stored at room temperature in the original plastic
container (glass containers interact with and destroy the fluoride in the solution). A slight darkening in the color of the
drops does not indicate a loss in potency of the vitamins or
fluoride; the solution can still be used safely. This medication
should not be refrigerated and should never be frozen.

USES

Multivitamins with fluoride are used to protect against dental caries (tooth decay) and vitamin deficiencies in children. Fluoride has been found to be helpful in preventing cavities.

TREATMENT

The tablets should be chewed or crushed before being swallowed. To provide maximum protection, the tablets should be given at bedtime after the teeth have been brushed. To allow the fluoride to work on the teeth, nothing should be eaten for at least 15 minutes after chewing the tablets.

The oral drop form of this multivitamin and fluoride supplement can be taken directly or can be mixed with juice or foods. The dose should be measured carefully with the dropper provided.

Milk prevents the absorption of fluoride from the gastrointestinal tract. Therefore, this product should not be taken with milk or other dairy products.

If your child misses a dose of this medication, administer the missed dose as soon as possible, unless it is almost time for the next dose. In that case, do not give the missed dose at all; just return to the child's regular dosing schedule. Do not double the next dose.

SIDE EFFECTS

Minor. This product seldom causes side effects, but can occasionally cause constipation, diarrhea, drowsiness, fatigue, loss of appetite, nausea, vomiting, or weakness. These side effects should disappear over time as the body adjusts to the medication.

To relieve constipation, increase the amount of fiber in your child's diet (fresh fruits and vegetables, salads, bran, and whole-grain breads) and encourage the child to drink more water (unless your doctor directs you to do otherwise).

Major. Tell your doctor about any side effects that are persistent or particularly bothersome. IT IS ESPECIALLY IMPORTANT TO TELL YOUR DOCTOR about bloody or black, tarry stools; difficulty in swallowing; discoloration of the teeth; excessive drooling; excitation; mouth sores; rash; stomach cramps; or tremors.

INTERACTIONS

This product should not interact with other medications if it is used according to directions.

WARNINGS

• Tell your doctor about any unusual or allergic reactions your child has had to vitamins, fluoride, or any medications.
• Tell your doctor if your child now has or has ever had bone, heart, kidney, or thyroid disease.
• The chewable tablets should not be used if the fluoride content of your drinking water is 0.7 part per million or more. The oral drops should not be used by children less than three years of age in areas where the drinking water contains 0.3 part per million or more of fluoride. If you are unsure of the fluoride content of your drinking water, ask your doctor or call the county health department.
• Vitamins with fluoride are often prescribed for infants who are not being given any source of fluorinated water. Once your infant is given fluorinated water consistently, be sure to ask your doctor if you should continue this medication.
• You should never refer to this medication as "candy" or "candy-flavored vitamins." Your child may take you literally and swallow too many.

---

vitamins, multiple, with fluoride

BRAND NAMES (Manufacturers)
Florvite (Everett)
Poly-Vi-Flor (Mead Johnson)
polyvitamins with fluoride drops (various manufacturers)
Polyvite with Fluoride Drops (Major)
Vi-Daylin F (Ross)

TYPE OF DRUG
Multivitamin and fluoride supplement

INGREDIENTS
vitamins A, D, E, C, B6, B12, folic acid, riboflavin, niacin, fluoride, and thiamine

DOSAGE FORMS

Chewable tablets (2,500 IU [international units] vitamin A; 400 IU vitamin D; 15 IU vitamin E; 60 mg vitamin C; 0.3 mg folic acid; 1.0 mg thiamine; 1.2 mg riboflavin; 13.5 mg niacin; 1.0 mg vitamin B6; 4.5 mcg vitamin B12; and 0.5 mg or 1.0 mg fluoride)

Oral drops (1,500 IU vitamin A; 400 IU vitamin D; 4.1 or 5 IU vitamin E; 35 mg vitamin C; 0.5 mg thiamine; 0.6 mg riboflavin; 8 mg niacin; 0.4 mg vitamin B6; 2 mcg vitamin B12; and 0.25 mg or 0.5 mg fluoride per mL)

Oral tablets (2,500 IU vitamin A; 400 IU vitamin D; 15 IU vitamin E; 60 mg vitamin C; 0.3 mg folic acid; 1.05 mg thiamine; 1.2 mg riboflavin; 13.5 mg niacin; 1.05 mg vitamin B6; 4.5 mcg vitamin B12; 0.5 mg fluoride)

STORAGE

The chewable tablets should be stored at room temperature in a tightly closed, light-resistant container. The oral drops should be stored at room temperature in the original plastic container (glass containers interact with and destroy the fluoride in the solution). A slight darkening in the color of the drops does not indicate a loss in potency of the vitamins or fluoride; the solution can still be used safely. This medication should not be refrigerated and should never be frozen.

USES

Multiple vitamins with fluoride added are used to protect against tooth decay and vitamin deficiencies in children. Fluoride has been found to be helpful in preventing cavities.

TREATMENT

The tablets should be either chewed or crushed before being swallowed. To provide maximum protection, the tablets should be given at bedtime after the teeth have been brushed. Nothing should be eaten for at least 15 minutes after chewing the tablets to allow the fluoride to work on the teeth.

The oral drop form of this medication can be taken directly, or can be mixed with juice or foods. The dose should be measured carefully with the dropper provided.

Milk prevents the absorption of fluoride from the gastrointestinal tract. Therefore, this product should not be taken with milk or other dairy products.

If your child misses a dose, administer the missed dose as soon as possible, unless it is almost time for the next dose. In that case, do not give the missed dose at all; return to the child's regular dosing schedule. Do not double the dose.

SIDE EFFECTS

Minor. Occasionally, this product causes constipation, diarrhea, drowsiness, fatigue, loss of appetite, nausea, vomiting, or weakness. These side effects should disappear as the body adjusts to the medication.

To relieve constipation, increase the amount of fiber in your child's diet (fresh fruits and vegetables, salads, bran, and whole-grain breads) and encourage your child to drink more water (unless your doctor directs you to do otherwise).

Major. Tell your doctor about any side effects that are persistent or particularly bothersome. IT IS ESPECIALLY IMPORTANT TO TELL YOUR DOCTOR about bloody or black, tarry stools; difficulty in swallowing; discoloration of the teeth; excessive drooling; excitation; mouth sores; rash; stomach cramps; or tremors.

INTERACTIONS

This product should not interact with other medications if it is used according to directions.

WARNINGS

• Tell your doctor about any unusual or allergic reactions your child has had to vitamins, fluoride, or any medications.

• Be sure to tell your doctor if your child now has or has ever had one or more of the following: bone, heart, kidney, or thyroid disease.

• The chewable tablets should not be used if the fluoride content of your drinking water is 0.7 part per million or more. The oral drops should not be used by children less than three years of age in areas where the drinking water contains 0.3 part per million or more of fluoride. If you are unsure of the fluoride content of your drinking water, ask your doctor or call the county health department.

• Vitamins with fluoride are often prescribed for infants who are not being given any source of fluorinated water. Once your infant is given fluorinated water consistently, ask you doctor if you should continue this medication.

• Never call this medication "candy" or "candy-flavored vitamins." Your child may take you literally and swallow too many.

---

vitamins, prenatal

BRAND NAMES (Manufacturers)
Prenatal-1 + iron tablets (various manufacturers)
Stuartnatal Plus (Wyeth-Ayerst)
TYPE OF DRUG
Multivitamin and mineral supplement
INGREDIENTS
Calcium, iron, folic acid, zinc, copper, niacin, riboflavin, thiamine, and vitamins A, D, E, B_6, B_{12}, and C
DOSAGE FORM
Tablets (200 mg calcium; 65 mg iron; 1.0 mg folic acid; 4,000 IU [international units] vitamin A; 400 IU vitamin D; 11 IU vitamin E; 1.5 mg thiamine; 3 mg riboflavin; 20 mg niacin; 10 mg vitamin B_6; 12 mcg vitamin B_{12}; 120 mg vitamin C; 25 mg zinc; 2 mg copper)
STORAGE
These tablets should be stored at room temperature in a tightly closed, light-resistant container. They should not be refrigerated.

USES
This product is a multivitamin and mineral supplement for use during pregnancy and nursing.

TREATMENT
In order to avoid stomach irritation, you can take this product with food or with a full glass of water or milk.

If you miss a dose of this medication, take the missed dose as soon as possible, unless it is almost time for the next dose. In that case, do not take the missed dose at all; just return to your regular dosing schedule. Do not double the next dose.

SIDE EFFECTS
Minor. Constipation, diarrhea, nausea, stomach upset, or vomiting. These side effects should disappear as your body adjusts to the medication.

To relieve constipation, increase the amount of fiber in your diet (fresh fruits and vegetables, salads, bran, and whole-grain breads), exercise, and drink more water (unless your doctor directs you to do otherwise).

Black stools are a normal consequence of iron therapy and do not indicate a problem.

Major. Tell your doctor about any side effects that are persistent or particularly bothersome. IT IS ESPECIALLY IMPORTANT TO TELL YOUR DOCTOR about bloody or tarry stools or severe abdominal pain.

INTERACTIONS

This product should not interact with other medications if it is used according to directions.

WARNINGS

• Tell your doctor about unusual or allergic reactions you have had to any medications, especially to any vitamins, minerals, or iron.

• Be sure to tell your doctor if you have ever had bone disease, liver disease, kidney disease, or stomach ulcers.

• Because this product may mask the symptoms of pernicious anemia, it should be used only under a doctor's supervision.

warfarin

BRAND NAME (Manufacturer)
Coumadin (DuPont)
TYPE OF DRUG
Anticoagulant
INGREDIENT
warfarin
DOSAGE FORM
Tablets (1 mg, 2 mg, 2.5 mg, 4 mg, 5 mg, 7.5 mg, and 10 mg)
STORAGE
Warfarin should be stored at room temperature in a tightly closed, light-resistant container. This medication should not be refrigerated.

USES

Warfarin is used to prevent blood-clot formation by decreasing the production of blood-clotting substances by the liver.

TREATMENT

You can take warfarin with a full glass of water. In order to become accustomed to taking this medication, try to take it at the same time each day.

If you miss a dose of warfarin, take the missed dose as soon as possible, unless it is almost time for the next dose. In that case, do not take the missed dose at all; just return to your regular dosing schedule. Do not double the next dose. If you miss more than two doses in a row, contact your doctor as soon as possible.

SIDE EFFECTS

Minor. Blurred vision, cramps, decreased appetite, diarrhea, or nausea. These side effects should disappear as your body adjusts to the medication. Warfarin may produce a red-orange discoloration of urine.

Major. Tell your doctor about any side effects that are persistent or particularly bothersome. IT IS ESPECIALLY IMPORTANT TO TELL YOUR DOCTOR about bloody or black, tarry stools; blood in sputum; fever; heavy bleeding from cuts; internal bleeding (signs of internal bleeding include abdominal pain or swelling and vomiting of blood or material that resembles coffee grounds); loss of hair; mouth sores; nausea; nosebleeds; rash; red urine; severe bruising; severe headache; swelling of joints; unusually heavy menstrual bleeding; or yellowing of the eyes or skin.

INTERACTIONS

Warfarin interacts with several other types of drugs:
1. Alcohol, allopurinol, amiodarone, anabolic steroids, antibiotics, chloral hydrate, chloramphenicol, chlorpropamide, cimetidine, clofibrate, danazol, disulfiram, erythromycin, glucagon, isoniazid, ketoconazole, methyldopa, methylphenidate, metronidazole, monoamine oxidase (MAO) inhibitors, nalidixic acid, propoxyphene, quinidine, quinine, salicylates, sulfamethoxazole and trimethoprim combination, sulfinpyrazone, sulfonamides, sulindac, tetracycline, thyroid

hormones, and tolbutamide can increase the effects of warfarin, which can be dangerous.

2. Azathioprine, barbiturates, carbamazepine, cholestyramine, colestipol, estrogens, ethchlorvynol, griseofulvin, oral contraceptives (birth control pills), phenytoin, propylthiouracil, rifampin, sucralfate, and vitamin K can decrease the effectiveness of warfarin.

3. Adrenocorticosteroids (cortisonelike medications), anticancer drugs, aspirin, diflunisal, dipyridamole, fenoprofen, ibuprofen, indomethacin, oxyphenbutazone, phenylbutazone, potassium, quinidine, quinine, and salicylates can increase the bleeding complications of warfarin.

4. Warfarin can increase the side effects of oral antidiabetic agents and phenytoin.

5. Diuretics may either increase the effects or decrease the effectiveness of warfarin. Be sure to ask your doctor about the safety of concurrent use of diuretics and warfarin.

Before starting to take warfarin, BE SURE TO TELL YOUR DOCTOR about any medications (both prescription and nonprescription) you are currently taking, especially any of those listed above.

WARNINGS

• Tell your doctor about unusual or allergic reactions you have had to any medications, especially to warfarin.

• Before starting to take this medication, BE SURE TO TELL YOUR DOCTOR if you now have or if you have ever had any condition for which bleeding is an added risk—an aneurysm, blood disorders, cancer, diabetes mellitus, congestive heart failure, edema, endocarditis, high blood pressure, indwelling catheters, intestinal infections, kidney or liver disease, malnutrition, menstrual difficulties, pericarditis, surgery, thyroid disease, tuberculosis, ulcers, vasculitis, or wounds and injuries.

• Before having surgery or any other medical or dental treatment, BE SURE TO TELL YOUR DOCTOR OR DENTIST that you are taking warfarin.

• Do not take any aspirin-containing products or any over-the-counter products while you are on warfarin, unless you first check with your doctor or pharmacist. Aspirin can increase the risk of bleeding complications from warfarin.

• Avoid any activity, such as a contact sport, that might lead to physical injury. Tell your doctor about any fall or blow that occurs. Warfarin can cause heavy bleeding from cuts.

• Use an electric razor while shaving to reduce the risk of cutting yourself, and be especially careful while brushing your teeth.

• Since factors as diverse as travel, diet, the environment, and your general health can affect your body's response to warfarin, your dosage level should be carefully monitored by your doctor.

• Do not stop taking warfarin unless you first consult your doctor. If you stop taking this drug abruptly, you may experience blood clotting. Your doctor may, therefore, want to reduce your dosage gradually.

• Do not change brands of this medication without consulting your doctor.

• Some of these products contain the color additive FD&C Yellow No. 5 (tartrazine), which can cause allergic-type reactions in certain susceptible individuals.

• Be sure to tell your doctor if you are pregnant. Warfarin has been associated with birth defects and bleeding complications in fetuses. Also tell your doctor if you are breast-feeding an infant.

---

zidovudine (AZT)

BRAND NAME (Manufacturer)
Retrovir (Burroughs Wellcome)
TYPE OF DRUG
antiviral
INGREDIENT
zidovudine (AZT, azidothymidine)
DOSAGE FORMS
Capsules (100 mg)
Syrup (50 mg per 5 mL)
STORAGE
Zidovudine capsules and syrup should be stored at room temperature in tightly closed, light-resistant containers. Zidovudine should not be refrigerated, and it should never be frozen.

USES
Zidovudine (formerly called azidothymidine), or AZT, is used in the treatment of human immunodeficiency virus (HIV) infection. HIV is the virus that causes AIDS. Zidovudine works by inhibiting the reproduction, or growth, of the virus, which slows down the progression of AIDS. Zidovudine does not cure AIDS, but this drug may delay the onset of other infections and diseases caused by AIDS.

TREATMENT
This medication works best when the level of medicine in your bloodstream is kept constant. It is best to take the drug at evenly spaced intervals throughout the day.

If you are using the zidovudine syrup, use a special measuring spoon to measure the doses.

If you miss a dose of this medication, take it as soon as possible. However, if it is almost time for your next dose, skip the missed dose and go back to your regular dosing schedule. Do not double the doses.

SIDE EFFECTS
Minor. Blue or brown bands on nails, difficulty sleeping, headache, muscle soreness, or nausea. Some of these side effects may go away during treatment as your body adjusts to the medicine.

Major. Abdominal discomfort, chills, confusion, convulsions, fever, loss of appetite, mania, muscle tenderness or weakness, pale skin, sore throat, or unusual tiredness.

INTERACTIONS
Zidovudine interacts with several other drugs:
1. Concurrent use of some other antibiotic, antifungal, or antiviral agents may increase toxicity of zidovudine.
2. Methadone and probenecid can interfere with your body's ability to eliminate zidovudine and may increase toxicity of zidovudine.
3. Zidovudine can alter the level of phenytoin in your body.

BE SURE TO TELL YOUR DOCTOR about any medication you are currently taking, especially any of those listed above.

WARNINGS

• Tell your doctor about unusual or allergic reactions you have had to any medications, especially zidovudine. Also tell your doctor about any allergic reaction you have had to any foods, preservatives, or dyes.

• You may require periodic blood sample checks at your physician's office to monitor the effects of zidovudine.

• Be sure to tell your doctor if you have anemia, liver disease, or vitamin deficiencies.

• Before having surgery or any other medical or dental treatment, tell your doctor or dentist that you are taking this drug.

• If you are infected with HIV, it is best to avoid any sexual activity involving an exchange of body fluids with other people. If you do have vaginal, anal, or oral sex, always use a latex condom.

• If you inject drugs, do not share needles with anyone.

• Be sure to tell your doctor if your are pregnant. Tell your doctor if your are breast-feeding an infant. It is not known if zidovudine passes into breast milk, but HIV or the AIDS virus can be transmitted through breast milk.

Canadian Brand Names

Following is a list of commonly prescribed Canadian brand-name medications and their manufacturers. Also listed are the profile names under which you can find information about each brand-name drug. Please note that in Canada acetaminophen is known as paracetamol, albuterol is known as salbutamol, metaproterenol is known as orciprenaline, and meperidine is known as pethidine.

BRAND NAME (Manufacturer) Profile

Acetazolam® (ICN)	**acetazolamide**
Ampicin® (Bristol)	**ampicillin**
Ansaid® (Upjohn)	**flurbiprofen**
Anturan® (Geigy)	**sulfinpyrazone**
Apo-Allopurinal® (Apotex)	**allopurinal**
Apo-Ampi® (Apotex)	**ampicillin**
Apo-Benztropine® (Apotex)	**benztropine**
Apo-Diazepam® (Apotex)	**diazepam**
Apo-Flurazepam® (Apotex)	**flurazepam**
Apo-Hydro® (Apotex)	**hydrochlorothiazide**
Apo-Ibuprofen® (Apotex)	**ibuprofen**
Apo-Pen-VK® (Apotex)	**penicillin VK**
Apo-Sulfinpyrazone® (Apotex)	**sulfinpyrazone**
Apo-Trihex® (Apotex)	**trihexyphenidyl**
Artane® (Lederle)	**trihexyphenidyl**
Bentylol® (Merrell)	**dicyclomine**
Benuryl® (ICN)	**probenecid**
Betaloc® (Astra)	**metoprolol**
Bonamine® (Pfizer)	**meclizine**
Canesten® (Miles)	**clotrimazole (vaginal)**
Carbolith® (ICN)	**lithium**

BRAND NAME (Manufacturer) Profile

Chlorpromanyl® (Technilab)	**chlorpromazine**
Claripex® (ICN)	**clofibrate**
Clavulin® (SmithKline Beecham)	**amoxicillin and clavulanic acid combination**
Corium® (ICN)	**chlordiazepoxide and clidinium combination**
Coronex® (Wyeth-Ayerst)	**isosorbide dinitrate**
Coumadin® (DuPont)	**warfarin**
Cytotec® (Searle)	**misoprostol**
Dalacin C® (Upjohn)	**clindamycin (systemic)**
Dalmane® (Roche)	**flurazepam**
Depen® (Horner)	**penicillamine**
Detensol® (Desbergers)	**propranolol**
Diuchlor H® (Medic)	**hydrochlorothiazide**
Dixarit® (Boehringer Ingelheim)	**clonidine**
Dopamet® (ICN)	**methyldopa**
Eltroxin® (Glaxo)	**levothyroxine**
Emex® (SmithKline Beecham)	**metoclopramide**
Erythromid® (Abbott)	**erythromycin**
Euglucon® (Boehringer Mannheim)	**glyburide**
Froben® (Organon)	**flurbiprofen**
Hibidil 1:2000 (Zeneca)	**chlorhexidine gluconate**
Hibitane® Gluconate 20% (Zeneca)	**chlorhexidine gluconate**
Hibitane® Skin Cleanser 2% and 4% (Zeneca)	**chlorhexidine gluconate**
Hip-Rex® (Riker)	**methenamine**
Hismanal® (Janssen)	**astemizole**
Impril® (ICN)	**imipramine**
Indocid® (MSD)	**indomethacin**

BRAND NAME (Manufacturer) Profile

Kwellada® (R & C)	lindane
Largactil® (Rhone-Poulenc)	chlorpromazine
Lenoltec with codeine No. 4® (Technilab)	acetaminophen and codeine combination
Levate® (ICN)	amitriptyline
Lidemol® (Syntex)	fluocinonide (topical)
Lithane® (Pfizer)	lithium
Lithizine® (Maney)	lithium
Loxapac® (Lederle)	loxapine
Maxeran® (Nordic)	metoclopramide
Minestrin ½0® (P.D.)	oral contraceptives
Min-Ovral® (Wyeth-Ayerst)	oral contraceptives
Mobenol® (Horner)	tolbutamide
Moduret® (MSD)	amiloride and hydrochlorothiazide combination
Myclo® (Boehringer Ingelheim)	clotrimazole (topical), clotrimazole (vaginal)
Nadopen-V® (Nadeau)	penicillin VK
Naxen® (SynCare)	naproxen
Neo-Codema® (Neolab)	hydrochlorothiazide
Novamoxin® (Novopharm)	amoxicillin
Novobutamide® (Novopharm)	tolbutamide
Novocimetine® (Novopharm)	cimetidine
Novocloxin® (Novopharm)	cloxacillin
Novodipam® (Novopharm)	diazepam
Novodoparil® (Novopharm)	methyldopa and hydrochlorothiazide combination
Novofibrate® (Novopharm)	clofibrate
Novoflupam® (Novopharm)	flurazepam

BRAND NAME (Manufacturer) Profile

Novoflurazine® (Novopharm)	**trifluoperazine**
Novohydrazide® (Novopharm)	**hydrochlorothiazide**
Novolexin® (Novopharm)	**cephalexin**
Novomedopa® (Novopharm)	**methyldopa**
Novomethacin® (Novopharm)	**indomethacin**
Novonaprox® (Novopharm)	**naproxen**
Novonidazole® (Novopharm)	**metronidazole**
Novopen-VK® (Novopharm)	**penicillin VK**
Novopoxide® (Novopharm)	**chlordiazepoxide**
Novopramine® (Novopharm)	**imipramine**
Novopranol® (Novopharm)	**propranolol**
Novoprofen® (Novopharm)	**ibuprofen**
Novopropamide® (Novopharm)	**chlorpropamide**
Novopyrazone® (Novopharm)	**sulfinpyrazone**
Novoridazine® (Novopharm)	**thioridazine**
Novosemide® (Novopharm)	**furosemide**
Novosorbide® (Novopharm)	**isosorbide dinitrate**
Novospiroton® (Novopharm)	**spironolactone**
Novospirozine® (Novopharm)	**spironolactone and hydrochlorothiazide combination**
Novotetra® (Novopharm)	**tetracycline**
Novothalidone® (Novopharm)	**chlorthalidone**
Novotriamzide® (Novopharm)	**triamterene and hydrochlorothiazide combination**
Novotrimel® (Novopharm)	**sulfamethoxazole and trimethoprim combination**
Novotriptyn® (Novopharm)	**amitriptyline**
Novoxapam® (Novopharm)	**oxazepam**
Nyaderm® (TARO)	**nystatin**
Orbenin® (Wyeth-Ayerst)	**cloxacillin**

BRAND NAME (Manufacturer) Profile

Oxycocet® (Technilab)	**acetaminophen and oxycodone combination**
Oxycodan® (Technilab)	**aspirin and oxycodone combination**
Penbritin® (Wyeth-Ayerst)	**ampicillin**
Peptol® (Horner)	**cimetidine**
Peridol® (Technilab)	**haloperidol**
Pertofrane® (Geigy)	**desipramine**
Phenazo® (ICN)	**phenazopyridine**
Ponderal® (Servier)	**fenfluramine**
Procytox® (Horner)	**cyclophosphamide**
Purinol® (Horner)	**allopurinol**
PVF® (Frosst)	**penicillin VK**
Reserfia® (Medic)	**reserpine**
Rivotril® (Roche)	**clonazepam**
Rofact® (ICN)	**rifampin**
Rogaine™ Topical Solution (Upjohn)	**minoxidil (topical)**
Roubac® (Rougier)	**sulfamethoxazole and trimethoprim combination**
Rounox® with Codeine (Rougier)	**acetaminophen and codeine combination**
Rynacrom® (Fisons)	**cromolyn sodium (nasal)**
Rythmodan® (Roussel)	**disopyramide**
Salazopyrin® (Pharmacia)	**sulfasalazine**
Solazine® (Horner)	**trifluoperazine**
Solium® (Horner)	**chlordiazepoxide**

BRAND NAME (Manufacturer) Profile

Somnol® (Horner)	**flurazepam**
Stemetil® (May & Baker)	**prochlorperazine**
Stieva-A® (Stiefel)	**tretinoin**
Sulcrate® (Nordic)	**sucralfate**
Tecnal® (Technilab)	**aspirin, caffeine, and butalbital combination**
Terfluzine® (ICN)	**trifluoperazine**
Transderm-V (Ciba-Geigy)	**scopolamine (transdermal)**
Triadapin® (Fisons)	**doxepin**
Uridon® (ICN)	**chlorthalidone**
Uritol® (Horner)	**furosemide**
Urozide® (ICN)	**hydrochlorothiazide**
Vivol® (Horner)	**diazepam**
Voltaren® (Geigy)	**diclofenac (sodium)**
Warfilone® (Frosst)	**warfarin**
Winpred® (ICN)	**prednisone (systemic)**

Index

This comprehensive index includes both brand names (in **boldface** type) and generic names in alphabetical order. To find information on a brand-name drug, first look up the brand name. The brand-name listing will give you the drug's generic name. Look up the generic name to find the page number of the appropriate drug profile.